Resolving Locational Conflict

Resolving Locational Conflict

edited by

ROBERT W. LAKE

CENTER
FOR URBAN
POLICY RESEARCH

Second Printing 1991

Published by the Center for Urban Policy Research
New Brunswick, New Jersey 08903

Printed in the United States of America

Library of Congress Cataloging-in-Publication Data

Resolving locational conflict.

   Bibliography: p.
   Includes index.

     1. Land use—Planning.   2. Building sites—Planning.
3. Industry—Location—Political aspects.   4. Public buildings—
Location—Political aspects.   5. Hazardous waste sites—
Location—Political aspects.   6. Conflict management.
I. Lake, Robert W., 1946–
II. Rutgers University. Center for Urban Policy Research.

HD108.6.R47   1986   338.6'042   86-17204
ISBN 0-88285-118-7

Contents

Part II. Process

Part III. Tools

Tables

Figures

Acknowledgments

This book was completed as part of a larger study on improving public participation in the siting of hazardous waste facilities, funded by the New Jersey Industry/University Cooperative Center for Research in Hazardous and Toxic Substances. I am grateful to Michael Greenberg, Director of the Public Policy and Education Division of the Cooperative Center, and to George Sternlieb, Director of the Center for Urban Policy Research, for their encouragement and support through all phases of the overall project. In developing the perspective that guided preparation of this book, I benefitted immeasurably from discussions with Ursula Bauer, Yvonne Chilik, and Lisa Disch, research assistants on this project, and with students in my graduate political geography seminar on Locational Conflict. I am grateful to the contributing authors and publishers for their kind permission to reprint these articles, and to Mary Picarella and Arlene Pashman for guiding this book through publication.

R.W.L.

About the Editor

Robert W. Lake, Associate Professor at the Rutgers University Center for Urban Policy Research, has a Ph.D. in urban geography from the University of Chicago. His research interests focus on the politics of geographical decision-making, and he is currently directing a three-year study on improving public participation in the siting of hazardous waste management facilities. He is the author of *Readings in Urban Analysis* and *The New Suburbanites: Race and Housing in the Suburbs,* and has published articles in the *Journal of the American Planning Association, Urban Geography,* the *American Journal of Sociology, Geographical Review,* and elsewhere.

Contributors

Nancy E. Abrams
Nicholas A. Ashford
Lawrence S. Bacow
Gail Bingham
D.J. Bjornstad
S.A. Carnes
Susan L. Carpenter
Stephen R. Cassella
Gerald W. Cormick
E.D. Copenhaver
Dennis W. Ducsik
Thomas N. Gladwin

Sam Gusman
Sheila Jasanoff
W.J.D. Kennedy
Howard Kunreuther
Joanne Linnerooth
S.M. Macgill
Douglas MacLean
James R. Milkey
David Morell
Dorothy Nelkin
Michael O'Hare
E. Peelle

Frank J. Popper
Joel R. Primack
J.H. Reed
Debra R. Sanderson
Peter M. Sandman
D.J. Snowball
E.J. Soderstrom
J.H. Sorensen
Lawrence E. Susskind
A. Dan Tarlock
James W. Vaupel

ROBERT W. LAKE

Introduction

"Once-rural Hillsborough mobilizes against hazardous waste proposal" (*Newark Star-Ledger,* March 2, 1986)

"Invitation withdrawn: South Amboy about-faces on hosting trash incinerator" (*Newark Star-Ledger,* March 11, 1986)

"Somerset moves to block toxic storage sites" (*Newark Star-Ledger,* March 19, 1986)

"Homes serving mentally disabled meet resistance" (*The New York Times,* March 24, 1986)

"Plans to build two waste plants upset many in poor section of North Carolina" (*The New York Times,* April 1, 1986)

Any one-month period in any region of the country contains multiple reports of local opposition to the siting of unwanted facilities. Nuclear power plants . . . high-rise developments . . . industrial plants . . . municipal landfills . . . toxic waste facilities . . . drug-treatment centers . . . shelters for the homeless . . . low-income housing . . . highways . . . prisons: from Westway to Love Canal to Three Mile Island, the siting of unwanted facilities generates locational conflict.

Locational conflict refers to the clash of interests generated by a site-selection decision. Locational conflict pits communities against corporations, local municipalities against state and federal agencies, environmentalists against industry, neighborhoods against regions—the broader society in need of a facility against the local community selected to site that facility. Local opposition often presents the greatest single hurdle to facility development, dwarfing technological problems and fiscal constraints.

The nature and intensity of conflict are markedly transformed when debate shifts from technological or fiscal matters to the geographical question of location. Conflicts over public/private-sector roles and responsibilities, agency jurisdiction, resource allocation, and facility design are seemingly resolved in the course of policy development only to resurface with a vengeance when the locational dimension is introduced in the course of selecting a site. Pinpointing a site brings all those prior decisions once again into question.

While technology, design, and capacity issues may be, and often are, raised by local opponents to disguise locational objections, the fact that these questions remain subject to debate suggests that seemingly objective, technical decisions contain far-reaching locational implications. What risks are imposed by the facility? How are risks distributed in space? Does the facility improve or aggravate the existing risk surface? Who pays and who benefits? Geography, often treated as an afterthought by facility designers and planners, is instead implicit and inescapable throughout the facility planning process. Locational conflict occurs when those geographical decisions implicit in facility planning and design are forced into the open and made subject to debate.

A Locational Conflict Perspective

This book examines the politics of conflict over the siting of major facilities. It aims to uncover the roots of locational conflict in order to facilitate its resolution. Individually and collectively, the readings assembled here suggest that resolution of locational conflict requires a considerable rethinking of commonly accepted practice in facility planning and site evaluation. Siting conflicts will not simply be accommodated through slight adjustments within a basically flawed process. Resolving locational conflict requires an explicit recognition of the siting implications that are too often left only implicit in facility planning and design.

As is usually the case, some disclaimers of intent are in order. This book is not a cookbook guide for avoiding or resolving conflict over a siting decision. It is not intended for either the siting official or the community activist embroiled in a siting controversy and searching for extrication. We suggest no simple techniques for the facility developer seeking public acceptance or the neighborhood association hoping to quash a facility proposal. Locational conflict is deeply rooted in the facility-development process and will not be expunged or avoided through treatment of surface symptoms or fine-tuning after the fact. (For practical approaches to facility siting, see Williams and Massa, 1983; Seley, 1983; and Mumphrey, Seley, and Wolpert, 1971). At the risk of cliché, there are no easy solutions.

If this book avoids facile answers, it also foregoes a comprehensive structural analysis of locational conflict as a political or a geographical process. Within the constraints of a policy-level discussion, we can offer little in the way of a theoretical unpacking of the causes of place-based conflict. Such an analysis requires a discourse on the fundamental sources of conflict (class, status, or party?); the nature of authority relations (public versus private, the state versus civil society, municipal/state/federal relations, etc.); and the complex interactions occurring between and among these various factors in the creation of a political geographical landscape (Cox and Johnston, 1982; Cox, 1978; Cox and Reynolds, 1974; Evans, 1976; Lake et al., forthcoming, 1987). Once again at the risk of cliché, analysis in these terms is well beyond the scope of this book.

The perspective informing this book interprets locational conflict as the inevitable emergence of unresolved political debates that have been submerged in earlier phases of policy development and facility planning. Locational conflict is public insistence that these unresolved debates be confronted and resolved, that basic assumptions be brought to light, and that policy (i.e., political) issues not be disguised as "objective" or technological questions.

POLITICS, PLANNING, AND TECHNOLOGY

Locational conflict arises from two false dichotomies that pervade the facility planning process. First, the potential for locational conflict arises from the tendency to separate facility planning and design decisions from the process of facility siting. Planners, developers, and officials too often engage in an elaborate facility planning process, and only then turn to the problem of deflecting or accommodating local opposition as a discrete policy objective.

The facility planning process contains within it multiple policy decisions regarding local impacts, the spatial distribution of risk, and similar inherent spatial implications that emerge and become manifest in a context of locational conflict. Attempting to separate facility planning from resolving locational conflict ignores the implicit spatial decisions already made in the former process.

This is not simply to argue the obvious point that different facilities have different locational requirements and spatial impacts. It is to say that the *pro-*

cess of facility planning and the *process* of resolving siting conflicts cannot be disaggregated. The seeds of locational conflict are sown in the earlier round of decision-making. Subsequent siting debates simply resurrect decisions that were avoided, ignored, or simply adopted without scrutiny in the course of facility planning. Locational conflict is a political process that demands that these policy decisions be debated and made explicit.

The second false dichotomy giving rise to locational conflict is the attempted separation of "objective" science from policy and politics. Facility planners and developers too often seek to portray planning and siting decisions as based on an objective, scientific process. The process instead is far from objective and value-free but rather contains innumerable political decisions and value judgments.

What standards are used for evaluating safety and health effects? How safe is safe enough? How much is safety worth? What priorities have been established among competing design, capacity, or siting criteria? What probabilities have been assigned to events? What assumptions underlie simulations or tests? How have results been interpreted? None of these questions is answerable in objective terms: all involve implicit policy decisions. Locational conflict is a statement that the public differs in its political and value positions from those implicit in the siting decision. Resolving locational conflict means addressing these political and policy issues openly and directly.

RESOLVING LOCATIONAL CONFLICT

It follows from this perspective on the politics of locational decisions that "resolving" conflict is by no means necessarily synonymous with deflecting, overpowering, or even accommodating opposition to siting. Resolution in many instances may well require the recognition that local objections are valid and that the facility and/or its location are ill-planned or poorly considered. We make no presumption here that a facility as planned, proposed, and sited is necessarily adequate and that opposition is simply a barrier to be overcome. The history of poorly planned facilities, of waste sites over aquifers and power plants near fault lines, is all too well developed. On many occasions, resolution of the conflict requires withdrawing the facility proposal.

By the same token, however, our perspective on conflict resolution also contains no presumption that all opposition is valid on its face or that opposition is successful only if it eliminates all grounds for complaint. Conflict is often highly self-serving, politically fortuitous, or motivated by concerns far removed from the issue at hand.

Ultimately, some measure of equity remains as the final arbiter of conflict resolution. While this is not the place for an extended discussion (see Kasperson, 1983, 1985; Kates and Kasperson, 1983), if equity is served, then remaining opposition is self-serving—if we have a sufficiently stringent standard of equity.

The equity problem in facility siting has become widely defined as a problem in the geographical correlation of costs and benefits: risks are concentrated in proximity to the site while benefits are dispersed throughout the state or region (National Governors' Association, 1981). A standard of equity sufficiently rigorous to distinguish "valid" opposition must move well beyond this relatively simplistic criterion. Geography is far more complex. Even if a perfect spatial correlation were achieved in the distribution of costs and benefits, all places are not equal. Some locations (or their residents) are better able than others to absorb costs, or are in greater need of benefits. A more stringent criterion of distributional equity may require a concentration of costs on those groups most able to bear them, regardless of the distribution of benefits (Kasperson, 1985).

As an example of where this logic might lead, this might require a state siting commission, for instance, to locate a hazardous waste incinerator in the most affluent community in the region, coupled with an extensive state-funded compensation package to buffer and disguise the facility in a park-like setting. The costs of such compensation might well substantially exceed the amount required by a less-affluent community willing to trade health risks for a smaller compensation package in order to get jobs and ratables. The excess costs are justified by equity considerations: the more affluent community is better able to absorb and offset the facility's negative externalities. The state commission should not automatically opt for the cheaper compensation package for the less-affluent community simply on the grounds of its lower cost; equity requires moving beyond fiscal efficiency in not burdening the poorer community less able to bear the added costs of hosting the facility.

This example, of course, offers just one possible scenario: many others could be suggested. The siting debate in the case just described pits efficiency against equity in a classic confrontation. *To opt for efficiency over equity by selecting the lower-cost alternative* (i.e., choosing the less-affluent community) *is a political decision that should be made publicly and explicitly in the context of the facility planning process.* As part of the public debate underlying the siting decision, explicit decisions are needed regarding the nature and distribution of equity, and relative priorities between equity and fiscal efficiency. Positions on these issues are implicit in all siting decisions, and emerge as locational conflict if the positions taken do not reflect a public consensus.

Issues

Facilities that are needed at a regional or national level but are objectionable to the people who live near them have been characterized by **Frank Popper** (Chapter 1) as LULUs: locally unwanted land uses. Popper cites the apparent political paradox arising from the increasingly effective opposition to these "pariah land uses." Safety, health, and environmental standards for facility design, construction, and operation have become stricter as environmentalists, community activists, and the public in general have become more aware of possible negative consequences of locally unwanted facilities. While facilities are becoming safer in response to public pressure, increased public awareness and intervention may have the unintended result that essential facilities are delayed or blocked entirely.

Popper examines some of the implications of "LULU blockage": Without hazardous waste treatment sites, wastes go to overburdened facilities or midnight dumpers; without new oil refineries, the U.S. remains dependent on foreign suppliers; without new low-cost housing, the poor are consigned to substandard housing or drift into homelessness; without new prisons, jails become more crowded or more criminals go free. Locational conflict is far from trivial. Its proliferation calls for political solutions to tough economic and social questions.

That locational conflict is indeed proliferating is documented by **Thomas Gladwin** (Chapter 2), based on data on 366 cases of conflict over industrial siting in the U.S. during the 1970s. (For a measure of the changing intensity and substantive focus of locational conflict from 1900 to 1980, see Cox, 1984.) According to Gladwin, controversy is shifting over time from existing to new facilities, from the Frostbelt to the Sunbelt, and from ecological or environmental concerns to a focus on social or quality-of-life issues. The terms of conflict seem more litigious in the U.S. than in Europe but less based on violent demonstration and protest, and outcomes, in the form of fines, compensation payments, shutdowns, and delays are proving increasingly costly to industry.

How, then, can this proliferation of conflict be explained, especially given the demonstrable costs of "LULU blockage" for society as a whole? In a provocative and tightly reasoned article, **Douglas MacLean** (Chapter 3) challenges us to think carefully about the nature of risks and the process of imposing risks on others in the context of centralized decisions about facility siting. His discussion explores the necessity but also the difficulty inherent in obtaining consent from those affected by centralized decisions. He weighs consent against other possible criteria, such as justice, rights, or efficiency, as workable standards for justifying centralized decisions regarding the distribution of risks.

Ultimately, MacLean arrives at the necessity of recognizing the *qualitative* element of risk in justifying siting decisions. Perceptions of and preferences for risks do not lend themselves to measurement through the convenient yardstick of rationality. Preferences are rarely transitive: a person may prefer A to B and B to C yet still prefer C to A—and have perfectly valid (to him or her) reasons for this preference structure. Most significantly for facility planners, there is little purpose in decrying the lack of rationality in risk perception. Attempting to counter moral or emotional concerns with scientific, technical, or "objective" reasoning is to run aground on the shoals separating fact and value.

The severity of this discrepancy is further increased by the circumstance that the scientific, technical dimension of risk measurement is itself shot through with value judgments and subjective decisions: about standards of measurement, tolerances for error, adequacy of data, setting probabilities, interpretation of results, and so on. None of these subjective elements can be resolved through yet more stringent scientific or technical analysis. They require hard policy choices, and they will continue to bedevil facility development, locational choice, and the imposition of risks until the policy decisions they embody are fully and directly resolved.

We can not expect to look to a scientific fix to resolve political debates over the imposition of risks. Technology can help reduce the incidence of overtly misguided siting decisions: e.g., the power plant built over a fault line. It cannot, ultimately, settle the questions of how safe is safe enough, how much is safety worth, or what risks people should be willing to accept. The limitations on technological solutions apply even more so in the case of conflict over human service (as opposed to technological) facilities: the half-way house, the homeless shelter, the drug treatment center. Here the issue is even more firmly ensconced in the emotional rather than the technological arena, and decisions are even more clearly political than scientific or technical.

This fundamental divide is addressed head-on by **Sheila Jasanoff** and **Dorothy Nelkin** (Chapter 4), in search of an institutional structure capable of bridging the "two cultures" of science and values. With the intrusion of science and technology into everyday life, judges and courts that traditionally deferred to experts on matters of substance are increasingly taking (or are being asked to take) positions on technical issues. In response, a "separatist" approach would have special institutions to deal with technological facts while the courts could maintain their traditional competence in the realm of law (Yellin, 1983). This approach assumes that it is possible to separate technical matters from political, ethical, and legal issues—that it is possible to identify certain questions as "scientific" and to assign them to appropriate, non-political institutions.

The difficulty, as Jasanoff and Nelkin assert, is that the boundary between fact and value, or science and policy, is entirely porous. Scientific and technological disputes have introduced non-scientific issues into the judicial arena. Problems of technical uncertainty, differential standards of proof, methodological incompatibility between science and policymaking, and the like complicate both the scientific and the judicial resolution of technical disputes.

For Jasanoff and Nelkin, however, proposals for judicial reform directed toward improving the "scientific literacy" of lawyers and judges evade the basic problem: "that the technical evidence presented for consideration is often inadequate, confused, and controversial." The problem is that "equipping the courts with scientific and technical support may . . . divert attention from the public responsibility for major policy decisions and encourage the conversion of moral and political questions into technical debates among experts." Political debates, in short, require political solutions. Political controversies concealed under a technological shroud eventually emerge as locational conflict.

Process

The question then becomes one of developing a *process* of facility planning and siting that explicitly confronts the political issues. This immediately raises the question of power: to establish the agenda, to frame the issues for debate, to participate in decision-making. Achieving *procedural* equity is of equal importance to attaining *distributional* equity (Kasperson, 1985). The institutional structure of the planning process determines "who decides."

Nancy Abrams and **Joel Primack** (Chapter 5) pursue the implications of the earlier chapters in outlining a process for policy development, termed "critical review and public assessment," *within* a traditional planning and siting procedure. Using the context of nuclear waste management, their approach is to (1) identify the major decisions that need to be made; (2) consider which of these decisions require public input; and (3) determine who constitutes the public (i.e., whose interests are at stake) at each critical decision point.

Decisions requiring public input are implicitly political decisions, i.e., decisions involving values, preferences, trade-offs, or some other subjective judgments. A process is needed that recognizes the political nature of these decisions and makes them explicit. In the case of a nuclear waste depository based on an extremely conservative design approach with very high performance standards, Abrams and Primack observe that "the price of such an approach could be enormous . . . but this is precisely the kind of decision that needs public input—from a public that understands the trade-offs. *This is not a scientific decision"* (emphasis added). The tendency by planners to play down the political debate is motivated at least in part by a desire for conflict avoidance and an unwillingness to espouse unpopular positions. Technological or scientific solutions are cleaner, less assailable, and contribute an aura of expertise. They are also illusory if sought as a substitute for political decisions.

The political *costs* of expanded public participation in decision-making are addressed head-on in **Dennis Ducsik's** (Chapter 6) discussion of power plant siting. Utilities studied by Ducsik oppose broader public participation, among other reasons, because they fear that premature disclosure will prejudice a project, opponents will be unwilling to compromise, laypersons are unqualified to participate in complex technological planning, and because expanded participation will still not eliminate all opposition. In short, the search for political solutions may simply open a "Pandora's box" of new and even more intractable problems. Ducsik proceeds to dismantle each of these arguments in turn. The biggest problem, he concludes, may be the tendency to evaluate public participation against too high a standard. "Open planning" is not a panacea. It is a necessary, if not necessarily a sufficient, condition of successful siting.

The theme of confronting the political dimensions of siting is continued in **David Morell's** essay (Chapter 7) on the politics of equity (see also Morell, 1984; Morell and Magorian, 1982). After listing the components of an effective siting strategy for hazardous waste facilities (i.e., balancing federal, state, and local authority; negotiating compensation with affected communities; achieving a regional distribution of facilities, etc.), Morell concludes: "While this may seem a set of impossible tasks, they should indeed be feasible if we soon begin to demand as much from our political system and our public policy makers as we are now beginning to demand from our engineers and scientists."

Some of the components of a political process for facility siting are sketched out by **A. Dan Tarlock** (Chapter 8) and by **Lawrence Bacow** and **James Milkey** (Chapter 9), again using the case of a toxic waste treatment facility. Within the context of an overall approach to siting, they examine the complex issue of state preemption of local land use controls, the political nature of siting criteria, the role of public participation, and the use of negotiation in siting decisions. Each of these components of a siting process raises thorny questions, and all have generated arguments on many sides of the issue. State preemption may streamline decision-making but it may also encourage local litigation and delay. Incentives and compensation may ease negotiations but some costs may simply not be compensable. Public participation may help assuage some opponents but others may be left out of the debate. The facility siting processes outlined in these chapters leave many of these issues unresolved, and other components of such a process could be identified. These chapters serve to suggest an overall framework and some of the components of an explicitly political siting strategy. More extended discussions of these and other issues follow in Part III of this volume.

Tools

INFORMATION

Perhaps the most important tool in both generating and resolving locational conflict is information. As **Michael O'Hare** (Chapter 10) suggests, what it is, who uses it, and how it is used can strongly influence the process of decision-making. Information is a public good with a marginal cost that varies by user and by the particular situation.

Several important policy implications derive from these (and related) characteristics of information, suggesting some significant alterations in current practice in the production and distribution of information used to guide locational decisions. O'Hare's analysis of information as a planning tool contrasts sharply with the usual "supply-side" approach of providing a massive environmental impact statement intended to cover all possible points of contention. Instead, O'Hare suggests focusing on the *demand side* to determine what information people need. Information should be packaged by user rather than by subject, since different users need different information. Most significantly, planners should forego the attempt to portray information as objective since "there is no report or study on a controversial matter *that will be used by the participants in debate as though it were objective*" (emphasis added).

His conclusion is to abandon "the supply-side impact statement process as a device to provide parties in conflict with the facts they need. . . . Instead of writing [an environmental impact] statement for use in debate, the debate [should be] structured as a negotiation and information exchange process organized to develop an impact statement." Rather than a starting-point "objective" report supplied to the participants in a debate, the impact statement should be considered the end-product of debate based on information generated by and for the participants. Information structured and used in this manner would radically alter the process of analysis, evaluation, and negotiation devoted to resolving locational conflict.

RISK ASSESSMENT

The contrasting uses of information are exemplified in the case of risk assessment as an evaluative tool. **S.M. Macgill** and **D.J. Snowball** (Chapter 11) discuss ten distinct "uses" of risk assessment, only three of which are technical in nature. Other uses of risk assessment are overtly political, intended to provide procedural validation, to add credibility to decisions and to the institutions that make them, or to justify the imposition of risk. Yet other uses of risk assessment identified by Macgill and Snowball are incidental to the issue at hand: the procedure can be used to legitimize existing positions, to create delay, or to substantiate demands for more far-reaching institutional reform.

Even overtly technical purposes of risk assessment—risk estimation (measuring the nature, probability, and consequences of risk); risk reduction (proposing planning and design modifications to reduce risk); and risk comprehension (developing and understanding of sources of risk)—are far from objective. **Howard Kunreuther, Joanne Linnerooth,** and **James Vaupel** (Chapter 12) use the term "trans-science" to indicate the subjective judgments incorporated in statistical estimates of the magnitude, probability, and consequences of risk.

The subjectivity of technical analysis has, of course, been widely noted. The difficulty, as Macgill and Snowball contend, is not so much the likelihood of bias in technical analyses but rather that the bias will be overlooked. Kunreuther and his associates point to the strong appeal of risk analysis—the comfort provided by precise numerical results—for policy-makers seeking a rational and scientific approach to public decision-making. That the public often rejects the results of such analyses is due, in **Frank Popper's** view (Chapter 13), to an insistence that the assumptions inherent in the process cannot easily be reduced to quantifiable measures. As Macgill and Snowball conclude: "The rapid development of quantitative risk assessment techniques has outpaced the evolution of the political and institutional framework wherein such analyses are examined and evaluated." Risk assessment is neither a substitute for political decision-making nor should it be used to manipulate the political process. It is a tool for gathering information that can be integrated into a decision process based on equity.

NEGOTIATION

Based on the frequency of its use and the size of its literature, negotiation has come of age as a dispute resolution technique (Bacow and Wheeler, 1983; Bingham, 1986; McCarthy and Shorett, 1984; Meeks, 1985; Susskind, 1980). Negotiation (and its various forms of mediation and arbitration) provides an institutional structure for bringing the full range of political interests into the debate. A negotiation framework provides an arena for the airing of the conflicting political positions that are inherent in any facility planning and siting decision. While it certainly carries no assurance of resolving extant conflicts, a negotiation process provides a means through which parties can have a voice, interests can be represented, assumptions can be probed, and conflicts can be addressed. Depending on the manner of its implementation, a negotiation approach represents a statement of how power is to be distributed in locational decision-making.

In Chapter 14, **Susan Carpenter** and **W.J.D. Kennedy** summarize a set of negotiation procedures based on their own experience in environmental conflict resolution. These procedures include identifying conflicting parties, discerning the relationships among the parties involved, discussing the substance of the issue, adopting an approach to conflict management, and implementing a resolution strategy.

Gerald Cormick (Chapter 15) further clarifies the various types of negotiation processes and discusses the prerequisites for successful mediation. He warns, however, against exaggerated claims and expectations, and exposes numerous misperceptions and misunderstandings regarding environmental mediation. Mediators do not resolve differences: they help parties reach accommodations that enable coexistence despite differences. Mediators do not avoid conflict: they help to settle conflict that has arisen. Mediation is often adversarial, and it is not simply or necessarily an alternative to litigation. As suggested above, mediation (or negotiation) provides a structure through which interested parties can participate in decision-making.

The role of parties in negotiation, and of negotiation in decision-making, depends on how the political process has been structured. Based on analysis of 162 cases of environmental mediation over more than a decade, **Gail Bingham** (Chapter 16) identifies conditions for successful resolution of environmental disputes. More important than the number of parties involved, the issues in dispute, or the presence of a deadline, the power and authority of the parties to the negotiation are primary determinants of successful conflict resolution through negotiation.

As with other tools of policy-making, negotiation is a medium for political empowerment, not a substitute. In a provocative essay, **Peter Sandman** (Chapter 17) outlines a negotiation strategy that recognizes the community's *de facto* veto power over facility siting. He offers nine maxims for negotiations that acknowledge the community's power and that allow the community to enter discussions without surrendering its power. The issue is not to structure negotiation in a manner that preempts community power; it is to recognize community power in the structure of negotiations. Ways of identifying all "stakeholders" to be represented in the negotiations are suggested by **Sam Gusman** (Chapter 18).

COMPENSATION, INCENTIVES, COST/BENEFIT ANALYSIS

One possible outcome of a negotiation process might be identification of incentives or compensation for the local community for accepting a facility. **S.A. Carnes** et al. (Chapter 19) discuss the possible use of incentives in the case of nuclear waste facility siting. Incentives may take three distinct forms: mitigation of anticipated adverse impacts; compensation for actual damages; and/or rewards for assuming societal risk. To be successful, an incentives approach must demonstrate a certainty of implementation and a consistency of policy, must be sufficiently comprehensive, and must be easy to administer.

Michael O'Hare and **Debra Sanderson** (Chapter 20) focus specifically on compensation as one form of incentive strategy. Their analysis highlights an important element of compensation as a means for equalizing the true distribution of costs and benefits associated with a facility:

> The decision to mine coal or convert it into electricity involves a comparison of the costs involved (bulldozers, labor, insurance, land acquisition, etc.) with the benefits (sales, for the most part). If some of the costs are ignored, too much coal will be mined or burned—it will appear "cheaper" than it really is. Thus efficiency requires that decision makers consider the costs of their development including the cost of inputs like small-town amenity which they consume in the production process. The obvious way to ensure that these costs are considered is to make energy developers pay for them, and then pass them on to consumers in the form of higher prices.

In addition to easing community acceptance of a facility, compensation thus helps to force an explicit recognition of facility costs. These costs may well lie hidden in the absence of a compensation approach, but more often it is precisely these hidden costs that generate locational conflict.

Compensation provides a means by which costs and benefits of a facility can be assessed and distributed within the political arena. It represents an answer to those implicit questions underlying every facility proposal: How much is safety worth? Who pays and who benefits? As the inevitable conflict demonstrates, these questions cannot simply be ignored, nor can their answers be imposed through policy preemption by higher levels of government (**Lawrence Susskind** and **Stephen Cassella,** Chapter 21). Costs and benefits, ultimately, fall upon someone and, as **Nicholas Ashford** (Chapter 22) concludes, are political and not simply monetary units of measure. Resolving locational conflict requires confronting that political calculus. The readings that follow provide some of the requisite tools.

References

Bacow, Lawrence and Michael Wheeler. 1983. *Environmental Dispute Resolution* (New York: Plenum Press).

Bingham, Gail. 1986. *Resolving Environmental Disputes: A Decade of Experience* (Washington, DC: The Conservation Foundation).

Cox, Kevin R. 1984. "Social change, turf politics, and concepts of turf politics," in Andrew Kirby, Paul Knox, and Steven Pinch (eds.), *Public Service Provision and Urban Development* (New York: St. Martin's Press), pp. 283-315.

Cox, Kevin R. (ed.). 1978. *Urbanization and Conflict in Market Societies* (Chicago: Maaroufa Press).

Cox, Kevin R. and R.J. Johnston (eds.). 1982. *Conflict, Politics, and the Urban Scene* (New York: St. Martin's Press).

Cox, Kevin R. and David R. Reynolds. 1974. "Locational approaches to power and conflict," in Kevin R. Cox, David R. Reynolds, and Stein Rokkan (eds.), *Locational Approaches to Power and Conflict* (New York: John Wiley), pp. 19-41.

Evans, D.M. 1976. "A critique of locational conflict," Discussion Paper No. 20, Department of Geography, University of Toronto.

Kasperson, Roger E. 1985. "Rethinking the siting of hazardous waste facilities," Center for Technology, Environment, and Development (CENTED), Clark University, Worcester, MA.

Kasperson, Roger E. (ed.). 1983. *Equity Issues in Radioactive Waste Management* (Cambridge, MA: Oelgeschlager, Gunn and Hain).

Kates, Robert W. and Jeanne X. Kasperson. 1983. "Comparative risk analysis of technological hazards (A Review)," *Proceedings of the National Academy of Science,* vol. 80 (November) 7027-7038.

Lake, Robert W., Ursula Bauer, Yvonne Chilik, and Lisa Disch. Forthcoming, 1987. *Paths to Participation: The Public Role in Hazardous Waste Management* (New Brunswick, NJ: Rutgers University Center for Urban Policy Research).

McCarthy, Jane E. and Alice Shorett. 1984. *Negotiating Settlements: A Guide to Environmental Mediation* (New York: American Arbitration Association).

Meeks, Gordon Jr. 1985. *Managing Environmental and Public Policy Conflicts: A Legislator's Guide* (Washington, DC: National Conference of State Legislatures).

Morell, David. 1984. "The siting of hazardous waste facilities in California," *Public Affairs Report,* vol. 25 (October) 1-10.

Morell, David and Christopher Magorian. 1982. *Siting Hazardous Waste Facilities: Local Opposition and the Myth of Preemption* (Cambridge, MA: Ballinger).

Mumphrey, Anthony J., Jr., John E. Seley, and Julian Wolpert. 1971. "A decision model of locating controversial facilities," *Journal of the American Institute of Planners,* vol. 33 (November) 397-402.

National Governors' Association. 1981. "Siting hazardous waste facilities," *The Environmental Professional,* vol. 3, 133-142.

Seley, John E. 1983. *The Politics of Public-Facility Planning* (Lexington, MA: D.C. Heath).

Susskind, Lawrence and Alan Weinstein. 1980. "Towards a theory of environmental dispute resolution," *Boston College Environmental Affairs Law Review,* vol. 9, 311-357.

Williams, Edward A. and Alison K. Massa. 1983. *Siting of Major Facilities: A Practical Approach* (New York: McGraw-Hill).

Yellin, Joel. 1983. "Science, technology, and administrative government," *Yale Law Journal,* vol. 92, 1300-1333.

Part I.   Issues

FRANK J. POPPER

1 *The Environmentalist and the LULU*

The United States faces a large, distinct, and rapidly growing class of development projects. They may be regionally or nationally needed or wanted, but are considered objectionable by many people who live near them. Examples of such pariah land uses include highways, hazardous waste facilities, power plants, airports, prisons, garbage disposal sites, low-income housing, and strip mines. The projects create political tension, for as a society we want them, but as individuals—and often as communities—we do not want them close to us. They are locally unwanted land uses, or LULUs.

Most Americans daily encounter LULUs large and small, existing and proposed, high- and low-tech. The LULU has become the central, shared, sometimes hidden subject of a great deal of city planning, law, economics, and political science, as well as of practical politics, government, and corporate administration. Big new kinds of LULUs loom, such as nuclear waste disposal sites, innovative high-tech factories, the MX missile system, and the many additional telecommunications towers necessitated by the AT&T breakup. LULUs strain a sense of fairness, since they gravitate to disadvantaged areas: the poor, minority, sparsely populated, or politically underrepresented localities that cannot fight them off and become worse places to live after they arrive. LULUs expose clear deficiencies in the nation's present devices for planning and regulating them.

From *Environment*, Vol. 27, pp. 7–11, 37–40 (March 1985). Reprinted by permission of the Helen Dwight Reid Educational Foundation. Published by Heldrof Publications, 4000 Albemarle Street, N.W., Washington, D.C. 20016. Copyright © 1985.

1

LULUs pose special problems for environmentalists. They are much of the reason the nation has environmentalists—and why it needs them. LULUs provide environmentalists with politically productive opportunities to rectify the imbalance between the local costs and regional benefits—chances to reduce what an economist would call the negative externalities of LULUs—and so benefit the public. On the other hand, LULUs place environmentalists in what seems to be their characteristic public stance of resisting proposed or operating LULUs, of defending the neighbors who object to the LULUs against the larger group of consumers who benefit from their output. This approach is often politically sensible for environmentalists, but not always. It allies them with groups that are inherently minorities, makes them look like selfish, inflexible obstructionists, and invariably puts them in an antidevelopment position—not the best of strategies in times or places that have weak economies, or even strong ones.

The temptation for environmentalists to resist LULUs almost instinctively is understandable, since such resistance has serious popular support. Over the last two decades, the American public has become more sensitive to the environmental consequences of LULUs, less willing to see them located or operated indiscriminately, and more demanding of stronger public control over them. But the result, often unintended by environmentalists or the public, has been that essential LULUs have been thwarted, stalemated, or delayed for years; built too small, too late, or in insufficient numbers; made too difficult, controversial, or expensive to manage—all situations that eventually foster antienvironmentalist sentiment among political moderates and conservatives. Environmentalists have simply gone too far in blocking LULUs. I would like to elaborate on the concept of LULUs, analyze some typical environmentalist defenses against them, explore the phenomenon of LULU blockage, and suggest some environmentalist solutions to it.

The LULU Concept

At the heart of every LULU lie large negative externalities. A LULU may be noisy (airports), dangerous (hazardous waste facilities), ugly (power plants), smelly (many factories), or polluting (all of the above). It may offend its neighbors because of such intrinsic features as its technology or occupants. Or it may offend because of its consequences—increased traffic, industrial by-products, or the problems its mismanagement could create.

LULUs impose costs on their neighbors, or are thought to do so. They often lower property values, especially residential ones. A big project—say, a power plant, a dam, or a military base—may be unpleasant even (or especially) during construction, particularly if the phase is lengthy and brings in large numbers of construction workers. Moreover, the many areas where land uses are primarily LULUs—slums; industrial neighborhoods; energy boom-towns; skid rows; red-light districts; some strip-development settings; and, on occasion, entire downtowns—are considered undesirable places. LULUs always threaten their surroundings by inflicting, or promising to inflict, nega-tive externalities on them.

In a trivial sense every land use is a LULU, in that it will be resisted because it is a change or because it is likely to do some kind of local harm to someone. An entirely praiseworthy residential development still inflicts what an economist would call an opportunity cost on the developer who did not get to build it, the neighboring local government that does not get to tax it, the environmentalist who concedes its merits but would rather have seen its land preserved, and the person who does not like the company that built it. Yet a true LULU is different: it always engenders a considerable, genuine local opposition.

Any existing or proposed LULU naturally has some local supporters—for example, the developers who build or the residents who live in low-income housing, or the actual or potential employees of a strip mine, or perhaps the local government that taxes the LULU. But the local opposition it provokes is environmental in the broadest sense because it focuses on the effects the LULU has on its surroundings. The development is a LULU when, although the opposition does not necessarily form a majority, it constitutes a substantial body of local opinion and cares enough to form an organization ("Apple Valley Coalition Against Interstate Highway 89").

Environmentalists and LULUs

Environmentalists have the social function, perhaps even the historic mis-sion, first to reveal the negative externalities of a project, and then to fight to reduce them. For example, much of environmental and land-use politics between the middle 1960s and the 1970s—a period favorable for environmentalists—amounted to an often successful society-wide attempt to find and diminish the negative environmental externalities of LULUs.

Reform laws—mostly at the state and federal levels of government, but also at local levels—legitimized negative externalities that had previously been under dispute, such as those of strip mines and all forms of power plants. The laws confirmed new negative externalities, such as those of nuclear power plants and hazardous waste facilities. They considered, essentially for the first time, externalities that crossed local boundaries, such as air and water pollu-tion. They invented new ways to limit the negative externalities of LULUs—for instance, environmental impact statements, designations of lands that were environmentally critical, and a wide variety of air- and water-pollution restric-tions. They created new centralized bodies—such as the Environmental Protection Agency (EPA) and the Council on Environmental Quality (CEQ) at the federal level and their counterparts at the state one—whose functions were to measure, research, and regulate the negative externalities. They gave legal standing to environmental groups to dispute the bodies' findings about these externalities through new citizen participation procedures.

But these measures produced a counterreaction, especially from the pro-development Reaganesque groups that had always sought to limit the exploration and reduction of negative environmental externalities. The thrust of environmental politics since the late 1970s—a relatively unfavorable period for environmentalists—has been to narrow the scope of the examined negative externalities by reversing and undoing the previous measures. For example, the Reagan administration has, for the most part, ignored some emerging externalities of LULUs (acid rain, groundwater contamination, ozone depletion), deemphasized previously accepted externalities, decentralized regulation to nonfederal levels of government, downgraded federal regulatory bodies (including the EPA and CEQ), and sometimes deregulated altogether. These 1980s measures convey a chilling message to environmentalists, as well as to other large portions of the public that oppose LULUs and their negative externalities: the United States now intends to build the LULUs despite the opposition and in the face of negative impacts.

At the personal level, inclinations about LULUs vary considerably. For the superstitious, cemeteries and funeral homes may be objectionable. Many residents of rapidly growing suburbs may dislike the few remaining local farms, with their pesticides, smells, escaping livestock, and slow-moving tractors on the roads. Conversely, environmentalists generally favor farmland preservation, growth control, and open space, and look askance at many commercial developments.

Additionally, one person's LULU is often another's livelihood. Environmentalists, not steelworkers or steamfitters, most object to living near factories. The employees of nuclear power plants, not necessarily their stockholders (who can always sell their holdings), most resist attempts to shut them down.

Rating Preferences

Market forces affect preferences for LULUs. "Manufactured housing"—trailer, modular, precut, or panelized housing that is built in a factory as distinct from conventional "stick-built" housing constructed on a site—was long a classic American LULU. Localities have historically shunned trailer parks. But when soaring prices and interest rates for conventional housing sent the industry into decline, manufactured housing began to thrive; by

1982 it had a 36 percent share of the nation's entire market for new homes, and it was no longer ugly, flimsy, unsafe, or considered tacky-cheap. In most parts of the country, a two-section, energy-efficient manufactured home with three bedrooms, two bathrooms, a garage, and 1,200 square feet of floor space sold for under $40,000, including land, and was hard to distinguish—inside or outside—from a standard single-family detached house. Manufactured housing was fast becoming recognized as permanent rather than transient shelter.

Many states and localities, particularly those with acute shortages of affordable housing, moved to revoke or loosen land-use laws that discriminated against trailers, trailer parks, and manufactured housing generally. In 1983 the Department of Housing and Urban Development began to offer to most people purchasing manufactured housing the same long-term mortgage insurance it offered to those buying other housing. Manufactured housing was not yet universally desirable, but in many places it was no longer a LULU. At the same time and for the same reasons, many homeowner suburbs began to reconsider their traditionally hostile attitudes toward other suburban housing LULUs, such as apartments and townhouses.

There seems to be a national consensus about which LULUs are least wanted. A 1980 poll, sponsored by CEQ and other federal agencies and conducted by Resources for the Future, found that only 10 to 12 percent of the population would voluntarily live a mile or less from a nuclear power plant or hazardous waste facility. By contrast, about 25 percent were willing to live at the same distance from a coal-fired power plant or large factory, and nearly 60 percent would live that close to a ten-story office building.

Although the poll assured respondents that the nuclear power plant and hazardous waste facility "would be built and operated according to government environmental and safety regulations" so that "disposal could be done safely and the site regularly inspected for possible problems," the facilities reached majority acceptance (51 percent) only when their distance from respondents passed 100 miles. Moreover, 5 and 10 percent, respectively, of the respondents stated that they would not voluntarily live at any distance from such facilities. Nuclear power plants and hazardous waste sites were utterly unacceptable to them.

Environmental Defenses

Environmentalists successfully use several lines of political resistance against proposed or operating LULUs. These defenses constitute arguments against particular LULUs or their negative externalities. Most LULU controversies involve several of the defenses, and some involve all of them.

The LULU is unneeded.   This is the most aggressive, absolute defense. It attacks the legitimacy of the LULU and denies its very right to exist on moral or economic grounds. It is used as the primary basis of opposition to nuclear power and synthetic fuel plants, the MX missile system, and many fossil-fuel power plants and strip-mine, dam, and highway projects. In its extreme form, the defense may lead to attempts to close down existing LULUs, as in the case of California environmentalists' partially successful attempts to decommission currently operating nuclear power plants and in New York citizens' completely successful efforts to close the Love Canal toxic waste dump.

This defense is politically risky for environmentalists, since its assertiveness or dogmatism may alienate potential supporters. It is also difficult to use against some proposed LULUs (for example, low-income housing projects or hazardous waste facilities) or against many that are already operating. Used cautiously, however, the defense can be highly effective.

The LULU doesn't belong in this region.   This defense concedes the need for the LULU but attempts to encourage its location in some other place more willing to accept it. In effect, the defense strives to export the LULU. The export is sometimes passive; much of the country is spared inconvenience, without taking deliberate measures, if a good deal of large-scale energy or mineral development happens to take place on western public lands, in Alaska, or on the Outer Continental Shelf—a long way from big cities or settled rural areas. More often, the export is active, as when polluting factories are forced to locate in poorer parts of the country or abroad, or when toxic substances, nuclear wastes, or sludge are shipped elsewhere rather than put into local repositories. LULUs may also be actively exported by prohibiting them within a given area, as when wealthy suburbs enact exclusionary zoning ordinances to keep out low-income housing, apartments, trailers, high-rises, or factories that then end up in poorer localities.

This defense seeks to capture the benefits of the LULU and evade its costs. Like "The LULU is unneeded," the defense cannot be applied to some proposed LULUs or to most existing ones. Yet it poses fewer regional political problems (much of the region and nearly all of the locality can unite around sending the LULU elsewhere) and has an undeniable escapist charm.

On the other hand, the defense is not always wise, practical, or ethical to pursue, for it does not limit negative externalities so much as transfer them. Indeed, it may increase them; the people of the regions to which the LULUs are exported inevitably suffer. And the people of the regions that export them do not benefit over the long run if they utterly lack factories, affordable housing, hazardous waste facilities, or other useful LULUs. Thus the defense has a potential for irresponsible, often self-defeating use.

The LULU is in the wrong place.   This defense accepts both the region's need for the LULU and for its placement somewhere in the region, but objects to a specific location. The LULU may be in or too near an environmentally critical area—say, a wetland. It may be too near other LULUs; for example, New Jersey's legendary reputation as a producer of LULUs and as an environmental black hole stems from the fact that most of the state's LULUs cluster within 10 miles of the central and northern sections of the New Jersey Turnpike (itself a LULU), around the chemical-processing towns (such as Elizabeth) on the Hudson River, or in Newark, Camden, or Trenton, rather than in the other nine-tenths of New Jersey. Alternatively, the LULU may be too distant from other LULUs; it may be objectionable because it is not in an area explicitly ratified (say, through zoning) or tacitly accepted as suitable, for instance, for industrial facilities, strip development, low-income housing, sex businesses, or halfway houses.

The LULU's siting [or operating] procedures are poor.   This defense aims at finding administrative flaws in the LULU's development or regulation that can be used to discredit it. Planning for it may be inadequate. The measures for consulting or informing the public may be nonexistent, perfunctory, tilted against the LULU's neighbors, or not sensitive to all of its negative externalities. The environmental impact statement (EIS) or similar required documents may be deficient or reveal good reasons to alter the LULU, or perhaps not to build it all. The documents may, for instance, suggest the impracticability of making the LULU subject to strong environmental standards. Or they may suggest that an emergency at the LULU, such as a toxic waste spill, is so likely or could be so serious that neither its developer nor the government could deal with it. The opposition can therefore always press for plausible new studies or regulatory reviews. This defense, which seeks to trap the LULU's developer in a combination of paperwork details, research uncertainties, and inchoate public fears, has worked well for environmentalists.

The LULU's effects will be harmful.   This defense, which nearly always appears in LULU controversies, treats the LULU's existence and location as givens, but tries to make adjustments in its operation. Stringent environmental, land-use, and public health regulations, for instance, may reduce the LULU's negative externalities. The locality may also insist on nonenvironmental forms of mitigation: the developers might be required to donate land for school buildings, generate their own electric power, make a beach on the site more accessible to the public, or pay high taxes that amount to a subsidy for the locality. Such mitigation measures can diminish the negative externalities of a LULU by ensuring that most of them are borne by those who receive the most benefits from it, usually because they develop or own it. (These parties may still tack on the costs of lowering the LULU's negative externalities to the consumers of its output: its customers.)

The main drawback of this defense is that the adjustment measures may not deliver on their promise—public acceptance is not certain, the developer may not carry out the measures in good faith, and these measures may not work in practice. If these obstacles can be overcome, this defense can be the one politically most attractive for local environmentalists, for it is the one least transigent toward the LULU. It allows all parties—both those in favor of the LULU and those opposed—to appear reasonable while getting much of what they want.

LULU Blockage

Public skepticism about LULUs and opinions such as those expressed in the CEQ poll have been intensified—indeed, justified—by such events as those at Three Mile Island, Love Canal, Bhopal, and by many smaller-scale environmental incidents. Partly for this reason, environmentalist defenses against LULUs have succeeded far better than most environmentalists would have expected 15 years age.

As a result of this success, many LULUs have been stymied. Numerous projects, some considered essential, are increasingly difficult and costly to site or operate. No new free-standing hazardous waste facility has been sited during the last five years. No new nuclear power plant has been undertaken since 1978, a year before the Three Mile Island accident, and every plant undertaken between 1974 and 1978 has been abandoned, no matter what its state of completion. No large metropolitan airport has been sited since the Dallas-Fort Worth facility was built in the early 1960s. The lack of locations for new prisons has caused such overcrowding in many existing jails that some cities (New York, Chicago, Pittsburgh, Grand Rapids) have had to release convicted criminals.

At least two dozen attempts since 1970 to site a new East Coast oil refinery anywhere from Maine to Georgia have failed. It is uncertain whether the one successful siting, in Hampton Roads, Virginia, will ever be built, for it is still in litigation. The fate of the MX missile system is unclear more than a decade after its first serious versions were proposed. Most big cities have not begun a major low-income housing, mass transit, or highway project in more than a decade. The completion of the final one-twentieth of the federal interstate highway system promises to be as difficult and expensive as the rest combined.

The 1980 Low-Level Waste Policy Act gave the states six years to negotiate compacts among themselves that Congress would approve to site multistate repositories for low-level—that is, less dangerous—commercial nuclear waste, but no compacts have yet come close to being approved. (For a more in-depth discussion of this topic, see Irvin L. White and John P. Spath, "Low-Level Radioactive Waste Disposal: How Are States Setting Their Sites," *Environment*, November 1984, p. 16.) The Department of Energy will be at least five years late in meeting the congressionally mandated 1985 deadline for selecting a site for the first permanent national repository for the more dangerous class of nuclear waste. Nevada, Texas, and Washington, the three leading candidates for the site, are all resisting it strenuously.

Even relatively harmless LULUs have been blocked. In many states— Virginia, for example—it is not possible to locate a new marina. The theme-park industry no longer attempts to build large amusement parks and is convinced that neither Disneyland in California nor Disneyworld in Florida could be built today. It would be impossible for a contemporary Gutzon Borglum to carve the four gigantic presidential faces into Mount Rushmore, for the mountain is sacred to the Sioux and today's laws—for instance, the 1978 American Indian Religious Freedom Act—protect such lands.

Environmental laws and environmentalist protests are not, of course, the only factors that have frustrated LULUs. In many cases additional factors play a part: recessions, inflation, straitened city or federal treasuries, high interest rates, regulatory inertia, fear of the new, exhaustion of easy or safe sites (e.g. the East Coast oil refinery), engineering uncertainties (the national nuclear waste repository), political uncertainties (the MX missile system, the multistate nuclear waste repository), labor shortages in the skilled trades that build and operate the LULU (nuclear power plants), projected declines in per capita demand for the LULU's output (all power plants), and excess capacity from existing LULUs (theme parks, power plants, and the East Coast oil refinery). These factors often combine with environmentalist objections to reinforce LULU blockage and turn more uses of land into LULUs. As a result, the number of locally *wanted* land uses is dropping fast, because more and more land uses are enmeshed in arguments as to their economic feasibility and environmental desirability. Perhaps the only land uses now universally acceptable to their neighbors are research parks and open space, not live options in most situations.

Effects of Blockage

Widespread LULU blockage has already had far-reaching consequences. It has helped to almost kill the American nuclear industry—a socially desirable outcome all around, since the economic arguments against nuclear power (for instance, the amount of time the plants are not in operation) are even more impressive than the environmental ones. Other cases of LULU blockage, however, present quite different problems. If new hazardous waste facilities cannot be sited, the waste must still go somewhere—to existing overburdened facilities, or often to organized-crime fronts, to midnight dumpers, or to the kind of company that has a truck driver open the stopcock and dump waste along 200 miles of rural roads (a real case in North Carolina).

Similarly, if oil refineries cannot be built, even in such desperate periods as from 1973 to 1981, the United States will remain dangerously dependent on foreign suppliers. If low-income housing cannot be constructed, the poor will have to live in even worse places; and as the problem of homelessness mounts, larger numbers of the poor will end up living nowhere at all. If sites for jails cannot be found, more convicted criminals will go free; or if they do not, the jails will become still more crowded and hellish and less rehabilitative. Alternatively, judges may sentence with excessive leniency.

If repositories for nuclear waste cannot be sited, the country will run out of interim storage places in a few years. If many kinds of big industrial, commercial, transportation, or even residential projects cannot be sited, the overall business climate may suffer.

In some cases, society's response has been simply to vacillate to gain time, often resulting in the worst of both alternatives, as is now the situation with many unfinished nuclear power plants. Most of the plants seem simultaneously too costly (and dangerous) to complete, too costly to dismantle, and too costly to do without. But the losses have been and will continue to be staggering. In just the first weeks of January 1984, the Marble Hill plant in Indiana was abandoned after expenditures of $2.5 billion, the Byron plant in Illinois ($3.4 billion) was denied permission to operate by the Nuclear Regulatory Commission, the Shoreham plant on Long Island ($4 billion) emerged as a candidate for cancellation, and the Limerick facility in Pennsylvania ($6.5 billion) was shut down.

The losses are sunk costs: they translate into higher charges and worse service for electricity consumers, lower dividends for investors, layoffs and curtailed opportunities for utility employees, weakened economies in towns near the plants, and possible utility bankruptcies and state or federal bailouts. The losses also produce higher interest rates, higher consumer charges, and lower dividends for utilities that continue to rely on nuclear power.

In hindsight, the plants probably should never have been undertaken; yet, to be fair, they have primarily been the victims of the long lead times needed to plan and build them. Unlike the case for most other blocked LULUs, there is no current alternative use for these great beached whales with cooling towers or for their sites. There can be no greater monument to economic schizophrenia, failed planning, and an ambiguous connection to nature than a permanently half-completed nuclear power plant.

Environmentalist Solutions

Environmentalists—and developers and American society at large—can do better. In particular, environmentalists, whose goals continue to have strong popular support in public opinion polls, need not conceive of their role as being forever in opposition to all LULUs. This stance promotes LULU blockage. It allows environmentalists' opponents to picture them as fearful pessimists largely responsible for a creeping paralysis in the nation's will to grow, to influence its future, and to achieve its legitimate developmental goals—a standard portrayed in, for instance, neoconservative rhetoric. The environmentalist posture also serves to encourage the Reagan administration's "build it anyway" attitudes, which are far more likely to lead to national disaster than is LULU blockage.

What environmentalists most need to do is to pull back from their hard-line position against LULUs. Instead of resisting every instance of LULUs, they should try to find (and encourage their opponents to find) more cases of middle ground—practical working relationships between valid national and regional goals and valid local ones, ways to mesh environmental and economic imperatives.

LULUs and their negative externalities create the seemingly impossible problem of having in our midst large numbers of projects that no one wants nearby. Yet the United States routinely and daily resolves the problem through familiar devices—our rituals to purify tainted taboo LULU objects, to draw the curse from structures and sites that would otherwise be in several senses polluting. Environmentalists support these devices and should work to make them deal more precisely with LULUs and their negative externalities.

One such device is the market. Occasionally, as with manufactured housing, the market makes quick adjustments that relieve LULU blockage. More often, the adjustments are long term; blockage of power plants is becoming less prevalent as energy demand slackens and fewer plants are proposed. Blockage of nuclear power plants has almost disappeared, since in recent years the nuclear industry has proposed no new ones and has begun to phase down some existing ones. Blockage of hazardous waste facilities will eventually become less prevalent as manufacturers find it in their interest to develop processes that create less waste. Blockage of landfills may diminish as more become resource recovery centers that produce energy.

Another device is to shrink the LULU, so that it becomes less objectionable and can be dispersed with some equality across a region's localities. For instance, small suburban airparks frequently preclude the need for a large new metropolitan airport, in the same way that scattered-site, low-income housing may supplant the large project, and small, decentralized soft-energy facilities replace large, centralized hard ones. In some lucky cases, alternatives can be found that do not need fixed land sites: the MX missiles can be put in bombers and submarines, mobile incinerators can be operated for hazardous waste, and energy conservation strategies can reduce the need for new power plants. As a last resort, the courts may have to step in to site LULUs that are blocked, as they are now beginning to do with jails, highways, and low-income housing.

These are piecemeal devices aimed at particular kinds of LULUs, but a broader device—planning—is needed to treat generically the large LULU as a distinct set of land uses requiring characteristic treatment. Local land-use plans, regulations, and ordinances could have sections devoted to the LULU, showing where specific kinds might and might not be located, and explaining why. Higher levels of government could do the same. For example, it was not until 1980, seven years after the first OPEC embargo, that the federal government published maps showing which East Coast sites were most suitable, from an environmental point of view, as locations for new oil refineries and other energy facilities. No such maps exist for other parts of the country or types of facilities, but they are needed.

There is also a necessity for stronger state and regional land-use planning bodies to regulate the siting of large LULUs with impacts that spill in complicated ways across local boundaries, thus placing the most important externalities of the LULU beyond the political purview and technical abilities of often parochial, underequipped local zoning boards. Models of higher level agencies that effectively regulate most kinds of big LULUs (and in some cases have done so for a decade) appear in Oregon, Vermont, Hawaii, New York's Adirondack Park, New Jersey's Pinelands, and in the coastal zone management programs of California, Massachusetts, North Carolina, and Wisconsin. These agencies, created during the 1960s and 1970s, the high tide of American environmentalism, are currently under heavy attack by conservatives, but there are convincing economic justifications (not just environmental ones) for their continuation. A helpful way to strengthen their initiatives would be to allow them to make "fair-share" allocations across all localities in their jurisdiction, either for one kind of LULU or by balancing off (even explicitly trading) different kinds against each other.

At the same time, environmentalists ought to work to streamline and simplify many regulatory procedures and requirements that have become too onerous or bureaucratic and therefore susceptible to abuse. Some citizen-participation procedures, for instance, amount to invitations to block LULUs. The requirements of some localities for environmental impact statements separate from zoning reviews seem unnecessary, particularly in situations in which state (and often federal) EISs are also needed.

There are many other opportunities to revise regulation productively, to make it easier to build vital LULUs without risking blockage or ecological catastrophe. LULUs challenge environmentalists to find ways to speed the siting of these projects and improve their operations, while at the same time allowing for the public's long-standing environmental concerns and the pro-development side's new economic ones.

THOMAS N. GLADWIN

2 Patterns of Environmental Conflict Over Industrial Facilities in the United States, 1970-78

Alaska, Baltimore Canyon, Creys-Malville, Fraser Island, Gorleben, Hopewell, Kairparowits, Kaiseraugst, Long Beach, Love Canal, Minamata Bay, Powder River Basin, Rotterdam, Sao Paulo, Seabrook, Seveso, Silver Bay, Snowdonia, Three Mile Island, Windscale . . . these are just a few of the many thousands of sites around the globe where major battles over the environmental impacts of existing or proposed industrial facilities were fought during the 1970s. Historians many years from now are surely going to label this decade the "golden age of environmental conflict." All of them will note how societies like the United States struggled with complex tradeoffs among job creation vs. clean air, energy development vs. wilderness preservation, growth vs. non-growth, risks vs. costs, hypotheses vs. facts, freedom vs. regulation, equity vs. efficiency, idealism vs. pragmatism, and even snail darters vs. dams. Some of the historians will undoubtedly argue that environmental conflict served to reduce economic growth, induce energy shortages, change industrial geography, burden the court system, foment civil disobedience, and divert valuable time and resources from truly creative and productive activity. Others, however, will just as vigorously stress that such conflict served to protect human health, conserve critical natural areas for the benefit of future generations, stimulate environmentally-oriented planning, enhance the quality of life, and bring about a new synthesis of development and

From *Natural Resources Journal,* Vol. 20 (April 1980), pp. 243-274. Reprinted with permission of University of New Mexico, School of Law.

14

environment more compatible with the limits of the Earth as a natural system. No matter what view is taken, all will certainly agree that environmental conflict was one of the most complex, difficult, pervasive, and consequential challenges ever faced by modern industrial society.

But we need not wait for the historians of the future, for environmental conflict is already being studied from many angles and in many ways.[1] Perhaps the most common approach is that of detailed individual case histories.[2] The case study method allows the observer to dig deep into the social psychology or political science of a particular dispute, and is thus of great value, particularly from the standpoint of generating hypotheses. The inherent limitations of the "micro" case study approach (i.e., absence of control, heavy reliance on subjectivity, many variables-small sample, etc.), however, have led many who investigate social conflict to move to "macro" quantitative studies. The study of a large sample of cases facilitates hypothesis testing, permits the use of statistical techniques, and can thus result in carefully controlled general empirical propositions.

This paper reports partial results from such a large-scale statistical study that has focused on the broad experience of environmental conflict over industrial facilities in the 1970s. This aggregate approach lends itself nicely to shedding some light on the question of "whither environmentalism." For waging conflict with the "industrial enemy" in order to prevent adverse, or compel beneficial, environmental impacts has obviously been one of the most important "social functions" of the environmental movement. By pinpointing patterns and trends in the nature of environmental conflict, therefore, we can gain useful insights regarding the possible future path of the environmental movement, particularly as it may find expression and perform on the "firing line."

The Environmental Conflict Project

The empirical survey reported here is a product of the "Environmental Conflict Project," under the direction of the author, at the Graduate School of Business Administration of New York University.[3] The overall purpose of the project, which is supported in part by a grant from the Rockefeller Foundation, is to provide empirical and theoretical generalizations of relevance to policy and practice in regard to the constructive management of environmental disputes. Much of the work to date has been aimed at empirically documenting temporal, spatial, and industrial trends in the emergence and character of such conflict around the world, and specifying patterns in the changing composition of issues, actors, tactics, resolution mechanisms, and outcomes involved. The ultimate objective is to develop a unified body of substantive theory regarding the causes, course, and effective management of environmental conflict.

The central methodology being employed can be described in summary and step-wise fashion as follows: (1) systematic, page-by-page scanning of a range of U.S. and foreign newspapers, journals, and magazines for the period 1970 to present; (2) clipping of every article and item pertaining to an environmental dispute; (3) creation of files for each and every site-specific conflict over an industrial facility; (4) bolstering of clippings files, where possible, with related books, hearing transcripts, court records, etc.; (5) development and testing of a standardized codesheet largely composed of a fixed set of close-ended questions (with answers convertible to machine-readable numbers); (6) "interviewing" of the data assembled on each dispute by trained graduate student "reader-analysts," and coding of information on three dozen characteristics of each dispute; (7) strict reliance in coding only on the explicit content of the assembled literature on each case; (8) careful monitoring, reliability testing, and rechecking of the coding operations; (9) keypunching of the coded case information, file editing, and creation of an operational computer data base; and (10) employment of computer-based descriptive and statistical methods in analyzing the data.

Environmental conflict has been operationally defined in behavioral, interorganizational, and observable terms along lines suggested by Katz and Kahn: "Two systems . . . are in conflict when they interact directly in such a way that the actions of one tend to prevent or compel some outcome against the resistance of the other."[4] Disputes described in the scanned literature entered the formal data base whenever evidence was provided of conflictful behavior (i.e., hindering, compelling, injuring against resistance) among two or more actors arising from impacts of a facility on the environment. Such was the case, for example, with regard to Dow Chemical Company's plans unveiled in 1975 for a $500-million petrochemical complex northeast of San Francisco. The proposal met with unremitting opposition from regulatory agencies such as the Bay Area Pollution Control District and environmental groups such as the Sierra Club and Friends of the Earth on air quality and other grounds. The title of one report on the case captured the essence of the struggle: "Can a Quiet Agricultural County on the Sacramento River Find True Happiness with a Huge, Messy Chemical Plant?"[5] Dow abandoned the project in 1977 after spending $4.5 million in a futile attempt to obtain 65 approvals needed for the plant that would have employed 1,000 workers.

As of 1979, data has been collected on approximately 3,000 such disputes spanning some 40 nations. Sector studies have guided the project's coding and computer analysis activities. The results reported here, for example, are from our "Chemical Process Industry" data set.[6] The composition of this set was determined by including every single site-specific environmental battle over an industrial facility ever mentioned in either *Chemical Week Magazine* or *European Chemical News* during the period January 1, 1970, through June 30, 1978 (442 weeks of coverage).[7] Data files bearing upon the 587 cases of conflict gathered from these two "base" information sources were supplemented by related articles drawn from two dozen other secondary literature sources, ranging from *The New York Times* and *Business Week* to *The Sierra Club Bulletin* and *Not Man Apart*.[8] Altogether, approximately 6,000 different articles were assembled on the pool of cases. Of the total sample, 366 of the disputes occurred in the U.S. and 221 of them overseas. The focus below is mainly on the U.S. subsample of this chemical process industry case collection and is largely limited to descriptive reporting. Analyses of the foreign data, as well as exploratory causal analysis efforts using multivariate statistical methods, are reported elsewhere.[9]

Some of the key strengths and limitations of the quantitative survey approach should be briefly noted. The systematic and replicable method facilitates the much-needed aggregative function. And the exhaustive acquisition of data on the entire universe of media-reported conflicts permits one to assess patterns and trends in the nature of environmental conflict which could not otherwise be done using more casual techniques of observation and sample selection. But the results of the survey are naturally of no better quality than the quality of the original secondary source data. Major reporting biases may in fact be present (i.e., toward environmental disputes of large size, high intensity, long duration, and in close proximity to wire service locations). Other problems include potential distortion in the content of assembled literature, including inaccurate reporting, along with differential completeness of data across conflict cases. The method, in its focus on aggregating general features of environmental conflict, may not give sufficient attention to the unique features of individual cases. General problems of reliability associated with massive coding operations and of validity associated with cross-sectional analysis (i.e., absence of detailed information about temporal sequences) are also confronted. These limitations should be kept in mind as we highlight some of the survey's findings.

The Sample

Table 1 shows the composition of the 366 U.S. environmental battles which resulted from our 1970 to mid-1978 scanning. As would be expected from the base chemical industry literature relied upon, nearly half of the reported conflicts were fought over chemical process facilities, while the remainder involved disputes in related industrial sectors. These latter conflicts found their way into the chemical industry literature mainly because of their input-providing (e.g., electric utility or mineral mining) or output-using or

TABLE 1

Composition of U.S. Environmental Conflict Sample (366 conflicts; 1970–78 scanning; % rounded off)

Type of Facility	Number of Cases	Percentage of Total Sample	Nature of Facility		Location of Facility					Year of Conflict Emergence			
			Existing %	Expansions and New Proposals %	North-East %	South-East %	Mid-West %	South West %	Far West %	1970–1971 %	1972–1973 %	1974–1975 %	1976–1978 %
Petrochemical	18	5	44	56	18	29	6	41	6	21	21	21	36
Oil Refinery	29	8	42	58	62	8	0	23	8	38	24	19	19
Nonferrous Metal	22	6	70	30	21	16	10	32	21	37	32	16	16
Ferrous Metal	26	7	96	4	43	9	22	26	0	29	35	29	6
Pulp and Paper	22	6	95	5	20	15	25	5	35	59	23	6	12
Nuclear Power	40	11	37	63	20	29	31	14	6	35	17	17	31
Electric Utility	11	3	44	56	20	20	20	20	20	50	0	37	13
Transport and Storage	33	9	18	82	48	10	7	14	21	28	11	33	28
Mineral Mining	40	11	36	64	6	34	0	37	23	19	25	38	19
Inorganic Chemical	62	17	81	19	35	29	17	15	4	46	26	15	13
Organic Chemical	40	11	100	0	44	19	22	14	0	29	29	12	29
Other	23	6	68	32	53	11	11	26	0	18	24	12	47
Total Sample	366	100	62	38	33	20	15	21	11	34	24	20	22

handling (e.g., ferrous metal, transport and storage) nature. In the nuclear power sector, therefore, the sample includes 40 cases of conflict that were deemed "significant" to the chemical process industry (i.e., were the subject of reporting in the chemical news). The sample, as such, may not be truly representative of the entire nuclear conflict scene in the United States.

Sixty-two percent of the battles in the sample were waged over environmental aspects of facilities already in existence, while the other 38 percent as shown in Table 1 involved either expansions of facilities at existing production sites or new "greenfield" plant proposals. Disputes involving nonferrous and ferrous metal, pulp and paper, and inorganic and organic chemical facilities were largely over impacts of existing operations. Conflicts over expansions or new proposals were concentrated in the petrochemical, oil refinery, nuclear power, (non-nuclear) electric utility, transport and storage facility, and mineral mining sectors. An important pattern discovered in this regard is that:

> *Environmental conflict is focusing on change*—the focus is shifting from old to new targets, from existing pollution problems to potential environmental impacts, and from "band-aid" remedies to preventive or risk reduction measures.

Over the years, there has been a definite shift in focus from existing to greenfield projects as targets of environmental concern; battles over expansions and new proposals rose from a 13 percent share in 1970-71 to a 53 percent share in 1974-75 (dropping back somewhat to 41 percent in 1976-78). This largely reflects the fact that pollution problems at many existing operations were apparently corrected as a result of citizen group and governmental pressure. Two-thirds or more of the conflicts in the Northeast, Southeast, and Midwest centered on existing facilities, while close to one-half of the Southwest and Far West battles involved new proposals. Another significant trend can be noted:

> *Environmental conflict is spreading*—locationally from the "Frostbelt" to the "Sunbelt" (although once conflict emerges in any particular region, it remains) and industrially to all types of facilities and phases of the production process (i.e., from extraction all the way through product disposal).

The top ten states for reported conflict, in descending order according to number of cases, were New Jersey, California, Texas, Pennsylvania, Illinois, Florida, Washington, New York, Delaware, and Ohio. These ten hotspots accounted for 58 percent of all reported conflict. Viewed on a regional basis, Table 1 reveals that 33 percent of the battles took place in the Northeast, 20 percent in the Southeast, 15 percent in the Midwest, 21 percent in the Southwest, and 11 percent in the Far West. Over time, however, the overall share of environmental conflict accounted for by the Northeast and Midwest declined markedly—from a combined share in 1970-71 of 59 percent to one in 1976-78 of 38 percent. This shift in the location of environmental disputes in favor of the "Sunbelt" is in accordance with the general shift of new industrial capital spending in that direction. But on a national basis, another finding must be emphasized:

> *Environmental conflict is continuing*—the amount of reported conflict over industrial facilities has not diminished since 1972, despite energy crises and recessionary conditions. The evidence indicates that environmental conflicts interact and feed forward via domino, contagion, diffusion, and learning processes.

As Table 1 reveals, one-third of the reported disputes over the entire eight and one-half year study period emerged during the first two years. The period 1970-71, of course, marked the "age of alarmed discovery and euphoric enthusiasm" regarding the environmental movement in the United States.[10] The remaining two-thirds of the battles were spread rather equally over the next six and one-half years. It should be noted, however, that our scanning operations revealed a significant lag in media reporting of conflicts, with coverage apparently dependent upon the disputes reaching some threshold level of media-attracting intensity. For this reason, the 1976 to mid-1978 share of 22 percent is somewhat understated. (Scanning since the computer data base cut-off date of July 1978 has indeed revealed four dozen battles which emerged in 1977 and early 1978 but did not make it into the computerized data base.) The key point is that the amount of reported environmental conflict over industrial facilities has evidently remained relatively constant since 1972. It has perhaps even increased, given that capital spending in the chemical process industries declined in constant value dollars in the United States from 1974 to 1977. And data for 1979 indicates a massive upsurge in reported conflict, particularly in regard to hazardous waste disposal sites and nuclear power plants, as a result of the Love Canal and Three Mile Island disasters respectively. Such incidents induced waves of related environmental battles by attracting media coverage and arousing public concern.

The Issues

Many kinds of issues can be found at stake in environmental conflicts, which have an important bearing on the intensity of the struggle, the duration of required interaction, and the general difficulty of reaching agreement. Research on conflict in general, for example, has shown that disputes tend to become more difficult to resolve the greater the extent to which the issues at stake are intangible, highly uncertain, irreversible in outcome, over large precedents, few in number with no tradeoffs among them possible, ideological in content, closely intertwined, generalized, broad and diffuse, abstract, similarly ranked in importance by both parties, difficult in terms of finding solutions, over general principles, and "winner-take-all" or zero-sum in character.[11]

We considered the following eight topical categories of issues in our survey: (1) *air quality* (pollution, visibility, odor); (2) *water quality* (degradable/nondegradable/persistent/residuals); (3) *land use* (landscape, scenery, wilderness, erosion, solid waste); (4) *biota* (vegetation, wildlife, biological effects, ecological balance); (5) *minerals* (fuel, nonfuel); (6) *human health and safety* (disease, noise, radioactivity, accidents, genetic and reproductive effects); (7) *social resources* (recreation, residential, cultural, life style, congestion, boomtowns); (8) *economic resources* (property values, tax, income, employment). The last three represent *primary issues* in the sense of being disputed in terms of manifest or direct human impacts, while the first five can be viewed as *secondary issues*, that is, those not necessarily or not yet translated into matters of direct human impact.

Table 2 provides summary data regarding issue type and number. On average, 1.8 issues were disputed per conflict in the United States, with the three most frequent types being water quality (present in 59 percent of the battles), air quality (31 percent), and human health (22 percent). An inspection of the data reveals a fundamental pattern found throughout this survey:

> *Environmental conflict varies tremendously in character*—the structure and substance of battles differ widely among nations, regions, types and natures of facilities, and times of emergence. No two environmental battles are totally alike, and variations in their characteristics are critically important in designing and applying appropriate methods of conflict management.

In comparison with the pool of 221 reported conflicts overseas (the bulk of which occurred in the Netherlands, United Kingdom, West Germany, Japan, Italy, France, Belgium, Canada, Spain, and Sweden), water quality issues were more frequent in U.S. battles, while air quality and human health issues were much less frequent. Variations were also discovered among regions of the United States, with air quality most frequent in the Southwest, water quality in the Northeast, human health in the Midwest, and land use, mineral base, social, and economic impacts in the Far West. Such variations reflect different kinds of environmental resources under heavy pressure.

The main determinant of issues, of course, was the type of facility involved (i.e., the nature of its environmental impacts). Air quality issues, for example, were most frequent in battles over electric utilities (e.g., the cancelled coal-fired power plant of Southern California Edison, et al., at Kair-

TABLE 2

Issues in U.S. Environmental Conflict (366 conflicts; 1970–78 scanning; % rounded off and means)

Categories and Conflict N	Types of Issues								Mean Number of Issue Types
			Secondary			Primary			
	Air	Water	Land	Biota	Minerals	Health	Social	Economic	
1. All U.S. Conflicts (366)	31%	59%	16%	18%	3%	22%	14%	18%	1.8
All Foreign Conflicts (221)	51	46	13	23	1	45	11	21	2.1
2. U.S. Location									
Northeast (121)	28	66	14	20	4	20	18	17	1.9
Southeast (73)	17	63	20	23	1	21	16	16	1.8
Midwest (55)	28	66	3	9	2	30	6	16	1.6
Southwest (77)	50	43	19	18	4	26	11	22	1.9
Far West (40)	30	49	27	21	6	6	21	24	1.8
3. Type of Facility									
Petrochemical (18)	56	63	19	25	0	25	25	31	2.4
Oil Refinery (29)	44	44	32	16	8	12	28	20	2.1
Nonferrous Metal (22)	80	35	25	20	10	35	10	25	2.4
Ferrous Metal (26)	67	43	0	5	0	14	0	0	1.3
Pulp and Paper (22)	20	90	0	10	0	0	0	0	1.3
Nuclear Power (40)	6	44	15	12	3	41	3	21	1.7
Electric Utility (11)	80	10	10	0	0	20	30	20	1.7
Transport and Storage (33)	11	68	21	46	4	21	36	50	2.6
Mineral Mining (40)	17	46	63	14	17	0	31	26	2.1
Inorganic Chemical (62)	41	57	4	16	0	25	8	14	1.7
Organic Chemical (40)	22	83	6	25	0	47	8	17	2.1
Other (23)	21	63	11	32	0	26	16	11	1.8
4. Nature of Facility									
Existing (227)	29	66	6	16	1	25	7	11	1.6
Expansion (14)	70	20	0	20	0	10	20	10	1.6
New Proposal (125)	32	46	39	24	9	18	31	36	2.3
5. Time of Emergence									
1970–71 (124)	27	73	7	16	2	18	9	12	1.6
1972–73 (88)	35	51	14	8	3	19	10	14	1.6
1974–75 (73)	34	38	27	27	9	29	21	23	2.1
1976–78 (81)	32	48	20	17	2	38	12	15	1.9

parowits, Utah), and metal facilities such as smelters and steel works. Water quality issues, in comparison, were at stake in 90 percent of all the pulp and paper disputes (e.g., International Paper's battle with the state of Vermont over the firm's mill at Ticonderoga, New York) and in a majority of the petrochemical, transport and storage, inorganic, and organic sector conflicts. Land use and mineral base issues were especially prominent in mining conflicts, while biotic impact issues were most frequent in transportation facility struggles (e.g., the epic Trans-Alaska oil pipeline battle of Alyeska Pipeline Service). Concerns of human health and safety were found most frequently in conflicts over inorganic chemical plants, nuclear power stations, and nonferrous metal facilities (e.g., Kennecott's difficulties in the early 1970s with its copper smelters in Utah, Arizona, Montana, and Nevada). Finally, concerns over adverse social and/or economic impacts were present most often in disputes over oil refineries, transport facilities, minerals mining, and electric utilities (e.g., classic "boomtown" struggles over power projects in Rock Springs, Wyoming, the Four Corners region, Colstrip, Montana, and Craig, Colorado).

But for the entire sample, this pattern stands out:

> *Environmental conflict is broadening*—the issues at stake are changing, with land use, social impact, and human health concerns rapidly on the rise as central matters in contention. The name of the game is no longer simple ecology, but rather the overall quality of human life.

Water quality issues have declined dramatically in prominence—from being involved in three quarters of all disputes in 1970-71 to only 38 percent in 1974-75 and 48 percent in 1976-78. The decline can perhaps be traced to considerable progress in cleaning up water pollution problems at existing facilities under the Federal Water Pollution Control Act Amendments of 1972, the most expensive and far-reaching effort ever undertaken by Congress in the field of environmental protection. Land use issues, on the other hand, have been on the rise, as have those of human health and safety. The control of land use, of course, has indeed undergone radical change in recent years, with the trend, at all regulatory levels and in the courts, towards ever greater constraints in the name of the overriding public interest in protecting environmental and esthetic values.[12] And the increased emphasis on health hazards, particularly in the area of environmental carcinogens, reflects a growing specification of what many consider to be the "bottom line" of the entire environmental movement. We should also note the rise over time in the number of types of issues involved in the average environmental battle. The trend, perhaps in large measure a product of the shift from "old" to "new" targets, may also reflect a broadening of the notion of the "human environment," with *primary* health, social, and economic impact issues increasingly being added to the more traditional *secondary* issues of general environmental quality.

The Opponents

Corporations have confronted many types of opponents in environmental disputes, with their characteristics varying in ways critical to the development, course, and resolution of the disputes. Some have been small and others very large; some have been novices and others old pros at waging conflict; some have been ad hoc and unorganized, while others long established and highly structured; some have been obsessed with a single issue, while others dallied in multiple issues; some have had abundant financial and human resources at their disposal, while others only had typewriters; some have been out for a little fun and excitement, while others have literally been willing to die or go to jail for their cause. We classified the opponents in our survey into nine topical categories: (1) *foreign governmental body;* (2) *national governmental body;* (3) *regional governmental body;* (4) *local governmental body;* (5) *national environmental groups;* (6) *regional or local environmental group;* (7) *local residents;* (8) *local industry;* and (9) *social action group.* For purposes of analysis these categories can be further classified into *governmental vs. nongovernmental* and *local vs. non-local.*

A few observations should be made before examining our opponent data. Most of the conflicts observed involved two or more opponents. An increase in the number of parties to an environmental dispute generally enhances the chances of communications failure, increases the difficulty of coordination, reduces the range of alternative solutions acceptable to all parties, and consequently increases the amount of time needed to reach agreement. Multi-party conflicts do show a persistent tendency, however, to reduce to two-party conflicts via coalitions and blocs. Parties which see themselves as sharing a common disadvantage at the hands of the corporation will often join forces and unify their resources in order to maintain or increase their individual strength. The firms, of course, just as often actively strive to prevent the formation of coalitions among weaker opposing parties.

Our focus below is on the opponents, but the involvement of other actors in the disputes should also be acknowledged. For example, the presence of interested and significant audiences has undoubtedly critically shaped the behavior of the direct protagonists in many conflicts. It is also clear that third parties have greatly influenced the course of many battles, entering into many environmental conflicts in several broad role categories: as possessors of superior powers to impose a settlement (e.g., judges, arbitrators), as reconcilers of disparate interests (e.g., fact-finders, conciliators, mediators), and as expert assistants to one or the other contending parties (e.g., attorneys, consultants, special envoys). Full-fledged analysis of environmental disputes must naturally take into account all the proponents, opponents, audiences, and third parties. The data provided in Table 3, however, focuses only on the opponent sector.

One point to note in the Table is the dramatically higher involvement of national and regional government agencies in U.S. disputes as compared to those overseas. Environmental battles abroad have been much more a local affair, with considerably higher involvement exhibited by local governments, residents, and industries. Within the United States, one should note that national groups were involved in 32 percent of the Far West disputes—a figure more than twice the average for the nation as a whole. Perhaps the most important pattern discerned in Table 3 is this:

> *Environmental conflict is characterized by a division of labor among opponents*—different types of opponents tend to wage conflict against different types of industrial facilities.

National and regional agencies were heavily involved in all types of facility disputes, but they found themselves without much company in the pulp and paper, ferrous metal, and organic chemical disputes. National environmental groups were strongly represented in only four of the twelve sectors: transport and storage, mineral mining, nuclear power, and (non-nuclear) electric utilities. This seems to suggest that such groups have devoted their time and energy vis-à-vis industry mainly to large scale, precedent setting, wilderness affecting, and/or highly threatening kinds of facilities. Regional and local environmental groups were also involved in these four, but exhibited a wider portfolio, with heavier involvement in many other sectors.

Likewise, local residents were present in roughly one-fifth or more of all the disputes in every category. The locals, who have to live with the effects of the facilities, thus appear more willing to oppose anything posing a perceived threat. Local industries and social action groups, according to the data, were more choosy in their targets. An example of the former is the victorious campaign of the Hilton Head Island Developers against the plans of the German chemical firm BASF for a petrochemical complex in South Carolina. A case of the latter is Ralph Nader's "Raiders" attacking Union Carbide's polluting ferroalloy plants in Ohio and West Virginia.

Another dimension of the division of labor is found in the data regarding nature of facility. Conflicts over expansions and new proposals attracted an average of 2.8 types of opponents, while existing facility disputes averaged only 1.8. The latter category of disputes largely involved only national or regional governmental opponents. "Greenfield" conflicts, on the other hand,

TABLE 3

Opponents in U.S. Environmental Conflict (366 conflicts; 1970–78 scanning; % rounded off and means)

Categories and Conflict N	Governmental				Nongovernmental					Mean Number of Opponent Types
	Foreign Govtal. Body	National Govtal. Body	Regional Govtal. Body	Local Govtal. Body	National Envtal. Group	Reg./Loc. Envtal. Group	Local Residents	Local Industry	Social Action Group	
1. All U.S. Conflicts (366)	1%	59%	54%	17%	15%	22%	30%	7%	7%	2.1
All Foreign Conflicts (221)	4	38	27	40	11	28	45	17	10	2.2
2. U.S. Location										
Northeast (121)	1	60	54	19	13	28	36	8	5	2.2
Southeast (73)	0	62	53	12	16	15	24	7	5	2.0
Midwest (55)	2	64	41	16	5	18	27	3	8	1.9
Southwest (77)	1	53	56	22	18	28	28	7	7	2.2
Far West (40)	6	56	71	12	32	15	32	9	9	2.4
3. Type of Facility										
Petrochemical (18)	0	29	47	18	12	35	41	12	18	2.1
Oil Refinery (29)	4	40	60	28	0	40	52	20	8	2.5
Nonferrous Metal (22)	5	50	85	30	0	20	25	10	10	2.4
Ferrous Metal (26)	0	69	83	22	9	4	17	0	9	2.1
Pulp and Paper (22)	0	70	50	0	5	5	20	0	5	1.5
Nuclear Power (40)	0	68	32	15	38	41	35	12	15	2.7
Electric Utility (11)	0	70	40	0	30	20	40	10	10	2.2
Transport and Storage (33)	7	66	52	38	52	48	45	17	7	3.3
Mineral Mining (40)	0	53	44	21	35	32	27	0	6	2.2
Inorganic Chemical (62)	0	62	60	14	10	21	19	4	4	1.9
Organic Chemical (40)	0	64	64	8	3	3	36	6	0	1.9
Other (23)	0	53	58	21	0	11	47	0	5	1.9
4. Nature of Facility										
Existing (227)	1	62	57	12	5	10	24	4	4	1.8
Expansion (14)	0	73	55	9	0	18	18	0	0	
New Proposal (125)	3	53	48	30	38	47	44	15	14	2.8
5. Time of Emergence										
1970–71 (124)	1	61	52	12	7	17	26	8	4	1.9
1972–73 (88)	0	56	52	14	10	19	18	1	3	1.8
1974–75 (73)	2	61	54	19	25	19	29	7	10	2.3
1976–78 (81)	2	54	51	18	11	21	41	5	6	2.1

attracted higher percentages of all other types of opponents. Local governmental bodies, environmental groups, residents, industries, and social action groups targeted much of their fire on new projects. National environmental groups, for example, exhibited about eight times as much involvement in conflict over proposed as against existing facilities. They thus appear to devote the bulk of their energies to opposing perceived adverse environmental consequences to the future rather than the present, which may perhaps be explained by their relatively greater power to oppose change than to effect corrections of existing problems.

A final pattern to note about opponents is that:

> *Environmental conflict is decentralizing*—battles increasingly involve local actors, and the mix of opponents is also shifting gradually from governmental to nongovernmental.

The trend data at the bottom of Table 3 shows recent declines in the involvement of national governmental agencies and environmental groups. It also reveals a gradually expanding role for local governmental bodies and increasingly greater involvement of local residents. The general trend is toward more frequent grass roots mobilization, perhaps as a result of growing disenchantment regarding the protection afforded by government bureaucrats or public interest groups in far-away locations.

The Tactics

Environmental opponents have pressed business firms with a wide range of tactics on practically every front: at construction sites, in the hearing rooms, in the courts, at shareholder meetings, in the media, on the streets, in city councils, state legislatures and Congress, as well as in the appointive bureaucracies of government at every level. We coded each case of conflict for the reported utilization of each of the following categories of tactics: (1) *governmental legal action;* (2) *governmental administrative action;* (3) *private legal action;* (4) *demonstration;* (5) *petition/referenda;* (6) *lobbying;* (7) *press campaign;* (8) *violence.* Tactics can be classified in many ways, but the distinction between *regulatory* and *social* tactics is particularly useful. Regulatory tactics involve governmental opponents through legal and administrative action, while social tactics encompass nongovernmental pressures such as those numbered (3) through (8) above.

What determines the tactics used by opponents of corporations in environmental battles? As with other aspects of conflict, it appears that many interrelated factors jointly affect preferences among, and choices of, different types of tactics by disputants. The nature of the issues giving rise to conflict are particularly important. So is the opponent group's ideology, leadership, resources, degree of organization, past experience in waging conflict, and perception of the relevant audiences' reactions. The nature of the preexisting relationship between the disputants may influence the choice of tactics, and so will the kinds of tactics employed by the other party. Corporate reliance, for example, on a strategy of power and tactics of threat, coercion, and deception is likely to elicit resistance, alienation, and similar types of countertactics on the part of its opponents.

Table 4 shows that regulatory tactics were the most frequent kind employed in the U.S. disputes. Administrative actions (e.g., delayed or denied permits, licenses, certificates, zoning variances, authorizations, etc.) were employed in nearly two-thirds of the battles. Legal actions (e.g., suits asking for civil or criminal penalties, citations, contingent injunctions, etc.) were undertaken by governmental bodies in 39 percent of the cases. Private legal actions (e.g., damage suits, class action suits, nuisance or trespass litigation, etc.) were initiated in 30 percent of the disputes. Table 4's comparative international data dramatically reveals that:

> *Environmental conflict is quite litigious*—governmental and private legal actions have been approximately twice as prevalent in U.S. conflicts as compared to those overseas.

Why so much litigation in the United States? On the surface one might simply note that the United States has three times as many lawyers per capita as England and 21 times as many as Japan.[13] But the roots surely lie deeper. The United States is a society of laws, a culture preoccupied with the assertion and maintenance of individual rights. Access to the courts to redress political grievances is relatively cheap and easy and an accepted part of American life. Litigiousness is naturally also stimulated by the orgiastic growth of complex and often deliberately ambiguous regulations, as well as by the legal profession itself. The traditions of adversarial politics and single-issue thinking are also deeply embedded. But litigiousness serves many positive functions. Note, for example, that violence has been three times, and mass demonstrations four times, as frequent abroad as compared to the United States. The tactics of opponents in Western Europe, particularly of antinuclear activists, have often been quite flamboyant and/or violent—extended plant site occupations in France, West Germany, and Switzerland; bombings and sabotage of plants, construction equipment, and high tension lines; terrorist attacks on executives of polluting corporations and officials of lax governmental agencies; and massive demonstrations, at times involving up to 50,000 protesters, led by a belligerent new breed of roving European "ecology troopers."[14] These kinds of tactics perhaps reflect high levels of frustration result-

TABLE 4

Tactics of Opponents in U.S. Environmental Conflict (356 conflicts; 1970–78 scanning; % rounded off and means)

Categories and Conflict N	Types of Opponent Tactics								Mean Number of Tactics Types
	Regulatory		Private Legal Action	Demonstration	Social			Violence	
	Gov'al. Legal Action	Gov'al. Admin. Action			Petition-Referenda	Press Lobbying	Campaign		
1. All U.S. Conflicts (366)	39%	64%	30%	4%	3%	8%	6%	1%	1.6
All Foreign Conflicts (221)	18	73	18	16	6	16	22	3	1.7
2. U.S. Location									
Northeast (121)	43	62	25	5	6	9	8	0	1.6
Southeast (73)	36	65	31	3	1	10	4	0	1.5
Midwest (55)	59	51	30	5	2	5	5	2	1.6
Southwest (77)	16	77	28	4	2	4	4	2	1.4
Far West (40)	38	69	47	0	0	9	9	3	1.8
3. Type of Facility									
Petrochemical (18)	27	60	14	0	0	0	7	0	1.3
Oil Refinery (29)	25	71	29	4	17	25	21	0	1.9
Nonferrous Metal (22)	33	67	33	11	0	6	6	0	1.6
Ferrous Metal (26)	74	70	9	0	0	0	0	0	1.5
Pulp and Paper (22)	40	55	35	0	0	5	10	0	1.5
Nuclear Power (40)	18	66	39	18	9	18	18	3	2.0
Electric Utility (11)	30	60	50	10	0	10	0	0	1.6
Transport and Storage (33)	25	68	43	4	4	11	14	7	1.8
Mineral Mining (40)	31	69	38	3	0	16	0	7	1.6
Inorganic Chemical (62)	44	68	26	2	2	2	0	0	1.4
Organic Chemical (40)	49	69	29	0	0	0	3	0	1.5
Other (23)	47	53	32	5	0	16	5	0	1.6
4. Nature of Facility									
Existing (227)	50	60	27	2	1	2	2	1	1.4
Expansion (14)	10	90	30	0	0	10	0	0	
New Proposal (125)	18	75	40	9	6	22	17	2	1.9
5. Time of Emergence									
1970–71 (124)	54	53	26	2	2	6	6	1	1.5
1972–73 (88)	39	67	23	3	1	6	1	0	1.4
1974–75 (73)	26	71	38	2	3	7	3	2	1.5
1976–78 (81)	26	70	34	7	4	4	5	0	1.5

ing from exclusionary political and corporate decision making processes, as well as the relative absence of means to redress grievances effectively.

Table 4 shows that different types of tactics have been utilized by opponents in different conflict situations. Governmental legal actions, for example, were employed in 74 percent of the ferrous metal conflicts—a figure almost twice the national average. Governmental administrative actions occurred in at least one-half of the cases in each facility category. The Far West, where groups such as the Sierra Club and Friends of the Earth have their headquarters, exhibited much higher use of private legal action (47 percent of all battles) as compared to the national average (30 percent). Demonstrations were found to be most frequent in the nuclear power sector (e.g., those orchestrated by the Clamshell Alliance in 1976-77 at the construction site of the controversial Seabrook, New Hampshire, nuclear power plant). The use of petitions and referenda was highly concentrated in the oil refinery sector, primarily in many of the ill-fated attempts to establish refineries along the coasts of states in New England with strong "home-rule" traditions. Opponents took their grievances directly to politicians, government bureaucrats, business executives, and/or corporate shareholders in the form of lobbying, particularly in the oil refining, nuclear power, and mining industries. Numerous firms, for example, have had to contend with proxy resolutions on environmental questions submitted by citizen lobbies for votes at shareholder meetings. Vigorous press campaigns have also been confronted. The long and acrimonious battle between Shell Oil and groups in Delaware over plans for an oil refinery is one case where a high-volume press campaign, with the slogan of "To Hell with Shell," won the day. Finally, it should be noted that violence or "ecological terrorism" has not been entirely absent from the U.S. environmental scene. The sabotage bombings of the Alaska oil pipeline and felled powerline transmission towers in a number of states are cases in point.

Existing facility disputes have largely attracted regulatory tactics, while new proposals have garnered the bulk of social tactics. The key pattern on the regulatory side is that:

> Environmental conflict is increasingly characterized by governmental administrative rather than legal action—the discretionary powers of government bureaucrats appear to have greatly expanded in the 1970s.

Perhaps the two most important time trends presented in Table 4 are the dramatic decline of governmental legal actions (54 percent to 26 percent) and the gradually rising role of governmental administrative actions (53 percent to 70 percent). The amount of government-initiated litigation linked to governmental regulations promulgated in the late 1960s and early 1970s has apparently leveled off, while the scope of discretionary action on the part of administrative agencies has widened. Other trends to note are the growing frequencies of private legal action, demonstration, and petitions/referenda—all mainly employed by public interest groups in their efforts to delay, modify, or block new industrial projects.

The Resolution Mechanisms

Various methods of dispute settlement (or termination) have been employed in the field of environmental conflict. The use of nine different resolution mechanisms was observed and coded in our study. They can be grouped into a smaller number of categories based on the relative amount of external participation in the resolution process: such outside intervention was at a maximum level when *public resolution mechanisms* (i.e., legislation, vote, public hearing) were employed; moderate level when traditional *third party resolution mechanisms* (i.e., autocratic governmental decision, adjudication, arbitration/mediation) were utilized; and very low level when *private resolution mechanisms* (i.e., bargaining/negotiation, joint problem-solving, private decision) were relied upon. Many of the battles in our sample involved only one of the nine mechanisms, but others involved two or more of them in sequential or simultaneous combination.

Much attention has recently been focused in the United States on ways in which the resolution of environmental conflicts might be made more "constructive" (i.e., fairer, faster, less costly, more sensible, more certain, etc.).[15] A serious national effort to bring about greater use of mediation and closely related techniques in resolving conflicts has been spearheaded by such organizations as RESOLVE (Center for Environmental Conflict Resolution), the American Arbitration Association, the Office of Environmental Mediation at the University of Washington, the Rocky Mountain Center on Environment, and the Environmental Mediation Project at the Wisconsin Center for Public Policy.[16] But even the most avid proponents of mediation acknowledge that it is not a panacea. The notion that there is "no one best way" to manage environmental disputes has begun to gain wide acceptance.

The focus, therefore, must be on contingencies which combine to suggest the most appropriate mechanisms of conflict management in particular situations. The notion of "appropriateness," of course, frequently depends on whether a private or a public policy perspective is involved, and on whether it is defined in terms of the outcomes of environmental conflict, the processes of conflict resolution, or both.[17] The character of environmental conflict naturally varies widely from case to case in regard to *situational features* and *decisional demands*. The characteristics of resolution mechanisms available also differ widely in regard to their *operating capabilities* and *resource requirements*. Constructive conflict resolution can thus be viewed as a function of the match or fit between procedure and dispute. The currently popular idea of mediation, for example, may best or perhaps only be suited for disputes reflecting low conflict of interest, a sense of shared goals, an absence of precedents at stake, relatively equal distribution of power, a relative lack of time pressure, a common interest in finding the "correct" or "best" solution, an acceptance of each party's legitimacy, issues which are relatively concrete, tangible, non-ideological, and negotiable, and a mature phase of conflict.[18] Mediation, in other words, may be appropriate or feasible in only a very small share of the nation's environmental disputes.

Table 5 provides data on the resolution mechanisms that were employed in the environmental disputes included in our sample. Courtroom adjudication was the most frequently used mechanism in the United States (46 percent of all cases), while autocratic government decision-making played a role in three-tenths of the disputes. Public hearings, bargaining, joint problem-solving, private decisions, and legislation were each evident in at least 10 percent of the battles. The least-used mechanisms were voting and arbitration/mediation. Third-party mechanisms have thus clearly dominated the U.S. scene, with public and private mechanisms each employed in only half as many cases.

In a fashion similar to what we found in regard to issues, opponents, and tactics above, the use of different resolution mechanisms varied according to location, type, and nature of facility. For example, unilateral decisions by government bureaucrats in such forms as sanctioning an environmental impact statement, authorizing a development, or approving a plan for regulatory compliance were evident in 30 percent of all the U.S. conflicts, but they were employed in nearly two-thirds of the disputes in the highly regulated electric utilities sector. Adjudication, often in the form of protracted litigation, was resorted to in six out of every ten battles over nonferrous and ferrous metal facilities (e.g., the long and bitter disputes between the EPA and such steel firms as U.S. Steel, Bethlehem Steel, Jones & Laughlin Steel, Republic Steel, National Steel, and Wheeling Pittsburgh Steel over their polluting facilities in states such as Pennsylvania, Ohio, and West Virginia). Other forms of third-party intervention, such as arbitration and mediation, were very rarely utilized in the kinds of industrial facility disputes included in our survey.

The most common public resolution mechanisms involved were public hearings or inquiries, employed most frequently in oil refinery and transport and storage facility battles, particularly in the Northeast. Legislation, at local, regional, and national levels, was called into play in helping to resolve 10 percent of all the conflicts, but significantly higher shares of the Far West, nuclear power, and transport and storage disputes (e.g., the Clinch River fast breeder reactor project and the Alaskan oil pipeline). Citizen voting was also

TABLE 5
Resolution Mechanisms Used in U.S. Environmental Conflict (366 conflicts; 1970-78 scanning; % rounded off and means)

Categories and Conflict N	Autocratic Govtl. Decision	Third Party		Public			Private			Mean Number of Resolution Mechanism Types
		Adjudication	Arbitration/ Mediation	Legislation	Vote	Public Hearing	Bargaining/ Negotiation	Joint Problem Solving	Private Decision	
1. All U.S. Conflicts (366)	30%	46%	1%	10%	6%	19%	13%	14%	11%	1.5
All Foreign Conflicts (221)	46	17	2	5	2	23	24	10	22	1.9
2. U.S. Location										
Northeast (121)	33	43	0	9	9	26	14	17	9	1.6
Southeast (73)	24	48	2	4	4	18	13	16	14	1.4
Midwest (55)	22	69	4	13	4	9	7	20	11	1.6
Southwest (77)	33	30	0	7	6	20	13	6	16	1.3
Far West (40)	38	50	3	22	0	19	16	13	9	1.7
3. Types of Facility										
Petrochemical (18)	23	39	0	8	15	23	8	0	8	1.2
Oil Refinery (29)	38	21	0	8	21	38	17	21	13	1.8
Nonferrous Metal (22)	17	61	0	0	0	28	28	28	11	1.7
Ferrous Metal (26)	32	59	0	5	0	9	32	9	5	1.5
Pulp and Paper (22)	13	50	0	0	0	13	13	31	19	1.4
Nuclear Power (40)	42	45	3	21	21	24	13	3	10	1.7
Electric Power (11)	63	50	0	0	0	13	13	13	13	1.6
Transport and Storage (33)	18	46	4	39	11	50	18	4	7	2.0
Mineral Mining (40)	30	40	3	7	3	7	17	13	20	1.4
Inorganic Chemical (62)	27	42	0	2	2	13	10	21	23	1.4
Organic Chemical (40)	38	45	3	10	0	14	14	21	7	1.5
Other (23)	47	41	0	6	0	18	0	6	6	1.2
4. Nature of Facility										
Existing (227)	29	52	1	6	2	10	13	17	12	1.4
Expansion (14)	40	30	0	0	0	50	20	10	0	
New Proposal (125)	34	35	2	19	13	35	12	10	12	1.7
5. Time of Emergence										
1970-71 (124)	25	55	0	6	2	11	5	12	15	1.3
1972-73 (88)	33	44	3	10	5	16	18	16	14	1.6
1974-75 (73)	24	42	2	12	6	24	14	18	0	1.5
1975-78 (81)	41	35	2	9	11	27	18	11	5	1.6

Types of Resolution Mechanisms

resorted to in those two sectors, as well as in cases of petrochemical plants and oil refineries.

Direct bargaining and negotiation among the disputing parties, unassisted by third parties, was employed in 13 percent of all the battles in the sample, but was evidenced in nearly one-third of all the nonferrous and ferrous metal disputes. Joint problem solving only transpired in 14 percent of the cases as a whole, but was more frequent in a number of sectors. Examples drawn from the mineral mining sector would include the "Experiment in Ecology" launched by AMAX in the planning of its Henderson, Colorado, molybdenum mine in the late 1960s and the same firm's agreement to participate in a joint review effort called the "Colorado Review Process" with regard to the planning of another molybdenum mining project near Crested Butte, Colorado, in the late 1970s. Both experiences, by opening up the planning process and bringing together people with widely divergent views to work on a practical development problem, represent innovative harmonizing approaches to environmental conflict management. Finally, private decisions, typically in the form of a corporation unilaterally deciding to shut down a facility or cancel a new project, were the way in which 11 percent of the disputes were terminated; about one-fifth of the pulp and paper, mineral mining, and inorganic chemical facility conflicts were handled in this way.

Table 5 also shows that:

> *Environmental conflict is moving out of the courts*—the relative amount of courtroom adjudication involving industrial facilities seems to be decreasing, while other resolution mechanisms such as voting, public hearings, and autocratic governmental decision making are on the rise.

We have recently witnessed a rise in (a) autocratic decision making, perhaps reflecting the stronger discretionary powers vested in administrative agencies; (b) citizen voting, indicating a rise in single-issue politics and perhaps a widening gulf between elected representatives and public opinion; and (c) public hearings, probably as a product of increased participatory activism and broadened acceptance of the notion of pre-project environmental impact assessment. Contrary to popular impressions, however, the relative amount of adjudication in U.S. industrial environmental disputes has been falling (from 55 percent in 1970-71 to 36 percent in 1976-78). The field of battle thus appears to be moving from the courtroom to the hallways of governmental agencies, town hall meeting rooms, and local ballot boxes.

The data on the number of different resolution mechanisms utilized per battle in Table 5, along with trends noted previously, indicates another important pattern:

Environmental conflict is growing in size—the average number of issues, opponents, and resolution mechanisms involved per battle is increasing, in large measure as a consequence of other trends above (e.g., the shift from existing facilities to new projects).

Table 2 revealed a rise in the number of types of issues involved in the average environmental battle (1.6 in 1970-71 to 1.9 in 1976-78), reflecting an expansion in the range of environmental impacts of concern to citizens. Table 3 indicated a rise in the number of opponent types per conflict (1.9 in 1970-71 to 2.1 in 1976-78) as a consequence of increased involvement on the part of local residents and governments. And Table 5 shows that an average of 1.3 resolution mechanisms were employed per battle in 1970-71. The figure in 1976-78, however, was 1.6, in part reflecting the increased use of public mechanisms as noted above. Shifting patterns in facility location, nature, and type also underlie these trends. Environmental battles in the Far West, for example, have led the nation in the number of opponents involved, tactics utilized, resolution mechanisms employed, and amount of time consumed (see Table 6 below). Likewise, conflicts over expansions and new proposals have entailed a significantly broader range of issues, opponents, tactics, and resolution mechanisms than disputes over existing facilities.

As one might expect, most of the conflict size variables mentioned above were found to be closely associated. A correlation analysis, for example, found that the number of opponents in a battle was strongly and positively associated with the number of issues (a zero-order correlation, significant at the .01 level, of .50), tactics (.63), and resolution mechanisms (.52) involved in the dispute, as well as its duration (.51).[19] This may suggest that the wider and deeper the environmental impacts of an industrial facility (i.e., the more varied the issues), the more numerous and diverse the actors which emerge in opposition and the tactics which they correspondingly bring to bear against the firm. The resulting complexity may, in turn, necessitate the use of more methods of conflict resolution. And channeling conflicts sequentially or simultaneously through a greater range of resolution mechanisms may thus eat up more time, lengthening the duration of the dispute.

The Outcomes and Durations

We now come to the outcomes of the environmental battles. As of the mid-1978 closing date of our survey, more than 40 percent of the sample conflicts were still ongoing. The data in Table 6 thus reflects intermediate outcomes reported for unresolved conflicts as well as both intermediate and final outcomes for disputes fully terminated or resolved. Final and/or inter-

TABLE 6

Outcomes and Duration of U.S. Environmental Conflict (366 conflicts; 1970–78 scanning; % rounded off and means)

Categories and Conflict N	Types of Outcomes										Mean Duration of Conflict (years)
	Opponent						Compromise		Corporate		
	Fine or Compensation	Jail Sentence	Shutdown/Capacity Reduction	Blocked	Postponed	Delay	Technical Modification	Relocated	Approved	Establishment	
1. All U.S. Conflicts (366)	16%	1%	19%	16%	2%	24%	36%	4%	22%	6%	1.8
All Foreign Conflicts (221)	13	2	19	18	4	32	39	14	22	9	1.5
2. U.S. Location											
Northeast (121)	22	2	13	18	1	14	47	7	17	7	1.8
Southeast (73)	16	0	18	11	0	24	28	4	22	4	1.4
Midwest (55)	17	0	29	6	0	23	43	0	17	6	1.8
Southwest (77)	15	0	26	16	8	23	28	5	23	7	1.7
Far West (40)	0	0	10	28	0	55	28	3	35	7	2.3
3. Types of Facility											
Petrochemical (18)	8	0	0	33	0	58	25	8	17	0	1.7
Oil Refinery (29)	20	0	5	50	5	10	25	25	15	0	1.6
Nonferrous Metal (22)	21	5	26	11	0	32	37	11	16	11	2.4
Ferrous Metal (26)	40	0	20	0	0	5	60	0	10	0	2.8
Pulp and Paper (22)	9	0	27	0	0	0	64	0	18	0	1.8
Nuclear Power (40)	4	4	20	20	0	36	20	0	44	8	1.4
Electric Utility (11)	11	0	0	44	0	44	33	0	0	0	2.0
Transport and Storage (33)	4	0	4	28	4	60	16	0	40	28	2.2
Mineral Mining (40)	3	0	24	14	14	48	17	0	28	10	1.4
Inorganic Chemical (62)	16	0	30	5	0	7	53	5	16	0	1.5
Organic Chemical (40)	42	0	42	5	0	0	47	5	0	5	1.8
Other (23)	15	0	8	23	0	23	39	8	31	8	1.2
4. Nature of Facility											
Existing (227)	26	1	28	3	0	5	50	1	13	3	1.8
Expansion (14)	0	0	11	33	0	33	22	0	33	0	
New Proposal (125)	2	1	5	34	6	56	17	10	35	12	1.8
5. Time of Emergence											
1970–71 (124)	19	0	20	12	1	11	43	4	10	1	1.9
1972–73 (88)	9	2	26	17	2	19	36	6	17	6	2.0
1974–75 (73)	12	0	12	19	2	33	26	0	33	2	1.7
1976–78 (81)	23	2	23	12	7	33	30	7	19	5	1.1

mediate outcomes were reported for 80 percent of the conflicts. The figures on duration, however, are limited to cases which had ended by the survey cut-off date.

For purposes of analysis, the outcomes of environmental conflict were grouped into three categories: (a) certain outcomes were generally of greater benefit to the *opponents* than to the corporations involved and would include fines and compensation, jail sentences, shutdowns and capacity reductions, blockages, and postponements; (b) other outcomes can be viewed as representing *compromises* offering partial satisfaction to each of the contesting parties and would include delays, facility modifications, and relocations; and (c) still other outcomes would generally indicate victory for the *corporation*, manifested in project approvals and establishments. The set of coded outcomes was thus limited to those which were tangible and of immediate consequence to the parties involved.

What determines the outcomes of environmental conflicts? The answer to this vital question is unfortunately not yet in hand on either a theoretical or an empirical basis. Whether a conflict ends in a clear victory for one side or a compromise obviously depends upon many aspects of the conflict process. Scholars have noted dozens of interacting variables which serve to shape the magnitude and distribution of conflict outcomes. Those shown in Table 6, for example, can perhaps be traced to characteristics of the parties involved, nature and magnitude of the goals in contention, nature of the issues at stake, past and anticipated relationship between the parties, strategies and modes of conflict behavior engaged in, differential power or resources among the parties, presence and influence of audiences, availability and use of third parties, and character of the resolution mechanisms employed.

An overall impression drawn from the data in Table 6 is that:

> *Environmental conflict is becoming more costly*—recently rising rates of fines/compensation and shutdowns in regard to existing facilities, and delays, postponements, and blockages with respect to new proposals, all translate into higher costs for industry. The costs of conflict over new proposals have generally been highest in the Far West.

Fines or compensation for damage were paid by corporations in 26 percent of the existing facility battles. Two well-known examples of this kind of outcome are General Electric's settlement of $7 million for PCB research and waste-treatment facility construction that terminated the New York State Department of Environmental Conservation's proceedings against the company's PCB pollution of the Hudson River and Allied Chemical's $20 million in fines, settlements, and donations related to its kepone ordeal at Hopewell, Virginia. Twenty-eight percent of the existing facility disputes ended with shutdowns or capacity reductions and 50 percent of such cases were resolved via technical modifications. Such "retrofitting" was especially prevalent in the ferrous metal battles in the Midwest—e.g., after years of emotionally fighting air and water cleanup regulations every inch of the way, U.S. Steel chose in 1978 pragmatically and comprehensively to negotiate its compliance with regulatory standards with the EPA. Twelve months of intensive negotiations between teams of U.S. Steel and EPA officials resulted in a 193-page landmark agreement in 1979 calling for the company to spend about $400 million on air and water pollution control projects—reportedly adding about $25 per ton to the cost of producing steel by the end of 1982.

The economic costs of conflicts over new proposals have also been staggering: 56 percent of such projects encountered substantial delay, while 10 percent of them were relocated, 6 percent postponed, and 34 percent blocked entirely. Delays of at least a half year due to environmental opposition were most pervasive in the mining, petrochemical, and transport and storage sectors; typical cases in the latter include proposals by the Louisiana Offshore Oil Port Authority for a $500 million deepwater port, Western LNG Associates for an LNG import terminal and storage facility at Port Conception, and Sohio for an oil import terminal at Long Beach, California. Fifty-five percent of all the battles in the Far West entailed significant delays for the firms involved; this helps to explain the recent emergence of an ABC (Anywhere but California) philosophy of industrial plant location. Site relocations, either attempted or realized, were most frequent in the oil refinery and non-ferrous metal sectors (e.g., Shell leaving Delaware in order to find a refinery site or Alumax abandoning Oregon after a ten-year aluminum smelter siting saga). Project postponements related to problems of environmental acceptance were most frequent in the mineral mining sector in the Southwest (e.g., deferred plans for oil shale development in Colorado involving Occidental, Ashland, Gulf, Shell, and Standard Oil of Indiana). Finally, we should note that one-third of the new proposal cases were successfully blocked as a result of opponent efforts; 50 percent of the oil refinery battles ended in this manner (e.g., proposals of Atlantic Richfield, Occidental, Maine Clean Fuels, Olympic Refining, and many others in the New England region).

The aggregate cost of these kinds of conflict outcomes, while impossible to estimate accurately, has surely been in the many billions of dollars. And while the jury is still out on many of the battles which emerged in 1976-78, the trend data presented in Table .6, in general, indicates no lessening of the cost burden of environmental conflict.

The far right-hand column in Table 6 provides data on the mean duration of those conflicts emerging in the 1970s which had reportedly been resolved or terminated by mid-1978 (only about one-half of the total pool of conflicts in the sample). Durations were calculated for each case in terms of the number of years between the first point of significant controversy (as marked by opponents engaging in interference or resistance) and the last point of controversy (usually associated with a symbolically important event or an explicit agreement between the contending parties indicating a resolution or termination of the dispute). The mean duration for the completed U.S. cases was 1.8 years, with the range extending from one to eight years. The determinants of conflict duration are numerous. Some of the key variables include the number of issues at stake, level of difficulty of the issues, presence of intangible or symbolic issues, number of parties directly involved, absence of prior and anticipated future relationships among the parties, absence of time limits and third party intervention, accountability of the parties to a greater number of salient audiences, presence of misunderstanding, faulty communication and hostile attitudes, availability and use of threats, high perceptions of stakes riding on the outcome, and involvement of competitively-oriented disputants of roughly equal power.[20] Such factors variously serve to deepen and broaden the conflict, increase the difficulty of coordination, and introduce barriers to the workings of resolution processes; thus they tend to increase the amount of time needed to resolve a dispute.

The duration data in Table 6, while heavily biased to the early and/or small and easily resolved disputes, reveals some interesting patterns. The Far West exhibited the longest mean duration of any region in the United States, while battles in the Southeast, where the environmental movement is probably weakest, showed the shortest average duration. Nonferrous metal, ferrous metal, and transport and storage sector conflicts lasted longer on average as compared to those in other sectors. (Note that many of the large-scale electric utility, nuclear power, and minerals mining conflicts are not yet resolved and thus did not enter into their sector's calculations.) Without the benefit of duration data on many of the disputes which emerged in 1976-78, it is difficult to tell whether conflicts today are being processed more or less quickly than those which erupted in the earlier part of the decade. Corporate and societal learning, along with institutionalization of dispute resolution processes, however, should be working to reduce the average duration of environmental conflicts.

Whither Environmental Conflict?

Where does environmental conflict over industrial facilities, and by implication the fighting arm of the environmental movement, appear to be headed? The 12 patterns already highlighted have noted some specifics, but a summary view can also be offered. Using the composite variables introduced in each section above (e.g., the *issues* were classified into two composite categories, *primary* and *secondary*), a correlation analysis was conducted to examine relationships between all pairs of such composites on issues, opponents, tactics, resolution mechanisms, and outcomes involved in environmental conflict.[21] We found, for example, that the role of non-governmental opponents (i.e., the "environmental movement" as it has traditionally been known) in environmental conflict in the 1970s could be characterized as follows. Such opponents were most often found to be involved in later rather than earlier disputes, active in battles over new proposals rather than existing plants, concerned with primary rather than secondary issues, local rather than non-local in origin, enmeshed in larger rather than smaller coalitions, employing social rather than regulatory tactics, displaying a broader range of tactics than governmental opponents, participating in public rather than third party or private resolution mechanisms, and scoring less clear-cut victories than the corporations.

We also discovered this overall pattern:

> *Environmental conflict is shifting from "regulatory" to "social" in general character*—as such the "environmental movement" is assuming an ever more central role in the process.

A formal factor analysis confirmed that many of the composite variables, particularly in regard to opponents, tactics, and resolution mechanisms, fall into clusters corresponding to two distinct types of environmental conflict. One seems to represent "social conflict," and the other might be described as "regulatory conflict." Table 7 shows the nature of the two clusters. Each includes items which were found to be more highly intercorrelated with each other in their own column than they were with items in the other.

The two types of conflict can be distinguished as follows. Primary issues (e.g., health and safety, economic and social impact) of deep concern to non-governmental and local opponents tend to be most prominent in social conflict, while governmental and non-local opponents mainly concerned with secondary issues of environmental quality (e.g., air and water pollution) tend to be more prevalent in regulatory conflict. Social conflict tactics such as demonstration, lobbying, and press campaigns confront firms planning new proposals, while governmental legal and administrative actions as applied to existing facilities characterize regulatory conflict. Social conflicts tend to encompass more issues, opponents, tactics, and resolution mechanisms than the regulatory variety. And the two types are dealt with in different ways—public resolution mechanisms are almost exclusively found in social conflict, while third-party mechanisms are mainly employed in regulatory disputes. Compromise and opponent outcomes appear to result in both types of disputes, but corporations generally fail to win regulatory battles, although they have better luck in the social ones. Finally, social conflicts have

TABLE 7
Types of Environmental Conflict

	"Social Conflict"	*"Regulatory Conflict"*
Types of Issues:	Primary (and Secondary)	Secondary (and Primary)
Number of Issues:	Higher	Lower
Types of Opponents:	Nongovernmental and Local	Governmental and Non-Local
Number of Opponents:	Higher	Lower
Types of Tactics:	Social	Regulatory
Number of Tactics:	Higher	Lower
Types of Resolution Mechanisms:	Public and Private	Third Party and Private
Number of Resolution Mechanisms:	Higher	Lower
Types of Outcomes:	Compromise, Opponent and Corporate	Opponent and Compromise
Facility Nature:	New Proposals and Expansions	Existing Facilities and Expansions
Time of Emergence:	Later	Earlier
Duration:	Longer	Shorter

emerged more recently, and typically have lasted longer, than the regulatory kind.

Our survey has focused on the 1970s. But the trends suggest that the country may be entering an even more difficult era in which growing demands and diminishing resources will increase the frequency and intensity of the "social" breed of environmental conflict. Yet it is evident from many recent episodes that we still know little about how to cope with such conflict in equitable and efficient ways. The urgent task confronting us all as we move into the 1980s is to develop and apply more systematic knowledge about constructive conflict management.

Notes

This research was supported, in part, by the Rockefeller Foundation and the Multinational Corporation Project of the Graduate School of Business Administration of New York University. Neither is responsible for the views expressed here. This paper benefited from the helpful discussions and research assistance of Ingo Walter, Kenneth Krieger, Judith Ugelow, Deborah Halliday, C. V. Pappachan, Greg Kiviat, Fred Wise, and Janis Bromfeld.

1. T. Gladwin, The Management of Environmental Conflict: A Survey of Research Approaches and Priorities (Jan. 1978) (Working Paper #78-09, Graduate School of Business Administration, New York University). *See also* L. Susskind, J. Richardson & K. Hildebrand, Resolving Environmental Disputes: Approaches to

Intervention, Negotiation and Conflict Resolution (June 1978) (Project Paper, Environmental Impact Assessment Project, Laboratory of Architecture and Planning, MIT).

2. *See, e.g.,* P. Baldwin & M. Baldwin, ONSHORE PLANNING FOR OFFSHORE OIL: LESSONS FROM SCOTLAND (1975); P. Bradford, FRAGILE STRUCTURES: A STORY OF OIL REFINERIES, THE NATIONAL SECURITY, AND THE COAST OF MAINE (1975); L. Caldwell, L. Hayes & I. MacWhirter, CITIZENS AND THE ENVIRONMENT: CASE STUDIES IN POPULAR ACTION (1976); L. Carter, THE FLORIDA EXPERIENCE: LAND AND WATER POLICY IN A GROWTH STATE (1974); R. Easton, BLACK TIDE: THE SANTA BARBARA OIL SPILL AND ITS CONSEQUENCES (1972); S. Ebbin & R. Kasper, CITIZEN GROUPS AND THE NUCLEAR POWER CONTROVERSY (1974); H. Feiveson, F. Sinden & R. Socolow, BOUNDARIES OF ANALYSIS: AN INQUIRY INTO THE TOCKS ISLAND DAM CONTROVERSY (1976); B. Gibbons, WYE ISLAND: OUTSIDERS, INSIDERS, AND RESISTANCE TO CHANGE (1977); R. Gregory, THE PRICE OF AMENITY: FIVE STUDIES IN CONSERVATION AND GOVERNMENT (1971); R. Kimber & J. Richardson, CAMPAIGNING FOR THE ENVIRONMENT (1974); R. Lewis, THE NUCLEAR POWER REBELLION (1972); A. Lovins, ERYRI: THE MOUNTAINS OF LONGING (1971); J. Mitchell, LOSING GROUND (1975); D. Nelkin, JETPORT: THE BOSTON AIRPORT CONTROVERSY (1974); J. Nicolson, SHETLAND AND OIL (1975); B. Richardson, STRANGERS DEVOUR THE LAND (1975); J. Roscow, 800 MILES TO VALDEZ: THE BUILDING OF THE ALASKA PIPELINE (1977); F. Schaumburg, JUDGMENT RESERVED: A LANDMARK ENVIRONMENTAL CASE (1976); W. Smith & A. Smith, MINAMATA (1975); A. Talbot, POWER ALONG THE HUDSON: THE STORM KING CASE AND THE BIRTH OF ENVIRONMENTALISM (1972); T. Whiteside, THE PENDULUM AND THE TOXIC CLOUD (1979).

3. For descriptions of the project see Gladwin, *supra* note 1; Gladwin, *Environmental Conflict*, 2 EIA REV. 48 (1978).

4. D. Katz & R. Kahn, THE SOCIAL PSYCHOLOGY OF ORGANIZATIONS 613 (2d ed. 1978).

5. Storper & DesRochers, *Can A Quiet Agricultural County on the Sacramento River Find True Happiness with a Huge, Messy Chemical Plant?* 1976 NOT MAN APART 1.

6. The assistance of Patrick P. McCurdy, Editor-in-Chief of *Chemical Week Magazine* in providing source materials for this data set is gratefully acknowledged. The "Environmental Conflict Project" has also constructed conflict data sets on minerals, mining, occupational health and safety, and energy supply facilities. The "Chemical Process Industry" set was the first one selected for conversion to a computer data base. It was chosen on grounds of prior research foundations, information availability, and pervasiveness of conflict episodes. We believe the set to be representative of all environmental conflict over industrial facilities. It may not, however, be representative of conflicts over public works projects such as highways or dams, given the different incentive systems under which governmental agencies, as opposed to private corporations, operate.

7. Only conflicts which emerged after January 1, 1970, were included in the trend analysis efforts. More than 100 conflicts which emerged in the 1960s but were mentioned in news reports in the 1970s were thus excluded from portions of the data analysis.

8. These secondary sources, drawn on for various time periods include: AMBIO, ATLAS WORLD PRESS REVIEW, AUDUBON, BUSINESS INTERNATIONAL, BUSINESS & SOCIETY REVIEW, BUSINESS WEEK, CHEMICAL & ENGINEERING NEWS, CONSERVATION FOUNDATION LETTER, THE ECOLOGIST, THE ECONOMIST, ENVIRONMENT, ENVIRONMENTAL ACTION, ENVIRONMENTAL POLICY AND LAW, ENVIRONMENTAL SCIENCE & TECHNOLOGY, EUROPE ENVIRONMENT, EUROPEAN BUSINESS, FORTUNE, THE INTERNATIONAL HERALD TRIBUNE, THE LIVING WILDERNESS, MANAGER MAGAZINE, NEW SCIENTIST, THE NEW YORK TIMES, NOT MAN APART, LE NOUVEL ECONOMISTE, NRDC NEWSLETTER, THE OIL & GAS JOURNAL, PETROLEUM ECONOMIST, SCIENCE, SIERRA CLUB BULLETIN, VISION, THE WALL STREET JOURNAL, and WORLD ENVIRONMENTAL REPORT.

9. For the foreign date *see* T. Gladwin & I. Walter, MULTINATIONALS UNDER FIRE: LESSONS IN THE MANAGEMENT OF CONFLICT (1980). For the multivariate causal analyses contact the author for recent working papers.

10. Downs, *Up and Down with Ecology—The "Issue-Attention" Cycle*, 28 PUB. INTEREST 38 (1972).

11. *See* M. Deutsch, THE RESOLUTION OF CONFLICT: CONSTRUCTIVE AND DESTRUCTIVE PROCESSES (1973); D. Druckman, NEGOTIATIONS: SOCIAL-PSYCHOLOGICAL PERSPECTIVES (1977); I. Morley & G. Stephenson, THE SOCIAL PSYCHOLOGY OF BARGAINING (1977); J. Rubin & B. Brown, THE SOCIAL PSYCHOLOGY OF BARGAINING AND NEGOTIATION (1975); P. Swingle, THE MANAGEMENT OF POWER (1976); I. Zartman, THE NEGOTIATION PROCESS: THEORIES AND APPLICATION (1978).

12. *See* M. Baram, ENVIRONMENTAL LAW AND THE SITING OF FACILITIES: ISSUES IN LAND USE AND COASTAL ZONE MANAGEMENT (1976); F. Bosselman & D. Callies, THE QUIET REVOLUTION IN LAND USE CONTROL (1972); F. Bosselman & D. Fevrer, THE PERMIT EXPLOSION (1977); J. Devanney, G. Ashe & B. Parkhurst, PARABLE BEACH: A PRIMER IN COASTAL ZONE ECONOMICS (1976); R. Healy, LAND USE AND THE STATES (1976); R. Linowes & D. Allensworth, THE POLITICS OF LAND USE: PLANNING, ZONING AND THE PRIVATE DEVELOPER (1973), R. Nelson, ZONING AND PROPERTY RIGHTS (1977); J. Noble, J. Banta & J. Rosenberg, GROPING THROUGH THE MAZE (1977); O'Hare, *Not on My Block You Don't: Facility Siting and Strategic Importance of Compensation*, 25 PUB. POLICY 407 (1977).

13. *See A Nation in Court,* THE ECONOMIST, November 5, 1977, at 44; *The Trouble with Lawyers,* THE NEW REPUBLIC, May 20, 1978, at 5; *The Chilling Impact of Litigation,* BUSINESS WEEK, June 6, 1977, at 58.

14. *See Whither Now the Ecolos?* VISION, March 1979, at 29; Spivak, *Nuclear Power Plans Unchanged in Europe Despite Rising Protests,* Wall St. J., April 3, 1979, at 6; Fernex, *Non-Violence Triumphant,* 5 THE ECOLOGIST 372 (1975); *Plump and Einfallslos,* MANAGER MAGAZINE, July 7, 1975 at 24; *Don't Tell Us Nuclear Power is Safe, We Don't Like It,* THE ECONOMIST, November 13, 1976, at 63.

15. Gladwin, *supra* note 1.

16. *See* P. Baldwin, ENVIRONMENTAL MEDIATION: AN EFFECTIVE ALTERNATIVE? (1978); RESOLVE, SELECTED READINGS IN ENVIRONMENTAL CONFLICT RESOLUTION (1978); M. Rivkin, NEGOTIATED DEVELOPMENT (1977); Carpenter & Kennedy, *Information Sharing and Conciliation: Tools for Environmental Conflict Management,* ENVT'L COM., May 1977, at 21; Clark, *Consensus Building: Mediating Energy, Environmental, and Economic Conflict,* ENVT'L COM., May 1977, at 9; Cormick, *Medi-*

ating Environmental Controversies: Perspective and First Experience, 2 EARTH L.J. 215 (1976); Cormick & Patton, *Environmental Mediation: Potentials and Limitations,* ENVT'L COM., May 1977, at 13; various issues of ENVIRONMENTAL CONSENSUS (published by RESOLVE, Center for Environmental Conflict Resolution); Greenburg & Straus, *Up-Front Resolution of Environmental and Economic Disputes,* ENVT'L COM., May 1977, at 16; McCarthy, *Resolving Environmental Conflicts,* 10 ENVT'L SCIENCE & TECHNOLOGY 40 (1976); O'Connor, *Environmental Mediation: The-State-of-the-Art,* 2 EIA REV. (October 1978); *Removing the Rancor from Tough Disputes,* BUSINESS WEEK, August 30, 1976, at 50; Straus, *Mediating Environmental, Energy and Economic Trade-Offs,* 32 ARBITRATION J. 96 (1977); Susskind, It's Time to Shift Our Attention from Impact Assessment to Strategies for Resolving Environmental Disputes, 1978 EIA REVIEW 4; Gladwin, *supra* note 1.

17. *Id. See also* J. Thibaut & L. Walker, PROCEDURAL JUSTICE: A PSYCHOLOGICAL ANALYSIS (1975).

18. Gladwin, *supra* note 1. *See also* Baldwin, *supra* note 16; Cormick & Patton, *supra* note 16; S. Mernitz, Mediation of Environmental Disputes: An Evaluation of Its Potential and Its Geographic Aspects (doctoral dissertation at the University of Wisconsin-Madison, 1978).

19. These measures for the interval scale data represent zero-order Pearson's product-moment correlations (ranging from -1 to +1) which assume symmetric and simple linear associations.

20. *See* note 9 *supra.*

21. Results of this correlation analysis can be obtained by writing to the author.

DOUGLAS MACLEAN

3 *Risk and Consent*

Philosophical Issues for Centralized Decisions

Introduction

At a typical conference on risk assessment or risk management, one session will be called something like "Social and Ethical Issues." It will usually be the last one on the program, and experts from the many professions who attend these conferences will then announce, with sincerity bordering on solemnity, that these issues are, after all, among the most important problems in the entire field. This session is as predictable as a litany. Members of the fraternity of risk experts, who may have quarreled for days, are now united in agreement. If nobody dissents, it is probably because nothing very substantive is being said.

Their sentiment is genuine and justified. Activities that involve great risks, and decisions that impose risks on other people, demand justification. This is an ethical or normative issue. If risk experts are not sure what to say about these issues, I believe the reason is that they involve philosophically difficult (or, as philosophers sometimes say, deep) problems. Let me announce at the outset that I shall not propose a method for solving ethical problems in risk management. In this paper, I will attempt, instead, to suggest a framework for thinking about some of them. This will involve identifying and relating certain philosophical concepts.

The concept that will focus this discussion is consent. Consent, I will argue, is a complex notion. First, there are different kinds of consent. This is

From Douglas MacLean, "Risk and Consent: Philosophical Issues for Centralized Decisions," in *Risk Analysis*, Vol. 2 (June 1982), pp. 59-67. Reprinted by permission of the Plenum Publishing Corporation and Douglas MacLean.

a virtue, since the most obvious and intuitive notion of consent—explicit, actual consent—will not apply where decisions are centralized and large numbers of people are affected. We will need to appeal, therefore, to more indirect versions of consent. Second, we will see that for consent to have normative or justificatory force, it will have to be conceptually linked to other concepts, most importantly, to the concept of rationality. As our understanding of consent becomes more indirect or hypothetical, the concept of rationality becomes more important and plays a stronger normative role. This is what I will argue. If I am correct, then we will see how the philosophical project might be linked to (and sometimes, perhaps, used to criticize) the work of economists and psychologists in this area, where rationality plays a central role.

In the next section I will give a general and abstract description of some risk-management problems for which the issue of consent is important and problematical. Then, in the following section, I will describe and relate three models of indirect consent. Finally, I will offer some speculations about how some other philosophical issues—aesthetic issues—are related to consent and deserve to be examined.

Centralized Decisions and Consent

A primary practical concern of risk assessors today is to determine how safe is safe enough in situations where individuals, acting individually, are not able to reach a satisfactory solution. Some of these situations involve isolation or coordination problems, where individuals can reduce a risk by their actions (which involve accepting a cost or foregoing a benefit) only if everybody acts similarly, but where no mechanisms exist to assure that others will cooperate. Or the situation may prohibit individual solutions because the transaction costs are too high, either because many different actors are each imposing slight risks which may be intolerable in their aggregate, or else because one actor imposes significant risks which are distributed thinly over very many individuals. Still other situations involve large-scale projects to provide public goods, where a social consensus about safety may be difficult or impossible to obtain.

In all these circumstances, decisions must be made by central authorities, usually governments. The problems are disturbingly general. They are dramatic because they involve life-and-death decisions that arouse considerable public concern. They are also complex, because the risks may be poorly understood, even by experts, thus raising further problems about determining and relying on public perceptions.

The work done in the area of risk assessment points explicitly to some deep philosophical problems. What special constraints are justified where risks are imposed on individuals (for example, members of future generations) for whom direct compensation may not be possible? And what is to count as compensation? Is compensation required only where the risks turn out badly—where they become actual costs—or should people be compensated for being subjected to risk? When do individuals have the right to reject a risk—or a risk-with-compensation package? When is it acceptable to impose a risk on others? Are there reasonable levels of risk that we can identify with analytical techniques and use to criticize individual perceptions? Or are individual perceptions the judge of reasonableness for the levels and kinds of risk that others may impose? And how do we accommodate fear? The fear surrounding many risks may be out of proportion to any reasonable measure of those risks (nuclear power and airplane safety, on the one hand, smoking and medical checkups, on the other). But fear is a cost, even where the risks do not turn out badly. We need to address problems such as these in a detailed and philosophically systematic way. My goal here is to lay some of the preliminary groundwork for discussing these more pressing issues.

The problems we are concerned with, where decision-making is centralized, will only occasionally yield noncontroversially to an "economic fix." An economic fix is a change in the structure of a situation that enables a satisfactory market solution. Where this is a desirable solution (and this point is often debated) it is because markets allow individuals to make their own choices, trading off values, as they see them, for their own advantage. People may regret their choices, but they take responsibility for the decisions that affect them.

In order to find a market or a quasimarket solution to problems involving risk, we may seek to "internalize" costs. This may not always be a desirable solution, even where it is a possible one, but especially when we are dealing with large-scale projects, latent effects, irreversibilities, and the like; it may not even be a possible solution. Moreover, individual perceptions about many of these risks, as individuals will candidly admit, are not always trustworthy. Eventually, however, a governmental agency or other centralized authority will have to make a choice and impose a decision. Since these choices are between competing values they require justification.

There are two very good reasons why we should think that consent, rather than some other concept, will play the crucial role in this justification. The first is that in less problematic cases involving risks, where the decisions do not have to be centralized and where fewer people are involved, consent is necessary. A physician or a medical researcher must obtain your explicit prior consent before she is allowed to impose risks by experimenting on your body. Detailed procedures are often required to certify that consent is obtained and to assure that some act or empirical procedure—like signing a form—truly counts as consent. A subject must, for example, be informed, uncoerced, and

in a normal frame of mind. We should take these simpler cases as our paradigm, and proceed from there to see how the nature or the role of consent
changes as the contexts of the risk decisions vary and become more complicated.

The second reason for examining consent is that no other concepts look
very promising. The requirements of justice or rights in this area demand a
separate and fuller treatment, but I can try to indicate briefly why I think
these other moral notions will not take us to the heart of the matter. Suppose,
for example, that we are wondering about how to justify standards for toxic-
waste disposal or standards for ambient air quality, and let us imagine that
after compensations are made, the risks and benefits are distributed more or
less equitably. The problem of justice or equity would not arise in this unreal-
istically utopian setting, yet the problems of setting and justifying an acceptable level of risk all remain.

Similar problems frustrate from the start any attempt to make progress
on these issues by invoking a theory of rights. Consider for a moment what
rights we would want to say individuals have in decisions that will affect their
safety or in determining the right balance between increased risk or safety,
added costs, and foregone benefits. People have the rights over decisions that
affect their property. Property, let us say, is to be distinguished into the *real*
and the *personal*. Most currently popular theories of rights include the right
of an individual to the use of his real property, and virtually all of them
include the right of the individual to his personal property, especially his body
and its parts.[1] A property right gives an individual veto power over decisions
that promote social welfare if they involve boundary crossings onto property
to which he has the right of use.

No theory, however, puts this forward as an absolute right. Over real
property the state has power of eminent domain; but this is restricted, and in
some ways defined, by the compensation clause of the Fifth Amendment. If a
person may lose his land, buildings, or some other investment, for example,
in a major mishap, must he be paid? Must he be paid even to bear such risks?
Or shall we say that property owners, who gain windfalls from public policy
(a highway near their store, for example) should bear the costs of mishap as
well? These are familiar problems.

The situation is different in respect to rights over personal property. Here
the right of the state to take what it needs for a public purpose is much more
circumscribed; indeed, it usually requires some emergency, such as a war.
The power of the state under eminent domain cannot be extended to the
bodies of persons without raising severe political, legal, and philosophical
problems. Hence the moral controversy over the military draft.

In some cases, an actor is not allowed to impose a cost, even with compensation, unless permission from the right-holder is obtained. In other cases,

costs, with compensation, can be imposed. Under which of these principles should we include society's risk decisions? Does it make any difference whether an individual or a firm or the government is imposing the risk? If we simply allow each individual the right to refuse, the results are intolerable. This analysis would imply, for example, that any individual has a veto power over any attempt to set standards for acceptable levels of air pollution. On the other hand, the right of eminent domain cannot be universal without posing too great a threat to the autonomy of individuals and communities. One's willingness to compensate, for instance, does not give him the right to play Russian roulette on an unwilling victim, even with a gun with thousands of chambers.[2] I know of no analysis of rights which does not ultimately appeal to the notion of reasonable consent that can sort out these cases.

Neither will efficiency be the central concept. In some risk contexts, it will not be clear what efficiency consists of, or how it could be measured. But even where we know what efficiency is, we cannot use it alone to justify our choices.[3] Consent to centralized decisions is crucial in a society that is nonauthoritarian.

There are many public policy decisions we *could* make to promote efficiency, but that we do not make because they would be wrong. No doubt it would be more efficient to dispense with elections in picking public officials, to dispense with jury trials in criminal proceedings, and to implement on a broad scale technologically sophisticated surveillance equipment as a better means to law enforcement. Of course it would violate our rights to do any of these things, but we also refuse to consent to these ways of being more efficient. In the area of reducing risks, it is an outstanding problem when and how we want to be more efficient than we are. Other values might conflict with efficiency. In the end, therefore, efficiency is a reason for doing something only when efficiency is supported by an argument from consent.

Before proceeding to describe some models of indirect consent, two further points should be kept in mind. The first is about risk assessment. One possibility for justifying a decision about risk is to make that decision on the basis of a method of risk assessment that measures and compares all the relevant factors. The argument, then, would have to show that ideally reasonable or rational people would consent to this decision because the method that generated it takes account of all the factors that matter. This argument would be based on conceptions of indirect consent that I will discuss below. Notice, first of all, that the idea of rationality is immediately prominent in this way of arguing. We should also notice what requirements this kind of argument would place on a method of risk assessment or evaluation that could be the basis of a decision. The risk-assessment technique must be abstract and general, so that estimations of different health risks, and also of the expected costs and benefits associated with accepting, eliminating, or controlling these risks, are comparable; at the same time, this information must be presented in such a way that it is rational for a person to choose on this basis.

These are stiff requirements. The problem is not simply to come up with just any common measure of risk that will homogenize all differences and present all factors on a single scale. It is no more difficult here than anywhere to cook up an artificial technique that will churn out an answer in any situation. The literature on risk abounds with them.[4] What we need are *acceptable* techniques for measuring and evaluating risks, ones to which reasonable people would consent, even if this means, in the end, that no single metric is entirely adequate.

The second point is about the connection between rationality and consent. Even in the simpler cases I mentioned, rationality plays a role in determining whether the necessary condition of consent is also sufficient. Sometimes an act that normally counts as consent may strike us as so crazy or irrational that we discount it. Now, I think that what we are likely to say in these cases is that the person had not "really" consented, but this way of speaking only demonstrates how some background of rationality is logically or conceptually connected to our understanding of consent. We may, occasionally, not even allow people to make certain choices because we are confident that no reasonable person could so choose. These are rare cases, no doubt, and consent is usually sufficient where people act individually with negligible effects on third parties, but the connection between consent and rationality is present even if it is not often noticed. I emphasize this because, as each successive model of indirect consent moves further from actual consent, the role of rationality becomes more important.

Three Models of Indirect Consent

It is useful, and not too distorting, to think of the different kinds of consent as situated along a continuum. At one end, consent is vivid, actual, and explicit, and the role of rationality in understanding the normative force of this kind of consent is present but minimal. As we move toward the other end of the continuum, consent becomes less explicit, more indirect, even entirely hypothetical, and the concept of rationality correspondingly becomes richer and takes on a more important normative role. The metaphor of a continuum should not, perhaps, be pressed too hard, for I doubt whether some conception of consent can be identified at every possible point or whether between any two conceptions of consent we might describe we can find another. Certainly there would be no interest simply in proliferating the number of such conceptions.

I will describe three conceptions or models of consent, but it is important to see how each successive model moves further away from the most explicit kind of consent, our paradigm. The reason this is important is that the last model is actually a suggestion for extending the "continuum" a bit, to the point where the concept of consent atrophies, playing a role in justifying risk decisions no more important than the role of the appendix in the functioning of the human body, while the concept of rationality bears the whole normative burden. I want to suggest at the end that the model that I will call "nonconsent" might help to justify some important risk decisions that today we find very difficult to justify.

IMPLICIT CONSENT

Some of the techniques that have been devised recently to evaluate the acceptability of certain risks rely on implicit consent. Revealed preference theory is one example.[5] The idea is that individual preferences for risk and safety trade-offs are revealed in certain areas, where markets function properly, so we can use data from these areas to justify decisions in other areas.

Market solutions to questions of risk are desirable, according to the defender of revealed preference theory, not because market solutions are efficient but because in a properly functioning market, as we have already suggested, people are supposed to consent to their transactions. Smoke detectors, for example, are sold to people who want to buy them. The costs of extra safety are known and individuals make their own decisions about how to balance costs and benefits in determining the level of safety they shall have. Since they make these decisions explicitly, they can thereby be said to consent to the trade-offs they accept. Likewise, we find studies purporting to show that evidence from the labor market indicates what extra benefits people demand in exchange for accepting the greater risks of hazardous work. These data, too, are used as a basis for generalizations about preferences for risk and benefit trade-offs.[6]

Once these general preferences for risk are determined, they are applied in contexts where market solutions are unavailable. Thus, safety standards can be set through centralized decisions that mimic the trade-offs market data reveal. These decisions are said to be justified because the public implicitly consents to them. What this means is that the decision establishes a level of risk or safety, at a cost and in exchange for benefits, identical to the level that people explicitly consented to accept in other areas. The assumption is that they would have consented here, had they been able to make a free and informed choice.

The development of a revealed preference approach to risk assessment was motivated in large part by the desire to resolve debates about adequate safety in nuclear power plants. Some people thought that criticisms of the risks of nuclear power were entirely irrational because the critics were advocating much more safety at much greater cost than they demanded in other areas, or so it was claimed. The particular version of implicit consent I have described was defended specifically in order to make this discussion more rational by advocating consistency in our treatment of risk.

Many controversial assumptions are needed to make a revealed preference version of implicit consent into a normative standard of justification. Since choices in the market are voluntary, in some sense, while centralized decisions are strictly imposed, we must assume that we are able to infer choices for imposed risks from choices for voluntary risks. It is further assumed that market data, which indicate past decisions, reflect people's attitudes toward the risks from such new, enormous, mysterious, potentially catastrophic, and symbolically significant technologies as a nuclear reactor. Some of these criticisms have led to an alternative implicit consent theory. This theory, called expressed preference theory, uses psychometric techniques to uncover current attitudes and preferences about these relevant factors.[7]

There are some important problems that arise in using implicit consent to justify decisions, especially in revealed preference theory. Can preferences revealed in markets be taken to reveal true and general preferences for balancing risks and benefits? In order for this to be true, consumers must be choosing on the basis of adequate information in a context of sufficient alternatives, and they must, furthermore, be satisfied with the choices they have made. Can we be certain that any of these conditions are met in the labor market, when people choose to accept hazardous work? The answer, clearly, is "no."

A related issue is this. People who might be willing to shop for safety in their homes and automobiles sometimes express a conviction that things like air and water should be treated differently. They do not regard these things as economic resources but tend to think that clean air and safe water are like social ideals or even rights. They want these things treated in different ways, even if the economic outcomes of this treatment will be different from the economic preferences they reveal for other things. We do not have to endorse this conviction in order to recognize that it is widely held. It is especially common where the costs of saving or of refusing to save extra lives are being considered. It is not so much that people believe we should forever be spending more for lifesaving, but that we should be considering these issues and making these decisions in other ways.[8] The belief is that the consent we reveal in a market, as consumers, is not implicitly consent to treating all allocation decisions as though they were market decisions. We might believe that some values require different procedures, and not just consistent outcomes, that it is not *reasonable* to treat all social decisions consistently *in this way*, as economic choices.

Again, I emphasize that I am not defending this view simply by describing it. An argument or justification for treating some values or goods differently must be given. The problem with implicit consent arguments, however, (or at least the revealed preference version of implicit consent) is that they simply beg the question about this socially important issue.

Revealed preference theory and its problems illustrate a point about the role of rationality in a model of implicit consent. Consent in one area is taken to justify a choice in another area. The assumptions about rationality that are needed to make this argument basically follow the formal constraints of rationality, common in economics for example, that rational preferences are consistent and transitive. These assumptions are beyond dispute, but what counts as consistency in behavior or in choice ultimately depends on how we interpret and judge certain background beliefs and values.

Are the critics of nuclear power who demand "excessive" safety really irrational, or are they only operating with some different assumptions and beliefs? Even the behavior of a schizophrenic can be seen as consistent, given the proper assumptions about his beliefs. At some point, clearly, we have to examine the background conditions that determine whether choices are consistent or not, and we must subject these beliefs and values to criticism and examine their rationality. This is a sense of rationality, of course, that is much richer and more substantial than the bare, formal (and noncontroversial) conception of rationality common in economics.

HYPOTHETICAL CONSENT

Hypothetical consent models attempt to evade the problem of determining people's actual preferences and generalizing from them. They do this by asking instead what people would consent to under certain favorable conditions. Hypothetical consent differs from implicit consent in two ways. First, consent, which was indirect in the implicit consent model, becomes even more shadowy. It is a complete idealization and never has to be based on any actual consent. Hypothetical consent is counterfactual, since it is based on an argument about what people would consent to under certain specified conditions, and these may be and often are completely unrealizable. What makes the model normative is the moral justification of these stipulated conditions. Thus, we might specify certain ideal conditions that model what the world would be like if everyone were treated fairly and equally, and then we might ask about some particular decision what people in that situation would choose to do.[9] Such an argument can be taken to support a conclusion about what we, in our current circumstances, ought to do.

The second difference is this: when we specify ideal conditions and ask what people in that situation would choose to do, we are not inviting ourselves to speculate about the effect of those stipulated conditions on human psychology. For all we know, humans are naturally perverse, so that in a morally ideal setting people would make bizarre choices that feed their neuroses in ways that the misery and injustice of our actual circumstances feed them now. I am not, of course, suggesting that our psychological makeup really is like this, but only that even if we had evidence that it was, this evidence would be irrelevant to the thought experiment that is supposed to generate hypothetical consent. What we are asking in that thought experiment is not how idealized conditions would affect the choices of actual people, but how ideal people would choose in those circumstances. We idealize the people, too, by making them ideally rational. What would a rational person do in those circumstances? That is our question. It is in this conception of rationality that we find the second major difference of the hypothetical consent model.

In order to yield any answer at all to the question of what a rational person would choose under ideal conditions, we must assume much more about that person than formal conditions of rationality, such as consistency. These further conditions will include assumptions about the values of a rational person, such as preferring happiness to misery, or perhaps desiring to have more rather than less of what we think of as good. Even with these assumptions, there may be no answer to what an ideally rational person would choose in many circumstances, but without such assumptions no answer could even be attempted.

To illustrate the hypothetical consent model, we can consider Pareto optimality, a principle basic to welfare economics, and examine how it is modified to apply to centralized decisions about health and safety risks. We define Pareto optimality in the following way. One allocation is (strong) Pareto-superior to another if and only if it makes no one worse off and at least one person better off. One allocation is (weak) Pareto-superior to another if and only if the gainers can compensate the losers and, after compensation, no one is worse off and at least one person is better off. A state of affairs is (strong or weak) Pareto-optimal if and only if it is technologically feasible and no Pareto-superior changes can be made. Pareto-superior moves produce only winners, no losers. Thus, they avoid a defect of utilitarian moral theories, which allow choices that involve sacrificing some people as means for producing overall social benefits.

In fact, however, this improvement is of little importance, because in many of society's risk activities the losers cannot be compensated. What, after all, compensates for death or permanent injury? It will not do to point to procedures for determining appropriate damages in negligence cases, for this is not the kind of compensation required by a Pareto justification, because it will not leave a person as well off as she would have been had the risk not ended up harming her. If compensation is impossible, a weak Pareto principle will not apply, but a strong Pareto principle would prohibit undertaking any risky activities that will result in real losses.

In order to avoid this difficulty, the Pareto principle must be modified. It is recast as a counterfactual principle that takes us back to the time when a risk is imposed, or perhaps even earlier, to a point where we will determine the procedures for deciding how, when, and where risks will be imposed (for example, procedures for determining where toxic-waste sites or MX missiles will be located). From some *ex ante* position the losers will be unidentified, and everyone will confront a situation in which there are only risks. Then, perhaps, compensation can be determined, and an efficiency argument can be made to work. This is *ex ante* compensation, as determined by an *ex ante* Pareto principle.

Why, though, should someone who actually faces a loss, or who has already suffered it, be persuaded by any such arguments?[10] In the end, it must be argued first that any reasonable person *would have consented* to the scheme that imposes these losses, and then that it is *fair* that these losses be suffered because of this hypothetical consent.

A virtue of the hypothetical consent model is that it might justify decisions in areas where there is now controversy and where there will undoubtedly be winners and losers. It does this by dividing risk decisions into two stages. The first stage establishes procedures that are regarded as fair to all for making decisions, and in the second stage the argument shows that a given decision would result from these procedures; it is therefore rational for a person to accept decisions made this way. On the basis of this kind of argument some theorists claim that people consent to their losses. This is quite misleading, for the word "consent" is being used metaphorically. It would be better to say that if a rational person, under conditions fair to all, would agree to procedures for making a decision, or to the decision itself, then the results of that decision are justified, even to the losers.

The problem with this model, of course, is in the argument that certain procedures are neutral and fair. If people know from the start how certain decisions are likely to affect them, they will not easily be convinced that procedures that will harm them are neutrally chosen. If we cannot find neutral procedures, then we must justify them on the basis of other principles we are willing to defend, principles that may have to endorse certain values. The issues will turn, then, on whether we can identify values that any reasonable person would accept, so that we are not unfair to some people by refusing to consider their legitimate interests.[11]

NONCONSENT

A hypothetical consent model, I believe, provides a promising way to justify some risk decisions. If we try to develop this model and make it powerful enough to have any practical applications for policy decisions, we will find ourselves paying more attention explicitly to rational values and less to actual consent. As we proceed down this road, we will probably be arguing in ways that those who have advocated hypothetical consent would be reluctant to accept. Perhaps, then, we should identify another model on our continuum and call it ultrahypothetical consent or, more simply, nonconsent.

A nonconsent model recognizes that the justification of some decisions might require direct appeals to the values we seek to secure, even though this might entail endorsing and ranking social values through philosophical arguments.[12] Proponents of this model would argue that not all individual preferences should be given equal weight in the arrangement of social institutions. If we need to interfere with liberty to promote our interest in equality or security or posterity, then we do this because one value is of greater weight or at any rate more urgent, than another in the area in question. Consent need not always be the basis of this claim.

The pitfalls of this model are too obvious to belabor. The arguments need to convince us that the decisions they imply are not authoritarian. Moreover, we would need to establish the political mechanisms for making these decisions. Currently, in fact, such decisions are coming to rest increasingly with the courts, but even there the problem of justification remains.[13] If we restrict ourselves to hypothetical consent, our arguments sometimes appear desperately ad hoc. There may, in fact, be good social reasons to draft 19-year-olds and expose them to a disproportionately high risk of death in war, but it is highly artificial to resolve our doubts about whether this is a proper way to treat our youth by arguing that, despite their protests to the contrary, they have consented to the system or the process that selects them for this service.[14]

Qualitative Determinants of Consent

I cannot attempt to pursue an argument about rational values in this paper, but I will mention one issue that a discussion of rational values would consider. Risks differ in their natures, and this raises some obvious problems for comparing risks and making decisions between them. Even where risks can be quantified, treating them merely as quantitative changes in a person's life prospects can obscure the qualitative aspects relevant to our social values. Extensive psychological research shows that risks are feared disproportionately to their dangers.[15]

The problem is this: we know that society demands greater safety, at greater cost, in some areas than in others. Airplanes must be safer than ground transportation; nuclear reactors must be safer than coal-fired plants. Sometimes we might choose to save fewer lives rather than more lives at equal cost because to do otherwise seems to value human lives in an unacceptable manner. The question is: "what makes these decisions acceptable?"

Some risk analyses try to be sensitive to these important "intangibles" and to factor them into the equations as "psychic costs."[16] More often than not, however, the attempt to do so is ad hoc. Most such attempts fail to base their claims successfully in any established theory of psychology or on any moral or philosophical basis. They appear more to be attempts to save a method of analysis than to demonstrate its explanatory power.

A typology of risk may help us to guide our use of decision techniques and our application of such concepts as the social value of human life. It will enable us to explain when it is acceptable to generalize from individual decisions to social decisions. Thus, a typology must explore the aesthetics of risk, the personal attitudes toward different risks that are relevant to formulating standards of social acceptability. Nobody wants a totally risk-free environment. In some activities we seek to concentrate risk, not to spread it, and this is essential to the value those activities have for us.[17] They exercise human abilities and test human potentials. Nobody wants to spend more on mountain-climbing safety; many people object to further safety measures on ski slopes or for motorcycles; and there is no shortage of test pilots or astronauts, though the compensation is often only standard military-officers' pay. How far-reaching are the implications of such phenomena? Do they tell us something about spending money to reduce risk in private airplanes? In automobiles? The Hell's Angels may refuse to wear helmets for macho reasons we dimly comprehend, but we do not imagine that their thrills include descending on Three Mile Island to breathe possibly contaminated air. This suggests that many factors determine socially acceptable risk, in addition to the probability that one will be harmed or killed from some given cause.

In some cases, such as mountain climbing, the risks themselves are essential to the value of the activity. In other cases, even when we restrict ourselves to risks that are voluntarily accepted, risks that are not essential to the value of the activity are accepted or rejected for different reasons. Someone may buy a smoke detector because he plans to take up smoking and he fears he might fall asleep with a cigarette lit.

We should also consider examples of the different kinds of risk that individuals choose to accept. The very few people who have discussed such cases invariably look at risks to life and limb. We naturally tend to think of activities that test one's physical limits, and the values that people find in these activities. But we should also think about a different kind of risk altogether, those that individuals take when choosing a course of action—say, a career path or a decision to marry—which may turn out well or badly, or will change one's life in unpredictable ways. Some people enjoy such gambles; some think the necessity of confronting such contingencies strongly determines our outlook on and appreciation of life. It may turn out that understanding these kinds of risk will prove very valuable to understanding social divisions over risk and safety. Perhaps the fear and opposition to certain large-scale projects has been misperceived because our attention has focused exclusively on safety risks; perhaps the source of the fear in some cases is about different kinds of risks to society or the opposition may be to the *way* these decisions are being made. These issues may be highly relevant to questions about the use of risk-assessment techniques in social decision-making.

References

For many helpful discussions, and for comments on an earlier draft of this paper, I am grateful to Mary Gibson, David Luban, and Susan Wolf. Research has been supported by the National Science Foundation, grant number PRA-80-20019.

1. For a discussion of different theories of rights, see: R. Dworkin, *Taking Rights Seriously* (Harvard University Press, Cambridge, 1977); R. Nozick, *Anarchy, State, and Utopia* (Basic Books, New York, 1974); and H. Shue, *Basic Rights* (Princeton University Press, Princeton, 1980).

2. For a sensitive discussion of these problems, see R. Nozick, op. cit., Chap 4.

3. This is argued in detail in R. Dworkin, Is wealth a value? *Journal of Legal Studies* **9**, 191-227 (1980); Why efficiency? *Hofstra Law Review* **8**, 576–578 (1981).

4. See L. Tribe, Policy science: Analysis or ideology?, *Philosophy & Public Affairs* **2**, 66-110 (1972).

5. See C. Starr, Social benefit versus technological risk, *Science* 165, 1232-1238 (1969).

6. For a review of this literature, see C. Brown, Equalizing differences in the labor market, *Quarterly Journal of Economics* **94**, 113-134 (1980).

7. B. Fischhoff *et al.*, How safe is safe enough? A psychometric study of attitudes towards technological risks and benefits, *Policy Studies* **8**, 127-152 (1978).

8. I have discussed this issue in detail in other essays. See "Quantified risk assessment and the quality of life," in *Uncertain Power*, Dorothy Zinberg, ed. (Pergamon Press, New York, 1983).

9. The most famous recent attempt to develop this model is J. Rawls, *A Theory of Justice* (Harvard University Press, Cambridge, 1971). Some of the extensive discussion of Rawls's version of hypothetical consent as a method of justification can be found in *Reading Rawls,* N. Daniels, ed. (Basic Books, New York, 1974).

10. See R. Dworkin, Why efficiency? op. cit.

11. In J. Rawls, op. cit., the discussion of the values that justify the principles of choice is contained mainly in the sections on primary goods (pp. 62, 90-95) and on the sense of justice and social union (pp. 520-529, 567-577).

12. In a series of articles, T. Scanlon has developed a version of a nonconsent theory. See Preference and urgency, *Journal of Philosophy* **72**, 655-670 (1975); and "Rights, goals, and fairness," in *Public & Private Morality*, S. Hampshire, ed. (Cambridge University Press, Cambridge, 1978), pp. 93-111. Classical utilitarian theories, of course, are another kind of nonconsent theory.

13. See O. Fiss, The Supreme Court: 1978 term, *Harvard Law Review* **93**, 1-58 (1979), for an enthusiastic view of the Supreme Court's role in making public policy. For a negative view, see J. Ely, *Democracy and Distrust* (Harvard University Press, Cambridge, 1980), Chap. 3.

14. See T. Nagel, "Ruthlessness in Public Life," *Public & Private Morality, op. cit.*, 75-92.

15. See B. Fischhoff *et al.*, op. cit. Extensive work in this area has been done by A. Tversky and D. Kahneman. See Judgment under uncertainty: Heuristics and biases, *Science* **185**, 1124-1131 (1974); The framing of decisions and the psychology of choice, *Science* **211**, 453-458 (1981).

16. For examples, see: W. Baumol and W. Oates, *The Theory of Environmental Policy* (Prentice-Hall, Englewood Cliffs N.J., 1975); M. Freeman *et al., The Benefits of Environmental Improvement* (The Johns Hopkins Press, Baltimore, 1979); and L. Tribe, Ways not to think about plastic trees, *Yale Law Journal* **83**, 1315-1348 (1974).

17. The positive value of risk is explored and discussed in many adventure stories. For example, see: T. Wolfe, *The Right Stuff* (Farrar, Strauss, Giroux, New York, 1979); H. Thompson, *Hell's Angels* (Ballantine, New York 1966). For a particularly good philosophical discussion, see W. Sayre, *Four Against Everest* (Tower Books, New York, 1964).

18. See B. Williams and T. Nagel, "A Symposium on moral luck," *Proceedings of the Aristotelian Society*, Supp. Vol. **50**, 115-151 (1976).

SHEILA JASANOFF AND DOROTHY NELKIN

4 Science, Technology, and the Limits of Judicial Competence

Resolution of scientific and technological controversies occupies an increasingly important position in the agenda of the federal courts. Government efforts to regulate problems related to technological advances have given rise to a new brand of litigation that focuses directly on issues debated among scientific experts. Legislation to control environmental and health risks, such as the National Environmental Policy Act, the Clean Air Act, and the Toxic Substances Control Act, require decisions based on the "best scientific information" as well as relevant social and economic considerations. Science itself has become a focus of litigation as advances in biomedical science lead to controversial research and clinical practices that are challenged in the courts. Thus, scientists are frequently called on to provide technical evidence in order to prove the rationality of administrative decisions or to establish the legitimacy of innovative research practices.

The resulting surge of science-related disputes into the judicial arena has produced a set of difficult and highly visible problems for the courts, and it is widely believed that the traditional processes of adjudication are no longer capable of handling many of these disputes. Introducing a panel on science and the law at the 1978 annual meeting of the American Bar Association, a legal scholar remarked:[1]

> Traditional legal techniques, education and institutions, may soon be the same kind of anachronism in an age of science-based technology that canon law

From *Science*, Vol. 214 (December 1981), pp. 1211-1215. Copyright 1981 by the American Association for the Advancement of Science. Reprinted by permission.

> institutions became with the decline of temporal religious authority. . . .
> What may be required is a reform of existing structures which is no less
> comprehensive than the reforms that freed Anglo-American law from the
> technicalities of writs and those that freed science from the grip of Aristotle.

Some scholars have argued that scientific and technical disputes fall outside the limits of judicial competence and that courts should therefore be content with a greatly reduced role in such controversies, limiting themselves to
reviewing the adequacy of procedures for collecting and analyzing scientific
evidence. Judge Bazelon, for example, has suggested that courts reviewing
actions of administrative agencies can do no more than verify that major
technical issues are addressed in agency decision-making, that decisions are
based on a consideration of all the relevant factors, and that the data and reasoning supporting administrative decisions are entered into the public record.[2]
Others seek a more substantive role for the courts, pointing out that it is virtually impossible in practice to avoid scientific and technical issues, because
courts have to acquire some understanding of the basis of agency decisions
simply to evaluate the adequacy of the underlying administrative procedures.[3]
Lawyers and scientists subscribing to this view have put forward a variety of
proposals designed to increase the scientific competence of judicial decision-
makers and provide better technical input into the judicial process.

In this article we consider some recent litigation in an effort to understand why controversies with a large scientific or technical component seem to
place an unusual burden on the adjudicatory process. These controversies fall
into two major classes: (i) those in which ethical issues have been raised by
scientific advances, particularly in the biological sciences, and (ii) those
involving societal risks and perceived deficiencies in the government's effort
to mitigate these risks through regulatory action. In part, the problems
encountered by the courts stem from the scale and complexity of the issues
involved. A "good" decision is hard to reach without evaluating trade-offs
whose ultimate consequences the courts are ill-equipped to consider in the
framework of a conventional adjudicatory proceeding. The high level of
uncertainty involved in the regulation of scientific and technological developments compounds the difficulty. Disagreements exist about the magnitude of
risk, the appropriateness of measuring techniques, and the reliability of data.
Because of its great visibility, the problem of technical uncertainty has
become the main focus of proposals intended to mitigate the difficulty of adju-
dicating scientific and technical disputes. We have examined some of these
proposed reforms and conclude that they frequently concentrate on the ques
tion of technical uncertainty to the exclusion of the conceptual and policy
issues at stake.

Scientific Disputes That Strain the Adjudicatory Process

Theoretical and technical advances, especially in the biological sciences, have made possible clinical applications and research procedures that are controversial on religious or moral grounds. Activities such as fetal research, in vitro fertilization, resuscitation of terminally ill patients, and the creation of living microorganisms through recombinant DNA techniques are perceived by some as having the potential to change the "normal" state of nature, alter the genetic structure of man, threaten cherished values, or even violate natural law. Opposition frequently crystallizes around particular applications of such research as attempts are made case-by-case to define limits through administrative appeals and, increasingly, through litigation. Opponents of particular applications seek judicial support for their moral or religious positions by invoking the traditional power of the courts to prevent or compensate for injurious activity.

In this kind of litigation the conflicting values that underlie a dispute are often masked by scientific issues, and the dynamics of adversary litigation seldom permit a separation or clear identification of the values at stake. This is what happened, for example, in the Del Zio case, in which a plaintiff sued Columbia University, Presbyterian Hospital, and the chairman of Columbia's department of obstetrics for refusing her permission to undergo a voluntary in vitro fertilization procedure. During the trial, the qualifications and scientific credentials of doctors who had agreed to perform the procedure became the subject of debate. Attention was focused not only on their past performance as researchers but also on particular technical decisions, such as the use of temperature charts to determine the time of ovulation and of test tubes rather than petri dishes for fertilization. Relatively little attention was paid to what some have seen as the basic issue in the case: the conflict between Mrs. Del Zio's desire to have a baby, even with the aid of controversial scientific techniques, and Columbia University's prior agreement with the federal government not to permit human experimentation without adequate review.[4] The litigation reduced the ethical issues involved in in vitro fertilization to a debate about what constitutes competent clinical work. This is ironic in view of the fact that adjudication is probably far better suited to weighing competing values and interests than to settling disputes among scientific experts.

A similar blurring of scientific, social, and moral concerns is evident in many of the "right to die" cases that are making their way into the courts. That courts have a legitimate role to play in this area is apparent from a careful reading of the Massachusetts Supreme Judicial Court's decision in the case of the *Superintendent of Belchertown State School v. Saikewicz.*[5] Here, the plaintiff was a 67-year-old, severely retarded man suffering from a fatal form of leukemia. The issue before the court was whether life-prolonging treatment should be administered to Saikewicz. Chemotherapy, the treatment routinely available to and accepted by most competent persons with the same disease, could have led to a remission lasting up to 13 months. The judges decided, after balancing the factors for and against treatment, that the plaintiff, acting through his guardian ad litem, could properly refuse such procedures. The central question in the case concerned the extent of an incompetent person's right to refuse life-prolonging treatment, taking into consideration the state's countervailing interest in preserving human life by any available means. Whatever one thinks of the particular balance struck by the court, it must be recognized that the weighing of competing interests carried out in this case constituted an appropriate functioning of the adjudicatory process.

Most "right to die" cases that reach the courts present considerably less clear-cut issues for adjudication. Typically, these cases arise when physicians refuse to discontinue treatment of terminally ill patients until they are assured by a court of law that the decision may be taken without fear of prosecution. Judicial approval is sought even though both the doctors and the patients' representatives agree from the outset that further treatment would be futile. One result is that the courts are converted into forums where litigants seek to establish the meaning of death in scientific terms. Moreover, it has been argued that resort to the courts in these cases is socially destructive, because court-ordered immunity from prosecution in effect permits the medical profession to escape the responsibility it should assume in making life or death decisions.[6]

No doubt the existence of legally valid definitions of life and death would make such decisions considerably less painful for doctors and for the families of patients, but it is questionable whether litigation is an appropriate avenue for establishing such definitions. For one thing, it would be unreasonable to expect sporadic litigation to aid the development of generally recognized biological criteria for defining concepts such as brain death. A scientific consensus could only be reached if the medical community worked actively toward establishing such criteria and ratified them through consistent professional practice. There is every indication that the courts would respect the results of such an effort and would not compel treatment beyond a point where responsible medical opinion would declare the use of life-prolonging techniques to be useless.[6] However, until a consensus exists, it is perhaps inevitable that a certain number of life-termination decisions will be challenged in the courts. In the meantime, by seeking protection against the threat of lawsuits, doctors may actually delay the attainment of a scientific consensus.

With respect to the ethical issues, although moral, social, or religious scruples may underlie the positions adopted by parties to a lawsuit, the technical rules of litigation virtually ensure that these will not themselves become the subject of courtroom debate. Most "right to die" cases essentially ignore the social or religious aspects of dying and focus instead on the technical definitions of death. In the Del Zio case, the social and ethical questions related to in vitro fertilization did not surface during litigation. Similarly, in the recent controversy over the patentability of living microorganisms, legal arguments have necessarily focused on the intended coverage of the patent laws and the distinction between an invention and a living organism, not on the morality of extending the concept of proprietary rights to the creation and commercial use of new life forms.[7]

Technological developments in areas outside the biological sciences do not directly interfere with the processes of life and death, but frequently pose risks to human health, safety, and welfare that generate controversies. Environmental groups and individuals have increasingly turned to litigation to prevent or minimize such risks, but for a variety of reasons, this type of litigation strains the adjudicatory process almost to the breaking point.

To begin with, such cases give rise to problems that have little to do with their scientific or technical dimensions. Courts are confronted with voluminous records and lengthy procedural wranglings, just as they are in large antitrust cases or other litigation involving major corporate entities and multiple parties. The special flavor of recent technology-related litigation, however, derives from its unique policy context. Government regulation of major technologies has to take into account a conflicting array of scientific, social, and economic considerations and of public and private interests. The trade-offs considered in the course of regulation are so complex that industry, private citizens, and special interest groups all find ample opportunity to raise questions about the scientific or technical validity and procedural fairness of individual decisions, as well as the underlying social values they seem to represent. Litigation growing out of this context takes many forms. Exposure limits for particular toxic substances, siting decisions and the environmental impact statements they are based on, methodologies such as cost-benefit analysis used to evaluate trade-offs, are all subject to challenge in the courts. And when technological failures occur, as at Love Canal or Three Mile Island, numerous and varied claims are filed against public and private entities by persons seeking compensation.

In the American legal system, basic rules of adjudication, such as those for determining standing or for assigning liability, have largely evolved out of a framework of two-party litigation. These procedures tend to break down in modern technology-related litigation, where the complexity of the issues makes it difficult to determine precisely who those affected are, how they have been injured, and by what agency. Liability is hard to apportion because of the confusion of public and private responsibility in the management of large technological enterprises. In the welter of facts, assumptions, and values represented in such litigation, it is almost impossible for judges to perform the painstaking analysis and balancing of conflicting values appropriate to the adjudicatory process.

The conceptual difficulties created for the courts by scientific and technical controversies are mirrored in the novel legal theories developed by the plaintiffs. For example, demonstrators at nuclear power plant sites have attempted to defend themselves against trespass charges by resurrecting the old "lesser of two evils" doctrine. In the course of judicial proceedings they have argued, with occasional success, that the crime of trespassing is less evil than the dangers of nuclear power and that trespassing is therefore justified as a means of dramatizing the greater evil. By invoking such a defense, litigants seek to ensure that some discussion of values will be injected into an otherwise routine proceeding for dealing with a minor infraction of the law. In another example, opposition to the use of nuclear energy resulted in nothing less than a "lawsuit to end atomic power." In *Honicker* v. *Hendrie*, the plaintiff's lawyers prepared a brief arguing that the harmful effects of ionizing radiation justify closing down all nuclear fuel cycle operations immediately.[8] Legal support for this position was derived from an array of national and international sources of law: principles adopted during the Nuremberg trials, covenants of the United Nations, provisions of the U.S. Constitution. As a social manifesto, and even as an indictment of nuclear power, the resulting document makes fascinating reading, but one does not have to engage in sophisticated legal reasoning to see why it could not carry the day in court. In its audacious reliance on litigation to effect large-scale social change, the *Honicker* case drastically, and perhaps intentionally, overstepped the dividing line between adjudication and policy making. Not unexpectedly, the Supreme Court rejected Honicker's petition against the Nuclear Regulatory Commission without comment, reaffirming its earlier, constitutionally based judgment that a policy decision concerning nuclear power must ultimately be left to Congress and the states.

Evidentiary Problems

The strains created by litigants wishing to compel policy formulation through the adjudicatory process are compounded by the uncertainty that pervades scientific and technological controversies. Efforts by the government to prevent or reduce harm from scientific and technological activities require decisions to be made at the frontiers of scientific knowledge, often on the basis of incomplete evidence. Challenges to these decisions bring into the courts disputes concerning the quality and interpretation of data that cannot be resolved definitively on the basis of current scientific knowledge. Examples of such questions abound: What is a "safe" standard for human exposure to low-level radiation? How can data from animal toxicity tests be extrapolated to human beings? How does noise affect human health and well-being?

Although issues like these are frequently raised in litigation, it is important to recognize that courts reviewing administrative decisions dealing with such questions are not themselves in the business of coming up with the "right" answer. It is not the correctness of the decision that is at issue, but the substantive and procedural adequacy of the record that supports it. The major function of the court is thus to ensure that the decision-making body, usually a federal regulatory agency, has not engaged in "arbitrary and capricious" action[9] and that due process has been afforded to all parties.

Basic authority to develop a scientific record and to make the necessary factual determinations in such cases is lodged in the administrative agency, which has at its disposal powerful procedures for generating evidence. As Judge Bazelon commented in reviewing the Atomic Energy Commission's rule-making process on nuclear waste disposal:[10]

> Many procedural devices for creating a genuine dialogue on these issues were available to the agency—including informal conferences between intervenors and staff, document discovery, interrogatories, technical advisory committees comprised of outside experts with differing perspectives, limited cross-examination, funding independent research by intervenors, detailed annotation of technical reports, surveys of existing literature, memoranda explaining methodology.

The role of the court is not to dictate the choice of particular procedures, but to make sure that the agency uses all the means at its disposal to generate a full record of relevant facts in support of its regulatory decision. Although it may often be difficult for the courts to determine what facts are most relevant and whether a "genuine dialogue" has been created by the agency, it seems clear that the reviewing court does not need independent access to the same fact-finding mechanisms that are available to the agency.

Too great an emphasis on the uncertainty of technological impacts can lead both scientists and regulators to recommend inaction, pending the development of better evidence of risk and causation. But decisions to protect human health and welfare need not invariably depend on scientific proof of harm. It is possible to obtain relief at common law from odors, noise, and other nuisances even when their effects on health or well-being are not scientifically understood. The California Supreme Court recognized this last year in upholding an award of damages for distress caused by airport noise. Compensation was approved for "a sense or feeling of annoyance, strain, worry, anger, frustration, nervousness, fear, and irritability" produced in neighbors of the airport.[11] By refusing to insist on medical evidence that exposure to noise causes ill health, the court confirmed that, at least in cases involving demonstrable harm from technological enterprises, a scientific rationale does not have to be provided to justify relief. In this case, judicial power was exercised to prevent an adjudicable conflict over values from being converted into a scientific dilemma.

However, the element of technical and scientific uncertainty often seems to encourage litigants to translate questions of social value into a technical discourse. It is assumed that the resolution of uncertainty will automatically clarify social choices and resolve value conflicts related to scientific and technological advances. Thus recommendations for improving the adjudication of scientific or technical disputes focus more and more on the technical competence of the courts.

Some Proposed Reforms

The courts face a diversity of problems as they are drawn into the resolution of problems related to scientific and technological advances. Technical uncertainty, a diversity of regulatory policies, and a complex array of social, moral and religious questions complicate the judicial resolution of such disputes. Yet almost all recent proposals for judicial reform are narrowly directed toward improving the scientific literacy of lawyers and judges and clarifying technical information used as a basis for judicial decisions.

Proposals to enhance the technical competence of the courts range from those suggesting basic changes in the adjudicatory process to those calling for the introduction of scientific advisory and training programs. It has been argued that the structure of litigation should be changed to recognize the crucial role of expertise; that because technical knowledge is necessary to evaluate risks and technical causation, interaction between lawyers and experts should take place at every stage in the process of litigation. The authors of one proposal for reform, in the area of product liability, seek a "seriated" trial format in which the question of technical causation would be debated before any claim for damages is considered. This would allow the theory of liability to develop consistently with an "expert" evaluation of the technical data; the intention is to make the litigation process "more responsive to technological realities."[12]

In another call for structural change, Judge Leventhal proposed setting up a cadre of scientific experts who would act as aides to appellate judges, helping them to understand problems of scientific methodology and to assess substantive data.[13] More extreme reformers would establish a system of special courts equipped to deal with technical matters and run by expert judges able to deal with questions of statistical reliability and the performance of complex technologies.[14]

Other suggestions for improving the ability of the courts to deal with technical information include the appointment of science advisers and special masters or changes in the training of lawyers, judges, and their clerks. Special masters or science advisers would be set up in ad hoc positions, depending on the need for special expertise. One proposal would extend a system now used in the Court of Customs and Patent Appeals to all the federal courts, buttressing them with a staff of technical advisers trained in both science and the law.[15] In effect, all these recommendations would equip the courts with sufficient expertise to consider scientific and technical claims more intelligently.

Such attempts to improve the competence of the courts, however, do not confront a common problem, namely, that the technical evidence presented for consideration is often inadequate, confused, and controversial. Accordingly, proposals have also been developed for clarifying technical issues and scientific arguments before they enter the courts. Their object is to create a scientifically sound basis for decisions, to develop criteria by which to assess the adequacy and competence of information, and to arrive at a consensus on controversial technical questions that represents the best judgment of the scientific community.

The science court, a well-publicized proposal for dealing with technical disputes, was intended as an adversary forum in which scientists with different views on controversial issues would argue in structured debates before unbiased scientific judges. Debate would be limited to questions of fact: judges would give opinions only of factual matters, leaving social value questions for the political or traditional legal arena. It was assumed, however, that the opinions of these judges would be authoritative enough to provide a basis for adjudicatory decisions. Indeed, proponents of the science court claimed that this procedure would make it possible "to find truth among the conflicting claims made by sophisticated advocates when there is serious controversy within the technological community."[16] Similar beliefs have generated calls for a "technological magistrature" and for a new profession of "certified public scientists" who would make independent technical evaluations of scientific disputes.[17]

Alternatively, legal scholars have proposed a systematic use of scientific bodies, such as the National Academy of Sciences, to resolve controversial technical questions. Their scientific findings and risk assessments would serve as a basis for judicial decisions.

A somewhat different approach, but one also intended to improve the technical information available to the courts, seeks to accommodate technical uncertainty rather than resolve it. Advocates of this approach stress that uncertainty requires open ventilation of the differences in expert opinion. For example, the decision in *Calvert Cliffs' Coordinating Committee, Inc.* v.

United States Atomic Energy Commission pointed out that poorly financed intervenors may lack the wherewithal to marshal technical evidence and thus be at a disadvantage in administrative proceedings and in the courts.[18] The problem could be ameliorated by distributing resources so as to allow all sides to air their concerns and to present expert data in support of their positions. Measures for promoting this include the funding of technical intervenors and the distribution of scientific resources to citizen groups.

Analysis

Are such reforms likely to resolve the problem of judicial competence? Will they enhance the ability of the courts to deal with the characteristics of science and technology that have strained the adjudicatory process? Although the proposals described above would certainly improve the technical competence of the courts, we believe that they hold little promise of solving the more basic problems involved in scientific and technological litigation.

We have suggested that advances in science and technology, especially in the biological sciences, have created new conceptual problems that cannot be resolved by analogy to existing legal precedents. Proposals to enhance technical competence do not confront these new problems. Furthermore, proposals that seek to develop factual justification for ethical decisions often represent an extension of scientific rationality to inappropriate areas. In an effort to provide legitimacy for judicial decisions, scientific data are used to resolve questions that have little to do with science at all. Questions of aesthetics, of human dignity, and of religious belief underlie many allegedly scientific disputes. Practices such as involuntary sterilization or fetal research threaten what Tribe[19] has called "fragile values"—values that are nonquantifiable, intangible, resistant to categorization. The empirical or logical deductive methods of science have little to do with such issues and may even "squeeze out" important values by subjecting them to precise definition. In such cases, using science to resolve disputes will not satisfy the parties involved.

Some proposals also seem to ignore the fact that the technical uncertainty underlying many disputes is genuine; in many cases the evidentiary basis for definitive resolution simply does not exist. In these cases, scientists operate less as neutral parties than as advocates, providing evidence on both sides of technical disputes. Proposals that enhance the role of scientists in adjudicatory procedures may bring areas of technical disagreement into sharper focus, but will not necessarily lead to resolution.

The use of expert forums in settling legal disputes can be questioned from still another perspective. The belief that scientific expertise is inherently removed from value considerations and that scientists are therefore political celibates is an anachronistic and even dangerous one. Expert forums may limit the role of dissent by giving a dominant place to establishment views on controversial topics. Such consensus-building procedures may also perpetuate misconceptions about the relation between facts and values in controversial areas where questions of value are difficult to distinguish from questions of fact. Furthermore, the need for urgent action in controversial areas may lead to undue reliance on expert opinion. When policy-makers and the courts need quick answers, tentative scientific judgments may be treated as definitive conclusions and the qualifications intended by scientists may be lost.[20]

In the end, proposals to bolster judicial competence in technical areas fall short, for the problems faced by the courts in dealing with controversies in these areas cannot be attributed simply to lack of judicial expertise. They also reflect the failure of the policy process to recognize fully the public and multifaceted character of modern scientific and technological development. In the absence of controlling policy principles, broad questions that follow from scientific and technological activities will continue to reach the courts in the artificial guise of two-party adversarial litigation. Equipping the courts with scientific and technical support may facilitate the adjudication of these issues; however, it may also divert attention from the public responsibility for major policy decisions and encourage the conversion of moral and political questions into technical debates among experts. As our strongest institution for defending fragile values, the courts should guard against such overextension of scientific expertise. However, the fundamental choices involved are not simply matters to be resolved by adjudication; they call for setting priorities and evaluating the public will, clearly a political, not a judicial, role.

Notes

1. G. Ahrens, paper presented at the annual meeting of the American Bar Association, New York, 4 August 1978.

2. D. Bazelon, "Coping with Technology Through the Legal Process," address at Cornell University Law School, 29 November 1976.

3. H. Leventhal, in *Ethyl Corp.* v. *Environmental Protection Agency*, 541 Fed. Rep. 2nd ser. 1 (1976).

4. T. Powledge, *Hastings Cent. Rep.* **8** (No. 5), 15 (1978).

5. *Superintendent of Belchertown State School* v. *Saikewicz,* 373 Mass. 728 (1977); G. J. Annas, *Hastings Cent. Rep.* **8** (No. 1), 21 (1978).

6. G. J. Annas, *Hastings Cent. Rep.* **8** (No. 3), 16 (1978).

7. *Patent Law Assoc.* **7** (Nos. 3 and 4) (1979); this is a special issue devoted entirely to the question of patenting new life forms.

8. U.S. District Court, Middle District of Tennessee, No. 78-3371. See *Honicker* v. *Hendrie, a Lawsuit to End Atomic Power* [A. Bates, Ed. (Book Publishing Co., Seattle, Wash., 1978)] for a review of the documents in the case.

9. *Administrative Procedure Act,* 5 U.S. Code, sect. 706.

10. *Natural Resources Defense Council* v. *U.S. Nuclear Regulatory Commission,* 547 Fed. Rep., 2nd ser. 633, 653 (D.C. Cir. 1976).

11. R. J. Smith, *Science* **207**, 1189 (1980).

12. H. R. Piehler, A. D. Twerski, A. S. Weinstein, W. A. Donaher, *ibid.* **186**, 1089 (1974).

13. H. Leventhal, *Univ. Pa. Law Rev.* **122**, 509 (1974).

14. See proposal in Federal Water Pollution Control Act Amendments of 1972 (Public Law 92-500, sect. 9) for special courts having jurisdiction over environmental matters.

15. This and other proposals were discussed at a Conference on the Use of Scientific and Technical Evidence in Formal Judicial Proceedings, Washington, D.C., September 1977 [see Working Paper by J. D. Nyhart, Sloan School, Massachusetts Institute of Technology (mimeographed)].

16. A. Kantrowitz, *Am. Sci.* **63**, 505 (September-October 1975).

17. See, for example, J. C. Glick, *Ann. N.Y. Acad. Sci.* **265**, 189 (1976).

18. *Calvert Cliffs' Coordinating Committee, Inc.* v. *United States Atomic Energy Commission,* 449 Fed. Rep., 2nd ser. 1109, 1118 (D.C. Cir. 1971).

19. L. H. Tribe, *When Values Conflict,* L. H. Tribe, C. S. Schelling, J. Voss, Eds. (Ballinger, Cambridge, Mass., 1975), pp. 61-92.

20. For a review of critiques of the science court concept, see A. Mazur, *Minerva* **15**, 1 (spring 1977); D. Nelkin, *Sci. Technol. Hum. Values No. 18* (January 1977), pp. 20-31.

Part II.   Process

NANCY E. ABRAMS AND JOEL R. PRIMACK

5 *Helping the Public Decide*

The Case of Radioactive Waste Management

Powerful individuals or groups affected by government decisions have always demanded and achieved influence in making those decisions. Now that large numbers of ordinary citizens in democracies such as the United States are educated and the mass media inform and connect them, they too are capable of becoming organized and therefore powerful when the right issues arise. The increase in the number of vocal interests is making government more difficult, but it may also lead to better considered and fairer decisions.

Public participation in decision making serves two basic functions: first, it adds to the legitimacy and public acceptance of government decision; and, secondly, what the public contributes—an outside perspective, unusual kinds of expertise, a longer-range view than most elected officials can afford, and on occasion basic moral demands—may actually lead to a better decision. This latter function is less recognized than the former by the government's own decision makers and experts, but there is no doubt that, at least in some cases, input from the public has saved us from some technological Vietnams, for example, the anti-ballistic missile system and the SST.

Government difficulty in winning public acceptance of nuclear power, combined with public frustration with existing procedures in this area, has led to various proposals for new forums and procedures that would permit more public input. But one cannot develop intelligent procedures in the abstract,

From *Environment,* Vol. 22, pp. 14-20, 39-40 (April 1980). Reprinted by permission of the Helen Dwight Reid Educational Foundation. Published by Heldrof Publications, 4000 Albemarle Street, N.W., Washington, D.C. 20016. Copyright© 1980.

even on a particular problem such as nuclear waste disposal, without first determining the nature of the issues for which the procedure is supposed to produce legitimate and wise decisions. As long as the framing of the questions is unexamined, the strong possibility exists that public participation appears to be difficult to obtain primarily because it is being sought on the least appropriate questions. We would argue that this is true in the case of nuclear waste disposal, based on the following considerations.

Public workshops and hearings sponsored by the Environmental Protection Administration (EPA), the Department of Energy (DOE), and the Nuclear Regulatory Commission (NRC) as well as NRC licensing experience indicate that these agencies permit public participation either too early, when plans are extremely vague, or too late, when the public is presented with a *fait accompli,* and also that the agencies have not thought through which of their decisions are the ones on which public participation is most essential or most feasible. The resulting confusion of issues makes most current public participation attempts frustrating and nonproductive.

Identifying the major decisions which must be made in nuclear waste management is a prerequisite to determining *which* of those decisions require public input and *who* constitutes the "public" in each case. This has never been done by the federal agencies.

The controversy we are seeing today is not simply over the choice among various possible methods of nuclear waste disposal; it also involves serious doubt, if not suspicion, about the government's real intentions in handling the whole problem. It would be highly desirable for the government to present as soon as possible a complete tentative plan of nuclear waste disposal. This plan should then be broadly discussed and criticized through government-funded studies by outsiders. Such a procedure would help to establish the main issues for public debate and thus facilitate informed and effective public participation. In this article we propose a new model for doing this—"critical review and public assessment," a two-tiered approach to public participation.

There have been attempts to develop "public participation mechanisms" but, with respect to the nuclear waste issue, these have been so premature that their use would prove not only worthless but diversionary. The public cannot respond to an enormous, vague technical question submitted to it directly. Members of the public have neither the expertise nor the patience. If government is serious about involving the public, it must first seek *and fund* expert comment and analysis from interested and independent experts on everything that could go wrong with a plan and allow this stage of criticism to establish the real issues and trade-offs for the public. It is well documented that again and again in public controversies over technologies it has been independent scientists who first effectively raised the issues which public activists came to understand and took over from there.[1]

Federal Agencies and the Public

The Environmental Protection Agency, the Nuclear Regulatory Commission, and the Department of Energy apparently believe public input on the nuclear waste disposal issue to be appropriate only as guidance on the most general issues before any real decisions have been made or as a challenge to a fully developed plan in a formal hearing. In other words, they do not know how to integrate public participation into an ongoing decisionmaking process where strong public input could really make a difference.

> If the EPA addresses unplanned events in its environmental protection criteria, what would be an appropriate and effective approach? What aspects of the disposal process and of the unplanned events should be addressed?

This was the first question participants at EPA's Albuquerque workshop on radioactive waste were supposed to consider. How they were supposed to know what "unplanned events" were, if EPA did not, is unclear.

> Can and/or should environmental radiation protection criteria be established on a generic basis addressing all forms and types of radioactive wastes if possible?[2]

This was the opener at EPA's Reston (Virginia) workshop. A few of the prepared papers dealt with questions like these, but a reading of the public comments shows one after another person expressing basically fear—fear that human beings will not handle radioactive waste with the care it demands, fear that the future of the earth is in danger—and ending with plaintive pleas to EPA to "take my statement into account." According to one participant at the Denver workshop, lack of travel funds meant that only the most dedicated antinuclear activists and the well-heeled nuclear industry representatives (who comprised about two-thirds of those attending) came, with a consequent polarization of all discussions and a premium placed on scoring points. Despite successes in getting some of their views reflected in the workshop proceedings, many antinuclear participants wondered what it was all for. Some demanded assurances on the record that they would be listened to.

NRC also held a series of workshops under specific instructions in their 1979 authorization act[3] that they prepare a report for Congress by March 1979 on the advisability of awarding grants to the states to fund development of "review capability," as they called it, and to make recommendations on better methods of participation by the states in the siting, licensing, and development of federal nuclear waste facilities. State officials and legislators thus made up the vast majority of participants at these workshops.

According to NRC's report,[4] a consensus was clear among the state representatives that states should have "consultation and concurrence" with federal authorities at every stage, but no ideas emerged as to exactly how this would be done. Another view on which the states all agreed was that NRC's preliminary site suitability criteria were far too vague to discuss usefully. The NRC report's recommendations to Congress, with the benefit of state input at four workshops, were basically that "a (federal-state) planning council be established" (as recommended already by the Interagency Review Group in their report to the President),[5] "a review capability [of states] be established," and "measures be taken to involve the states."[6]

The main subject of discussion in the report, and apparently a central NRC concern, is how to proceed with siting a federal waste dump if state concurrence cannot be obtained voluntarily. Many arguments are provided to justify a federal right to proceed "in the national interest," creating a reasonable doubt in the mind of the reader as to the seriousness of NRC's concern with genuine state involvement. In NRC's own words, the purpose of state involvement is twofold: it serves as a "channel for informing the states," and "it enables federal decision makers to solicit and receive a more or less authoritative expression from policy-making officials of the states with respect to those matters which are of direct concern to them."[7] In other words, state participation is basically for information exchange, not a sharing of power.

The IRG report also discusses the "state veto" issue but, while determining that a recommendation for or against a state veto would be premature, it concludes that "consultation and concurrence" would be more in the interests of the *states* than a state veto right. Both these rationalizations miss the point that a "veto" need not be over the flat question of siting or not siting but could be over part of the issue—namely, the acceptability of incentives offered for siting and of the criteria according to which the facility is guaranteed by contract to be built. Only by separating out the specific issues can one move beyond the standard legalistic approach of each party attempting to preserve its rights for a future dispute.

DOE's draft Environmental Impact Statement (EIS) on "Management of Commercially Generated Radioactive Waste"[8] weighs about seven pounds. It gives no indication what DOE plans to do; instead, options within options are all duly presented. DOE has held several public hearings around the country to elicit the public's reactions to its EIS, but the San Francisco hearing[9] was not even conducted by DOE's own employees. Instead, some outside consultants with unspecified, if any, connections to DOE policy making had been hired to take care of this apparent nuisance of a task.

EPA, NRC, and DOE discuss generalities and numberless options, presumably in the hope that somehow a solution will emerge. Their jurisdictions and missions are limited in such a way that no one of them is in a position to take charge or even to take an overview of the whole process. This contributes to public confusion because it is impossible to tell what solution is emerging, if any, or who is responsible and, consequently, where one's efforts and concern should be focused. As the NRC itself says:

> One reason that State participation at the present time may be poorly focused is that there is no effective way to determine exactly what the Federal policies and programs consist of. To a large extent, this may reflect the fact that activities at the Federal level are themselves still in the process of being worked out and, further, that the participation of several Federal agencies creates inevitable problems of coordination.[10]

Without sorting out this admitted confusion, the agencies would like to "involve the public," as if *they* could help clarify matters. But involving more people in a confused effort merely magnifies the confusion; it also creates ill feelings. The "State Planning Council" proposed by the IRG will have the same problem. It is supposed to develop "criteria for evaluating proposed nuclear waste management activities."[11] Meanwhile, DOE determines "site selection criteria"; NRC determines "site suitability criteria";[12] and EPA determines "environmental protection criteria."[13] Since development of criteria is the area most in need of public participation, something basic must be done to give the public half a chance to participate.

The "Public"

Before discussing public participation further, it is important to define "public." Of course, the public is not a monolith with a single point of view. For our purposes the public is composed of all the people outside the federal agencies and the nuclear industry (representatives of the nuclear industry have never lacked channels through which they can and do influence government decision making). All individuals or groups with a contribution to make to the national debate or to a local debate on radioactive waste management are considered to be legitimate spokespersons for the public, even if they do not represent anyone else.

Peter Montague has pointed out that there are two major unrepresented interests in the radwaste controversy: the uninformed and the unborn.[14] It is important to consider these groups, to be sure, because they are the largest in number, yet the least likely to be heard from. But there is another unrepresented group far easier to reach, whose input could be of great value: the informed and concerned public. This last category of the informed, concerned, and uninfluential includes:

- people who oppose nuclear energy anytime, anywhere;
- people who oppose nuclear powerplants near their homes;
- people like the authors of the Kemeny Report, who have no objections to nuclear power in principle but insist that, if it is used, it must be made much safer;
- labor organizations mostly concerned with jobs;
- nuclear proponents outside the nuclear industry;
- businesspeople, especially those concerned about the relationship between nuclear power and the national economy, or between nuclear power and their local economy;
- public interest scientists, lawyers, economists, energy analysts, and other independent experts;
- civil liberties advocates;
- environmental organizations;
- foreign policy experts or others concerned about the relationship between nuclear energy and proliferation;
- state officials concerned about additional responsibilities nuclear facilities may place upon them (such as transportation monitoring, evacuation planning);
- and other concerned persons.

The Crucial Decisions

CRITERIA THE PROGRAM MUST MEET

Short-term safety. Short term safety may turn out to be the most important question of all. How much safety will we require in the transportation, handling, interim storage, and burial operations of the spent fuels and other waste forms? Most attention has been paid to the long-range effects of nuclear waste because frontiers of science are more interesting than such mundane issues as how to get the waste safely off a truck. But these are not only the chief concerns of workers and unions; they are precisely the concerns of greatest importance to the people living in the region of the site and will also be the first public test of the competence of the entire operation.

Transportation, handling, and burial operations could become to nuclear waste disposal what the waste disposal issue has become to nuclear power: the "trivial" but recalcitrant engineering problem that threatens to undermine the whole venture.

Long-term safety. How safe should the disposal facility be in relation to people living nearby, people who will live there in the future, and the environment?

Design specifications. How much radioactivity can be released in various forms, both before burial and after? What degree of certainty will be required? Salt, for example, might really work as a storage medium. But there are so many uncertainties about it that it just might not. We do not have the necessary scientific knowledge now to predict with assurance the fate of cannisters, glass, or other physical barriers, water flow, etc., and therefore cannot do *realistic* calculations. The usual engineering approach in such circumstances is to do "conservative" computer simulations (use conservative values for parameters), although the computer simulations themselves are of uncertain validity because the whole approach might be wrong. The real question is, thus, how much scientific understanding will we demand before proceeding.

How much scientific verification of the procedure will we require? How much hydrologic, seismic, and other geologic data and understanding? How much certainty about the long-term behavior of the physical barriers, the sorption of various radioactive elements by the rock? Will we require that all relevant tests be performed at the actual site? Must waterflow rates be measured on-site? This is an extremely important question.

If it were decided that everything must be done very conservatively, then DOE, when they thought they had a site, would have to drill each exploratory hole as if they were starting the real construction, since it is not possible to drill a lot of test holes without ruining a site. Yet in beginning measurements in these holes they would have to be open to the possibility of having to abandon the site as inadequate. The price of such an approach could be enormous, both financially and in delay, but this is precisely the kind of decision that needs public input—from a public that understands the trade-offs. This is not a scientific decision.

How reliable or robust should the technology be? In other words, if the technical designers forget to take some parameter into account or careless workers mess up some aspect of construction, will it still work reasonably well? Is it failsafe, like the Italian dessert, appropriately called "Il Diplomatico," whose recipe says:

You can put in a little less rum or a little more chocolate, add or subtract an egg, and you'll still come up with a successful and delicious cake. It's practically foolproof.[15]

Nuclear technology is not known for its robustness. Nuclear power plants are so complicated that they are out of service much of the time for one cause or another, and it gets harder to service them as they grow older and become increasingly contaminated with radioactivity. Can we afford a temperamental nuclear waste disposal technology?

Time and cost. Despite all protestations that safety comes first, time and cost are the major trade-offs in all decisions about waste disposal. How soon do we demand that final disposal operations begin? How much are we willing to spend on the whole venture, now and in the future?

GEOLOGIC MEDIUM

Salt has been the "preferred" geologic storage medium for over 20 years, and DOE inherited the idea with so much momentum behind it because no alternatives were seriously studied until recently. The particular public whose input is badly needed on this decision is independent scientists.

TECHNOLOGY

Given a choice of geologic medium, there are still many decisions to be made about technologies. Should the waste be left in the form of fuel rods, or should it be physically or chemically reprocessed? Should reprocessed waste be combined with glass or ceramics; and, if so, with what dilution and in which chemical form?[16] What materials should the waste be encased in? How many layers and which metals? Should the waste forms be surrounded by something which will still be there in thousands of years when the long-lived isotopes like plutonium come out, to be sure they emerge with the proper valence to be sorbed by the surrounding rock and not dissolve in groundwater? The decisions made under "Criteria" above are crucial for guidance on such questions and, if there has been substantial and meaningful public input into the decisions about criteria, then there may be no need to involve the general public in this kind of technical choice. The need to involve public interest scientists and other outside experts remains, however.

MANAGEMENT

How should the waste program be set up? Should a federal agency manage it directly? Should it be managed by a private corporation? A public corporation?[17] This is a valid question for public participation by management experts, knowledgeable businesspeople, and public interest lawyers, among others. And it should be discussed with the recognition that the short-term and the long-term tasks involved in nuclear waste disposal present very different management problems which might best be handled by different schemes.

RIGHT TO NEGOTIATE

Who will negotiate for the potential victims? As the NRC Report puts it:

> A State may have sound economic motivation for welcoming the location of nuclear power reactors within its boundaries; the incentive for accepting high-level wastes, on the other hand, is hardly so clear.[18]

It is admittedly a no-win proposition, involving unknown risks but no conceivable gain; therefore the government will have the choice of either negotiating incentives to encourage a region to accept siting of a nuclear waste repository or of forcing it to do so by a near-totalitarian exercise of power. The IRG and the NRC, as mentioned earlier, are clearly concerned about what will happen if "consultation" does not lead to "concurrence," so it is probably safe to assume that at least an attempt at negotiation will be made.

The local people—and exactly what constitutes "local" will have to be determined case by case—should have a strong say in who represents them in these negotiations. It should not be automatically assumed that officials elected for entirely different reasons, such as mayors or governors—officials who may never have taken any public positions on nuclear issues—should represent the public in such a capacity. Probably no one would want to be represented by an official like the mayor of Carlsbad, New Mexico, who was quoted in the *International Tribune* in 1978 as saying about the Waste Isolation Pilot Project, which was to have been built in Carlsbad: "Well, I guess it'll be good for the economy if it doesn't kill us all."

NRC has already discussed the issue of incentives with state representatives in its workshops, and apparently Western states oppose "special incentives" while Central and Eastern states want them. However, all states have agreed that the federal government should pay what they call "compensation for the direct and indirect costs of repository siting."[19] When DOE finally points the finger, "indirect costs" may very well be indistinguishable from "special incentives."

Suppose, for the sake of argument, that a negotiating team agreed, in a region that did not want a nuclear waste facility, that they would accept such a facility if the government promised to fulfill certain publicly determined criteria (of safety, etc.); to guarantee full property insurance (no Price-Anderson type arrangements), with strict liability and a 100-year statute of limitations;

to provide parks, a civic center, a library, assurance of gasoline supplies, and other benefits.

It would still be extremely important, regardless of the method by which the negotiating team was selected, that the public concerned also approve the contract, just as most labor unions require membership approval of contracts. This approval could take the form of a referendum where the choices were simply "yes" or "no"—possibly with a required two-thirds vote. This is probably the only issue of those we have discussed where the public should not only have its say but should actually make the decision.

LEGAL ISSUES

Should sanctions be specified in advance for gross incompetence in managing the wastes? How? Imposing sanctions would require independent monitoring of performance and is related to the question of management. What would the appropriate remedies be?

Another concern is, who will protect the dangerous materials during transport and while they are collected at the site? Since siting cannot be near a big population center, it will have to be in a rural, relatively quiet area of the country which is not accustomed to a large police presence and the kind of security arrangements which may be necessary. Local police, furthermore, will be too few in number and not trained to handle these matters alone. What kinds of civil liberties problems are posed by the possibility of a federal police force and surveillance to avert terrorist or other attempts at sabotage or theft? These are matters for public debate.

CONTINUING PUBLIC INPUT

Finally, but perhaps most fundamentally, the question arises: How much public participation does the public want? The federal government should not look for a single "final solution" to the public participation problem. This, above all other problems, is not one which could be solved "if only we had enough information." For example, would the region around a site want a local nuclear waste board to monitor activities at the site, or would they rather leave it to the federal experts? Some areas probably would want such a board, like a school board or a police supervisory board, that would not only monitor but keep the whole process open, especially to the media. Other regions might prefer to leave matters to the experts, but the *region in question* should have the choice. People in a given region may even want different things at different times because more participation will always be sought at times when trust in the main actors is low. Rather than trying to establish a single policy on public participation, therefore, the federal government should recognize by law the right of regions in which a site is proposed or constructed to determine the extent of participation in the waste management program that they consider to be necessary. They should also have the right to review their decision periodically.

One Plan Is Better Than a Thousand Options

The number of important decisions to be made in nuclear waste management is large, and it is always dangerous to make such interconnected decisions in a vacuum, each separate from the others. The confusion among the agencies, and between the agencies and the public, has created a situation where we will be lucky if there even *is* a conscious decision made on each of the questions discussed above. The fundamental flaw in the process is that *no one sees the big picture*. There is a solution, however.

In Sweden in 1977 a law was passed preventing utilities from starting up new nuclear power plants until they had shown that a safe plan for nuclear waste disposal existed. With five operating reactors and two newly completed reactors ready to go into operation, the Swedish utilities formed a study group called KBS ("Nuclear Fuel Safety" in Swedish) which in one year put together a detailed plan for nuclear waste disposal. This was not the plan which *would* necessarily be used, since actual waste disposal was not within the power of the utilities to control; it was instead an existence proof—a plan to show that a safe plan could be devised. The Swedish government then had the plan reviewed by about 25 Swedish and 25 foreign organizations. In addition, the government had its own Energy Commission, a politically appointed body with limited lifespan, perform an extraordinary technical review according to a new procedure called "scientific mediation," which Nancy Abrams and Steve Berry had developed a year earlier.[20]

The KBS Report laid out a complete scenario: fuel rods would be removed from reactors, stored in a central facility in Sweden, then shipped to France for reprocessing, including vitrification (conversion to glass) of the high-level liquid waste. The vitrified blocks would then be returned to Sweden, stored for 30 years in a middle-term facility which was described in detail, then encased in various layers of metals and buried 500 meters deep in tunnels cut into solid granite and irrigated for cooling until the depository was ready to be closed; it would then be sealed with a bentonite clay and quartz-sand mixture. Computer models were used to predict the long-range behavior of the waste form, the containers, the groundwater movements, and so forth.

There were enormous problems with such a complex plan. Many were discovered by the various reviewers. They might never have been foreseen given the piecemeal planning now going on in the United States. Furthermore, during the entire period since 1977, this plan and a subsequent one proposed for disposal of unreprocessed spent fuel have been central topics of public controversy and political debate at the highest levels of government in Sweden.

The enormous value of preparing the KBS Report and having it reviewed independently by so many organizations and individuals was that Sweden got a real sense of the big picture. Ironically, the United States, with the biggest collection of nuclear waste in the world, has not even attempted an exercise on the scale of the Swedish effort. It should and it can.

A single overall nuclear waste management and disposal plan should be designed, including a complete scenario for the fuel rods from the reactor to the waste forms that will exist thousands of years from now. The scenario should be understandable and visualizable, not a list of options. However, unlike the KBS Report, it should also contain an explanation of the reasons behind the main technological choices in the scenario and upfront, unvarnished worst-case analyses.

This plan, representing the best thinking of its makers, should be published and open for criticism. Numerous independent critical reviews funded by the government would ensure that the plan would become a focus of national and international scientific interest as well as of public debate. It is always easier to rewrite a draft than to start from scratch, and this plan would be the nation's first draft.

Who should prepare the plan? No U.S. government agency is in a position to do this. In Sweden the utilities prepared it and the government reviewed it. This could be a good idea for us, too. If the U.S. utilities want to continue building and operating nuclear power plants, they should be able to provide a plan for nuclear waste disposal. The advantages of such an approach would be:

Public support.   There is already considerable enthusiasm for imposing such a condition on the utilities, both in the Congress and at the state and grassroots level.

The utilities' self-interest.   The utilities under current plans will be charged for a depository DOE is supposed to develop. Given the tendencies of the federal government toward cost overruns and inefficiencies of every kind, it is in the interest of the utilities to be the ones to develop the first plan, and therefore they may very well welcome the challenge.

No jurisdictional problems.   Unlike EPA, DOE, NRC, DOT, etc., the utilities are not limited in their planning capacity by jurisdictional divisions. They may therefore be in a better position than the government to prepare a complete scenario now.

Government review. Government agencies are incomparably better at regulating industry than at regulating each other. The chances are much greater that NRC or its successor agency will exercise critical judgment over a utility plan than over a DOE plan.

The utilities might decide to form a special consortium to prepare the plan, but their already existing research organization, the Electric Power Research Institute (EPRI), seems the logical candidate.

Once the plan is released, the independent critical reviews should be funded and published. At least one review, possibly sponsored by the White House or, as in Sweden, by an independent commission, should be performed according to the procedure of scientific mediation, since this is the only procedure specifically designed to bring out the real trade-offs, both qualitative and quantitative, in such a technical plan.

The various reviews[21] should then be presented at a national conference on nuclear waste management, held in Washington to assure attendance by the largest possible number of relevant decision-makers. This would become a focus of world attention and an opportunity for experts with different views to meet each other face to face in a civilized way. If properly arranged, the conference could provide a forum for discussion not only of the technical issues and alternatives but also of all the major questions discussed in the "Decisions" section of this article, including methods of effective public participation.

Through the EPRI Report and the round of reviews, the big picture could emerge. It is not only the general public that needs to see such a picture; the agencies too would have an easier time, especially in communicating with everyone outside—including Congress. The general understanding that would arise from an effort of this kind, not only of the technical issues involved but of the scope of the program contemplated for disposal of nuclear waste as well, is a prerequisite both to development of an adequate long-range plan and to meaningful public participation in the process. Outside scientists would probably be called upon by EPRI, but the review stage particularly would involve many scientists all around the country and probably the world, thus greatly increasing the chances for eventual development of a well-examined and well-thought-through technical plan. As long as the initial plan was understood to be only a first draft, the critical reviews could be recognized as constructive and not merely political in motivation. The process could thus be one of convergence rather than of confrontation.

The question of how to involve the general public would remain, however; for this, additional steps could be taken. For instance, one reputable public interest group with special expertise in the energy area could follow, step by step, the development of EPRI's plan, with assured access to all relevant information and the right to ask questions. They would be there to be educated, however, not to interfere. They would later be able to explain the reasoning and choices embodied in the EPRI plan. Although EPRI would have to provide an explanation, as mentioned before, of the reasons behind its technological choices, it is always hard for outsiders to try to reconstruct a complicated process from this kind of explanation alone, and the experience and observations of the public interest group could fill in the gaps in the EPRI statement.

In addition, it might be a good idea to involve a small citizens' committee in observing the step-by-step development of the plan. They would be people who had been involved in energy issues from the point of view of informing the public, not as scientists. Between EPRI and the public interest experts, the citizens' committee should gain a good general understanding of the plan, the reasoning behind it, and possible objections to it. They could then write a book about the plan for the general public.

It would add to their independence if both these groups were funded by an outside foundation rather than by the government.[22]

Critical Review vs. Intervention

So far we have explained the "critical review and public assessment" model as a means of obtaining a high quality technical plan while preparing the public to participate effectively in the decision-making process. Viewed another way, however, the model solves a separate problem of comparable importance. The main channel for public participation today is through intervention in the proceedings of government agencies. To finance themselves, environmentalists and others have for many years sought "intervenor funding" from the agency before which they would appear. Although this is now mandated by statute in a few cases, it has on the whole been difficult if not impossible to obtain. As a general strategy for raising needed funds, the quest for intervenor funding has not been successful.

Intervention itself has problems: intervenors are usually restricted to raising only those issues which the law already empowers or requires the agency to take into account in its decision; and, furthermore, much of the hard-raised money spent by the intervenors must go to lawyers to fight the up-hill, stylized battles inevitable in such a forum. At a higher level, however, intervention does not seek to challenge the decision-making process, which is itself essentially flawed. Since an agency decision, as explained earlier in this article, is frequently a *fait accompli* by the time of intervention, there is no real opportunity for intervenors to do anything but create delay. Consequently, they are regarded by both their industrial opponents and the agency before which they appear as obstructionists.

"Critical review and public assessment" can be seen as an alternative strategy to intervention, a strategy which challenges the decision-making process and which, ironically, may be less objectionable to the agencies and industry for several reasons. First, money paid out by the relevant agency (or possibly through a separate agency set up specifically for this purpose) would go directly for constructive critical reviews, not to hire lawyers. Second, scientists representing many points of view would be funded, not just environmentalists. Third, raising new technical issues or problems, so difficult in agency hearings, would be encouraged as one of the main goals of the entire process. Finally, the use of "critical review and public assessment" would, in a relatively short time, substantially increase the number of scientists who contribute to public issues generally, broadening the base of the public-interest science movement with beneficial results across the board for technology politics.

The Need for Public Participation

The legitimacy that public participation can lend to decision making on nuclear waste disposal is not mere sugarcoating. The alternative—the federal preemption-rush approach—may work to obtain the first dump site, but as things inevitably go wrong, mounting public anger and distrust will prove incomparably harder to deal with thereafter. The other central purpose of public participation—improving the quality of the decision—may also turn out to be of incalculable value. The public has already saved us from several technological quagmires, and a disastrous nuclear dump could be harder to pull out of than Vietnam.

The fear of some people that public participation will lead to endless delay is based on the mistaken belief that the "public" is comprised of only those totally committed antinuclear people who are fighting the possibility of safe nuclear waste disposal on the grounds that the existence of such a technology will encourage the production of more waste and more nuclear plants. This group certainly exists and is highly vocal. However, there are many others who could understand, if real efforts were made to clarify for the public the issues and trade-offs involved, that the price of preventing development of safe nuclear waste disposal (or even of demanding such excruciatingly high standards of safety and conservatism as to put off such development indefinitely) is an increased probability over time that the wastes will never be disposed of properly. Instead, as the public loses interest in the issue, the problem will be inherited by lower and lower levels of bureaucracy as the wastes themselves age, leak, and become more dangerous. Like the other toxic wastes that litter the countryside, nuclear waste, once the national attention shifts, will become just another kind of garbage to be taken care of whenever someone has the time.

Public participation need not cause interminable delay. To the contrary, if no waste disposal technology is developed in the next few years, delay—the traditional tool of the environmentalists—may well be intentionally appropriated by the pro-nuclear forces, who understand the difficulty of safe nuclear waste disposal and would like to put it off till no watchful eye remains. This was the approach before environmentalists got the public interested, and there is every reason to expect that this will be the approach again if environmentalists and the public lose interest.

Notes

1. Joel Primack and Frank von Hippel, *Advice and Dissent: Scientists in the Political Arena*, Basic Books, 1974; New American Library, 1976.

2. *Proceedings: A Workshop of Policy and Technical Issues Pertinent to the Development of Environmental Protection Criteria for Radioactive Wastes*, Albuquerque, New Mexico, April 12-14, 1977, U.S. EPA, Office of Radiation Programs; *Proceedings: A Workshop on Issues Pertinent to the Development of Environmental Protection Criteria for Radioactive Wastes*, Reston, Virginia, February 3-5, 1977, U.S. EPA, Office of Radiation Programs; *Proceedings of a Public Forum on Environmental Protection Criteria for Radioactive Wastes*, March 30-April 1, 1978, Denver, Colorado, U.S. EPA, Office of Radiation Programs.

3. Sec. 14(b) P.L. 95-601.

4. *Means for Improving State Participation in the Siting, Licensing and Development of Federal Nuclear Waste Facilities: A Report to Congress*, U.S. NRC, Office of State Programs, March 1979 (NUREG-0539). Hereinafter called NRC Report.

5. *Report to the President by the Interagency Review Group on Nuclear Waste Management*, March 1979 (TID-29442), pp. 93-95. Hereinafter called IRG Report.

6. NRC Report, p. 27.

7. NRC Report, p. 15.

8. Draft Environmental Impact Statement, *Management of Commercially Generated Radioactive Waste*, vols. 1-2, April 1979, Department of Energy, (DOE/EIS-0046-D).

9. Nancy Abrams testified at this hearing.

10. NRC Report, p. 15.

11. IRG Report, p. 90.

12. NRC Report, pp. 6-7.

13. EPA, Preface to Albuquerque workshop proceedings.

14. Peter Montague, "Representing the Unrepresented In Radioactive Waste Management Decisions," unpublished paper presented to the AAAS Symposium on Radioactive Waste Management, Houston, Texas, January 1979.

15. Marcella Hazan, *The Classic Italian Cook Book*, Knopf, 1976, p. 436.

16. Richard A. Kerr, "Nuclear Waste Disposal: Alternatives to Solidification in Glass Proposed," *Science* 204, 289 (April 20, 1979).

17. Mason Willrich and Richard Lester, *Radioactive Wastes Management and Regulation*, Free Press, 1977.

18. NRC Report, p. 3.

19. NRC Report, p. 10.

20. Nancy E. Abrams and R. Stephen Berry, "Mediation: A Better Alternative to the Science Court," *Bulletin of the Atomic Scientists*, April 1977.

Scientific mediation is a procedure for advising government agencies on the technical aspects of a policy question when scientists are apparently in disagreement on the scientific questions. Very briefly, two or more scientists, one representing each main technical viewpoint, are brought together and, with the help of a mediator, they write a joint paper explaining their areas of agreement, their areas of disagreement, and the reasons why they disagree on each point. The focus of the effort is on illuminating their grounds of disagreement rather than on arriving at consensus.

A more complete account of how scientific mediation was used in Sweden appears in Nancy Abrams, "Nuclear Politics in Sweden," **Environment**, May 1979. Nancy Abrams served as a consultant to the Swedish Energy Commission during the entire review.

21. Judy Hurley of the Center for Non-Violence, Santa Cruz, California (and a participant at the EPA Denver workshop on radioactive waste criteria) has suggested that some of the grants given to outside scientists to review the EPRI plan should be for scientists who will work with a citizens group, explain the plan to them, and perform with them a review in which the technical aspects are not isolated from value questions (personal communication).

22. The idea of involving both a public interest group and a small citizens' committee in this way was suggested by Harriet Barlow, Institute for Local Self-Reliance, Washington, D.C. (personal communication).

DENNIS W. DUCSIK

6 Citizen Participation in Power Plant Siting

Aladdin's Lamp or Pandora's Box?

For over a decade now, one of the most intractable problems on the energy–environment scene has been rancorous political opposition to the construction of big power plants. Born in the late 1960s at places like Storm King Mountain, Turkey Point, Bodega Head, and Four Corners, the resistance movement has snowballed to the point where it is now rare for a major project involving an electric generating facility to go unopposed. This lack of public acceptance has even been institutionalized in the form of national organizations such as the Environmental Action Foundation, to which groups all over the country turn regularly for help in fighting utility expansion plans.[1]

Although the reasons for political resistance to power plants are many and complex (especially in the case of nuclear reactors), concern over the choice of site and its environmental and social implications usually plays a key role. Indeed, with the possible exception of "No to Nukes," the most familiar cry to a utility executive's ears is almost certainly "Don't Put It Here." It is a cry, moreover, that seems likely to be heard with increasing frequency throughout the '80s and beyond. Electric companies are already hard pressed to come up with locations that are technically capable of development as well as suitable on economic, environmental, and political grounds.[2] As the tradeoffs involved become even more acute in the future, it follows that confrontation between the industry and affected interest groups can be expected to intensify as well.

From *Journal of the American Planning Association,* Vol. 47, No. 2 (April 1981). Reprinted by permission of the *Journal of the American Planning Association* and Dennis W. Ducsik.

The ultimate source of difficulty, of course, is that no large-scale power facility can be designed to completely avoid imposition on a landscape, an airshed, or a body of water in its vicinity. The laws of thermodynamics together with engineering and economic realities simply preclude it. Nor is it realistic to think that siting disputes are a thing of the past in light of recent progress in reducing the nation's consumption of electricity. Even load growth at the modest annual rate of two percent translates into a significant need for additional generating capacity, and there will always be older plants to replace irrespective of the rate of increase in demand. Some would argue, in fact, that it is desirable to *accelerate* the retirement of certain oil-fired units as a means of reducing dependence on foreign petroleum products and improving air quality in cities, where many of these units are located. Thus, a sizable complement of new sites must still be found in the years ahead.

Can anything be done to avoid the grim prospect of more disruptive conflict over the location of power plants? In this author's view, the time has come to give serious consideration to an idea that has actually been around since the early '70s and found useful application in fields such as highway location and water resources development,[3] but not to any significant extent in the electricity sector. This is the concept of "open" planning, which calls upon electric companies to voluntarily incorporate some form of citizen participation into the site selection process. Many variations are possible, but the key feature of this approach is that interaction with concerned citizens should take place *during* the process of elimination that is commonly used in the evaluation and choice of alternative locations. Such collaboration would occur, moreover, well in advance of the regulatory process which now provides, in the form of licensing hearings, the principal opportunity for persons affected by a siting decision to influence it directly. Under the participatory scheme, a formal public hearing would mark the end point of dialogue between the company and the public at large, not the beginning.

Over the years this notion of citizen involvement in site planning has gained the endorsement of prominent individuals and organizations outside of industry circles,[4] and has even been written into proposed legislation such as the Department of Energy's (now defunct) Nuclear Siting and Licensing Act of 1978.[5] On the whole, however, it has yet to penetrate the thinking of those in the best position to initiate new approaches to the politics of siting, i.e., the utilities themselves. Instead of reconsidering the long-standing policy of keeping sites confidential until license applications are ready to be filed, most companies take the position that legislative reform is needed to ensure that siting disputes will be settled more expeditiously within the framework of federal and state certification procedures. As to suggestions that the company might try to get together in a constructive fashion with environmentalists and other citizen advocates, typically these have either been greeted with the utmost skepticism or dismissed as altogether outlandish.

With the climate of alienation that has long prevailed between utilities and their ardent antagonists, this attitude on the part of the electricity industry is perhaps understandable. The problem, however, is that for several years now the idea of collaborative siting has been so negatively prejudged that very few companies have been willing to experiment with it, even on a limited basis, and there has been practically no careful evaluation of it in the industry literature.[6] As a consequence of this unfortunate lack of attention, very little is really known as to whether citizen participation might be a viable means of stemming controversy over where to put future power plants, or, for that matter, any major energy facility likely to engender serious environmental opposition.

This article is intended as a first step toward better understanding the relative merits of the participatory approach to siting. The principal objective is to develop a realistic and balanced perspective on the matter, one that accounts in particular for issues that are important from the standpoint of the power industry (who, after all, must take on the bulk of the risks before any benefits can be realized). After a brief review of the rationale advanced on behalf of collaboration, the discussion concentrates on the major concerns a utility might be expected to have with respect to its operational implications. These concerns have been identified by the author in a series of informal (though extensive) communications with thirty-two persons with experience in the siting domain, over half of whom are executives or technical professionals employed by major electric companies. A systematic appraisal of the data generated in this study has been completed,[7] and it is hoped that the effort has yielded some insightful propositions that can serve as a guide to future inquiry on the subject.

The Rationale for Collaboration

Advocacy of citizen participation in power plant siting is, in large measure, an outgrowth of nearly universal dissatisfaction with adjudicatory hearings as the basic forum for communication among those with a stake in the decision process. The source of consternation from the utility standpoint is that intervenor groups, capitalizing on the procedural complexity of the regulatory system, have turned such proceedings into the "marathons among legal track meets."[8] The resulting delay and uncertainty can wreak havoc on facility planning efforts which, because of the technical complexity and vast financial commitments involved, must proceed in an orderly fashion. Equally distressing to the industry is the tendency for disputes to wind up in the courts, before judges who are ill-equipped to engage in technology assessment and who are inclined, therefore, to base decisions on strictly procedural considerations instead of the substantive merits of the project.[9]

Environmentalists, too, are disillusioned with the traditional hearing process, albeit for very different reasons. Coming as it usually does at the end of the licensing process—which itself does not begin until after facility plans are ready to be consummated by the utility—the hearing is widely regarded as an exercise in futility.[10] This breeds frustration, distrust, and anger on the part of concerned citizens, who sense quite rightly that many important options have been foreclosed[11] and that their involvement comes too late to have a meaningful influence on the project (except perhaps to stop it altogether). Contention thus tends to gravitate naturally away from issues of substance and toward questions of procedure.

Such difficulties have precipitated much discussion and debate as to how the rules of practice governing hearings might be modified to make them less vulnerable to dilatory tactics on the one hand,[12] and to facilitate effective contributions from intervenors acting in good faith on the other.[13] There is another school of thought, however, which holds that political turmoil over electricity decisions will never be obviated within the context of agency hearing rooms, where the heavily legalistic and distinctly adversarial climate by itself induces polarization of views and inhibits compromise solutions. More importantly, by the time a hearing convenes it is simply too late for mutual adjustment to occur on any matters except the relatively minor details of plant layout and design. The basic problem, in other words, lies not so much with what goes on during the hearing itself, but rather with what does *not* transpire in the way of communication during the earlier stages of the planning process.

It is against this background that suggestions arise to the effect that citizens be invited to participate directly in site selection, beginning at a time when options are open and plans can be developed in a way that accounts fully for environmental and social concerns. In theory, this creates an opportunity to avoid a great deal of unnecessary conflict and to take corrective measures well in advance of the eleventh hour, when changing plans can result in a dramatic escalation of overall project costs. Front-end costs, of course, would almost certainly go up with the implementation of a collaborative approach, and some additional time might even be needed. However, if the process succeeds in narrowing the range of issues to be hashed out at the licensing stage, the probability of inordinate delay at this crucial point—where the financial penalties of slippage are particularly severe—seems likely to decline.

Even without the potential for smoother scheduling, there is another and probably more important benefit that could accrue to a utility in the wake of a successful interactive endeavor, i.e., an increase in its general credibility in the public's eye. If nothing else, a more open process would seem to be a good way to ameliorate problems of misinformation and confusion that so often in the past have served to erode public confidence.[14] The resulting goodwill might even spill over in the long run into the arena of price regulation, where any relaxation of political tensions would be a most welcome development to beleagured utility executives attempting to secure timely rate relief.

Underscoring this line of argument is the fact that the political context within which investor-owned utilities operate has undergone profound change in recent years, and even the most friendly critics of the power industry agree that it should adopt new modes of behavior in response to present circumstances. Mason Willrich, for example, has asserted in a major trade journal article[15] that all the key assumptions underlying the "old utility politics" are now invalid—including consensus on growth, technological optimism, confidence in government, and deference to business judgment. To him, therefore, the key question facing the industry is how to operate in an ambivalent, volatile, and potentially hostile political environment, and his answer is that each power company should take an active role in efforts to form a "new political consensus." Among the specific steps Willrich advocates, interestingly, is that utilities should first involve affected interest groups in the development of methodology and criteria to guide the siting process, and then join with these same groups in an open-ended search with the aim of establishing an inventory of acceptable sites for various types of plants.

At least on the surface, these and other exhortations on behalf of citizen participation appear perfectly logical and reasonable. Why, then, has the concept yet to be embraced by the electric utility industry? One possible explanation, usually espoused by those with a perspective untempered by field experience, is that such reluctance is merely a reflection of hide-bound conservatism on the part of utility executives. While there may be a grain of truth in this view, it must also be said that many of the proponents of collaboration are equally guilty of taking its efficacy completely for granted, as if it were an Aladdin's Lamp. Before attempting a judgment on the matter, therefore, it seems advisable to try to appreciate the misgivings of those most familiar with the particulars of how the siting process operates in practice.

The Nature of Utility Concerns

As any utility planner or consultant will readily attest, finding sites that are capable of development and potentially licensable—in engineering, economic, and environmental terms—is an exacting task that takes several years of effort, costs millions of dollars, and often produces documentation which occupies an entire bookcase.[16] Further complicating the situation is the fact that site selection has become almost as much a political process as it is a technical one. Indeed, the continuing mobilization of opposition forces and the increase in hostility toward utilities generally has led the industry to weigh questions of public acceptance heavily against other relevant parameters, beginning even with the evaluation of broad candidate areas during the early stages of reconnaissance.[17]

Against this background one might reasonably expect that both the political and technical implications of collaborative planning would be of concern to the electric companies. As it turns out, this was precisely the case among the utility respondents with whom this author has communicated. From the political standpoint, the idea actually seemed antithetical to what most considered a rational response for those who come under siege, i.e., to "pull in the wagons" and do whatever else seems necessary to minimize vulnerability to attack. From the technical standpoint, the idea seemed equally at odds with the conventional notion of what is required in solving vastly complicated planning problems. The kneejerk reaction, in other words, was not what one might call favorable.

These general misgivings on the part of utility respondents can be translated into six distinct (though interrelated) statements of concern. It is appropriate now to review them, one by one.

Concern no. 1: Will early disclosure of planning information put the company at a political disadvantage, and thereby prejudice its ability to purchase and/or license a preferred site? By its very definition, collaborative planning suggests that information about alternative plant locations and their potentially adverse impacts should be made available in advance to persons outside the utility itself. The desirability of sharing information in this manner, however, was seriously called into question by several respondents. One comment frequently made was that early disclosure of potential sites would stir up the public unnecessarily and wouldn't allow the company enough time to prepare an adequate defense against irresponsible or incorrect allegations. Why risk embarrassment by opening the files before you have all the appropriate answers, knowing that critics will be quick to capitalize on the situation to bolster their own position and credibility, and that the press (which thrives on controversy) will probably blow things way out of proportion?

Another concern about providing ammunition to utility opponents is that it will ultimately be used to complicate the licensing process, or, worse yet, to preclude the purchase of a preferred site altogether. The latter possibility is especially worrisome in states where utilities do not have access to the power of eminent domain, in which case there is nothing to prevent an opposition group (or, for that matter, a wealthy individual opposed in principle to industrial development of any kind) from buying critical parcels of land and then refusing to sell. Even in states where utilities have the power of condemnation, moreover, there is a reluctance to use the process because it is perceived negatively by the public at large, provides another opportunity for procedural delay, and can result in higher acquisition costs due to speculation (which is viewed as a rip-off to customers and stockholders alike).

Concern no. 2: Can environmentalists behave in a rational and constructive manner and be willing to accept compromise solutions? Underlying the foregoing reservations about early disclosure is a fear that citizen activists would continue to engage in zero-sum political struggle, regardless of any attempt on the part of the company to initiate a constructive dialogue. This in turn seems based on a set of perceptions regarding the motives and behavioral characteristics of environmentalists. They are accused, for example, of having a parochial, hands-off mentality that fails to acknowledge the existence of tradeoffs ("can't they say anything but no?"). Another prevalent image is that advocacy groups constitute a disloyal opposition, i.e., they have no stake in seeing a broad public interest served and do not feel accountable for the consequences of their actions. Many utility respondents also assert the "intervenor types" are protecting vested interests at best, and are power-hungry, ego-tripping, or out to discredit the establishment at worst.

In addition to characterizing the opposition as inflexible, irresponsible, and self-serving, many respondents indicated that citizen activists have highly emotional tendencies and are therefore inclined to overreact in ways that will undermine an open planning process. A final concern was that "manipulative" environmentalists would use the open planning platform as a means of attracting public attention, and might not even participate if they thought their ability to selectively control the flow of information to the media would be diminished.

Concern no. 3: Can laypersons participate effectively in a complicated planning process without having the skills and qualifications normally required of the technical professional? Foremost in the minds of several respondents was the issue of whether and how participating citizens would be able to cope with a planning problem of enormous scope and complexity. Some felt, to begin with, that the highly technical nature of power plant siting simply precluded direct participation by anyone other than qualified professionals, who alone have the specialized knowledge and experience necessary for intelligent planning. These respondents seemed to feel that the involvement of unsophisticated laypersons would inevitably lead to chaos, and is therefore totally inconsistent with the need to maintain an orderly and efficient site evaluation process. Others were more willing to entertain the possibility that concerned citizens could be educated on key technical issues, but saw the task as a monumental one consuming an inordinate amount of time and resources.

Concern no. 4: Will environmental advocates recognize that there are no perfect solutions, given that planning operates in the presence of numerous constraints and ambiguities? A second technical issue raised by several respondents arises from the fact that site planning is a process fraught with constraints and imperfections. Two recurring comments were that the range of potential sites might not be sufficiently wide to satisfy concerned citizens,[18] and that the prevailing legal and institutional framework might also limit the planner's range of motion in developing suitable alternatives.[19] Another common worry expressed by utility respondents was how participating citizens might react in the face of environmental information that is qualitative, diffuse, incomplete, or otherwise intangible. Such information, it was noted, is not only hard to get a handle on but also resists comparison to more easily quantified engineering and economic considerations (the so-called "apples and oranges" problem).

Being keenly aware of these limitations and ambiguities, the experienced planner realizes that the search for ideal solutions can be unending. Will environmentalists be indecisive in the face of this reality, or unwilling to balance the need for more and better information against resource and time constraints? What some respondents seemed to fear most is "paralysis by analysis," where "pipe-smoking alternative-posers" argue interminably for keeping options open and for studying each and every site in great detail.

Concern no. 5: Is it possible to keep the focus on site selection when many environmentalists are more interested in larger, generic issues such as need for power and the future of nuclear technology? A fact often pointed out by respondents is that environmental groups these days are concerned not only (and perhaps not even primarily) with specific impacts, but also with a number of larger questions surrounding the future expansion of power supply systems (e.g., need for power, use of nuclear technology, etc.). Is it possible, however, for such matters to be dealt with in the context of an open planning forum, oriented as it is toward the resolution of specific site-related conflicts? Utility representatives see little hope for this, in part because some of the most important issues are generic ones and beyond the company's control altogether. They argue, consequently, that some means must be found to keep the focus on site selection per se, or else the collaborative process will fail. At the same time, they fear this may constitute a wholly unacceptable pre-condition for the environmentalist concerned with the more general implication of long-range power system plans.

Concern no. 6: Will the company get burned in the end anyway, due to the impossibility of achieving universal happiness with the outcome of the planning process? Quite apart from the issue of what should be on the agenda for discussion is whether, in any event, a cooperative effort would be fruitless because of the difficulty utilities and concerned citizens seem to have in agreeing on anything at all. Several respondents pointed out that the basic difference between the industry and even its most "reasonable" opponents is at the level of values and perspectives, a fact which all but guarantees that everyone cannot be made happy with a final decision. To some this is particularly troublesome because, with the present legal context, there may be little to prevent a tyranny of the minority in the form of protracted court battle, regardless of the outcome of the collaborative planning exercise. With this in mind, a few respondents suggested that there be a quid pro quo for open planning, perhaps in the form of limits on the right of participants to challenge decisions after a certain point.

All in all, if the above reactions to the concept of public involvement in siting were to be characterized in a single word, that word would have to be "dubious." To most respondents it seems palpably irrational to attempt to build a collaborative relationship when there is little hope of arriving at accommodation but a very real possibility of creating chaos and intensifying conflict. Would this not, in effect, be playing right into the hands of one's enemies? Thus, it is the prospect that open planning could well turn into a Pandora's Box that stands as the major disincentive to its use by the electric utility industry, for whom citizen participation is simply too much of a gamble.

Considering the high stakes involved in making power plant investment decisions, one can hardly call into question this desire to avoid risk. However, it does seem reasonable to ask if the utilities, who have grown accustomed to operating in an intensely adversarial mode, have an accurate perception of the risks to begin with. The opinion here is that probably they do not. In contemplating the difficulties they envisage, in fact, a number of potential mitigating factors have come to mind, along with some thoughts as to how specific problems might be avoided through careful process design. The concatenation of misgivings put forth by utility respondents is thus deserving of a closer look.

Political Objections Evaluated

Of the six basic concerns articulated by utility respondents, the first two are closely related and reflect a basic fear that going public at an early stage would somehow backfire in a purely political sense. Without confidentiality, it is argued, opposition to potential sites will be stimulated before the company is ready to meet it, and intransigent activist groups will simply have additional opportunities for disruption. Would not an open process, then, make siting even more contentious and vulnerable to intervenor tactics than it already is?

Consider first the assertion that premature disclosure will give rise to unnecessary public concerns and embarrassment on the part of an ill-prepared utility. While this is certainly a plausible scenario under business-as-usual conditions (where the utility announces and defends a single, preferred site), one wonders if such difficulty would really be encountered within the open planning context. Since the whole idea is to begin interaction with affected interests at a time when a range of options exists and adjustments can still be made in response to expressed concerns, it seems unlikely that anyone would expect the utility's data and analyses to be anything other than preliminary.

This is not to say that advance notice of conceivable facility locations would be received by the public with total equanimity. Nor can one guarantee that the free flow of information associated with collaborative planning will not give rise to misconceptions about the alternatives available and their impacts. Nevertheless, at least there is an opportunity to deal constructively with the public's fears and mistaken impressions. It is difficult to imagine how such an effort could give rise to anything like the anxiety engendered by the conventional "decide-announce-defend" process, in which dialogue tends to polarize shortly after affected persons learn of the project and begin to sense that most key decisions, for all intents and purposes, have already been made.

A second argument that seems less than persuasive is that site planning information must be kept secret lest it eventually be used against the company in some manner. First of all, it is hard to see how this might pertain to the case of environmental data, considering that extensive impact statements are required in connection with the regulatory process at both state and federal levels. Also seemingly overdone is the fear of speculation, insofar as even a two or three million dollar increase in land cost—which is often occasioned, by rumor in any event—is quite small relative to overall project expenditures. While this is by no means an insignificant amount, neither is that which the utility loses for each day or week that a new power plant is delayed as a result of public opposition that might have been avoided.

One issue that cannot be dismissed so easily is land availability, which is crucial and, in some states, must be handled very delicately. No utility will disclose a preferred site if there is a chance that acquisition will be precluded by a landowner who refuses to sell, or by a zoning change made at the behest of opposition forces. It helps, of course, that most electric companies have access to the power of eminent domain and can request a state override of local zoning ordinances by the public utilities commission. While neither of these legal devices have ever been politically palatable to the industry, they both would seem to be important prerequisites for effective open planning. In fact, using them to implement a siting decision arrived at through a collaborative means, and thus more easily identifiable with collective interests, may even help remove the traditional stigma of "big brotherism" that has made the public uncomfortable with such proceedings in the past.

This line of reasoning, to be sure, offers little comfort to the utility professional who subscribes to the second major type of political concern identified in this study, that having to do with the alleged motives and behavior of "extremists." With environmentalists expected to exploit every available opportunity for subversion, it is understandable that the industry would see little to be gained (and much to be lost) in attempting a collaborative siting process. The obvious question to be raised here, however, is whether the problem of extremism is as widespread or as threatening to the viability of a cooperative effort as the statements of utility respondents make it seem. Without denying that there is a darker side to human nature which creates some difficulty for open planning, this author is inclined to doubt that such a highly pessimistic view is warranted.

It is important to note at the outset that some respondents seemed to view the environmental community in terms just as monolithic as environmentalists have always viewed the power supply establishment. Indeed, many of the adjectives chosen to characterize intervenors (intransigent, self-serving, irresponsible, and so on) seem borrowed from the very lexicon activists have long employed with reference to utility actions. Drawing this parallel is useful because it serves to remind us not only that reasonableness is a very subjective thing, but also that neither side in a polarized debate is likely to have a very accurate perception of the other. Such perceptions, after all, are based on observations of behavior that may be idiosyncratic to an adversarial context. Any sociologist will confirm that even the most docile citizen can be transformed into an activist if the circumstances are right; witness, for example, how parents angry over the busing of school children and farmers aroused by governmental food policies have taken to the streets in recent years. In this light one might argue that much of the extremism decried by the utilities is really a natural response on the part of concerned citizens to a perception that unless they resort to unorthodox tactics their strongly held values will be excluded altogether from the decision process.

These observations suggest that the key issue is not whether environmentalists are capable of acting rationally, but whether they have come to view cooperation as a viable alternative to confrontation. Utility respondents often asserted that activists possess a vested interest in the adversarial process, but other factors seem to belie this notion. Thoughtful environmentalists recognize, for example, that prolonged radical behavior can diminish their credibility and be self-defeating in the long run, and that the best way to influence decisions is usually to participate in them directly on a constructive basis. Citizen groups have even been known to seek interaction with utilities on their own initiative,[20] and some recent reports show that traditional adversaries in the business and environmental communities generally are making concerted attempts to identify common ground.[21] Thus, while the environmental movement certainly has a permanent stake in *advocacy*, there is no reason to think this necessarily stands in the way of a collaborative relationship with those responsible for the siting process.

Still, it would be naive to suggest that the problem of extremism will disappear altogether. Some will undoubtedly enter the participatory arena bent on opposition, and there will be others for whom no amount of interaction in the spirit of accommodation would make a difference. What is to prevent such persons from disrupting an otherwise useful process of interaction among parties willing to seek compromise? Is it desirable, as has been suggested, to simply exclude them and/or put constraints of some kind on subsequent legal challenges?

The inclination here is to reject such limitations on a number of grounds, not the least of which is that environmentalists would probably decline to participate at all, and for good reason. First of all, as has been noted above, it is by no means clear how one distinguishes the extremists from the responsible parties, given the relative nature of such characterizations. Moreover, a so-called open process that is available to some and not others is a contradiction in terms, and would probably give rise to legitimate skepticism about the utility's motives (e.g., "this must be a clever attempt to divide and conquer"). This would discourage participation, as would the pressure those excluded from the process seem likely to put on those inclined to stay (via charges of selling out, etc.).

Likewise, fairness will always require an adjudicatory procedure for those who are adversely affected (even after open planning) because one cannot assume that the requirements of due process will automatically be met in the course of such an informal undertaking. In the alternative, if elaborate procedures were devised to police the process, flexibility would be reduced in a manner reminiscent of the highly structured adversarial approach that colla borative planning is designed to supplant in the first place. Thus, once again it seems likely that a restrictive participatory policy would only serve to aggravate the existing climate of distrust and thereby reduce the chances for success.

At first glance this appears to be a Catch-22 situation: without certain parties participation won't materialize, and with them it can only degenerate into confrontation. What is being overlooked, however, is the possibility that the open planning process itself might create an unfavorable climate for extremism. One should remember that charges of secrecy, double-dealing, and other deceitful practices rely heavily on emotional appeal and are most effective when the utility is perceived as a villain. Extremists also benefit when there is confusion as to the facts of the case, and often rely on outright distortion and obfuscation. With open planning, however, insofar as it seeks to dispel alienation and clarify the issues of choice, much of the basis for radical political action might well be removed.

This concept of reduced vulnerability to extremist action seems equally applicable in the case where dissatisfied participants undertake legal action after open planning has concluded. Both regulatory officials and members of the judiciary, who are not unaware of the prevailing political climate, may be much less sympathetic to continuing challenges in the face of an obvious good faith effort by the utility to incorporate all views and suggestions into the siting process. This is particularly true if a negotiated settlement has been reached, in which case the company would have the support of a constituency much broader than it had ever enjoyed in the past in connection with its siting decisions.[22] Such political capital, in fact, would in all likelihood prove valuable in almost any area of utility endeavor that is much in the public eye.

Technical Objections Evaluated

Proceeding in a manner similar to that of the foregoing section, there are a number of points that can be made in response to the third and fourth concerns utilities seem to have about citizen participation. Here the prevailing view is that the process could just as easily break down in the technical sense, either because of an inability on the part of concerned citizens to grasp the analytical complexities of the subject matter, or because of an unwillingness to accept the ground rules by which site selection normally operates. Is it not impossible, respondents ask, to "democratize" an endeavor that is complicated and needs to be conducted in a very structured and orderly fashion? Clearly there is a special paradigm of planning underlying this concern, and its basic premises need to be scrutinized.

To begin with, consider the issue of disparity in expertise. Respondents have argued that because the siting process is highly technical, it should be reserved for technical professionals who have acquired the necessary experience and expertise. This is an argument subject to criticism, however, on grounds that it underestimates the capabilities of laypersons and overestimates those of experts. The fact is that many planning issues can be dealt with only through careful reasoning and common sense—not expert analysis—and in this regard the engineer is no less prone to stupid mistakes than anyone else. Further, on certain matters it is the average citizen who is the true expert, and in such cases direct interaction with the public at large could be of real value to the planning team and improve the overall quality of the siting effort.

One topic a utility staff might not be completely familiar with, for example, is that of the socio-cultural conditions related to land use. Impacts in this domain often have significance only for those who live in a particular area and possess knowledge and understanding that no outsider has. Such information is rarely obtainable by surveys, polls, and other consensus-oriented techniques, which are not sufficiently disaggregated to reliably foresee public acceptance issues, judge their severity, and direct planner attention to local problems and opportunities.[23]

This is not to say, on the other hand, that one should expect citizens to participate directly in the sort of detailed ecological or meteorological studies that utility specialists carry out. Indeed, this is far from the real objective of participation, which is to incorporate a broader set of values and perspectives into the process of making the difficult tradeoffs that have been confronted heretofore in a vacuum by the utility, only to be challenged at some later (and much more inconvenient) time. Most planners would readily admit that the siting process, however complex, is at root a matter of judgment and even intuition; witness, for example, the "apples and oranges" problem often mentioned as a key difficulty in making site comparisons. Here it is the purely *technical* methods of analysis that tend to break down, and it is also where collaboration with affected interests—a dialectic inherently capable of operating on subjective information—could be most advantageous.

Establishing that concerned citizens have a legitimate role to play in siting, of course, says nothing about whether or not the process can be made to go smoothly. Achieving effective two-way communication between technical professionals and laypersons is rarely a straightforward matter, particularly when there is a good deal of anticipatory mistrust present (as there would be in the power plant siting case). Also, it is clearly preposterous to suggest there should be an environmentalist looking over the shoulder of every siting engineer, an image that quite understandably makes utility people shudder ("don't ask the people to help you plan, you'll not know whether you're coming or going."). How, then, should participation be structured to be workable?

No obvious answers can be given, although one point which needs to be brought out is that collaboration does not necessarily connote a truly joint effort. What seems most important is that the public not be totally insulated from the technical work, because a lack of understanding of the thought processes followed and judgments made by planners can easily give rise to a perception that the weak or questionable aspects of various alternatives are being concealed in technical jargon. Thus, it is essential that lay participants at least be informed of what is being done, and be encouraged to make whatever observations or suggestions they feel are appropriate (e.g., as to new lines of inquiry, the criteria to be applied in making tradeoffs, and so on). Beyond this baseline the degree of interaction can vary considerably as a function of what is expected from the participants, what sort of capabilities they exhibit, or where their major interests lie.

Another problem to be faced is that of educating participants on the idiosyncracies of site selection, for there can be no constructive dialogue unless all parties to the process have achieved a modicum of literacy on its substantive aspects. This could be a prodigious task requiring considerable investment of time and effort on the part of the utility. Here again, though, one must not overlook the fact that many concerned citizens are intelligent, serious students of the issues who could rather quickly comprehend at least the broad technical dimensions of the situation (if not the specific engineering details). Even if this were not the case, what is wrong with an endeavor that helps those outside the utility gain deeper appreciation of the nature of the siting problem? Rather than bemoan it as too costly an investment, it seems the industry should welcome this educational opportunity as one that is entirely consistent with its long-standing (though yet to be achieved) public relations goals.

The final issue at the interface between participation and planning involves the manner in which imperfections in the real world of planning are to be dealt with in the collaborative context. The hope, of course, is that citizens working on a cooperative basis with the utility would come to realize that decisions are never made under ideal circumstances, and that it is necessary to bound the problem and even muddle through on occasion in order to maintain a timely and efficient evaluation process. Realizing this goal is still not easy, however, and much will depend on the extent to which a spirit of give and take develops in the course of interaction. Can anything be done to foster flexibility and otherwise loosen up the planning process? There are no set formulas to prescribe, but certain steps and gestures do come to mind as being necessary in this regard.

It would be important, for example, to ensure that the project schedule allows sufficient time for planner-citizen interaction, recognizing that environmentalists might be inclined to approach the impact assessment process in a more cautious manner than experienced site planners. Planning lead times already span a couple of years or more, and as long as participation begins at an early point this would seem to allow the necessary breathing room. If not, perhaps the objective should be to find potential sites for generic plant types, rather than a specific unit for which a target construction date has been established. In either event, one must take care that the time available is not used in an undisciplined way, perhaps by adopting a mutually agreeable timetable together with procedures by which it can be modified in the event of unanticipated circumstances.

Aside from arranging an appropriate time horizon, it is important that the utility be sensitive to the fact that if the alternatives presented are not sufficiently broad to present real choices, participation will be suspected of being a thinly-disguised effort to market a decision that has already been made (even if it has not!). If such a perception is to be avoided, attempts must be made to broaden the range of options to the point where there is room for compromise. It might be desirable, for example, to begin with a reconnaissance of broad regions of interest instead of narrowing the focus immediately to evaluation of a small number of final candidate sites.

Yet, it will not be so easy to relax other types of constraints or to remove certain ambiguities from the impact assessment process—what then? Here it would seem that the utility's attitude toward such difficulties, and not the difficulties themselves, is the most important factor in determining the viability of the collaborative approach. It may well be, for example, that questions involving uncertainty will not become bottlenecks if the company acknowledges that there are good and bad ways to deal with incomplete information and employs methodologies that are designed to explicitly support a judgmental approach. Likewise, having a wide range of options available may not be so crucial if the company shows it will actively seek to develop new alternatives and to ease particularly burdensome constraints. It might even be the case, ultimately, that all parties could work together to effect legal and institutional changes that would ease the siting dilemma, changes that might not otherwise be possible without the support of a bipartisan constituency.

What is being argued here, really, is that in most cases the substance of planning need not pose major difficulties for a collaborative effort if the *style* of planning is adjusted in appropriate ways. What seems essential is that participating citizens come to feel that the company is keeping an open mind and is trying, in the face of imperfect circumstances, to be responsive to environmental and social concerns. If this can be achieved, the notion of blending citizens into a highly technocratic planning process seems not so disquieting after all.

On the Search for Common Ground

Several arguments have now been made to the effect that constructive interaction between utilities and concerned citizens is not a wholly implausible scenario. Nothing has been said, however, about whether the process can actually converge on a mutually acceptable course of action, an issue quite apart from political and technical considerations per se. Respondents noted in their fifth and sixth concerns that discussions could founder at the very beginning—over nonsiting questions like need for power or choice of plant technology—as well as subsequently when disagreements emerge as to the relative merits of specific locations. Thus, if the parties involved will never see eye to eye and impasse is inevitable sooner or later, why bother with collaboration at all?

Consider, first, the dilemma posed by the fact that advocacy groups will probably raise a number of larger, generic issues unrelated to the siting problem itself. On the one hand, to broaden the scope of inquiry to include such matters is to create additional potential for contention, especially where nuclear plants are concerned. On the other hand, insofar as the specification of capacity requirements and plant types predetermines to a large extent the options and impacts in siting, it is understandable that environmental groups would vigorously object to any attempts to decouple these underlying decisions from the process.

In light of strongly held sentiments to this effect, it seems clear that questions of power demand and alternative means of supplying it must be dealt with somehow if a collaborative siting process is to proceed. Ideally, such questions should be debated and resolved in a separate forum and at a more appropriate level of policy making, and it is perhaps encouraging to note in this regard that state and federal regulatory agencies have begun to implement new procedures for review of utility demand forecasts and supply plans.[24] It is highly problematical, though, as to whether the environmental community will have confidence in these new mechanisms to the point where plant-related issues would not prove distracting to a participatory siting process. For one thing, not all states have adopted legislative provisions enabling evaluation of long-range system plans. For another, there is evidence that few states are truly capable of effecting a comprehensive overview of utility planning and its relationship to other programs and policies having to do with environmental resource management.[25]

It is conceivable, therefore, that existing forums for consideration of long-range plans will prove unacceptable to citizen advocates in some respects. What then? One possible strategy might be to obviate the need to consider this aspect of decision making altogether by involving citizens in a broad reconnaissance effort aimed, not at siting a specific facility, but at identifying suitable locations for a variety of generic plant types. The attractive feature here is that, because no final decisions have been made as to when or even whether a plant will be built, the situation might be less threatening than it would be if the utility were committed to bringing a particular facility on line at a preordained time. Most utilities maintain an inventory of potential sites anyway, and seeking public input to modify or expand that inventory could provide public acceptance information useful to system planners and project designers alike.

Not to be overlooked, however, are several potential disadvantages to this site inventory approach. One of these stems from the fact that a site may look good at one time but be unacceptable later as technology, environmental understanding, or regulatory requirements change. Unless the open planning effort is a continuous one (perhaps it should be!), changing conditions could render moot any tentative agreements reached. Another, probably more severe, obstacle is that land banking proposals are often disdained because they evoke the image of a self-fulfilling prophecy. Some people, for example, might think twice about endorsing a site for a larger generating facility, even tentatively, for fear of prejudicing the utility's attitude toward mitigating demand or exploring alternative energy sources. While it is most unlikely that a utility would build a plant merely because a suitable site is available, the symbolic and perceptual significance to the environmentalist of being associated with a utility site inventory is, nonetheless, not to be discounted.

Thus, a utility may well have no choice but to direct a participatory process toward siting an actual facility. In this case, perhaps the only way to keep the focus on the issue of location is to start with a plant that seems least likely to raise the hackles of the environmental constituency. It certainly seems unwise, for example, to apply a collaborative approach for the first time to the siting of a nuclear reactor, considering the ongoing debate over radioactive waste disposal and the change in public attitudes toward accidents in the wake of Three Mile Island. One need not be so pessimistic, however, over the prospects for effective cooperation in the case of other major facilities such as coal-fired or hydroelectric plants, which at least do not suffer from a deep-seated mistrust in the basic technology that is employed.

An even better way to minimize attention to broader issues in electricity planning might be to choose a station of intermediate size (e.g., a 500 megawatt cycling coal plant) for the initial outreach effort. To be sure this is not the type of plant the industry usually has great difficulty siting; but the real objective is to break the ice of mutual distrust and begin to develop a cooperative working relationship, and to achieve this it seems best to start with a rather limited participatory experiment that has a reasonable chance of success. Thereafter it might be possible to tackle the issues associated with larger facilities, where the stakes are higher and the conflicts more difficult to resolve. Indeed, the best course of action would probably be to follow up the initial siting endeavor with joint deliberations on how a future collaborative siting process might be structured, in light of the experience gained.

With this basic strategy of working up to the more controversial projects, one begins to wonder if it might not be feasible after all to address, as an adjunct to the site selection process, the questions of need for power and alternative supply strategies. Certainly there is no a priori reason why some issues like, say, the validity of load forecasts or the prospects for purchasing power cannot be scrutinized in an open forum, at least to some extent. Without the opportunity to engage in such deliberations, there may be little inclination on the part of citizens to attend to the question of siting at all. Is there any hope of resolving anything? This author, for one, is not about to underestimate what can be accomplished if only the present atmosphere of hostility and suspicion can be dispelled.

This is not to say that compromise solutions which enjoy substantial bipartisan support will be easy to come by, and this brings us to the final impediment to effective open planning, i.e., the problem of honest disagreement. Utility respondents argued in the end that, if nothing else, severe polarization of views would ultimately preclude closure on whatever issues are brought under consideration. In their opinion, then, the mere fact that reasonable minds can be expected to differ is a compelling argument against interaction. Is it really so? Only, it would seem, if one believes that either (1) it is necessary for *all* conflict to be resolved as a result of the process, or (2) it is

unlikely that *any* significant amount of conflict can be resolved. To subscribe
to these propositions, however, would be to lose sight of some of the most
basic concepts upon which all attempts at compromise are based.

One important premise is that it is often possible to achieve substantial
agreement on a course of action without reaching consensus on underlying
goals and values. The history of decision making in our pluralistic society is
fraught with examples where those with seemingly irreconcilable differences
at the level of broad principles have come to terms within a context of specific
proposals. One must take care to remember, in addition, that universal happiness is not the criterion upon which any process of conflict resolution should
be judged. The ultimate goal, rather, should be to avoid unnecessary conflict
and seek accommodation wherever possible, and to have all participants feel
comfortable with the way the process was conducted. This view of what is to
be expected of collaboration readily admits that dissatisfaction cannot be
totally forestalled. The hope is that those whose interests suffer will not only
be fewer in number, but also more equitably treated and less inclined, therefore, to turn their disagreement into overt resistance. Is this not, after all, the
classically conceived essence of democratic methods for managing the clash
of opposing views?

To be sure, avoiding impasse within an atmosphere of divergent interests
and long-standing mistrust will still be a formidable task, requiring most careful attention to a number of behavioral realities. One cannot assume, for
example, that a utility company would abandon the position of advocacy
which grows out of the very nature of its business; nor is it reasonable to
expect that concerned citizens will be responsive to all goals and interests, or
even have confidence in their ability to make balanced judgments. For
environmentalists, moreover, participation in a so-called balancing process
may not ring true because they fear co-optation and a resulting loss of consti-
uency. One can easily appreciate the awkward position of a citizen advocate
who is asked to make a transition virtually overnight from watchdog to collab-
orator, especially when there are extremists about who would be quick to
make the charge of selling out.

These observations make it clear that one cannot rely on a simplistic
"goody-two-shoes" approach which says that, if people are just nice to each
other and lay their cards on the table without playing games, agreements will
eventually be reached. Given human nature, it seems more pragmatic to conceive of interaction in terms of hard-nosed bargaining, in which participants
are asked only to seek a compromise consistent with their own interests. In
this way accommodation can often be reached even if the respective parties
don't accept each other's facts, figures, or line of reasoning, because each side
is motivated at least initially by the realities of what can be gained from
compromise. If a sense of collegiality develops in the course of rubbing

elbows (as it often does), all the better, but a relationship of grudging respect can do almost as well.

To argue that partisanship is important even in collaborative planning, of course, says nothing about how conflict should be handled at the operational level. Those familiar with the route to compromise know that it is tortuous even under the best of circumstances, in which all participants feel pressure to reach a decision and have clear incentives to give ground. Still, there is every reason to believe that traditional adversaries *can* find courses of action that each can live with if the circumstances are right, and it is heartening that more is being learned all the time about how to make this process work. Consider, for example, the work that is being done with techniques such as compensation[26] and environmental mediation,[27] with the latter being applied to a variety of disputes around the country. As these efforts toward improving the state of the art of conflict resolution multiply, it seems reasonable to be optimistic about the prospects for convergence in an open planning endeavor.

Concluding Remarks

In a sense, this discussion of the relative merits of citizen participation in power plant siting has now come full circle. The hopeful note sounded at the outset soon gave way to a formidable litany of objections which, on their face at least, made collaboration seem a classic example of an idea that sounds good in principle but is patently unworkable in practice. However, further examination of the "can of worms" scenario put forth by utility respondents makes one realize that some concerns are probably overstated or based on questionable premises, and that others might be obviated through appropriate groundrules to guide the interaction process. There is reason to believe, in other words, that the participatory approach has more to commend it than the electricity industry has heretofore been able to envision.

This author has noted, in fact, a rather distressing tendency on the part of utility respondents to view the concept of collaboration almost exclusively through the jaundiced eye of the political game theorist, and to evaluate it in terms of an unreasonably stringent criterion, i.e., whether or not it constitutes a panacea that could eliminate all political conflict and technical ambiguity from the siting process. Clearly it cannot. What it does offer is a means of approaching these inherent difficulties in a manner far more constructive than is possible in an adversarial context where there is every incentive to polarize debate and exploit uncertainty. The industry also seems inclined, unfortunately, to view proponents of participation as wild-eyed idealists who harbor the naive expectation that consensus is attainable through gentle persuasion. Yet this, too, is far from the truth, as most professionals in the field of collaborative problem solving recognize full well the realities of value conflict and the need, therefore, to select modes of interaction specifically designed to operate under such circumstances.

This is not to say that issues of concern to the electric companies should be taken lightly, or that the lines of reasoning advanced on behalf of open planning constitute a mandate for immediate adoption. Many of the counterarguments presented in response to industry misgivings are admittedly laced with "ifs," "mights," and "coulds," and while plausible they hardly comprise a definitive rejoinder to the utility position. It seems clear, moreover, that in some ways collaboration is a delicate balancing act that requires a great deal of practice before it can be performed with regularity and precision. Thus a substantial burden of proof remains to be satisfied before one can conclude that citizen involvement should become a principle of operation in all siting endeavors.

The central thrust of this article, however, has not been to demonstrate conclusively the wisdom of opening up the site selection process. Such a determination can never be made with confidence on the basis of a priori arguments which are intrinsically speculative on *both* sides as to what sort of scenario might unfold in practice. The only answerable question, then, is whether collaboration should be taken more seriously as a legislative alternative to the conventional means of dealing with public acceptance problems. In this author's mind the response should most definitely be in the affirmative, for the proposition is obviously defensible and even persuasive in many respects.

Where does one go from here? Since the basic theoretical issues are now well-drawn, it seems best to proceed with inquiries of a more empirical nature. A body of experience is needed to serve as the testing ground for the various hypotheses that have been articulated so far, both pro and con, and to provide insight on a host of issues in the category of process design. How open is open enough? Who should (or will) participate, and how does one deal with the issue of representation? Which participatory techniques are more useful than others? What are the sources of funding and other resources necessary to support the effort? What should be the role of government officials with ultimate responsibility for granting licenses and permits? Clearly, the particulars of mobilizing a pluralistic planning process must be carefully attended to; indeed, the extent to which the technical and political issues addressed herein become significant will probably depend more than anything else on operational details such as these.

As it turns out, an evidentiary base of sorts already exists because a handful of innovative utilities have experimented in the last ten years with various forms of citizen participation in siting. Some have simply allowed early access to documents prepared in connection with a preferred site,[28] while others have actively solicited the opinion of environmentalists on the relative merits of candidate sites.[29] One company—Pennsylvania Power and Light—has even gone so far as to establish a permanent siting advisory task force whose deliberations began, in 1977, with a critique of the general methodology PP&L and its consultants were using in the evaluation of potential sites.[30]

These cases, while limited in number, present a golden opportunity to learn more about the intricacies of open planning. The problem, however, is that the literature at the moment is woefully inadequate in this area. Accounts of utility experiments are typically sketchy and anecdotal, appearing for the most part in a scattered array of trade journals, workshop proceedings, and company reports of limited distribution.[31] Thus, although considerable data has been generated the bulk of it remains little studied and poorly understood. Until this information is brought to light more effectively, collaborative siting will remain an unknown (and, to the utilities, fearful) quantity whose true risks and benefits can only be the subject of speculation.

What this suggests is that it is no longer worth trying to decide in the abstract whether citizen participation is a Pandora's Box or an Aladdin's Lamp, for in fact it is probably neither. What it may be is an idea whose time is coming, because the institutional reforms of the '70s have failed to quell electricity–environment controversies, and because other potential solutions have been too few and far between. The participatory approach, in sum, deserves a lot more systematic analysis in the decade of the '80s than it has just received in the decade past.[32]

Notes

1. See R. Morgan and S. Jerabek, "How to Challenge Your Local Electric Utility: A Citizen's Guide to the Power Industry," Environmental Action Foundation, Washington, D.C. (March, 1974).

2. See, e.g., G. A. Brown et al. *Power Plant Site Considerations at Charlestown, Rhode Island*, University of Rhode Island, Marine Technical Report No. 23, Kingston, Rhode Island (1974); see also R. H. Ball et al., *California's Electricity Quandary: II. Planning for Power Plant Siting*, Rand Corporation Report R-1115-RF CSA, Santa Monica, California (September, 1972).

3. See, e.g., A. K. Sloan, *Citizen Participation in Transportation Planning: The Boston Experience*, Ballinger Publishing Co., Cambridge, Massachusetts (1974); J. O'Riordan, "The Public Involvement Program in the Okanagan Basin Study," 16 *Natural Resources Journal* 177-196 (January, 1976).

4. See, e.g., Committee on Power Plant Siting, *Engineering for Resolution of the Energy Environment Dilemma,* at 12, National Academy of Engineering, Washington, D.C. (1972); Special Committee on Electric Power and the Environment, *Electricity and the Environment: The Reform of Legal Institutions,* at 8-9, Association of the Bar of New York City, New York, N.Y. (1972).

5. S. 2995, introduced to the 95th Congress on March 17, 1978, included a provision directing the Nuclear Regulatory Commission to encourage or require utilities to engage in open and advance planning for the addition of generating capacity as well as the evaluation of potential sites.

6. One of the better pieces on the subject that has appeared in recent years is an interview with Robert I. Hanfling of the Department of Energy, "Utility Decisions: What Voice for the Public?," *Electrical World* (December 1 and 15, 1977).

7. D. Ducsik and T. Austin, *Citizen Participation in Power Plant Siting: An Assessment,* Energy Studies Group Report No. 2, Center for Technology, Environment, and Development, Clark University, Worcester, Massachusetts (May, 1979). These communications took place during 1974 and 1975, with information collected in the form of notes taken during face-to-face interviews and telephone conversations, letters, tape recordings, and marginal notations received in response to concept papers describing the open planning process.

8. T. J. Dignan, "Licensing Hearings: A Modest Proposal," *Nuclear News,* at 45 (May, 1974).

9. For a good discussion on this point, see Barton, "Behind the Legal Explosion," 27 *Stanford Law Review* 567 (February, 1975).

10. See, e.g., Ebbin and Kasper, *Citizen Groups and the Nuclear Power Controversy,* MIT Press, Cambridge, Massachusetts (1974).

11. The necessity of committing to studies and making equipment selections for a given site prior to knowing whether that site would be acceptable is described in J.L. Leporati, Envirosphere Company, "Expanding Role of States in Power Plant Regulation," presented at the 47th Annual Executive Conference, New York, N.Y. (October, 1976).

12. One measure that is often proposed, for example, is the use on a res judicata standard to preclude the rehearing of issues for which there was a prior opportunity for hearing.

13. See, e.g., Boasberg, Hewes, Klores, and Kass, *Policy Issues Raised by Intervenor Requests for Financial Assistance in NRC Proceedings,* NUREG 75/071, Nuclear Regulatory Commission, Washington, D.C. (July 18, 1975).

14. The inverse relationship between public confusion and public confidence has been documented by Clark and Brownell in *Electric Power Plants in the Coastal Zone: Environmental Issues,* American Littoral Society Special Publication No. 7, Highlands, New Jersey (October, 1973).

15. M. Willrich, "The Electric Utilities and the Energy Crisis," *Public Utilities Fortnightly,* vol. 95, no. 1, pp. 22-28 (January 2, 1975); vol. 95, no 2, pp. 25-34 (January 16, 1975). Professor Willrich is now vice-president for corporate planning of Pacific Gas and Electric Company.

16. See Nagel and Vasseld, "Power Plant Siting Requirements," *Planning,* Vol. 39, No. 2, at 24 (February, 1973); Brown, "Power Plants—Picking the Sites," *Consulting Engineer,* Vol. 40, No. 3, at 133 (March, 1973).

17. Commonwealth Associates, Inc., *Nuclear Power Plant Siting—A Generalized Process,* prepared for the Atomic Industrial Forum, Inc., Washington, D.C. (August, 1974).

18. Nuclear plants, for example, are subject to stringent regulatory criteria with respect to seismology, distance from population centers, and so on.

19. Among the limitations known to this author are the lack of compensatory mechanisms to mitigate adverse effects (e.g., liability problems that preclude recreational access to sites; tax laws that confine payments to one town) and legal constraints on the region of interest for siting purposes (e.g., statutes that disallow out-of-state investment in the rate base; charter provisions and/or pooling agreements that restrict siting to the service territory only).

20. Sierra Club Press Release, "Environmental Groups Form Wisconsin Utilities Advisory Coalition," Office of the Midwest Representative, Madison, Wisconsin (August 22, 1972).

21. See H. Leonard, J. Davies III, Gordon Binder, eds., *Business and the Environment: Toward Common Ground,* The Conservation Foundation, Washington, D.C. (1977).

22. As it was put nearly a decade ago, "a political compromise with expert and responsible ecology groups capable of representing the public's interest would be a large step toward securing a solid mandate upon which to rest long range construction plans." D. Jopling and S. Gage, "The Pattern of Public Political Resistance," *Nuclear News,* at 32 (March, 1971).

23. The advantage of citizen participation in providing more disaggregated information on public acceptance has been noted in Calvert and Heilman, "New Approach to Power Plant Siting," *Journal of the Power Division,* Proceedings of the American Society of Civil Engineers (June, 1972).

24. For a detailed compilation of siting legislation in the fifty states, see *Energy Facility Siting in the United States,* Southern States Energy Board, Atlanta, Georgia (February, 1978). See also Stevens, "State Perspectives on Energy Facility Siting: Current State Practices," report for the National Governors' Association, Washington, D.C. (December, 1978).

25. See "Survey of Current State Practices for Evaluating Utility Power Supply/Demand Planning," in *Electricity Planning—Today's Improvements Can Alter Tomorrow's Decisions,* EMD-80-112, Appendix I, U.S. General Accounting Office, Washington, D.C. (September 30, 1980).

26. See, e.g., M. O'Hare, "Not on My Block You Don't: Facility Siting and the Strategic Importance of Compensation," 25 *Public Policy* 407-458 (Fall, 1977).

27. See, e.g., D. O'Connor, "Environmental Mediation: The State-of-the-Art," 2 *EIA Review* 9, MIT Laboratory of Architecture and Planning (October, 1978).

28. Examples are Florida Power & Light Co., Potomac Electric Co., and Washington Public Power Co.

29. Examples are Northeast Utilities Co., Northern States Power Co., San Diego Gas & Electric Co., Ontario Hydro, and Duke Power Co.

30. See Pennsylvania Environmental Research Foundation, *Public Involvement in Corporate Policy Decisions: A Report on the Experience of the Public Advisory Committee of Pennsylvania Power & Light Company,* Philadelphia, PA (March, 1979).

31. One major work in progress that will begin to fill this gap is D. Myhra, *Public Involvement in the Introduction of Power Plants,* forthcoming, John Wiley & Sons, New York, N.Y. (1981).

32. In New England, the author is happy to report, two efforts are underway that promise to shed some additional light on questions of collaboration in power plant siting. The New England River Basins Commission has convened a 30-member working Task Force comprising utility executives, regulatory officials, and environmental advocates with the common aim of improving the site selection process as it currently exists in the region. Further, the regional office of the General Accounting Office has undertaken a study of how early public and government involvement can alleviate energy facility siting disputes in general. At the time of this writing, however, published reports are not available for either of these projects.

DAVID MORELL

7 *Siting and the Politics of Equity*

Introduction: The Siting Imperative

As America plunges ever further into the depths of her hazardous waste crisis, the critical dilemma of siting new waste management facilities in the face of intense public opposition becomes ever more apparent. These wastes must be managed, by the millions of tons per year. Thousands of old dumpsites must be cleansed, groundwater must be decontaminated. All this requires hundreds of new facilities, primarily for treatment of liquid wastes and contaminated soil but also for disposal of the treatment residuals and of the untreated (or untreatable) wastes. But where are these facilities to be sited? Can a new system adequate to provide effective management of the nation's hazardous wastes be developed in the 1980s in the face of the common refrain expressed so vigorously every time a new hazardous waste management facility is proposed in a particular location: "Not in *my* backyard"?[1]

Success in waste management, nationally and in every region of the country, founders on the impasse of today's siting paralysis. Facilities are needed, desperately; but they cannot be sited. As a result, the Superfund cleanup effort is failing to attain its objectives. Responsible parties in industry are reluctant to cooperate in site cleanups which would require redisposal at other dumps likely to leak at some future date, rendering the firm liable once

Reprinted from David Morell, "Siting and the Politics of Equity," *Hazardous Waste,* Vol. 1 (1984), pp. 555-571, by courtesy of Mary Ann Liebert, Inc., publishers. Reprinted by permission of the publisher, Mary Ann Liebert, Inc., and David Morell.

again to pay for the second cleanup. The RCRA effort (and its state equivalents) enforces much more stringent standards on new facilities as opposed to existing ones. How can we actually close today's landfills, inadequate though they may be, if new treatment and disposal facilities are simply not available?*

Innovative land disposal phaseout efforts, in California and soon nationally through the reauthorized RCRA statute, evidence huge gaps between their rhetoric and the reality of continued land disposal. Since new treatment facilities are unavailable, how can pits, ponds, lagoons, and other surface impoundments really be closed? Without the intertwined economic and regulatory pressures of an effective phaseout effort, new onsite and offsite treatment facilities fail to amass sufficient force to overcome siting obstacles. And as a result, incentives for gradual reduction in the volumes of hazardous wastes being generated remain primarily an illusion. Millions of tons of new wastes overwhelm today's set of grossly inadequate land disposal facilities, but with no realistic alternative in sight. In sum, our inability to site new facilities is at the core of our continuing inability to manage hazardous wastes successfully. The intense national pressures to gain effective control over these wastes have, to date, failed to be translated into forces of sufficient power to overcome local siting resistance to each proposed new facility.

This siting dilemma can be resolved through implementation of an overall waste-management strategy based on the politics of equity. The reasons for local resistance need to be understood, so that they can be confronted honestly . . . not overwhelmed or preempted or ignored. An effective balance of federal, state, and local siting authority; a focus on treatment rather than continued dumping on the land; an emphasis on onsite rather than offsite waste treatment; an acceptance of the need for fair patterns of compensation negotiated with the local communities selected; simultaneous siting of numerous new facilities in accordance with regional needs and with local patterns of equity; and a firm commitment to reestablish the integrity and credibility of both government and industry. These are all crucial components of an effective strategy to site new hazardous waste management facilities, and therefore to achieve responsible waste management. While this may seem a set of impossible tasks, they should indeed be feasible if we soon begin to demand as much from our political system and our public policy makers as we are now beginning to demand from our engineers and scientists.

---

* This issue is posing serious problems in Southern California, as well as elsewhere. Wastes and contaminated groundwater and soil from the McColl site (Fullerton, Orange County) and the Stringfellow site (Glen Avon, Riverside County) cannot be taken to the BKK site in West Covina (Los Angeles County) for redisposal because of EPA enforcement actions there under both RCRA and CERCLA.

Coping With the Causes of Local Opposition

If the siting impasse is ever to be ended, policy makers will have to comprehend the various causes of local opposition, and then deal with each on its own terms. Because local citizens' concerns arise from several different genuine motivations, no single response by government or by industry should be expected to "solve" the siting problem. That is, there is no "magic wand" in siting; public policies predicated on the search for one are thus doomed to fail.

FEAR

In dealing with the reality of local siting opposition, it is vital to recognize that people are afraid. This fear takes many forms, and in the vicinity of proposed new hazardous waste management facilities it emanates from complex dynamics. While public health risks from these chemicals are real, perceptions of danger are far more intense than this reality. The specter of Love Canal and of Stringfellow stalks the landscape. People see dangers in the very terms "hazardous wastes" and "toxic waste." They ask "Is my water safe to drink?"* Most believe that new facilities will be equally as dangerous as were the old ones. Given credibility problems, assertions by industry and government to the contrary carry little weight in the emotion-ridden dialogue.

Such fears certainly won't dissipate in the near future; and realistic siting programs ought not to aspire to such a miraculous goal. Nevertheless, government and industry can do a great deal both technologically and institutionally to counter public fears. Design standards for new treatment, storage, and disposal facilities can assure better technical performance. Buffer zones can be designated, and then enforced through effective land use controls. Open programs of public participation can build confidence. Public availability of reliable data on patterns of waste generation can assure a common basis for debate over the need for a proposed new facility. Clarity about ultimate liability can induce industry to shift rapidly from reliance on disposal to investment in waste treatment. Siting of treatment facilities in industrial areas where they are compatible with existing land use patterns would lessen concerns over their safety, in contrast to a new facility in an undeveloped area. Finally, risk assessments comparing the impact of new facilities with those of the facilities operating today should indicate the large marginal improvements

---

* A non-scientific survey taken in Santa Clara County, California, in 1984 indicated that 75 percent of all respondents considered their water "unsafe to drink." In reality, three public water supply wells in the entire county had been tested and found to contain low levels of chemical contamination; all three had been immediately closed by the public health authorities. All the water being provided to the public in this area was being tested carefully to assure its safety.[2]

in safety associated with the new waste management system. While still imperfect, perhaps, they would represent a tremendous improvement over the present situation.

Taken alone, none of these steps would be sufficient. In the context of a broader siting strategy based on equity and balance, however, these actions can place fear of health effects from a new facility in proper perspective.

EQUITY

While fear of cancer and of other chronic diseases lies behind public opposition to proposed new facilities, the principal force comes from perceptions of injustice, of exploitation, of unfairness. Any site is in someone's backyard. That person or group naturally shouts out: "Why me? Why not someone else?" The facility's proponents typically find themselves at an enormous disadvantage in responding to such queries, particularly as the level of emotion escalates. The arcane jargon of siting criteria and of hydrogeochemistry, and simplistic notions of market forces and corporate decision-making, all fail miserably in the face of "Not Here." No reasonable person wants to host a new hazardous waste facility in his or her town; and if it's a large facility designed to manage wastes from a whole region, rather than just meeting the waste management needs of the immediate community, opposition based on equity rapidly assumes extraordinary proportions.*

Response to equity concerns is vital to any successful siting strategy. This will require a major shift in the traditional siting paradigm. Instead of locating one facility at a time, simultaneous siting of multiple facilities provides the only realistic way to respond to the equity challenge.

DISPARITY IN COSTS AND BENEFITS

An inherent imbalance between localized costs and dispersed benefits is integral to the equity question. These facilities typically manage wastes from a relatively large area: a county, or region, or entire state or even interstate area. The larger or more specialized the facility, the more extreme this principle of dispersed benefits becomes.

In contrast, the facility's costs are, without exception, concentrated within the local area. Noise or odors, air emissions, groundwater leachate—

* In Santa Barbara County, the City Councils of both Santa Barbara and Santa Maria (near the Casmalia hazardous waste landfill) passed resolutions in mid 1984 calling for an end to extensive reliance on this facility by trucks carrying wastes from the Los Angeles industrial complex. With the growing enforcement actions against the BKK landfill, many hazardous wastes were being transported to Casmalia instead. The city resolutions did recognize the need to continue access to this facility for wastes generated within Santa Barbara County.

whatever—all threaten the facility's immediate neighbors, not people hundreds of miles away who may well benefit from its daily operations.

This imbalance helps explain why the "not in my backyard" syndrome can be anticipated in each and every siting attempt. It will not disappear. Instead, mechanisms of compensation (monetary and other) must be employed to redress the imbalance. Several states, including California, require a hazardous waste facility to provide ten percent of its gross receipts as a tax payment to the local community, in addition to normal property tax payments. Other actions may be taken to compensate the community for hosting a "locally unwanted land use," or LULU.[3]

DISTRUST

Opposition also results from generalized public distrust of the institutions of government and industry. In this sense, Vietnam and Watergate have left their scars on the American political psyche. Given the intensity of emotions aroused whenever a new hazardous waste management facility is proposed in any community, responding honestly and openly in a climate of distrust becomes as important as it is difficult.

Provision of sound information, over time, is a vital step in a successful siting process. "What *is* this facility being proposed? How would it operate? Why is it necessary? Where would all these wastes come from? How do I know that it would operate safely?" These, and dozens of other typical questions, require answers by the facility's proponents early in the siting process. A full Environmental Impact Statement or Environmental Impact Review document, provided at the end of the siting process, is far from an adequate substitute for continual information. Public meetings are also vital; not formal hearings, but a continuing pattern of public involvement from the inception of the siting proposal. Once again, these actions will not dispel local distrust entirely. They should, however, serve to open effective channels of communication between local skeptics and facility proponents.

COMMUNITY IMAGE

So often, local residents perceive the new facility in negative terms. They see it as tarnishing the community's image. "We don't want to become the dumping ground for the whole region," they argue. Such images typically reinforce the equity concerns inherent in the imbalance between costs and benefits.

The principal counter to this component of local opposition arises in the distinction between treatment facilities—which resemble modern industrial plants—and land disposal facilities: dumps. Located in an area already zoned for industry, a modern hazardous waste treatment facility should bring no disrepute to the community's image. This distinction may take some time to be communicated well to a distrustful public; but in the end, the fundamental facts should prevail.

PROPERTY VALUES

People across the country are concerned about possible declines in their property values whenever a LULU is proposed nearby. While such concerns may often be cloaked in a rhetoric of fear or the verbiage of equity, an economic calculus seldom lies far from the surface of the explicit debate.

Once again, siting of treatment facilities in industrial areas should be a very different matter from siting landfills in rural communities. Moreover, various schemes of insurance and compensation can be devised to ensure protection of a community's economic values throughout the lifetime of the waste management facility.

NUISANCE

Often the proposed facility is also seen as a nuisance by the local community, and thus deserves to be opposed. Trucks transporting wastes might have to traverse city streets; smells from landfills are certainly unpleasant; noise from an industrial or waste-disposal facility is undesirable.

In a sense, these are all specific aspects of the local costs associated with hosting a waste management facility. They can be countered in several ways. The facility can be specially designed and operated to minimize its nuisance impacts. Trucks can be directed to special routes, away from residential streets. Operating hours can be restricted. Noise abatement procedures can be required. Furthermore, the distinction between waste treatment and land disposal is again significant. A treatment facility in an industrial area need not involve any additional nuisance to its hosts.

These various aspects of local opposition, once identified clearly in a particular siting controversy, can be addressed directly by the facility's proponents. But who has the power to make the ultimate siting approval decision? Who's in charge? If local opposition is intense, should the state simply assume control?

Authority and the Myth of Preemption

Many concerned observers, frustrated by the siting paralysis so evident today, have advocated some way to shift siting authority from local into state hands through the creation of some kind of super siting agency.[4] In fact, some

25 states have already created some form of preemptive structure to site hazardous waste facilities. Among these states are Arizona, Connecticut, Florida, Kansas, Maryland, Minnesota, New Jersey, New York, Ohio, Pennsylvania, and Tennessee.[5] The preemptive aspects of all such state agencies derive from their legislatively-established power to ignore local zoning and impose needed sites for facilities within selected communities.

A master siting agency and preemptive state power are seductively attractive to anyone frustrated with the ability of local governments to pursue their parochial interests and thereby thwart statewide needs. This approach seemingly guarantees a means to obtain needed sites for new facilities, since it removes the local zoning obstacle.[6] While the preemptive approach may eventually prove successful in obtaining some new sites, analysis of recent siting controversies and exploration of the concepts underlying state preemption suggest that such state power may well prove illusory in the face of determined local opposition.[7] Preemption may thus be a myth.

Continuing difficulties with siting are to be expected; indeed, local opposition will only intensify when states rely on preemption. If a locality's residents are vehemently opposed to a proposed hazardous waste facility, the project may simply not succeed. Legal measures can be used to delay and eventually defeat the project. Alan Farkas has warned that:

> . . . although state preemption may remove one mechanism to stop a proposed facility, citizens may be able to find other mechanisms such as the National Environmental Policy Act of 1969 or similar state requirements which can be used to delay or even stop a proposed development.[8]

Angry local residents can cause great difficulty for a facility even after it is constructed. The case of Earthline's landfill in Wilsonville, Illinois, provides a graphic example of this phenomenon. The town, frustrated in its legal activities, managed effectively to halt the facility's operations by digging a trench across its access road—ostensibly as part of municipal culvert repair efforts.[9] Lawrence Bacow has concluded that:

> If people are fervently opposed to a hazardous waste facility in their town, they will find some mechanism for making their feelings known.[10]

Because of the considerable range of means—legal, quasi-legal, and extralegal—available to local opponents to prevent siting of unwanted facilities, preemptive measures asserting exclusive state power are not likely to enjoy much long-term success. While they may achieve administrative efficiency, it comes at a very high price in terms of political equity and popular acceptance of the siting process.

This does not mean that the states should play no positive role in the siting process. Although political realities may dictate against relying on preemption, the alternative of continued reliance on parochial local decisions in which facilities of statewide benefit may be rejected without due cause is also unacceptable. Some balance must be found between the extremes of preemption and local veto power.

As an overall objective, the decision-making *process* must be perceived as legitimate by the residents of the local area. Some of them may never fully accept the presence of the new waste facility in their town; but if they come to agree that the siting process was fair, their effectiveness in continuing to oppose the facility will greatly diminish.

With this objective in mind, a siting process based on state override seems to have a much greater chance to gain local respect than does a process based on state preemption. This distinction is admittedly slight, and rather subtle. The fundamental principle involves the explicit grant of authority by the state legislature to the local community to say "yes" or "no" to the proposed hazardous waste facility. A local decision of this kind is vastly different from local participation in state preemptive decisions, in which the actual authority rests with a state agency, board, commission, or administrative law judge. Citizens feel isolated from such decisions. They resent the way in which preemption places priority on administrative efficiency over political sensitivity. They become angry at the evident lack of state accountability to local interests.

Given the intensity of emotions fed by fear of hazardous waste, retention of explicit local decisionmaking authority over siting seems imperative. The local government must be allowed to examine the siting proposal, conduct necessary studies, hold its own hearings, and reach its own decision. Starting the siting process with an unambiguous local decision provides far more opportunity for effective participation by local citizens than do typical public hearings.

While a balanced siting process can thus provide a crucial role for the affected local government, it must also include authority for state override of any parochial local veto. This override can be rendered difficult, formally and politically (just as a two-thirds vote from both Houses is required for Congress to override a president's veto of legislation). If adequate pressure is to be placed on local decisionmakers to consider a siting proposal on its true merits, however, the existence of some kind of state override power seems essential.[11] Otherwise, simple parochialism will prevail.

Creating a balanced process to reach decisions on siting new hazardous waste management facilities will not automatically resolve all the siting problems, of course. The entire wide range of controversial issues which affect local attitudes toward proposed facilities must be addressed. The politics of siting, however, lie at the core of the dilemma. In distinct contrast to preemptive schemes, a balanced siting approach is likely to be perceived as legitimate by local residents. In essence, the path to legitimate yet successful location of needed new waste management facilities appears to lie in the establishment of an undeniable state siting presence, balanced against the preservation of a meaningful local role and structured through equitable allocation of these facilities throughout the overall society which is responsible for generating the wastes in the first place.

Regional Siting Strategies and the Politics of Equity

The balance of authority to make siting decisions—override rather than preemption—along with programs of negotiated compensation are necessary prerequisites to success in siting these controversial facilities. They are not sufficient to achieve the siting goal, however.

In addition, the traditional approach of siting single facilities one-at-a-time typically must be replaced by a bold and complex innovation: simultaneous siting of numerous individual hazardous waste management facilities, all within the context of a regional siting strategy. Such an approach is essential if the dynamics of equity and exploitation which lie at the heart of local siting opposition are to be addressed. Without regional equity as the core of a new approach to siting, marvelous advances in facility technology, in siting authority, and in negotiated compensation may all fail when put individually to the test of intense local opposition. Communities will still argue persuasively: "why here?", "why us?", "why not over there instead?"

A regional siting strategy would rest on a few key principles, and would be based on a clear and comprehensive analysis of the region's patterns of hazardous waste generation.

- Each jurisdiction within the region would agree to accept at least one new facility.
- Each jurisdiction would agree to accept a set of facilities appropriate in scale and type to its own relative proportion of the region's overall waste volume.
- The entire strategy would focus on treatment of wastes rather than their disposal, untreated, on the ground.
- The region, however, would require at least one facility for the ultimate disposal of treatment residuals, along with adequate capacity to dispose of wastes during the transition to maximum waste treatment.
- A clear policy preference would be established to locate facilities primarily on the grounds of existing industrial waste generators (onsite treatment).

EQUITY IN SITING

The regional siting strategy would be designed to lead to a multi-county negotiated agreement. Since each of the cooperating jurisdictions would be expected to accept at least one new hazardous waste management facility, the "not in my backyard" syndrome would be blunted. Each participant would know in advance that at least some local commitment to siting would transpire; no jurisdiction would be able to argue completely "not here." Even an area with very small volumes of waste generation would be able to justify a modest transfer station to accumulate economically-transferable quantities for treatment and disposal elsewhere. Larger waste-generating areas, of course, would be expected to accommodate more than one facility; and they would recognize this reality at the inception of the negotiations.

Equity principles also require each participating jurisdiction to accept a set of facilities appropriate to its own proportion of the overall regional volume. Siting numerous facilities at one time is the key here. This concept protects smaller, remote areas from becoming the "dumping ground" for wastes from industrial areas, while giving industrial areas access to the broader regional arena needed to site a complete set of facilities. The process envisions each community being responsible for managing its own share of the regional waste stream—but without the autarky characteristic of "you make it, you keep it." A relatively large area like Southern California or New Jersey, for example, might require 20 or 30 new neutralization/precipitation units to handle its inorganic wastes; one or two new incinerators to handle its incineratable organic wastes; and one new landfill to manage the sludges and ashes from treatment, plus stabilized wastes from Superfund site cleanup activities.

In the siting dialogue, each community would see how its proposed share of the region's new facilities would fit in with all the rest; each would be participating equitably in effective management of the region's overall waste volume. Local residents would be able to see the appropriateness of those facilities proposed for their own area, as part of their basic responsibility to manage that volume of wastes equivalent to the amount generated by taxpaying and job-creating industries in their own community. While some local residents might still understandably prefer to send these wastes elsewhere—anywhere—simultaneous siting based on inter-jurisdictional equity renders rather hollow the appeal of such an argument.

This concept can be implemented by private construction and operation of needed new facilities, or by a public agency. Once each jurisdiction agrees to its appropriate share of the overall set of facilities needed by the region as a whole, and commits to issuing the required building and land use permits, it could issue a Request for Proposals from private corporations, or await private initiative. Evidence from across the country suggests that such proposals will usually be forthcoming, once waste management firms gain confidence that they will not be thwarted by local opposition. Other firms would propose their own new onsite waste facilities, with confidence that they will receive approval from the city council or county board of supervisors. Alternatively, public corporations could be formed to build the new facilities; or innovative public/private hybrid systems could emerge. The crucial issue is to break the siting impasse, allowing various versions of private or public entrepreneurship to flourish.

While large states like New York, Texas, and California could certainly arrange such regional systems of negotiated interjurisdictional siting within their own boundaries, elsewhere in the country new interstate systems may be preferable. These could resemble the emerging interstate structures for siting new radioactive waste management facilities. In many regions, some kind of interstate arrangements may be necessary to ensure that states which choose to pursue aggressive interjurisdictional siting arrangements will not simply have their new facilities overwhelmed by wastes imported from their neighbors who pursue inaction instead.

TREATMENT OF WASTES

California was the first state to ban the land disposal of certain categories of hazardous wastes, requiring their treatment instead.[12] This approach is now incorporated in the version of RCRA passed by the Congress in late 1984.

A rapid transition from a national emphasis on land disposal to a focus on waste treatment is essential if the overall paralysis in facility siting is to come to an end. The public will not easily tolerate large numbers of new landfills whatever their design standards and monitoring provisions. Siting opposition will grow rather than dwindle over time, leading to increasingly intense confrontations over use of preemptive authority. Moreover, siting of new landfills accepting the full range of liquid hazardous wastes would undercut the basic economics of waste treatment. A regional hazardous waste management system based on treatment cannot compete easily with large new landfills nearby (unless liability provisions for groundwater contamination are strictly enforced). Furthermore, industry's growing liability concerns are shifting us gradually away from unreliable land disposal, and into waste treatment.

Siting of waste treatment facilities is no easy task, in the face of public emotions about anything associated with "toxic wastes." However, a growing body of evidence suggests a general tolerance for siting approval of industrial facilities designed to dewater, oxidize, neutralize, or incinerate hazardous wastes.

LAND DISPOSAL: THE RESIDUALS REPOSITORY

While a regional system of new waste treatment facilities seems feasible to develop, it is vital to recognize that all this treatment leaves a residue of some kind: a metal hydroxide sludge from neutralization/precipitation; an ash and a scrubber sludge from incineration; solidified materials from a stabilization process. These residues all require land disposal. While they could be taken to a traditional hazardous waste landfill, a preferable alternative exists: the "residuals repository."[13] This new kind of landfill would accept only dried residues from waste treatment (no untreated wastes); it would be designed and operated to keep these residues dry in perpetuity (using a cover of some kind). As a result, the wastes would lack mobility—no dangerous leachate could be formed to threaten nearby groundwater.

In addition, the repository could be designed to segregate metallic sludges of various kinds in terms of their metal contents. While the economics of waste recovery do not presently favor recycling of such sludges to reclaim their metal values, this certainly seems feasible in the early 21st century. Different disposal cells for different ores would allow ease of future mining.

The residuals repository offers several advantages as a key component of a regional siting process. First, it would reinforce and complement all of the new treatment facilities—onsite and offsite. The repository would offer a reliable place for them to dispose of their treatment residues. Without the possibility of leachate to endanger groundwater, industry's liability concerns would be lessened greatly. In contrast, taking even a dewatered treatment residue or fully stabilized materials to a traditional landfill leaves the generator potentially responsible for enormous costs under CERCLA's joint and several and strict liability provisions. Once the local public comprehends its innovative characteristics, they should be willing to consider siting proposals for a residuals repository, in contrast to their intense opposition to traditional landfills. The repository's ability to confidently avoid groundwater contamination, its contribution to the overall regional waste management system, and its future orientation toward reclaiming metal values, all render such a facility at least worthy of serious discussion within the local community where siting is proposed.

Finally, the repository could be envisioned as a fully cooperative public/private venture, in recognition of its vital role in waste management. A governmental body—state, county, or special district—could provide the land for the new facility, greatly reducing overall operating costs. A private corporation could then build and operate the residuals repository on a profit-making basis (perhaps with some constraints on fees charged, as with an investor-owned utility regulated by a Public Utilities Commission). The eventual profits from mining of waste metals thirty or forty years hence could then be split 50/50 between the public and private sectors.

ONSITE TREATMENT

For maximum success in siting, and for efficient public waste management policy, the regional strategy should focus on onsite treatment facilities. The basic principle is: if the wastes can be treated economically onsite, that should be done. The only wastes which should be shipped offsite for treatment are those which require highly specialized treatment (e.g., high temperature incineration of PCB's, now accomplished only in Arkansas and Texas), or those from small firms with low waste volumes.

This focus has several advantages relevant to siting. Transportation risks to the overall community are far less, since most wastes do not leave the plant (except in the form of dewatered sludges). Opposition to siting based on fear of waste transportation would thus be minimized. Second, no one community is being selected as the host for a large, centralized offsite waste management facility. Equity concerns are thus minimized by this onsite focus, as wastes are being managed primarily within the very areas where they were originally generated. Finally, by definition, the onsite strategy means that siting takes place in already-industrialized areas, rather than in remote locations. Concerns over incompatible land uses are thereby minimized as well.

Southern California: The Politics of Equity In Practice

Activities underway in Southern California during the past four years illustrate these basic siting principles. A special local-state-federal intergovernmental effort was begun here in early 1981. The Southern California Hazardous Waste Management Project involves all the relevant interest groups—state and local, public and private—in this region of some 15 million people and their associated industry and its hazardous wastes.

In 1980, four of the area's five Class I hazardous waste land disposal facilities closed unexpectedly within a few months of one another. As a consequence, a sense of urgency permeated discussions by local officials and waste management planners. The one remaining landfill—a large facility owned by the BKK Corporation in West Covina, on the eastern edge of Los Angeles county—itself seemed increasingly vulnerable to closure by a variety of political and environmental pressures. Nearby residents—7,700 within one mile, 60,000 within two miles—were vociferously demanding that it be closed.

Political officials throughout Southern California reacted sharply to a situation they found intolerable: reliance on a single landfill for all hazardous waste disposal, a landfill itself vulnerable to sudden closure. They formed the regional siting project, based on six paramount principles:

1. A cooperative state-local effort was needed. Neither the cities and counties on the one hand, nor the state agencies on the other, could

be successful on their own in coping with the siting crisis.

2. A regional perspective was essential. Los Angeles County's industries generate approximately 75 percent of the region's total wastes, but could not manage them entirely within this county alone. But neither could Los Angeles expect to ship all these wastes to other points in the region.

3. While a growing proportion of the region's wastes would be amenable to treatment, significant capacity within the region for land disposal of toxic substances remained imperative. Reliance on a single, potentially vulnerable disposal site was deemed unacceptable as a long-term public policy.

4. Clear criteria for selection of new sites had to be devised, and then applied throughout the region. For reasons of equity, the initial phase of the project explored plausible locations in each county, as a set from which final selection could be made.

5. A comprehensive approach to hazardous waste management was essential, encompassing air quality, surface water and groundwater pollution, solid waste management, and public health.

6. While government would take the lead in the planning and siting effort, extensive participation by the concerned public, the waste generating industries, and the waste management industry was needed. The private sector would own and operate most if not all of the new facilities, but local public consent for their siting would be required as part of the local permit process.

Funds from the U.S. Environmental Protection Agency, the California Department of Health Services, and the Los Angeles County Sanitation Districts were used to carry out the project's initial activities. Criteria for siting a new land disposal facility were initially developed.[14] Applied throughout the region through hydrogeologic and population analyses, these criteria were used to identify 448 potential locations, which were then further narrowed to 28 (four in each of the seven counties). Extensive public participation activities were initiated.

In 1981, California announced its new approach to phasing out the land disposal of selected types of hazardous wastes; they were to be treated instead. Landfills were no longer the focus of state policy, nor the priority siting task. Energies within the Southern California Hazardous Waste Management Project therefore shifted toward siting of numerous new treatment facilities, both onsite and offsite, in order to implement the land disposal phaseout effort.

Project participants prepared a comprehensive statement of regional goals and policies designed to guide the overall waste management and siting effort.[15] This innovative regional policy statement, shown as Table 1, was formally adopted by the regional Councils of Government and by several of the area's counties and cities.

The siting project also stimulated preparation by the state Department of Health Services of siting criteria for waste treatment facilities.[16] In contrast to the criteria earlier devised for new land disposal sites, these criteria pointed toward siting treatment facilities near the sources of initial waste generation; here the new facilities would be compatible with existing land uses, and truck transportation would be minimized. The overall equity implications of targeting new waste treatment facilities for urban/industrial areas, and new waste disposal facilities for remote areas, enhanced the probability of siting for both.

TABLE 1

Regional Goals and Policies for the Safe Management of Hazardous Wastes

Goals	*Policies*
Develop a comprehensive program for the safe management of all hazardous wastes.	Promote comprehensive planning. Provide adequate treatment and disposal capacity for all generators. Improve safety precautions and emergency response capabilities. Strengthen law enforcement.
Promote the use of proven and safe hazardous waste management technologies.	Encourage waste recycling, reduction, and treatment. Reduce dependence on land disposal.
Accelerate the siting and permitting of safe waste management facilities	Develop appropriate siting criteria. Facilitate the local siting process. Consolidate the permitting process.
Involve the public in decisions on hazardous waste issues.	Educate the public on all issues concerning hazardous wastes. Consult the public on the siting of facilities. Involve the public in hazardous waste management planning.
Encourage cities and counties to ensure the safe management of hazardous wastes within their jurisdictions.	Promote local responsibility for locally generated hazardous waste. Encourage local hazardous waste management planning and programs.
Encourage industry to construct and manage a system of high quality waste management facilities.	Promote cooperative planning by industry and local government. Encourage the equitable distribution of responsibilities and risks.

Source: Southern California Hazardous Waste Management Project, *Regional Goals and Policies for the Safe Management of Hazardous Wastes* (Los Angeles: SCHWMP), June 1982.

The siting project also conducted a comprehensive regional analysis of waste generation patterns. Existing and projected treatment and disposal facilities were studied to determine the resultant requirements for new waste treatment facilities of various kinds. An analysis of these complicated topics was completed in 1983,[17] and then updated in 1984.[18] Summary data on Southern California's patterns of hazardous waste generation are shown in Table 2. These became the basis for subsequent allocation of facility siting requirements among each of the region's counties, roughly proportional to their individual share of the overall waste volume.

The project's revised scope also included an implementation strategy designed to identify the institutional, legal, financial, and political issues involved in siting new facilities in Southern California. The state's regulatory responsibilities and the counties' role in planning for hazardous waste management formed the core of this analysis. Siting decisions were viewed in the context of a continuing balance of state and local authority.

The project's public participation efforts brought a wide range of groups into the siting debate. Some 130 meetings were held with groups as diverse as the Los Angeles and the Orange County Chambers of Commerce, the Sierra Club, the League of Women Voters, and the Imperial Valley Association of Governments. Public workshops and meetings reached concerned citizens directly. Extensive contacts with the communications media helped publicize

TABLE 2
Patterns of Hazardous Waste Generation in Southern California (tons/year)

Area	Generation of Wastes Managed Onsite	Generation of Wastes Sent Offsite	Total Waste Generation
Los Angeles County	1,070,403	424,824	1,495,227
Upper Coastal Los Angeles	(188,197)	(148,206)	(336,403)
North Los Angeles	(499,332)	(24,846)	(524,178)
Central Los Angeles	(132,726)	(31,782)	(164,508)
Northeast Los Angeles	(83,509)	(37,110)	(120,619)
Southeast Los Angeles	(7,860)	(26,274)	(34,134)
Long Beach	(158,779)	(156,606)	(315,385)
Orange County	445,950	40,242	486,192
San Diego County	290,688	25,614	316,302
San Bernardino and Riverside Counties	44,001	11,610	55,611
Ventura County	11,025	15,486	26,511
Southern California Total	1,862,067	517,776	2,379,843

Source: Morell, D. and Bergin, K.; *Hazardous Waste Generation and Facility Development Requirements in Southern California: A Policy Analysis* (Los Angeles: Southern California Hazardous Waste Management Project) July 1983, p. 8.

the siting issue. All of this activity enhanced the public's understanding of the hazardous waste problem, although the intensity of public interest associated with an actual siting proposal in their own community could not be replicated in these informational sessions.[19]

By 1984, the effort was moving beyond planning and analysis, and toward implementation. EPA and the state's Department of Health Services initiated further enforcement actions against the West Covina landfill, thereby intensifying pressures on local officials to gain siting approval for new facilities. In June, 19 families had to be evacuated from their houses on the edge of the landfill due to high levels of methane and vinyl chloride air emissions. The BKK Corporation announced that it would cease accepting hazardous wastes at the landfill on November 30, 1984; BKK withdrew from EPA its RCRA permit application. An intercounty agreement for the siting process was being considered by each county Board of Supervisors, in advance of formal negotiations on siting anticipated in early 1985. Specific siting options for each participating jurisdiction were being identified. A total of perhaps 50 new treatment facilities were seen as likely to be sited, along with transfer stations in each county and a new regional residuals repository. While success certainly cannot be assumed, the process was well underway.

Political pressures in Southern California illustrate many of the dynamics typical of hazardous waste management, and of siting hazardous waste facilities. Research for effective compromise was continuing in the face of apparently irreconcilable interests: state vs. local, treatment vs. land disposal, government vs. the private sector, waste generators vs. waste managers, competitive waste management firms vs. one another, residents near hazardous waste facilities vs. those living elsewhere. While the potential for politicization and conflict remains high, federal, state, and local agencies are searching cooperatively for a consensus based on equity through their Southern California Hazardous Waste Management Project.

Conclusion: Siting from an Optimist's Perspective

Siting new hazardous waste management facilities is one of the toughest tasks facing environmental managers, and the American political system as a whole. Most people would agree that such facilities are needed—but nearly everyone wants them located in someone else's town. Pressures to clean up abandoned dumpsites and manage new wastes better are intensifying: from the Congress, nearly every state's legislature, and the citizenry as a whole. The revised Resource Conservation and Recovery Act (RCRA) passed in late 1984 sets forth powerful new constraints on previous patterns of waste management. These actions all require siting of new facilities, however, if they are to succeed.

Siting can be accomplished, even in the face of the "not in my backyard" syndrome. Principles outlined in this paper, in tandem with one another, can provide a sense of optimism that approval of the needed set of new facilities can be accomplished, throughout the country. A balance of siting authority between local decisionmakers and state agencies is essential; neither abject local parochialism nor total state preemption are warranted. Adequate patterns of negotiated compensation are also essential, to redress the inherent imbalance between regionwide benefits and localized costs. Finally, a process of equity must be introduced into siting—through simultaneous consideration of multiple treatment, storage, and disposal facilities, so that each area is asked to host structures roughly proportional to its own share of the broader overall waste stream. To receive siting approval, waste management facilities must meet a true social need—not simply a corporate interest. And government agencies at all levels must communicate genuine honesty, sincere credibility, and complete integrity to the public if they aspire to success in gaining local commitments to host these locally-unwanted land uses.

No system of hazardous waste management will satisfy everyone's interests; too many divergent pressures and intense emotions are always at stake in this policy realm. No matter what is said and done, some people will feel aggrieved that the facility ended up in their town rather than elsewhere. But their minority viewpoint need not always prevail. Siting processes can ensure that at least the way decisions are made can be perceived as fully legitimate. Certainly, some level of parochial animosity will remain whatever the rationality of the arguments amassed by the facility's proponents. Opposition based on this factor alone needs to be identified, recognized, and then accepted for what it is. A few opponents in a community can always be isolated (though never silenced), and thereby rendered ineffective by the majority viewpoint. Here again the politics of equity are critical to success in siting. By avoiding "sacrifice areas" and locating most waste management facilities proportional to areas of waste generation, logic can reasonably be expected to prevail over parochialism.

Finally, hazardous waste policy makers, legislators, and the public at large must come to accept the blunt reality that hazardous wastes *will* be managed. If not placed in well-designed new treatment facilities and residuals repositories, then they will go to traditional landfills and surface impoundments. Or, worse yet, these wastes will be "managed" via illegal dumping in sewers, abandoned lots, along roadsides, in people's "front yards." Hazardous wastes do not disappear simply because proposed new facilities are defeated in the local siting process, as victims of "not in my backyard" emotionalism. By the millions of tons every year, they are being generated; and they must be managed somehow, somewhere. This unfortunate truth provides strong impetus to achieving success through an innovative new siting process centered on the politics of equity.

References

1. This phrase was first popularized in O'Hare, M.; *Public Policy* 25: 407, (1977).

2. Communication from Betty Roeder, President, Great Oaks Water Company, June 1984.

3. For a detailed analysis of compensation issues, see the chapter "Who Pays? Compensation and Siting," in Morell, D. and Magorian, C.; *Siting Hazardous Waste Facilities: Local Opposition and the Myth of Preemption* (Ballinger; Cambridge, MA), 1982, pp. 149-182.

4. See Murray, W. and Seneker, C.; *Hastings Law Journal* 30: 318 (1978). Also see Baram, M.; *Environmental Law and the Siting of Facilities* (Ballinger; Cambridge, MA), 1976, p. 144.

5. See Hadden, S.; Veillette, J.; and Brandt, T.; "State Roles in Siting Hazardous Waste Disposal Facilities: From State Preemption to Local Veto," in *The Politics of Hazardous Waste Management* (J. Lester and A. Bowman, eds.) (Duke University Press; Durham, N.C.), 1983, pp. 196-211.

6. Farkas, A.; *Capital University Law Review* 9: 456 (1980).

7. See U.S. Environmental Protection Agency, *Siting of Hazardous Waste Management Facilities and Public Opposition*, SW-809 (Centaur Associates report) (Washington, D.C.: U.S. EPA), November 1979.

8. Farkas, op. cit.

9. See U.S. EPA, op. cit., p. 310.

10. Bacow, L.; *Mitigation, Compensation, Incentives, and Preemption*, report prepared for the National Governors' Association, November 1980, p. 13.

11. See California statute A.B. 3119, introduced by Assemblywoman Sally Tanner, May 1984; passed by both the Assembly and Senate, but vetoed by Governor George Deukmejian in September 1984.

12. Governor Edmund G. Brown, Jr., Executive Order B-8881, October 13, 1981; California Governor's Office of Appropriate Technology, *Alternatives to the Land Disposal of Hazardous Wastes: An Assessment for California* (Sacramento: OAT, 1981); and California Department of Health Services, *Notice of Proposed Changes in Regulations of the Department of Health Services Regarding Hazardous Waste Land Disposal Restrictions* (Sacramento: August 18, 1982).

13. Southern California Hazardous Waste Management Project, *Residuals Repository: Conceptual Design and Feasibility Study* (D'Appolonia Consultants report) (Los Angeles: SCHWMP), February 1984.

14. _____ , *Status Report* (April 15, 1982).

15. _____ , *Regional Goals and Policies for the Safe Management of Hazardous Wastes* (June 1982).

16. California Department of Health Services, *Criteria for the Siting of Treatment Technologies* (Sacramento: June 1982).

17. Morell, D. and Bergin, K.; *Hazardous Waste Generation and Facility Development Requirements in Southern California: A Policy Analysis* (Los Angeles: Southern California Hazardous Waste Management Project), July 1983.

18. In 1984, SCAG issued a contract to a consortium of Louis Berger, Inc. and ERM Associates, Inc. to conduct additional technical analyses of the patterns of waste

generation, probable requirements for new treatment facilities, and siting criteria for such facilities. Work was to be completed by November 1984.

19. Southern California Hazardous Waste Management Project, *Report on November Meetings and Evaluation of Regional Workshops*, November 24, 1982.

A. DAN TARLOCK

8 State Versus Local Control of Hazardous Waste Facility Siting

Who Decides in Whose Backyard?

Introduction

The issue of siting hazardous waste treatment, storage, or disposal (TSD) facilities involves a complex interplay of federal, state and local laws. In brief, federal law, regulations and policy leave the site selection process to the states. In those states that have regulatory programs mandated by federal law, site selection is governed by local zoning and other land use regulatory programs unless a court concludes that state legislation implicitly preempts local regulation. Many of the states that generate large quantities of hazardous wastes have enacted special siting legislation that deals with local land use vetoes in a variety of ways from state preemption of local authority to the preservation of local control.

A hazardous waste facility is an industrial use. Some zoning ordinances allow a TSD facility to locate as a matter of right in a heavy industrial zone, but most modern ordinances make all TSD facilities conditional uses/special exceptions or subject them to similar site permit requirements. For example, in *State ex rel. SCA Chem. Waste Services v. Koinsberg,* 636 S.W.2d 430 (Tenn. 1982), the power of a county to pass an interim ordinance requiring a special permit for a TSD facility was upheld. Under special siting acts that preempt local zoning authority, such facilities remain, in effect, conditional uses/special exceptions; but the state decides whether the facility is consistent with local land use plans and the range of relevant issues becomes much broader. Not only must the local impact of a TSD facility be assessed, but this impact must be balanced against statewide considerations. The issues remain complex if local communities retain their land use authority. These communities must perform the scientific assessment function that other states assign exclusively to the state. In Illinois, for example, local communities are charging up to $100,000 for permit application fees to allow the community to assemble sufficient siting information.

Federal Hazardous Waste Policy

Federal hazardous waste policy has three goals at the present time: (1) to clean up existing "orphan" sites; (2) to bring existing operating TSD facilities up to minimum safety standards and then to impose progressively higher levels of technology-based standards on them; and (3) to impose more stringent safety standards on new or expanded TSD facilities. The first goal is addressed through the Comprehensive Environmental Liability Response Act, 42 U.S.C. §§ 9801 et seq. (CERCLA or "Superfund"). The last two goals are addressed through the Resource Conservation and Recovery Act of 1976, 42 U.S.C. §§ 6901 et seq. (RCRA). RCRA currently allows a hazardous waste generator the freedom to choose among all management options so long as federal and state standards are met. Because of the diversity among waste streams, RCRA is less technology-forcing than either air and water pollution legislation. Therefore, a hazardous waste generator can choose the less environmentally sound management option—land disposal—over environmentally preferable ones such as treatment or resource recovery. These options are only indirectly encouraged. Pending amendments to RCRA would greatly circumscribe a waste manager's options by phasing out land disposal, but for the present, land disposal remains the preferred permissible, and controversial, management option.

Land disposal has acquired an increasingly bad name, especially after the federal Environmental Protection Agency published its 1982 landfill regulation, 47 Federal Register 32373 (July 26, 1982), which candidly admitted that all landfills may leak no matter how well lined and operated. Because the agency's policy is to leave the TSD site selection process to the states, siting decisions are made either through local land use controls or state agencies where local authority has been preempted. RCRA does not preempt local control over siting. See *City of Philadelphia v. New Jersey,* 437 U.S. 617, 620 n.4 (1978).

Judicial Curbs on Local Vetos

Any decision to site a hazardous waste management facility must accommodate two conflicting interests. These are: (1) the state interest in reconciling industrial growth and public health protection through the provision of an adequate number of safe facilities and (2) the local interest in the health and safety of those who will be most directly exposed to the facility. The two interests are likely to conflict because the state, with its dual objectives, will have a higher tolerance for safety trade-offs. Another factor is that hazardous waste management facilities are capital-intensive operations and generally do not offer much of a tax bonanza to local communities.

Absent an express legislative preemption, local units of government have great discretion to veto the entry of a hazardous waste facility since such a facility is simply another land use to be regulated by applicable zoning ordinances. A persistent theme in local government and land use law is that a community's first duty to its citizens is to protect their health and welfare. This theory of local self-interest has been sustained by the U.S. Supreme Court and state courts. As a result, it will be difficult for courts to develop an effective law of local duties which would require municipalities to consider extra-local interests.

What relevant law exists must be drawn from two related lines of cases. The first derives from those cases that deal with the question of whether an "intruder" governmental unit or licensed private entity wishing to enter a community that has prohibited the activity by its zoning ordinance is immune from the "host" community's land use controls. The second line comes from scattered precedents that impose some duty on a community to take regional or statewide interests into account in its land use policies.

Immunity From Local Land Use Controls

Traditionally, immunity from local land use controls was determined by a series of abstract tests that focused on the grant of the power of eminent domain, whether the function was governmental or proprietary, and the rank of the intruder in the hierarchy of governmental units. Now many courts have responded to the argument that the abstract tests for immunity do not take into account the legitimate interests of the host government in using its land use control powers to protect the health and welfare of its citizens. Recent decisions have replaced the abstract tests with a more functional balancing approach, but balancing means different things to different jurisdictions. One line of cases, stemming from a landmark 1972 New Jersey case, *Rutgers, State University v. Piluso,* 60 N.J. 142, 286 A.2d 697 (1972), balances several factors to determine if the legislature intended to grant immunity or if the intruder should be immune regardless of legislative intent. The factors are weighted toward a finding of immunity, and the practical effect of the New Jersey balancing test is to create a rebuttable presumption of immunity. A host community may only rebut the presumption by showing that the intruder's land use choice is unreasonable as measured either by the host's existing land use patterns or, one would assume, by the exposure of the public to unreasonable risks.

A second line of balancing cases, from Florida, places a burden on the intruder to show that the host community acted unreasonably in applying its zoning ordinance. See *City of Temple Terrace v. Hillsborough Ass'n for Retarded Citizens,* 322 So. 2d 571 (Fla. App. 1975), *aff'd,* 332 So.2d 610 (Fla. 1976). The intruder must show that "the public interests favoring the proposed use outweigh those mitigating against a use not sanctioned by the zoning regulations of the host government. To rebut an exclusion, the intruder can show that there was no good-faith effort to accommodate the use, that suitable sites for the use exist in the community, and that mitigation measures are possible at the chosen site." 322 So. 2d at 578-79.

Duty of Localities to Consider Regional Interests

If an intruder use is not granted immunity, it may still be able to claim entry under the judicial doctrines developed in the late 1960s and 1970s to combat so-called "exclusionary zoning." Judicial activism to force communities to admit new uses has been bolstered by the U.S. Supreme Court decision of *City of Philadelphia v. New Jersey,* 437 U.S. 617 (1978), which held that a state ban on the import of wastes generated out-of-state violates the Commerce Clause. *City of Philadelphia* thus suggests that states have an affirmative duty to accept a fair share of hazardous waste TSD facilities.

State courts have invalidated exclusionary ordinances either on state constitutional grounds or on a theory that exclusionary zoning is *ultra vires* because the essence of zoning is the division of territory among different land uses. This second line of cases is more applicable to hazardous waste siting decisions, as illustrated by the Pennsylvania cases that shift the burden of justification to the excluding community. See, *e.g., Beaver Gasoline Co. v. Zoning Hearing Bd.,* 445 Pa. 571, 285 A.2d 501 (1971). Pennsylvania remained hostile to zoning long after most states accorded local ordinances a presumption of validity and the state's anti-exclusionary rules illustrate the state's continued skepticism of the benefits of zoning.

Although Pennsylvania has excepted noxious uses from its anti-exclusionary doctrine, at least one community has been forced to accept a hazardous waste facility. In reversing the local zoning hearing board's decision to exclude the facility, the commonwealth court made the following statement: "Under these circumstances, we conclude that waste disposal facilities do not have the obvious potential for polluting air or water or otherwise creating uncontrollable health or safety hazards. Nor do common knowledge and experience suggest other clear deleterious effects which would inevitably be visited upon the public in general." *General Battery Corp. v. Zoning Hearing Bd.,* 29 Pa. commw. 498, 371 A.2d 1030, 1032 (1977). Local vetoes are now preempted in Pennsylvania.

One recent exclusionary zoning case illustrates the potential for an argument that communities have a duty to accept a fair share of TSD facilities while another illustrates the potential for a community to argue that the location of facilities elsewhere in the region has already fulfilled that duty. In *Associated Home Builders v. City of Livermore,* 18 Cal. 3d 582, 557 P.2d 473, 135 Cal. Rptr. 41 (1976), the California Supreme Court suggested that substantive due process requires cities to justify growth control ordinances likely to be exclusionary. Ordinances "must have a real and substantial relationship to the public welfare. . . ." 557 P.2d at 489.

The state of Washington, however, gave California's regionalism theory an interesting and reverse twist. A 1978 case suggests that a community may have a duty to exclude a use which is environmentally detrimental from a regional perspective. In *Save A Valuable Environment (SAVE) v. City of Bothell,* 89 Wash. 2d 862, 576 P.2d 401 (1978), the state's supreme court found that a community's decision to allow a regional shopping center in a rural but growing area of the Seattle metropolitan area "was arbitrary and capricious in that it failed to serve the welfare of the community as a whole." Once adverse regional environmental impacts are disclosed, a city "may not act in disregard of the effects outside its boundaries. Where the potential exists that a zoning action will cause a serious environmental effect outside jurisdiction borders, the zoning body must serve the welfare of the entire affected community. If it does not do so it acts in an arbitrary and capricious manner. The precise boundaries of the affected community cannot be determined until the potential environmental effects are understood." 576 P.2d at 404.

State Preemption of Exclusive Local Authority

Most states have chosen the preemption issue directly in TSD facility siting legislation. However, a few states rely only on RCRA qualifying legislation that gives a state agency the authority to issue permits for TSD facilities. In these states, the preemption issue must be decided by courts since the legislation is usually silent on the issue. *Stablex Corp. v. Town of Hooksett,* 456 A.2d 94 (N.H. 1982), is a typical case. The court there held that New Hampshire's permit statute preempted local authority to deny a TSD facility site approval, because "the options offered by the federal government in the Resource Conservation and Recovery Act of 1976 devised a comprehensive and detailed program of statewide regulation, which on its face must be viewed as preempting any local actions having . . . the effect of frustrating it." 456 A.2d at 100.

Other courts have similarly rejected the argument made by local communities that constitutional or statutory home rule grants them irrevocably vast land use authority. Hazardous waste management is a problem that affects entire states and regions and all states have the power to enact general laws on matters of statewide concern that preempt local laws. See, *e.g.*, *Clermont Environmental Reclamation Co. v. Wiederhold*, 2 Ohio St. 3d 44, 442 N.E.2d 1278 (1982). In addition to the state's power to preempt, federal constitutional limitations such as the negative commerce clause restrict the power of local communities to control the location of TSD facilities. See, *e.g.*, *Browning-Ferris Inc. v. Anne Arundel County*, 428 A.2d 269 (Md. 1981) (ordinance prohibiting the disposal and transportation of hazardous wastes not generated in county held invalid).

State Approaches to Preemption

The law of TSD facility preemption is just emerging. Most of the major industrial states have either passed special siting legislation that deals explicitly with local autonomy or have singled out siting for specific legislative treatment. A variety of preemption approaches have been adopted. Many foreclose the exclusive exercise of traditional land use powers at the local level in return for a special voice in the state-administered siting process. Localities thereby retain some influence over the siting decision.

Five basic approaches have emerged. These are: (1) straight state preemption; (2) state preemption of local vetoes upon state review and an extraordinary majority of the state siting authority; (3) state preemption after extensive local involvement; (4) straight preservation of local veto authority; and (5) a requirement that the operator and the local community negotiate an agreement that offers rules to the community with arbitration as a last resort—a model much favored by consultants and others who find the adversary process too crude.

Opposing Choices: Straight Preemption or Exclusive Local Authority

Maryland and Michigan have made the cleanest opposite choices. Maryland's legislation, Md. Nat. Res. Code Ann. § 3-705(d), states that local units of government are given sufficient protection through the state siting review process and preempts all local land use controls. Similar legislation exists in Ohio, Ohio Rev. Code § 3734.05(D); and Utah, Utah Code Ann. § 26-14a-8.

In Michigan, on the other hand, the power of local governments was sufficient to amend the siting act the year after it was passed, preserving local land use authority and legislating a double veto system. See Mich. Comp. Laws Ann. § 299-516. New York requires the siting board to deny an application for site approval if the site is inconsistent with local zoning in force on the date of the application. N.Y. Envtl. Conserv. Law § 21-1107.

Preemption After State Administrative Review

Connecticut and Flordia permit local communities to make initial decisions, but provide for state review and preemption. In Connecticut, a two-thirds vote of the siting board is necessary to override a local veto. Conn. Gen. Stat. Ann. § 228-124. In Florida, local governments have 90 days to veto a proposed site subject to a three-stage appeal process. Fla. Stat. Ann. § 403.723 (1)-(4). First, the disappointed operator must apply for a local variance. If the variance is denied, he goes to the appropriate regional planning council, which may recommend that the governor and cabinet approve or deny the variance. To recommend a variance, the regional planning council must make five findings, including a determination that the facility will not have a significant adverse impact on the environment and natural resources of the region. The governor and cabinet have the authority to consider a wide range of relevant factors, including the need for the facility and alternative sites, but the discretion to issue a variance is severely limited. Fla. Stat. Ann. § 403.723 (7)(c).

Pennsylvania's override procedure is less cumbersome, but state officials are equally exposed to political liability if a local veto is reversed. The state may refuse to follow a local government's recommendation to deny a facility permit, but if it does, a "written justification" must accompany the decision. Pa. Stat. Ann. tit. 35, § 6018.504.

Two recent cases from Pennsylvania return to local communities some of the ability to influence the siting of a TSD facility taken away by the legislature. *Susquehanna County v. Department of Environmental Resources*, 458 A.2d 929 (Pa. 1983) and *Franklin Township v. Commonwealth*, 452 A.2d 718 (Pa. 1982), hold that units of local government have standing to challenge both the issuance and enforcement of hazardous waste facility permits. The state has a four-part test for the standing. With respect to the first part, whether a plaintiff possesses a substantial interest in the subject matter of the litigation, the *Franklin Township* court observed: "Aesthetic and environmental well-being are important aspects of the quality of life in our society, and a key role of local government is to promote and protect life's quality for all of its inhabitants. Recent events are replete with ecological horrors that have damaged the environment and threatened plant, animal and human life. We need only be reminded of the 'Love Canal' tragedy and many like situations faced by communities and local governments across the country to recognize the substantial local concerns." 452 A.2d at 720.

Illinois has opted for a system of concurrent state and local vetoes of new TSD facilities with state administrative review. This statute, Ill. Rev. Stat. ch. 111½, § 1001 *et seq.*, requires both state and local approval of all new regional pollution control facilities. A regional pollution control facility is any waste management site that serves an area that extends beyond the boundaries of any local unit of government. Denials are reviewable by the Pollution Control Board, a state administrative agency that hears appeals from decisions of the Illinois Environmental Protection Agency, which is charged with implementing and enforcing state environmental policy. A recent survey indicated that local governments have approved 23 non-hazardous regional pollution control facilities and three hazardous waste facilities. Local governments have vetoed seven non-hazardous facilities and three hazardous facilities. Two of the three local approvals were in industrial areas of Cook County, and the third was for an incinerator-storage facility that accepted both non-hazardous and hazardous wastes. Various appeals are working their way through the administrative and judicial systems so it is too early to tell how the Illinois law is working, but preliminary indications are that the concurrent veto scheme will make it very difficult and costly to site new TSD facilities.

Preemption in Florida and Pennsylvania gives considerable weight to local objections, and Illinois gives conclusive weight to these objections. In other states, local units of government have not fared quite so well with preemption. Indiana created a solid waste facility site approval authority in 1981 that consists of five permanent statewide members and four local ad hoc members chosen from the county and town closest to the proposed site for a facility. The authority's function is to issue certificates of environmental compatibility. These certificates are issued after local authorities and planning boards are given notice of a proposed facility and a formal public speechmaking hearing is held. After these steps, however, all local land use authority is preempted, subject to a duty on the part of the authority to consider local plans and ordinances and, "to the fullest extent practicable," integrate local ordinances into state certificates. Ind. Code § § 13-7-8.6, 13-7-13. The duty to give weight to local interests becomes significant when combined with the authority's duty to provide a written explanation for its decision and the Indiana doctrine that due process guarantees a review of administrative decisions regardless of whether a statutory basis exists. Thus, while preemption in Indiana is complete, it must be justified to avoid a reversal in court.

Preemption with Expanded Public Participation

Minnesota and New Jersey have completely preempted local land use controls, but have attempted to reduce the sting by giving local communities adequate opportunity for input in a multi-step siting process.

Minnesota has established an elaborate two-tier siting process that can serve as a model of both industry and citizen representation, but can also serve as a prescription for excluding waste facility sites. Minn. Stat. Ann. § 115A.09. A waste management board prepares plans, reports, and "preferred" site inventories with the assistance of a broad-based hazardous waste advisory council. The board's specific duty is to select six "candidate" sites across the state, each in a different county. Local communities are entitled to an "early warning" that a site in their area has been selected as a candidate site. Localities cannot bar the entry of a facility, but they can impose reasonable "construction, inspection, operation, monitoring, and maintenance" conditions. It appears that a reasonable condition is any one not reversed by the board.

New Jersey's more technically oriented siting statute, N.J. Stat. Ann. tit. 13, § 13:1E-49 *et seq.,* also tries to enhance the weight given local concerns. The Department of Environmental Protection must first adopt technical siting criteria. The Department then prepares and adopts a plan that includes a determination of needed TSD facilities and designates new sites based on the projected needs. State grants are available to affected municipalities to conduct site availability and safety studies and an adjudicatory hearing is held after the study is completed and prior to the inclusion of the site on a list of recommended sites. Further, when an applicant applies for a state permit, the affected local community has the right to review the application and to receive funds from the applicant to finance the review.

Preemption with Negotiated Bribes

Massachusetts has also enacted a two-tier siting process. Although the regulatory authority of local communities appears to be quite strong on paper, the statute creates pressure on the state's cities to accept a facility. Basically, Massachusetts siting decisions rely on state and local site review councils supplemented by developer bribes to the community. (Rhode Island has adopted a similar approach, codified at R.I. Gen. Laws § 197-5). The key permission under the Massachusetts procedure is not approval by the state siting council, although such approval is required, but rather a siting agreement negotiated between the operator and the second-tier siting authority—the local assessment committee formed after an operator proposes a facility. The officials of both "host" and abutting communities are represented on the local committee and the statute contemplates substantial "bribes" for both, such as services and transfer payments. If the local assessment committee and the developer cannot negotiate an agreement, they may ask the state siting council to find that an impasse has occurred. If the council agrees, the issues may be referred to binding arbitration before either a single arbitrator or a three-person panel.

The success of bribes as an alternative to regulatory mechanisms that address the preemption issue is not assured. Cities are relatively immune to bribery on this issue because the risks are unquantifiable and no substantial economic return is immediately forthcoming. As the authors of a study of the Massachusetts law concluded: "Whether the combined efforts of the educational campaign and incentives offered through the negotiation process are sufficient to overcome local opposition remains to be seen." Bacow and Milkey, "Overcoming Local Opposition To Hazardous Waste Facilities: The Massachusetts Approach," 6 Harv. Envtl. L. Rev. 265, 303-4 (1982).

The statute, Mass. Ann. Laws ch. 21D, § 12, precludes a community from amending its zoning laws after an applicant has filed a notice of intent with the Hazardous Waste Facility Site Safety Council. It has been held not to violate the state constitution's home rule amendment. *Town of Warren v. Hazardous Waste Facility Site Safety Council*, No. 82-21740 (Worcester Super. Ct. 1983).

Common Law Challenges to Siting Decisions

Neither local nor state approval of a hazardous waste site will be effective unless that approval acts as a shield against future litigation. Aside from arguments that a site has violated a statutory siting standard, see, *e.g.*, *Pioneer Processing, Inc. v. Illinois Environmental Protection Agency*, 444 N.E.2d 211 (Ill. App. 1983) (statutory 1,000 foot buffer zone measured only from active area of site), common law challenges are likely to be the most effective. Legislative approval of an activity is generally not a defense to a common law nuisance action. The apparent justification is a judicial conclusion that the legislature did not consider all possible adverse effects of an activity.

Despite this rule, most new land uses cannot be enjoined because plaintiffs will be unable to show that the proposed use causes the requisite imminent irreparable injury. See *Green v. Castle Concrete Co.*, 181 Colo. 309, 509 P.2d 588 (1973). This doctrine rests on the theory that an activity is not ripe for evaluation as a nuisance until the operators have had a chance to prove that it can operate reasonably. If the facility is a public one, a second doctrine virtually immunizes public or licensed activities from preconstruction injunction suits. There is an almost conclusive presumption that the balance of equities lies with the public interest in the operation of the facility. See *Brent v. City of Detroit*, 27 Mich. App. 628, 183 N.W.2d 908 (1970).

These doctrines are still good law, but in recent years courts have begun to accept a showing of risk rather than demanding proof of cause in fact, and the doctrine of imminent irreparable injury has begun to change accordingly. The initial decisions related to legislative and administrative discretion to protect the public from proven health risks such as cancer. Now it appears that courts may be willing to lower the quantum of proof necessary to prove future harm in actions for injunctive relief.

A recent Illinois Supreme Court decision, *Village of Wilsonville v. SCA Services, Inc.*, 86 Ill. 2d 1, 426 N.E.2d 824 (1981), illustrates the developing law of equitable risk-benefit analysis. The village sued to require the removal of a hazardous waste landfill that had been approved by federal and state agencies. The trial court granted an injunction after a 104-day trial on the merits. As is usual in such cases, expert testimony was sharply divided on the risk of future harm that the landfill in fact posed, but the trial court granted the injunction, even though it found that the likelihood of substantial future harm was remote. An intermediate appellate court affirmed because of the nature of the hazard involved. The state supreme court affirmed in the face of an argument that the two lower courts had incorrectly "failed to require a showing of substantial risk of certain and extreme future harm." The court's reasoning will create some confusion, however. Instead of directly addressing the question of when a court may base an injunction on proof of risk as opposed to relatively certain injury, the court found that the evidence met the conventional standards of "real and immediate" danger. Nevertheless, the court's summary of the evidence and of the law leaves little doubt that courts now have more discretion to resolve the uncertainty issue in the public's favor when hazardous wastes are involved: "In this case there can be no doubt but that it is highly probable that the chemical waste disposal site will bring about a substantial injury. Without again reviewing the extensive evidence adduced at trial, we think it is sufficiently clear that it is highly probable that the instant site will constitute a public nuisance if, through either an explosive interaction, migration, subsidence, or the 'bathtub effect,' the highly toxic chemical wastes deposited at the site escape and contaminate the air, water, or ground around the site. That such an event will occur was positively attested to by several expert witnesses. A court does not have to wait for it to happen before it can enjoin such a result. Additionally, the fact is that the condition of a nuisance is already present at the site due to the location of the site and the manner in which it has been operated. Thus, it is only the damage which is prospective. Under these circumstances, if a court can prevent any damage from occurring, it should do so." 426 N.E.2d at 836-37.

The specter of *Wilsonville* suits has led at least one state to preempt common law actions. See Utah Code Ann. § 26-14a-7. Utah's attempt to reinforce the integrity of the siting process has generated controversy because landowners' rights are sharply reduced. However, while a landowner does have a constitutional right to some form of nuisance remedy, the U.S. Supreme Court has made it clear that a property owner has no constitutional right to any particular remedy so long as the available remedy does not deny him due process. *Duke Power Co. v. Carolina Envtl. Study Group,* 438 U.S. 59 (1978). It would seem to be well within a legislature's discretion to decide that allowing private suits for injunctive relief thwarts the public interest in obtaining sufficient disposal capacity in the state; that the planning and permit process adequately protects the public against unreasonable risk; and that landowners, the most obvious parties adversely affected, are adequately compensated if they can obtain damages for demonstrable injuries. (Cities, of course, have no constitutional rights against the state, so the state may provide them with whatever remedies it chooses to protect the health of their citizens.) Finally, it is significant that the U.S. Supreme Court has recently endorsed inverse condemnation as a remedy superior to specific relief in many cases involving damages from land use regulation. *San Diego Gas & Elec. Co. v. City of San Diego,* 450 U.S. 621 (1981).

State preemption of local land use authority to site hazardous waste facilities is a response to the intense opposition to these uses. Preemption, even if local interests are given great weight, can resolve specific siting disputes, but will not quell local opposition to new and expanded TSD facilities. Local opposition will manifest itself by opposition at the state level, see, e.g., Browning-Ferris, Inc. v. Texas Dep't of Health, 625 S.W.2d 764 (Tex. 1981) (permit denial upheld), or common law suits to enjoin the facility. In the end, preemption will work only if the entire siting process is perceived as a legitimate mechanism by a large segment of the public.

Siting Criteria: Hard or Soft?

Siting statutes are based on the assumption that the ultimate objective of the siting process is to ensure a safe facility. While this goal seems uncontroversial, experience has shown that it is not. For instance, statutory definitions of "safety" are positive: a facility is safe simply because a duly constituted agency deems it so. Positive definitions of safety implicitly define safety as the minimization, rather than the elimination, of public health and other risks. Thus, such definitions are also relative: To many rational people, risk minimization is the best that can be achieved. Many opponents of TSD facilities, however, refuse to be so "rational." They either refuse to believe that safety data prove that risk exposure has been adequately minimized or argue that one is entitled to live in a risk free environment. A recent report by the Keystone Center's Hazardous Waste Management Study Group concluded that because of the uncertainties that surround hazardous waste decisions, "some people's exaggerated perceptions about risk . . . may be the most serious obstacle to successful siting of new facilities." Public fear of TSD facilities has significant implications for siting processes because the fear—justified or not—removes the siting issue from the realm of purely technical considerations.

Technical Criteria

While public perceptions must be addressed, the fact remains that technical criteria are essential to evaluating site safety; the siting process, therefore, is still regarded as primarily a technical issue. There is a growing body of literature, mostly written by consulting firms, on siting criteria. After an inventory of an area's waste management needs is made, screening criteria are applied to the target sites. The purpose of the first screen or series of screens is to exclude certain sites from further consideration. These screens focus on such factors as terrain, the geological and hydrological conditions of the soil, the site's proximity to population concentration and water supplies, and its potential for supporting higher land uses. (Naturally, there are some problems with the exclusion process. For example, an effort to exclude flood plains from the list of potential site locations is difficult in some regions, where the whole area has been classified as a flood plain.) After the screens have excluded certain locations, then an attempt is made to find sites that can physically support the facility and will not excite too much public opposition.

The primary emphasis on technical factors is also reflected in state siting statutes. New Jersey's statute, N.J. Stat. Ann. § 13:1E-57 (West), is an example of faith in the ability of technical siting standards to screen out unsafe sites. The state's Department of Environmental Protection is directed to adopt standards implemented by general and specific performance criteria. The statute calls for standards that "prevent any significant adverse environmental impact" and mandates specific siting prohibitions. Under the law, TSD facilities are prohibited within:

(1)   2,000 feet of any structure which is routinely occupied by the same person or persons more than 12 hours per day, or by the same person or persons under the age of 18 for more than 2 hours per day, except that the commission may permit the location of a major hazardous waste facility less than 2,000 feet, but in no case less than 1,500 feet, from such structures upon showing that such a location would not present a substantial danger to the health, welfare, and safety of the persons occupying or inhabiting such structures;

(2)   Any flood hazard area . . . ;

(3)   Any wetlands designated [pursuant to state law];
(4)   Any area where the seasonal high water table rises to within 1 foot
      of the surface, unless the seasonal high water table can be lowered
      to more than 1 foot below the surface by permanent drainage meas-
      ures approved by the department; and
(5)   Any area within a 20-mile radius of a nuclear fission power plant at
      which spent nuclear fuel rods are stored on-site."

Michigan's siting statute, Mich. Comp. Laws Ann. § 299.520 (7)-(8),
contains a typically inclusive list of technical and environmental factors that
must be considered. These factors include the risk and impact of an accident
during waste transport; the risk and impact of ground or surface water contamination by leaching or runoff; the risk of fires or explosions from improper
storage or disposal; the impact on the affected municipality in terms of
health, safety, cost and consistency with planned and existing development;
and the "nature of the probable environmental impact. . . ."

Non-Technical Criteria

Public fear has created an atmosphere in which compliance with state and
federal site selection and operational standards will not necessarily ensure
community acceptance of a site. In this sense, a modern TSD facility is more
like a nuclear power plant than it is its predecessor, an old sanitary landfill.
The hard, if not impossible, question for regulators and TSD facility operators
is how non-technical factors can be properly factored into the siting process.

The easiest method is to add them to the laundry list of other relevant
criteria. For example, the Michigan legislature added the following catch-all
obligation to the end of the list of factors noted earlier: "The board also shall
consider the concerns and objections submitted by the public. The board shall
facilitate efforts to provide that the concerns and objections are mitigated by
establishing additional stipulations specifically applicable to the disposal facility and operation at that site. . . ."

While Michigan's statute expresses the hope that technical measures will
overcome public opposition, Kentucky's seems to have gone farthest in recognizing the legitimacy of non-technical factors divorced from mitigation. The
licensing agency there is required to consider "community perceptions and
other psychic costs." Ky. Rev. Stat. § 244.866(1)(c).

Of course, merely mandating consideration of a factor such as community fear is not sufficient to persuade people that their fears are groundless. If
this can be done at all, it must be through procedures that convince all those
interested that a decision is legitimate. Lawyers have always paid a great deal
of attention to procedure, but they have viewed procedural legitimacy in very

formal and ultimately narrow terms. In this view, decisions are classified as either adjudicative or legislative. Thus, when the truth of evidentiary facts is at issue, an affected person is generally given the right to a trial-type hearing. If the issues are more ones of policy than fact, the right to be heard is generally limited to a speech-making hearing. In recent years, courts and legislatures have collapsed the adjudicative-legislative distinction and have experimented with a variety of hybrid procedures to promote greater fairness and legitimacy.

TSD facility siting legislation continues the legislative search for procedural fairness and ultimate legitimacy by moving beyond the classic adjudicative-legislative dichotomy and the recent hybrids and seeking "effective public participation." While some statutes continue the classic distinction and others deem certain formerly legislative decisions to be adjudicative, many of the most progressive statutes seek to create opportunities for enhanced public input as a means of assuring that equal weight is given to technical and non-technical factors.

Models of Enhanced Public Participation

There are at least six models of public participation suitable for the siting of TSD facilities: (1) minimum formal public participation; (2) enhanced formal public participation; (3) enhanced formal participation in a planning process that precedes regulatory decisions; (4) formal due process; (5) direct electoral participation; and (6) interest representation in mediation and arbitration processes.

Minimum formal public participation describes a nonadjudicatory, or speechmaking, hearing, with or without a record. This model is widely used, but the defects are obvious. Citizens seldom feel that such a hearing adequately involves them in the decision. In enhanced public participation, the public is involved in the proceedings at relatively early stages of decision-making. This technique is being increasingly used in the consideration of environmental impact statements, for one example, and is required in the TSD facility siting statutes in Massachusetts, see Mass. Gen. Laws Ann. ch. 21D (West), and Minnesota, see Minn. Stat. Ann. § 115A.11 (West). The salient features of enhanced public participation include targeted notice, advance distribution of relevant documents and multiple hearings held in the locality of the proposed facility.

A few states have sought to involve the public in the process prior to the regulatory decision by allowing public input to the planning and site identification process. In this model, guidelines can be established to weed out sites that are technically and politically unacceptable and to locate sites that are more acceptable under both of these criteria.

Formal due process is simply an adjudicatory hearing. Some siting statutes require an adjudicatory hearing before a permit is granted. See, *e.g.*, Ohio Rev. Stat. Ann. § 3734.05(c)(3) (Page). Parties who meet the jurisdiction's rules for standing or intervention may become formal parties to the proceeding. However, since the burden rests on the interested party to incur the costs of joining the proceedings, the presence of litigants opposing a permit will often depend on the existence and interest of a citizen's organization.

Direct electoral participation through the initiative and referendum process is perhaps the most favorable means of public participation for those who oppose a facility. There is no requirement that the electors vote at all rationally. The absence of voter rationality is a problem with any election, but the problem is magnified with single issue, limited electorate elections. State courts, following the lead of the U.S. Supreme Court's decision in *City of Eastlake v. Forest City Enterprises, Inc.,* 426 U.S. 668 (1976), have generally sustained referendums on specific rezonings against due process challenges. See, *e.g., Margolis v. District Court,* 638 P.2d 297 (Colo. 1981). Compare, however, California's approach, which subjects referendums to judicial review. *Arnel Dev. Co. v. City of Costa Mesa,* 28 Cal. 3d 511, 620 P.2d 565 (1980), *opinion on remand,* 126 Cal. App. 3d 330, 178 Cal. Rptr. 723 (1982) (initiative was arbitrary because it was designed to benefit a small number of adjoining property owners rather than the "general public welfare"). New Hampshire, moreover, recently held that a local attempt to exclude a facility through a referendum election was preempted by state legislation. *Stablex Corp. v. Town of Hooksett,* 122 N.H. 1091, 456 A.2d 94 (1982).

Interest representation has developed as a response to the adversary process, which many say focuses on the wrong issues. Since the mid-70s, some people have been searching for ways to involve more people in a process that produces a wider range of options in a less hostile atmosphere. Two options currently being explored are mediation and arbitration. Mediation may involve either "intervention" before a situation becomes a focused conflict or an attempt to reach agreement among parties with well-defined adverse interests. It attempts to find a relevant negotiating group to approve a solution that may or may not be in the group's power to implement; as one practitioner of the art has said, "the only basis for mediating disputes is fear—fear that something worse will happen. . . ." Mediation is an evolving art that is highly dependent on the trust placed in the mediators by the participants, so at the present time there are scattered case studies, but no rules as to how the process should work.

Arbitration is a more formal process in which the relevant parties (one hopes) voluntarily submit the dispute for a binding decision. Considerable effort is now being made to arbitrate disputes in which the many parties that are necessary to a final resolution have no formal representative in the decision-making process. Three states, Massachusetts, Rhode Island and Wisconsin, apply this evolving dispute-management process to the siting of hazardous waste management facilities.

Comprehensive Facility Site Planning

Another means of promoting community acceptance of a new TSD facility is through development of a comprehensive facility site plan to guide siting decisions. The plan identifies acceptable and nonacceptable sites prior to a specific decision. This allows a state to avoid intense controversies by eliminating the worst sites in advance. It is easier to respond to public concerns when all the options are actually open.

The federal Resource Conservation and Recovery Act (RCRA) requires each state to prepare an inventory of existing hazardous waste sites, 42 U.S.C. § 6933, but there is no requirement that a state devise a process for selecting acceptable future sites. Some states have chosen to go beyond RCRA and require the preparation of a facility plan or inventory for new sites. For example, Michigan requires the preparation of a plan that provides an inventory of existing facilities and "a projection or determination of future hazardous waste management needs." Mich. Comp. Laws. Ann. § 299.509(3)(c). New Jersey's 1981 siting statute makes the Major Hazardous Waste Facilities Plan the major referent for subsequent siting decisions. N.J. Stat. Ann. § § 13:1E-58, 59 (West). The plan consists of data on the amounts and composition of hazardous wastes generated in the state, an inventory of all TSD facilities and projections of TSD needs for the future. In addition, the statute requires consideration of non-storage and disposal options or, at the least, the most efficient storage and disposal options. The plan must include: "(7) Procedures to encourage codisposal of solid and hazardous waste, source reduction, materials recovery, energy recovery, [and] waste exchanging and recycling, . . . to discourage all inappropriate disposal techniques, and to minimize the amount of hazardous waste to be treated, stored or disposed of in this State; and (8) A regional analysis of existing and necessary major hazardous waste facilities and recommended procedures for coordinating major hazardous waste facilities planning on a regional basis."

Maryland distinguishes more sharply between an inventory and a plan, because that state's siting legislation contemplates state construction of facilities. Md. Nat. Res. Code Ann. § 3-710. The Maryland Environmental Service, the state agency responsible for sewer and other environmental management facility construction, must prepare an inventory of sites suitable for TSD facilities. The plan is prepared by the state's Department of Natural Resources.

Preparation of a statewide inventory or plan is one of those sensible ideas that may not work because the final product cannot perform its intended function. Ideally, technical criteria can be applied to screen out undesirable sites and select desirable sites, and relevant non-technical concerns can be addressed at a stage where the consideration of alternatives is still feasible. But, ironically, the better the plan or inventory, the less effective it may be in the end. If specific sites are identified as suitable, as a report prepared by the National Governors' Association has noted, the plan or inventory "may trigger vigorous local opposition at a time when there is little mobilized force to counteract the opposition. The opposition force can [cause] loss of sites before their merits are fully explored or before meaningful and, perhaps, effective mitigations can be offered."

Michigan tries to deal with this problem by requiring that the plan provide for "a reasonable geographic distribution of disposal facilities" within the state, Mich. Comp. Laws Ann. § 299.509(2)-(3), and by allowing the specification of "general locations." Minnesota's approach to the geographic diversity and alternatives issues is more direct. The inventory must include at least three sites each for a commercial chemical processing facility, a commercial incinerator and a commercial transfer and storage facility. Minn. Stat. Ann. § 115A.11 (West).

If mandated plans are to be effective, they must be specific and they must be followed. The dynamics of the planning process generally lead planners to hedge their bets so that final plans seldom delineate hard recommendations for specific tracts of lands. A vague plan has little value as a guide for decision-making, since a wide range of decisions is consistent with it.

Moreover, an effective siting plan must control the permitting decision. Some states have nullified the effectiveness of a site plan by failing to specify the relationship between the plan and subsequent permits. In this sense, hazardous waste site plans are similar to comprehensive land use plans. In recent years some courts and legislatures have bought the planners' argument that land use controls should be subordinated to planning, but the evidence to date suggests that mandating consistency between planning and land use regulations will not increase the quality of plans or the weight given them.

It would seem easier to enforce compliance with the mandates of a TSD facility site plan than with a comprehensive land use plan. The Michigan siting statute requires consistency with the site plan, so in theory, the plan controls the permit stage. Minnesota, on the other hand, has attempted to avoid the problems of mandating consistency by using the planning process not to make a final selection of sites, but to identify those sites that will be subjected to intensive evaluation with substantial public participation. Utah, while not requiring consistency, does encourage it by waiving statutory protections for operators who deviate from the plan. The state's 1981 siting statute, Utah

Code Ann. § 26-14(a)-6(6), provides: "After adoption of the final plan, an applicant for approval of a plan to construct and operate a hazardous waste [TSD] facility who seeks protection under this act shall select a site contained on the final site plan. Nothing in this act, however, shall be construed to prohibit the construction and operation of an approved hazardous waste [TSD] facility at a site which is not included within the final site plan, but such a facility is not entitled to the protections afforded under this act."

Siting Boards: Composition and Challenges Thereto

Regulation of TSD facilities is primarily shared among the U.S. Environmental Protection Agency, state environmental protection agencies and local units of government (to the extent that their authority is not preempted). In most states, other state agencies also have a role in the regulatory process. The consensus among the states is that these existing regulatory authorities have neither the legitimacy nor the proper perspective on siting to design effective siting regulations. Thus, states have created either permanent or ad hoc siting boards. See, *e.g.*, N.Y. Envtl. Conserv. Law § 27-1105 (McKinney). These new boards or commissions are modeled after power plant and industrial facilities boards that emerged in the 1970s in response to the problem of fragmented regulatory authority over large-scale public and private facilities.

The composition of a siting authority is the key to its legitimacy. It must have widespread public appeal plus the capability to make intelligent and timely decisions. The dilemma facing legislators is finding the proper balance. If the board reflects the interests of the most interested groups, expertise may be gained at the expense of legitimacy. A board weighted too heavily in favor of industry or environmental community groups will only engender distrust by the other side. If special interests are disregarded altogether, "citizen" boards which lack expertise may be distrusted by both industry and industry opponents and may have difficulty reaching any decision. Many states have tried to resolve this tension by separating interest and expertise from the power to site. To accommodate demands that various special interests be given a formal role in devising siting policy, advisory commissions may be established that consult with public bodies, but which lack the power to site facilities. See, *e.g.*, N.J. Stat. Ann. § 13:1E-54 (West).

In practice, siting and advisory boards are generally a mix of interested and presumptively neutral parties. Interested parties predominate in many states, although those representing facility operators and waste generators and transporters are in the minority. The general pattern is to select a board composed of members of the scientific community, generally hydrologists and geologists, industry representatives, state and local officials, and token members of the general public. See, *e.g.,* Md. Nat. Res. Code Ann. § 3-703(b). Massachusetts has departed from this model by creating a 21-member board composed of state officials, a "representative of the public knowledgeable in environmental affairs," and six other members of the public. Mass. Gen. Laws Ann. ch. 21D, § 4(13). Industry officials are expressly excluded from the council.

Siting boards that are composed of interested parties—either for or against—might be vulnerable to the challenge that they deny due process of law to applicants or to the public on the ground that contested issues have been prejudged or the public has been systematically unrepresented. In California, the public's right to a fair decisional process has been recognized in a case holding that a forestry board partially charged with environmental regulation but dominated by industry representatives was created by an invalid delegation of legislative power to private parties. *Bayside Timber Co. v. Board of Supervisors,* 20 Cal. App. 3d 1, 97 Cal. Rptr. 431 (1971). However, it is unlikely that courts will conclude that the very structure of a siting board denies due process to applicants or to the public at large. The U.S. Supreme Court has indicated that regulatory officials are presumed to act fairly. See *Withrow v. Larkin,* 421 U.S. 35 (1975), and *United States v. Morgan,* 313 U.S. 409 (1941). Furthermore, regulatory boards are usually representative of enough interests to ensure that diverse viewpoints will be heard. This decreases the risk that issues will be prejudged.

Courts will probably follow the lead of the Supreme Court of Maine and reject a challenge to a siting board's "compositional" unfairness. In *In re Maine Clean Fuels, Inc.,* 310 A.2d 736 (Me. 1973), the court considered a challenge to the decision of the Maine Environmental Improvement Commission (EIC) denying a permit to a proposed petroleum refinery on Penobscot Bay. The disappointed refinery operator argued that the composition of the EIC was biased because it was too pro-environment, but the court's reasons for rejecting the claim apply equally to a challenge that a board with too many industry representatives is structurally unfair: "The composition of the EIC is necessarily broadly based because we deem the legislature found it reasonable that many factors would necessarily have to be considered in regulating the location of any development. . . . It seems clear to us that the legislature considered a variety of interests which it felt could best make the important decisions delegated to this commission. Its conclusion that the five types of interests delineated in the statute could best serve the public is completely reasonable." 310 A.2d at 750.

If, of course, an applicant or a member of the general public with standing to raise the matter can prove that issues regarding a specific facility were prejudged, then the court would invalidate the decision and try to find a remedy that ensures a fair reconsideration of the issues.

Negotiating an Acceptable Site

Massachusetts, Rhode Island and Wisconsin are pioneering the use of bribes and other concessions by facility operators to promote community acceptance of new or expanded TSD facilities. All three states preempt local land use controls, but then throw the facility operator and affected communities into a procedure combining mediation, negotiation and arbitration. The theory is that through the use of neutral or self-interested parties, all interested parties can come together, identify areas of common interest and reach a solution that is fair and mutually acceptable. The prerequisites for successful negotiation in siting a TSD facility may at times be difficult to meet. For starters, a facility is not a large employer, so the possibility that the host community will be amenable to bribes is more limited than in the case of a large plant. In addition, it may be difficult to find negotiators who will be accountable to all interests opposing a facility.

Massachusetts was the first state to move beyond mere preemption to the negotiation approach to TSD facility siting. Under the law, Mass. Gen. Laws Ann. ch. 21D, § 12, a developer may apply to a state siting council for permission to construct a facility in an area locally zoned for industrial uses. If the council decides that the proposed facility is feasible, the "host" community is brought into the siting process and becomes eligible for state grants. The key power granted to local communities to protect themselves from adverse environmental risks is the formal siting agreement. This agreement is negotiated between the operator and host community and is a necessary condition to construction of a TSD facility. If the parties cannot come to an agreement, the matter goes to binding arbitration. Abutting communities may also petition the state for developer-funded compensation if they demonstrate adverse effects from the facility. Rhode Island's law is similar. See R.I. Stat. Ann. § 19-5.

Wisconsin permits any host community to compel negotiation or arbitration (assisted by a mediator) by enacting a siting resolution. Wis. Stat. Ann. § 144.445 (West). The local negotiating committee is composed of city and county officials. The only subjects that are statutorily excluded from negotiation are waivers of state standards and the need for the facility.

Arbitration, on the other hand, is run by the state and is limited to final offers made by both sides in negotiation and to a list of seven subjects. These subjects are: compensation to persons sustaining substantial economic harm as a direct result of the facility; reimbursement of reasonable costs incurred by the local negotiating committee; screening and fencing of the facility; such operational concerns as noise, debris, odors and hours of operation, but not design capacity; traffic; uses of the site after the facility is permanently closed; economically feasible methods of recycling or reducing the flow of wastes to the facility; and the applicability of preexisting local controls.

Wisconsin's statute not only pioneers a new approach to siting, but it also attempts to use the siting process to deal with a problem that is just beginning to be addressed at the state and federal level. A few states, California and Minnesota among them, have adopted legislation that provides for administrative compensation for those injured through exposure to toxic chemicals. Similar federal legislation is pending. See generally Trauberman, "Statutory Reform of 'Toxic Torts': Relieving Legal, Scientific and Technical Burdens on the Chemical Victim," 7 Harv. Envtl. L. Rev. 177 (1983).

Environmental mediation is a new experiment. Unlike labor mediation and arbitration, the relevant issues have not been defined in a prior contract or collective bargaining agreement, so it is not certain that the parties can even set an agenda. Once this hurdle is overcome, though, environmental mediation raises many of the same issues that have been faced in labor law.

Arbitration involving local government has been challenged as an invalid delegation of power to private parties, but the courts have generally upheld the procedure. See, *e.g., Town of Arlington v. Board of Conciliation & Arbitration,* 370 Mass. 769, 352 N.E.2d 914 (1976). An equally fundamental issue is determining who is bound by a decision. Although the Massachusetts statute speaks of binding arbitration, the reference is not accurate since TSD facility siting involves other permits that are open to challenge. In general, it seems unlikely that a negotiation-arbitration procedure can eliminate all possible third party challenges to the TSD approval process. The courts may still have to define the range of arbitrable issues and the scope of judicial review, as well as resolve the various procedural due process and evidentiary issues that arbitration raises.

Conclusion

The new TSD facility siting laws surveyed in this article have the potential to accommodate the demand for safe new or expanded hazardous waste management facilities. However, there is still a high risk that the siting approach adopted in these statutes will not work. Industry may reject participation in the process by claiming that the procedures of adequate risk assessment are merely vehicles for delay. On the other side, environmental groups and other critics of present hazardous waste management practices may become disillusioned with siting controversies, because the "real" issues—the actual need for a facility, front-end modifications of the waste stream and non-land disposal treatment options—are not seriously addressed in the siting process.

LAWRENCE S. BACOW AND JAMES R. MILKEY

9 Overcoming Local Opposition to Hazardous Waste Facilities

The Massachusetts Approach

Finding sites for new hazardous waste treatment and disposal facilities is one of the most challenging problems facing society today. For years, we have been careless about disposal of hazardous wastes,[1] and this carelessness has led to environmental disasters such as Love Canal.[2] In response, both state[3] and federal[4] governments have imposed strict controls on the handling, transport, and disposal of hazardous wastes.[5] Although these regulations have forced unsafe facilities to close,[6] they also have increased the amount of waste that must be processed in off-site facilities.[7] Consequently, legal disposal facilities have become scarce in many regions,[8] and developers must find new sites.[9]

Unfortunately, the same public concern that prompted new legislation governing hazardous waste has also frustrated development of new facilities. Local residents, fearing that their community could become another Love Canal,[10] have thwarted most recent efforts to find additional sites for hazardous waste disposal facilities.[11] In fact, as a result of public opposition, no new off-site hazardous waste treatment facilities have been approved during the last three years.[12] The success of local opposition has created a dilemma. Efforts to end "midnight dumping"[13] and to eliminate unsafe disposal sites are doomed to failure unless new, safe disposal facilities can be built,[14] but no community appears willing to accept a new hazardous waste facility.

Reprinted with permission from *Harvard Environmental Law Review*, Vol. 6 (1982), pp. 265-305. Copyright © 1982 by the *Harvard Environmental Law Review*.

In an attempt to resolve this dilemma, several states[15] have enacted measures to assist developers in finding new sites. This article examines several approaches that states have adopted, particularly the novel Massachusetts statute.[16] Section I describes the causes of the local opposition which states must address in their hazardous waste facility siting laws. Section II analyzes two approaches in state siting laws, preemption of local authority and payment of incentives to local communities. Section III discusses the innovative Massachusetts siting statute, which requires developers to negotiate compensation agreements with host communities.

I.   Local Opposition to Hazardous Waste Facilities[17]

Proposals to build hazardous waste disposal facilities typically inspire intense local opposition, which may delay or prevent the siting of the facility.[18] Industry's past failures to use environmentally sound waste disposal techniques[19] have received widespread publicity[20] and have aroused public anxiety about the dangers associated with hazardous wastes.[21] Even though stringent hazardous waste regulations are mandated by the Resource Conservation and Recovery Act,[22] many local residents lack confidence in industry's and government's ability to protect public health and safety from the major, long-term risks posed by such facilities.[23]

Furthermore, because of the patterns in which the costs and benefits of such facilities occur, rational economic action often results in local opposition. The social costs associated with hazardous waste facilities fall most heavily on those who live nearby.[24] These costs include the potential risks to health and the environment from accidents and improper operation of the facility, the noise and congestion associated with transportation of hazardous material, and the stigma associated with being labelled "the region's dump." To the extent that these costs are capitalized by the real estate market, property values fall, thereby reducing the community's tax base and limiting the ability of residents to sell their homes at previous market values.[25]

By contrast, the dispersed benefits of a hazardous waste facility accrue to the entire region served by the facility. Such benefits include reduced midnight dumping, decreased transport distances for hazardous wastes, and increased disposal capacity to serve the many industrial activities that produce hazardous wastes. Those few benefits that are concentrated locally, increased tax revenues and new jobs, are typically modest in comparison to the concentrated social costs. Thus, from the perspective of the neighbors of a proposed hazardous waste facility, the costs of a new facility are almost always greater than the benefits. As a result, local residents are usually better off if the facility is built somewhere else.

The distribution of benefits and costs also affects the pattern of public participation in the siting process.[26] Because the benefits are broadly distributed, no individual has an incentive to advocate that any given site under consideration is the best site. Local opponents dismiss as self-serving the developer's attempts to make this argument. Consequently, society's need for safe hazardous waste facilities is generally poorly represented in the siting process. By contrast, because the social costs are large and concentrated, neighbors of the proposed facility have a substantial incentive to get involved. Local opponents organize carefully, attend meetings, lobby politicians, and hire lawyers if necessary to defeat an unwanted facility.[27] This activism may be effective enough to defeat all facilities, including those providing net benefits to society.[28] Thus, finding sites for the safe disposal and processing of hazardous materials is largely a problem of managing local opposition.[29]

II.   Traditional Approaches of State Siting Laws

The most potent weapon available to facility opponents is the local police power, particularly the power to establish land use policies.[30] Local government officials, reflecting citizen sentiments,[31] may pass laws to exclude proposed facilities from their jurisdiction.[32] If construction of a proposed facility requires amendment to existing law, such as a zoning amendment, the path of facility opponents is even easier.[33]

The need for new hazardous waste facilities requires that states take action to overcome these exclusionary tactics.[34] To date, states have used two techniques to manage local opposition to hazardous waste facilities. Some states attempt to bypass or quash local authority in matters dealing with the siting of hazardous waste facilities.[35] Other states attempt to address the causes of local opposition by redistributing the benefits and costs associated with the facility while leaving substantial local autonomy over siting decisions.[36]

PREEMPTION OF LOCAL AUTHORITY

The Approach.   Sixteen of the twenty-five states with statutes governing hazardous waste facility siting have adopted some procedure to preempt local regulatory authority over hazardous waste facilities.[37] The processes used to invoke preemption and the extent of the preemption, however, vary from state to state. The most comprehensive statutes automatically exempt qualifying facilities from all local regulations.[38] All but one of the remaining preemption statutes authorize either the state legislature or a state board to overrule local authority on a case-by-case basis.[39] The remaining statute does not establish a procedure for direct state preemption of local regulations, but permits local jurisdictions to regulate qualifying facilities only if the regulation is less restrictive than and not duplicative of state regulation.[40]

Preemption statutes attempt to accommodate local interests in a variety of ways. Michigan requires the state approval board to integrate local regulations into the siting decision "to the fullest extent practicable."[41] North Carolina allows preemption "only to the extent necessary to effectuate the purposes of [the act]."[42] In Florida, state preemption can occur only with the approval of the regional agencies and a finding of public necessity by the Governor and the Cabinet.[43] Connecticut leaves intact all initial local authority, but subjects all local permit decisions to state review.[44] In New York, the state siting board can override only those local zoning or land use regulations enacted after the developer has filed a formal application to site a facility.[45] Washington exempts land acquired by the appropriate state agency from local land use regulations, except to the extent inconsistent with comprehensive local plans enacted prior to January 1, 1976.[46]

Because preemption of local regulatory authority is a sensitive political issue, these statutes all provide for public participation in the preemption decision. Each statute requires a state agency to hold a public hearing before local authority is preempted.[47] Furthermore, several states allow members of the public to sit on the state siting body.[48]

A Critique.   Preemption represents legal disarmament. It removes some obstructionist tactics from the hands of facility opponents, but does not render them powerless or remove their incentive to fight the facility. More specifically, there are three weaknesses of the preemption approach.

First, states cannot preempt all forms of local opposition. It is difficult to anticipate every exercise of the local police power that opponents might use to thwart construction of an unwanted facility. Most state siting statutes preempt only the authority of local governments to withhold needed zoning or other permit approval. Opposition to unwanted hazardous waste facilities, however, can be based on subtler strategies. For example, a town can amend the maximum weight limit on a bridge maintained by the town in order to limit truck access to a proposed site.[49]

Second, a preemption statute may encourage opponents of a proposed facility to turn to litigation. The preemption statute itself may become grist for the mill of litigious facility opponents.[50] Facility opponents may also seek judicial review of permit decisions under state and federal health, safety, and environmental laws.[51] Although these litigants may lose individual battles over specific issues, they may ultimately win the war if the costs of delay are sufficient to defeat unwanted facilities. Public participation procedures may offer similar opportunities for delay.[52]

Third, local governments can often use their power in the state government to defeat or prevent the operation of a preemption statute. In Massachusetts, for example, the results of a state study on locations for hazardous waste facilities were released while a bill to preempt local authority was before the legislature. State legislators for the three sites which were ranked highest in the study introduced bills to exempt their communities from further consideration. They garnered support for the bills by asking their fellow legislators whether they would like such a facility forced upon their districts.[53] The legislature subsequently enacted a statute based on compensation; preemption was not politically acceptable in Massachusetts.

The politics of hazardous waste in other states are similar to the politics in Massachusetts. Because the benefits of a hazardous waste facility are diffuse and the costs of a facility are concentrated, there are few rewards and many potential headaches for politicians who try to force an unwilling community to accept a hazardous waste facility.[54] The beneficiaries of a hazardous waste facility are unlikely to notice, but the politicians are sure to incur the wrath of the potential host community. Although a state may succeed in passing a preemption bill when no specific sites are under active consideration, once the process of selecting sites begins, local governments can exert their influence with state officials to avoid application of state preemption to their regulations.[55]

Finally, even when legal and political tactics fail, facility opponents can resort to civil disobedience to thwart unwanted development. In Michigan, local residents put nails and tacks on the highways in order to prevent the state from burying cattle contaminated by polybrominated biphenyls.[56] In other jurisdictions, residents have threatened to dynamite existing facilities,[57] and have taken public officials hostage to vent their anger over policymaking processes that failed to adequately address their concerns.[58] If people feel that their health or safety is jeopardized or that their investment in their home is threatened, they will resort to extreme measures to prevent the construction of hazardous waste facilities.

Conclusion. Because states have only recently passed preemption statutes, it is perhaps too early to tell whether preemption will work in practice.[59] Analysis of the preemption approach, however, suggests that states cannot control local opposition solely by overriding local regulatory powers. Preemption does not reduce the risks associated with hazardous waste facilities and does not compensate the host community for these risks. Thus, preemption operates only on the symptoms of local opposition, not on the causes. Although states can neutralize some of the many tactics available to facility opponents, they cannot eliminate all of these tactics. Furthermore, by shutting off legitimate channels for expressing fears and concerns, preemption may encourage facility opponents to use extra-legal means to gain a hearing for their grievances.

THE INCENTIVES APPROACH

The Approach.   Compensation can be an effective technique to eliminate the causes of local opposition to a hazardous waste facility. Most local residents oppose the construction of hazardous waste facilities out of self-interest. They perceive that the local benefits from such facilities, such as increased tax revenues and new jobs, are outweighed by the local costs, such as health and environmental risks, noise, congestion, and reduced property values.[60] In theory, if the benefits obtained by the community from the project are increased so that they offset the residual social costs, the community should no longer have any incentive to oppose. Indeed, if the benefits to the community are large enough, it might actually desire the facility.[61]

Statutes requiring compensation for social costs should improve the facility siting process in a number of ways.[62] First, the prospect of compensation should encourage discussions between the community and the developer. Under current practices, the host community has every reason to fight a proposed facility. If the only alternatives under consideration are to build or not to build the facility, and if building the facility invariably leaves the host community worse off than not building, the community and the developer will be at loggerheads. When there is a possibility of compensation, the parties at least have something to talk about: the terms under which the community might accept the facility. Second, compensation promotes efficiency by allowing projects to proceed only if their social benefits outweigh their social costs. Furthermore, by requiring the developer to compensate for social costs, compensation creates an incentive for the developer to minimize these costs.[63]

The developer who wanted to compensate a community could first seek to mitigate adverse impacts by, for example, siting a facility in an area compatible with its purpose, creating a buffer zone around the facility, and providing necessary infrastructure, such as a transportation network or a sewer system.[64] Then the developer could compensate the local community for remaining impacts through cash payments, taxes, payments in lieu of taxes, and indirect payments, such as property value guarantees, parks, and jobs and job training.[65]

In other contexts, developers have used compensation with mixed results to site otherwise unwanted facilities.[66] These efforts reveal potential weaknesses in the incentives approach.

A Critique.   The incentives approach assumes that compensation for all costs can render an individual neutral towards a hazardous waste facility. This assumption may be valid; people implicitly make trade-offs between health or environmental values and other values all the time.[67] For example, workers often receive wage premiums for performing hazardous work.[68] Similarly, land values reflect environmental amenities; houses with water views typically sell for more than houses without water views.[69] Other factors being equal, land values usually are higher in pristine than in polluted areas. Because people implicitly value their health and their environment in making employment and housing decisions, in theory it should be possible to reverse the process and compensate people when the construction of a hazardous waste facility places their health or environment slightly at risk.

Prior experience with compensation, however, suggests that the social costs of hazardous waste facilities may not be compensable.[70] Many people blanche at the suggestion that they explicitly surrender part of their safety or tranquility in return for compensation.[71] Indeed, offers of compensation have occasionally increased local opposition; opponents of a proposed facility have attacked compensation as an immoral bribe.[72] Ironically, where communities have requested compensation, developers have labelled such requests extortion.[73]

There are at least three reasons why the costs of hazardous waste facilities may not be compensable. First, consumers do not always conduct the rational risk-benefit analysis that is attributed to them by economists. Many individuals never explicitly calculate the cost, for example, of living in a less polluted neighborhood. Instead, they merely choose a desired neighborhood, and look for the best house they can afford in that neighborhood.[74]

Second, many people object to the concept of putting a price on health or environmental amenities.[75] These people believe that the environment is to be valued for its own sake; thus, rivers and streams should be protected from pollution not because they are a source of drinking water, but because of their place in the natural order. These people are unimpressed, and may be offended, by developers' offers of compensation for environmental degradation.[76]

Third, even if social costs are compensable at the individual level, it may not be possible to reach a community consensus on the appropriate form or amount of compensation. Different constituencies within a community may have different views on what constitutes fair compensation, and thus a community may reject a facility because its members cannot agree on the terms that would render the facility acceptable.

Compensability is not the only potential barrier to the successful negotiation of a compensation agreement. Developers have little incentive to negotiate unless agreements can curb opposition. Compensation agreements, however, are binding only upon those who sign the agreement. Thus, for example, a developer who signs an agreement with an ad hoc opposition group may find that other members of the community still oppose the facility. Similarly, a developer who signs an agreement with a municipality may find that courts will not enforce the agreement because common law rules generally prohibit municipalities from bargaining away their policymaking powers.[77] In sum, even if developers could compensate people for the costs of a proposed hazardous waste facility, they would have difficulty finding all these people and negotiating an effective compensation agreement with them.

Applications in State Siting Laws.   Several states now require compensation as part of their process for siting hazardous waste facilities,[78] either as the sole approach to overcoming local opposition, or in combination with preemption of local authority.[79] Some states fix compensation as a function of the gross receipts or amount of wastes processed at a facility.[80] Other states allow the local community to assess a special tax or licensing fee up to a specific amount.[81] Ohio does not require compensation from the developer, but authorizes the relevant state agency to make incentive payments to the host community.[82] It is too early to tell whether these statutes will work in practice,[83] but there is reason to question whether they will be able to overcome local opposition. With the exception of the Massachusetts and Connecticut statutes, the goal of these statutes seems to be to enable communities to recover only the direct expenses associated with a facility, rather than to compensate communities for all public health, environmental, and intangible harms of a facility.[84]

Some states have developed variations on the compensation approach. Connecticut allows the host community to choose between receiving compensation through a set statutory formula or negotiating a package of incentives with the developer.[85] North Carolina allows local communities to assess an annual licensing fee based on the costs incurred as a result of the facility's existence.[86] Ohio establishes a dispute resolution mechanism, called an "adjudication hearing," which includes the developer, affected individuals, and officials of the state, county, and local governments.[87] Because these statutes offer a wider range of options to local communities, they may have a greater chance of overcoming local opposition.

III.   Incorporating Incentives Into the Facility Siting Process: The Massachusetts Approach˙

The Massachusetts Hazardous Waste Facility Siting Act[88] is the most sophisticated statute adopting the incentives approach.[89] There are five critical elements of the Massachusetts approach. First, the Act gives a developer the right to construct a hazardous waste facility on land zoned for industrial use if the developer obtains the required permits and completes a negotiated or arbitrated siting agreement with the host community.[90] The siting agreement describes the steps which the developer will take to mitigate adverse impacts associated with the facility and to compensate the community for remaining impacts.[91] Second, the Act limits the ability of local communities to exclude hazardous waste facilities without first showing that such facilities pose special risks.[92] Third, the state provides potential host communities with technical assistance grants to promote local participation in the siting process and effective negotiation with developers.[93] Fourth, the Act requires that deadlocks between developers and host communities be submitted to an arbitrator.[94] Finally, the Act provides for compensation to abutting communities that are likely to be affected by new hazardous waste facilities in adjacent jurisdictions.

The Massachusetts Act does not attempt to increase state control over local decisions; instead, it seeks to eliminate the causes of local opposition to hazardous waste facilities.[95] Compensation should help internalize the external costs of the facility.[96] Negotiations create a forum for addressing the concerns of local residents who oppose a proposed hazardous waste facility. This process is intended to minimize harm to the community, avoid formation of adversary relationships, and increase public confidence in the siting decision.[97] Thus, the Massachusetts approach may indeed be able to eliminate the causes of local opposition.

This section discusses the Massachusetts siting process in detail, examines the major legal issues that might be raised in court challenges to the Act, particularly the validity of preemption of local authority through the arbitration clause, and explores the practical and theoretical implications of the Act.

THE SITING PROCESS

The State Role. The developer and the host community have the primary role in the siting process; state agencies oversee the process, but have no independent authority to site facilities or to override local decisions.[98] Three state agencies share that oversight role. The Department of Environmental Management is responsible for attracting developers to Massachusetts, for planning, and for assessing the state's requirements for hazardous waste storage, treatment, and disposal facilities.[99] The Department of Environmental Quality Engineering grants the necessary permits and licenses and enforces the relevant regulations.[100] Because of their mandates, these two agencies lack the neutrality necessary to referee negotiations between developers and communities. The legislature therefore created a new agency, the Hazardous Waste Facility Site Safety Council, to oversee and facilitate the negotiation process.[101] The Council has twenty-one members[102] and includes representatives for all parties involved in and affected by the siting of hazardous waste facilities.[103]

Initiating the Siting Process.   A prospective developer initiates the siting process by filing a notice of intent with the Council.[104] The notice of intent describes the proposed facility, the projected site, the wastes to be processed, and the compensation which the developer would offer to the host community.[105] Alternatively, a developer may submit a proposal without naming a site and rely upon a statutory process to locate potential sites.[106]

Within fifteen days of receiving a completed notice of intent, the Council must determine whether the proposal is "feasible and deserving" of state assistance.[107] This review is a rough screen; its purpose is to eliminate projects that are infeasible, illegal, unnecessary, or proposed by disreputable or financially insecure developers.[108]

If the Council decides that the proposal is feasible and deserving, both the host and abutting communities become eligible to receive technical assistance grants to support their participation in the siting process.[109] If the Council decides that the proposal is not feasible and deserving, the developer may petition for reconsideration.[110]

Within thirty days of the filing of a notice of intent, the chief executive officer of the host community must form a local assessment committee, the local body that participates in negotiations with the developer.[111] The local assessment committee has the power and duty to represent the host community in negotiations with the developer, to negotiate specific mitigation measures and obtain compensation for remaining adverse effects, to enter into a binding siting agreement, and to appoint two local residents to serve as voting members of the Council.[112]

Within thirty days of a decision that a proposal is feasible and deserving, the Department of Environmental Management conducts public briefing sessions to "maximiz[e] the participation of interested persons [and] more fully inform the public about every proposal."[113] During those sessions, communities and individuals may question state officials and the developer about the proposed facility, the siting process, and the benefits and protections afforded host and abutting communities.[114]

Once potential sites have been identified, the developer must prepare a preliminary project impact report.[115] This report, which discusses the facility's environmental, economic, and social impacts, coordinates the siting process with the disclosure requirements of the Massachusetts Environmental Policy Act.[116] The report forms the basis for the negotiations between the developer and the host community.[117] After a public comment period, the Council reviews the adequacy of the report.[118]

Negotiations and the Siting Agreement.   Formal negotiations between the developer and the local assessment committee begin after the Council approves the preliminary project impact report.[119] The negotiations should result in the formal "siting agreement" that must be concluded before the developer can construct a facility.[120] The siting agreement must specify the "terms, conditions, and provisions" under which the developer will operate the facility and the mitigation and compensation measures[121] that the developer will take.[122] The Act states these requirements in general terms, however, and they serve more to illustrate the potential range of negotiations rather than to constrain the shape of the final agreement.

Arbitration. If the host community and the developer fail to establish a siting agreement, the Council may declare an impasse and compel the parties to submit all unresolved issues to "final and binding arbitration."[123] The parties jointly select the arbitrator, or, if they fail to agree, the Council appoints one.[124] The arbitrator "resolve[s] the issues in dispute between the local assessment committee and the developer"[125] in accordance with standards and procedures set out in the regulations.[126] The provisions of the Uniform Arbitration Act for Commercial Disputes govern the arbitration proceedings and judicial review of the arbitration decision.[127]

State and Local Permit Requirements. Before constructing a hazardous waste facility, the developer must obtain a license from the Department of Environmental Quality Engineering and a site assignment permit from the local board of health.[128] The Department of Environmental Quality Engineering cannot issue a license unless it finds that the facility "does not constitute a significant danger to public health, public safety, or the environment, does not seriously threaten injury to the inhabitants of the area or damage to their property, and does not result in the creation of noisome or unwholesome odors."[129]

Communities cannot impose new permit requirements on hazardous waste facilities after the effective date of the Act, July 15, 1980.[130] Thus, the only local permit required of a developer in most Massachusetts jurisdictions is the site assignment permit from the local board of health.[131] A local board of health must assign a site if the proposed facility "imposes no significantly greater danger . . . than the dangers that currently exist in the conduct and operation of other industrial and commercial enterprises in the Commonwealth not engaged in the treatment, processing or disposal of hazardous waste, but using processes that are comparable."[132] The initial site assignment permit is subject to rescission, suspension, or modification by the Department of Environmental Quality Engineering or the local board of health if either agency determines "that the maintenance and operation of a facility has resulted in significant danger to public health" or determines that the developer has not complied with the siting agreement.[133]

The statute also limits the power of localities to exclude hazardous waste facilities in one other important way: it amends the Zoning Enabling Act to permit hazardous waste facilities to be built as a matter of right on land which is zoned for industrial use at the time a developer initiates the siting process.[134] A locality can rezone such land only before a notice of intent is filed or after a proposed facility is finally disapproved.[135]

The Act also places restrictions on the power of the state to seize property for a facility site through eminent domain.[136] The most important restriction is that the state cannot use the power of eminent domain without an assenting vote of the city council, board of aldermen, or board of selectmen.[137]

Declaration of an Operational Siting Agreement. After completion of a siting agreement either through negotiation or arbitration, the Council reviews the agreement. Proposed regulations require the Council to approve the agreement if it contains all provisions mandated by the regulations and complies with the terms of the Act.[138] If the Council approves the agreement, the developer prepares a final project impact report, which is similar to the preliminary report, but includes comments received by the developer, responses to these comments, a copy of the siting agreement, and relevant data derived from the negotiations.[139] After the appropriate agencies approve the final report, the Council decides whether to declare the agreement "operative and in full force and effect."[140] This declaration establishes the siting agreement as "a non-assignable contract binding upon the developer and the host community, and enforceable against the parties in any court of competent jurisdiction."[141] Abutting communities also become directly involved in the siting process.[142] They are invited to the initial briefing sessions and are eligible for technical assistance grants.[143] Moreover, abutting communities may petition the Council for compensation to be paid by the developer for "demonstrably adverse impacts" imposed upon the community by the proposed facility.[144] Unlike compensation for the host community, which is determined through bilateral negotiations with the developer, the Council fixes the compensation to be paid abutting communities after a public hearing.[145] If the abutting community is unsatisfied with the Council's award, it may request that the compensation issue be submitted to impartial arbitration.[146] The developer, however, has no comparable right of appeal.

LEGAL ISSUES

Statutory ambiguity is the bane of legislative initiative. Many innovative statutes have been hailed at the time of their adoption only to founder later in the courts. This section explores some of the legal issues raised by the Massachusetts Hazardous Waste Facility Siting Act.

State Preemption and Home Rule. Although incentives are central to the structure of the Siting Act, the Act also incorporates significant preemption provisions. The relationship of these provisions to the grant of municipal police powers under the Massachusetts Home Rule Amendment[147] is a critical issue.

Municipalities possess no inherent rights, but instead derive their powers of self-government from state grants in home rule provisions and enabling statutes.[148] The Massachusetts Home Rule Amendment gives local governments powers "not inconsistent with the constitution or laws enacted by the [legislature] in conformity with powers reserved to it . . . and which [are] not denied . . . to the city or town by its charter."[149] The legislature retains "the power to act in relation to cities and towns but only by general laws which apply alike . . . or to a class of not fewer than two."[150]

In the absence of state law governing hazardous waste facilities, municipalities would have broad power under the Home Rule Amendment to impose use restrictions or permit requirements on those facilities.[151] The Siting Act, however, is a general law affecting all cities and towns alike, and thus preempts any local powers that are inconsistent with it.[152]

The Siting Act contains three explicit preemption provisions. First, the Act gives developers a right to build facilities on land zoned for industrial use at the time the developer files the notice of intent if "all permits and licenses required by law have been issued to the developer and a siting agreement has been established."[153] Second, the Act prohibits local communities from requiring new permits or licenses that were not required before the effective date of the Act.[154] Third, the Act allows local boards of health to deny a site assignment permit only when the facility poses a significantly greater danger to the public health or public safety than do comparable enterprises.[155]

Despite these explicit limitations on local authority, an argument still remains that communities retain some power to exclude facilities that otherwise meet the relevant safety standards.[156] For example, the Act does not expressly bar a community from passing an ordinance that prohibits the construction of a hazardous waste facility.[157] The legislature clearly intended, however, to proscribe such action. If a community could bar facilities in this fashion, it would render meaningless the provision giving developers a right to build facilities on land zoned for industry.[158]

Moreover, the basic purposes of the Act are to expedite the siting of hazardous waste facilities and to protect the public health;[159] these purposes restrict by implication communities' independent police powers. The Massachusetts Supreme Judicial Court has stated that the police powers "cannot be exercised in a manner which frustrates the purpose or implementation of a general or special law enacted by the Legislature."[160] If state and federal regulations adequately protect the public health, additional local requirements are preempted because they frustrate the expediting function of the Act. Even if state and federal regulations were in some way inadequate to protect the public health, these inadequacies should be addressed exclusively through the

Department of Environmental Quality Engineering licensing process, not through local regulation. Local regulation would frustrate the purposes of the Act and lead to a patchwork quilt of regulations.

The Powers of the Arbitrator. The Siting Council's power to declare an impasse in negotiations between the developer and the local community and to refer the unresolved issues to "final and binding arbitration"[161] is a unique feature of the Massachusetts statute. The characterization of this arbitration procedure as "final and binding," however, is deceptive. The terms of the arbitration award are not binding on either party in the conventional sense. A developer who finds an award excessive can simply decline to construct the proposed facility.[162] Similarly, an arbitration award is not binding on a host community because the community can subsequently attempt to withhold the site assignment permit[163] or challenge the state's grant of a construction and operation license. Consequently, the arbitration award only defines the terms under which the proposed facility can be constructed and operated if the developer still finds the prospect economically worthwhile and obtains the necessary state and local health permits.

The Act offers little guidance to the arbitrator charged with rendering a decision. It allows the Siting Council to declare an impasse and "frame the issues in dispute between the Local Assessment Committee and the developer" and empowers the arbitrator to "resolve the issues in dispute" within forty-five days.[164] The Act is silent on the standards or criteria that the arbitrator should employ.[165] The Council has attempted to fill this gap by drafting regulations to guide the arbitrator's decision.[166] Although these regulations provide some guidance, they fail to establish true decision standards.[167]

Despite the absence of explicit statutory standards, the discretion granted to the arbitrator does not constitute an unlawful delegation of legislative authority. Massachusetts courts have construed the delegation doctrine narrowly, stating that legislative standards for agency action "may be found not only in the express provisions of a statute but also in its necessary implications."[168] In one recent decision, the Massachusetts Supreme Judicial Court expressed its reluctance to use the delegation doctrine to invalidate compulsory arbitration provisions where the arbitration follows negotiation and fact-finding.[169]

Some provisions of the Act do supply implicit guidance for the arbitrator. For example, by specifying the contents of a siting agreement, the Act implies that an arbitration award must meet certain minimum levels.[170] Furthermore, the arbitrator must have some discretion to tailor specific "remedies" to the individual situation, as intended by the Act. Courts have generally recognized that standards need not be specific where the problems to be resolved are complex and the need for flexibility is great.[171] Moreover, the proposed regulations will further limit the discretion of the arbitrator, even if they do not ultimately settle the issue of what is "fair compensation." Courts are moving to the position that a delegation is valid if administrative discretion is limited, whether or not it is limited by the legislature.[172]

Although the delegation doctrine will not invalidate the statute, the arbitrator still needs normative standards to guide his or her judgment. In practice, an arbitrator is likely to be called upon to make three types of judgments: (1) the mitigation measures, operating controls, and post-closure management techniques that the developer must use, (2) the services that the host community must provide to the developer, and (3) the compensation that the developer must pay to the host community.

In determining which measures the developer must employ to safeguard health and the environment, the arbitrator should be guided by the same standard that governs the local health board's issuance of the site assignment permit: the arbitrator should require that the facility not create risks greater than comparable industrial facilities.[173] If the arbitrator fails to require the developer to meet this standard, the local board of health can justifiably refuse to issue the site assignment permit, and the entire siting process ends.

It is much harder to identify standards for the other two aspects of an arbitration award. Ordering the host community to provide services is troublesome because it intrudes upon local autonomy. In theory, for example, an arbitrator could compel a community to increase the capacity of its municipal sewage system so that it could provide necessary sewage services to the facility. Because of the difficulty of supervising such awards, however, the arbitrator should use sparingly the power to compel provision of services. In assessing the reasonableness of a developer's request for services from the host community, the arbitrator should examine the need for such services, their availability from sources other than the host community, the legal and institutional capacity of the host community to provide the services, and the standard practices of other communities hosting similar industrial facilities.

In practice, the services issue will be intimately bound up with the compensation issue. Under Massachusetts law, the state cannot require local expenditures without establishing a funding mechanism for them.[174] Thus the arbitrator cannot compel a municipality to deliver services without simultaneously providing funding for these services. In most cases, user charges or tax receipts generated by the new facility will provide that funding. Nothing in the Act, however, prevents the state from compensating the community directly.

In deciding on compensation for costs that are not related to services, the arbitrator should be guided by the theory of the Act: that communities should be made whole, to the extent possible, for the social costs associated with a hazardous waste facility. The project impact report, the studies prepared with technical assistance grants, and other information produced by the parties and the state should provide the arbitrator with a qualitative assessment of the social costs. Putting a price on these costs is a much more difficult and subjective task. In rendering such a judgment, the arbitrator essentially sits as a court in equity and accordingly should have wide latitude in fashioning an award.

Although it is difficult to articulate a single rule to guide the arbitrator in deciding compensation questions, the following five suggestions might prove helpful. First, the arbitrator should try to structure the compensation award to respond to the concerns of the host community. For example, if the community objects to the facility because it will inhibit recreational opportunities, the arbitrator should look for ways to restore these opportunities. Second, the arbitrator should make extensive use of contingent compensation awards. The health and environmental costs of hazardous waste facilities are often impossible to predict. It is therefore better to fix the level of compensation per unit of damage and provide for damage assessment at future dates than to fix the award based on what may turn out to be an inaccurate prediction of the project's effects.[175] Third, when assessing impacts that may be fundamentally noncompensable, such as increases in risk to human health, the arbitrator should resist the temptation to award excessive compensation. By definition, such awards do not make the community whole. Moreover, they defeat the legislative determination that the slight risks to human health posed by legal hazardous waste facilities are preferable to the larger risks posed by illegal dumping. Fourth, the arbitrator should consider the benefits as well as the costs of the facility. Thus, the arbitrator should balance the benefits that occur naturally to the host community and the benefits to which the developer has already agreed against the remaining adverse impacts. Finally, the arbitrator should not limit compensation to what the developer can afford. Compensation helps to screen out facilities that should not be built because of their excessive social costs. If the arbitration award is constrained by the financial capabilities of the developer, this important screening function will be lost.

The Powers of the Siting Council. The Siting Act includes both a specific enumeration of the Council's powers[176] and, in a separate section, a statement that "no facility shall be constructed, maintained or operated unless a siting agreement has been established . . . and said agreement has been declared to be operative and in full force and effect by the council."[177] The statute and the regulations are silent on whether the Council may withhold this declaration from a developer who has obtained a license from the Department of Environmental Quality Engineering, received a site assignment permit from the local board of health, and obtained either a negotiated or an arbitrated siting agreement. Thus, the Act is ambiguous about the Council's ability to impose additional public safety requirements beyond those already embodied in the Act, the siting agreement, and the required permits.

The language of the Act suggests that the Council has the power to review the substance of the siting agreement. In construing a statute, each part of a statute should be interpreted to give it meaning and effect.[178] The only way to give meaning to the Council's power to declare siting agreements operative is to assume that, under some circumstances, the Council would withhold the declaration.

On the other hand, the Act's explicit enumeration of the Council's powers[179] does not include any power to review the substance of a final siting agreement. One provision does state that the Council has authority to "review all proposals for the construction and operation of hazardous waste facilities [and] reject proposals which the council finds to be unacceptable."[180] This language, however, refers to "proposals," not final siting agreements; it only allows the Council to reject, at the beginning of the siting process, proposals that are not "feasible and deserving."

The legislative history of the Act is also ambiguous on this question. The report of the commission that drafted the statute states that the Council should "oversee the facility siting process and . . . ensure the protection of public health and safety."[181] This language suggests that the Council should review the substance of a siting agreement before declaring it operative. The same report, however, also states that "[t]he development function [of the Department of Environmental Management] is kept separate from [the Department of Environmental Quality Engineering's] regulatory and permit granting function, and separate from the process management and public safety functions of the [Council]."[182] This "separation of powers" language suggests that the Council should not impose additional requirements prior to declaring the siting agreement operative because this would overlap with the permitting powers of the Department of Environmental Quality Engineering.

The structure of the statute suggests that the purpose of the Council's declaration that the siting agreement is operative is not to create a level of substantive review but rather to signal the end of the siting process and certify its procedural validity. The declaration recognizes the siting agreement as a binding, non-assignable contract between the developer and the host community.[183] Thus, the Council, because it is entrusted with overseeing the entire siting process, would be justified in withholding the declaration until all other aspects of the process were completed. For example, the Council should delay issuing the declaration if the siting agreement is established prior to conclusion of the licensing and environmental review procedures that parallel the negotiation of the siting agreement.[184] Similarly, the Council should withhold its declaration if the procedural requirements of the negotiation process have been violated in a way that prejudiced the rights of a party to the siting process.[185]

The Legal Status of a Siting Agreement.   Under the Act, a developer can force a community to accept a hazardous waste facility against its will. For example, the developer generally selects the host community in the notice of intent. After the Council has declared the proposal feasible and deserving of state assistance, the Council can require the community to form a local assessment committee by threatening to appoint members to the committee if the chief executive officer refuses to do so.[186] If the local assessment committee refuses to negotiate with the developer, the Council may declare an impasse and refer the task of formulating a siting agreement to an arbitrator.[187] And if, after the arbitration award, the community refuses to issue to the developer the public health permit, the developer can obtain it through court action.[188]

If a community resists the siting process, the arbitrated siting agreement that results bears little resemblance to a traditional contract because there has been no mutual assent.[189] Nonetheless, the Act treats a siting agreement established through arbitration as a "non-assignable contract binding and enforeable against the parties in any court of competent jurisdiction."[190] This language gives the developer contractual remedies to enforce the agreement.

The Act does not indicate, however, what kinds of contract remedies are available. Ideally, a community that declines to provide a developer with services mandated by an arbitrator should be liable for both damages and specific performance. Damages might include additional financing costs on construction loans, the cost of obtaining the services elsewhere, and lost profits from delayed operations. The threat of a damage action establishes incentives for reluctant communities to fulfill their obligations in good faith; limiting a developer's remedies to specific performance would only encourage a community to delay providing essential services until the courts have resolved all other legal issues. Of course, a skillful arbitrator could achieve the same result by structuring the compensation award in a way that rewarded efforts by the community to expedite the siting process.[191]

The statutory language also makes contractual defenses available to the parties. For example, the host community may assert the defense of illegality or impossibility to excuse non-performance of mandated services. Because of the lack of mutual consent in an arbitrated siting agreement and the limited scope of review of such an agreement,[192] litigants are more likely to assert these defenses than in typical contracts litigation.

A siting agreement not only defines the community's obligations to the developer but also defines and limits the community's claims against the developer. Allowing the community to impose additional obligations upon the developer outside of those agreed to would harm the integrity of the siting process. For example, although there is no explicit statutory language on the subject, the legislature would not have required arbitration of the compensation issue[193] unless it intended for arbitration finally to decide that issue. Similarly, in forbidding communities to impose new permit requirements after the effective date of the Act,[194] the legislature intended to limit the power of local governments to impose obligations on developers beyond those explicitly stated in the Act. The purpose and theory of the Act is to provide an integrated package of mitigation, compensation, and monitoring measures for the host community; additional obligations are thus inconsistent with the Act.

Judicial Review.   The Massachusetts Act attempts to replace the prevailing pattern of extensive litigation over every siting proposal with a consensual process based on negotiation and compensation, or, if a consensus cannot be reached, with arbitration. Nonetheless, given the high stakes involved in siting hazardous waste facilities for both community and developer, some litigation is inevitable. Litigation may follow each of the major decisions mandated by the Act: the Council's decision on whether a project is feasible and deserving, the permit decisions of the local health board and the Department of Environmental Quality Engineering, the arbitrator's award, if any, and the Council's declaration that a siting agreement is operative. This part of this article discusses the scope of judicial review of each of these decisions.

The "Feasible and Deserving" Decision.   The Council must decide whether the proposal is "feasible and deserving of state assistance" within fifteen days after a developer submits a notice of intent.[195] The short time given the Council to make this decision indicates that the legislature did not intend the Council's review to be searching. The purpose of the review is only to screen out obviously inappropriate proposals using the criteria delineated in the regulations.[196] An affirmative decision merely allows the siting process to proceed; full economic, environmental, and social review does not occur until later in the siting process.[197]

The consequence of a negative decision is less clear. The proposed regulations suggest that the Council's feasibility determination is a necessary prerequisite to obtaining the assistance and using the procedures established by the Act.[198] Although nothing in the Act prevents a developer from negotiating a siting agreement with the host community without state assistance, such negotiations would probably fail if only because of the effect of a negative Council decision on local public opinion.[199] Moreover, if the proposal cannot survive the relatively modest hurdle provided by the feasible and deserving decision, it probably would not qualify for the necessary state permits and licenses.[200]

Judicial challenges to the Council's feasible and deserving decision are likely to come from two sources: a potential host community attacking an affirmative decision and a developer attacking a negative decision.[201] The Massachusetts Administrative Procedure Act makes judicial review available to any person aggrieved by a final agency decision.[202] This provision should bar a potential host community from seeking review of an affirmative decision. At this early stage of the siting process, the community is not aggrieved because it has suffered no injury. An affirmative decision merely requires the community to form a local assessment committee and negotiate with the developer; the state must underwrite the cost of this participation through technical assistance grants.[203] From the perspective of a community seeking to thwart construction, a final decision is not rendered until the Council declares that a siting agreement is operative and in full force and effect.

By contrast, after administrative appeals are exhausted, the developer should be able to obtain judicial review of a negative decision by the Council.[204] A negative determination has the effect of a final decision which terminates the statutory siting process.[205]

State and Local Permits.   Under the Siting Act, the Developer must obtain a site assignment permit from the local board of health.[206] If the board of health denies the permit, judicial review is available under an arbitrary and capricious standard.[207] If the board grants the permit, administrative review is available by an appeal to the Department of Environmental Quality Engineering.[208] If the Department rescinds or modifies the permit, its decision is reviewable in court under the arbitrary and capricious standard.[209] The statute is silent about judicial review of a decision by the Department to affirm the site assignment permit. The Siting Act, however, does not preclude review, and the agency action meets the other requirements of the Massachusetts Administrative Procedure Act, and hence courts would presumably grant judicial review and apply an arbitrary and capricious standard.[210]

After the developer acquires this initial permit, it is subject to rescission, suspension, or modification by the Department of Environmental Quality Engineering or the board of health.[211] This action is likewise reviewable in court under the arbitrary and capricious standard. There is similar review of the initial decision by the Department of Environmental Quality Engineering to grant a construction and operating license.[212]

Arbitration Awards.   Judicial review of an arbitration award under the Act differs substantially from review of state and local permit decisions. By incorporating the judicial review provisions of the Uniform Arbitration Act for Commercial Disputes,[213] the legislature sharply curtailed judicial review.[214] Unlike the Massachusetts Administrative Procedure Act, which permits a court to reverse agency action under the arbitrary and capricious standard, the Uniform Act allows courts to vacate an award made during compulsory arbitration only if the arbitrator has committed fraud, has shown demonstrable partiality, or has exceeded his or her powers.[215] The leading Massachusetts case interpreting this standard of review states that, absent this finding, courts will not overturn an arbitrator's award even if it contains gross errors of law or fact.[216] Thus, if courts apply the case law of commercial arbitration to the Siting Act, the awards will stand, absent fraud or demonstrable partiality, unless the arbitrator exceeded his or her powers by deciding an issue not submitted by the Council. The legislature apparently limited judicial review in this way in order to shorten the already lengthy siting process.[217]

The extensive judicial review of other decisions in the siting process alleviates concern that judicial review of the arbitration award is inadequate. For example, a community can withhold the facility's public health permit if it believes that the arbitrator's decision does not adequately protect the public health or safety.[218] If the developer contests this denial,[219] the community will have an opportunity to attack the arbitration award collaterally by showing that the facility does not meet the "comparable processes" standard for site assignment[220] or the standards for obtaining permits from the Department of Environmental Quality Engineering.[221] Similarly, if the community believes that it cannot comply with the arbitrator's order to provide services to the developer, it can plead illegality or impossibility as a defense in a contractual action brought by the developer to enforce the siting agreement.[222] In practice, therefore, the only part of the arbitration award not subject to collateral judicial review is the arbitrator's award of compensation to the community.

Case law reviewing other arbitration statutes, however, suggests that courts may require full judicial review of the arbitration award despite the statutory limitations. Courts have generally upheld the limited judicial review of arbitration because the parties voluntarily agreed to submit their dispute to arbitration.[223] Under the Siting Act, however, the parties do not agree to submit their differences to an arbitrator; arbitration is compulsory once the Council finds that negotiations have failed.[224] Courts have generally required a fuller review of compulsory than of voluntary arbitration.[225] For example, in upholding the Massachusetts compulsory labor arbitration statute, the Supreme Judicial Court emphasized availability of judicial review as an important safeguard against arbitrary action.[226]

Under closer scrutiny, however, the analogy between the Massachusetts Siting Act and the other compulsory arbitration statutes proves false. For example, the Massachusetts compulsory labor arbitration statute binds both the municipality and the union.[227] An egregious award could bankrupt the municipality or, conversely, threaten the integrity of the union. The Supreme Judicial Court was justifiably reluctant to sustain this substantial grant of power to a private arbitrator without the safety mechanism afforded by judicial review.[228] By contrast, the siting process does not impose affirmative obligations on the host community;[229] the community is deprived of property only to the extent that the social costs of the facility are not fully covered by the compensation agreement.

Because the case law construing arbitration statutes is inapplicable to the Siting Act, any challenge to the restrictions on judicial review of compensation agreements must be based on general due process grounds. An analysis of this argument must consider the nature of the community's interest in the compensation and the process, if any, that is due.

The due process clause applies when there has been a deprivation of a liberty or property interest.[230] Under recent Supreme Court cases, the community cannot obtain due process safeguards for its interest in being compensated under the Siting Act unless the Act created a "legitimate claim of *entitlement.*"[231] The Act suggests, but does not explicitly declare, that host communities are entitled to compensation.[232] Whether the statute's lack of specificity bars such a claim of entitlement[233] remains an open question.

Even a sufficiently clear entitlement, however, may not trigger the requirements of due process. Under the "bitter with the sweet" doctrine,[234] statutes which create an entitlement can also define the procedures by which those benefits are bestowed.[235] If courts applied this doctrine to the Siting Act, they would probably find that the legislative intent to minimize delay took precedence over the local community's claim of entitlement. Thus, the due process clause would not invalidate the Siting Act's restriction on judicial review.

Even if the local community has a constitutionally protected entitlement to compensation to which all procedural protections attach, however, full judicial review is not necessarily required. To determine what process is due, courts will balance the local community's interest in obtaining additional review of the compensation agreement against the interests of the state in expeditiously locating sites for hazardous waste facilities.[236] In these circumstances, the state interest is strong; each delay resulting from more stringent judicial review imposes substantial environmental costs and frustrates the statutory purpose to expedite siting. By contrast, the local community's interest in additional judicial review is relatively weak because of the other procedural protections in the Act: during negotiation, community participation is not only allowed but is funded by the state; during arbitration, the community participates in the selection of the arbitrator[237] and has the right to be heard, to be represented by counsel, to introduce evidence, and to cross-examine witnesses.[238] Furthermore, the Act already provides for extensive judicial review. The arbitration award is directly reviewable for fraud, demonstrable bias, and extension of the award beyond the issues rightfully submitted to arbitration. Mitigation measures to protect the public health are subject to de facto collateral review.[239] Thus, the due process clause should not impose additional judicial review requirements on the siting process.

Declaration that a Siting Agreement is Operational. Individuals or groups in a host community may challenge the siting agreement by attacking the Council's declaration that the agreement is operative.[240] There is, however, little in the Council's decision for a court to review. The Council should not impose additional conditions on a negotiated siting agreement beyond those specified in the permits and licenses issued by the relevant regulatory bodies.[241] Courts should thus limit their review of the Council's declaration to determining whether the negotiation process was conducted according to the procedural requirements of the Act. The legislature carefully designed a process for ensuring balanced representation on the local assessment committee and exposing the fruits of the committee's labor to public scrutiny. The courts should respect this process.

THE MASSACHUSETTS APPROACH IN PRACTICE: A CRITIQUE

As of early 1982, potential facility developers have filed three notices of intent with the Council.[242] The project that has advanced the farthest is a proposal to build a solvent recovery facility on the banks of the Merrimack River in Haverhill.[243] The developer completed the preliminary project impact report in January and negotiations are expected to begin sometime in the spring.[244] The local government formed a local assessment committee for the Haverhill site, which so far has received $40,000 in technical assistance grants from the Council.[245] The second notice of intent is a proposal by IT Corporation to build a multipurpose waste processing facility in Warren.[246] The developer is considering two sites, one of which is on state-owned land.[247] The third notice of intent was a proposal by Cyclotech Corporation to construct a hazardous waste recycling facility in Gardner.[248]

Local groups and governments have attacked all three proposals as well as the Siting Act itself. In Gardner, local opposition led the developer to agree to abide by the results of a referendum on the proposed facility. Gardner voters rejected the proposed facility by nearly a three to one margin. The developer is now seeking an alternative site in Massachusetts or a neighboring state.[249] In Haverhill, the city has sought judicial review of the Council's affirmative "feasible and deserving" vote.[250] In Warren, the town has tried to exploit an apparent loophole in the Act by adopting a by-law that prohibits hazardous waste facilities within its boundaries.[251] These first three proposals have revealed one of the major shortcomings of the Act: the feasible and deserving decision.

The legislature intended that the feasible and deserving decision would screen out only obviously inappropriate proposals,[252] and that substantive review on the merits of a proposal would occur later in the siting process. Accordingly, the legislature gave the Council only fifteen days to determine whether a proposal is feasible and deserving of state assistance; the consequence of an affirmative decision is simply to make the local assessment committee eligible for technical assistance grants and to allow the proposal to proceed into the next stage of the siting process.

Unfortunately, however, the Council has been unable to convey to the public the limited nature of this initial review. Residents of both Haverhill and Warren urged the Council to resolve important substantive issues before making the "feasible and deserving" decision. The Council has declined to do so, citing the substantive review that the Act provides in later stages of the siting process. Facility opponents, however, have harshly criticized the Council for giving its "approval" to proposals while ignoring legitimate concerns raised by the interested public.

This problem is not unique to the Massachusetts statute. Because of the publicity attending hazardous waste disasters like Love Canal, local residents are understandably wary of proposals to build new facilities. They tend to form judgments about the merits of proposals quickly and permanently. Moreover, questions on the merits of a proposal are more easily raised than answered. Consequently, criticism of preliminary screening devices is inevitable. Perhaps a better means of screening out frivolous proposals would be to require that the developer pay an initial fee when filing the notice of intent.[253] By delaying the first administrative review of the merits of a proposal until later in the process, the fee might have the salutary effect of discouraging formation of adversary relationships at an early stage.

Massachusetts is trying to create a public climate conducive to siting new facilities through a statewide educational campaign that stresses the benefits provided by safe, legal disposal as well as the hazards from continued illegal dumping.[254] Furthermore, the state has tried to legitimize the use of compensation negotiations in the siting process. Whether the combined effects of the educational campaign and the incentives offered through the negotiation process are sufficient to overcome local opposition remains to be seen.

The intense criticisms of the first three proposals filed under the Massachusetts statute should not be interpreted as an indictment of the Massachusetts approach. None of the proposals under consideration has yet reached the negotiation stage. Moreover, the Massachusetts statute, unlike the preemption statutes, does not attempt to ignore local opposition but rather to incorporate it into the siting process. If the costs of a proposal outweigh its benefits, then it should be defeated by local opposition.

In practice, only allowing the siting process to run its course will prove or disprove the central assumption of the Massachusetts statute: that the costs associated with hazardous waste facilities are compensable. Because Massachusetts is interested in developing only a handful of sites, it is not necessary that social costs be compensable in each of the Commonwealth's 351 cities and towns for the Act to fulfill its purposes. If that assumption ultimately proves erroneous, then states will face the difficult question of whether to force communities to accept facilities. The answer may be that the state has no other choice. Nonetheless, efficiency and fairness suggest that even unwilling communities should receive compensation. Even if it is impossible to make a community whole, the state should not impute a zero value to the social costs incurred. If a state must ultimately rely upon some form of preemption, it should still incorporate some provision for compensation. The Massachusetts statute does this by providing for compensation even in the event of an arbitrated siting agreement.

Conclusion

This article began by contrasting two different approaches to the problems posed by local opposition to the siting of hazardous waste facilities: preemption and compensation. Preemption addresses only part of the problem; it inhibits local opposition by stripping away some of the most effective tactics of facility opponents, but it does not render them impotent. "Solving" the local opposition problem through the blunt instrument of preemption may ultimately prove ineffective if it encourages facility opponents to turn to other tactics such as litigation, political organization, and civil disobedience.

By contrast, the incentives approach attempts to come to grips with the underlying causes of local opposition. In theory, this approach is superior in terms of equity, efficiency, and political acceptability. It is much easier, however, to articulate the rationale behind this approach than it is to design an administrative mechanism to make it work. The Massachusetts statute, while ambitious, rests on theoretical assumptions of questionable empirical validity and contains enough ambiguity to keep the Massachusetts courts busy for some time to come.

With all of its faults, the Massachusetts statute is still an admirable attempt to solve one of society's most perplexing problems. A final judgment of the relative merits of the various approaches to the problem of local opposition will have to await complete implementation and evaluation. If each fails, we will have to reexamine seriously the institutional capacity of state and local governments to address this crucial environmental problem.

Notes

This research was supported by a grant from the Center for Energy Policy Research of the Massachusetts Institute of Technology.

1. Over 90% of the industrial hazardous wastes in the United States have been disposed in a manner actually or potentially harmful to the environment. U.S. Envtl. Protection Agency, Draft Environmental Impact Statement for Subtitle C, at V-36 (Jan. 1979). Major hazards resulting from improper hazardous waste disposal include explosions and fires, M. Brown, Laying Waste: The Poisoning of America by Toxic Chemicals 155-56 (1979), and contamination through leachate of the underground aquifers that feed city water supplied, *id.* at 100-27. Such contamination has forced 29 public water supplies in Massachusetts to close. Menzies, *In Search of a Waste Solution,* Boston Globe, Jan. 18, 1982, at 15, col. 4. Other ways hazardous wastes cause damage include surface contamination from runoff, air pollution through open burning, evaporation, direct contact with hazardous substances, and contamination of the food chain. Subcomm. on Transportation and Commerce of the House Comm. on Interstate and Foreign Commerce, 94th Cong., 2d Sess., Materials Relating to the Resource Conservation and Recovery Act of 1976, at 40-42 (Comm. Print No. 20, 1976) [hereinafter cited as 1976 House RCRA Materials]. The public health dangers of hazardous wastes are substantial: "Hazardous wastes can be toxic, carcinogenic, mutagenic, teratogenic, radioactive, flammable, explosive, biologically persistent, and can accumulate in living organisms." Wolf, *Public Opposition to Hazardous Waste Sites: The Self-Defeating Approach to National Hazardous Waste Control Under Subtitle C of the Resource Conservation and Recovery Act of 1976,* 8 B.C. Envtl. Aff. L. Rev. 463, 467-68 (1980).

2. Love Canal is an abandoned waste dump at Niagara Falls, New York. New York State was forced to evacuate six residential blocks that had been contaminated by toxic fumes and leachate escaping from 20,000 tons of chemical wastes. M. Brown, *supra* note 1, at 5, 28-40. Residents suffered property damage and severe health effects, including chemical burns, chromosome damage, high incidence of spontaneous abortion, and a cancer rate 30 times the national average. Cleanup costs are in the hundreds of millions of dollars. *See Hazardous and Toxic Waste Disposal: Joint Hearings Before the Subcomm. on Environmental Pollution and the Subcomm. on Resource Protection of the Senate Comm. on Environmental and Public Works Part 1,* 96th Cong., 1st Sess. 8-25, 104-232 (1979) [hereinafter cited as *1979 Senate Hearings*]: Wolf, *supra* note 1, at 467 n.13; [10 Curr. Dev.] Env't Rep. (BNA) 27 (May 5, 1979).

3. *See* National Conference of State Legislatures, Hazardous Waste Management: A Survey of State Laws 1976-1980, at II-1 (1980).

4. Resource Conservation and Recovery Act of 1976, 42 U.S.C.A. §§ 6901-6987 (West 1977 and Supp. 1981). Subtitle C of RCRA, *id.* §§ 6921-6931, directs EPA to establish a "cradle to grave" program for regulating hazardous waste, including their transportation, storage, treatment, and disposal.

5. Nationally, about 47.5 million metric tons of the 344 million metric tons of total industrial wastes generated yearly are potentially hazardous. U.S. Envtl. Protection Agency, *supra* note 1, at VI-2. In Massachusetts alone, 100 million gallons of hazardous waste are produced annually. Massachusetts Dep't of Envtl. Management, Preliminary Hazardous Waste Facility Siting Guide 3 (Oct. 1981).

6. *See* U.S. Envtl. Protection Agency, *supra* note 1, at VII-32 to -38.

7. Specifically, the Resource Conservation and Recovery Act will increase the amount of wastes defined as hazardous. U.S. Envtl. Protection Agency, *supra* note 1,

at VII-32 to -38; U.S. Gen. Accounting Office, How to Dispose of Hazardous Waste— A Serious Question That Needs to Be Resolved 9-10 (1978) (Doc. No. CED-79-13). Furthermore, EPA has emphasized enforcement against on-site facilities, thereby deliberately forcing waste to off-site facilities. [9 Curr. Dev.] Env't Rep. (BNA) 2295 (Apr. 6, 1979). Even equality of regulation and enforcement between on-site facilities, however, would eliminate the earlier cost advantages of under-regulated on-site facilities, and, in fact, economics of scale may favor off-site facilities. Subcomm. on Oversight and Investigations of the House Comm. on Interstate and Foreign Commerce, 96th Cong., 1st Sess., Report on Hazardous Waste Disposal 26 (Comm. Print No. 96-IFC31, 1979) [hereinafter cited as 1979 House Report]; U.S. Envtl. Protection Agency, *supra* note 1, at VII-33.

8. Statistics point to the acute shortage of environmentally suitable hazardous waste facilities. Wolf, *supra* note 1, at 465. In 1977, EPA estimated that the capacity shortfall for off-site facilities stood at 1.7 million tons. U.S. Envtl. Protection Agency, *supra* note 1, at V-35; U.S. Gen. Accounting Office, *supra* note 7, at 5-7. The Massachusetts Special Commission on Hazardous Waste estimates that only eight percent of Massachusetts' waste can be properly disposed in-state. Massachusetts Special Comm'n on Hazardous Waste, Procedures and Guidelines for Siting Hazardous Waste Facilities in the Commonwealth at xi-xii (June 25, 1980) (First Interim Report). Furthermore, projected increases in hazardous waste production will exacerbate the shortage. During the period 1974-1983, total waste generation from the 14 major industrial hazardous waste generating groups is expected to grow 29%. 1976 House RCRA Materials, *supra* note 1, at 22-25.

9. EPA projected that, by 1984, the shortfall in off-site hazardous waste capacity will increase to 2.6 million metric tons unless at least 46 new off-site facilities are built. U.S. Envtl. Protection Agency, *supra* note 1, at V-35; *see also* U.S. Gen. Accounting Office, *supra* note 7, at 5-7. More recently, Representative James J. Florio, citing an EPA study, estimated that 50 to 125 new off-site waste disposal facilities will be needed by 1985 as new regulations force old facilities to close and old waste sites are cleaned up under Superfund. [12 Curr. Dev.] Env't Rep. (BNA) 315 (July 3, 1981).

10. *See* Massachusetts Special Comm'n on Hazardous Waste, *supra* note 8, at xiii.

11. *See* Centaur Assoc., Siting of Hazardous Waste Management Facilities and Public Operation 9-16 (Nov. 1979) (report prepared for the Office of Solid Waste, EPA).

12. *Siting of Hazardous Waste Management Facilities: A Major Problem Facing Industry and States,* [12 Curr. Dev.] Env't Rep. (BNA) 871, 872 (Nov. 13, 1981) (Special Report, citing claim of EPA and the National Solid Waste Management Association) [hereinafter cited as *BNA Special Report*]. Two on-site facilities in Michigan, however, have recently been sited. *Id.* at 873.

13. Midnight dumping refers to intentional, illicit disposal of hazardous wastes; for example, dumping on property of others, stockpiling wastes on leased land which is subsequently abandoned, and discarding wastes in sewer systems, lakes, or rivers. *See* M. Brown, *supra* note 1, at 243-53, 260-65; National League of Cities, Unwitting Disposal Imperils the Chain of Life (Apr. 23, 1979) (Environmental Report).

Spectacular examples of illegal hazardous waste dumping abound. *E.g.,* 1979 House Report, *supra* note 7, at 9-18 (description of the "Valley of the Drums" in Shepardsville, Ky., where a waste dealer illegally dumped over 17,000 barrels of hazardous waste on a 23 acre site); *1979 Senate Hearings, supra* note 2, at 84-85 (statement of Thomas C. Jorling, Assistant Administrator for Water and Waste Management, EPA, about the dumping of PCBs along 210 miles of rural North Carolina highways).

14. *BNA Special Report, supra* note 12, at 872.

15. States have become the primary government level involved with siting; the federal government has no direct authority to become involved because RCRA is silent on the siting issue. *Id.* at 871 (statement of Jeffrey Goodman, Chief, Analysis Branch, Office of Solid Waste, EPA). Local governments do not adequately represent the need for sites because they have a vested interest in representing the viewpoint of the surrounding community. *Id.* at 872.

16. Massachusetts Hazardous Waste Facilities Siting Act, ch. 508, 1980 Mass. Acts 673 (codified in scattered chapters of Mass. Gen. Laws Ann. (West)).

17. This discussion is adapted from M. O'Hare, D. Sanderson & L. Bacow, Sticks, Carrots and the Siting Problem, ch 5 (forthcoming).

For other general discussions of local opposition to hazardous waste facilities, see J. Duberg, M. Frankel & C. Neimczewski, Understanding Public Concern Over Hazardous Waste Disposal Sites (1979) (prepared by Centaur Associates); U.S. Gen. Accounting Office, *supra* note 7. Local opposition is generally successful. *Id.* at 13-15. "[W]e know no one wants a landfill program in their backyard and that communities object to hazardous waste facilities in their midst." *Resource Conservation and Recovery Act: Oversight Hearing Before the Subcomm. on Resource Protection of the Senate Comm. on Environment and Public Works,* 95th Cong., 2d Sess. 2 (1978) (statement of Sen. Culver).

18. *See supra* text accompanying notes 11-12; U.S. Envtl. Protection Agency, Hazardous Waste Facility Siting: A Critical Problem 3 (July 1980).

19. Over 90% of the industrial hazardous wastes in the United States have been disposed in a manner actually or potentially harmful to the environment. U.S. Envtl. Protection Agency, *supra* note 1, at V-36. *See also* U.S. Council on Envtl. Quality, Environmental Quality—1980, at 214-16 (1980) (11th Annual Report); Wolf, *supra* note 1 at 467 n. 13.

20. *See, e.g.,* Wolf, *supra* note 1, at 467 n. 13 (descriptions of the Love Canal incident). Patrick P. McCurdy, public issues manager of Dow Chemical Company, has stated that the press often "inflames" the hazardous waste issue, thereby exacerbating local opposition, [12 Curr. Dev.] Env't Rep. (BNA) 316 (July 3, 1981). *See also* U.S. Gen. Accounting Office, *supra* note 7, at 10.

21. Wolf, *supra* note 1, at 467.

22. 42 U.S.C.A. § § 6901-6987 (1976 & West Supp. 1981).

23. [12 Curr. Dev.] Env't Rep. (BNA) 283 (June 26, 1981) (statement of James R. Janis, ICS Inc.). An EPA policy paper states that "[t]his opposition is based on fear, and is generally characterized by extremely strong emotions, broad participation, and a willingness to commit time and resources in the effort to forestall or close a site." U.S. Envtl. Protection Agency, *supra* note 18, at 3.

24. National Governors' Ass'n, *Siting Hazardous Waste Facilities,* 3 The Envtl. Prof. 133, 134 (1981).

25. National Conference of State Legislatures, *supra* note 3, at II-1.

26. *See* M. Olson, The Logic of Collective Action: Public Goods and the Theory of Groups (1971); Wilson, *The Politics of Regulation,* in Social Responsibility and the Business Predicament (J. McKie ed. 1974); L. Bacow, Creating Markets for Development Externalities 2 (July 1980) (M.I.T. Energy Laboratory Working Paper).

27. *BNA Special Report, supra* note 12, at 871.

28. Another disincentive to public support for hazardous waste facilities is that the facilities are a collective good whose benefits cannot be denied to non-participating consumers. Consequently, rational consumers will undertake no effort to obtain the good. *See, e.g.,* R. Stewart & J. Krier, Environmental Law and Policy 107-09 (2d ed. 1978).

29. *See* Massachusetts Special Comm'n on Hazardous Waste, *supra* note 8, at x-xi; Cohen & Derkics, *Financial Responsibility for Hazardous Waste Sites, 9 Cap. U.L. Rev.* 509, 509-10 (1980); [12 Curr. Dev.] *Env't Rep.* (BNA) 283 (June 26, 1981). There are also technological aspects to siting hazardous waste facilities, especially landfills. *See generally* Senkan & Stauffer, *What to Do with Hazardous Waste, Tech. Rev.,* Nov.-Dec. 1981, at 34, 46.

30. The existence, locus, and nature of such authority, of course, varies with the jurisdiction.

31. Local public officials have a vested interest in the community and generally represent the local consensus. *BNA Special Report, supra* note 12, at 872.

32. *See* Wolf, *supra* note 1, at 485.

When a facility was recently proposed in the town of Warren, Massachusetts, residents quickly passed a by-law prohibiting hazardous waste facilities within town limits. For an account of the Warren siting effort, see *infra* text accompanying notes 246-47, 251. For a discussion of the legality of such a by-law, see *Infra* text accompanying notes 157-60.

For a useful overview of various siting efforts across the country, see Centaur Assoc., *supra* note 11. One conclusion the report reached is that "[i]f these [local regulatory] controls can hold veto power over site development, then the primary role of local jurisdiction will be to block siting attempts." *Id.* at 31.

Because most proposals to site hazardous waste facilities are dropped before full litigation by the parties, it is difficult to identify any one cause of each failed attempt. Still, local regulatory control appears to have been a major factor in many instances. For example, Minnesota recently abandoned its attempts to site a facility, after the commissioners for the proposed host counties passed resolutions banning site development in their areas. U.S. Gen. Accounting Office, *supra* note 7, at 13. The state siting agency dropped all plans to use any of the sites. *Id.*

In at least one case, a town was able to block facility development solely through the use of its regulatory powers. Even in the face of a statute that reasonably could be interpreted to preempt local authority, the Wisconsin courts held that a town could block a proposed facility through local zoning. *See* Nelson v. Department of Natural Resources, 88 Wis. 2d 1, 276 N.W. 2d 302 (Wis. Ct. App. 1979), *aff'd,* 96 Wis. 2d 730, 292 N.W.2d 655 (Wis. 1980).

33. In Brentwood, California, for example, IT Corporation seems to have dropped its plans for a proposed facility because the county planning commission denied a needed land use permit. Centaur Assoc., *supra* note 11, at 233.

34. U.S. Gen. Accounting Office, *supra* note 7, at 12. For a discussion of incentives for state to undertake such a role, see Florini, *Issues of Federalism in Hazardous Waste Control: Cooperation or Confusion?,* 6 Harv. Envtl. L. Rev. 307, 324 (1982).

35. *See infra* text accompanying notes 37-48.

36. *See infra* text accompanying notes 78-87 (other states), 88-146 (Massachusetts).

37. *See* National Conference of State Legislatures, *supra* note 3; National Governors' Ass'n, Abstracts of State Hazardous Waste Siting Laws (Oct. 1981). These statutes vary substantially: under some statutes, states initiate the siting process; under others, the developer initiates the process. Typically, the statutes establish siting approval procedures, which may include approval boards, preemptive authority over local laws, state acquisition, construction, operation, and maintenance of facilities, negotiations between communities and developers, and economic incentives. *BNA Special Report, supra* note 12, at 873.

The states with preemption authority include: Arizona, Ariz. Rev. Stat. Ann. § § 36-2801 to -2805 (supp. 1981); Connecticut, Hazardous Waste Facilities Siting Act, Pub. Act No. 81-369, 1981 Conn. Legis. Serv. 1153 (West) (to be codified at Conn. Gen. Stat. tit. 22a, ch. 445); Florida, Fla. Stat. § 403.723 (1981); Indiana, Ind. Code § 13-7-8.6-13 (Supp. 1981); Iowa, Hazardous Wastes Act, ch. 152, 1981 Iowa Acts 509 (to be codified at Iowa Code § 455B); Kansas, Kan. Stat. Ann. § § 65-3430 to -3448 (Supp. 1981); Maine, Me. Rev. Stat. Ann. tit. 38, § 1305-A (Supp. 1981); Maryland, Md. Nat. Res. Code Ann. § § 3-701 to -713 (Supp. 1981); Michigan, Mich. Comp. Laws Ann. § § 299.501-.551 (Supp. 1981); Minnesota, Minn. Stat. § § 115A.18-.30 (1980 & Supp. 1981); New Jersey, Major Hazardous Waste Facility Siting Act, ch. 279, 1981 N.J. Sess. Law Serv. 814 (West) (to be codified at N.J. Rev. Stat. § § 13:1E-49 to -91); New York, N.Y. Envtl. Conserv. Law § § 27-1101 to -1107 (McKinney Supp. 1981); North Carolina, N.C. Gen. Stat. § 104E-6.2 (Supp. 1981); Ohio, Ohio Rev. Code Ann. § 3734.02 (Page Supp. 1981); Pennsylvania, Pa. Stat. Ann. tit. 35, § § 6018.101-.1003 (Purdon Supp. 1981); Washington, Wash. Rev. Code § § 70.105.010-.140 (1981); Wisconsin, Wis. Stat. § § 144.44-.445 (1980). The Massachusetts statute includes some preemptive aspects, but it takes an innovative approach. *See infra* text accompanying notes 88-146.

Other hazardous waste siting statutes include: Georgia, Ga. Code Ann. § § 43-2901a to -2914a (Supp. 1981); Illinois, Environmental Protection Act Amendments, Pub. Acts No. 82-572, 1981 Ill. Legis. Serv. 2541 (West) (to be codified at Ill. Rev. Stat. ch. 111.5, § 1039); Kentucky, Ky. Rev. Stat. § § 244.855-.884 (Supp. 1980); Nebraska, Neb. Rev. Stat. § § 81-1521.02 to .07 (Supp. 1980); Oregon, Or. Rev. Stat. § § 459.410-.690 (1979); Tennessee, Tenn. Code Ann. § § 53-6301 to -6306 (Supp. 1981); Utah, Utah Code Ann. § § 26-14a-1 to -9 (Supp. 1981).

38. *See* Ind. Code § 13-7-8.6-13 (Supp. 1981); Hazardous Wastes Act, ch. 152, § 11, 1981 Iowa Acts 509, 514; Kan. Stat. Ann. § 65-3438 (Supp. 1981); Md. Nat. Res. Code Ann. § 115A.29(2) (Supp. 1981); Major Hazardous Waste Facility Siting

Act, ch. 279, § 15, 1981, N.J. Sess. Law Serv. 814, 825 (West) (to be codified at N.J. Rev. Stat. § 13:1E-63); N.C. Gen. Stat. § 130-166.17B (Supp. 1981); Ohio Rev. Code Ann. § 3734.05(D)(3) (Page Supp. 1981); Wash. Rev. Code § 70.105.040 (1981); Wis. Stat. § 144.64(4)(1980). The severity of this comprehensive preemption is mitigated in various ways. *See infra* text accompanying notes 41-48.

39. *See* Ariz. Rev. Stat. Ann. § § 36-2801 to -2805 (Supp. 1981); Hazardous Waste Facilities Siting Act, Pub. Act No. 81-369, § 13(b), 1981 Conn. Legis. Serv. 1153, 1171 (West) (to be codified at Conn. Gen. Stat. § 22a-124(b)); Fla. Stat. § 403.723 (1981); N.Y. Envtl. Conserv. Law § § 27-1101 to -1107 (McKinney Supp. 1981); Pa. Stat. Ann. tit. 35, § 6018.105(g) (Purdon Supp. 1981).

40. Me. Rev. Stat. Ann. tit. 38, § 1305-A (Supp. 1981). The lack of an explicit administrative override appears to necessitate judicial intervention to resolve state-local disputes.

The North Carolina statute also directly limits the positive authority of localities, but establishes a mechanism that can override the state preemption. N.C. Gen. Stat. § 130-166.17B (Supp. 1981).

41. Mich. Comp. Laws Ann. § 299.520(8) (Supp. 1981). *See also* Kan. Stat. Ann. § 65-3434(g)(4) Supp. 1981); Me. Rev. Stat. Ann. tit. 38, § 1305-A(1) (Supp. 1981); Mich. Comp. Laws Ann. § 299-.520(7)(d) (Supp. 1981).

42. N.C. Gen. Stat. § 130-166.17B (Supp. 1981). The developer petitions the Waste Management Board to have the state exercise its preemption authority. The Board makes a recommendation to the Governor, who has the final decision.

43. Fla. Stat. § 403.723 (1981). An advisory council recently recognized the need to change the override authority to include the preemption of the regional councils, which are in fact composed of local officials. *See* National Governors' Ass'n, State Siting Programs in Effect as of January 1, 1982, at 3 (Jan. 25, 1982).

44. *See* Hazardous Waste Facilities Siting Act, Pub. Act No. 81-369, § 13(b), 1981 Conn. Legis. Serv. 1153, 1171 (West) (to be codified at Conn. Gen. Stat. § 22a-124(b)). The state council does have exclusive authority "in regard to any question of public safety and necessity." *Id.* § 13(a).

45. N.Y. Envtl. Conserv. Law § § 27-1105(2)(f), -1107 (McKinney Supp. 1981).

46. Wash. Rev. Code § 70.10.040 (1981).

47. There are several variations on public hearing requirements. For example, in Arizona there is no special hearing before preemption by the legislature, but there must be a hearing prior to the site selection process. Ariz. Rev. Stat. Ann § 36-2802 (Supp. 1981). In Connecticut, hearings are provided for in the state permitting process, but no hearings are required for the explicit override procedures accomplished through appeals to the relevant state agency. Hazardous Waste Facilities Siting Act, Pub. Act No. 81-369, § § 22a-119, -124).

48. Hazardous Waste Facilities Siting Act, Pub. Act No. 81-369, § 3, 1981 Conn. Legis. Serv. 1153, 1155-56 (West) (to be codified at Conn. Gen. Stat. § 16-50) (both general public and local representation); Ind. Code § 13-7-8.6-3 (Supp. 1981) (local representation); Hazardous Wastes Act, ch. 152 § 4, 1981 Iowa Acts 509, 511 (to be codified at Iowa Code § 455B.135) (local representation); Kan. Stat. Ann. § 65-3432 (Supp. 1981) (general public representation); Me Rev. Stat. Ann. tit. 38, § 1305-A(2) (Supp. 1981) (local representation); Md. Nat. Res. Code Ann. § 3-703 (Supp. 1981)

(general public representation); Mich. Comp. Laws Ann. § 299.517 (Supp. 1981) (local representation); Minn. Stat. § 115A.05, .22, .34 (1980 & Supp. 1981) (local representation); Major Hazardous Waste Facilities Siting Act, ch. 279, § 4, 1981 N.J. Sess. Law Serv. 814, 816 (West) (to be codified at N.J. Rev. Stat. § 13:1E-52) (general public representation); N.Y. Envtl. Conserv. Law § 27-1107(2)(d) (McKinney Supp. 1981) (local representation); N.C. Gen. Stat. § 130-166.17B(9) (Supp. 1981) (local representation); Pa. Stat. Ann. tit. 35, § 6018.507(b) (Purdon Supp. 1981) (general public representation).

Some states have more than one siting body. In New Jersey, for example, both the Hazardous Waste Facilities Siting Commission, which has public representation, and the Department of Environmental Protection have regulatory power over a proposed facility. Major Hazardous Waste Facilities Siting Act, ch. 279 §§ 3-12, 1981 N.J. Sess. Law Serv. 814, 815-25 (West) (to be codified at N.J. Rev. Stat. §§ 13:1E-51 to ¯60).

In general, the public representatives serve as full voting members; the only exception is Maine, in which the legislative body of the affected community appoints four non-voting local representatives.

49. Some state statutes, however, prohibit localities from placing undue restrictions on transportation of waste to the facility. *E.g.,* Ind. Code § 13-7-8.6-13 (Supp. 1981); Hazardous Waste Act, ch. 152, § 11, 1981 Iowa Acts 509, 514 (to be codified at Iowa Code § 455B).

50. Substantive ambiguity in the preemption statute may lead to litigation. *See e.g.,* Nelson v. Department of Natural Resources, 88 Wis. 2d 1, 276 N.W.2d 302 (Wis. CT. App. 1979) aff'd, 96 Wis. 2d 730, 292 N.W.2d 655 (Wis. 1980).

51. For example, the Resource Conservation and Recovery Act requires that all owners and operators of hazardous waste facilities obtain permits. 42 U.S.C. § 6925(a) (1976 & Supp. III 1979). Other possible litigation theories include challenges to permits under the Clean Water Act, 33 U.S.C. §§ 1251-1376 (1976 & Supp. III 1979), and compliance with the ambient air quality standards of the Clean Air Act, 42 U.S.C. §§ 7401-7626 (Supp. III 1979). For a discussion of the use of environmental disclosure requirements as a tool of delay, see Bacow, *The Technical and Judgmental Dimensions of Impact Assessment,* 1 EIA Rev. 109 (1980).

52. For an example of legal battles arising from the public participation process, see the Bordentown, New Jersey case study in Centaur Assoc., *supra* note 11, at 157.

53. Langier, *Voluntary Approach to Hazardous Waste Disposal,* Boston Globe, July 7, 1980, at 13, col. 2. Representative Nicholas Costello (D-Amesbury), Representative Theodore Alexio (D-Taunton), and Senator Robert Wetmore (D-Barre) introduced legislation to exempt Amesbury, Taunton, and Sturbridge from consideration as potential locations for hazardous waste facilities.

54. *See* Wolf, *supra* note 1, at 491. This problem is exacerbated if representatives of local interests sit on state siting boards, *see supra* note 48, or if state siting statutes require consideration of local interests, see *supra* text accompanying notes 41-46.

55. For example, three Massachusetts legislators succeeded in exempting communities they represented from the preemption approach. *See supra* text accompanying note 53.

56. *See PBB (Polybrominated Biphenyls) Pollution Problem in Michigan: Hearings Before the Subcomm. on Water Resources of the House Comm. on Public Works and Transportation,* 96th Cong., 1st Sess. (1979); U.S. Council on Envtl. Quality, Environmental Quality—1977, at 3 (1977) (8th Annual Report).

57. Centaur Assoc., *supra* note 11, at 307.

58. M. Brown, *supra* note 1, at 62.

59. Only two preemption statutes predate 1980. No off-site disposal facility has been sited, however, since 1979. The only documented use of preemption authority under the siting statutes took place in Michigan in late 1981 when the state siting board approved two on-site facilities, a landfill in the town of Midland and an incinerator in the town of Muskegon. *See supra* note 12; National Governors' Ass'n, *supra* note 43, at 11. At the time of the writing of this article, these facilities had not yet been built.

60. *See supra* text accompanying notes 17-29.

61. For example, two communities in Massachusetts competed to obtain a regional resource recovery facility after the state offered compensation to the host community; communities had shunned the proposed facility before the state made the compensation offer. *See* L. Bacow & D. Sanderson, Facility Siting and Compensation: A Handbook for Communities and Developers 75 (Sept. 1980) (M.I.T. Energy Laboratory Working Paper).

62. Even without a state statute the developer and the public at large that benefited from the proposed facility could in theory bargain with the neighbors of the proposed facility to compensate them for accepting it. *See* Coase, *The Problem of Social Cost,* 3 J.L. & Econ. 1 (1960); R. Stewart & J. Krier, *supra* note 28, at 133-40 (an application of Coase's analysis). Transaction costs, however, prevent this bargaining from actually taking place. In the absence of a state statute, the developer would first have to organize the parties for negotiation, which is particularly costly given the dispersed beneficiaries of the project, and would then need to propose terms for agreement and conduct the actual negotiation.

63. Essentially, the incentive approach internalizes the external costs of the facility by requiring the developer to compensate for those costs, thereby bringing about a more efficient allocation of resources. *See* R. Stewart & J. Krier, *supra* note 28, at 113-16.

64. *BNA Special Report, supra* note 12, at 874.

65. Centaur Assoc., *supra* note 11, at 22-23; Farkas, *Overcoming Public Opposition to the Establishment of New Hazardous Waste Disposal Sites,* 9 Cap. U.L. Rev. 451, 458 (1980).

66. *See* Bacow & Cohen, *Avoiding the Trials of Big Development,* Tech. Rev., Jan. 1982, at 42 (discussion of attempts to mitigate the effects of large-scale development by compensation and negotiation).

67. *See, e.g.,* R. Ridker, Economic Costs of Air Pollution (1967); R. Thaler & S. Rosen, The Value of Saving a Life: Evidence from the Labor Market, NBER Conference on Income and Wealth, Household Production and Consumption, Washington, D.C. (Nov. 30, 1973).

68. R. Thaler & S. Rosen, *supra* note 67.

69. *Id.*

70. This argument is developed in more depth in L. Bacow, *supra* note 26, at 6-12.

71. *Id.* at 10-12.

72. *See* M. O'Hare, D. Sanderson & L. Bacow, *supra* note 17.

73. *See* L. Bacow & D. Sanderson, *supra* note 61, at 42-43.

74. In economic terms, they maximize subject to a constraint without ever explicitly calculating its shadow price.

75. *See* R. Stewart & J. Krier, *supra* note 28, at 183-95; Stone, *Should Trees Have Standing?—Toward Legal Rights for Natural Objects,* 45 S. Cal. L. Rev. 450 (1972).

76. Other people believe that it is correct to pursue economic efficiency, but argue that discounting future benefits to present value is not appropriate in the environmental context. *See* T. Page, Conservation and Economic Efficiency (1978); R. Stewart & J. Krier, *supra* note 28, at 173-79; Ehrenfeld, *The Conservation of Non-Resources,* 64 Am. Scientist 648 (1976). Instead, there may be an obligation to save and preserve environmental goods for future generations. *See* J. Passmore, Man's Responsibility for Nature 78-80, 87-88 (1974). For a general discussion of the issue of intergenerational sacrifice, see J. Rawls, A Theory of Justice 284-93 (1970).

77. *E.g.,* Opinion of the Justices, 341 Mass. 760, 168 N.E.2d 858 (1960); *see also* D. Kretzmer, Legal Problems of Binding Communities to Compensation Agreements for Adverse Effects of Energy Facilities (1979) (M.I.T. Laboratory for Architecture and Planning).

78. The state siting statutes adopting the incentives approach are:

Connecticut: An applicant facility pays a filing fee of up to $30,000, which is disbursed to the local project review committee to obtain technical assistance for their review. Hazardous Waste Facilities Siting Act, Pub. Act No. 81-369, § 15, 1981 Conn. Legis. Serv. 1153, 1175 (West) (to be codified at Conn. Gen. Stat. tit. 22a, ch. 445).

An operating facility either pays an assessment based on gross receipts or negotiates a package of incentives with the local project review committee. *Id.* § 16, 1981 Conn. Leg. Serv. at 1175-76 (West) (to be codified at Conn. Gen. Stat. tit. 22a, ch. 445).

Georgia: The host county receives a one percent gross receipts tax. Ga. Code Ann. § 43-2905a (Supp. 1981).

Indiana: The host county receives $.50 per ton of waste disposed in the county. Ind. Code § 6-6-6.6 (Supp. 1981).

Kentucky: The host county may collect a license fee from off-site hazardous waste facilities of up to two percent of gross receipts to defer general revenue requirements. Ky. Rev. Stat. § 68.178 (1980).

Maine: The host municipality may, by ordinance, levy a fee on a commercial hazardous waste facility of up to two percent of the facility's gross receipts. Me. Rev. Stat. Ann. tit. 38, § 1305-A(3) (Supp. 1981).

Massachusetts: The host community and the developer negotiate a compensation package. Mass. Gen. Laws Ann. ch. 21D, § 12 (West 1981); *see infra* text accompanying notes 88-146.

New Jersey: The affected municipality may collect a five percent tax on a facility's gross receipts to fund local fire, police, inspection, road repair, and other expenses directly related to the facility. The state siting commission may change the amount. Major Hazardous Waste Facility Siting Act, ch. 279, § 32, 1981 N.J. Sess. Law Serv. 814, 830 (West) (to be codified at N.J. Rev. Stat. § 13:1E-80).

North Carolina: Cities and counties may collect a license tax based on the amount needed to compensate for incurred expenses such as loss of property tax revenues, monitoring costs, and other costs associated with the facility. N.C. Gen. Stat. § § 153A-152.1, 160A-211.1 (Supp. 1981).

Ohio: The state provides grants to local governments to encourage facility siting, Ohio Rev. Code Ann. § 3734.25 (Page Supp. 1981), and there is a four percent state tax on the gross receipts of hazardous waste facilities, *id.* § 3734.18.

See National Governors' Ass'n. *supra* note 37.

79. States that combine preemption with a compensation component include Connecticut, Indiana, Maine, New Jersey, North Carolina, and Ohio. Non-preemption states that include some provision for compensation include Georgia and Kentucky. *Compare supra* note 37 (preemption) *with supra* note 78 (compensation).

80. Hazardous Waste Facilities Siting Act, Pub. Act No. 81-369, § 16, 1981 Conn. Legis. Serv. 1153, 1175 (West) (to be codified at Conn. Gen. Stat. tit. 22a, ch. 445); Ind. Code § 13-7-8.6-1 (Supp. 1981); Major Hazardous Waste Facility Siting Act, ch. 279, § 32, 1981 N.J. Sess. Law Serv. 814, 830 (West) (to be codified at N.J. Rev. Stat. § 13:1E-80).

81. Me. Rev. Stat. Ann. tit. 38, § 1305-A(3) (Supp. 1981). For non-preemption statutes adopting this approach, see Ga. Code Ann. § 43-2905a (Supp. 1981); Ky. Rev. Stat. § 68.178 (1980).

82. Ohio Rev. Code Ann. § 3734.25 (Page Supp. 1981).

83. Only the Ohio statute has an effective date prior to 1981.

84. The statutes may inadequately perform even this limited role. The National Governors' Association has noted that the Ohio four percent gross receipts tax "cannot pay for the administration of the hazardous waste program. . . , much less pay for abandoned site cleanup or grants to local governments for siting." National Governors' Ass'n, *supra* note 43, at 20.

85. Payments under the negotiated package are not to exceed the amount set by the statutory formula. Hazardous Waste Facilities Siting Act, Pub. Act No. 81-369, § 16, 1981 Conn. Legis. serv. 1153, 1175 (West) (to be codified at Conn. Gen. Stat. tit. 22a, ch. 445).

86. The developer must pay the assessed fee but can appeal it to the appropriate state agency. N.C. Gen. Stat. § § 153A-152.1, 160A-211.1 (Supp. 1981).

87. Ohio Rev. Code Ann. § 3734.05(c)(4) (Page Supp. 1981). The North Carolina statute has an arbitrated compensation component similar to that of the Massachusetts provision, but it lacks a formal negotiation component. *See* N.C. Gen. Stat. § § 153A-152.1, 160A-211.1 (Supp. 1981).

88. Ch. 508, 1980 Mass. Acts 673 (codified at Mass. Gen. Laws Ann. chs. 21D, 40A (Zoning Enabling Act), 111 (public health regulations), 21C (Massachusetts Hazardous Waste Management Act)).

89. Connecticut has a negotiation procedure similar to that of Massachusetts, but the Connecticut statute gives the state government a larger role and limits the payments of the negotiated agreement. Hazardous Waste Facilities Siting Act, Pub. Act No. 81-369, § 16, 1981 Conn. Legis. Serv. 1153, 1175-76 (West) (to be codified at Conn. Gen. Stat. tit. 22a, ch. 445).

90. Mass Gen. Laws Ann. ch. 40A, § 9 (West Supp. 1981).

The negotiation element of the Massachusetts approach is critical. *See generally* D. Kretzmer, *Siting Hazardous Facilities: A Compensation and Mediation Model,* 1 Hazardous Waste Rep. 4 (no. 5, 1979). Successful conflict resolution through negotiation requires these elements: identifying the interested parties, assisting those parties in designating representatives, clarifying the critical issues, providing independent expertise, establishing a forum for negotiation, and developing a mechanism to enforce settlements. Farkas, *supra* note 65, at 457.

91. Mass Gen. Laws Ann. ch. 21D, § 12(5) (West 1981). Possible mitigation and compensation techniques include limiting the hours of operation, providing the increased community services required, establishing off-site park lands, and direct monetary payments. *See supra* text accompanying notes 64-65; *cf.* Hazardous Waste Facilities Siting Act, Pub. Act No. 81-369, § 16(C), 1981 Conn. Legis. Serv. 1153, 1176 (West) (to be codified at Conn. Gen. Stat. tit. 22a, ch. 445) (statutory description of possible mitigation techniques).

92. *See* Mass. Gen. Laws Ann. ch. 21C, § 7 (West Supp. 1981).

93. *See id.* ch. 21D, § 11 (West 1981).

94. *Id.* ch. 21C, § 15 (West Supp. 1981).

95. Massachusetts Special Comm'n on Hazardous Waste, Massachusetts Hazardous Waste Facility Siting Act 5 (Aug. 8, 1980).

96. Consequently, the negotiation and compensation approach is more equitable because one town will no longer have to bear the full costs of a facility whose benefits are shared by many, and the approach is more efficient because developers must consider the full social cost when choosing where to site a facility. *See supra* text accompanying notes 62-63.

97. The compensation scheme is more politically acceptable because localities will bargain for compensation, rather than having facilities forced upon them. Consequently, it will address legitimate local concerns in advance. Massachusetts Special Comm'n on Hazardous Waste, Minutes 1 (Apr. 10, 1980).

98. Massachusetts Special Comm'n on Hazardous Waste, *supra* note 95, at 3.

99. Massachusetts Special Comm'n on Hazardous Waste, *supra* note 8, at vi-vii; Mass. Gen. Laws Ann. ch. 21D, § 3 (West 1981). The Department of Environmental Management also studies the risks and impacts of hazardous waste sources and management technologies, solicits and evaluates construction proposals, and disseminates information to the public. *Id.*

100. Massachusetts Special Comm'n on Hazardous Waste, *supra* note 8, at vi-vii.

101. Mass. Gen. Laws Ann. ch. 21D, § 4 (West 1981).

102. *Id.* The Council is composed of nine state officials or their designees, six representatives from various interest groups, including scientists, and several representatives of the general public. In addition, two temporary members from the

affected community can be appointed "for the purpose of participating in and voting upon matters relative to the site selection in said community." *Id.*

103. Massachusetts Special Comm'n on Hazardous Waste, *supra* note 95, at 3.

104. Mass. Gen. Laws Ann. ch. 21D, § 7; Hazardous Waste Facility Site Safety Council & Massachusetts Dep't of Envtl. Management, Proposed Siting Regulations § 4 (Jan. 1982) (public hearing draft) [hereinafter cited as Proposed Regulations]. The primary purposes of the notice of intent are to inform the public and to provide the Council with the information necessary for its preliminary review. *Id.* § 4(A).

105. Proposed Regulations, *supra* note 104, § 4(A).

106. The site selection process can be quite complex. *See* Mass. Gen. Laws Ann. ch. 21D, § 9 (West 1981); Proposed Regulations, *supra* note 104, § § 4(C), 7.

107. Mass. Gen. Laws Ann. ch. 21D, § 7 (West 1981); Proposed Regulations, *supra* note 104, § 5(A). For a discussion of the scope of this administrative determina tion, see *infra* text accompanying notes 195-200. For a discussion of judicial review of this determination, see *infra* text accompanying notes 201-05.

108. Proposed Regulations, *supra* note 104, § 5(C). If a notice of intent names a specific site, the developer must meet several additional criteria relating to the attainability and environmental suitability of the land. *See id.* § 5(D).

109. Funds are awarded at the discretion of the Council, subject to specified criteria, upon application from the host or abutting community. Mass Gen. Laws Ann. ch. 21D, § 11 (West 1981); Proposed Regulations, *supra* note 104, § 9. The local assessment committee spends the funds. *Id.* § 8(G)(4).

110. *See* Proposed Regulations, *supra* note 104, § 5(F).

111. Mass. Gen. Laws Ann. ch. 21D, § 5 (West 1981); Proposed Regulations, *supra* note 104, § 8. The local assessment committee members are the local chief exec- utive officer, who acts as chairman, the chairman of the local board of health, the chairman of the local conservation commission, the chairman of the local planning board, the fire chief, four local residents, and four members nominated by the local chief executive officer and approved by the city council. *Id.* § 8(B).

112. Proposed Regulations, *supra* note 104, § 9(B).

113. Mass. Gen. Laws Ann. ch. 21D, § 8 (West 1981); Proposed Regulations, *supra* note 104, § 6. The Council retains the power to revoke its decision, in certain circumstances, until the siting agreement is established. *See id.* § 5(G).

114. Massachusetts Special Comm'n on Hazardous Waste, *supra* note 95, at 4.

115. Mass. Gen. Laws Ann. ch. 21D, § 10 (West 1981); Proposed Regulations, *supra* note 104, § 10(B).

116. Mass. Gen. Laws Ann. ch. 21D, § 10 (West 1981).

117. Massachusetts Special Comm'n on Hazardous Waste, *supra* note 95, at 4.

118. Proposed Regulations, *supra* note 104, § 10(B)(6).

119. *Id.* § 11(A).

120. Mass. Gen. Laws Ann. ch. 21D, § 12 (West 1981).

121. Curiously, unlike the provision that entitles abutting communities to compensation for "demonstrable adverse impacts," host communities have only an implied, not an express, entitlement to compensation. This disparity is puzzling. Section 12, which enumerates the elements of a siting agreement, including a provision

for "compensation, services and special benefits that will be provided to the host community by the developer," *id.* § 12(5), but fails to specify a standard for determining the level of compensation. The second part lists the optional elements of a siting agreement, including "provisions for direct monetary payments from the developer to the host community in addition to payments for taxes and special services and compensation for demonstrable adverse impacts." *Id.* Ambiguity results from the grammatical construction of this sentence. If the words "in addition" relate not only to the clause "to payments for taxes and special services" but also to "compensation for demonstrable adverse impacts," then by implication the host community would be entitled to such compensation. If the words "in addition" relate only to the first clause, however, and not to the second, then it would appear that a provision dealing with "demonstrable adverse impacts" is optional and not an entitlement for the host community. The former interpretation is more consistent with the theory of the Act. Furthermore, such an interpretation would place the host community on the same footing as abutting communities in its entitlement to compensation, an outcome that seems only fair.

122. *Id.* § 12. Specifically, each siting agreement must contain terms, provisions, and conditions governing: (1) facility construction and maintenance procedures, (2) operating procedures, (3) monitoring procedures, (4) the services to be provided to the developer by the host community, (5) the compensation, services, and special benefits that will be provided to the host community by the developer, (6) the services and benefits to be provided to the host community by agencies of state government, (8) provisions for renegotiation of any of the terms of the siting agreement, (9) provisions for resolving any disagreements in the construction and interpretation of the siting agreement, and (10) the compensation to be paid abutting communities. *Id.*

123. *Id.* § 15.

124. *Id.* The statute provides for either an arbitration panel of three, with one arbitrator chosen by each party and one agreeable to both, or a single arbitrator agreeable to both. The Council reserves the power to name any arbitrator necessary to fill a three person panel if the parties do not make their selection within 30 days after an impasse has been declared. *Id.*

125. *Id.*

126. Proposed Regulations, *supra* note 104, § 12. The arbitrator may consider factual stipulations of the parties, specified host community and developer interests, management and operational history of the developer, abutting community interests, and other relevant information. *Id.* § 12(E). For further discussion of the arbitrator's decision, see *infra* text accompanying notes 161-75.

127. Mass. Gen. Laws Ann. ch. 21D, § 15 (West 1981). These procedures are codified at *id.* ch. 251. For a discussion of judicial review of the arbitrator's decision, see *infra* text accompanying notes 213-39.

128. Mass. Gen. Laws Ann. ch. 21D, § 7 (West 1981).

129. *Id.*

130. *Id.* § 16.

131. *Id.* § 4.

132. *Id.* ch. 111, § 150B (West Supp. 1981). For a discussion of judicial review of this decision, see *infra* text accompanying notes 206-12.

133. Mass. Gen. Laws Ann. ch. 111, § 150B (West Supp. 1981). This process may be initiated by the local board of health or the Department of Environmental Quality Engineering upon complaint by any person aggrieved by such assignment, or by the Department of Environmental Quality Engineering upon its own initiative. This action, by either agency, is subject to judicial review under the arbitrary and capricious standard. *Id.*

134. *Id.* ch. 40A, § 9.

135. *Id.* This provision reflects a change made by the House Ways and Means Committee in the initial version of the bill. As originally proposed, the bill prohibited all zoning changes after the effective date of the Act that operated to prohibit hazardous waste facilities. S. Jaffe, A Multiple Perspective Analysis of the Massachusetts Hazardous Waste Facility Siting Act 25-26 (1980) (unpublished M.I.T. Thesis).

136. Mass. Gen. Laws Ann. ch. 16, § 19 (West Supp. 1981).

137. The developer must meet two additional criteria before the state can use eminent domain: (1) he or she must obtain all necessary permits and negotiate a siting agreement, and (2) he or she must have made a "good faith effort" to acquire the site and failed. *Id.*

138. Proposed Regulations, *supra* note 104, § 11(G).

139. *Id.* § 10(C).

140. Mass Gen. Laws Ann. ch. 21D, §§ 10, 12 (West 1981); Proposed Regulations, *supra* note 104, § 13.

141. Mass. Gen. Laws Ann. ch. 21D, § 12 (West 1981).

142. *Id.* § 14.

143. *Id.* §§ 8, 11.

144. *Id.* § 14; *see* Proposed Regulations, *supra* note 104, § 11(H).

145. Mass. Gen. Laws Ann. ch. 21D, § 14 (West 1981).

146. *Id.*

147. *Id.* ch. 43B, §§ 1-19 (West 1968 & Supp. 1981).

148. *See* Board of Appeals of Hanover v. Housing Appeals Comm., 363 Mass. 339, 357, 294 N.E.2d 393, 407 (1973). In the absence of state constitutional provisions establishing municipal rights of self-government, municipalities are mere departments of the state, which can grant or withdraw privileges and powers as its sees fit. City of Trenton v. New Jersey, 262 U.S. 182, 187 (1923).

149. Mass. Gen. Laws Ann. ch. 43B, § 13 (West 1968).

150. Mass. Const. Art. of Amend., art. 89, § 8.

151. The zoning power is part of the Home Rule Amendment's "broad grant of powers to adopt ordinances or by-laws for the protection of the public health, safety, and general welfare." Board of Appeals of Hanover v. Housing Appeals Comm., 363 Mass. 339, 359, 294 N.E.2d 393, 409 (1973).

152. For an example of state preemption through the use of compulsory arbitration, *see* Town of Arlington v. Board of Conciliation & Arbitration, 370 Mass. 769, 352 N.E.2d 914 (1976); for an example of preemption of local zoning powers, see Board of Appeals of Hanover v. Housing Appeals Comm., 363 Mass. 339, 294 N.E.2d 393 (1973).

153. Mass. Gen. Laws Ann. ch. 40A, § 9 (West Supp. 1981). After a developer files a notice of intent naming a particular community, that community cannot amend its zoning ordinances to exclude the proposed facility. *Id.*

154. *Id.* ch. 21D, § 16 (West 1981).

155. *Id.* ch. 111, § 150B (West Supp. 1981).

156. For an example of a court decision finding that a community had this power, even though the applicable statute had similar preemption language, see Nelson v. Department of Natural Resources, 88 Wis. 2d 1, 276 N.W.2d 302 (Wis. Ct. App. 1979), *aff'd.* 96 Wis. 2d 730, 292 N.W.2d 655 (Wis. 1980).

157. *See infra* text accompanying note 251.

158. It appears, however, that a municipality can avoid having a hazardous waste facility by not zoning any land industrial or by declining to grant a zoning change to a developer. The Act may limit preemption to land zoned for industrial use because siting is less likely to include local opposition when a facility can be "hidden" among other industrial development. This provision may also seek to ensure that communities that open themselves up to the gains of industrial development do not close themselves to its associated burdens.

159. *See, e.g.,* New England LNG Co. v. City of Fall River, 368 Mass. 259, 331 N.E.2d 536 (1975) (comprehensive state regulation of gas companies evidence an intent to preempt local regulations). This contrasts with other situations where courts have held that the existence of mandatory health standards did not itself preempt local authority to enact more stringent standards. In Decoulos v. City of Peabody, 360 Mass. 428, 274 N.E.2d 816 (1971), for example, the court found that towns can adopt health standards that are more stringent than the state's sanitary code. The court stated that the uniformity of the state health laws did not demonstrate an "intention to preclude a city from including appropriate, more specific and stringent health protection measures in a zoning ordinance." 360 Mass. at 429, 274 N.E.2d at 817. Here, the statute's limit on the local health board's role to the comparable industry test and the statute's purpose to expedite siting manifest this very intention.

160. Board of Appeals of Hanover v. Housing Appeals Comm., 363 Mass. 339, 359, 294 N.E.2d 393, 409 (1973). In this case, the court upheld state override of local zoning regulations. The court stated that the challenged statute's "grant of power . . . to override local zoning ordinances . . . which would otherwise frustrate the statute's objective . . . does not violate the Home Rule Amendment." 363 Mass. at 360, 294 N.E.2d at 409-10.

The key factor is whether the legislature intended to create a comprehensive, state-wide statutory scheme. *See* County Comm'rs v. Conservation Comm'n, 405 N.E.2d 637, 643 (1980) (a home rule challenge "is neither a 'town's rights' case, nor a 'county's rights' case, but rather a question of legislative intent"); Town of Arlington v. Board of Conciliation & Arbitration, 370 Mass. 769, 353 N.E.2d 914 (1976); Bloom v. City of Worcester, 363 Mass. 136, 155, 293 N.E.2d 268, 280 (1973) (a statute demonstrates legislative intent to override local regulation if it "deals with a subject comprehensively, describing (perhaps among other things) what municipalities can and cannot do").

161. Mass. Gen. Laws Ann. ch. 21D, § 15 (West 1981).

162. "The siting agreement shall specify the terms, conditions and provisions under which the facility shall be constructed, maintained and operated *if the developer chooses to construct, maintain and operate a facility on said site. . . ." Id.* § 12 (emphasis added).

163. *Id.* ch. 111, § 150B (West Supp. 1981).

164. *Id.* ch. 21D, § 15 (West 1981).

165. *Id.*

166. Proposed Regulations, *supra* note 104, § 12(E), "The arbitrator shall determine the terms, conditions, and provisions of a siting agreement. . . ." *Id.* In making this determination, the arbitrator may consider the factual stipulations of the parties, a broad range of community and developer interests, all relevant information available to the arbitration panel, the past management and operational history of the developer, and abutting community interests. *Id.*

167. These criteria may, however, be enough to protect the statute against constitutional attacks. *See* Town of Arlington v. Board of Conciliation & Arbitration, 370 Mass. 769, 352 N.E.2d 914 (1976).

168. Massachusetts Bay Transp. Auth. v. Boston Safe Deposit & Trust Co., 348 Mass. 538, 205 N.E.2d 346, 351 (1965); *see also* Massachusetts Hous. Fin. Agency v. New England Merchant Nat'l Bank, 356 Mass. 202, 249 N.E.2d 599 (1969); Opinion of the Justices, 330 Mass. 713, 113 N.E.2d 452 (1953). In *Massachusetts Housing Finance Agency,* a subsidized housing program was upheld despite a broad statute that allowed the agency to determine tenant selection and income criteria under a "reasonableness" standard. The court ruled that though the standards might have been stated with "greater definitiveness. . . , it is reasonably apparent from the Act what those standards are." 356 Mass. at 214, 249 N.E.2d at 607.

Furthermore, Massachusetts courts have used the delegation doctrine to invalidate a statute only in unusual circumstances. *See, e.g.,* Corning Glass Works v. Ann & Hope, Inc., 363 Mass. 409, 294 N.E.2d 354 (1973). There, the overriding issue seems to have been the delegation to a private group that had a strong pecuniary interest in the outcome.

169. *See* Town of Arlington v. Board of Conciliation & Arbitration, 330 Mass. 769, 776, 352 N.E.2d 914, 1919 (1976). In upholding the compulsory arbitration statute, the *Arlington* court emphasized: (1) that the act had set out specific standards, (2) that the Board had promulgated procedural regulations, (3) that arbitration followed negotiation, mediation, and fact-finding, and (4) that judicial review was open to both parties. *Id.* Although this approach does not establish a "hard and fast" rule on what constitutes proper delegation, the Siting Act seems to meet the requirements. One possible exception is judicial review of the arbitrator's decision. *See infra* text accompanying notes 213-41.

170. *See supra* note 122.

171. *E.g.,* City of Amsterdam v. Helsby, 37 N.Y.2d 19, 332 N.E.2d 290, 371 N.Y.S.2d 404 (1975) (examining the validity of a New York statute that provides for compulsory labor arbitration); Massachusetts Bay Transp. Auth. v. Boston Safe Deposit & Trust Co., 348 Mass. 538, 205 N.E.2d 346 (1965) (the size and regional scope of the MBTA make it suitable to receive a broad delegation of authority).

172. *See* Town of Arlington v. Board of Conciliation & Arbitration, 370 Mass. 769, 352 N.E.2d 914 (1976); 1 K. Davis, Administrative Law Treatise §§ 3:14-:15 (2d ed. 1978).

173. *See* Mass. Gen. Laws Ann. ch. 111, § 150B (West Supp. 1981).

174. *Id.* ch. 29, § 27C (effective Nov. 4, 1980). The statute, popularly known as Proposition 2½, states that "[a]ny law imposing any direct service or cost obligation upon any city or town shall be effective . . . only if such law is accepted by vote or by the appropriation of money for such purposes . . . for the assumption by the commonwealth of such cost." *Id.*

175. For example, noise is a common problem in the operation of waste facilities. One source of noise is trucks delivering wastes to the site. The level of truck traffic varies with market conditions, and thus might be difficult to predict at the time of arbitration. An arbitrator might therefore tie the level of compensation for noise to the actual number of truck deliveries to the site.

176. The powers of the Council are: (1) to observe the operation of the siting process and advise the participants, (2) to review the rules, regulations, procedures, and standards of the Department of Environmental Quality Engineering and to recommend changes needed to carry out the Act, (3) to review and comment on the state environmental impact report, (4) to administer the economic impact appendix of the preliminary project impact report in cooperation with the Secretary of Environmental Affairs, (5) to award technical assistance grants, (6) to consult with the Executive Office of Communities and Development in awarding grants, (7) to obtain information and recommendations from other agencies of state and local government, (8) to review proposals for hazardous waste facilities and reject those found to be unacceptable for the siting process, (9) to establish compensation for abutting communities, (10) to facilitate negotiations between the developer and host and abutting communities, (11) to determine if an impasse exists in negotiations, (12) to encourage cooperation between a host and abutting communities, and (13) to adopt needed rules, regulations, procedures, and standards. Mass. Gen. Laws Ann. ch. 21D, § 4 (West 1981).

177. *Id.* § 12.

178. *See* P. Maxwell, The Interpretation of Statutes 36 (12th ed. 1969).

179. Mass Gen. Laws Ann. ch. 21D, § 4 (West 1981).

180. *Id.* § 4(8).

181. Massachusetts Special Comm'n on Hazardous Waste, *supra* note 8, at vii.

182. *Id.* at vi-vii.

183. Mass Gen. Laws Ann. ch. 21D, § 12 (West 1981).

184. *See id.* § 10.

185. Furthermore, if an arbitrator neglects to rule on an issue submitted by the Council or rules on issues not properly before him or her, the Council should withdraw its declaration. *See* Proposed Regulations, *supra* note 104, §§ 12, 13.

186. "If the chief executive officer of said city or town fails to take appropriate action to establish a local assessment committee . . . the council shall establish and appoint the membership of said committee." Mass. Gen. Laws Ann. ch. 21D, § 5 (West 1981).

187. *Id.* § 15.

188. *Id.* ch. 111, § 150B (West Supp. 1981).

189. In an arbitrated siting agreement, there is no offer and acceptance, no exchange of promises, indeed no promises are made at all. The arbitrator merely declares the conditions that will govern the construction, operation, and maintenance of the facility if the facility is built.

190. Mass. Gen. Laws Ann. ch. 21D, § 12 (West 1981).

191. For example, additional compensation could be awarded to a community that satisfied its obligations under the siting agreement within a specified time period.

192. *See infra* text accompanying notes 213-39.

193. Mass. Gen. Laws Ann. ch. 21D, § § 12, 15 (West 1981).

194. "No license or permit granted by a city or town shall be required for a hazardous waste facility which was not required on or before the effective date of this chapter by said city or town." *Id.* § 16.

195. *Id.* § 7.

196. Proposed Regulations, *supra* note 104, § 5(C).

197. Mass Gen. Laws Ann. ch. 21D, § 10 (West 1981).

198. Proposed Regulations, *supra* note 104, § 5(B).

199. Furthermore, the developer would have to persuade the community to proceed without the benefit of technical assistance grants and other aid typically provided by the state.

200. In determining whether a proposal is technically feasible or conflicts with other environmental regulations, the Council relies heavily on the advice of two of its members, the Commissioner of Environmental Quality Engineering and the Commissioner of Environmental Management. The Commissioner of Environmental Quality Engineering is ultimately responsible for issuing the state regulatory permits and licenses required by hazardous waste facilities.

It is possible that the Council could reject a proposal which met all technical permit and licensing requirements but which did not offer capacity needed by the state. The state should license such a facility, however, if the host and abutting communities are willing to accept it. In other words, rejection because of excess capacity should only act as a bar to state assistance in the siting process, not as a final bar to the facility itself.

201. Conceivably, a host community should also attack a negative decision if it desired the facility.

202. Mass. Gen. Laws Ann. ch. 30A. § 14 (West Supp. 1981).

203. *See supra* note 174.

204. Within 15 days of notification of a negative decision by the Council, the developer may file a written request for reconsideration to the Council. The request may include any information that the developer desires the Council to consider. The Council must decide within 45 days of the request. Proposed Regulations, *supra* note 104, § 5(F).

205. Furthermore, judicial review is available according to the standards articulated in the Massachusetts Administrative Procedure Act because the substantive statute does not explicitly bar review. Mass Gen. Laws Ann. ch. 30A, § 7 (West 1979).

206. *Id.* ch. 111, § 150A (West Supp. 1981). If the facility is being developed by a state agency, the statute requires the Department of Environmental Quality Engineering to conduct the site assignment review. *Id.* ch. 21C, § 7.

207. *Id.* ch. 111, § 150A.

208. *Id.* The Act is silent on the standard to be used by the Department of Environmental Quality Engineering in this review. To be symmetrical it would have to be the arbitrary and capricious standard.

209. *Id.*

210. *See id.* ch. 30A, § 14.

211. *Id.* ch. 111, § 150A. This process may be initiated by the local board of health or "upon complaint by any person aggrieved by such assignment, or by [the Department of Environmental Quality Engineering] upon its own initiative or upon complaint by any person aggrieved by said assignment." *Id.*

212. The Siting Act provides for an adjudicatory hearing before the Department of Environmental Quality Engineering, and then for judicial review under the Massachusetts Administrative Procedure Act. *Id.* ch. 21C, § 11.

213. *Id.* ch. 251.

214. *Id.* ch. 21D, § 15 (West 1981).

215. *Id.* ch. 251, § 12(a) (West Supp. 1981).

216. Trustees of the Boston & Me. Corp. v. Massachusetts Bay Transp. Auth., 363 Mass. 386, 390, 294 N.E.2d 340, 343 (1973).

217. There is a conflict between the Massachusetts Administrative Procedure Act and the review provided by the Siting Act. The Administrative Procedure Act provides that "[w]here a statutory form of judicial review or appeal is provided such statutory form shall govern in all respects, except [that] [t]he standards for review shall be those set forth in paragraph (7) of this section." Mass. Gen. Laws Ann. ch. 30A, § 14 (West 1979). Thus, although another statute may govern the procedural aspects of review, the scope of review must follow paragraph (7), the "unsupported by substantial evidence, arbitrary or capricious" standard. The Siting Act, by attempting to provide limited judicial review rather than wholly precluding review, apparently contradicts the Administrative Procedure Act. Nonetheless, because the Administrative Procedure Act was last amended in 1976, there is a strong argument that the legislature implicitly amended its standard of review with the passage of the Siting Act.

218. *Id.* ch. 111, § 150A (West Supp. 1981).

219. *See id.*

220. *Id.*

221. *Id.* ch. 21C, § 7.

222. The language of section 12 of the Siting Act seems to allow contractual defenses such as illegality and impossibility. *Id.* ch. 21D, § 12 (West 1981). Section 12 allows the arbitrator to retain jurisdiction to resolve future controversies arising over interpretation and implementation of the siting agreement; where this occurs, a community's access to the courts for a hearing on these defenses would be reduced, because chapter 251 allows reversal of an arbitrator's decision only in instances of fraud or partiality. Thus, an arbitrator's decision on issues such as impossibility would be dispositive. This result should not occur, however, if the community pleads

illegality. While an arbitrator might rule that a community has the legal authority to discharge its obligations under the siting agreement, such a decision should not be binding on a subsequent court if it involves interpretation of something other than the siting agreement itself, such as the community's charter or an enabling act for a municipal agency. Illegality should be treated differently than impossibility because impossibility generally involves purely factual considerations that fall within the scope of the arbitrator's expertise, whereas illegality requires a determination of whether a particular action is ultra vires under the applicable law. Even if an arbitrator ruled that a particular action was legal, his or her decision would not prevent a local resident from obtaining an injunction blocking implementation of the provision in question. Because such an action would not be brought on the contract, the chapter 251 provisions for deference to the arbitrator would not apply.

223. See Trustees of the Boston & Me. Corp. v. Massachusetts Bay Transp. Auth., 363 Mass. 386, 294 N.E.2d 340 (1973). The court stated that the rationale for the limited scope of review in commercial arbitration is that the parties "received what they agreed to take, the honest judgment of the arbitrator as to a matter referred to him." 363 Mass. at 390 91, 294 N.E.2d at 344 (citation omitted).

224. Mass. Gen. Laws Ann. ch. 21D, § 15 (West 1981).

225. See Division 540, Amalgamated Transit Union v. Mercer County Improvement Auth., 76 N.J. 245, 386 A.2d 1290 (1978); Mount St. Mary's Hosp. v. Catherwood, 26 N.Y.2d 493, 260 N.E.2d 508, 311 N.Y.S.2d 863 (1970).

In Division 540, the New Jersey Supreme Court upheld a compulsory arbitration statute that was silent on review only by concluding that judicial review must be available: "Because [arbitration] is compulsory, principles of fairness, perhaps even due process, require that judicial review be available to ensure that the award is not arbitrary or capricious and that the arbitrator has not abused the power and authority delegated to him." 76 N.J. at 253, 386 A.2d at 1294. Similarly, in Mount St. Mary's Hospital, the New York Court of Appeals concluded that "[d]ue process of law requires . . . that the contract imposed by the arbitrator . . . have a basis not only in his good faith, but in law and the record before him." 26 N.Y.2d at 507, 260 N.E.2d at 515, 311 N.Y.S.2d at 873 (citations omitted).

The manner in which the Mount St. Mary's Hospital court took review is particularly important for present purposes. The New York statute that authorized review in that case is similar to chapter 251 of the Massachusetts Siting Act. Acknowledging that the New York statute was written for voluntary arbitration, the court held that, in the context of compulsory arbitration, review to see whether the arbitrator exceeded his or her power includes "substantial evidence" review of the arbitrator's decision. The court reasoned that otherwise the statute would not be constitutional. A Massachusetts court could similarly discover full judicial review within the wording of the Siting Act and the Uniform Arbitration Act.

226. Town of Arlington v. Board of Conciliation & Arbitration, 370 Mass. 769, 352 N.E.2d 914 (1976).

227. Id.

228. Similarly, a New Jersey court found that, because a compulsory arbitration statute required the municipality to fund the award, the constitution required judicial

review to assure that the statutory scheme did not deprive the municipality of property without due process of law. Division 540, Amalgamated Transit Union v. Mercer County Improvement Auth., 76 N.J. 245, 386 A.2d 1290 (1978).

229. The affirmative obligations of mandated services to the developer are not relevant to this discussion because: (1) they are subject to broad judicial review in a contractual action brought by the developer to enforce the arbitrator's award, and (2) there is no deprivation of property because Proposition 2½ requires that these services be funded by the state. *See supra* note 174.

230. Board of Regents v. Roth, 408 U.S. 564, 570-71 (1972).

231. *Id.* at 576-77 (emphasis added). Municipalities have no general property interest in avoiding risks and stigmas that tend to reduce individual property values. For example, some statutes leave the siting of other undesirable facilities to the discretion of state agencies, subject to approval by the governor. Mass. Gen. Laws Ann. ch. 123, § 8 (West Supp. 1981) (authorizing the Department of Mental Health to select sites for state mental hospitals); *id.* ch. 124, § 10 (West 1974) (authorizing the Department of Corrections to select sites for state prisons).

232. The section of the Siting Act that describes the terms of the siting agreement, Mass. Gen. Laws Ann. ch. 21D, § 12 (West 1981), is divided into two parts. The first part, which describes the terms, conditions and provisions that the agreement "shall" contain, includes "the compensation, services, and special benefits that *will* be provided to the host community by the developer." *Id.* (emphasis added). The second part, which contains provisions that the siting agreement "may" contain, does not include compensation. This dichotomy, and the strong language of the first part, implies that the Act entitles the host community to compensation. Furthermore, a purpose of the Act is to make facilities attractive to potential host communities and to avoid state override of local decisions; compensation is consistent with this purpose. *See* Massachusetts Special Comm'n on Hazardous Waste, *supra* note 95, at 2. *See also supra* note 121.

233. *Cf.* Griffeth v. Detrich, 603 F.2d 118 (9th Cir. 1979). The court held that a hearing was required for an initial denial of welfare benefits, but did so only because of the mandatory nature of welfare in California and because the agency's discretion was narrowly limited.

234. Arnett v. Kennedy, 416 U.S. 134, 153-54 (1974) (plurality opinion).

235. Although only a plurality endorsed this doctrine, *id.,* and the doctrine is controversial, *see* L. Tribe, American Constitutional Law § 10-12 (1978), the Siting Act may present an appropriate case for its application. The concept of moral entitlement forms the basis for the attack on the rights-privileges distinction. The entitlement established by the Act, however, is less infused with a sense of moral obligation than cases involving individual welfare or civil liberties. Therefore, the legislature should have a freer hand to define the process that will accompany entitlements that they create.

Moreover, there are good reasons to apply the "bitter with the sweet" doctrine when a municipality claims the entitlement. *See* Williams v. Mayor and City Council, 289 U.S. 36 (1933). In fact, *Williams* suggests that federal procedural due process might not be implicated at all.

236. *See* Goldberg v. Kelly, 397 U.S. 254, 263 (1970).

237. Mass. Gen. Laws Ann. ch. 21D, § 15 (West 1981).

238. *Id.* ch. 251, § § 5-7 (West Supp. 1981).

239. *See supra* text accompanying notes 218-22.

240. Because this is a final action and the Act does not prohibit judicial review, such review is available under the Massachusetts Administrative Procedure Act.

241. *See supra* text accompanying notes 176-85.

242. National Governors' Ass'n, *supra* note 43, at 9.

243. *Id.;* Garland, *New England Braces for Its First Toxic Waste Landfill Site, Christian Sci. Monitor,* Nov. 10, 1981, at 6, col. 1.

244. National Governors' Ass'n, *supra* note 43, at 9; Blake, *Waste Plant Site Decision Near, Boston Globe,* Oct. 12, 1981, at 1, col. 4.

245. National Governors' Ass'n, *supra* note 43, at 9.

246. *Id.*

247. *Id.*

248. Ziegler, *Hazardous Waste Plant Rejected by Nearly 3-1 Ratio in Gardner, Boston Globe,* Mar. 10, 1982, at 35, col. 4.

249. *Id.*

250. City of Haverhill v. Hazardous Waste Facility Site Safety Council, Civ. Action No. 82-683 (Mass. Dist. Ct. filed Feb. 9, 1982).

251. Town of Warren v. Hazardous Waste Facility Site Safety Council, Civ. Action No. 82-21740 (Mass. Dist. Ct. filed Jan. 17, 1982). For a discussion of the legality of such an action, see *supra* text accompanying notes 156-60.

252. *See supra* text accompanying notes 107-08.

253. Connecticut has adopted this approach. *See supra* note 78.

254. *See* Menzies, *supra* note 1. The Executive Office of Environmental Affairs, the parent agency of the Department of Environmental Management and the Department of Environmental Quality Engineering, is spending $375,000 on an educational campaign.

Part III.   Tools

MICHAEL O'HARE

10 Improving the Use of Information in Environmental Decision Making

How Information is Used in Decision Making

Information is often wasted, perhaps because it is peculiar stuff with only partial similarities to other goods. Therefore, reasonable behavior on the part of information users will appear quirky or irrational by comparison to the way we produce, use, and exchange other things of value.

According to an eclectic but conventional model of enlightened choice, a decision is an irretrievable commitment of resources (time, money, goods, a vote), either by society, or by an individual seeking to affect a societal decision. Each decision maker, choosing his action to maximize something called *expected utility* (the utility of society is often called *social welfare*) estimates the utility of different alternatives by predicting the respective futures that would result from them. *It is in this prediction process that information is used.* In the simplest version of this model, often used by economists, the decision maker has as much information available to him as he wants at no cost. It was long recognized, mostly in footnotes, that this simplification was usually wrong, and in the last twenty years useful models have appeared that recognize the real cost of information and the resulting consequence that the decision maker's first nontrivial decision is whether to get more of it.

Information has a cost at least in production: consultants, professors, and computers are real resources with real alternative uses. If this were all that

From Michael O'Hare, "Improving the Use of Information in Environmental Decision Making," in *Environmental Impact Assessment Review*, Vol. 1 (September 1980), pp. 229-250. Reprinted by permission of the Plenum Publishing Corporation and Michael O'Hare.

mattered, it would be relatively straightforward for a government agency to estimate the cost of information that might be produced (taking appropriate account of uncertainty), compare it to the benefits that might be gained if it existed, and arrange for the production of an efficient amount and type.

Unfortunately, this simple model ignores several other qualities of information that, taken as a group, make it unique among goods. Seven of these are especially important for public or collective allocation decisions; some bear on the likelihood that a potential producer will produce efficient amounts, and some suggest doubt that consumers will use what is produced efficiently. I list them as a group, and then discuss each in more detail.

SUPPLY-SIDE CONSIDERATIONS

- Information is a public good at small scale, and some information is a public good in the most general sense. *Why should Millville pay for that expensive impact assessment when Mudville will probably have one done and Millville can just read theirs?*
- The value of information varies with its quantity and in a complicated and lumpy way (in fact, an indifference curve in the usual sense cannot even be defined for it). *Why should Mudville pay for the impact assessment when it will probably just confirm what it already thinks to be the case—though if it were opposite in its implications and convincing it would be very much worth having!*
- It is often impossible to know whether information has been consumed. (The consumption of information is *not* the same as the purchase of the document that contains it.) *Ten copies of the assessment were sent, but who knows if their representative read it?*

DEMAND-SIDE CONSIDERATIONS

- Knowledge about the value of information at the time of its acquisition is likely to be worse and harder to obtain than knowledge about other goods. *Why should Mudville pay for an impact assessment when it doesn't even know whether it will answer its question or even whether reading it and commenting on its conclusions will affect the final decision anyway?*
- There are externalities in the use of information. *If Mudville has a study done, it can be used to convince Millville to vote with Mudville, since the project will be shown to benefit them too.*
- Demand is limited by special considerations involving the consumer's investment of time. *The mayor would like to be informed about the project, but the impact assessment is hundreds of pages long and he can only spend a couple of hours on it.*

A TWO-EDGED SWORD

- The quantity of information is undefined except as regards a particular user at a particular time. *How can you say the impact assessment was informative? It was full of stuff I already knew—not a new idea in it!*

INFORMATION AS A PUBLIC GOOD

It is commonplace that public goods are undersupplied, and there is an ample body of theory and experience that indicates what might be done about it. A particular piece of information (the content of a consultant's report is a good example) may be of value to several parties in a public decision, even if it is relatively more valuable to one than another. In such cases consumers may not be able to offer an amount of resources that will buy (1) any research at all, or (2) an efficiently extensive or complicated study. Even in the case in which any one of the parties would gain enough from the research to buy it for himself, the study may have the nonexcludability property: a report written for a public agency, or a part of the public record of debate, cannot be withheld from those who didn't pay for it. Or, the report may not be purchased at all as the various parties who would like to have it wait for each other to be the first. Government agencies, such as the National Science Foundation, recognizing that information is a public good, buy basic research on behalf of the population as a whole.

MARGINAL VALUE OF ADDITIONAL INFORMATION

I assume here that information provides no utility by itself, but only as a way to improve decisions. (Anyone who has tried to read an environmental impact statement will understand the justification for this assumption.) Consider the case of the binary decision whether to support or oppose a proposal by vote: an individual who has already decided to vote *yes* has done so on the basis of some amount of knowledge that leads him to think that proposal best for him. The most likely nature of the information he might obtain is, of course, to be consistent with what he already knows—in other words, he expects that information he might obtain will support the decision he's already made. If this turns out to be the case, the information won't change his decision and will have been (to a first approximation) worthless,[1] though there is always some probability that the "next piece of information" will contradict the individual's current intentions persuasively and thus save him from what he would then see as a misguided choice.

An individual considering whether he should obtain more information is not in a paradoxical state, of course. The complication arises when a third party, such as a government, is trying to estimate the value to B of information produced by A. What the next increment will appear to be worth to B depends on B's probabilities when it is offered, which in turn depend on what B already knows, and neither of these is usually ascertainable from outside B's head.

The relationship between an individual decision and a public decision is also a complicated one. In many cases, it's rational for an individual decision maker to expect none of the alternatives open to him to affect a public decision.[2] If this is the case, no information he can obtain will affect the utility he obtains from the public decision and any information will appear worthless.

The importance of this uncertain relationship between quantity of information and its value to the consumer is that many of the usual public-good supply strategies will not work, because even a public body trying to produce an efficient amount cannot know how much to produce.

UNCERTAIN CONSUMPTION OF INFORMATION

A bookseller need only know how many copies of a book he sells, but suppliers of information in the public decision process are in a position similar to the book's author, who wants to know not only that the book is sold, and not only that it is read, but whether it has been persuasive. Some partial data of this kind are available, as for example when the developer of a large project mounts a public relations campaign and sees the town referendum on his zoning proposal come out favorably. Much more typical is the uncertainty familiar to every public speaker unable to tell whether the impassive audience for his argument is really convinced.

Note that this uncertainty is about the consumption of information as distinct from its acquisition. This is especially important in the case of a project proposer trying to convince a decision maker. If A can supply information to B that will make B's behavior more favorable to A, the market for information is improved, because A will invest an amount that matches the total social product it generates (see [Spence 1972] where this behavior is modelled for several private transactions). But uncertainty about whether the leaflet slipped under B's door has also slipped into his consciousness makes this desirable behavior on A's part less likely. To make matters worse, a policy that supplies information that is not consumed doesn't even reveal its failure by growing physical inventories in the supplier's warehouse.

The effect of these uncertainties is to cause information to be underproduced unless special measures are taken.

KNOWLEDGE ABOUT INFORMATION

If information has a real cost, then we must consider the price at which an information user obtains it. If he creates his own information, he must consider the real cost; the same is true if he contracts for it to be produced. If he buys a book, he pays at least some fraction of the production cost. But even if a package containing information arrives in his lap, he can only obtain the information at a cost of effort and time in absorbing it. We conclude that information is only available at a nonzero price to the consumer; therefore, obtaining it is a consumption decision. I will call what the information consumer knows at a trivial cost, somewhat awkwardly, *public knowledge,* and restrict *information* to mean what can only be known at a significant cost to him.

The public knowledge used in consuming information about the public choice problem is probably worse, in a particular though unquantifiable way, than the public knowledge used in consumption decisions for "ordinary" goods. Figure 1 illustrates the consumption decision with the formalism of decision analysis. At point A the decision maker chooses among several consumption alternatives. Each of these, as C_1 and C_2 illustrate, will give rise to a spectrum of outcomes whose attractiveness is described by their respective utilities and whose likelihood of occurrence (given the particular consumption decision) is described by probability. Thus, if C_1 is chosen, utility U_{11} will be obtained with probability P_{11}. The knowledge bearing on the decision at point A in this diagram is simply the array of utilities and probabilities associated with each alternative in the decision. In Figure 2, the model is abstracted into a simpler form. The knowledge pertaining to the purchase of an ordinary good is the description of what is inside the dotted line: knowledge describes the causal arrow connecting the acquisition of a good or service and the utility it provides.

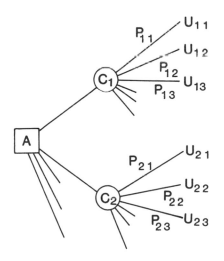

FIGURE 1.

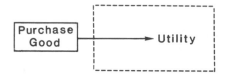

FIGURE 2.

Figure 3 illustrates the situation for the participant in a public decision process who is a step removed from actually making the final decision. In this case, the cost of the information might be the price of a consulting report purchased by a town government, or it could be the time required to read through an environmental impact statement already prepared by someone else. Information about public planning decisions is likely to be overdemanded or underdemanded because the arrows in Figure 3 are so difficult to understand and analyze when the consumption decision must be made. The two arrows that give rise to the greatest analytic difficulty connect information to the individual's decision, and the individual's decision to the public decision. It is the uncertainties in these relationships that make the value of information so ill-defined.

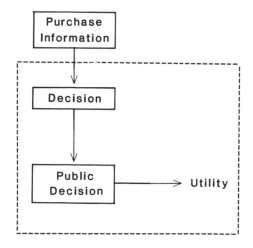

FIGURE 3.

EXTERNALITIES IN INFORMATION CONSUMPTION

Information shares with education the property that many believe its consumption to have positive externalities. If someone becomes more knowledgeable about an investment project, parties to the decision (on both sides!) often expect he will be more likely to join their side. If the consumer is a swing vote, the benefits expected to flow from the decision that results from his joining a side may far exceed the benefits he himself obtains from a better public decision. One manifestation of such externalities—or at least the perception that they exist—is propaganda: A subsidizes B's access to information in hopes of inducing B to favor an alternative favored by A. Another is the existence of public education and libraries. An information user will underconsume information to the extent that some of the benefits of his consumption accrue to others.

USERS' INVESTMENTS OF TIME

Information is further distinguished by the time it takes to consume. The decision at hand for such an individual involves commitment of time in two different ways: he can spend time gaining information about the project to learn which actions are most advisable for him and which alternative he should favor, and he can invest time in action that will change the likelihood that the alternative he favors will be selected.

If an individual is rational, the value of time invested in thinking about the project and acting to affect its outcome should not be greater than the intrinsic utility of learning and action, plus the difference between the best and worst values of the project.[3]

If information becomes available after an individual has committed the maximum rational amount of time to informing himself, he might well regard his previous commitment of time as a sunk cost and start the meter again at zero. But a public decision-making process in which this behavior is common is obviously inefficient. I will concentrate on the case in which decision makers try to allocate their time budgets in advance on the basis of some reasonable initial understanding about a project and about the information that might be forthcoming. The important point here is that information use will be limited not only by the cost of production as compared to the benefits it provides, but by rational limits on the costs individuals must incur to receive it.

The behavior I describe is often obscured by voiced regret at having employed it in particular cases. A decision maker may occasionally wish he had better informed himself, especially in cases when the decision's outcome was a high-cost one, initially perceived as unlikely, that would have been avoided by investing more in information. But there is usually no way to identify these cases *ab initio:* the decision maker can only follow a general policy of investing in information for each decision up to the point that the expected marginal net gain from information is zero.

These considerations suggest that information users will not be induced to consume more information simply by having a richer spread set before them. They can be expected to underconsume information by ignoring externalities, and to exhibit a distinct point of satiety (different for each, of course) as a result of competition for time.

TYPES OF INFORMATION

What people use to improve their decisions is not only scientific evidence, but also the news that the next-door neighbor is against the new power plant. More precisely, four types of information are apparently useful in public debate:

1. **Data** comprise facts susceptible of testing in a universally acceptable way. The quintessential example of a datum is the accepted value of a physical constant.
2. **Models** are explanations or mechanisms that (usually) involve a causal relationship. They are not subject to proof or demonstration of the fundamental sort we assume for data. For our discussion the line between data and models is less clear than in the technical context in which these terms are usually met. An example of a model is an econometric relationship between jobs and income, with or without estimated values for the parameters.
3. **Preferences** are properties of individuals, and subject to change. A demand curve is a formal statement of a set of preferences: "low income families need housing more than they need art museums" is a less formal one.
4. **Conclusions** are decisions recommended by others, like "the mayor thinks we should build a museum rather than another housing project."

USER BEHAVIOR

In studying facility siting through several case studies and by abstraction from a variety of other empirical work, I have identified five types of information users. I cannot estimate the frequency with which each type is met, but every one is exemplified in almost every real dispute. Though the categories overlap, they are useful as paradigms.

Some information users behave in a way that could be called rational even in the narrowest sense. These *fact respecters* form their opinions, insofar as they can, on substantive information concerning a proposal at hand and expect to do their own analysis of the data they collect.

Expertise takers adopt opinions (usually a "favorable" or "unfavorable" view of a particular proposal) from other individuals who presumably have special expertise in the area of concern. While these information users think rational analysis appropriate to the decision, they do not expect to perform the analysis themselves. They accept the result of an analysis performed by someone whose conclusions they have already determined to accept.

Within this category two types of expertise takers can be distinguished. The *rational* expertise takers select the expert to whom they will listen on the basis of specific criteria, probably taking into account education, employment, access to information, and honors and distinctions. Another type of expertise taker looks for an expert with some *official* approval. An information user of this type is more likely to be impressed by the Staff Director of the President's Commission on Energy Safety than by one professor of nuclear engineering among many others.

Another type of information user forms his opinion as an *attitude taker;* again, two classes can be distinguished. *Ideology takers* weigh more heavily outcomes that reinforce their previously established ideology. For example, a project widely promised to provide more jobs will be favored by those who consider unemployment a major issue. We shouldn't be surprised to find attitude takers of this type ready to accept a project that promises high employment, even if the promise can be demonstrated to be unlikely of fulfillment. The distinguishing characteristic is that a concern "that the things that happen are good ones" swamps the user's interest in "whether the good things will happen at all."

Another type of attitude taker, a leadership taker, adopts, without a review of the facts of the case at hand, the position of a publicly visible individual whose ideology is known to be sympathetic on other issues.

A fourth important category of information users can be called *majority viewers.* Members of this group take their positions from the "predominant" view of certain groups of individuals; when a bandwagon comes by, they jump aboard. The particular majority chosen may differ from one person to another. For example, some people will adopt the opinions of their friends or peer group; if three out of four people in the carpool oppose a new power plant, the user will oppose it also. Another kind of majority viewer looks for the dominant view in a local or national polity; the sentiment at town meetings or the results of a public opinion poll will influence such an individual to join the revealed majority.

Information users in the last category take their opinions from an individual or individuals on entirely personal grounds. These *personality takers* are to be distinguished from the leadership takers by their lack of interest in expressly ideological or public interest concerns: they follow a particular opinion leader because they "like him" in a personal rather than ideological or rational way.

Every one of these approaches to information use represents an effort on the user's part to balance the cost of obtaining information of various types and at various levels of detail against the benefits to be obtained by doing so. They are roughly ordered on a scale of decreasing predicted value of analysis: the fact respecters invest the most resources in obtaining data, making their own models, and doing their own analysis; the expertise taker invests— perhaps once for several decisions—in an evaluation of experts and then uses the experts' conclusions; majority viewers and personality takers commonly use easily obtainable information about sources of opinions and then adopt conclusions at second hand. Not only individuals but also agencies and firms can be placed in one of these categories. Government agencies, however, usually have special responsibilities to behave like fact respecters (and also to collect data on preferences of affected populations).

INFORMATION AND PARTICIPATION

Planners have vigorously and successfully advocated allowing parties "most affected" by various public decisions to be involved in the planning process, only to be perplexed at the tendency of people to display "apathy" towards the opportunities so created. What often happens is that the project or proposal "most affects" the planners (in fact, it occupies their whole attention!) and a few special interests, and its consequences for the community are so widely diffused that the value of involvement for any individual is probably quite small. The *individual* members of the community in such cases are not well advised—at least as regards their respective self-interests—to invest much effort in being informed.

Recognition that much information is a public good, and a less frequently explicit realization of the efficiency (for the many individuals who see only modest gains and losses at stake) of ignoring public choices, is presumably the delegation of decision making to government agencies: in cases in which it's not worth anyone's while *in particular* to invest much effort in a problem, but in which much is at stake for the society *as a whole,* we invent, fund, and empower a government service of expert, informed, evaluation and choice.[4] These services have probably failed, as advocates of participation have asserted, but the principal failure is one of imperfectly obtaining or integrating information about preferences, and not one of depriving the people of influence. Interesting indirect support for this perception is found in such studies as Stewart and Gelberd's (1976) demonstration that public officials predict the judgments (preferences) of relevant interest groups very badly, suggesting ignorance that could only damage their ability to serve their decision-maker function. Regulatory agencies are to some extent captured, of course, but accusations of favoritism affect planning agencies and government units, such as legislatures, with very broad constituencies. In such cases the institutional design errors that cause the wrong interests to be served are more subtle than simply allowing a concentrated interest group to shoulder the public interest aside.

An important class of such errors is the design of information management systems for public choice that ignore the properties of information elucidated above. A public involvement process constructed as though everyone is a fact respecter will not work in the real world. But even if an affected party involves himself in a public decision and is willing to commit enough time to make a difference, there are paradoxical properties of information that will discourage its use. To the extent that someone has formed a strong opinion on an issue from information already processed, the likelihood that further information will contradict what he already knows is small and therefore the expected value of obtaining any is reduced. Again, this is not irrational. In fact, such devaluation of future information is the only logical result consistent with the fact of having an opinion, which in turn is just what a responsible person should have if he has processed some information!

The nature of available information will have a great bearing on the likelihood that someone uses it. Consider our hypothetical citizen confronted with an EIS that will take more time to read than he thinks worth committing. First, the EIS might generate descriptive data about the project as part of a sequence moving from elementary to sophisticated. For example:

1. The project will injure some wildlife.
2. The species affected will be birds, rather than animals.
3. Central estimators for the number of each species killed are: etc.
4. The variances of these estimates for each species are: etc.
5. New technologies available with probability 0.2 will reduce these estimates by 8 percent on the average.

If absorbing the five items listed above exceeds the efficient information processing time of an actor, the last fact adduced will never be consumed since its understanding requires that the first four have been appreciated. If consumers know that information is being supplied in this fashion, however, not much harm is done other than the waste of the analysis that generated item number 5.

But suppose information is supplied with increasing quality, thus:

1. This project is harmful to birds and other living things.
2. Actually, it's only harmful to birds.

3. In fact, it makes fish poisonous to eat and the effect on bird popula-
    tions will be temporary.

Processing information of this kind is likely to make an information
user's overall judgment about the project swing back and forth as he con-
sumes it. Furthermore, there is no particular sequence in which it must be
consumed; one would be as well off to read only the last (most authoritative)
report as to read the entire sequence. The order of provision is important for
reasons opposite to the case above: we would like to know which paper came
out last so we can *ignore* the previous ones rather than wanting to know so
we can be sure to read them. If research and public investment could be
organized so that only the last (best) research is done, that would obviously be
preferable to simply doing more research at any given time. But conflicting
sources of information of this kind are typically not provided to the user in
any sequence or ordering. What the individual sees is a quantity of information, separated into parts that he can expect to be more or less independent,
each of which will turn his decision in a different direction, and all of which
will exceed his rational time budget for the project. Such an information user
is in a very difficult situation indeed. He must either overrun his rational
investment of analysis or run a serious chance of missing most or all of the
valuable information available to him if he stops after having processed what
he has time for. It is easy to construct cases in which the rational response of
the consumer is to do without information entirely, adopting his opinion from
someone else or even choosing at random. He may also excuse himself from
participation in the decision making process entirely.

OPPORTUNISTIC USE OF INFORMATION

Participants in public choice who have formed firm opinions as to the
merits of the alternatives available are principally concerned with getting what
they want. Among the variety of ways to do this is to demand more information about the project. This strategy is especially effective in the form of a
lawsuit or administrative appeal on the adequacy of an environmental impact
statement. Redrafting the statement and including more impacts sometimes
imposes delay on a project's developer that can sometimes stop a project cold
through cost increase, or sometimes such techniques form part of a mul-
tipronged strategy to defeat it. The legal process by which information is
managed can in such ways provide levers that participants have incentives to
pull for reasons unrelated to information's typical use. The analogy to dilatory
or bullying use of discovery in litigation is direct. Frieden (1978) describes
such uses of environmental protection levers to avert local population growth.

The importance of such opportunistic uses of information is evidenced by
Bardach and Pugliarese (1977) in their description of the effort invested by

public agencies in anticipating exactly such attacks on impact statements. The reason this opportunism is so often successful lies in the impossibility of assessing the amount of information in a signal without reference to the receiver's probabilities; an information user can claim to be underinformed without the independent review possible, for example, when a purchaser of a commodity claims to be shortweighted.

Policy Implications

The foregoing analysis provides a basis for several policy recommendations. The ones I offer are illustrative; it is not necessary to make these reforms en bloc, nor is the process proposed the only one that will work.

FOCUS ON THE DEMAND SIDE

Supply-side strategies for information provision require someone to guess what someone else would find useful to know. This conclusion challenges the entire impact statement process as currently practiced, and the challenge is a powerful one. It's hard enough for an information user to obtain the information he should; for someone else to anticipate his needs and those of other differently situated parties with different interests is simply hopeless. The only chance an agency has to supply what the various interested parties care to know is to supply everything it can—but the result will provide too much information for any but the most profoundly affected party, and will hence not be worth the minimal investment of effort required to get anything out of it! As we have seen, overprovision of information is not only wasteful, but can easily decrease the amount of information used by many parties with no irrationality on the users' parts.

The Council on Environmental Quality guidelines for EISs (1979) recognize the problem of information overload, but with the greatest crudeness (i.e., a 150-page length limit). As long as party A is compelled to provide information for B1, B2, B3, etc.,—especially at the beginning of a dispute—he will err seriously one way or another. Resources committed to informing participants in a public choice process should be concentrated on the users themselves.

Furthermore, trying to push a string, as impact-statement requirements of law do, has consequences more serious than waste; someone else can pull on the string and deflect the information search towards ends that have nothing to do with information. In particular, we have become accustomed to intervenors in the public decision process demanding in court that an agency provide more information in the EIS; it may be that the agency guessed wrong about what the public wanted to know, but the same events can be explained as intervenors using the opportunity as a means to delay the project, and the latter interpretation has in many cases poisoned the well of constructive debate.

Reorientation of our attention to information demand rather than supply has two subsidiary implications for information providers.

Government Should Provide Only Public Good Information. For a particular proposed project, most information about the futures to be expected from different alternatives is valuable to only a minority of affected parties. However, there are a few things everyone wants to know. Among these are an initial identification of the *kinds* of impacts the project's alternative versions might cause (to allow specific impacts to be predicted by the parties respectively concerned with them), and descriptions of fiscal impacts on a government (since these are spread by the tax system over all citizens of the polity). But there is no advantage to the government's role being expanded; the information it provides will be poorly matched to consumer demand for all the reasons we have seen. What people can be expected to gather for themselves will be better suited to its purpose.

This principle does not unduly restrict the role of government in making public decisions better informed. While it has no business providing information that does not meet the conventional test for public goods, it can often be appropriate for a unit of government to subsidize potentially affected parties to obtain their own information (Steeg 1976), and management of the decision process itself can have profound effects on information use.

Package Information by User Rather Than Subject. The fundamental question a decision maker asks of a proposal is "what does it mean for me?" He knows who *me* is, but seeks information to partly explain the *what.* An ideal source for the information user would allow him to look up his own characteristics (e.g., "plumber, more than three children, income between $15,000 and $20,000, good health . . .") and find descriptions of his future life with and without the proposal in question, including how his health would change, what would happen to his taxes, etc. If information is organized by subject, on the other hand, the user either has to know at the start that his taxes, for example, might change and that he should look under "fiscal effects," or he must browse at random at a cost that may well exceed what he is wise to invest. Short of the ideal, there is much room for achievable improvement on the conventional impact statements. At the least, information can be presented in a variety of "bite" sizes.

Because it is so difficult to know how much information a document contains for the next user, much less how valuable it will be to him, and because differently affected parties have different rational information-processing budgets, information is much more likely to be used if it is provided with a conscious recognition that different users will use it in different ways. A modest example would be thorough indexing and summarization of impact statements; an existing example, although not an EIS, deserving emulation is the New England River Basin Commission's study of oil development on the New England coast (1976). It offers its results in at least three levels of detail, with imaginative cross-referencing and "road maps." Current practice works in almost exactly the opposite direction, perhaps because the operational criterion for an impact statement is that it withstand a court test of its completeness imposed by someone who is looking specifically for faults rather than trying to use it (Bardach and Pugliarese 1978).

DISCOURAGE STAKING OUT POSITIONS

The planning process should be designed to discourage parties from taking positions, especially binary "pro" or "con" positions, until the last possible moment. People who adopt such positions are unlikely to invest time or effort in using information, and a planning process in which the various parties take firm sides and try to bargain each other towards a total victory position will ensure poorly informed participants. Furthermore, many projects, especially industrial developments, don't allow intermediate positions as usually formulated: half a nuclear power plant is not a feasible compromise. If the feasible actions are widely separated, there is little to bargain since one side or the other will obviously end up near-total losers. In such cases, it is especially important to keep the possibility of persuasion alive. If everyone agrees that a certain solution is pretty good, no one feels like a loser. But if the parties have taken sides early on, such an outcome will be especially difficult to attain.

The existence of majority viewers and personality takers gives special importance to public figures and local leaders in this regard. In facility siting conflicts, for example, a proposal can be permanently derailed if a local official takes a position in opposition to a new proposal early in the debate: in the first place, he often cannot gracefully change his mind, and in the second place, a bandwagon of opposition develops carrying a great many people who are no longer processing information.

Keeping participants uncommitted depends on the gross structure of the planning process, and in particular on two factors. First, many different alternatives should be on the table early, and for as long as possible. One of the wrong ways to site a prison or hazardous waste landfill is to choose a single "best" location and advocate it.

Second, the alternatives should be described with as many parameters as possible that can be adjusted over a wide range of values. Another wrong way to site an unpopular facility is to present a fixed design on a take-it-or-leave-it basis. Sometimes continuously variable parameters, such as local compensation for disamenity (O'Hare 1977), have to be purposely built into the design. If the only possible outcomes of a dispute are "a power plant" or "the status quo," someone who favors the status quo will have to expect overwhelming evidence contradicting what he knows before he will rationally invest in more information. But if compensation, or some other dimension of the project, allows for more outcomes distributed between these poles, a modest amount of information favoring the pole opposite his can be expected to move him to a feasible, nearby solution. A modest amount of such information is much more likely than overwhelming evidence, so the user will have incentives to process more information at any point and to suspend judgment as to exactly where along the "scale" he wants to take his stand until he has more data.

DON'T USE PUBLIC CHOICE MECHANISMS THAT REQUIRE OBJECTIVE ANALYSES

A tradition of social choice is embodied in the study by a "blue-ribbon" or "expert" or "broadly representative" commission, or an engineer's technical evaluation of alternatives. This tradition may be the modern expression of oracular or priestly decision making, or it may be a new development; in any case it produces the same schismatic effect. Appeal to an expert evaluation, or trust in an "objective" impact statement, is grounded in the expectation that the resulting study will be perceived as objective, and treated as objective, by the participants in the debate. This expectation is confounded so universally that I can propose a general principle exactly contrary:

> *There is no report or study on a controversial matter that will be used by the participants in debate as though it were objective.*

The results should not be surprising for several reasons. In the first place, many controversial issues cannot be settled with an outcome superior to the *status quo ante,* much less with a solution that dominates all others. This means that some interests will think themselves worse off under the proposed solution than they would be otherwise: motivation therefore exists to attack the report. The means are usually at hand as well: (1) complicated problems are at best analyzed under uncertainty and on the basis of arguable assumptions; (2) experts achieve their expertise by involvement in the industry or practice under study on one side or another, and bias is easy to assert; (3) preferences are difficult to assess, and an expert study deliberately removes logrolling from the political process that was invented to balance interests. One faction or another will present the report as evidence for one side—a seizure which afflicts the document itself with the appearance or suspicion of hidden bias.

The policy implication is accordingly that public choice mechanisms should not require objective information in order to function properly, since there is no operational definition of "objectivity" and hence no such information. Much useful information is ignored by the parties it might best serve because it is mistrusted, and such mistrust is more likely to vitiate the information if the provider makes claims to objectivity. Because of the acceptance of the "capture" theory of regulators, or because of a more general mistrust of government, this fate often befalls impact statements. Designed to nourish information-hungry citizens, they are more often dismembered by litigants. In fact, the parties to the dispute often have more influence with frankly self-serving statements and reports, since a user can correct them for known bias and doesn't fear deception by indeterminate distortions.

If tendentious information had a formal place in the decision process, it would be less important to try to select or produce "objective" material; trials exemplify decision processes in which all information is presented to favor one side or the other, and explicit confrontation is trusted to separate truth from falsehood. One obvious way to provide this place is to enable each party to obtain his own information, noting that the public good information that a central authority might provide is most often (but not always) of the type that will not attract challenge. I will present a more complicated mechanism in the next section.

How to Proceed

What would a decision process designed to satisfy these criteria look like? Much variation is possible; I draw one possible outline. Two central goals motivate it. First, all participants should where possible be empowered and encouraged to obtain information that they respectively find useful; second, the incentives to use information provision as a delaying or bullying tactic should be countered.[5]

INITIAL STEPS

When a project or policy is initially conceived, the proposer describes it in a document of specified form, providing technical material or access to it, and such predictions of its effects as he cares to offer. A supervisory government agency draws up a schedule for hearings and debate, notifies the interest groups likely to seek participation, and prepares and circulates a preliminary impact statement that outlines the kinds of significant impacts such a project is likely to have, without attempting to estimate their magnitude. This statement is not subject to judicial review.

The agency also provides planning grants, preferably at the proposer's expense, to governments and interest groups meeting a legislated set of criteria including proximity, record of previous participation, etc. These grants will be recognized as a form of the "intervenor compensation" that has been frequently proposed. An important feature of the grants, however, is that they are not matched to costs actually incurred in participation; they must be given without strings. They represent the cost imposed on these actors by the proposal itself (not the project that might or might not proceed) through its demand for analysis, and unfortunately must be estimated according to some parameters of the proposal itself. (If the compensation were conditioned on intervention or actually obtaining information, there is no reason to expect that the intervention would be legitimate or that the information would be worth obtaining even for the producer, since nothing would need to be given up for it.)

INFORMATION MANAGEMENT

The regulatory agency manages a process of debate, discussion, and, importantly, negotiation, which can take a variety of forms. As it proceeds, the various parties are invited to submit what they please in the form of information, analysis, exhortation, or evidence. This information is continuously aggregated and sorted according to the individuals or groups to whom each submitter claims his information will be of interest; the supervising agency serves as an information retrieval system operated according to rules specified (item by item) by the participants. The only grounds for litigation are that the agency did not classify an offering as its submitter asked. Information users are provided, for a small nuisance charge, the submissions that have accumulated to date under the headings they specify;[6] each item is labelled by provider to allow discounting for expected bias as the user sees fit. Note that a variety of technical devices, such as microfilm and computerized indexing, are available to reduce the cost of this process to a trivial level.

NEGOTIATION

The decision mechanism does not concern us here with the exception of two characteristics: First, it is important for the set of alternatives to be dense, or for at least one dimension of the project to vary continuously or nearly so. The amount of compensation that might be paid to affected groups—"side payments"—is one such variable (O'Hare 1977), and allowing for such compensation is important in the case of intrinsically lumpy projects for just this reason. As we have seen, alternatives that are very far apart, especially binary "all-or-nothing" choices, encourage all parties to harden their positions as "pro" or "con" very early.

One way to put such variables on the table is for the supervising agency to include them as types of impacts in its initial statement. Alternatively, they can be legislated as a condition of permit granting, as is done for energy facilities in Washington State (Sanderson 1979).

Second, debate is not restricted to a finite set of alternatives; the information management process we have described obviously permits any party to propose new alternatives, at any level of analysis, at any time. This is important because current choice processes seem to do very badly at forcing an appropriate set of alternatives to the surface; the developer has no incentive to identify alternatives other than those he found necessary in order to choose his favorite, and no practical means is available to compel him to do so with even minimal enthusiasm—much less success.

DECISIVENESS

The multiplication of alternatives, however, obviously raises the specter that so many will be in question that none can command a decisive coalition. The problem of balancing between inclusiveness and decisiveness is a general one: the legal process that grants everyone the right to be sure his other rights have been observed in court is especially liable to misuse as a technique of delay. There seems to be no elegant mechanism by which to align everyone's incentives in these cases; sooner or later, a supervisory authority (by offering slightly different versions of existing ones), or the likelihood that a useful and fundamentally different proposal will be presented, are no longer worth investing time in waiting for.

Collapsing a cloud of slightly different alternatives into a few distinct ones probably can't be done except by fiat (note that the incentives that motivate legislators, for example, to cluster around a few distinct alternatives do not motivate parties that want a project, in any form, killed). But deadlines announced in advance help. For example, the process we have described will probably lead to litigation; it would be very useful to empower the judge in the first such case to declare it a class action in the sense that anyone not joining it with whatever objection he wanted to make to the process would be precluded from any subsequent litigation. A single case would then be dispositive, or nearly so, and sequential litigation could not be used to impose delay.

Similarly, a deadline for the information exchange and debate process, analogous to the scoping process used by Massachusetts for impact statements (Massachusetts 1978), improves the incentive structure of the process greatly. It should be extremely difficult to delay this schedule; the agency's or a court's response to an intervenor asking for a suspension of events should be (1) the intervenor has had funds and opportunity to obtain the information he wants, and (2) all decisions are made with less than full information. Just because not everything that could be known about this one is known does not justify prolonging the status quo.

DISCOVERY

The mechanism we have outlined provides appropriate incentives for actors to inform themselves, and efficient means by which to inform each other. What about its incentives for one side to disclose what it doesn't want the other side to know? It is difficult to design a mechanism that forces A to reveal things to B, because B (on whom it obviously falls to enforce his rights) usually doesn't know that there is something there to demand, nor can he prove its existence if he suspects it. In law, this problem is dealt with by stringent punishment (voiding a conviction or worse) on the occasions when concealment of exculpatory evidence is revealed, and by not allowing evidence withheld by either party to be presented in a trial. Neither scheme promises to help much in our case; we will have to be content with the various parties' shrewdness in getting the facts they need to make their own case, and with a rather limited set of rules obliging the developer to disclose technical data about the project that is needed for others' models.

In particular situations, it may be possible to force information to the surface by demanding or negotiating for warranties: a developer might, by way of providing credible information about air pollution, warrant that his emission will be within certain limits with appropriate remedies for nonperformance, e.g., fines, conditional compensation payments, or agreement to correct shortfalls (Arrow 1974).

We should be cautious, in any case, about empowering any parties to demand information from others; such rules violate our conditions for operating on the demand rather than the supply side. Analogies to the many cases in which A can practically be forced to provide X to B are faulty because of the impossibility of observing what B has actually received, either in type or amount, when the information is at issue. Since B's satisfaction cannot be ascertained, there is no way to know whether his continued claim for information is merely a delaying device or evidence of real ignorance. Notice that B is not prevented from using A's reticence persuasively. An effective argument in many cases is, "we have reasons x, y, and z, to believe that A knows something that would make you reject his proposal, but he won't tell us about it—isn't that suspicious?"

Summary

The mechanism described above can be characterized in a nutshell as abandoning the supply-side impact statement process as a device to provide parties in conflict with the facts they need; instead the parties themselves are expected to get their own facts, and enabled to do so; the impact statement is then simply the record of debate itself. Instead of writing a statement for use in debate, the debate is structured as a negotiation and information exchange process organized to develop an impact statement. The participants are using a collective and inclusive impact statement writing process as a decision tool, rather than relying on the product of an exclusive and selective one. To the extent possible such a process anticipates the things people are likely to do anyway, rather than what they might be implored to do, and rather than trying to prevent these things, incorporate them into the choice process in a constructive way.

Notes

1. The approximation is that we ignore the psychological cost of uncertainty. Information may be consumed somewhat more than a simple efficiency calculation would suggest in order to reduce anxiety, but this additional consumption is unrelated to the phenomenon at issue here.

2. The well-known paradox of voting is an example of this problem; see also the analysis by Olson (1971) of the disincentives to act to obtain collective goods.

3. In this discussion we omit entirely considerations of the type explicated by Olson (1971), indicating in many cases that a member of an affected group will not rationally invest *any* time or effort in obtaining the outcomes he desires. But it should be noted that such behavior on the part of the group members makes their effective demand for information go to zero. We are also ignoring the possibility that information will be consumed for its own sake, as when people read history books for recreation.

4. For a thorough discussion of this type of economy or analysis, see Kelman [forthcoming].

5. Massachusetts has recently passed hazardous waste facility siting legislation that embodies most of these recommendations (Chapter 508 of the Laws of 1980).

6. Obviously, indexing can be done by topic and otherwise as well as by expected user.

References

Akerlof, G. 1970. The Market for Lemons. *Quarterly Journal of Economics.* 84:488-500.

Alchian, A. 1969. Information Costs, Pricing, and Resource Unemployment. *Western Economic Journal.* 7:109-128.

Arrow, K. 1973. *Information and Economics Behavior.* Federation of Swedish Industries, Stockholm.

————. 1974. *The Limits of Organization.* New York: Norton.

Bacow, L. and O'Hare, M. 1980. "Means and Ends in Evaluating Public Choice Mechanisms." Project Paper. Laboratory of Architecture and Planning, Massachusetts Institute of Technology, Cambridge, Massachusetts.

Bardach, E. and L. Pugliarese. 1977. The Environmental Impact Statement Versus the Real World. The Public Interest. Fall: 22-38.

Boulding, K.E. 1966. The Economics of Knowledge and the Knowledge of Economics. American Economic Review 56, no. 3:1-13.

Demsetz, H. 1969. Information and Efficiency: Another Viewpoint. Journal of Law and Economics. 12:1-12.

Downs, A. 1957. An Economic Theory of Democracy. New York: Harper and Row.

Frieden, B. 1979. The Environmental Hustle. Cambridge, Massachusetts: MIT Press.

Green, P.E. et al. 1967. Experiments on the Value of Information in Simulated Marketing Environments. Boston: Allyn and Bacon.

Haefele, E.T. 1973. Representative Government and Environmental Management. Baltimore: Johns Hopkins.

Kelman, S. Regulation and Paternalism. Public Policy, in press.

King, L.R., and Melanson, P.H. 1973. Knowledge and Policy. In Knowledge, Politics, and Public Policy, ed. P.H. Melanson. Cambridge, Massachusetts: Winthrop Publishers.

Machlup, F. 1962. The Production and Distribution of Knowledge in the U.S. Princeton, New Jersey: Princeton University Press.

Massachusetts, Commonwealth of, 310 C.M.R. 10.05.

McDonough, A. 1963. Information Economics and Management Systems, pp. 68-118. New York: McGraw-Hill Book Company.

McHale, J. 1971. The Changing Information Environment. In Information Technology: Some Critical Implications for Decision Makers, pp. 183-238. The Conference Board.

Michael, D. 1968. On Coping with Complexity: Planning and Politics. Daedalus 97:1179-1193.

——. 1971. Democratic Participation and Planning. In Information Technology in a Democracy, ed. Alan Weston, pp. 291-310. Cambridge, Massachusetts: Harvard University Press.

Mundel, D.C. 1979. Personal communication. Congressional Budget Office.

New England River Basins Commission. 1976. Onshore Facilities Related to Offshore Oil and Gas Development. Boston, Massachusetts.

O'Hare, M. 1977. Not on My Block, You Don't. Public Policy 25:407-458.

Olson, M. 1971. The Logic of Collective Action. Cambridge, Massachusetts: Harvard University Press.

Popkin, S., et al. 1976. Comment, What Have You Done For Me Lately? Toward an Investment Theory of Voting. American Political Science Review 70:753-778.

Reutlinger, S. Techniques for Project Approval under Uncertainty. Baltimore, Maryland: Johns Hopkins Press.

Rubin, D.M. 1974. Directions for Environmental News Coverage. In The Environment, eds. J. Cairng, Jr. and K.L. Dickson, pp. 139-150. New York: Marcel Dekker.

Sanderson, D.R. 1979. "A Case Study of Four Negotiated Compensation Settlements." Laboratory of Architecture and Planning, Massachusetts Institute of Technology, Cambridge, Massachusetts.

Shubik, M. 1976. Information, Rationality and Free Choice in a Future Democratic Society. *Daedalus* 96:771-778.

Skjel, S. 1973. *Information for Collective Action.* Lexington, Massachusetts: D.C. Heath and Company.

Spence, A.M. 1974. An Economist's View of Information. In *Annual Review of Information Science and Technology,* ed. C. Curadra, Vol. 9.

Spence, M. 1972. "Marketing Signaling." Discussion Paper No. 4, Kennedy School of Government, Harvard University, Cambridge, Massachusetts.

Steeg, R.M. 1976. Federal Agency Compensation of Intervenors. *Environmental Affairs* 5:697-719.

Stewart, T.R. and Gelberd, L. 1976. Analysis of Judgment Policy: a New Approach for Citizen Participation in Planning. *AIP Journal,* January:33-41.

Stigler, G. 1961. The Economics of Information. *Journal of Political Economy* 69:213-255.

––––––. 1962. Information on the Labor Market. *Journal of Political Economy* 70, no. 5:94-105.

U.S. Council on Environmental Quality. 1978. Implementation of Procedural Provisions: Final Regulations: National Environmental Policy Act––Regulations. *Federal Register* 43, no. 230.

Weiss, C. 1977. Research for Policy's Sake: The Enlightenment Function of Social Research. *Policy Analysis* 3:531-545.

S.M. MACGILL AND D.J. SNOWBALL

11 *What Use Risk Assessment?*

Introduction

Risk assessment emerged as something of a growth industry in the late 1970s, the product of an age of increasing risk potential and risk awareness (Dierkes *et al.* 1979; Goodman and Rowe 1979; Conrad 1980; Schwing and Albers 1980; Griffiths 1981). This paper examines various features of the current use of written risk assessments in conjunction with planning decisions for potentially hazardous installations in the United Kingdom. These are installations which pose a potential threat to the health and safety of the public in their vicinity due to the possibility of rare but catastrophic (low probability, high consequence) accidents. Such installations include chlorine plants and liquefied petroleum gas facilities posing, respectively, the threat of release of toxic gas and of cataclysmic fire.

Risk assessment can be viewed as an aid to decision-making for the siting of such installations, with the general aim of improving the quality of the decisions (by increasing the base of information on which decisions are taken) and probing the acceptability of them (by demonstrating something about the safety of the proposed installations). These are very general statements of why risk assessments are undertaken; the significance of these broad uses and the extent to which they might be considered to be fulfilled may depend on who one is—applicant (industry), planner, or politician (local or national govern-

From S.M. Macgill and D.J. Snowball, "What Use Risk Assessment?" in *Applied Geography*, Vol. 3 (1983), pp. 171-192, copyright © Butterworth Scientific, Ltd. Reprinted with permission.

ment), guardian (Health and Safety Executive), adviser, public participant, or observer. It is far from obvious that risk assessments successfully perform their intended roles. Moreover they may perform other, less obvious, roles that are not subsumed in the above statements.

The assessment of risk raises intrinsically difficult and emotive issues, and the different agencies referred to above view different moral, statutory and democratic rights to be at stake. Moreover, judgements on risk are often embedded in a complex web of costs and benefits from other impacts of particular installations. In order to get beyond rather general statements such as those above about the uses that risk assessments serve, the interests of all parties involved with a decision must be appreciated, and also the way parties typically interact with each other. This is because the different parties involved may each attach different degrees of importance to the roles that risk assessments can serve.

This paper aims, critically and explicitly, to identify the range of roles which risk assessments can fulfil. Ten are specified. These are examined and, where appropriate, related to the broad responsibilities, aims and interests of parties who are typically concerned with planning decisions for potentially hazardous installations.

Geographers have long been involved with risk and hazard issues, and, as Otway (1980) notes, the roots of contemporary academic concern with risk assessment for potentially hazardous installations lie in the two disciplines of geography and of chemical engineering. The contribution from the former field stems from the long history of work concerned with perception of and adaptation to natural hazards (see, for example Parker and Harding 1979), and from the latter field from safety engineering and loss prevention (Lees 1980).

It is debatable whether consideration of risk assessment in planning decisions can be separated from the broader and currently fashionable concern with environmental impact analysis (Clark *et al.* 1980; O'Riordan and Sewell 1981). The view underlying the work below is that risk and hazard issues are sufficiently distinctive for risk assessment to be considered separately. This view has ample precedent, for instance in the deliberations of the officially recognized Advisory Committee on Major Hazards (Health and Safety Commission 1976, 1979) and the work of the recently established Major Hazards Assessment Unit within the Health and Safety Executive (Barrell 1981). Notwithstanding the separation in the present paper of risk assessment from environmental impact analysis, it may be possible to broaden the interpretation of the 10 roles that are examined below to the broader field of environmental impact analysis.

The paper is based on UK experience. While a broader international perspective might have been more desirable, this is difficult due to different cultural and institutional environments. Nuclear installations are not of immediate concern, though the greater attention they have attracted elsewhere may be noted, and some of the discussion developed below will be of relevance to them.

Context

Risk assessment in the planning (as opposed to the operational) phase of hazardous installations is of particular interest because decision-making is open to publicly acknowledged scrutiny, and there is an opportunity for the planning system to exert a measure of control over the siting of the installations in relation to their environment. Such decisions may be concerned with applications for hazardous facilities on greenfield sites, or for major alterations to existing facilities. Most existing hazardous installations are not involved, however, as these are typically no longer within the sphere of planning control. An additional category of development which is of relevance below is for certain changes in land use in the vicinity of hazardous installations. An indication of "events" in a typical decision process is given in Fig. 1.

The risk assessments alluded to in the present paper arise either from information presented by the developer in support of a planning application, from the official consultation activity by the planning authorities, or by other parties in response to publicity about the proposed facilities. Thus they may be either official or unofficial, but in all cases are the written evidence on safety that is available before a decision is taken.

To the non-bureaucrat, the safety scrutiny occurring during a decision process for hazardous installations is by far the most visible evaluation of safety for these plants. This may or may not involve acknowledged public debate, either through the formal proceedings of a Public Inquiry (increasingly questioned about their effectiveness; Pearce et al. 1979; Edwards and Rowan-Robinson 1980; Wynne 1980a), or less formal public meetings, where arguments for and against applications can be presented and cross-examined (McRea and Greaves 1981).

Kates (1978) gives a vivid classification of the roles of parties or agents involved in decisions on risk as hazard-makers, risk-takers, guardians and assessors. Industry, as applicants and would-be operators of the installations in question would appear to be the main hazard-makers, whilst the public in the vicinity of such plants are the main risk-takers, though the host local authorities and industry could also be included in this category. The Health and Safety Executive are the main guardians, with the local authorities and industry also potentially important in this capacity. All parties are likely to undertake some role as assessor. When attempting to appraise the use of risk assessment by such agencies it is useful to appreciate at the outset that each

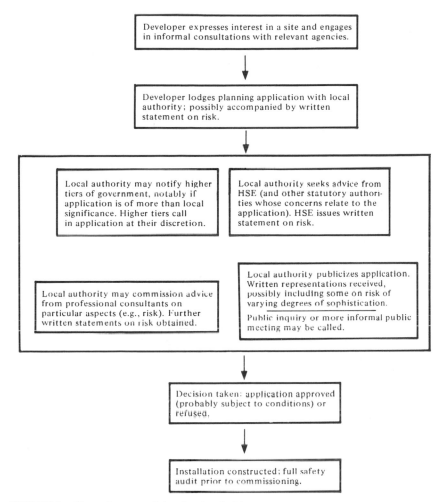

FIGURE 1. The main stages of the planning decisic ..

has its own (1) role in the decision process; (2) responsibility for different aspects of safety; (3) technical competence and expertise; (4) accountability to and degree of independence of others. These matters are addressed before considering the 10 roles of risk assessment.

ROLE IN THE DECISION PROCESS

The applicant seeking official planning approval will typically be strongly committed to a project. This does not mean that plans are finalized, though there might be a great deal at stake if efforts to obtain permission are unsuccessful. Planning approval is more likely to be viewed as a hurdle to be overcome than as a beneficial experience.

The decision-taker (Secretary of State or local authority council, or those civil servants and planning officers acting on his or its behalf) is expected to make a political decision in the "public interest" on the whole package presented by a planning application—safety, economics, employment, environment, possible sterilizing effects on adjacent land via its designation as a buffer zone, and liability for indemnity in the event of an accident. The imposition of planning conditions allows the decision-taker a broad measure of hazard control in the event of approval being granted.

The Health and Safety Executive, the statutory guardians of safety, and professional risk consultants, act in an advisory capacity to other parties. They ostensibly judge safety only, as far as this is possible, and have no material interest in any single decision outcome.

The broad goal of public participants is for safety to be seen to be achieved—a cause which, in view of its intrinsic nature, will always give room for debate. It is difficult and probably not useful to identify the public as a distinct entity; participation may arise through the actions of individuals, of ephemeral pressure groups, or through established interest groups (O'Riordan 1981a: 254-256, alternatively groups them as ideological, civic and private). As such objector groups tend to be articulate, self-funded, often middle-class, and able to draw on their own expertise (it is often essential that they can), this suggests that the expression of public opinion is sometimes as much a function of social fabric as it is an indication of strength of feeling. Although safety may be the main concern of public participants, their campaign will often not be confined to this issue.

Public participation is voluntary (unlike other parties there is no professional obligation to participate) and arises from a feeling that certain views would otherwise not be adequately represented, in particular, not accounted for in the planning authority's view of the "public interest." As a minority, it might reasonably be argued that the unequal standing with other parties which may be experienced is justified (disadvantaged over time, financial and information resources). However, whether the substance of any arguments should carry correspondingly less weight (an often-heard complaint) is a more contentious point. Public participants are sometimes viewed rather patronizingly by other parties, and sometimes as irrelevant nuisances, but it can also be argued that they make a positive long-term contribution to societal risk management, at their own expense, by forcing other parties not only to recognize their existence but also to provide evidence in favour of contrary opinions and thereby contribute towards more exhaustive decision-making procedures. They can also serve an additional function of keeping regulatory bodies on their toes.

RESPONSIBILITY FOR SAFETY

Safety is a double-edged commitment for industry. On the one hand employers are responsible under the 1974 Health and Safety at Work Act to ensure the safety of their employees and the surrounding community "so far as is reasonably practicable," and indeed in many cases they exceed what is required under this Act; on the other hand, if a major accident occurred there could be a considerable loss of capital, revenue and prestige for the operator involved.

The main responsibility of the Health and Safety Executive lies outside the planning system, namely in the enforcement of the provisions of the Health and Safety at Work Act and its subsequent regulations for installations under construction and in operation. As suggested above, however, they are also involved in an advisory capacity on planning applications, advising the statutory planning authorities as to the broad acceptability in principle of planning applications.

The explicit responsibilities for safety by local authorities are more difficult to pinpoint. They are obliged to have regard for issues of safety before planning approval is judged. Although this gives them some kind of responsibility as guardians of the community at risk, it gives no indication of their explicit responsibilities. It is a moot point, for instance, as to whether they or the Health and Safety Executive ought to have the final word in allowing (or refusing) an application on grounds of safety, in suggesting planning conditions relating to safety and in defining the terms of Heads of Agreement on buffer zones. The Health and Safety Executive have greater technical expertise, but the planning authorities are more directly related to the local community. Moreover, safety is only one of many considerations, and often reduces to a matter of priority rather than principle.

TECHNICAL COMPETENCE AND EXPERTISE

A high level of technical competence and expertise permits safety discussions to be conducted at a sophisticated level (for example, between industry, the Health and Safety Executive, and consultants) but may also foster a sense of alienation or impotence in those groups who do not have access to the necessary resources to produce detailed balancing opinions.

The technical expertise of public participants can range from the highly sophisticated to the barely articulate. While not necessarily covering such an extreme range, the technical competence and experience to identify and estimate hazards may sometimes be beyond the ability of planning authorities. It is clearly important for planners and local authority councillors to be able to assimilate advice obtainable from expert sources at both local and national level which in some cases may be conflicting (both in terms of technical content and recommendations made). Mann (1979), speaking from experience of onshore oil and gas-related developments in NE Scotland, has suggested that there is a growing sophistication on the part of officials who regularly deal with these sorts of planning applications, a theme which is apparently echoed in the experience of planners in Cheshire where there is a heavy concentration of major hazard industry (Payne 1981). Elsewhere, experience is less rich. Several planners have written about the difficult position they occupy; see for example Brook (1980).

ACCOUNTABILITY AND INDEPENDENCE

The parliamentary accountability of a Secretary of State, in those cases where he is involved, is divorced from local considerations and overrides the concept of local sovereignty in an area where there are often some difficult local versus national conflicts to judge (local safety versus the national interest, for instance). Local authorities are accountable to local populations via their democratically elected representatives, but the record of an authority in dealing with hazardous industries is unlikely to be a burning election issue, and the spatial resolution of constituencies is too small adequately to represent the spatial divergence of opinion that may arise. The Health and Safety Executive are indirectly accountable to Parliament (via the Secretary of State for Employment), but not for individual decisions.

As the independent statutory guardians of safety, the Health and Safety Executive are swift to deny any collusion on their part with industry. That questions in this connection are sometimes raised is perhaps predictable given the nature of the system in the UK which emphasizes self-control with minimum external interference (the Robens philosophy, Cmnd 5034). The Executive are similarly anxious to promote their independence of government policy and immunity to unseen government interference, pointing out that any attempt at interference from this source would automatically be "public."

The position occupied by private consultants, whoever their clients are, can lead to claims of bias (giving their clients what they wish to hear) which are hardly made any simpler by the nature of the subject under consideration but which, in a broader sense, expose equally vital questions about the ethics underpinning specialist advice and the possible sacrifice of expert judgement to short-term political appeasement. It would be futile to deny the importance of expert opinion but apposite to question anyone's infallibility, and even to try to determine the possible vested interests that any of the different parties have in decisions when assessing the significance of their contributions.

Ten Roles of Risk Assessment

Various roles that risk assessment can serve have been widely referred to or alluded to in different sources in the literature. Kates (1978), for example, cites the classic three stages of risk estimation, risk evaluation and risk reduction (or control). Other authors (for example, O'Riordan 1981b) concentrate on political and accountability functions, or longer-term institutional issues. Others still are preoccupied with risk estimation only (for example Institute of Chemical Engineers 1982; Lees 1982). The aim below is to attempt to be comprehensive in explicitly identifying the roles that risk assessment can serve. The evidence drawn on is taken largely from existing sources in the literature rather than direct case-study work. However, familiarity with particular case studies has conditioned the authors' interpretation of the litera ture. (In a forthcoming paper, Snowball and Macgill 1982, five individual case studies are examined in more detail.) The 10 broad roles to emerge from this work and to be considered below are:

1.	Risk estimation	
2.	Risk reduction	Technical
3.	Risk comprehension	
4.	Accountability of procedure	
5.	Accountability of income	Political
6.	Credibility of institutions	
7.	Risk evaluation	
8.	Legitimation of interests	
9.	Delay	Incidental
10.	Institutional reform	

Each is examined in turn and, where relevant, the significance of each to the main agencies typically involved with risk assessment in planning decisions is brought out.

RISK ESTIMATION

This is the most immediate function of written risk assessments—the provision of a written description of the nature of the risk and hazard posed—the probability of occurrence of adverse events, and the nature of their consequences,* with particular reference in the present context to effects that may

---

*In some sources, the word "risk" is used strictly to refer to the probability of occurrence of adverse events, and "hazard" is used to refer to their consequences. In the present paper, however, the authors have chosen not to be bound by these strict definitions. This, for instance, allows the use of "risk assessment" and "hazard assessment" interchangeably, and recognition that "risk-benefit" embodies issues of "hazard" as well as "risk."

extend beyond the site boundary and possible interaction (domino) effects with other installations. There are various types of written risk assessment, from general (verbal) statements (Political Ecology Research Group 1980) to those involving complex (fault tree) calculations (Cremer and Warner 1980), mirroring varying levels of technical expertise on the part of the authors, different methodologies, different briefs from the clients, different aims of the authors, or differences in the amount of information available.

The results of risk assessments may be given either quantitatively or qualitatively, in the former case quantifying either or both of the probability of occurrence of events, and the magnitude of their consequence. Ideally, quantitative assessment would appear to be preferable, ostensibly achieving more precision and objectivity. Although it may be difficult to distinguish, say between a 10^{-7} and 10^{-8} result, it is nevertheless useful to know the order of magnitude involved (10^{-3} or 10^{-8}) rather than a description "small" or "very small" which involves an implicit value judgement by the assessor and may be difficult to interpret (Russell 1981). Confidence intervals and sensitivity analysis may be appropriate for some of the uncertain elements, and, for maximum relevance of results, the risk assessment should be both plant specific and site specific (Farmer 1981).

For a risk assessment on a planning application these represent ideals that are likely to be neither feasible nor appropriate, and go far beyond what is statutorily necessary. Permission sought is that of approval in principle; specific design detail is unlikely to be made available, and may not be binding even if it is. Thus risk estimation will typically relate to a generic plant rather than the actual plant to be built, and the representation of the actual plant may not be sufficiently close for results to be meaningful. The plant design may, for example, be changed between planning approval and construction stages unless unusually detailed planning conditions are specified. Thus there are a number of grounds for scepticism over the relevance of a risk estimation exercise at the planning application stage.

Risk estimation problems are by no means confined to those centred on the available level of detail on plant design. Other problems include the following. Scientific knowledge on, say, heavy gas flow, is inadequate for a full risk profile to be determined (McQuaid 1982). Operating experience (the only, albeit second-best, source of information about the performance of such plants) although achieving a good record is still relatively short. Important safety features may be overlooked, or particular geological information (Jones and Sands 1980). Moreover, the potential for sabotage is capable of undermining even the best risk estimation exercise. Extreme skill and perception is therefore required to produce and interpret a useful risk assessment and, far from being a simple objective decision aid, risk estimation is a complex subjective activity, the results of which may be as varied as the authors. Consecutive reports for a given installation produced by a single party may not always concur—as seen, for instance, in two official risk assessment reports for Canvey (Health and Safety Executive 1978, 1981) the latter using modified techniques as well as allowing for recent improvements at the complex. (Typically, the Health and Safety Executive produce considerably less detailed risk estimations than these on planning applications.)

The significance of risk estimation to different parties varies widely. Industry is likely to be firmly convinced in principle of the safety of proposed installations. The type of risk estimation study of most use to industry is an internally conducted hazard analysis or loss prevention study when a plant is being constructed and operated (some time after the planning decision). The required technical design data for such an assessment may not be finalized until after planning approval has been obtained (Bell 1980), it being argued, though not always accepted by other parties, that long lead times from the initial feasibility study of a project to its ultimate operation preclude "freezing" of details at the planning approval stage (Bell 1980). Moreover, considerations of commercial confidentiality and sheer expense may also mitigate against making public more information. Not all applicants take an equally hard line on this matter, there being notable differences in the amount of detail made available by potential developers at the planning approval stage.

Public participants are likely to argue that considerably greater detail than is currently made available is required in order to provide a rich enough base for a risk debate on a planning decision, this being, after all, the only phase of publicly acknowledged scrutiny of hazard potential. The more technically competent public participants may produce their own formal risk estimation studies, despite limitations outlined above. Others prefer to concentrate on other aspects of the risk debate. There may be vehement arguments over the relative merits of qualitative or quantitative assessments (Rasbash and Drysdale 1977; Scottish Development Department 1978; Department of the Environment 1982) which are prone to futility, if taken too far, in the light of the observations made above about the level of plant detail. This in turn, somewhat paradoxically, implies that apparently detailed and sophisticated quantitative assessments may be no more relevant than rather generalized judgements.

The Health and Safety Executive readily acknowledge the limited nature of risk estimation that is possible at the planning stage (Barrell 1981) (though they have recently moved from a general qualitative description of risk to an estimation of the hazardous consequences of worst case events). As with industry, their prime concern lies with scrutiny of the design and operation of actual plant, this obviously occurring *after* planning approval. Planning authorities may rely on risk estimates available from the Health and Safety Executive or may privately commission professional consultants who, in spite of the above-mentioned limitations, often present quite elaborate risk estimation reports. Support for quantitative versus qualitative assessments seems to vary considerably between planning authorities. Some would apparently not know how to interpret the results of a quantitative assessment; others see quantitative estimation as a vital basis on which to found their judgements on acceptable risk.

Risk estimation is fundamental: all subsequent risk assessment roles rest on it. The nature of risk estimation may determine the nature of the risk debate during decision-making. If the estimation is qualitative, argument may focus on the need for quantitative assessment; if the estimation is already quantitative, argument may be pitched at a more sophisticated level, for example focusing on confidence limits and sensitivity analysis for various of the risk estimates produced (it being argued that risk estimation without sensitivity analysis is worthless; Ravetz 1979), or on other than technical issues (see below).

RISK REDUCTION

Risk assessment may be used as a basis for designing plant or granting permission to a self-imposed risk target (10^{-6} or whatever), or for providing specific advice to the decision-maker as a guide for framing suitable planning conditions. Modifications in plant layout and design, additional containment measures, suggested management practices, and evacuation measures may all be recommended on the basis of a written risk assessment (in light of weak points, suboptimal layout, susceptible populations, etc.), and in this way obvious problems may be eliminated early on. Risk assessment can also be used in a site-screening forward-planning role (Cremer and Warner 1978).

Recommendations for getting the design right first time are made notwithstanding the observation (Flint 1981: 178) that relatively few reported failures stem from oversight in design, the larger remainder (human error) defying mathematical modelling. At the outline planning stage such recommendations would be at a relatively coarse level (plant layout, quantities of materials, secondary containment buffer zones), due to a lack of design detail, and the inappropriateness of forcing certain design features onto an operator. There may be considerable differences between parties regarding what is required in this respect, and what is actually specified (for example in planning conditions and heads of agreement) is unlikely to satisfy all.

Consultants may suggest the nature of containment or safety systems which a developer with considerable experience in operating a given type of plant may see as unnecessary external interference. It might even be thought that such suggestions should have been made by the Health and Safety Executive (Brough 1981). Thus planning and safety are among the many spheres in which definite statutory responsibilities cannot be defined. There is much overlap and, despite all parties claiming to act in the public interest, not always agreement. Consultants and the Health and Safety Executive may disagree over prudent buffer zones (as was brought to light at a recent public inquiry, see Milne 1981), over prudent evacuation, or over basic features of plant layout. Sections of the public may also venture to offer suggestions on prudent locations (especially NIMBY groups, an acronym for *Not in my back yard*; see, for example, Thompson 1981). What is specified in the final planning decision is either a compromise, or a judgement over party differences and over possible difficulties within parties. For instance, a local authority may encounter problems over compensation for loss of development land if it wants to establish a buffer zone (Walsh 1979).

RISK COMPREHENSION

Although the end result of a risk assessment may be its most obvious characteristic, the process of carrying it out is hardly less important (as argued for example by Lees 1980: Ch. 1). The preparation of a risk assessment may force onto the author a more rigorous understanding of the system than might otherwise be the case. This might include knowledge of broad geographic features of the area as well as industrial process information and explicit recognition of areas of uncertainty. Clients of any reports prepared for the assessment are also given the opportunity of a better understanding. For "lay" parties, however, this will not necessarily be productive: they may not understand or believe the more technical material. For parties opposing the development in question, explicit recognition of uncertainty may seem grounds for remote siting. Thus although risk comprehension is a necessary prerequisite for informed dialogue, and to increase the comprehension of risk by all parties may be a laudable aim, it is not necessarily a means of reconciling interparty differences. The most acceptable risk is the one about which people are most ignorant (see also Ravetz 1979); the knowledge whereby this ignorance is dispelled may be used irrationally or antagonistically rather than productively. Kletz (1980), for example, argues that the public involved in risk debates are often still risk illiterate, and do not seem to appreciate that risk assessment is about priorities, not principles. Such remarks shift the focus from risk comprehension to risk evaluation, discussed more fully under a separate heading below.

ACCOUNTABILITY OF PROCEDURE

It is self-evident that the very act of risk assessment on a planning application involves publicity of information and invites publicly acknowledged debate, and hence a degree of procedural accountability that would otherwise not occur. This may be of particular significance to planning authorities and to public participants for whom the planning decision is a particularly crucial step. Implicit remarks on safety from "risk experts" have apparently been found increasingly unsatisfactory by these parties, for whom understanding technical matters is not necessarily the daunting prospect of times past.

In theory, greater accountability should promote better-informed decision-taking and more orderly and structured deliberations. Greater expertise may be brought to bear, parties may question assumptions and whether all sources of hazard have been identified. As suggested above, the resulting debate may be either more or less acrimonious. Notwithstanding these considerations, increasing procedural accountability may not necessarily have an effect on the decision outcome and the operating safety of a given plant: thus, for instance, industry and the Health and Safety Executive may consider it to be of marginal value in this respect, other than in a public relations capacity.

O'Riordan and Sewell (1981:4) distinguish in increasing levels of procedural accountability between: (a) closed decisions (no consultation with wider interests); (b) consultation—where selected interests are informed of impending decisions and asked to state their views, but with no guarantee that their views will be taken into account (political whitewash?); and (c) influential participation (where a wider array of interests are not only consulted, but are directly involved in negotiations and creative discussions that lead to generally acceptable outcomes). Clearly of importance here is the extent to which all relevant information is made available in detail and in sufficient time to allow for adequate response to it.

Although the UK apparently fits into categories (b) and (c) (relative to other countries rather than in any absolute sense), other authors (e.g. Wynne 1980a) have noted that discussion is often terminated rather than resolved, questions raised need not be answered, and new evidence is not necessarily considered. Elsewhere, criticisms have been made about a mismatch of resources between the public and other parties—over time, money, expertise and information available (OCPU 1979). A recent article *(Planning 440)* suggests that some, albeit modest, modifications to the current Public Inquiry system may be forthcoming in this respect.

As noted above, it is not only on behalf of the public that calls for increasing procedural accountability may be made. Planners have also made calls for more explicit advice, and sometimes complained that the generalized statements made by the Health and Safety Executive are an inadequate basis for their own decisions (ENDS 1981). The fact that such dissatisfaction has apparently been expressed must be at least in part due to the tantalizing nature of the subject of risk. Moreover, since it is not generally spelled out what has to be established as regards safety before a decision is taken (whether it is to be "brought out," risk ascertained to lie below a given quantitative level, or achievable within what is reasonable and practicable—the first vague, the second undermined by deficiencies noted under the risk estimation heading, and the last affording considerable ambiguity and dispute) it might be difficult for planners (and others) to know whether or not it has been achieved. This further undermines the ideals of "accountability."

ACCOUNTABILITY OF DECISION

Distinct from procedural accountability is the accountability of the final decision, namely whether criteria of safety and justification for the decision are given alongside the decision itself. The Advisory Committee for Major Hazards has emphasized the importance of safety not only being achieved, but being seen to be achieved (Health and Safety Commission 1979:24) and publications from the Major Hazards Assessment Unit (for example, Barrell 1982) suggest that material ought to be available to a wide audience despite problems of time, expense and commercial confidentiality.

Notwithstanding such positive qualities, there is no guarantee that any decision justification that might be given will be complete in terms of coverage of the range of issues at stake, or that the weight of consideration given to different issues is matched by their relative importance. Despite these caveats, it would seem to be more in line with democratic principles for criteria of safety and decision justification to be seen than not.

Decision accountability without procedural accountability is of limited benefit. In this regard, the relatively recent innovation (following Cremer and Warner 1976) which seems to be becoming established as standard practice (Barrell 1982) of stipulating as a planning condition that a hazard and operability audit* has to be undertaken to the satisfaction of the Health and Safety Executive before an installation can be commissioned, does not answer calls for increasing procedural accountability, although increasing the apparent accountability of the decision.

CREDIBILITY OF INSTITUTIONS

Risk assessments may be used as a vehicle for judging institutions who manage risk. Whereas under the previous headings the focus was on the substance of risk assessments and procedures within which they are used, the

---

*A detailed safety auditing conducted on completed plants and pioneered by chemical companies (see, for example, Chemical Industries Association 1977); usually to be done to the satisfaction of the Health and Safety Executive.

focus now turns to the parties who produce and refer to these assessments. Wynne (1980b:186) has noted:

> Since we cannot in any significant sense assess the technology itself for its full 'factual' impact, we have to assess the institutions which appear to control technology.

"We" in this quotation would appear to refer to academics or observers, but it can just as well refer to parties directly involved in a decision, as they have probably always judged each other, perhaps subconsciously, as much as the substance of each others' arguments. This may be particularly important to the public, whose criteria of risk acceptability may include their level of confidence in their guardians of safety (Otway 1980; Macgill 1982).

Positive involvement with risk assessment during a decision process enables the basis of the Health and Safety Executive's judgements on safety to be made explicit and hence provides a basis for the public's confidence (or lack of it) in their own guardians of safety. Consistency and stringency of Health and Safety Executive judgements may be two factors of particular importance, though their criteria of risk acceptability are rarely given explicitly, and whether they should be open to suggestion or above criticism in their involvement during the decision process is a matter of debate. A more positive involvement by the Executive that has recently become evident (Barrell 1981) may enable others better to judge their position in this respect. Similar judgements may be made of other parties (e.g. by the public of local authorities, of Secretaries of State, or of Industry). Neither arrogance nor incompetence is likely to win the respect or confidence of other parties, but rather considered argument presented at a level to which others can relate. This is not to suggest that party judgements of each other are or should be related only to their handling of the risk debate: the long-standing public image of industry and its reputation in its history of operating installations of the type being considered here is also likely to be relevant, for instance.

Party judgements of institutions depend not only on their own direct communication with them, but also observation of the interaction of these institutions with others. In the case of one recent risk debate the observer had the opportunity of witnessing exchanges between the statutory guardians of safety and expert private consultants (and the latter's clients) in which the judge (the Secretary of State for the Environment) had to make a judgement on his own safety advisers (Milne 1981; Department of the Environment 1982; *New Scientist* 1982).

Elsewhere it has been noted that the relationship between planners and the Health and Safety Executive has not always been a comfortable one, and inconsistencies in judgements by the Health and Safety Executive have been suspected (Payne 1981). The recently streamlined structure within the Health and Safety Executive (Barrell 1981) may avert future criticism on the latter (and hopefully also on the former) count.

RISK EVALUATION

Risk assessment (estimation and reduction) is likely to be followed by a judgement or evaluation about the acceptability, or otherwise, of the potential risk and hence the suitability of sites for the application in question, with or without appropriate risk reduction measures. This judgement may be made either in its own right, for example against some suitable quantitative yard-stick which might include results of other risk assessments already available, or in qualitative comparison with other man-made or natural risks (a method of evaluation strongly favoured by industry; see, for example, Kletz 1980). It may thus perform an absolute site-screening function: sites posing an unac-ceptable residual risk may be deemed unsuitable, sites falling within an acceptable range may be deemed suitable even to the extent that risk is not considered detrimental. Alternatively the result may be used as part of a wider cost–benefit appraisal of the development in question (seen to be the only way such assessments can be used by many economists, for example Pearce 1981). In this case, tolerance or acceptability of residual risk, however small, may depend on, and be positively related to, expected benefits to be derived. Similarly a comparative cost–risk–benefit analysis of several alternative sites may be undertaken. These criteria for risk evaluation are summarized elsewhere by Kates (1978).

It is a statement of the obvious that parties evaluate risk quite differently. Nevertheless, it is an apparent source of exasperation to industry that there is general mistrust about their criteria of publicly acceptable risk and that they are expected to exhibit high moral and ethical standards which are not neces-sarily observed in other sections of society. Furthermore, it is argued, an imposition of further requirements is not only unjustified by events, but may not automatically bring any beneficial impacts (Eberlein 1978). Green (1981:165), however, remarks of the dangers of confusing perceived risk with preferences:

> . . . of assuming that if the public demand a small risk to be made smaller, then this must be because they overestimate risk. The public might, however, see it more important to reduce some risks rather than others, despite relative magnitudes.

Risk-takers may show considerable resentment and hostility to hazard-makers and guardians who are apparently using them as sacrificial pawns in a cost–risk–benefit appraisal. The latter, aware of the emotive issue involved, are often keen to avoid any hint that a trade-off of any kind is made in this respect, though at the same time they may accuse the public of seeking immortality. Some such trade-off between risk and benefit is inevitable, however, given that the *raison-d'être* of such plants is economic, and there is no such thing as absolute safety. Pearce (1981) suggests that the cost–risk–benefit trade-off should be made explicit, as the most reasonable way of using the result of a risk assessment. If this is attempted, however, tantalizing problems in assessing benefit and in aggregation arising from unequal distribution of costs, risk and benefits are then superimposed on existing technical problems of estimating risk noted under the first heading above.

The decision-taker has to reconcile society's high ideals with what is reasonable and practicable. There may be inconsistencies between different decision-takers—local authorities and Secretaries of State. These might be difficult to discern because criteria for evaluation are rarely made explicit. Broad conclusions can be drawn and examples of inconsistencies shown, but it is hard to prove, for instance, that the key trade-offs made in decisions are risk versus employment, the impact of new risks on existing risky situations, or risk versus likely spread of direct benefits. Decision-takers' risk evaluations may depend on the risk assessment reports of their safety advisers. In some such cases, the decision-taker is virtually obliged to take such expert advice literally. Various problems may be identified: the report that the local authorities receive from private consultants will frequently contain the authors' own evaluation of the acceptability of the risks posed, thus contravening the theoretical model in which private consultants provide information about levels of risk and hazard on the basis of which publicly elected representatives independently formulate their view of risk acceptability. It is at least debatable whether uncritical acceptance of such advice is valid. The Health and Safety Executive will also typically have given their judgement on risk acceptability, and it is again a moot point as to whether they or local authorities should decide on risk acceptability on behalf of the local community. A rather more perverse situation arises, as noted above, when the statutory decision-taker is judge (and not only client) of his own statutory safety advisers.

LEGITIMATION OF INTERESTS

There would appear to be a strong correlation between the results of risk assessments for particular installations, or different interpretations of the same results, and parties' overall positions either in favour of or against approval of those installations. These may be cynically regarded as strategic discrepancies in order to advance party self-interests (legitimation of decisions already taken by the respective parties—Majone 1982—the endorsement of site selection, for instance), or may be genuine determinants of party positions in the first place. Reynders (1982:6) has coined the descriptors "Valium" or "doomsday" risk assessments in this context. The difficulties of risk estimation and comprehension aid this legitimation role.

In the light of issues raised under earlier headings, it would be naive to assume that totally impartial assessment was possible, since every assessment will contain some value judgements. There is therefore the possibility for risk assessments to reflect what their authors want. The danger is that this will go unnoticed. In some ways the rapid development of quantitative risk assessment techniques has outpaced the evolution of the political and institutional framework wherein such analyses are examined and evaluated. This, of course, provides further reasons for using risk assessment as a way to legitimate or justify precarious positions in an uncertain environment. Since the relevant arguments have, moreover, so far been difficult if not impossible to verify against well-established scientific criteria, such a situation may maintain its own inbuilt momentum and aversion to change. That, in turn, would preserve the current perceived inadequacies of risk assessment use.

It is not necessarily a matter of questioning party integrity to ask whether risk assessments are sometimes used for more than they were either capable or intended: can a generic risk assessment based on a broad design that may subsequently be changed be a rigorous or legitimate input to a cost–benefit calculus? The scope for inadvertent legitimation is particularly wide in cases where risk assessments are not subject to expert scrutiny. This may not be uncommon, since planning authorities may lack the necessary expertise.

DELAY

The preparation of risk assessments may increase the time taken in decision-making. The significance of this delay may be appraised in a number of ways. Time allows reflection on and assimilation of the complicated issues at stake; time may change perceptions; time may heal or increase party divisions; time may allow additional issues to arise, safety or economic, and these could be crucial to the validity of a decision in a field where new research findings are frequently emerging. Time taken for risk assessment may overrun the deadline for decision-taking, resulting in a decision being taken without the benefit of a risk assessment; time taken for risk assessment may be more than repaid in terms of improved risk management, or appeasement of, say, the fears of the public. However, whether or not a lengthy decision process is in fact more legitimate than a swift one, can be examined case by case only.

Delay is clearly of more strategic importance to those who do not share the view that safety decisions are purely routine affairs to be conducted by industry and the Health and Safety Executive. Predictably perhaps, spokesmen for industry concerned to minimize delay have urged careful consideration of EC legislation in the environmental field as this is seen as providing further opportunities for large-scale projects to be blocked (House of Lords 1981:160). Indeed, the expense of delay may prompt consideration of withdrawal from a given site, a continued repetition of which could ultimately lead to a degree of economic instability and greater long-term risk.

INSTITUTIONAL REFORM

Various authors (Sandbach 1980; Cotgrove 1981; O'Riordan 1981b) have put forward the thesis that risk assessment, along with other forms of holistic assessment such as cost–benefit analysis and environmental impact appraisal, may represent a focus for attention and action that could be used to adapt or restructure bureaucratic and political activity as a whole. Dissatisfaction engendered by perceived inadequacies of risk assessment (from the adherence to other roles described above) may thus trigger objection at a deeper level. As such, risk assessment has a symbolic focus for reform. Public participants are in the vanguard for such change. Their concern extends much further than outright objection to a specific development; ideological issues about the way society is run assume importance. Several ideological stances are apparent (O'Riordan 1981b). The traditional technocentrist believes in maintaining the status quo of political power and social democracy and the resolution of risk issues through the application of science and technology. McAuslan (1980) suggests that planning law endorses and enhances the technocentrist status quo. At the other end of the continuum, the ecocentrist argues that any society relying on centralized control of science and technology and technical solutions to technical problems does not cater adequately for genuine human concerns. A range of intermediate stances can also be identified exhibiting variations on these themes. Such classifications are not, of course, rigid. They merely illustrate dominant characteristics of various agencies and interest groups in decision-making, and may be usefully related to the present context.

It is open to question whether risk assessment for the types of major hazard industries covered here has produced the same sort of symbolic reaction that has become all too obvious in the nuclear debate, or whether, conversely, certain types of risk assessment are looked upon as the logical, pragmatic way to handle certain problems.

Risk assessment would appear to have played at least a modest role as an agent of institutional reform. Recent changes in the official use of risk assessment, notably in the more positive advisory role of the Health and Safety Executive, may be interpreted as changes, albeit minor ones, in government secrecy and agency accountability. Such change is accomplished painstakingly slowly and paralleled by the length of time for draft notification regulations to be legalized (Health and Safety Commission 1978), only now before parliament for enactment during 1983. They herald (i) a change in the relationship between outline and full planning permission, if further design detail accompanying a planning application is to be stipulated; and (ii) a change in institutional responsibility for planning where significant issues of public safety are concerned—the overlap between planning authority and Health and Safety Executive responsibility referred to earlier.

A further type of reform may be identified as follows. In many cases applications are for plants of a type which are already operating throughout the UK. However, the questions raised about new planning applications implicitly challenge not only safety criteria for the plants under consideration, but also the basis for the nation's hazard control policy and stringency in general. Thus the processing of a planning application can have an important function that goes rather beyond what it might be deemed reasonable to establish about safety at the planning stage for any particular plant, though not as far as the ideological stances cited earlier in this section. If the analysis for a given plant turns out to be unusually complex and detailed, it may reach the status of being "new research." Thus the function of risk assessment on a planning application merges with a broader ongoing risk research, whether technical, again political or psychological. Moreover, although it may be possible for such new results to be incorporated in a given decision, it is less easy to relate them to the status quo for existing installations, which will concomitantly have been brought into question.

Conclusion

We have attempted to provide a framework whereby the relative utility of risk assessment in planning may be gauged. Three criteria that would appear to be suitable for drawing some general conclusions both about the individual roles and the overall utility of risk assessment are those of effectiveness, efficiency and equity.

The criterion of effectiveness is intended for present purposes to focus attention on the actual safety of a plant. The primary controls in this respect are industry self-regulation (being a function of in-house management, state of equipment, and specific design features, and varying across different firms) and Health and Safety Executive scrutiny, neither of which is necessarily related to what might be evident during the decision process for such an installation. This is because the risk estimation and hazard control relevant to operational safety are conducted in confidence and on a level of plant design detail that is unlikely to be available during the decision process. Corresponding criteria adopted for risk evaluation are those of reasonableness and practicability as judged by the Health and Safety Executive, and again not necessarily observable. Only occasionally is this detailed scrutiny open to wider interference—for instance, if specific design detail is suggested for planning conditions, but even then, only weakly.

The criterion of effectiveness does not rest only on detailed design specifications, however. Given that risk management involves not only guarding against the possibility of disaster, but also minimizing possible consequences, functions of risk evaluation (and hence, indirectly, risk estimation and risk reduction) based on more general features are important in determining the effective safety of an installation (notably the stipulation of buffer zones and *cordons sanitaires,* to a lesser extent in terms of the broader spectrum of expertise that is involved in the risk debate). As remarked above, there is ample scope for disagreement as to who should have the final responsibility in this area. The mixture of safety and planning thus poses a problem with which the institutions in the UK can currently only grapple with some difficulty.

The criterion of efficiency may be used to judge whether a given level of plant safety is achieved by the most parsimonious means. Judicious use of risk assessment during the decision process and before construction commences, communicated between industry and the Health and Safety Executive, can increase efficiency by avoiding broad design features that the latter might later find unacceptable (thus drawing on roles 1, 2 and 4). The benefits of delay (role 9) during decision-making while contentious aspects of safety are debated between parties may exceed short-term costs and hence also be efficient if they enable a degree of reconciliation not otherwise achieved. It is not obvious, however, that this will happen and that roles 4, 5 and 6 will "succeed." The inherently ambiguous nature of risk may stimulate disagreement and conflict. For example, where the foundations of the arguments used to oppose risk decisions can be identified as predominantly ideological, then the symbolic focus on risk assessment could persist. No amount of wider debate (role 4) or more stringent health and safety or planning legislation (role 10) will necessarily produce appeasement in this case, but they may all be rejected simply as more elaborate versions of the same procedures that were opposed in the first place. Thus, again, problems which the current institutions in society are unable to treat may persist.

Consideration of equity raises notions of natural justice, in particular, regarding decision procedures and decision outcomes that may be seen to be fair. The accountability roles (4-6) are important here, as are the incidental roles they herald (9 and 10). Equity in decision outcome may be a utopian ideal, as it requires that criteria of safety are both agreed and implemented. Agreement is bound to be difficult on an issue (safety) which cannot be defined and about which there are many different value judgements: Ravetz (1979) and Fischoff *et al.* (1981) argue that the latter have to be confronted if any progress is to be made. Wherever an installation is sited there may be an unequal distribution of costs and benefits and no effective mechanism whereby the beneficiaries can compensate those who must tolerate costs; costs in this case are an, albeit irrational, belief in unacceptable, involuntary exposure to risk.

Some amelioration towards equity in decision outcome may be possible here if it is believed (see, for example, OCPU 1979) that people will accept decisions inimical to them if arrived at by procedures that can be seen to be fair. Thus the emphasis shifts from equity in outcome to equity in procedure. An alternative view, however, is that procedures will always be criticized by parties dissatisfied with their outcomes.

Equity in procedure requires adequate publicity of planned developments, opportunity for participation, and significant response to reasonable inquiries. Increased use of risk assessment enables criteria of safety to be seen, despite residual doubts about what is supposedly being established, and the amount of detail and expertise that is brought to bear. However, recurrent criticisms of UK procedures (OCPU 1979; Macgill 1982) undermine a sense of fairness to (usually minority) interests, as do weaknesses indicated under roles 5 and 6, and under "efficiency." Much may be a reflection of a lack of respect accorded by some groups for the guardians of the public interest and safety (though it is not only on behalf of the "public" that complaints arise). The challenge is to ameliorate these criticisms without necessarily jeopardizing other party interests: a Pareto improvement. Proposed EC draft regulations for Environmental Assessment and for Major Hazard Industries are being met with guarded reactions from industry and government, who maintain that the British system is adequate, but derive support from other parties who wish to see an improvement in the opportunities for greater participation and ultimate fairness in decisions.

Risk assessment roles and the extent to which they are fulfilled are not static. Procedural changes, both in terms of planning and in terms of health and safety legislation, change the formal backcloth and are sometimes accompanied by significant internal institutional reorganization. Any such deliberate changes occur against a more general evolution in risk awareness and sophistication of risk argument. At a more general level still, changes in the macroclimate alter the significance of risk on the agenda of societal problems.

It would seem appropriate to end by making a number of comments about the future use of risk assessment in the light of the material discussed in this paper (see Table 1). Given the conflict of interests and range of difficulties identified, the recommendations in Table 1 are presented somewhat tentatively and are heavily qualified (see column 3). Thus, notwithstanding the recommendations made, the aim of this paper is to sharpen general awareness of the multifaceted nature of risk assessment, and to pinpoint various flaws and

TABLE 1
Current problems in the use of risk assessment and possible directions for improvements

Problems	Suggested Directions for Improvement	Some Implications and Complications
Paucity of failure data	Common and accessible data bank	Confidentiality of certain information; no guarantee of completeness
Modelling limitations	Further research; common and accessible bank of models; spectrum of applicable models to be used	Why should a commercial firm freely share out its research findings?
Lack of sensitivity analysis alongside results	Confidence intervals and sensitivity analyses should be given	Method oversophisticated *vis-à-vis* available information base
Lack of detail of plant design	Results of risk estimation at planning approval stage must subsume results of a later risk estimation on the actual plant	Legal status needed for original assessment; unwieldy?
One-site decision process: relative merits of alternatives inadequately probed and considerable incentive to approval	Consider several alternative sites	Significant change to current UK planning system; is expense justified by aim: blighting of alternatives, time consuming; increases uncertainty

Problem	Suggestion	Comment
Vested interest of parties who produce risk assessments (Valium and doomsday)	HSE to take a more positive role as arbiters	Overlap with the role of decision-taker; change in the general nature of HSE activities
Questionable technical competence of users of written risk assessments	HSE to scrutinize significant risk assessment reports, and publish findings	Beginning to be done; occasional lack of confidence in HSE; may be overruled politically
Risk evaluation bound up with risk estimation	Authors should keep the two aspects distinct	Clients may prefer the two combined, even if others do not
Basis for risk evaluation obscure: what is an acceptable risk?	Explicit criteria should be given where they have been used; admit intuition or ambiguity otherwise	Do minimum criteria exist that are acceptable to all agencies? Risk acceptability philosophically unresolved
Major disasters are credible	Greater incentives for remote siting	UK land-use already heavily constrained; perhaps some scope
Inadequate mechanism for public participation (time, information, expense)	Implement some recently suggested improvements	Is public participation a right, or a favour; how can its value be gauged?
Approval in principle too slack a consent; Robens philosophy inappropriate	Comprehensive cultural, political and institutional reform (revolution?)	(not a serious suggestion) There may always be winners and losers. It may require continual vigilance for safety to be achieved; even more difficult for it to be seen to be achieved

inadequacies. Improvement in current practice is more likely to evolve from a gradual learning process than from an attempt directly to transplant particular recommendations. As Fischoff *et al.* (1981:197) note:

> There is no way to get the right answer to many risk problems; all that we can hope for is to avoid the mistakes to which each of us is attuned; the more perspectives involved, the more local wisdom is brought to bear on the problem.

References

Financial support given to D. Snowball by the Department of Education for Northern Ireland is gratefully acknowledged.

Barrell, A. C. (1981) The work of the major hazards assessment unit. In Scientific and Technical Studies, *Planning for major hazards,* pp. 34-43. London: Oyez Publications.

Barrell, A. C. (1982) Future directions for siting decisions. In *Liquefied energy gases facility siting: international comparisons* (H. Kunreuther *et al.*, eds). Laxenburg, Austria: International Institute for Applied Systems Analysis, CP-82-S6.

Bell, W. E. (1980) Planning legislation: striking a balance. In *Petroleum development and the environment,* pp. 30-39. London: Heyden.

Brook, C. A. (1980) Planning legislation: industry/government interface. In *Petroleum development and the environment,* pp. 40-51. London: Heyden.

Brough, C. W. (1981) Dealing with hazard and risk in planning (2). In *Dealing with risk* (R. F. Griffiths, ed.). Manchester: Manchester University Press.

Chemical Industries Association (1977) *A guide to hazard and operability studies.* London: CIA.

Clark, B. D., Chapman, K., Bissett, R. and Wathern, P. (1980) *Assessment of major developments—a manual.* London: HMSO.

Cmnd 5034 (1972) *Safety and health at work, Report of the Committee 1970-72* (Chairman: Lord Robens). London: HMSO.

Conrad, J. (ed.) (1980) *Society, technology and risk assessment.* London: Academic Press.

Cotgrove, S. (1981) Risk, value conflict and political legitimacy. In *Dealing with risk* (R. F. Griffiths, ed.). Manchester: Manchester University Press.

Cremer and Warner (1976) Report on environmental impact of the proposed Shell UK (Expro) NGL plant at Peterhead. London: Cremer and Warner.

Cremer and Warner (1978) *Guidelines for layout and safety zones in petrochemical developments.* London: Cremer and Warner, Report prepared for Highland Regional Council (C2056).

Cremer and Warner (1980) *Safety assessment of a proposed gas reception terminal and SNG plant, St. Fergus, Scotland.* Aberdeen: Cremer and Warner, C2276.

Department of Environment (1982) Town and Country Planning Act 1971, Application by Broseley Estates, PNW/5063/219/16.

Dierkes, M., Edwards, S. and Coppock, R. (1979) *Technological risk. Its perception and handling in the European community.* Boston, MA: Oetgeschlager, Gunn and Hain.

Eberlein, A. J. (1978) Considerations for siting a major hazard plant. In *Harwell environmental seminar: Major chemical hazards,* Harwell, Oxford.

Edwards, L. and Rowan-Robinson, J. (1980) Whatever happened to the Planning Inquiry Commission? *Journal of Planning and Environmental Law,* May, 307-315.

ENDS (1981) Can planners control major hazards? *Environmental Data Services 65,* 9-11.

Farmer, F. R. (1981) Quantification of physical and engineering risks. *Proceedings of the Royal Society, London, A 376* (1764), 103-119.

Fischoff, B., Slovic, P. and Lichtenstein, S. (1981) Lay Foibles and expert fables in judgements about risks. In *Progress in Resource Management and Environmental Planning 3* (T. O'Riordan and R. K. Turner, eds). Chichester: Wiley.

Flint, A. R. (1981) Risks and their control in civil engineering. *Proceedings of the Royal Society, London, A 376* (1764), 167-179.

Goodman, G. T. and Rowe, W. D. (eds) (1979) *Energy risk management.* London: Academic Press.

Green, C. (1981) Discussion comments. *Proceedings of the Royal Society, London, A. 376,* 165.

Griffiths, R. F. (ed.) (1981) *Dealing with risk: the planning, management and acceptability of technological risk.* Manchester: Manchester University Press.

Health and Safety Commission (1976) *Advisory committee on major hazards, First Report.* London: HMSO.

Health and Safety Commission (1978) *Hazardous installations (notification and survey) regulations, 1978, Consultative Document.* London: HMSO.

Health and Safety Commission (1979) *Advisory committee on major hazards, Second Report.* London: HMSO.

Health and Safety Executive (1978) *Canvey: an investigation of potential hazards from operations in the Canvey Is./Thurrock area.* London: HMSO.

Health and Safety Executive (1981) *Canvey: a second report. A review of potential hazards from operations in the Canvey Island/Thurrock area three years after publication of the Canvey Report.* London: HMSO.

House of Lords 69 (1981) *Select Committee on the European Communities. Environmental Assessment of Projects, Session 1980-81, 11th Report.* London: HMSO.

Institute of Chemical Engineers (1982) *The assessment of major hazards.* Rugby: Institute of Chemical Engineers, Symposium Series No. 71.

Jones, C. and Sands, R. L. (1980). *Great balls of fire.* Exhall, Coventry: Jones and Sands Publishing.

Kates, R. W. (1978) *Risk assessment of environmental hazards, Scope 8.* Chichester: Wiley.

Kletz, T. A. (1980) Benefits and risks: their assessment in relation to human needs. *International Atomic Energy Authority Bulletin 22* (5/6), 2-12.

Lees, F. P. (1980) *Loss prevention in the process industries* (2 vols). London: Butterworth.

Lees, F. P. (1982) The hazard warning structure of major hazard plants. *Transactions of the Institute of Chemical Engineers 60*, 211-221.

Macgill, S. M. (1982) *Case study of the Mossmorran: Braefoot Bay decision.* International Institute for Applied Systems Analysis Research Report, CP-82-40.

McAuslan, P. (1980) *The ideologies of planning law.* Oxford: Pergamon.

Majone, G. (1982) *The uses of policy analysis.* Laxenburg, Austria: International Institute for Applied Systems Analysis.

McRea, M. and Greaves, J. (1981) Nigg Bay petrochemical developments. A successful alternative to a public inquiry? *Scottish Planning Law and Practice 2*, 8-10, 19.

McQuaid, J. (1982) Future directions of dense gas dispersion research. *Journal of Hazardous Materials 6*, 231-247.

Mann, G. (1979) Implications of preferred sites at district level. In *Planning Exchange Forum Report 16, Site selection for large industry.* Glasgow: Planning Exchange.

Mehta, R. (1980) *A local view of terminal siting.* International Institute for Applied Systems Analysis Liquefied Energy Gases Task Force Meeting (mimeo).

Milne, R. (1981) Inquiry to probe safety issues. *Planning 433*, 5.

New Scientist (1982) Test case decision brings homes into danger zone. *New Scientist 95* (1310), 760.

O'Riordan, T. (1981a) *Environmentalism.* London: Pion.

O'Riordan, T. (1981b) Societal attitudes and energy risk assessment. In *European transitions from oil—societal impacts and constraints on energy policy* (G. T. Goodman, L. A. Kirstoferson and J. Hollander, eds). London: Academic Press.

O'Riordan, T. and Sewell, W. R. D. (1981) From project appraisal to policy review. In *Project appraisal and policy review* (T. O'Riordan and W. R. D. Sewell, eds). Chichester: Wiley.

Otway, H. (1980) *A perspective on risk perception. Confessions of a disillusioned analyst* (mimeo).

Outer Circle Policy Unit (1979) *The big public inquiry. A proposed new procedure for the impartial investigation of projects with major national implications.* London: Outer Circle Policy Unit.

Parker, D. J. and Harding, D. M. (1979) Natural hazard evaluation and adjustment. *Geography 64*, 307-316.

Payne, B. J. (1981) Dealing with hazard and risk in planning (1). In *Dealing with risk* (R. F. Griffiths, ed.). Manchester: Manchester University Press.

Pearce, D. W. (1981) Risk assessment: use and misuse. *Proceedings of the Royal Society, London A 376*, 181-192.

Pearce, D. W., Edwards, L. and Beuret, G. (1979) *Decision-making for energy futures: a case study of the Windscale inquiry.* London: Macmillan.

Planning 440 (1981) Funds for major inquiry objectors? p. 1.

Political Ecology Research Group (1980) *Barrow hazards survey.* Oxford: PERG.

Rasbash, D. J. and Drysdale, D. D. (1977) *Fire and explosion hazard to Dalgety Bay and Aberdour associated with the proposed Fife Natural Gas Liquids plant.* Edinburgh: University of Edinburgh, Department of Fire Safety Engineering.

Ravetz, J. R. (1979) Public perceptions of acceptable risks as evidence for their cognitive, technical and social structure. In *Technological risk. Its perception and handling in the European Community* (M. Dierkes, S. Edwards and R. Coppock, eds). Boston, MA: Oetgeschlager, Gunn and Hain.

Reynders, L. (1982) Societal interests. In *Liquified energy gases facility siting* (H. Kunreuther *et al.*, eds). Laxenburg, Austria: International Institute for Applied Systems Analysis, CP-82-S6.

Russell, R. (1981) Discussion comments. *Proceedings of the Royal Society London, A 376*, 99.

Sandbach, F. (1980) *Environment, ideology and policy.* Oxford: Blackwell.

Schwing, R. C. and Albers, W. A. (eds) (1980) *Societal risk assessment. How safe is safe enough?* New York: Plenum Press.

Scottish Development Department (1978) *Report of the Public Inquiry into the Shell/Esso Mossmorran/Braefoot Bay proposals, New St. Andrews House, Edinburgh.* Edinburgh: Scottish Development Department.

Snowball, D. J. and Macgill, S. M. (1982). Liquefied energy gas facilities in Scotland: risk assessment in five recent decisions. Working Paper 346, School of Geography, University of Leeds.

Thompson, M. (1981) *A cultural analysis of a risk debate.* Laxenburg, Austria: International Institute for Applied Systems Analysis, WP-81-17.

Walsh, P. M. (1979) Major hazard premises: the problems of "nearby developments." *Local Government Review 143* (38), 551-553, 560.

Wynne, B. (1980a) Windscale: a case history in the political art of muddling through. In *Progress in resource management and environmental planning 2* (T. O'Riordan and R. K. Turner, eds). Chichester: Wiley.

Wynne, B. (1980b) Technology, risk and participation: on the social treatment of uncertainty. In *Society, technology and risk assessment* (J. Conrad, ed.) London: Academic Press.

HOWARD KUNREUTHER, JOANNE LINNEROOTH AND JAMES W. VAUPEL

12 *A Decision-Process Perspective on Risk and Policy Analysis*

Introduction

This paper explores how risk analysis and policy analysis can improve the decision process associated with the siting of potentially hazardous facilities. A principal purpose of risk analysis is to estimate the probabilities and consequences of a catastrophic accident. For various reasons, two risk analyses of the same potential hazard may yield radically different risk estimates. Such discrepancies may significantly influence the course of the siting decision process. We suggest the importance of rules of evidence for encouraging more constructive analyses.

Policy analysis is broadly concerned with providing decision makers with useful information and procedures, but to date has not been widely used to facilitate mutually advantageous agreements. We investigate how compensation programs for sharing gains and losses may help resolve conflicts in the siting process.

The use of risk analysis and policy analysis for improving outcomes is highly correlated with the interplay of the various stakeholders involved in the decision process. Siting actions are *not* taken by a single decision maker; rather they are a product of conflict resolution between the various interested parties, each with a different set of objectives and concerns (Fischhoff *et al.* 1981, Vaupel 1982b.) Some of these stakeholders have commissioned their own risk analysis to defend their position. Others rely on published documents.

Consider the following illustrative example associated with estimating the public safety risk of a proposed liquified natural gas (LNG) terminal at Oxnard, California. One risk assessment prepared by a private consulting firm for the gas companies showed that a person living in Oxnard has between a 10^{-4} and 10^{-7} chance per year of dying from an LNG accident. A second risk analysis commissioned by the Oxnard City Council concluded that the risk to a citizen in the community was somewhere between 10^{-7} and 10^{-10}. These two ranges differ by three orders of magnitude. However, it was difficult to determine the basis for these discrepancies because the risk analysis did not clearly state their assumptions nor discuss the limitations of the data employed.

The Oxnard example is not an isolated case. As a study on the siting of LNG terminals in four countries (Kunreuther, Linnerooth *et al.* 1983) has shown, widely varying risk estimates for the same event are pervasive. The politics of the risk management process discourage the risk analyst from revealing the uncertainties inherent in making probabilistic estimates and has inhibited the pursuit by the policy analyst of programs such as compensation that involve explicit tradeoffs.

We will illustrate the current role of risk analysts and policy analysts through a set of concrete examples primarily related to the siting of liquefied natural gas terminals.[1] The next section sketches key events in the siting process of an LNG terminal in California and highlights several features of the decision process which appear to be common in most siting controversies. The third section then considers the role of risk analysis in the siting process. The fourth section is devoted to how policy analysts can play a role in negotiating conflicts with particular emphasis on the use of compensation. The final section presents a brief set of conclusions.

Policy as Process: LNG in California

The decision processes associated with the siting of LNG terminals are roughly similar to the processes associated with locating other kinds of hazardous facilities, such as nuclear power plants and hazardous waste storage sites (Keeney 1980). Each of these problems involves multiple parties with different agendas and concerns.

In the California case, in September 1974 Western LNG Terminal Company, a firm representing the siting interests of several gas distribution companies, applied to the Federal Power Commission for approval of three sites on the California Coast: Point Conception, Oxnard, and Los Angeles. These applications generated considerable controversy on the federal, state, and local levels concerning the need for natural gas and the safety of locating a terminal at the populated Los Angeles and Oxnard sites. The most frightening possibility was that the storage tanks would fail catastrophically, releasing a large quantity of natural gas which would vaporize into a cloud that might travel over a neighboring population center and then ignite. Many questions concerning the plausibility of this scenario were left unanswered. The conflicts among the many groups involved were exacerbated by the different results of the risk analyses commissioned by different groups.

By the summer of 1977, it appeared likely that none of the three sites would be approved by all the necessary local, state and federal authorities—the Oxnard and Los Angeles sites because of safety considerations, and the beautiful Point Conception site because of environmental considerations. Hence, the utility companies turned to the state legislature for help. The resulting legislation, the California LNG Terminal Siting Act, was a compromise between the interests of the utility companies and the interests of those concerned about safety and the environment. The process was streamlined to facilitate the identification and approval of a site within a prescribed time interval. The environmentally minded California Coastal Commission was given the authority to rank the sites but the energy-minded California Public Utility Commission would make the final choice. The Federal Energy Regulatory Commission must also approve the application.

Following this procedure, the remote Point Conception site was tentatively selected: its final approval was made conditional on the site being seismically safe. A seismic Review Board appointed by the California Public Utilities Commission found that the earthquakes did *not* pose an unacceptable risk. Nonetheless, at the end of this ten-year process, Western LNG Terminal Company withdrew its application. Following the deregulation of domestic natural gas prices in 1978, it appears that California does not now need an LNG terminal.

This brief description of the siting saga in California reveals the following features of the decision process which are worth noting.

MULTI-PARTY, MULTI-ISSUE PROCESS

There was no single person, group or institution that decided on the Point Conception site. The final choice evolved from a variety of actions taken by the many authorities involved at the federal, state and local government levels as well as interactions between the applicant, citizens groups and environmentalists (Kunreuther, Lathrop and Linnerooth 1982). The objectives of each group and their explicit mandates are narrowly focused so that conflict is bound to emerge. For example, the California Coastal Commission is explicitly authorized to protect the coastline; the local city councils are primarily concerned with creating jobs for their constituents and preventing accidents; the California Public Utility Commission is primarily concerned with assuring an energy supply to the state.

A second complicating feature of siting decision processes is that the institutions involved are usually dealing with many issues in addition to the siting question. According to Majone (1984) a public policy question, such as siting energy facilities, leads competing stakeholders to take stands on policy issues consistent with objectives related to the long-term survival of their institutions. While the problem may be formulated as approving a certain site, other institutional concerns related, for instance, to energy policy or regional development may determine a party's position on the narrower agenda item. For example, what appeared as irrational behavior on the part of Western LNG Terminal Company in pursuing the earthquake fault issue at Point Conception when California no longer needed the terminal may be rational when viewed from the perspective of Western's long-term objectives; an approval of this site clears the path for an LNG facility in the future should the gas utilities want it.

The government politics model proposed by Allison (1971) comes closest to our view of the siting process. Allison points out that each of the actors in the game focuses on multiple problems rather than a single issue. Since the parties share power and have conflicting preferences it is necessary to identify the various issues deemed important to determine why certain bargains and compromises emerge.

SEQUENTIAL PROCESSING OF ISSUES

The siting of technological facilities is not solved systematically once and for all through the use of large-scale decision analyses and similar tools. Rather, the decision process moves sequentially through a set of questions: at each stage only segments of the problem are addressed.

Braybrooke (1974) has developed a model of the decision making process which captures this kind of siting process.[2] Over time issues are resolved, dismissed or transformed as new information or new alternatives emerge. Not only are the larger problems—whether and where to site an LNG facility—broken down into smaller subproblems, but these subproblems are usually dealt with sequentially by agencies with different and sometimes conflicting responsibilities. Constraints due to legislative and legal considerations may dictate the order in which certain actions must be taken.

Resolution of the question whether an LNG terminal is needed usually precedes the site selection phase which, in turn, usually precedes the licensing phase. Occasionally, the end result may differ from the original intent. For example, in California, the applicant originally stressed the risk of an interruption in the supply of natural gas as a major reason for importing LNG to three separate sites. During the course of the decision process, the three sites were reduced to one, and the number of storage tanks at that site were reduced from four to two. Because of this concentration in one small area, and the possibility of routine closures or nondelivery due to bad weather conditions, the net result of the sequential decision process was that a project originally meant to decrease supply interruption risk was shaped over time into a project that may have increased that risk.

AGENDA SETTING

If the process is sequential in nature, then the setting of an agenda is likely to play a role in determining the final outcome as well as the length of time it takes to reach it. Agenda setting determines the order in which different subproblems are considered. Empirical evidence from the field as well as from laboratory experiments (Cobb and Elder 1972, Levine and Plott 1977) suggests that different agendas for the same problem frequently lead to different outcomes.

There are two principal reasons for this. A particular decision made on a subproblem serves as a constraint for the next subproblem. If the order of the subproblems is reversed, then there would likely be a different set of choices to consider. Secondly, each subproblem involves a different set of interested parties who bring with them their own set of data to bolster their cause. The timing of their entry may have an effect on later actions. For example, citizen groups normally enter the siting debate only when their own community is being considered as a possible candidate.

SALIENCE OF EXOGENOUS EVENTS

While different parties are concerned with many aspects of the siting decision, the risk issue nonetheless often arouses special concern. This concern is fueled by the perplexing moral and symbolic dilemmas that arise when a large number of lives may be at stake. Low probability events are frequently ignored until an exogenous event, such as a disaster, structures the political agenda by calling attention to the dangers associated with a particular technology. The small data base for judging the frequency of low probability phenomena increases the impact of these salient events on the decision process (Nisbett and Ross 1980, Slovic *et al.* 1983). Controlled laboratory experiments by psychologists have illustrated this type of estimation bias (Lichtenstein *et al.* 1978). Tversky and Kahneman (1974) describe this bias as resulting from an availability heuristic whereby one judges the frequency of events by the ease with which specific examples can be retrieved from memory. However, opposition to large-scale technology may be due to other concerns of protestors that are unrelated to the psychological biases described in the literature (Otway and von Winterfeldt 1982).

In a study of legislative decision-making, Walker (1977) suggests the importance of graphically and easily understood evidence of trouble as an important factor in setting the discretionary agenda of the U.S. Congress or a governmental agency. He also contends that the political appeal of dealing with a specific problem is increased if it has an impact on many people. To support these points, Walker presents empirical evidence on the passage of safety legislation in the U.S. The recent Tylenol scare in the United States illustrates Walker's point. Numerous examples of this process are also provided by Lawless (1977) through a series of case histories of problems involving the impact of technology on society. He points out that frequently

> new information of an "alarming" nature is announced and is given rapid and widespread visibility by means of modern mass communication media. Almost overnight the case can become a subject of discussion and concern to much of the populace, and generate strong pressures to evaluate and remedy the problem as rapidly as possible (p. 16).

In the case of decision processes involving the siting of hazardous facilities, exogenous events such as an LNG explosion or an oil spill may be sufficiently graphic and affect enough people to cause a reversal of earlier decisions, inject other alternatives into the process, and change the relative power of parties interested in the decision outcome. The mass media may play a critical role by focusing attention on these specific events and by exaggerating their importance. For example, in December of 1976 the Los Angeles City Council voted to allow work to begin on an LNG terminal in San Pedro Bay. The following day an explosion destroyed the oil tanker in Sansinea in Los Angeles harbor, leaving 9 dead and 50 injured. A week later the City Council commissioned a study of the relative safety of the proposed site. The explosion, although it had nothing to do with liquified natural gas, alerted many Californians to the potential dangers of LNG (Kunreuther and Lathrop 1981).

Risk Analysis in Decision Processes

Interested parties often disagree on the nature of the risks associated with health, safety, and environmental policies. Differences are created at even the most elemental level since the word "risk" has many interpretations. In the case of LNG siting in California the utility companies were concerned about the risk of insufficient supplies of gas. They expressed the belief that the importation of LNG from foreign countries would reduce this risk. The Sierra Club and local citizen groups, on the other hand, expressed concern about environmental and safety risks from a new facility. They were each using a language of "risk" in relation to this particular issue as part of their vague and broader set of interests and objectives. Most risk analyses have focused on the threat to life or health as a potential consequence of a given activity (Fischhoff *et al.* 1981). This is the notion used in the following discussion.

TRANS-SCIENCE AND RISK ESTIMATION

Weinberg (1972) was one of the first scientists to call attention to the difficulty of estimating low-probability events. He proposed the term "trans-science" to indicate that there is no practical basis for precisely estimating the statistical chance and consequences of the occurrence of certain types of accidents.

The trans-science nature of risk estimation is aptly illustrated by the LNG analyses done in California. Consider first some examples of differences in the choices made by analysts in defining the boundaries of the risk problem they were addressing. One study of the Oxnard site focused on a geographical area that put 15,000 people at risk; another study considered a broader area that put 90,000 people at risk. Two of the three risk assessments done for the Point Conception site considered risks involving transport ships, the transfer of LNG to shore, and the storage tanks on shore; the third study considered only risks involving the transport ships. One major risk to an LNG facility is sabotage and another is war; none of the various California risk assessments, however, included either possibility. The chapter by Mandl and Lathrop in Kunreuther, Linnerooth *et al.* (1983) provides more details on the risk studies.

Analysts also have to make judgements about how to model complex phenomena. Simplifications have to be made—but which simplifications? A risk analyst's time is spared if various events are assumed to be independent—but when are such convenient assumptions of independence justified? How likely is it that the human operator of a hazardous facility will err and prove yet again Murphy's law? Should best-guesses or prudently conservative estimates be used for the various parameters in the risk assessment? Risk analysis is a craft that requires analytical judgements on a series of questions like these.

As a result, it can happen that two analysts portray the same hazard very differently. For example, one California LNG analysis indicated a probability of about one in 100 million per year of a ship collision in the harbor, whereas another analysis indicated a probability of one in 2000—a series of differing analytical judgements produced a 50,000-fold difference.

THE USE OF RISK ANALYSES

Institutions of all sorts battling in the political arena quite naturally seize upon the estimates that aid their cause. Utility companies advertise the risk assessments with narrow problem limits by analysts which rely on the best-available scientific estimates and leave out nebulous factors. Environmentalists and nearby residents prefer broad risk assessments done by analysts who are willing to use subjective judgements, who strive to be prudent by cascading conservative estimates, and who can vividly imagine a myriad of possible errors and disasters. Advocates, in general, exploit the statistics that support their arguments and interests (Vaupel 1982a).

The opportunities for conflicting interpretation of risk assessments are widened because advocates not only can pick their study but can also choose their numbers and figures from a study. For instance, one Oxnard risk study included, among many other estimates, a worst case scenario that indicated that a spill of 125,000 cubic meters of LNG from all five tanks on the tanker would cause a vapor cloud which might kill up to 70,000 people. Any resident could look on a map to determine whether the cloud covered his own house (Ahern 1980). Although no estimate of a probability was attached to this scenario, the chances were miniscule. Nonetheless, the graphic depiction of those consequences generated a strong public reaction by groups of local citizens. The California legislature was influenced by this public reaction. One legislative staff member stressed that it was not possible to allow a site that could lead, no matter how remote the chance, to a catastrophe (Kunreuther and Lathrop 1981). This report was influential in persuading the state legislators to rule out Oxnard as a possible site by including the remote siting provision into the California LNG Terminal Siting Act. Thus, the risk number and the map that the analyst calculated had a large political impact due to the way the data were presented.

THE MYTH OF OBJECTIVITY

Several authors have discussed how and why an analyst's values color his or her methods and results (see, for example, Quade 1975, Majone 1980). Wynne (1982) suggests that these biases be recognized as part and parcel of science, and not lapses from rational scientific analysis.

> There is a pervasive myth about the nature of science which supports this false approach to the question of "analytic bias." The tendency in the literature is to regard bias or mistakes as individual and isolated in origin, which suggests that ideal objective scientific knowledge can be attained in professional practice and as an input to policy issues. . . . This gives a funda-

mentally misleading and politically damaging picture of the role of expertise. . . .

The myth of objectivity, especially where policy sciences are concerned,
has led to a dual perspective on risk analyses. On the one hand, because the
analyses are quantitative they appear to be factual and objective. On the other
hand, the large uncertainties involved necessarily preclude the assessments
from being definitive. This *dual nature* of a formal risk study has fogged discussions of its role in the policy process. The numbers produced by a risk
analysis are not exact or "hard." They incorporate a number of judgements,
but hardly anyone in our culture is capable of handling inexact quantities or
"soft" numbers as has been pointed out by Ravetz (Kunreuther, Linnerooth,
and Starnes 1982, p.402).

In many ways, science has served to maintain the authority and legitimacy of our public institutions. The full objectivity of scientific investigation
has been, and remains, a concept necessary for upholding authority. As
scientific investigation moves into areas with a clear subjective element, there
is a danger that the myth of full scientific objectivity will be exposed and that
institutional authority will be threatened. Thus, institutional leaders, in guarding this myth, are reluctant to expose the uncertainty and subjectivity inherent
in risk analyses. The analyst, himself, is caught in a system that offers little
choice but the cloaking of results in a veil of scientific objectivity.

This pretense of objectivity has been observed by Moss and Lubin
(1980), who emphasize the appeal of risk analyses that present a rational and
scientific approach to public decision making. Precise numerical results provide comfort by concealing such inherent and fundamental uncertainties as
those reflected in the millionfold difference between risk estimate for saccharin or in the Inhaber-Holdren debate (Inhaber 1979, Holdren *et al.* 1979) concerning the risks of nuclear power plants. Even at an institution like the
National Research Council (NRC), where analysts are somewhat insulated
from political pressures, it is difficult to avoid biases in risk assessments. A
concern over this was expressed recently in a report surveying the way in
which risk analyses are prepared by the NRC.

> Science is strongly biased towards numbers, for when numbers can be justly
> employed they denote authority and a precise understanding of relationships.
> Because this is so, there is an equally important responsibility not to use
> numbers, which convey the impression of precision, when the understanding
> of relationships is indeed less secure. Thus while quantitative risk assessment
> facilitates comparison, such comparison may be illusory or misleading if the
> use of precise numbers is unjustified. (NRC Governing Board Committee on
> the Assessment of Risk 1981, p. 15.)

According to this view, it appears that the responsibility for exposing the imprecision of risk estimates lies with the analyst. But it is mistaken to suppose that the analyst can be removed from the social and political setting in which he or she is bound. In our adversarial system of policy making, the livelihood of consultants depends on their ability to prepare persuasive analytical arguments. Piehler (1974) provides an interesting example of this phenomenon in the context of a court case involving product liability.

CONSTRUCTIVE ROLES OF ANALYSIS

One possible direction for reform is discussed by Ackerman *et al.*(1974). They note that differences of opinion are often exacerbated by simultaneous studies of the same phenomenon and that traditional approaches, such as agency hearings and judicial reviews, are inherently limited in evaluating these conflicting assessments. To deal with this problem, they advocate establishing rules of evidence for scientific studies used in legal proceedings, in much the same spirit as a science court. These rules would encourage more uniform analyses so that the debate could focus on the alternatives themselves rather than the particular assessment or presentation promoted by an interested party. Lathrop and Linnerooth (1982) provide a suggested set of guidelines with respect to establishing rules of evidence. In particular, they stress the importance of defining the risk being assessed and clarifying the assumptions and error bounds, as well as indicating the conditional nature of specific analyses which are undertaken.

Without questioning the validity of our adversarial system of policy making, which has certain advantages over other political systems, we should recognize that analysts are constrained by the realities this system imposes on them. From this decision-process perspective, it is illusory to expect substantial changes in analytical practices without changes in the institutional foundations on which the system rests.

A Role for the Policy Analyst: Negotiating Conflicts

If each of the individual parties focuses on different attributes in judging the attractiveness of a particular site and if risk analysts differ widely in their risk assessments, then it is not surprising that proposed options, like the California LNG sites, may be rejected after a debate that is more heated than it is illuminating. Policy analysts may be able to make an important contribution by developing creative processes for resolving conflicts in mutually advantageous ways.

Conflict negotiation may be facilitated if policy analysts can develop programs for sharing gains and losses from a proposed project. By arranging for winners to compensate losers, by monetary payments or by payments in kind such as a recreation park, all parties may feel they are better off after the siting of a new technological facility.

A distinction can be made between *ex ante* compensation, by which payments in money or in kind are made at the time a facility is approved or constructed, and *ex post* compensation, by which reimbursement is paid to individuals or groups who suffer losses from an accident. In this section we illustrate several types of *ex ante* and *ex post* compensation arrangements which have been considered in siting facilities in different countries. The most difficult aspect of designing these compensation agreements is the problem of misrepresentation of preferences and concerns by some of the parties for personal gain. Designing systems which encourage parties to tell the truth independent of what others do (truth dominant procedures) or to tell the truth when others are also telling the truth (incentive compatible procedures) requires some ingenuity (Raiffa 1982). Here we will provide illustrative examples of the types of compensation systems which appear to have worked well and others which have had their problems.

EX ANTE COMPENSATION MEASURES

In siting power plants, an applicant may propose to reduce electricity rates to residents within a certain distance of the hazardous facility in order to compensate them for the increased risk or unpleasantness. Such a system has recently been introduced in France with respect to nuclear power plants. People living within approximately 15 km of a facility can apply to the local authority for a reduction of up to 15-20% in electricity rates. (Personal conversation with Gaz de France 1982.) Another example of *ex ante* compensation relates to the construction of a 1500 MW coal-fired power plant in Wyoming. A law suit had enjoined construction of the plant because of its potential damage to the surrounding environment. The suit was settled when the utility companies agreed to set up a $7.5 million trust fund for the express purpose of preserving a 60-mile stretch of the Platt River, the habitat of migratory birds, including the whooping crane. The coal plant was completed in 1981 and is fully operational today. (Personal conversation with Patrick Pateneau, National Wildlife Federation, 1982.)

We have been able to find only a single case where direct monetary compensation was given to individuals and this provoked a very strong reaction from others. In West Germany, the utility company STEAG (Steinkohle-Elektrizitatswerke AG) announced plans in 1976 to construct a 1400 MW coal power plant in the city of Bergkamen in the Ruhr area. A citizen action group protested the project and threatened to delay the licensing procedures. In March 1977 a contract was signed between the utility company and three representatives of the action group: the group would be reimbursed with a payment of $750,000 if they agreed not to oppose the project. However, a court case was provoked when the city of Bergkamen refused to distribute the money. The federal court decided that the contract was valid because the citizen group should be compensated for legitimate rights, but the decision was greeted with negative reactions by German public opinion. Concerns were voiced in the media that health and safety were citizens' inalienable rights that could not be bought off.

EX POST COMPENSATION

In *ex post* compensation the key question is who is responsible for the damage should an accident occur. To encourage safer designs there is good reason to have the applicant responsible for any damages from an accident. Pfennigsdorf (1979) points out that for ultra-hazardous or abnormally dangerous activities, such as an LNG terminal, public policy supports the doctrine of strict liability whereby the operator of the facility is liable for damages regardless of fault. Whether the developer actually will have to pay for these losses in the event of a catastrophic LNG accident in the future remains to be seen. If the courts hold the applicant responsible, then some form of public or private insurance appears to be attractive on the surface since, to the extent premiums are based on risk, it creates incentives for firms to make their facilities safer. Yet, as we have discussed above, experts often disagree on the chances and consequences of a catastrophic accident; this makes it difficult for an insurance company to set premiums. For this reason and because premiums are small compared to the potential losses should an accident occur, insurance and reinsurance companies are reluctant to provide protection against these low probability, high consequence events. A unique set of *ex post* compensation arrangements between the developers, insurance firms, government and victims may well emerge depending on the exact characteristics of the accident. In fact, we could not determine for any of the four case studies of LNG siting what fraction of the damage would be shared by each of the interested parties should an accident occur.

Rather than using direct monetary payments to make *ex post* compensation, it may be attractive for all parties to arrange for payment in kind. A landmark case in this spirit was the settlement by Allied Chemical in Virginia after being found guilty of polluting the James River with the pesticide kepone. Rather than paying a fine, the company proposed paying $5.2 million and establishing an $8 million trust fund to be used for environmental grants in Virginia. In essence, the firm provided *ex post* compensation in the form of support for research to prevent future damage to the environment (1982 Annual Report of Virginia Environmental Endowment).

These types of compensation arrangements may be important tools in the analyst's repertoire if certain individuals or groups have the power to block the approval of a facility that promises to increase general social welfare.

Conclusion

Viewing siting decisions from a decision-process perspective leads to some insights that might not be apparent from the simplifying vantage point of a single decision maker resolving a single decision once and for all.

Most risk analysts recognize that risk estimation involves vague uncertainties and subjective judgements and that two risk analysts may therefore produce widely differing assessments of the same hazard. The decision-process perspective highlights a key consequence of such discrepancies: interested parties seize the assessments that favor their position and try to use them as conclusive arguments rather than as a bit of incomplete evidence. Furthermore, from a decision-process perspective it seems naive to expect that such misuse of risk analyses can be curtailed by exhorting analysts to reform their practices. Institutional changes, including perhaps rules of evidence, are required.

The decision-process perspective also suggests that a major role for policy analysts is to help negotiate conflicts. One promising approach that deserves more careful study is to facilitate agreement by using various compensation strategies to redistribute gains to losers. Transfer payments either in monetary form or more likely through payments in kind may lead groups who opposed a facility to favor its construction. How well these tools are likely to work depends upon the nature of the problem, degree of opposition and the view which society has on satisfying all interested parties. In the end it comes down to how society deals with tradeoffs between parties when there is imperfect information on both the risks and the benefits.[3]

Notes

1. We choose this technology because most of the ideas in this article arose in the context of a collaborative study of LNG siting decision processes. The study was conducted at the International Institute for Applied Systems Analysis in Laxenburg, Austria. See Kunreuther, Linnerooth *et al.* (1983). As background it may be helpful to know that:

> Liquefied natural gas (LNG) is a potential source of energy which requires a fairly complicated technological process that has the potential, albeit with very low probability, of creating severe losses. For purposes of transporting, natural gas can be converged to liquid form at about 1/600 its gaseous volume. It is

shipped in especially constructed tankers and received at a terminal where it undergoes regasification and is then distributed. The entire system (i.e., the liquefication facility, the LNG tankers, the receiving terminal, and regasification facility) can cost more than $1 billion to construct (Office of Technology Assessment, 1977).

2. This model is in the spirit of the incrementalism approach to political decision making developed by Lindblom (1959).

3. This research was funded in part by Bundesministerum fuer Forschung und Technologie West Germany Contract No. 321/75911RGB8001, NSF Grant No. 5-22669, and ICSAR funding to IIASA. We would like to express our appreciation to Baruch Fischhoff and an anonymous referee for their helpful comments.

References

Ackerman, B., S. Rose-Ackerman, J. Sawyer, and D. Henderson, *The Uncertain Search for Environmental Quality*, The Free Press, New York, 1974.

Ahern, W., "California Meets the LNG Terminal," *Coastal Zone Management J.*, 7 (1980). 185-221.

Allison, G., *Essence of Decision*, Little, Brown and Company, Boston, 1971.

Braybrooke, D., *Traffic Congestion Goes Through the Issue Machine*, Routledge and Kegan Paul, London, 1974.

Cobb, R., and C. D. Elder, *Participation in American Politics: The Dynamics of Agenda Building*. Johns Hopkins University Press, Baltimore, 1972.

Fischhoff, B., S. Lichtenstein, P. Slovic, R. Keeney and S. Derby, *Acceptable Risk*. Cambridge University Press, Cambridge, 1981.

Holdren, J. P., K. Anderson, P. Gleick, I. Mintzer, G. Morris and K. Smith, "Risk of Renewable Energy Resources: A Critique of the Inhaber Report," U.S. Department of Energy, Washington, D.C., Contract No: W-7405-EW6-45, 1979.

Keeney, R. L., *Siting Energy Facilities*, Academic Press, New York, 1980.

Kunreuther, H. and J. Lathrop, "Siting Hazard Facilities: The Case of LNG Terminals," *Risk Analysis*, 1 (1981), 289-302.

———, ——— and J. Linnerooth, "A Multi-Attribute Multi-Party Model of Choice," *Behavioral Sci.*, (July 1982).

———, J. Linnerooth, J. Lathrop, H. Atz, S. Macgill, C. Mandl, M. Schwarz and M. Thompson, *Risk Analysis and Decision Processes: The Siting of LEG Facilities in Four Countries*, Springer Verlag, New York, 1983.

———, ——— and R. Starnes, *Liquefied Energy Gas (LEG) Facility Siting: International Comparisons*, Proceedings of the IIASA Task Force Meeting, September 23-26, 1980, Laxenburg, Austria, 1982.

Lathrop, J. and J. Linnerooth, "The Role of Risk Assessment in a Political Decision Process," in P. Humphreys and A. Vari (Eds.), *Analysing and Aiding Decision Processes*, North-Holland, Amsterdam, 1982.

Lawless, J., *Technology and Social Shock*, Rutgers University Press, New Brunswick, N.J., 1977.

Levine, M. and C. R. Plott, "Agenda Influence and its Implications," *Virginia Law Rev.,* 63, 4 (1977).

Lichtenstein, S. et al., "Judged Frequency of Lethal Events," *J. Experimental Psychol.: Human Learning and Memory,* 4, (1978) 551-578.

Lindblom, C., "The Science of Muddling Through," *Public Admin. Rev.,* 19 (1959), 79-88.

Majone, G., "An Anatomy of Pitfalls," in G. Malone and E. Quade (Eds.), *Pitfalls and Analysis,* IIASA series on Applied Systems Analysis, No. 8. Wiley, Chichester, U.K., 1980.

————, "Policies vs. Decisions," to appear in Majone G., *The Use of Policy Analysis,* 1984 (forthcoming).

Moss, T. and B. Lubin, "Risk Analysis: A Legislative Perspective," in C. R. Richmond, P. Nalsh, and E. Copenhaven (Eds.), *Health Risk Analysis,* The Franklin Institute Press, Philadelphia, 1980.

National Research Council Governing Board Committee on the Assessment of Risk, "The Handling of Risk Assessment in NRC Reports," Report to the Governing Board, U.S. National Research Council, Washington, D.C., 1981.

Nisbett, R. and Ross, L., *Human Inference: Strategies and Shortcomings of Social Judgment,* Prentice-Hall, Englewood Cliffs, N.J., 1980.

Office of Technology Assessment, *Transportation of Liquified Natural Gas,* Washington, D.C., 1977.

Otway, H. and D. von Winterfeldt, "Beyond Acceptable Risk: On Social Acceptability of Technologies," *Policy Sci.,* 14, 3 (June 1982).

Pfennigsdorf, W., "Environment, Damages and Compensation," *Amer. Bar Foundation,* 2 (1979), 347-448.

Piehler, H. "Product Liability and the Technical Expert," *Science* 186, (1974), 1089-1093.

Quade, E. S., *Analysis for Public Decision,* Elsevier, New York, 1975.

Raiffa, H.,*The Art of Science and Negotiation,* Harvard University Press, Cambridge, 1982.

Slovic, P., B. Fischhoff and S. Lichtenstein, "Characterizing Perceived Risk," in R. W. Kates and C. Hohenemser (Eds.), *Technological Hazard Management,* Oelgeschlager, Gunn and Hain, Cambridge, Mass., 1983.

Tversky, A. and D. Kahneman, "Judgment Under Uncertainty: Heuristics and Biases," *Science,* 185 (1974), 1124-1131.

Vaupel, J. W "Statistical Insinuation," *J. Policy Anal. and Management,* 1 (1982a), 261-263.

————, "Analytical Perspectives on Setting Environmental Standards," report prepared for U.S. Environmental Protection Agency, contract number ID2290-NASX, 1982b.

Walker, J., "Setting the Agenda in the U.S. Senate: A Theory of Problem Selection," *British J. Political Sci.,* 7 (1977), 423-445.

Weinberg, A. M., "Science and Trans-Science," *Minerva,* 10 (1972), 209-222.

Wynne, B., *Rationality and Ritual: The Windscale Injury and Nuclear Decision in Britain,* The British Society for the History of Science, 1982.

FRANK J. POPPER

13 *LP/HC and LULUs*

The Political Uses of Risk Analysis in Land-Use Planning

The LULU as a Public Issue

A recent Environmental Protection Agency examination of the siting of hazardous waste facilities analyzed 21 case studies and came to the following "major conclusions":

> public opposition to the siting of hazardous waste management facilities, particularly landfills, is a critical problem. It is the most critical problem in developing new facilities, in the opinion of most government and industry officials interviewed.[1]

The study maintained that the consequences of such public opposition could be "enormous." Yet the 1976 Resource Conservation and Recovery Act, which the EPA and the states are just now beginning to carry out, requires a large number of new, safer disposal sites. These sites, whether found by the EPA or the states, will typically meet stiff public resistance—no one wants to live near them. But, the EPA found, "if public opposition continues to frustrate siting attempts, there may be no place to put all this hazardous waste, and the national effort to regulate hazardous waste may collapse."[1]

Such public opposition is not new; federal, state, and local governments, along with industry, have faced this apparently awesome problem many times before. Hazardous waste facilities are merely an extreme instance of a common—and increasingly prevalent—land-use situation. They are one of a distinct group of development projects that are regionally or nationally needed, but whose location or operation is undesirable to many of their neighbors. There is no accepted term for such projects, but they have a defining characteristic: they are Locally Unwanted Land Uses, or LULUs.

LULUs abound. There are nuclear power plants, refineries, airports, strip mines, highways, low-income housing projects, power and rail lines, halfway houses, dams, prisons, military installations, hospitals, and fossil-fuel power plants. Many public parks, factories, and residential developments (especially high-rises, suburban apartments, and trailer parks) may qualify. The most visible LULUs are typically large, based on medium to high technology, and regulated by several levels of government. Many such LULUs have a technology, scale, or other features (for example, materials or transportation requirements) that call for LP/HC (low-probability/high-consequence) risk analysis.

There seems to be a general consensus on which LULUs are most unwanted, and these are in fact the ones prone to produce LP/HC events. A 1980 poll, sponsored by the Council on Environmental Quality and other federal agencies, found that only about 10–12 percent of the population would voluntarily live a mile or less from a nuclear power plant or hazardous waste disposal site; see Fig. 1. By contrast, approximately 25 percent would be willing to live that distance from a coal-fired power plant or large factory, and nearly 60 percent that near to a 10-story office building.

The nuclear power plant and the hazardous waste site reached majority acceptance (51 percent) only when their distance from the respondents passed 100 miles, despite assurances in the poll questions that the facilities "would be built and operated according to government environmental and safety regulations" so that "disposal could be done safely and the site regularly inspected for possible problems." And 5 and 10 percent, respectively, of respondents stated that they would not voluntarily live at any distance from the plant or site—that is, they said the LULU was utterly unacceptable to them.[1]

Yet the LULUs likely to produce LP/HC events are only partly distinguishable from other kinds. Indeed, the two sets of LULUs blend into each other and have no clear point of separation. To take the CEQ poll examples, a coal-fired power plant, big factory, or large office building can in principle pose LP/HC risks formally comparable to those of a nuclear power plant or hazardous waste site.[2] A walkway could collapse or a fire occur in any of these structures. But there is a difference, however blurred, between the most unwanted LULUs and the others: the most unwanted ones are judged by the public (and sometimes by the real estate market, lenders, and insurers) to have higher overall probabilities of seriously harming their neighbors, in a way that a walkway collapse or even a fire would not. The perceived greater

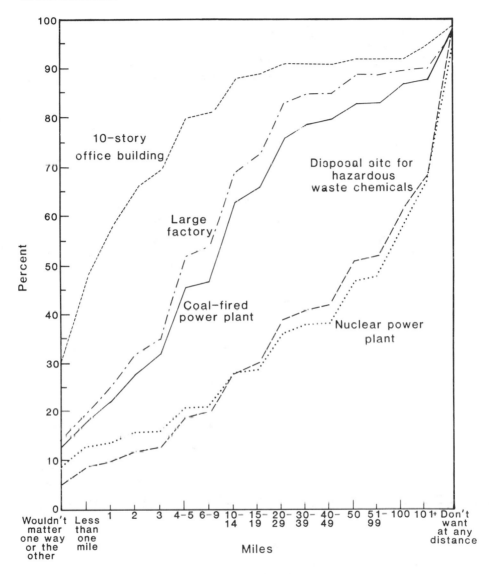

FIGURE 1. Cumulative percentage of people willing to accept new industrial installations at various distances from their homes.

Source: Council on Environmental Quality, Department of Agriculture, and Environmental Protection Agency, Public Opinion on Environmental Issues: Results of a National Public Opinion Survey (Washington: U.S. Government Printing Office, 1980), p. 31.

likelihoods of wide-area, large-scale damage mean that the LULUs with the potential of creating them will be wanted less and opposed more.

In the language of the economist, the most unwanted LULUs threaten the largest negative externalities—the highest economic and environmental costs to parties other than the producer and the consumer of the LULU's output, such as neighbors. The larger costs do not affect the probability of an LP/HC event, but greatly increase its consequences. For parties likely to be hurt by the increased consequences of an LP/HC event—such as neighbors—the value of the LULU will be quite low. In technical terms, for the neighbors the LULU's expected value—the total of multiplying the subjective probabilities of the various LULU outcomes by the subjective costs and benefits (that is, the consequences) assigned to each outcome—will be extremely negative. The result will be, the CEQ poll indicates, that the LULUs that most seem to threaten LP/HC events will be the most objectionable to the public.

By definition a LULU satisfies a strong nonlocal public need or private demand. A LULU offers (or appears to offer) large regional or national benefits. The difficulty is that its costs fall mainly on its locality or neighborhood. The asymmetry between costs and benefits, which is often inequitable—and may become catastrophic if LP/HC events occur—sometimes cannot be rectified. The claims of the local few must be weighed against those of the regional many. This is the essence of the public problem posed by LULUs. It is posed in its most extreme, politically and emotionally wrenching form by those LULUs most likely to create LP/HC events.[3]

Risk Analysis in Land-Use Planning

Most persons engaged in land-use planning—not just city planners, but also developers, environmentalists, members of planning commissions and zoning boards, other government officials, and the lawyers for all these groups—do not explicitly use LP/HC or other risk analysis approaches in their work. Indeed, most such persons barely know of the existence of these approaches unless they happen to be economists. To the extent that any economic model at all underlies contemporary land-use planning, it is probably cost-benefit analysis rather than risk analysis.

But even the most rudimentary form of cost-benefit analysis cannot really be said to be the basis of the eclectic, often jumbled mix of activities—drawing up master plans, regulating land uses, designing projects, collecting information, preparing capital budgets, coordinating different levels of government, and negotiating policy—that is the daily lot of those who do land-use planning. A good deal of this work, including the portion that ostensibly deals with "reducing hazards," is not even site-specific—that is, it deals with large undifferentiated zones of land or standard administrative issues rather than particular projects.[4] It is therefore not always pointed toward specific LULUs, even those that most clearly threaten LP/HC events.

Still, if land-use planning does not typically employ or appreciate technically sophisticated risk analysis and LP/HC methods, it does employ the questioning LP/HC cast of mind: it looks, as any responsible discipline would, at how its efforts that should work in principle could go wrong in practice. In particular, when it deals with LULUs that might result in long-shot disasters, it does not hesitate to use versions, however rough, of LP/HC techniques. It thinks in terms of worst cases. It tries to weigh the relative probability of diverse worst cases. It makes crude attempts at fault trees. It works to separate necessary, inevitable uncertainties from unnecessary, avoidable ones and to minimize both. It attempts to imagine perverse consequences of unlikely combinations of unlikely accidents.

In addition, it studies the record of the other instances of the kind of LULU in question. It draws whatever comparisons and analogies are relevant from other kinds of LULUs. It tries to figure out how governments and industry might respond to an LP/HC event at the LULU. It worries about the economic consequences—especially the cost, practicality, efficiency, and equity—of the alternatives before it. Above all, it aims for a tough-minded, conservative skepticism. Land-use planning does not invariably succeed at all of these praiseworthy efforts, for what discipline does? But it tries, usually very hard.[5]

The demands that land-use planning makes of LULUs prone to LP/HC events show up clearly in the requirements planners, environmentalists, and government officials, including regulators, routinely place on proposed or operating LULUs. The LULUs are often expected to survive withering scrutiny so as to allay deep-seated, environmentally oriented suspicions. For instance, the LULUs must usually be justified—generally in applications, environmental impact statements, hearings, and the like—not simply in terms of their benefits, which are almost always prospective and so inherently conjectural. The LULUs must also be shown to be socially preferable to all realistic development alternatives—that is, to both other possibilities on the intended site and possibilities that would put the LULUs elsewhere. The LULUs must also be shown preferable to doing nothing, to not developing.

LULUs that pose LP/HC risks are not always held to all of these standards, but they are held to them often and searchingly enough to annoy the parties that build and operate them. The LULUs are held to these standards more often than they were in 1970 or 1960; and any Reaganesque attempt to undo the standards typically finds institutional, legal, and political barriers that prevent dropping them to where they used to be.[6] Meeting the standards remains, to be diplomatic, a challenging task, in part because it amounts to a requirement to prove a negative—that the LULU at issue will not lead to an LP/HC incident even under the most hard-to-imagine, bizarre, unpredictable circumstances. As LP/HC analysts know, such a task is humbling.

Yet consider the many lines of political resistance available to environmentalists and their allies, including land-use planners, during controversies over the siting of LULUs with LP/HC possibilities. For example, the opposition will typically argue that a proposed LULU's benefits are illusory, maintaining that the LULU is totally unneeded anywhere (as in the case of nuclear power plants) or unneeded by the region (many dams, highways, and fossil-fuel power plants). Such attacks, which inevitably and understandably focus on a LULU's potential for LP/HC events, can make siting difficult and often impossible.

Alternatively—and by no means inconsistently—the opposition may argue that the proposed LULU is located in the wrong place within the region, sited by means of defective procedures, or likely to produce harmful effects, including LP/HC events, that cannot be mitigated. These three attacks in fact appear nearly universally in siting controversies over LULUs that pose LP/HC risks. A comparable set of attacks is available to the opposition once the LULU is in operation and may culminate in actually closing the LULU—as in the case of Love Canal and, at least temporarily, several nuclear plants. Environmentalists can be depended on to make land-use planners aware of a LULU's LP/HC risks, and to make them take steps to counter the risks.

So, for instance, the Nuclear Regulatory Commission encourages utilities to locate new power plants in lightly populated areas and usually will not approve a plant in a densely populated area if another site is available in a less populated one. A large buffer zone between the plant and its surroundings is always required. In the case of some plants, there has been sentiment in the Commission for making agreements with local governments to limit population beyond the buffer zone—in a radius of five or ten miles around the plant.[2]

In addition, the possibilities of earthquakes, floods, tornadoes, and tidal waves are explored, even in places with no history of them. A Commission study, using case studies of plants in Florida, Illinois, Mississippi, and Indiana, shows sedulous attention to the potentially catastrophic effects of such unlikely events as misdirected water outflows, unintended impacts on weather, grotesquely improbable transportation accidents, and combinations between cooling tower plumes and the effluents of distant fossil-fuel plants to produce dangerous sulfur compounds. The study also shows the Commission and utilities taking land-use measures, often expensive ones, to anticipate and prevent these events.[3]

The Concept of Risk in Land-Use Planning

Although land-use planners for LULUs are willing to think in terms of LP/HC events and to take measures to forestall them, they are not interested in the fine details or exotic manipulations of LP/HC risk analysis. Nor would they be more concerned with these intricacies if they knew more about them. The disinclination springs not from the education they have received so much as from the temperament their work later induces in them. For land-use planners—whether formally trained in the discipline or recruited to it by the demands of professional or civic life—tend to view risks, especially the long-shot ones posed by an LP/HC event, as facts of life that are often inexplicable but cannot be totally avoided or suppressed. They do not see risks as problems to be explained, mitigated, or solved by technical devices such as LP/HC analysis.[7]

Land-use planners and their associates will thus act to prevent risks and LP/HC events at LULUs, but will do so fatalistically—without firm expectation that they will succeed. They are simply and unapologetically operating in the cautious, common-sensical spirit of what the law calls the prudent man. They do not seek a regulatory perfection that covers all eventualities. They are impatient with the abstraction of LP/HC analysis. For them, a large buffer zone will frequently be all that is needed to deal with LP/HC events at LULUs.

Specialists in LP/HC risk analysis, such as economists, scientists, and engineers, tend to see risk differently. In their view, what economists call the expected value criterion ought to play a more prominent role in land-use planning. More precisely, an LP/HC event at a LULU such as a meltdown at a nuclear power plant should be formally comparable to a high-probability/low-consequence (HP/LC) event such as continuing, non-serious water pollution by the plant. Similarly, the risks of an LP/HC LULU such as a nuclear plant should be comparable to those of an HP/LC LULU such as a coal-fired power plant. In all these cases formal comparability need not, LP/HC specialists would argue, be the sole guide to public policy or land-use planning, but it ought at least be taken into account. Some attempt should be made to maximize the expected value of the LULU.

As a result, LP/HC specialists are often quite discomfited by the evidence that the public and its decision-makers, including land-use planners, do not act in accord with the expected value criterion—which, of course, they have never heard of. The specialists are bothered when, as in the CEQ poll, the public shows a plain preference for coal-fired power plants over nuclear ones. Charles A. Zraket, for instance, of the MITRE Corporation told a 1979 MITRE symposium on risk assessment:

Public perceptions of comparative risks and of the magnitude of risks seem
to be widely at variance with the actuarial fact base. . . . Conventional risk
assessment, as measured by the product of probability times the consequences, is not valid with respect to the public view. For the public, high-
consequence/low-probability events (such as nuclear accidents) are often perceived as more serious than low-consequence/high-probability events, even
though the first moments of the consequence's distribution may be the
same.[4]

LP/HC specialists are equally uneasy with the many well-designed
psychological experiments that show a clear public unwillingness to multiply
"probability times the consequences."[8]

Yet in refusing to do the multiplication—or at least to act on it—the public, its decision-makers, and land-use planners are probably being more realistic about LULUs than are LP/HC specialists. The multiplication is far too
simple and mechanical to serve as a basis for policies on projects as complex
and organic as LULUs. The multiplication neglects the uncertainties inevitable
in both the probabilities and the consequences it is manipulating. It ignores the
fear, ignorance, and hostility that palpably surround any LP/HC risk. It
assumes that experts, who differ obscurely with each other and disconcert-
ingly with the public, know something important that the rest of the population does not—something important enough to make the public and governments take steps that may be counter-intuitive or against their better judgment.

The multiplication also presumes that "the actuarial fact base" is deeper
than it usually is for LP/HC events. Perhaps worst of all, the multiplication
seems to imply if an event is sufficiently improbable, it will not really cause
any damage if it occurs. An extremely low probability, multiplied by any
level of negative consequences, will still yield an expected value that is negative but quite near zero, vanishingly small. It is as if the multiplication
wishes away the damage—a nonsensically optimistic posture, and a politically
indefensible one. So the public and its decision-makers do not do the multiplication, at least in a politically perceptible sense.

What they do instead is think and act in terms of the consequences of an
LP/HC event at a LULU. Operating in terms of consequences, rather than
probabilities or probabilities times consequences, means that decisions about
LULUs—whether by politicians, regulators, or land-use planners—are made
with defensive gingerness. They are made as they would be by anyone who
has just suffered a disaster, believes they might be about to suffer one, or
knows that they will be held accountable if someone else suffers one. Operating consequentially means ignoring the probability-times-consequences multiplication. More precisely, it means assuming that the consequences variable
has a high multiplier while the probabilities variable has none, or—more
radically—that there is such a total disjuncture between the variables that any

multiplication of them is meaningless. Such rejections of the expected value criterion do not come easily to LP/HC specialists, especially economists.

Yet some LP/HC specialists are evidently bothered by the way the complexity of their work does not register with decision-makers or the public. Such specialists have grasped that in many public and political situations, including land-use planning for LULUs, the technicalities of LP/HC and similar risk analyses look like—and probably are—dim academic approaches to the eternal, inherent difficulties of life. As a result, these specialists have begun to emphasize the importance of operating consequentially. For instance, at the 1979 MITRE symposium Marvin R. Gustafson of the University of California's Livermore Laboratory said:

> I find I have to go back to fairly simple things to keep from getting lost. The first of these rather simple things is that actions have consequences. And as soon as I start to partition them into goods and bads, the benefits and the risks, I am already inserting value judgment. It seems to me, to be absolutely honest with myself, that all I can do is to calculate consequences.[5]

Similarly, Nathaniel Barr of the U.S. Energy Department said:

> To the extent that you can describe with a reasonable degree of confidence an uncertainty and what the consequences are, the public is more likely—we are talking about many uses—to react to uncertainty in the consequences than to uncertainty in the probability of occurrence . . . The question has always been the public asking, "We accept this as a low-probability event, but are you sure that, if it should happen with extremely low probability, that we will not be wiped out?"[9][5]

Barr's question is a good one. It is made even more pointed when we realize that LP/HC and similar risk analyses do not offer analytic frameworks for decision-making that do not depend on the expected value criterion. Perhaps they will someday be able to offer them. But at present such analyses are merely an input—a flawed, technical contribution among other, more politically cogent ones—to the world of the public decision-making process.[10] The inhabitants of this political world have idiosyncratic customs: they make up their own minds, are not bothered by seeming subjective rather than objective, are not often totally swayed even by expert analysis far more convincing than the LP/HC approach provides, and—above all—use a less optimistically perfectionistic concept of risk than that of LP/HC analysis. In short, the political world—including, most particularly, the land-use planners for LULUs—operates on the basis of consequences. If LP/HC and other risk analysts want to be more influential, they should begin to do likewise.

A Political Interpretation

As public environmental sensitivity has grown, LULUs of all kinds and sizes have become increasingly difficult and expensive to site and operate. American society is experiencing what one could call environmental/economic blockage. For instance, since 1970 at least 12 attempts to place an oil refinery somewhere on the East Coast, from Maine to Georgia, have resulted in only one successful proposal (in Portsmouth, Virginia).[6] No new nuclear power plant has been undertaken in five years—well before the Three Mile Island incident—and no metropolitan airport in thirteen. Most big cities have not begun a large highway, mass transit, or low-income housing project in more than a decade. In many states projects as relatively innocuous as marinas and theme parks provoke intense controversy and are often stymied.

Put another way, the number of locally *wanted* land uses is dropping fast. Perhaps the only land uses left that are almost always acceptable to their neighbors are open space and research parks, which in most cases are not live options or LP/HC risks. The public considers more projects LULUs. In addition, the public—and not just the environmentalist portions of it—shows a growing reluctance to have LULUs located or operated indiscriminately, especially nearby.

Yet many big new LULUs loom ahead: nuclear waste disposal sites and innovative kinds of high-technology factories, possibly the MX missile system—all in addition to the many LULUs that already bedevil us. Moreover, a tight economy makes some projects previously considered LULUs more desirable. In 1982 twenty-two depressed rural Illinois towns were competing to be the site of a new state prison; none had been willing to compete for another prison five years earlier.[7] In Niagara Falls, New York, there was a strong demand for the homes abandoned by the residents of Love Canal.[8]

In its present form LP/HC and similar risk analysis does little to illuminate these difficult land-use problems. Indeed, it may sometimes make them worse, both by making some worthwhile LULUs seem more objectionable than they deserve and by appearing to sanction other LULUs that may be truly objectionable. We are reaching a point where the very use of LP/HC and similar risk analysis of LULUs will often create an uncertainty distinct from that created by the actual risks posed by the LULU. Nuclear power plants probably reached this point several years ago, but many LULUs—as the examples of environmental/economic blockage indicate—are catching up. Consequently, LP/HC risk analysis and the modes of thought associated with it are fast becoming a political liability.[11]

In part, the difficulty is simply one of public presentation. LP/HC and other forms of risk analysis seem to the public to be bloodless, unrelated to real life, and a complicated euphemism that fools no one. The experts espousing such analysis are distrusted, often seem to distrust each other, and sometimes to distrust their own expertise, which in any case rarely seems sufficient to justify their influence. They inspire little confidence. The public would prefer not to trust them, and resists being placed in a position where it must.

But a larger part of the difficulty is—there is no other word for it—moral. LP/HC and other risk analysis frequently assumes that the problem of LULUs is primarily one of production—of producing the LULUs in the optimum or near-optimum number, size, timing, and arrangement. The more basic question of whether the LULU should be produced at all—whether it should exist—never gets a fair hearing. Any LULU admittedly meets some non-local public need or private want. Yet if a nuclear power plant, hazardous waste disposal site, or missile system is consistently impossible to site, or too costly, or acrimonious to operate anywhere, the market—more exactly, the population—is sending a clear message. In such cases government and the private sector might better respond not by pushing the LULU harder, but by seeking substitutes for it—other sources of energy, industrial processes that create less toxic waste, new military strategies, and the like. Not all demands for LULUs need be met, but LP/HC risk analysis often operates as if they should.

To make the point another way, LP/HC risk analysis almost always deals with LULUs—such as nuclear power plants or dams—whose risks come from their technology or scale. Why does it never deal with LULUs—such as prisons, low-income housing projects, or halfway houses—whose risks come from the occupants? There is nothing in the method that makes it inherently more suited to engineering problems or less suited to people problems. Indeed, as some LP/HC risk analysts point out, the engineering problems are often people problems in thin disguise. So why can't we treat the true people problems as if they were engineering problems? The answer is that we are reluctant to treat people—even feared and despised people such as prisoners or the poor—as if they were simply inanimate variables in some abstract engineering, environmental, or land-use equation. A similarly humane reluctance runs through much of the current grassroots movement to prevent a nuclear detonation, which represents the ultimate LULU.

How can LP/HC and similar risk analysis approaches be made more politically effective? More precisely, how can LP/HC risk analysts and their associates begin to operate consequentially rather than in terms of the expected value criterion? Several possibilities come to mind, all applicable to LULUs. First and most basically, LP/HC risk analysts should make an honest attempt to learn more about how land-use planners and political decision-makers think, and why they think that way. Such attempts might take idiosyncratic form—ranging from private meetings to personal sabbaticals, from after-hours reading programs to bureaucratic exchange arrangements—but the exact form is probably less important than the sincerity of the attempt to view one's profession from another perspective.

A number of subsidiary initiatives would follow. LP/HC risk analysts should, wherever possible, try to keep in mind that there may be alternatives to the LULU at issue that could be preferable to it—ones that may do less harm to its neighbors or that achieve its objectives without creating its problems. The analysts should do what they can to speed and simplify the siting of LULUs in a way that will still allow adequate investigation of their dangers. They should do more to probe the physical, psychological, and economic effects of living next to a LULU, about which we know surprisingly little. Finally, the analysts should do more to explore the potential of economic incentives to compensate the neighbors of a LULU for the difficulties it causes them. Such incentives can take an unusual number of forms—grants, loans, bond guarantees, taxation devices, cash payments, in-kind contributions, improvements in public services, perhaps property tax reductions or even auction bidding for (or against) a LULU—that with imagination can be adapted to suit almost any site, government, developer, political climate, or opposition.

Notes

1. Council on Environmental Quality, Department of Agriculture, Department of Energy, and Environmental Protection Agency, *Public Opinion on Environmental Issues: Results of a National Public Opinion Survey* (Government Printing Office, Washington, 1980), pp. 29-32. Figure 1 appears as p. 31. The study was prepared by Resources for the Future.

2. For a discussion demonstrating the formal comparability, see T. Page, "A Generic View of Toxic Chemicals and Similar Risks," *Ecology Law Quarterly*, **7**, 208-216 (1978).

3. For further discussion of LULUs, see F. J. Popper, "Siting LULUs," *Planning* **47**, 12-15 (April 1981); Popper, "How to locate a LULU," *American Land Forum* **2**, 6-7 (Summer 1981); Popper, "When the Development is a LULU. . . ," *Resources* **1**, 14-15 (Spring/Summer 1981); Popper, "LULUs," *Resources* **73**, 2-4 (June 1983); R. G. Healy and Popper, Speeding Industrial Siting: the False Promise of Procedural Reform, *Sloan Management Review* **22**, 47-54 (Fall 1980); and Popper, *The LULU: Coping with Locally Unwanted Land Uses* (forthcoming).

4. See, for example, American Planning Association, *Reducing Landslide Hazards: A Guide for Planners* (APA, Chicago, 1981) and *Reducing Earthquake Risks: A Planner's Guide* (APA, Chicago, 1981).

5. See, for example, D. Morell and C. Magorian, *Siting Hazardous Waste Facilities: Local Opposition and the Myth of Preemption* (Ballinger, Cambridge, Massachusetts, 1982).

6. For a detailed case study of this phenomenon in state land-use planning, see F. J. Popper, *The Politics of Land-Use Reform* (University of Wisconsin Press, Madison, 1981), pp. 154-170, 193-208, and 233-235.

7. See, for example, F. S. Chapin, Jr., and E. J. Kaiser, *Urban Land Use Planning* (University of Illinois Press, Urbana, third edition, 1979).

8. For examples of such experiments, see B. Fischhoff, P. Slovic, and S. Lichtenstein, Weighing the risks, *Environment,* **21,** 17-20 and 32-38 (May 1979); P. Slovic, B. Fischhoff, and S. Lichtenstein, Why study risk perception?, *Risk Analysis,* in press; and D. Kahneman and A. Tversky, Prospect theory: an analysis of decisions under risk, *Econometrica* **47,** 263-292 (May 1979).

9. For an application to the LULU of nuclear waste disposal sites, see H. S. Burness, "Risk: Accounting for an Uncertain Future," *Natural Resources Journal* **21,** 723-734 (October 1981). For a general application of this approach, see National Academy of Sciences, *Regulating Pesticides* (NAS, Washington, 1980), pp. 75-77.

10. For comparable opinions, see MITRE Corporation, *Risk Assessment and Government Decision Making,* pp. 14, 175, 377, 597, and 605. On the more general case of scientists and engineers advising decision-makers, see D. K. Price, *The Scientific Estate* (Oxford University Press, Oxford, 1965).

11. For confirmation, see MITRE Corporation, *Risk Assessment and Government Decision Making,* pp. 488, 489, 494, and 495-496.

References

This paper was completed while the author was a Gilbert F. White Fellow at Resources for the Future in Washington, D. C. Philip Herr, Paul Slovic, and an anonymous reviewer offered useful comments on earlier drafts.

1. EPA Office of Water and Waste Management, *Siting of Hazardous Waste Management Facilities and Public Opposition* (EPA, Washington, 1979), p. 3.

2. W. Toner, Nuke Siting the EROS Way, *American Land Forum,* **2,** 4, (1981).

3. W. Ramsay and P. R. Reed, *Land Use and Nuclear Power Plants: Case Studies of Siting Problems* (Atomic Energy Commission, Washington, 1974).

4. MITRE Corporation, *Risk Assessment and Government Decision Making: Symposium/Workshop on Nuclear and Nonnuclear Energy Systems—Proceedings* (MITRE Corporation, McLean, Virginia, 1979), p. 3.

5. MITRE Corporation, *Risk Assessment and Government Decision Making,* p. 624.

6. R. G. Healy and F. J. Popper, Speeding Industrial Siting: The False Promise of Procedural Reform, *Sloan Management Review* **22,** p. 47.

7. Jay Mathews, "Midwest Towns Hunt for Unlikely Saviors," *Washington Post,* p. A1 (April 5, 1982).

8. "Potential Buyers Clamor for Abandoned Love Canal Homes," *Washington Post,* p. A7 (April 29, 1982).

SUSAN L. CARPENTER AND W. J. D. KENNEDY

14 *Environmental Conflict Management*

In December 1979, 27 members of the Colorado state legislature, the body responsible for developing a vehicle emissions control plan, sued the Environmental Protection Agency (EPA) over the constitutionality of threatened federal sanctions. In the same month, a separate lawsuit was filed in Denver against the EPA by the National Wildlife Federation and citizens challenging the EPA's possible approval of the regional air quality plan. If the EPA did impose sanctions, the loss of federal funds to the state of Colorado would exceed $300 million. While injunctions are sought and the court deliberates on legal details, Denver's air grows dirtier.

"A promising effort to ready Colorado's burgeoning Front Range region for the challenges of the '80s may be stalled because local officials mistrust Governor Dick Lamm's motives." (*The Denver Post,* December 16, 1979). "The Front Range Project was to build consensus about how development can continue, reducing negative impacts and increasing positive contributions to qualities of life." The project was launched in the spring of 1979. By fall, it was producing newspaper headlines such as "Lamm Takes Growth-Curb Step," "Lamm Tries to Pressure Commissioners," "Counties Dubious of Lamm's Growth Project," and "Governor Lamm, County Panels Intensify Land-Use Conflict."

The Denver Water Board's plans for delivering water to a rapidly growing metropolitan area depend on an extremely complex system of water

From *The Environmental Professional,* V2(2):67-74, 1980. Copyright © 1980 by The National Association of Environmental Professionals, Washington, D.C. Reprinted by permission.

storage reservoirs, transmountain diversion structures, and water treatment plants which have had a substantial influence on water management throughout the entire state of Colorado. An important component of the Denver Water Board's system is the Williams Fork Project, a series of dams and ditches to be built near a potential wilderness area in scenic mountain country. The project has come to a halt because of specific objections of the U.S. Forest Service to construction plans. Williams Fork is now the focus of another round of disputes that involves a broad group of interests including the American Wilderness Alliance, the Grand County Commissioners, the Colorado Open Space Council, the Colorado River Water Conservation District, and the Sierra Club Legal Defense Fund.

The courts are now dealing with suits involving the Water Board and the Grand County Commissioners, the Water Board and the Forest Service, requests for injunctions and requests for transfers of proceedings from one court to another. Other actors are involved in various legal ways.

As we enter the 1980s, increasing and competing demands for dwindling supplies of natural resources are creating more and more environmental conflicts, and these conflicts are becoming increasingly complex and severe. Many people in government, business, public interest groups, and other sectors of our society are realizing that new methods are needed to manage environmental conflicts in the '80s.

The primary issues in the three controversies described are air pollution, land use, and water management, or at least that is what they seemed to be at the beginning of each dispute. Air pollution, especially, was considered to be a solvable problem. Once its technical dimensions were clearly delineated, it was thought, Denver would get on with clearing up the air. After some years in which the mountains disappeared behind a brown haze for days on end, the city fathers acknowledged the possibility that Seattle's pollution could not really be blamed for all of the smoke. Later, motor vehicles were identified as the cause of 90% of the air pollution in Denver, which by then was second only to that in Los Angeles, and still is. A blue ribbon committee was formed by the governor; the Chamber of Commerce took an interest, and much sound was heard in the state legislature. Three years ago, we at ROMCOE initiated a program to design alternative transportation approaches at the neighborhood level, as an effort to anticipate conflict situations that we expected to develop. We were told that air pollution was not likely to cause conflict in the future because everyone was opposed to dirty air. What the EPA, the governor, the legislature, and the prestigious committee failed to assess adequately were the values, perspectives and motives of the people who would have to create alternatives to the problem.

The Front Range Project mentioned in the second example is managed by persons of outstanding credentials in public administration, economics, and political science, among others. The idea is sound—to plan for growth and distribute its effects in ways that will protect the quality of life in the 13 counties of metropolitan Colorado—but the issue of land use and growth was lost in a storm of opposition from local officials the instant the program was made public. Although carefully designed technically, the project did not acknowledge the essential relationships on which success would depend. Urban-rural differences, Democratic–Republican hostilities, suspicion of land use controls, and most important of all, resentment against state intervention in local prerogatives were ignored in the project plans—or at least so it seemed to the county commissioners. Local governments were brought in at the end of the design process, not in the beginning, and thus had no stake in the success of the program. The critical need to plan ahead for growth and change was buried because human and political relationships were not given equal weight with conventional technical planning procedures.

Transmountain water diversion, the transfer of water from agricultural and recreational use to the domestic needs of large metropolitan areas, is a major cause of conflict all over the West. The Williams Fork dispute described above is one of a series of intensely emotional conflicts that have revolved around the Denver Water Board for decades. The issue of what is the wisest use of water in the water-short West is in the hands of lawyers representing every conceivable interest from oil companies wanting to develop oil shale, to farmers, to fishermen and kayakers, to federal agencies managing public resources. The familiar adage that "water flows toward money" is both an assurance of job security for an army of legal advisors, and a cause of deeply entrenched animosity among those whose interests and values doubt the ability of the market system alone to allocate this essential natural resource in society's best interests. The courts are making the decisions on legal precedents that are unlikely to take into account the goals of the contending parties, the use of water supplies to control growth in the metropolitan area, wilderness and other ecological values, and the needs of rural people who hold a deep-seated hostility toward urban demands for this natural resource. Continued and intensified conflict is inevitable until the broader questions of goals and interests are addressed.

ROMCOE's primary task as a third-party intervenor is to expand the range of available choices people use to make decisions. Our approach to conflict management is based on the premise that better decisions are made when all the affected parties join in defining the issues and developing alternatives. In fact, people must feel a sense of ownership in both problem and solution if lasting solutions are to be found. We have learned that the earlier people begin working together, the lower the social, financial and physical costs are likely to be and the better the chances will be of achieving long-term solutions rather than short-term gains. Most, if not all, environmental controversies involve technical questions, and it is easy to assume that if technical solutions can be identified, a conflict will be resolved. Our experience indicates that problems are a mixture of substantive issues, personal motives, and current and past relationships. *To be effective, conflict management strategy must address all of these areas.*

While accurate and consistent data are essential to understanding technical issues, efforts to solve environmental problems in terms of purely technical criteria often cause more conflicts than they resolve. As we have suggested in describing three examples of typical environmental conflicts over air, land and water, the substance of the original problem often becomes overwhelmed by other factors, and management of the conflict depends on their resolution. Since we are looking for long-lasting solutions, not temporary peace, we try to find ways in which all parties are benefited by the outcome.

Before developing any conflict management process, we feel it is important to do a careful analysis of the situation. The analysis should include three categories of information: people, relationships and substance. If we were to focus only on the substance, we might miss the essential elements of the conflict. We might, for example, fail to realize that the parties have mutually acceptable goals and do not disagree on the means of getting there, but because of poor communication, they have developed misconceptions about each other that have convinced them that they are adversaries.

Analysis

ENTRY

The way in which a third-party intervenor enters a conflict situation is critical for the success of the conflict management process. Power relationships and attitudes and even the issues may not be what they first seem to be. Although most of the formal analysis is done after the conflict management process is underway, care must be taken to understand people and relationships before public intervention is made. If the wrong people are talked to first, if the wrong questions are asked, systems of suspicion and hostility may take over, and rational discussion may be impossible. The entire program may lose its credibility and attention may never get to the essential problem.

PEOPLE

We begin by acquiring information about the main and potential interest groups affiliated with a dispute. We need to identify the main interest groups, the secondary groups and key individuals, and to become familiar with the attitudes, values, perceptions, motivations, style, basis of power, and goals of each of the groups. For each of the categories mentioned, we can ask a series of sub-questions. For example, under *main interest groups* we want to know not only who the main interest groups are, but what groups have a lesser stake in the problem and what other groups may become involved for reasons outside the specific issue. A dispute over the siting of a new highway may include, in addition to the highway officials, affected property owners and local planning staffs and officials, as well as the local garden club which is concerned about the aesthetics of transportation corridors.

We want to know the main spokespeople for each of the major groups, what other individuals have become publicly identified with the issue, who the opinion-makers are, and who could have a major influence on the participants.

In Delta County, Colorado, we had great difficulty obtaining the necessary support of the three county commissioners for a conflict management project. We knew the commissioners had the highest respect for two former elected officials in the next county. One of the individuals had served eight terms in the U.S. Congress and the other had been governor of the state. One major reason for the commissioners' eventual support of the project was the letters from these two officials enthusiastically endorsing the project.

In every joint problem-solving project we look for some *goals* which can be supported by all interest groups and an understanding of basic *values* held by the parties. Under the subject of values, we identify the major values of each of the parties, such as growth vs no growth, capitalism and private enterprise vs perceived public welfare, local self-control vs federal government regulation. We also must determine if any major religious or ideological differences exist.

The problem of air pollution in Colorado has caused a bitter fight between the state legislature and the Environmental Protection Agency. The value of self-determination or states' rights has been offered as one explanation for the conflict. No public agreement has been reached on other values, such as the right to a healthy environment, which might provide a common goal among the disputing interests.

Under the category of *motivation,* we want to understand the forces motivating each group, what role past grievances play in a conflict, how the desire to belong to a group motivates a person's involvement in a conflict, and how the personal interests of the leaders might affect the motivation of the different groups.

If, in a current dispute between a group of environmentalists and a federal agency, environmentalists feel they have been unfairly treated in a previous encounter, they will be more suspicious and less willing to consider options offered by the federal agency, especially if they feel that they had opened up to good-faith negotiations and had been taken advantage of.

It is important to know what *perceptions* the parties have of each other. One party may see another as identical to other parties outside the immediate conflict and expect it to act identically. The issue may be seen as an isolated event or as part of a larger conflict.

A mining company that has worked with an environmental resource council in one state may assume that a resource council in an adjoining state has identical interests and will respond in a similar fashion. This type of stereotyping is a common problem among conflicting interests. Accurate perceptions by each group of the other's goals and needs is an essential basis for developing workable solutions.

RELATIONSHIPS

A second category of analysis questions concerns those associated with relationships, the associations conflicting parties have with each other. It is important that each set of relationships be looked at separately. If five major parties are involved in a dispute we must look at the relationship each group has with each other separate group.

Relationships can be divided into: (1) the history of each relationship, (2) the relationship's current status, and (3) the trends which seem to be emerging.

Under *history,* we would want to know what types of *power* each party has used against the other, the styles of *communication* that have been used, the levels of *awareness* of the problem, and what *negotiations* or efforts to solve the problem have occurred.

The history of each relationship affects the current perceptions and attitudes each party holds toward the other. The historical relationship between the Denver Water Board and the Colorado West Slope water users has been characterized by decades of bitter struggle. Until recently, the Water Board's style in negotiation has been unyielding and arrogant. Future efforts to discuss problems rationally must recognize the accumulation of hostile feelings before any progress on substantive issues can be made.

We would have similar questions about *current forms* of power which are being exercised; what style, form and frequency of communications are being applied now; to what degree the parties are aware that a conflict exists; and the form of current negotiations, if any.

For example, the use of coercive power by one party against another may cause the other group to take a more rigid position against the opposing side. When the EPA threatened to impose sanctions on the Colorado state legislature for not passing a satisfactory inspection and maintenance (I&M) law, many legislators became more adamant in their opposition to the EPA and to passage of any form of an I&M law. Even after EPA announced that sanctions

would be imposed, some legislators felt compelled to resist passage of legislation in order not to appear that they had been forced to submit to a federal
agency. In this particular example, the communications between the parties
had been infrequent, very formal and often abrasive.

In the National Commission on Air Quality Conference described at the
end of this paper, we recognize that many of the participants' only previous
contact with each other had been in some form of an adversarial
relationship—in the courtroom or in hearing sessions. We recognized the need
to create opportunities for collaboration.

Analysis of *trends* in a relationship is important because one must know
the direction in which the relationship is moving—whether the relationship is
improving because communications are opening up, or if it is deteriorating
because one side feels more threatened and therefore feels compelled to hard-
en its position. If the relationship does appear to be worsening, we need to
identify reasons why it is deteriorating as quickly as possible and develop
strategies to reverse the trend.

SUBSTANCE

The third area for analysis is the substance of the issue. In addition to
information about people and relationships, we must have a precise understanding of central issues in the conflict, what options are available, what
secondary issues exist, and what major events have occurred. We want to
understand how each party describes the *central issues* and how these issues
may have changed over time. We want to recognize what *options* have been
proposed, and to assess how realistic they are in terms of each parties' needs.
We want to look at *secondary issues* to see what influences they may have on
the outcome of the dispute. Finally, we want to know what *major events* have
occurred in the conflict, in particular, whether there was an event or series of
events that triggered the conflict.

Looking at options, for example, we want to know if realistic options
have been developed, if the options seem to reconcile the concerns and
interests of all parties, if they are simple enough to be workable, and if they
can be broken down into simpler, more manageable units.

Developing A Strategy

Analysis of questions about people, relationships and substance offers
essential information to the third-party intervenor. It provides the basis for
developing an appropriate strategy for managing the conflict. For example, if
there are very few options, and opinions are polarized on an issue, the problem may lie not in the lack of ability to generate alternatives, but in the
unwillingness of parties to talk with one another. In this case, some form of

conciliation must occur before parties can be brought together to discuss possible alternatives.

The three categories of information—people, relationships and substance—must be thoroughly understood by the intervenor before the parties begin to develop a conflict management strategy.

In the case of the Front Range Project, what seemed like a logical design for a process was immediately challenged by local officials not because the process was inadequate or inappropriate, but because the local officials were suspicious of the motives of the state officials who had developed the process. By failing to recognize the importance of identifying the motives of the individuals who were to become involved in the project, the designers of the project jeopardized the success of the effort.

Environmental problems can arbitrarily be categorized in two ways: as generic or site-specific issues and as potential or manifest conflict situations (Table 1). Generic problems include the development of natural resource policies and regulations for administering them. Site-specific problems usually address changes in the local use of a natural resource—land, mineral, air, or water. Manifest conflicts have been recognized as conflicts by the affected parties. Potential conflicts are situations in which conflict will occur if no action is taken.

TABLE 1
Categories of Environmental Problems

Situation Type	Generic	Site Specific
Manifest	Example: Western water rights	Example: Siting a power plant
Potential	Example: Conversion of agricultural land	Example: A county's land-use plan

We use three general approaches to conflict management: *conflict anticipation* for potential conflicts, *problem solving* for disputes that are acknowledged but not highly polarized, and *mediation* for highly polarized situations.

We enter each new conflict situation with no preconceptions about what set of tools should be used. In some cases our role may be limited to improving communications. After talking with the affected parties, we may determine that a carefully managed half-day discussion of the problem will allow the parties to begin working together effectively. In other situations, we organize and manage a comprehensive problem-solving effort—identifying parties; sharing data, issues and concerns; developing alternatives; and negotiating a resolution. This kind of effort may take a few weeks or it may require a year or more, depending on the number and complexity of the parties and issues. In each situation, we work with the parties to determine the most appropriate process for them and the most effective role for ROMCOE as a third party intervenor.

Implementing A Strategy

One of the first activities in a conflict management effort is to *review* with all the participants the *procedures* to be used. Included in such a review would be a definition of the substantive and procedural boundaries for the discussions, a statement of expectations, guidelines for behavior, and the establishment or review of a group contract.

In clearly establishing boundaries and guidelines which are agreed to by the participants, the facilitator gains a tool for controlling difficult individuals and managing relationship problems that may occur during a discussion. (See the Plateau Uranium Mine example.)

After agreeing on the procedures, the parties must *understand* the *needs* and *concerns* of each of the other parties before they can proceed to a discussion of the substantive issues. Articulation of needs and concerns provides a base for evaluating the desirability of alternative solutions.

The parties should also establish a precise *definition* of the *issues* as each party sees them. Differences in perception need either to be resolved, or at least publicly acknowledged. An agreement on how differences will be handled should also be reached.

The process of *generating, assessing* and *selecting alternatives* acceptable to all parties must also take into account the nature of parties and their relationships to each other. Throughout an entire conflict management session, a facilitator must be prepared to respond to comments that may seem to have no relevance to the issue's substance or are provoked by angry feelings that have not found a previous outlet.

If discussions do deteriorate, it may be desirable to separate the parties into their respective interest groups to allow them to vent angry feelings without causing a complete breakdown in the discussion. On the other hand, it may be preferable to arrange an informal break in the session, such as a half-hour intermission or a meal together in a local restaurant. When one is uncomfortable asking questions before a large group, it is often easier to do so in a less structured setting. The following three case examples illustrate some of the ideas we have suggested in this paper.

The National Commission On Air Quality Workshop

Although everyone wants clean, breathable air, legislation designed to maintain acceptable air quality has produced countless disputes and little progress toward solution of the main problem. The National Commission on Air

Quality was established by Congress to evaluate the Clean Air Act and examine additional means of achieving air quality standards. The Commission is now compiling and assessing available information on environmental, scientific, technological, economic, and social issues related to air quality policy. ROMCOE was asked to design and manage a workshop on procedural changes in the permitting process. The topic was chosen because it includes many of the difficult and controversial issues associated with air quality regulation.

We knew that the entire subject of air quality regulation had become intensely polarized and that positions on every element had long since become rigid. We decided to acknowledge that condition explicitly and then try to break through the fixed positions of the groups. Our letter of invitation included this paragraph:

> It is likely that you have already developed and advocated positions on many issues to be discussed at the workshop. We look forward to hearing these ideas. But we will also be asking you to develop new ideas which may also meet your needs but may never have been suggested before. Through a collaborative process, we will be seeking alternatives which address the needs of all three constituency groups.

Ten representatives from each of three constituency groups, industry, public interest organizations, and state and local government, attended the three-day conference, held in February 1980. At all times, the greatest hazard to success was the possibility that factions would form and revert to previous publicly expressed positions on solutions.

Our printed materials and comments throughout the three days of the workshop emphasized terms such as "creativity," "collaborative problem solving," and "desirable alternatives." We were urged by some of the principal people involved not to use a collaborative process. They said we should "get down to facts right away."

Instead, we designed a process in which *needs* of the constituency groups were listed by the members. We then reshuffled the groups so that working groups were formed of three or four representatives from each of the interests. These people worked together for most of the three days. They proceeded to list concerns and then to compare the needs and concerns with the issues that had been identified before the conference began. After acknowledging needs and concerns, the groups worked independently of each other on alternatives.

By an extremely tightly structured process, which participants resisted occasionally, we avoided forming fixed positions on solutions before the participants could understand each other's interests and goals. In the NCAQ workshop, investigation of relationships and people was as important as substance and it was essential that it be done *first,* before discussion of alternative procedures began. We managed to avoid the instant polarization that had been predicted, by giving people a chance to reassess their perspectives and form new opinions about their historical adversaries. Each working group reported its findings and made specific recommendations to the Commission. A frequently repeated suggestion was that this workshop should be the first of several that should be held under Commission sponsorship.

The Plateau Uranium Mine

Plateau Resources Ltd. is proposing to mine and mill uranium in an area of southern Utah, just north of the Glen Canyon Recreation Area. ROMCOE was asked by Plateau Resources to organize a meeting with company officials and representatives from environmental and public interest groups to discuss plans for the mine and mill, and to provide an opportunity for the groups to voice their concerns. The meeting was held in Salt Lake City, Utah, in March 1979.

Twenty persons representing national, state and local citizen groups attended the meeting. Company executives and engineers were present to answer questions about the radiological impacts of the mine and mill, the design and adequacy of the tailings impoundment area, the long-term responsibility for reclamation, the potential for contamination of surface water and aquifers, the economic feasibility of mining and milling uranium at the proposed site, and the social and economic effects of a proposed new town.

ROMCOE's purpose here was to design a system by which information could be exchanged for the benefit of both sides. We knew that there were special considerations that would make the project difficult, and that the potential for a truly explosive confrontation existed. The proximity of the National Recreation Area was a factor, and so was the history of warfare over siting in southern Utah of very large coal-burning power generating plants. One leading environmentalist said he could not attend the proposed meeting because he had been threatened on numerous occasions and was physically attacked several times because of his opposition to large energy projects in southern Utah.

Of much greater potential for open confrontation was the nature of the material to be mined—uranium. Southern Utah is down wind of the Nevada nuclear test site and many residents have lost family members to illnesses thought to be caused by radiation. One of our participants had lost a brother to leukemia after he had been exposed to a radioactive cloud. Furthermore, the area has unusually high levels of natural radioactivity. We made several stipulations to the company: (1) That top company officials would be at the meeting with adequate engineering staff support so that all questions could be answered without delay or apparent evasion; (2) That participants be fully informed about technical details of the project *before* the meeting; (3) That ROMCOE would design a process by which information would be exchanged, but it would be up to the company to make a thorough presentation of data and handle the questions. Plateau agreed to all stipulations, even going to the considerable expense of reprinting the Draft Environmental Impact Statement and mailing it to all the participants in advance of the meeting.

As plans for the meeting went forward, we began to receive requests that invited participants be permitted to bring along friends. We refused. We did not want any one interest to dominate the discussion.

In our opening remarks, we addressed the issue of nuclear warfare explicitly by pointing out that it was unlikely that we would solve that problem in one day, but it could easily absorb the entire time we had available. We suggested that the group agree not to address the nuclear warfare issue because we wanted to know about the plans for the uranium mine. The participants agreed that it was in their best interests to conduct the meeting as a joint problem-solving enterprise. The discussion was emotional at times; the person who had lost a brother to leukemia broke into tears at one point, but at no time was there a personal attack on the integrity of individuals or on their motives.

The meeting began with a description of the project by Plateau officials using slides, maps and graphs. We then went around the room recording on large sheets of newsprint the categories of concerns of each individual. The sheets were displayed on the walls around the room so that everyone could be sure that we had covered every topic. We listed the questions that the participants had about each concern and then, with the help of the group, clustered them into discussion areas. In focusing and sharpening the questions, the ROMCOE staff members carried on an active dialogue with each other and with the group. Every action was made clear and tested for agreement. ROMCOE facilitators were conscious of the danger of appearing to exercise too much control over the discussion, but from time to time the conversation had to be brought back on track. After the meeting, Plateau officials followed up inquiries by sending whatever additional material was needed to fully answer a question.

This meeting provided a nonconfrontational atmosphere for the constructive exchange of viewpoints and reasonable discussion of specific issues. More important, it opened lines of communication which did not previously exist.

Delta County

In January 1977, ROMCOE was asked to assist citizens of Delta County, Colorado, in developing a program in which all major interests would share in constructive responses to expanding coal development. At least 11 coal companies are considering developing underground mines in the county. Many local elected officials were indifferent to the problems of rapid growth and some were actively hostile toward any program that was designed to identify and deal with them. Our purpose was threefold: (1) To assess the situation in Delta County and to anticipate problems and work with the residents in designing methods for developing alternative courses of action; (2) To move beyond the small group of citizens who were concerned about the future and actively involve a broad range of public interests; (3) To persuade elected officials that the program would support, rather than threaten them, and that they ought to become active participants.

The culminating event of the first phase of the Delta County Project was a workshop in March 1978, but the year-long process leading to that event was as important as the workshop itself because it brought together potentially conflicting interests—coal company executives, ranchers, farmers, and orchardists—in a collaborative effort for mutual benefit. A steering committee, made up of Delta County citizens of diverse interests, was formed early in the project. A series of open planning meetings for the workshop was held throughout the fall of 1977, in which citizens of Delta County decided that the theme of the program would be "Quality of Life in Delta County—The Price Tag?"

Citizen and official participation in these meetings was continuously and aggressively sought by personal telephone calls, letters and newspaper articles. Simultaneously, the support of respected leaders was obtained by personal visits in which the purposes of the project were carefully explained. We acknowledged the crucial part that the county commissioners and city officials would play in the implementation of project programs and we made their active involvement a major goal. The long and difficult business of gaining the confidence of conservative local officials was handled by local people using their own persuasive methods. We, as outside intervenors, acted only to reinforce the arrangements worked out by our local partners with these officials.

The March workshop was designed to give the participants a means by which they could, for the first time in this county, meet and discuss their future. It is our experience that citizens of a community come to a problem solving event with very different levels of awareness about the problem and understanding of available alternatives. In addition to general publicity, the purpose of the newspaper articles and the slide show was to bring the citizens of Delta County to approximately the same level of knowledge so that the workshop itself could take off on problem solutions.

We organized the workshop around an extremely tight agenda in which the 250 participants were moved gently but firmly from rooms in which they were exposed to new ideas about alternatives, to general working sessions in which they were assigned to tables of mixed interests where everyone had to speak and share the responsibility for the success of the workshop. We wanted them to feel that they had worked hard and had produced solid tangible accomplishments. Throughout the Delta County Project, it was clear that the issues were difficult enough, but if alternatives to conflict were to be found and put into effect, substantial changes in perception and attitudes would have to take place.

In the 14 months of the first phase of the project, the community moved from a condition of general unawareness that any problem existed to a precise understanding of some of the implications of explosive population growth. In the second phase, citizens are carrying out workshop recommendations through task groups. Subjects being addressed include economics, human services, planning and environment, and sense of community.

In each case study described in the previous sections, ROMCOE carefully assessed the personal motives, the current and past relationships, as well as the substantive issues before it designed an appropriate conflict management strategy. Any tool developed to manage or resolve an environmental dispute which does not pay adequate attention to these three areas risks the danger of provoking more controversy.

GERALD W. CORMICK

15 *The Myth, the Reality, and the Future of Environmental Mediation*

The first explicit effort to mediate an "environmental dispute" began in the fall of 1973 when the author and a colleague, Jane E. McCarthy, initiated discussions with parties to a flood-control/land-use planning conflict in Washington state. In December 1974, that lengthy and difficult mediation effort culminated in unanimous, written agreement between the dozen or so parties at interest. That widely documented and discussed mediation effort has become the prototype for a variety of similar efforts by the Institute for Environmental Mediation, its predecessor—the Office of Environmental Mediation—and other emerging organizations.

Since 1973, mediators with the Institute have discussed the application of mediation with disputing parties in scores of environmental/economic conflicts. About two dozen complex disputes have been successfully resolved. And, equally important, the Institute is presently exploring with state, federal, and regional governmental agencies ways in which mediation may be made available in a more regular manner.

Environmental mediation has evolved from an interesting and novel concept to an accepted but often misunderstood part of the environmental decision-making lexicon. Successful efforts to resolve long-standing disputes make "good copy"; the notion of solving problems to everyone's relative

From *Environment*, Vol. 24, pp. 14-17, 36-39 (September 1982). Reprinted by permission of the Helen Dwight Reid Educational Foundation. Published by Heldrof Publications, 4000 Albemarle Street, N.W., Washington, D.C. 20016. Copyright © 1982.

satisfaction is an appealing one. There is a reservoir of persons acting as consultants in the field of public involvement who see mediation as a possible new vocation.

It is hardly surprising, then, that the bandwagon has attracted a large and diverse group of riders. This popularity has been accompanied by claims for mediation and suggested applications of the process that appear to be beyond reasonable expectations, based on experience with the mediation process in other contexts.

Intervention Processes

Mediation, a particular approach to conflict resolution used for centuries in international relations and extensively for the past five decades in labor disputes, has become a "buzz word" used to describe a bewildering array of conflict-intervention processes and styles. A danger we now face is that the overselling of the process and its misapplication by inexperienced intervenors anxious to enter the field will result in costly failures that could broadly discredit the mediation process. This concern has led the Institute for Environmental Mediation to be particularly careful that potential parties to the negotiation/mediation process have a clear understanding of what the process entails, where it is most effective, and what it can reasonably be expected to achieve.

There are a variety of intervenors presently active in environmental/economic disputes, all of whom claim three essential characteristics:

- They are impartial or "neutral" as to the specific disposition of the issues in dispute.
- Their focus and expertise relate to process rather than to scientific or technical knowledge.
- The intervention process which they practice seeks to achieve mutually derived and mutually acceptable outcomes.

However, it has also been found that there are at least three different types of intervention processes being practiced:[1]

Consensus building is a problem-solving approach grounded in small-group process which emphasizes the common interests of disputants in jointly defining and solving problems.

Mediation is an approach adapted from labor relations which seeks to identify—through negotiation—the limited but real cooperative actions possible for mutually interdependent parties having different long-term interests and objectives.

Policy dialogues are a problem-solving and negotiation approach developed on a pragmatic, ad hoc basis by leaders of environmental groups and representatives of industry. Dialogues are intended to identify joint positions which can be advocated in the public policy arena by interest groups that are normally opposed to one another.

While their practitioners may share the three essential characteristics outlined, each process differs substantially in the basic assumptions which underlie its development; the means by which the services of the intervenor are made available; the specific activities of the intervenors; and the process outcomes that can be anticipated. It is critical that the parties and the intervenor have a clear and consistent understanding of the process and their relative roles and responsibilities if the always difficult problem of settling their differences is to proceed to a successful conclusion.

The "Mediation Process"

The term *mediation,* used in its strictest sense, is nothing more nor less than a device for facilitating the negotiation process; negotiations can and do occur without a mediator, but mediation can never occur in the absence of negotiation. The Institute for Environmental Mediation uses the following definition when discussing the mediation process:

> Mediation is a voluntary process in which those involved in a dispute jointly explore and reconcile their differences. The mediator has no authority to impose a settlement. His or her strength lies in the ability to assist the parties in settling their own differences. The mediated dispute is settled when the parties themselves reach what they consider to be a workable solution.

A number of important considerations are implicit in this definition: (1) Involvement of the parties in the mediation process and their acceptance of the mediator(s) is *voluntary.* (2) The parties will *jointly* explore and debate the issues, both in joint sessions and in caucuses of one or more of the parties with the mediator. (3) The mediator has *no authority to impose settlement.* (4) The mediator facilitates the negotiation process assisting the *parties* to *reach a settlement acceptable to them.* (5) An agreement requires the support of *all* of the parties: It is a *consensus,* not a majority decision. (6) The mediator shares with the parties the responsibility of ensuring that any agreement reached represents a *viable solution* that is technically, financially, and politically *feasible to implement.*

In environmental/economic disputes, the parties are seldom able to proceed directly to negotiation of the issues dividing them. They must first reach an understanding of the framework within which they will negotiate;

have some assurance of the "good faith" intent of all involved to reach a mutually successful conclusion through accommodation; and have confidence in the skills, objectivity, and independence of the mediator(s).

To Mediate or Not?

To assist the parties and the mediator in making a determination of when and whether to use the mediation process, the Institute suggests eight questions which should be explicitly and mutually addressed:[2]

- Are all parties who have a stake in the outcome of the negotiations represented? Is any party excluded that could prevent an agreement from being carried out?
- Have all of the parties reached general agreement on the scope of the issues being addressed?
- Are the negotiators for each party able to speak for their constituency? Is there a reason to believe that, if the negotiators reached an agreement, the agreement will be honored by the groups they represent?
- Have the immediate parties and the eventual decision makers committed themselves to a good faith effort to reach a consensual agreement?
- Has a realistic deadline been set for the negotiations?
- Are there reasonable assurances that affected governmental agencies will cooperate in carrying out an agreement if one is reached?
- Does the mediator operate from a base that is independent of both the immediate parties and the decision makers with jurisdiction over the dispute?
- Do all parties involved trust the mediator to carry messages, when appropriate, and to honor confidential remarks?

Clearly, it is impossible for either the parties or the mediator to determine the answers to all of the above questions at the outset. Therefore, it is appropriate and necessary that there be extensive exploratory discussions between and among the parties and the mediator before any commitment is made to negotiate the issues.

These discussions should culminate in a clear and mutual understanding of such matters as the parties to be involved; the specific and, perhaps, differing roles of private groups and organizations, government agencies, and elected officials; the scope of the issues to be addressed; elected deadlines for showing progress and/or achieving agreement; sponsorship and commitments necessary to help ensure implementation; and the projected form any agreement which is reached will take—for example, written contract, proposed legislation, signed joint recommendations. Agreement on at least these items should be achieved before moving to a formal discussion of the issues if necessary misunderstandings are to be avoided during the difficult negotiation phase.

Mediation Successes

Where these necessary conditions have been met, mediation can be a powerful tool in reconciling even the most difficult situations. During the first ten months of 1981, for example, mediators from the Institute helped conflicting parties reach agreements in five diverse disputes located in four western states.

The Briones Park Dispute—A long-standing dispute in northern California over access to and development of a major regional park was settled when negotiators representing the regional park district, local governments, neighborhoods most directly impacted by the type and location of park development, and user interests reached agreement on a mutually acceptable development plan.

The Queets Sewer Lagoon Dispute—A dispute in Washington state between an Indian tribe, local government, private interests, and federal agencies over arrangements for the protection of a sewage treatment facility which was threatened with imminent destruction by a changing river course. The issue was settled after a relatively brief period of intensive and difficult negotiations.

The Homestake Pitch Mine Dispute—In Colorado, the Homestake Corporation and seven environmental organizations and coalitions reached an agreement which settled their differences over the operation and reclamation of an open pit uranium mine in the Gunnison National Forest. State and federal agencies concurred with the agreement.[3]

The CREST Dispute—In Oregon, Institute mediators assisted two towns, a county, a port authority, four state agencies, and four federal agencies in reaching a mutually acceptable plan for the location, nature, and timing of development, protection, and mitigation for loss of habitat in the estuary of the Columbia River. The controversy had for years pitted development interests against conservation interest.[4]

The Riverside Solid Waste Siting Dispute—Institute mediators helped representatives of ten local organizations reach agreement on a package of recommendations to submit to the Riverside County, California, Board of

Supervisors. The agreement recommends a replacement site for two landfills scheduled to close, steps for strengthening county management of solid waste disposal, and programs to recover valuable resources and reduce the need for landfill space. The effect was sponsored by the California State Solid Waste Management Board.[5]

Misperceptions about Mediation

There are a variety of widespread misconceptions and misperceptions regarding the mediation process and its application. Dealing with these misunderstandings may be as important as definitions and descriptions in providing real insights into how the process works.

MEDIATION CAN RESOLVE DIFFERENCES

Mediation does *not* lead to a resolution of the basic differences that separate the parties in conflict. Rather, in situations where none of the parties perceives that it is able to gain its goals unilaterally, mediation can help the parties agree on how to make the accommodations that will enable them to co-exist despite their continued differences. Labor and management, for example, have never reconciled their basic disagreement over the share of profits that should go to labor versus capital. As the Homestake Pitch Mine Dispute demonstrates, environmental coalitions may negotiate standards for revegetation, site reclamation, and water quality maintenance of an open pit mine when they realize it cannot be completely blocked, even though they would never agree that the mine is desirable or even necessary.

A mediated agreement, therefore, cannot be construed as an indication that two or more conflicting parties have resolved their divergent priorities or reconciled their differing perceptions. Rather, it is an indication that, in the immediate situation which confronts them, they have found a solution upon which they are able to agree despite their basic differences. Those who would espouse mediation as a means by which society can forge a new consensus, making future conflicts unnecessary, are doomed to failure and frustration. Mediation can best be seen as a process for *settling* disputes, not for *resolving* basic differences.

MEDIATION CAN AVOID CONFLICT

Conflicts are *settled* through the mediation process. Until the conflict emerges, and the parties are confronted with limits to their unilateral options and mutually desire to find some settlement of specific issues, there is no basis for negotiation. It is the conflict that provides the awareness of the problem, the acceptance of the need to find other than unilateral solutions, and even the leadership necessary to represent often ad hoc interest groups. Avoiding the conflict not only makes negotiation unlikely in the short run but may also serve to delay and make more painful the ultimate confrontation.

MEDIATION IS NON-ADVERSARIAL CONFLICT RESOLUTION

Since it requires the presence of a conflict, mediation is decidedly *not* "non-adversarial." Indeed, it has been the experience of mediators at the Institute that unless the parties remain mindful of their conflicting self-interests, they are unlikely to strike a bargain that is viable when faced with the difficult realities of implementation; both the parties and their agreements will be repudiated by their constituents. Established, confident adversaries aware of their own self-interest make the best negotiators and work out the best agreements.

MEDIATION IS AN ALTERNATIVE TO LITIGATION

Although mediation is sometimes touted as an alternative to litigation, this claim is intended to appeal to those who see proposed projects frustrated by interminable court delays. It is a much less appealing claim to citizen and environmental organizations who oppose such projects and who see the courts as a critical line of defense. Actual or threatened litigation is often a necessary prerequisite to the willingness of a party proposing some action to negotiate; it is the source of power and influence that brings the parties to the table and to mediation.

Rather than being an alternative to the courts, mediation often relies on them for its viability. While the parties to a conflict may at some point choose to negotiate in lieu of initiating or continuing court action, mediation cannot reasonably be expected to supplant or negate the need for litigation until such time as protesting constituencies are provided with some other basis for their power and influence.

SUCCESSFUL MEDIATION IS WHERE THE NEGOTIATORS LEARN TO "LIKE," TRUST, AND AGREE WITH EACH OTHER

Statements such as this are usually based on a misunderstanding not only of the mediation process but of the nature of environmental/economic conflicts. Such disputes typically involve a number of groups and organizations, many with large constituencies. The purpose of mediation is to assist representatives of these various organizations and interest groups in formulating a mutually acceptable agreement which will be ratified by their constituents.

Where the focus is primarily on the relationships and understandings between negotiators who are "at the table," there is a danger that they will begin to "like," trust, and understand each other to the point where they forget that their constituents have not had the benefit of the same intensive and cooperative interaction.

Solutions that are not politically viable may gain credence in the rarified atmosphere of cooperative discussions, but later be repudiated as a "sell-out" by constituents. Some intervention processes have their roots in small group methodologies or the settlement of inter-personal disputes where all of the actors *can* be gathered around the table and where the intervenor and participants need not be concerned with the need for ratification.

The mediation process works best where the parties have sufficient mutual trust to negotiate in "good faith," mixed with a continued realization that agreement among the negotiators is only the beginning. Indeed, for the negotiators to reach an agreement which one or more of the parties' constituents fails to ratify will only exacerbate the conflict. Successful mediation agreements can be concluded even when the interactions merely confirm the breadth of the basic disagreements between the parties.

MEDIATION IS WHERE EVERYONE SITS AROUND A BIG TABLE AND NEGOTIATES

In mediation, the most critical action—orchestrated by the mediator—often occurs away from the table. As has already been outlined, a critical role played by the mediator in environmental conflicts is creating the framework for negotiations: this is likely to take at least as long as the actual negotiation of the issues. During the negotiations per se, the mediator is likely to spend the majority of his or her time in individual caucuses with one group or subgroups of the parties, helping them to explore positions and formulate alternatives, advising on mediation process, carrying messages, and "trying out" offers on behalf of the parties. Indeed, if the mediator is effective in this part of the task, his or her role in the joint meeting may be minimal. (In one recent joint negotiation, the mediation team spoke less than a hundred words—including a check of whether anyone wanted coffee—during a three and one-half hour meeting.)

THE MEDIATOR SHOULD HAVE TECHNICAL EXPERTISE IN THE ISSUES

It has been the experience of the Institute that where a mediator has personal expertise regarding the issues in a dispute, he or she may be less effective: First, "experts" have a tendency to rely on their own assumptions and values, rather than allowing the parties to "teach" them about the dispute. Second, there is an inclination to filter information and communication based on their independent assessment of the facts. Third, the discussions tend to move away from the underlying sets of values and perceptions which led to the dispute, and end up focusing on technical concerns. This can result in solutions that are technically appropriate yet do not represent a real accommodation of the more basic value differences.

Finally, the greater the technical expertise of the mediator in the subject area, the more the agreement is likely to be a result of the mediator's "leading" the parties and the less committed the parties will be to the difficult task of implementing the agreement. However, the mediator *does* have a responsibility to become sufficiently conversant with the issues in dispute and the legislative, legal, and organizational environment within which they occur to be able to communicate effectively with the parties and to assist them in devising viable solutions.

Where the parties to conflict are aware of these common misperceptions and misconceptions of the mediation process, it can provide an additional basis for judging both the appropriateness of the process and the qualifications of the mediator.

Future Directions

Our experience to date suggests that mediation can play a role in settling many environmental/economic disputes. However, a number of specific steps must first be taken if mediation is to evolve from an interesting idea to a more broadly available option. (While it is possible to discuss these required actions, this article does not argue that experience with the mediation process in environmental conflicts yet justifies a full-fledged national commitment. Rather, continued experiments with more formal application of the process in specific issue areas may be the prudent course.)

Encourage Negotiated Solutions—The reluctance of representatives of government agencies to become involved with mediation efforts—as they are apprehensive about a lack of support at higher levels in their agency—is an important factor impeding the development of environmental mediation. A clear statement of public policy which encourages mutual solutions based on the interaction of public and private parties will, at some point, be necessary.

Public-policy support for negotiations between labor and management was embodied in executive initiatives and national legislation during the 1930s. In the environmental arena, such support might be made clear and effective by such actions as providing special alternatives and funding for mitigation for loss of habitat, where mutual agreement is achieved between normally disputing interests, or by providing that such agreements "go to the front of the line" for further processing. Of course, to qualify such agreements would have to fall within the bounds of established laws and regulations.

Establishing a Viable Power Base for all Parties—The negotiation/ mediation process requires that all parties have sufficient power to influence the action of each other party. Government organizations and private corporations are endowed with such power or influence by our existing political/ economic system. Citizen and environmental groups, however, often must develop their power resources on a situation-by-situation basis, through legal challenges and the delay and uncertainty which they represent. For mediation to become more broadly and regularly applied, it may be necessary to develop less transitory sources of influence for protesting constituencies.

In the labor/management analogy, this power was conferred by a combination of legitimizing the strike and establishing legislative requirements to bargain. In environmental/economic disputes, one approach might be to require that government agencies calculate into their benefit-cost ratios the cost of delay in cases where they are unable to demonstrate the broad support of interest groups.

The Problem of Conferring "Recognition"—Recognition is often termed a "threshold issue": It frequently requires greater "clout" to enter the decision-making process than to influence it once entry has been achieved. Labor originally achieved recognition through such economic actions as strikes, boycotts, or even the physical takeover of production facilities. Today, recognition is conferred through representation elections. In environmental/ economic disputes recognition is conferred by real or threatened court challenges or political action. The alternative is difficult to perceive.

It might be argued that the labor/management history teaches that a more orderly route to the recognition of unions was achieved only after existing authorities realized that such recognition was inevitable. If the analogy holds, we may be approaching the stage in environmental/economic disputes where there is similar inability to avoid dealing with parties who oppose proposed projects. The best approach may lie in some combination of the political process, as applied in union representation elections, and the concept of "standing," as applied by the courts.

Identifying Appropriate Points for Intervention—Most projects or proposals that become "environmental disputes" require a lengthy decision-making, permitting, and public-involvement process. Typical legislation providing for mediation of labor-management conflicts identifies a point *after* extensive negotiations should have occurred but before the direct economic action is permitted. The mediation agency is informed of the status of the negotiations and *may* intervene. The intent is to avoid interfering with negotiations between the parties while recognizing the public interest in avoiding unnecessary disruptions.

Similarly, in environmental disputes, it may be possible to identify points in the decision-making process where a mediator has an opportunity to discuss confidentially with the parties the current status of a dispute and possible alternatives for settling it. It may be possible to build into such a system a provision that particular actions—such as filing for administrative or court review—automatically "trigger" consideration of the use of a mediator. There are two critical factors which must be recognized here: First, mediation must avoid becoming just another "hoop" for the parties to jump through before they get down to serious consideration of their differences. Second, an actual mediation effort, beyond initial discussions of the process and whether it is appropriate, must be kept voluntary.

Provision of Mediation Services—Here again, the labor/management analogy provides a useful point of departure. Virtually all mediation services are supported and/or provided by state or federal governments as a matter of public policy. Except in unusual circumstances, the parties do not directly pay for mediation services, either singly or jointly.

There are a number of reasons why a similar reality will operate in environmental/economic disputes, including: (1) the disparate nature of the conflicting parties and their differential ability to finance the cost of mediation services; (2) the absence of any pre-existing relationship through which the parties could agree to share the cost of mediation services; and (3) the inordinate amount of time which a mediator must routinely spend developing a possible negotiating relationship without any assurance that a particular dispute will, in fact, progress to negotiation of the issues.

Of paramount concern in the long-term provision of mediation services for environmental disputes is where such services should be located. Here the labor/management analogy suggests the need for some entity independent and insulated from operating departments and agencies. Unlike the labor/management sector, where disputes occur and services are provided at either the federal or state level, many environmental conflicts involve combinations of local, state, and federal concerns and agencies. For this reason, the Institute has been particularly interested in exploring the use of regional and joint state-federal bodies as an appropriate location for environmental mediation services.

Realizing the Potential

It is both possible and desirable to explore further these and other initiatives on an experimental basis in order to further determine their viability. It must be recognized, however, that unless such experiments, and any resulting initiatives, proceed with the support of all of those parties and interests involved in environmental/economic conflicts, they are unlikely to succeed.

The mediation process holds exciting potential for settling difficult environmental/economic conflicts. Where appropriately applied by capable mediators, it has resulted in innovative and mutually beneficial agreements. Where misapplied, it can exacerbate already thorny situations. The next few years will determine whether and how this potential will be realized.

Notes

1. Kai N. Lee, "Intervention by 'Neutral' Third Parties: An Analytic Report," *Working Paper,* Institute for Environmental Studies, University of Washington, 1982.

2. The Institute for Environmental Mediation, brochure, 1982; For a more complete discussion of the intervenor's responsibility to the parties, see Gerald W. Cormick, "Intervention and Self-determination in Environmental Disputes: A Mediator's Perspective," *Resolve,* The Conservation Foundation, Winter, 1982, pp. 1 ff.

3. Orville Tice, "But What Does a Mediator Really Do? The Pitch Mine Case," The Institute for Environmental Mediation, August 1981, Mimeo.

4. This dispute and the mediation effort which led to its settlement are described in the case study, "The CREST Dispute: Negotiated Settlement Through Mediation," by Verne Huser.

5. This mediation experience and a series of workshops and discussions with persons involved in disputes over the management of solid waste were part of a study funded by the California State Solid Waste Management Board. The results of that study are reported in *Siting Solid Waste Management Facilities: Approaches to Dispute Settlement,* Recommendations to the State Solid Waste Management Board, The Institute for Environmental Mediation and The Wisconsin Center for Public Policy, October 1981.

GAIL BINGHAM

16 *Resolving Environmental Disputes*

A Decade of Experience

The Growth of the Environmental Dispute Resolution Field

The use of environmental dispute resolution approaches has grown exponentially in little more than a decade. In 1973, Daniel J. Evans, then governor of the state of Washington, invited mediators Gerald W. Cormick and Jane McCarthy to help settle a long-standing dispute over a proposed flood control dam on the Snoqualmie River. Nationally, by the end of 1977, 9 disputes had been mediated. Another 9 were mediated in 1978, and 18 more were mediated in 1979. By mid-1984, mediators and facilitators had been involved in over 160 disputes in the United States. Compared to 1973, when only two individuals were beginning to develop a mediation practice for environmental disputes, there are now organizations and individuals in 13 states, the District of Columbia, and Canada offering environmental dispute resolution services. Others, elsewhere, are attempting to establish similar practices.

In addition, and relatively recently, the practice of environmental dispute resolution has grown beyond the resolution of disputes on a case-by-case basis to the institutionalization, by statute, of procedures for resolving environmental disputes. Statutes in Massachusetts, Rhode Island, Virginia, and Wisconsin authorize or even require negotiation of hazardous waste facility siting disputes. A statute in Virginia specifies procedures for negotiation and mediation of intergovernmental disputes triggered by annexation proposals; in late 1985, the Pennsylvania legislature was considering a bill proposed a few years earlier to authorize mediation of any local land-use or zoning dispute.

The track record of the field has grown with time, so that environmental dispute resolution organizations now provide services that are not reflected by the number of cases in which they have been involved. Many conduct training courses in the effective use of environmental dispute resolution techniques. All provide consultation and technical assistance to parties in disputes wishing to explore the feasibility of an alternative approach in a particular controversy. Other services offered include newsletters, conferences, and consulting to various organizations, particularly government agencies, wishing to develop organizational capabilities for more effective dispute resolution.

There is striking diversity among the cases that comprise the cumulative track record of the environmental dispute resolution field. The primary issues involved in these cases fall into six broad categories. Some cases involve site-specific disputes over a particular project or plan; others involve disputes over questions of state or national environmental policy.

Land-use. About 70 site-specific and 16 policy-level land-use disputes have been resolved with the assistance of a mediator. They have involved neighborhood and housing issues, commercial and urban development issues, parks and recreation, preservation of agricultural land and other regional planning issues, facility siting, and transportation.

Natural resource management and use of public lands. Mediation has been used in 29 site-specific and 4 policy-level controversies, involving fisheries resources, mining, timber management, and wilderness areas, among others.

Water resources. Among the 16 site-specific cases and 1 policy-level case that involved water resources, the issues in dispute included water supply, water quality, flood protection, and the thermal effects of power plants.

Energy. In this area, 10 site-specific and 4 policy-level cases involved such issues as siting small-scale hydroelectric plants, conversion of power plants to use coal instead of oil, and geothermal development.

Air quality. Odor problems, national air quality legislation, and acid rain were the topics of 6 site-specific cases and 7 policy dialogues.

Toxics. National policy on the regulation of chemicals, plans for removal of asbestos in schools, pesticide policy, and hazardous materials cleanup were among the issues discussed in 5 site-specific cases and 11 policy dialogues.

When people think of environmental disputes, they commonly think of cases in which environmental groups challenge proposals made by private industry. Most environmental dispute resolution cases do not fit that model, however. Many mediated environmental disputes have involved only public agencies. In others, citizen groups were engaged in disputes with their local government, or a mix of government agencies were in dispute with one another and a variety of interest groups.

Environmental groups were at the negotiating table in only 33 percent of the site-specific cases that were examined. Private corporations also were involved in 33 percent of the cases studied. Surprisingly, environmental groups and private companies were involved in negotiations with each other in only 18 percent of the site-specific cases studied, whereas federal and state agencies and units of local government were involved in 81 percent of these cases. Local citizen groups were involved in 44 percent of the cases.

For the most part, environmental dispute resolution processes have been used on an ad hoc, case-by-case basis. Recently, however, efforts to encourage and routinize the practice have emerged. Negotiation and mediation procedures have been written into statutes governing solid and hazardous waste facility siting, annexation, and coastal zone management issues. The Administrative Conference of the United States (ACUS) adopted a resolution in 1982 recommending that federal regulatory agencies incorporate negotiation into the rule-making process under certain circumstances, and three federal agencies have experimented with negotiated rule making. Further, the National Institute for Dispute Resolution is supporting statewide offices of dispute resolution in five pilot states—Hawaii, Massachusetts, Minnesota, New Jersey, and Wisconsin.

How Successful Have Environmental Dispute Resolution Processes Been?

Although people's strategies for resolving environmental disputes may vary depending on their views about social conflict and the characteristics of a particular dispute, individuals and groups care about similar factors. They care about the outcome and the extent to which it satisfies the real issues in dispute, as they see them. They care about the process—its fairness, its efficiency, and the opportunities it provides them for influencing a decision. And to the degree that the parties have or desire a continuing relationship, they care about the quality of that relationship and their ability to communicate with one another.

An assumption inherent in environmental dispute resolution alternatives is that the parties are good judges of what the real issues are and whether they are resolved adequately. Another is that the voluntary nature of the process, both in deciding whether to participate and whether to concur in an agreement, allows the parties to exercise their judgment freely. In theory, therefore, environmental dispute resolution processes allow broader attention to the real issues in dispute, because the parties set the agenda and because they decide what the terms of the agreement will be. Thus, the first and most simple measure of how successful these processes have been in resolving the issues is how often agreements have been reached.

A second test of how well the agreements reached have resolved the real issues in dispute is the extent to which the parties have supported the agreement through the implementation process. It is during implementation that other shortcomings of a dispute resolution process may emerge. Were all the parties with a stake in the issues involved? If not, although an agreement may have been reached, it may not have addressed the issues of concern to unrepresented parties. These parties may take action to block the implementation of the agreement. Does the agreement satisfy community norms of fairness? Were the parties well informed during the process so that the agreement is technically sound? Was a mechanism established for dealing with unanticipated events after the agreement was reached and the negotiations terminated? How were the parties able to handle disputes that may have arisen during the implementation process?

Other, intangible factors are also likely to be important to parties in dispute. Sometimes, as part of reaching an agreement, and sometimes in spite of *not* reaching an agreement, the participants report that the process itself was valuable. They may feel that they have gained valuable insights into their opposition's point of view on the issues and have created more open lines of communication. For example, in one policy dialogue sponsored by The Conservation Foundation, the parties reported more than a dozen instances in which one or another of them contacted others on issues outside the scope of the dialogue group's discussions. They had not done so in the past, although many had been involved in these issues for many years. Even when parties have decided not to participate in mediated negotiations, studies have shown that they often believe that the contacts by the mediator have helped them to clarify the issues and to better understand the dynamics of the dispute, thus helping them to deal with one another more effectively through more traditional decision-making processes.

In 133 of the 162 cases documented in this study, the parties' objective was to reach an agreement with one another. Of these cases, 100 involved site-specific issues and 33 involved policy issues. Overall, agreements were reached in 104, or 78 percent, of the cases; no agreements were reached in the remaining 29 cases (table 1).

- Little difference between site-specific and policy-level disputes was evident in the study. The parties were successful in reaching agreement in 79 percent of the site-specific cases and in 76 percent of the policy dialogues.

TABLE 1
Success in Reaching Agreements (broken down by parties' objectives)

		Site-specific disputes		*Policy dialogues*	
	All cases	*To reach a decision*	*To agree on a recommendation*	*To reach a decision*	*To agree on a recommendation*
Agreement	78% (104)	81% (52)	75% (27)	100% (4)	72% (21)
No agreement	22% (29)	19% (12)	25% (9)	0% –	28% (8)
Total	100% (133)	100% (64)	100% (36)	100% (4)	100% (29)

(Numerals in parentheses represent actual number of cases.)

- When the parties at the table had the authority to make and to implement their agreements, they were able to reach an agreement in 82 percent of the cases. When the agreements took the form of recommendations to a decision-making body that did not participate directly in the negotiations, the parties reached agreement 74 percent of the time.

Reaching an agreement does not mean that it sticks. The problem with litigation and administrative proceedings usually is not that decisions are not *reached* but that these decisions are frequently *appealed*. In theory, if the parties themselves have voluntarily agreed to a decision, they are more likely to be satisfied with it. Thus, agreements reached through an environmental dispute resolution process should be more likely to be implemented. How well is the claim borne out in practice?

- For site-specific disputes, of those cases in which agreements were reached and implementation results are known, the agreements were fully implemented in 80 percent of the cases, partially implemented in 13 percent, and not implemented in 7 percent.
- There has been more difficulty in implementing the results of policy dialogues than in implementing agreements reached in site-specific disputes. Of the policy dialogues in which agreements were reached and implementation results are known, agreements were fully implemented in 41 percent of the cases studied, partially implemented in 18 percent, and not implemented in 41 percent.

What Affects the Likelihood of Success?

There are few absolutes in predicting whether parties involved in any specific dispute will be successful in reaching an agreement or, if one is reached, in implementing it. There are several principles, however, that appear to increase the likelihood of success. Some of these principles are based on qualitative observations, while others are backed up by more quantitative analysis. But all remain hypotheses that require further study.

A particularly important reason for the relatively high success rate in dispute resolution efforts probably is that, as an accepted part of professional practice, the mediators conducted dispute assessments at the beginning of each case, as a first step in helping the parties decide whether to proceed with a voluntary dispute resolution process and, if so, what the nature and the ground rules of the process should be. Environmental disputes are so varied that different forms of assistance are appropriate in different cases, depending on the circumstances and the wishes of the parties. Mediators spend time discussing the possibility of a voluntary dispute resolution process with each of the parties, identifying and bringing to the parties' attention those conditions that may make it difficult to resolve the dispute, and helping the parties decide how they wish to proceed. Logically, this initial screening, if done well, will improve the likelihood that, once an informed decision to negotiate has been made, the parties will be successful in reaching an agreement. Until comparable samples of negotiated settlements without the assistance of mediators are available, however, this will remain a hypothesis.

The parties must have some incentive to negotiate an agreement with one another. The willingness of all parties to a dispute to participate is a major factor in the success of a voluntary dispute resolution process, if one expects an agreement reached to be both fair and stable. But the parties are unlikely to participate, let alone agree to a settlement, if they can achieve more of what they want in another way. It is difficult to assess the importance of incentives, however, because mediators generally do not convene negotiations unless the parties are at least somewhat interested in attempting to resolve the dispute.

The way the negotiation or consensus-building process is conducted also appears to be an important factor in whether agreements are reached. Mediators often refer to the difference between "interest-based" negotiation and "positional" bargaining in discussing what makes negotiations effective. In particular, the ability (and willingness) of the parties to identify the interests that underlie one another's positions, and to invent new alternatives that satisfy these interests, helps enormously in resolving disputes. At times, however, the parties can find no common ground regardless of their skill in negotiating with one another or the assistance of a mediator. Again, it is difficult to evaluate how well a negotiation or consensus-building process is conducted.

Among the factors that can be more easily measured, the likelihood of success is not clearly affected by the number of parties involved in the dispute, the issues themselves, or the presence of a deadline. There is no evidence that a larger number of parties makes reaching agreement more difficult. In fact, the average number of parties for cases in which the parties failed to reach an agreement was lower than the average number of parties in cases in which agreements were reached. Also, the evidence does not show that the issues in dispute have a significant effect. More study, done perhaps at a more detailed level, may show different results. The influence that the kind of issue has on the likelihood of success also may be linked to other factors, such as whether the particular dispute has precedent-setting implications. Finally, it appears that the presence of a deadline does not affect the likelihood of reaching an agreement.

The most significant, measurable factor in the likelihood of success in implementing agreements appears to be whether those with the authority to implement the decision participated directly in the process. When those with the authority to implement decisions were directly involved, the implementation rate was 85 percent; when they were not, only 67 percent of the agreements reached were fully implemented. Agreements were not implemented in about 7 percent of the cases in both categories. The difference in the implementation results is that when those with the authority to implement the recommendations were not at the table, the terms of the agreement were more likely to be modified. Agreements were partially implemented in 27 percent of the cases in which those with the authority to implement the agreements were not at the table as compared with 7 percent of the cases in which those at the table had the authority to implement their agreements.

Few factors are absolute preconditions for success. In many situations, the combined positive effect of some factors can offset potentially negative factors. Also, many factors may be subject to modification by the parties and the mediator before and during the dispute resolution process. If no deadline exists, the parties may be able to create one. If one side lacks sufficient incentives to negotiate, another may raise the ante with assurances about implementation, mitigation, or compensation offers contingent on an agreement, or with reminders of ways the dispute could be escalated. If there are an overwhelming number of parties, coalitions may be possible. If those with power to implement the agreement are not direct participants in the process, the mediator may be able to provide an appropriate link between the parties and the eventual decision maker.

How Efficient are Environmental Dispute Resolution Processes?

Perhaps the single most common assertion made about environmental dispute resolution processes—indeed, about alternative dispute resolution processes generally—is that they are cheaper and faster than litigation. There has been little empirical evidence to support this assertion, however. Very little information exists about how long it takes either to mediate or to litigate environmental disputes, and there are several conceptual problems in making comparisons between environmental dispute resolution alternatives and litigation.

Most individuals and organizations involved in environmental disputes can cite at least one occasion in which the parties became so locked in a legal stalemate that there seemed to be no way out. These stories have served to underscore the weakness in relying solely on litigation for settling disputes, but they also may have oversimplified the image both of litigation and of environmental dispute resolution alternatives. A lawsuit that goes to trial may take a very long time, but few lawsuits go to trial. Some mediated environmental disputes have been resolved quickly, but voluntary dispute resolution processes are not necessarily fast if the issues are complex. In addition, although mediators generally charge less than attorneys, this does not necessarily mean that one can be substituted for another. It is also important to consider other costs associated with resolving disputes. The costs of preparing for negotiation, for example, may be as high as or higher than the costs of preparing for some kinds of litigation, particularly for public interest groups.

A simple comparison of the costs of litigating a complex dispute that later was mediated can be misleading. First, it is unrealistic in many situations to begin counting the costs of mediation at the time that the parties agreed to negotiate, if the previous period of contention, litigation, or clarification of relative power contributed to the parties' willingness to negotiate a voluntary settlement. A simple comparison of costs also leaves out a major part of the equation—the nature and quality of the outcome. A more efficient process may not be more desirable if it leads to significantly poorer decisions in the view of one or all of the parties. The other, major conceptual problem in asking whether environmental dispute resolution processes are really cheaper and faster than litigation is the problem of finding comparable samples of cases.

Environmental disputes, on the average, do take longer to resolve through litigation than do civil suits generally, although the median durations of both are relatively short. For example, the median number of months from filing to disposition of all civil cases in U.S. district courts terminated in the

12-month period ending June 30, 1983, was 7 months, whereas for the same period the median duration of all environmental cases was 10 months. For cases that went to trial, the median duration of civil suits generally was 19 months; for environmental disputes, it was 23 months.

More interesting than the median duration of these lawsuits, however, is the range among the cases: 10 percent of all civil litigation in this sample took more than 28 months from the time of filing to disposition; 10 percent of the environmental litigation took more than 42 months. For those cases that went to trial, 10 percent of the environmental cases took longer than 67 months—or over five and a half years—not counting any possible appeals to a higher court. It is likely, therefore, that it is the *threat* of protracted litigation, not the length of the standard case, that creates the popular conception that mediation is faster than litigation.

In documenting environmental dispute resolution cases for this book, some information was available about the length of the dispute resolution process. This information is not complete, but one can get some idea about the duration of cases. Not only is this information incomplete, it is definitely *not* comparable to the statistics about litigation given above. Keeping that in mind, the median duration of the environmental dispute resolution cases in this sample was between 5 and 6 months, and 10 percent of the cases took over 18 months to resolve. Information about the costs of these cases is too sparse to report with any confidence.

Looking Ahead to the Next Decade

During the next 10 years, it will be important to identify and to put into practice mechanisms that encourage the use of environmental dispute resolution processes, increase the likelihood that disputes are resolved successfully, and protect the parties from potential abuses of these processes. To accomplish this without losing the flexibility that is a basic strength of voluntary dispute resolution processes will be a challenge. In addition, several important questions remain unanswered. How will the services of mediators be funded? Can citizens' groups and public interest organizations afford to use these processes? To whom are mediators accountable, to whom should they be accountable, and how should such accountability be maintained?

In the future, the institutional mechanisms for implementing environmental dispute resolution processes are likely to include: a continuation of the role that independent mediators now play in responding to the needs of parties on an ad hoc basis; court-referred or court-linked programs; mediation services provided by local, state, or federal agencies; and the incorporation of voluntary dispute resolution procedures into state or federal statutes. These options are not mutually exclusive, but the choices do have important implications with respect to who pays the mediator, to how these processes become widely available, to the flexibility of the approach, to the accountability of the mediator, and, ultimately, to how successful voluntary dispute resolution processes will be as an innovation in public decision making for environmental issues.

During the first decade in which mediators helped parties to environmental disputes resolve issues directly with one another, the mediators' services were paid for principally by foundation grants. Corporate donations, government contracts, in-kind support from citizen groups and public interest organizations, and fees made up the rest. For the most part, however, the mediators' services were free of charge to the parties. The question of how these services will continue to be paid is pressing. Foundation officials and others in the field raise a legitimate question: has this first decade of experience established the value of mediation services sufficiently that someone—the government or the parties themselves—is willing to pay for them? The data in this report begin to provide a basis for making such an evaluation. Looking ahead, additional case experience along with institutional mechanisms to encourage the resolution of environmental and other public policy disputes will create a framework for a more detailed assessment of environmental dispute resolution processes.

PETER M. SANDMAN

17 *Getting to Maybe*

Some Communications Aspects of Siting Hazardous Waste Facilities

I. Introduction

The United States generates roughly fifty million metric tons of non-radioactive hazardous wastes annually.[1] While much can be done to reduce this figure, a healthy economy will require adequate facilities for transporting, treating, storing and disposing of hazardous wastes for the foreseeable future. Current facilities are far from adequate; new ones and safer ones must be sited and built. The alternatives are dire—economic and technological slowdown on the one hand, or "midnight dumping" and similar unsafe, illegal and haphazard disposal practices on the other.

The principal barrier to facility siting is community opposition: "not in *my* backyard." Experience amply justifies this opposition. Communities have learned, largely from the media, that hazardous waste facilities endanger public health, air and water quality, property values, peace of mind and quality of life. They have also learned, largely from the environmental movement, that they can mobilize politically to block the siting of a facility, eminent domain statutes notwithstanding.

Technical improvements have reduced, though not eliminated, the risk of "hosting" a hazardous waste facility. State governments have learned how to regulate facilities more effectively. Responsible hazardous waste generators have come to terms with the need to reduce waste flow and handle remaining wastes properly. Responsible environmentalists have come to terms with the need to accept some waste and some risk in its disposal. A government-industry-environmentalist consensus is emerging in behalf of state-of-the-art facility design, development and siting. However, this consensus is not enough. The community typically rejects the consensus, and may well enforce its dissent through its exercise of a *de facto* veto.[2]

The comments that follow are predicated on several assumptions: (1) A facility can be designed, managed and regulated so that risks are low enough to justify community acceptance (without this, the task of siting is unethical); (2) Community acceptance is more desirable and more feasible than siting over the community's objections (without this, the task of meeting with a community is unnecessary); and (3) The positions of the siting authority and the developer are sufficiently flexible—legally, politically and economically—to permit meaningful concessions to community demands (without this, the task of gaining community approval is unachievable).

II. Acknowledge the Community's Substantial Power to Slow or Stop the Siting Process

Despite the preemption and eminent domain provisions of New Jersey's Major Hazardous Waste Facilities Siting Act,[3] many observers are convinced that a facility cannot be sited over a community's objections. The resources in the community's hands are many: legal delay, extralegal activities, political pressure, legislative exemption, gubernatorial override. The subtitle of one of the leading books on the siting problem testifies to the conviction of authors David Morell and Christopher Magorian that the community has something close to a veto. The book is entitled *Siting Hazardous Waste Facilities: Local Opposition and the Myth of Preemption*.[4] Moreover, in a January 25, 1985 interview with *The New York Times,* Department of Environmental Protection (DEP) Commissioner Robert E. Hughey agreed. "Siting," he said, "will be fought everywhere. I think everything else but this has an answer."[5] At the Seton Hall Symposium on siting, Douglas Pike of Envirocare International acknowledged the veto power of communities when he stated: "We have to operate as if there is no eminent domain."

Ironically, nearly everyone is impressed by the community's power of opposition—except the community, which sees itself as fighting a difficult, even desperate uphill battle to stop the siting juggernaut. From a communication perspective, this is the worst possible state of affairs. Suspecting that the "fix" is in, the community judges that it simply cannot afford to listen, to consider alternatives, to negotiate modifications. Intransigence looks like its best shot, perhaps its only shot. But suppose the Commission and the developer were to acknowledge *to the community* its considerable power: "Look, we probably can't site this thing unless you agree, and there are plenty of chances for you to stop it further on down the pike. Why don't we put the possible battle on ice for now and explore whether there is any possible agreement. If the talks fail, you can always go back to the fight." It will not be easy, of course, to persuade the community that this is not a trick, that it is forfeiting nothing by negotiating now, that it can switch its stance from "no" to "maybe" while protecting the road back to "no." It will take some effort not to *over*state the community's power. Though more powerful than it thinks, the community is not omnipotent, and the risk of override is real. The goal is to let the community know, publicly, what other participants already know privately: that it will be extremely difficult to site a facility over community objections, and that the siting authority would greatly prefer not to try. Formal acknowledgments of community power, such as a developer's pledge to honor a community referendum on any agreement that might be negotiated, are sometimes possible. But even an informal acknowledgment will reduce intransigence and encourage open discussion.

Acknowledging the community's substantial power will have three other desirable impacts. First it will reduce community resentment of what is seen as a power imbalance, an outrageous imposition of state control over local self-determination. This resentment and the deep-seated feeling of unfairness that accompanies it are major factors in community rejection of hazardous waste facilities. Residents look at New Jersey's siting law and note that in the final analysis, state action prevails over local preference. Angrily, they resolve to resist. Open acknowledgment of *de facto* power will lessen the anger at the imbalance of *de jure* power.[6]

Second, acknowledging community power will reduce fear about the health effects of a hazardous waste facility. One of the best documented findings in the risk perception literature is that we fear voluntary risks far less than involuntary ones. According to one study people will accept *one thousand times* as great a risk if it is chosen than if it is imposed by others.[7] Therefore, to the extent that the community feels itself in control of the siting decision, the risks of the facility become much more acceptable and much less fear-arousing.

Third, acknowledging community power will put the dialogue on a more frank footing than the classic "one-down/one-up" pattern that tends to dominate siting discussions. Under this pattern a community tries to prove itself the equal of the developer and the siting authority, while secretly feeling that it is not. The developer and the authority adopt a parental "the-decision-is-not-yours-but-we-value-your-input" attitude, while secretly fearing the community's *de facto* veto. Negotiations are much easier when the parties are acknowledged equals.

III. Avoid Implying that Community Opposition is Irrational or Selfish

Nothing interferes so thoroughly with the settlement of a dispute as the suggestion from either side that the other is being irrational or selfish. Yet developers, siting authorities and their expert consultants often aim this charge at community opponents. The acronym "NIMBY"—Not In My Back Yard— has become a sarcastic code, implying that opponents approve of siting in principle but oppose it in their neighborhoods for insupportable reasons. Some community groups, by contrast, still use the phrase as an anthem of their battle to prevent the Love Canals of the future. For example, Nicholas Freudenberg's book on how to organize community opposition is entitled *Not In Our Backyards.*[8] But the sarcastic meaning prevails. Opponents now take offense when developers or siting authorities start talking about "the NIMBY syndrome"—and they are correct to be offended.

Some opponents disapprove of siting new facilities anywhere, but choose to fight only in their own communities where their stake is greatest and their power base strongest. Some argue that source reduction and recycling can eliminate the need for new facilities, or that facility siting should be conditioned on policies that will reduce the waste stream, or that expansion of existing facilities is a wiser alternative, or that we should wait for improvements in waste treatment technology. Some take the position that the type of facility proposed is unduly dangerous, or that the site chosen is environmentally inappropriate, or that the developer's record is unsatisfactory. Others assert that equity dictates a different location. Rural dwellers argue that they should not serve as host to a facility because they did not produce the waste in the first place. Urbanites argue, on the other hand, that they have suffered enough pollution already. These are *all* coherent positions that deserve respectful responses. Dismissing them as a manifestation of the NIMBY syndrome is not fair, accurate nor strategically wise.

Similarly, community distrust of risk estimates by experts is not irrational. The experts generally work for interests with a stake in reassuring answers. Even with total integrity, non-resident experts in pursuit of a site can be expected to reach less cautious conclusions than residents with no special interest in siting. Moreover, there is ample precedent in the last several decades of siting experience to justify fears of a lack of integrity, or of incompetence or callousness. At best, the field is new and risk estimates are inherently uncertain. It is rational to distrust the experts even without any expertise of one's own. People who are trying to sell a hazardous waste facility are no different from people who are trying to sell, say, insulation for a home. One does not have to understand what they are saying technically to suspect that they are not to be trusted.

Furthermore, many siting opponents have acquired impressive expertise of their own. They have sifted the evidence in pursuit of technical arguments to support their position. In some cases, the opponents have become impressively knowledgeable. When pro-siting experts dismiss *all* objections as ignorant because *some* are without foundation, they are fighting *ad hominem,* inaccurately and unfairly.

It is important to note that many siting questions have no technical answers: How much risk is too much? What should you do when the answers are uncertain? These are "trans-scientific" questions, sometimes couched in technical language but unanswerable by technical methods.

Sociologists divide people into the categories "risk-aversive" and "risk-tolerant." What separates them is a fundamental values difference. The risk-aversive believe that if you are not sure of what you are doing you should not do anything, that meddling usually makes things worse. The risk-tolerant believe that problems should be solved incrementally, that the new problems caused by their tinkering will be solved later by someone else's tinkering. Neither position is unreasonable, and neither can be supported or refuted by technical information.

It takes courage for community activists to pit their newly acquired knowledge and deeply felt values against the professional stature of the experts. Unsure of their technical ground, these activists defend it all the more tenaciously, sensitive to the merest hint of disrespect. They deserve respect instead and they will not listen until they feel they have it.

IV.   Instead of Asking for Trust, Help the Community Rely on its Own Resources

Most of the people working to site a hazardous waste facility consider themselves moral and environmentally responsible people. Many are incredibly dedicated to meeting society's need for a decent facility. They also view themselves as professionals, as careful specialists who know what they are doing. In both of these roles they feel that they deserve at least trust, if not gratitude. They experience community distrust—sometimes even community hatred—with great pain. The pain often transforms into a kind of icy paternalism, an "I'm-going-to-help-you-even-if-you-*don't*-know-what's-good-for-you" attitude. I suspect that much of the rhetoric about community irrationality, selfishness and the "NIMBY syndrome" has its origins in hurt feelings. It is entirely reasonable for socially responsible experts to want to be trusted, to feel that they deserve to be trusted, and to resent the fact that they are not trusted.

It is sometimes said that the solution to the siting problem is to build trust. To be sure, the siting authority and the developer must make every effort not to trigger still more mistrust. For example, any hint of *ex parte* discussions between the siting authority and the developer must be avoided. But just as it is reasonable for siting experts to expect to be trusted, it is also reasonable for local citizens to withhold their trust, to insist on relying on their own judgment instead. The Commission must not only accept this, but also encourage and facilitate it.

Information policy is an excellent case in point. As noted earlier, one need not understand a technology in order to distrust experts with a vested interest. One, however, *must* understand the technology in order to decide whether the experts are right despite their vested interest. There is wisdom in the Siting Act's provision of research grants to the community at two stages in the siting process.[9] Methods should be found for the Commission to help the community inform itself even earlier in the process, when positions are still relatively fluid. The advantage of an independently informed community is not only that citizens will understand the issues, but that they will be *satisfied* that they understand the issues, and thus feel less pressure to construct a rejectionist front. A community that believes it has the knowledge to decide what should be done and the power to do it can afford to be reasonable. A community that believes it lacks sufficient knowledge and power, even if it has them, must conclude that the undiscriminating veto is the wisest course.

Similarly, communities want to know that if a facility *is* built they will not need to rely on outside experts for monitoring and enforcement. Many mechanisms can provide this autonomy:

(1) training of local health authorities, and citizen activists, to monitor effluents,
(2) funding for periodic assessments by consultants accountable to the community;
(3) duplicate monitoring equipment in a public place, so citizens can check, for example, the incinerator temperature for themselves;
(4) establishment of a trust fund, with trustees acceptable to the community, to supervise compensation in the event of accident, so citizens need not rely on the state courts.

Do not underestimate the depth of community disillusionment. Modern society depends on letting experts decide. When experts fail to decide wisely we are jolted into belated and reluctant attention. We feel betrayed. We are angry because we must now pay attention. We feel guilty for having relinquished control in the first place. We do not know what to do but are convinced we cannot trust others to decide for us. Above all, we fear that others will impose their unwise decisions on us even now that we are paying attention.

When the community grimly demands its autonomy, it is too late to ask for trust. Experts must instead presume distrust while helping the community exercise its autonomy wisely.

V. Adapt Communications Strategy to the Known Dynamics of Risk Perception

When people consider a risk, the process is far more complex than simply assessing the probability and magnitude of some undesired event. Departures from statistical accuracy in risk perception are universal and predictable. Communications strategy can therefore take the departures into consideration. It is crucial to understand that the following patterns of risk perception are "irrational" only if one assumes that it is somehow rational to ignore equity, uncertainty, locus of control and the various other factors that affect, not "distort," our sense of which risks are acceptable and which are not. Rational or not, virtually everyone considers getting mugged a more outrageous risk than skidding into a tree on an icy highway. And virtually everyone is more frightened by a hazardous waste facility than by a gasoline storage tank. Our task is not to approve or disapprove of these truths, but to understand why they are true and how siting communication can adapt to them.

The points in the following section deal with why communities fear hazardous waste facilities more than technical experts judge that they "should," and how communication can be used to reduce the discrepancy. It might be possible to employ this counsel to the exclusion of all else in this article, hoping to pacify community fears without acknowledging, much less honoring, community power. Such an effort would, I think, fail abysmally. Communications strategy must be part of fair dealing with the community, not a substitute for it.

PATTERNS OF RISK PERCEPTION

1. *Unfamiliar risks are less acceptable than familiar risks.* The most underestimated risks are those, such as household accidents, that people have faced for long periods without experiencing the undesired event. The sense of risk diminishes as we continue to evade it successfully. Thus, the perceived riskiness of a hazardous waste facility is, in part, a reflection of its unfamiliarity. Stressing its similarity to more familiar industrial facilities can diminish the fear; so can films, tours and other approaches aimed at making the facility seem less alien. Even more important is to make the wastes to be treated seem less alien. Detailed information on the expected

waste stream—what it is, where it comes from and what it was used to make—should reduce the fear level considerably.

2. *Involuntary risks are less acceptable than voluntary risks.* As mentioned earlier, some studies show acceptance of voluntary risks at one thousand times the level for involuntary risks.[10] Eminent domain, preemption and the community's general feeling of outside coercion thus exacerbate the level of fear. Acknowledging the community's power over the siting decision will lessen the fear and make siting a more acceptable outcome.

3. *Risks controlled by others are less acceptable than risks under one's own control.* People want to know that they have control over not only the initial decision but also the entire risky experience. To some extent this is not possible. Once a facility is built it is difficult to turn back. But credible assurances of local control over monitoring and regulation can be expected to reduce risk perception by increasing control. Similarly, trust funds, insurance policies, bonds and such contractual arrangements can put more control in local hands. Quite apart from any other advantages, these arrangements will tend to diminish the perception of risk.

4. *Undetectable risks are less acceptable than detectable risks.* A large part of the dread of carcinogenicity is its undetectability during its latency period. As a veteran war correspondent told me at Three Mile Island, "In a war you worry that you might get hit. The hellish thing here is worrying that you already got hit." While it is not possible to do much about the fear of cancer, it *is* possible to make manifest the proper, or improper, operation of the facility. For instance, a local monitoring team, or a satellite monitoring station in the City Hall lobby, can make malfunctions more detectable, and can thereby reduce the level of fear during normal operations. Not coincidentally, these innovations will also improve the operations of the facility.

5. *Risks perceived as unfair are less acceptable than risks perceived as fair.* A substantial share of the fear of hazardous waste facilities is attributable to the fact that only a few are to be sited. A policy requiring each municipality to manage its own hazardous waste would meet with much less resistance. A more practical way of achieving equity is to negotiate appropriate benefits to compensate a community for its risks and costs (this is, of course, after all appropriate health and safety measures have been agreed to). In a theoretical free market, the negotiated "price" of hosting a facility would ensure a fair transaction. The point to stress here is that

compensation does not merely offset the risk faced by a community. It actually *reduces* the perceived risk and the level of fear.

6. *Risks that do not permit individual protective action are less acceptable than risks that do.* Even for a very low-probability risk, people prefer to know that there are things they can do, as individuals, to reduce the risk still further. The proposed protective action may not be cost-effective, and the individual may never carry it out, but its availability makes the risk more acceptable. Discussion of hazardous waste facility siting has appropriately focused on measures to protect the entire community. Some attention to individual protective measures may help reduce fear.

7. *Dramatic and memorable risks are less acceptable than uninteresting and forgettable ones.* This is generally known as the "availability heuristic": people judge an event as more likely or frequent if it is easy to imagine or recall.[11] The legacy of Love Canal, Kin-Buc, Chemical Control and the like has made hazardous waste dangers all too easy to imagine and recall. A corollary of the availability heuristic is that risks that receive extensive media treatment are likely to be overestimated, while those that the media fail to popularize are underestimated. The complex debate over media handling of hazardous waste goes beyond the scope of this article.

8. *Uncertain risks are less acceptable than certain risks.* Most people loathe uncertainty. While probabilistic statements are bad enough, zones of uncertainty surrounding the probabilities are worse. Disagreements among experts about the probabilities are worst of all.

   Basing important personal decisions on uncertain information arouses anxiety. In response, people try either to inflate the risk to the point where it is clearly unacceptable or to deflate it to the point where it can be safely forgotten. Unfortunately, the only honest answer to the question "Is it safe?" will sound evasive. Nonetheless, the temptation, and the pressure, to offer a simple "yes" must be resisted. Where fear and distrust coexist, as they do in hazardous waste facility siting, reassuring statements are typically seen as facile and self-serving. Better to acknowledge that the risk is genuine and its extent uncertain.

9. *Cross-hazard comparisons are seldom acceptable.* It is reasonable and useful to compare the risks of a modern facility to those of a haphazard chemical dump such as Love Canal. The community needs to understand the differences. It is also reasonable and useful to compare the risks of siting a facility with the risks of not siting a facility—midnight dumping and abandoned sites. This comparison

lies at the heart of the siting decision. On the other hand, to compare the riskiness of a hazardous waste facility with that of a gas station or a cross-country flight is to ignore the distinctions of the past several pages. Such a comparison is likely to provoke more outrage than enlightenment.

10. *People are less interested in risk estimation than in risk reduction, and they are not interested in either one until their fear has been legitimized.* Adversaries who will never agree on their diagnosis of a problem can often agree readily on how to cope with it. In the case of facility siting, discussions of how to reduce the risk are ultimately more relevant, more productive and more satisfying than debates over its magnitude. Risk reduction, however, is not the only top priority for a fearful community. There is also a need to express the fear and to have it accepted as legitimate. No matter how responsive the Commission is to the issue of risk it will be seen as cold and callous unless it also responds to the *emotional* reality of community fear.

VI. Do Not Ignore Issues Other Than Health and Safety Risk

The paramount issue in hazardous waste facility siting is undoubtedly the risk to health, safety and environmental quality. But this is not the only issue. It is often difficult to distinguish the other issues so they can be addressed directly especially if legal and political skirmishes have thrust the risk issue to the fore.

Negotiated compensation is especially useful in dealing with these other issues. Moreover, negotiation helps to distinguish them from the risk issue. It is not uncommon, for example, for a community group to insist in adversary proceedings on marginal protective measures at substantial expense. In negotiations where other issues can more easily be raised, the group may reveal that it is also worried about the possible fears of prospective home purchasers and the resulting effect on property values. The developer may find it easy to bond against *this* risk. The homeowners have thus protected their property at a cost that the developer, who plans to establish an excellent safety record, expects will be low. It is extremely useful, in short, to probe for concerns other than risk, and to establish a context, such as mediated negotiation, where such concerns can be raised.

Aside from health risk, the impacts of greatest concern are: (1) the decline in property values; (2) the inability of the community to keep out other undesirable land uses once one has been sited; (3) the decline in quality of life because of noise, truck traffic, odor and the like; (4) the decline in the image of the community; (5) the overburdening of community services and community budgets; and (6) the aesthetically objectionable quality of the facility.

Apart from these possible impacts, a number of non-impact issues may create adverse community reaction to a proposed facility:

1. Resentment of outside control, including the threat of preemption and eminent domain.
2. The sense of not being taken seriously; resistance to one-way communication from planners and experts who seem to want to "educate" the community but not to hear it; perceptions of arrogance or contempt.
3. The conviction that the siting process is unfair, that "the fix is in."
4. The conviction that the choice of this particular community is unfair, that the community is being asked to pay a high price for the benefit of people who live elsewhere, and that it would be fairer to ask someone else to pay that price. This feeling is especially strong in communities that are poor, polluted or largely minority. These communities see their selection as part of a pattern of victimization.
5. Support for source reduction and recycling instead of new facilities.

Another issue that often surfaces is whether the facility will accept non-local waste. In a recent Duke University poll of North Carolina residents, only seven percent approved of allowing out-of-state waste to be disposed of in their county.[12] By contrast, thirty-eight percent would allow waste from other North Carolina counties and forty-nine percent would allow waste from within the county.[13] Technically, it may well be impractical to require each community to cope with its own waste. Psychologically, however, this is far more appealing than central facilities, for at least three reasons: (1) It seems intrinsically fairer to have to dispose of one's own waste than to be forced to dispose of everyone else's; (2) A strictly local facility will not earn a community an image as the hazardous waste capital of the state or region; and (3) Local wastes already exist, either stored on-site or improperly dumped, and a new local facility thus represents no net increase in local risk. Enforceable guarantees to limit "imported" waste should alleviate in part at least one source of opposition to a facility.

VII. Make All Planning Provisional, So That Consultation With the Community is Required

A fatal flaw in most governmental public participation is that it is grafted onto a planning procedure that is essentially complete without public input.

Citizens quickly sense that public hearings lack real provisionalism or tentativeness. They often feel that the important decisions have already been made, and that while minor modifications may be possible to placate opponents, the real functions of the hearing are to fulfill a legal mandate and to legitimize the *fait accompli*. Not surprisingly, citizen opponents meet what seems to be the charade of consultation with a charade of their own, aiming their remarks not at the planners but at the media and the coming court battle.

This scenario is likely even when the agency sees itself as genuinely open to citizen input. For legal and professional reasons, experts feel a powerful need to do their homework *before* scheduling much public participation. In effect, the resulting presentation says to the citizen: "After monumental effort, summarized in this 300-page document, we have reached the following conclusions. . . . Now what do you folks think?" At this point it is hard enough for the agency to take the input seriously, and harder still for the public to believe it will be taken seriously. Thus, Siting Commission Chairman Frank J. Dodd complained that the siting hearings "have turned into political rallies. The last thing that was discussed was siting criteria. It was how many people can you get into an auditorium to boo the speakers you don't like and cheer for the ones you support."[14]

The solution is obvious, though difficult to implement. Consultations with the community must begin early in the process and must continue throughout. Public participation should not be confined to formal contexts like public hearings, which encourage posturing. Rather, participation should include informal briefings and exchanges of opinion of various sorts, mediated where appropriate. The Commission must be visibly free to adjust in response to these consultations, and must appear visibly interested in doing so. Above all, the proposals presented for consultation must be provisional rather than final—and this too must be visible. A list of options or alternatives is far better than a "draft" decision. "Which shall we do?" is a much better question than "How about this?"

This sort of genuine public participation is the moral right of the citizenry. It is also likely to yield real improvements in the safety and quality of the facilities that are built. As a practical matter, moreover, public participation that is not mere window-dressing is probably a prerequisite to any community's decision to forego its veto and accept a facility. This is true in part because the changes instituted as a result of public participation make the facility objectively more acceptable to the community. Public participation has important subjective advantages as well. Research dating back to World War II has shown that people are most likely to accept undesirable innovations, such as rationing, when they have participated in the decision.[15]

Much in the Siting Act and in the behavior of the Commission represents important progress away from the traditional "decide–announce–defend" sequence, whereby an agency ends up justifying to the public a decision it has already made. Holding hearings on siting criteria instead of waiting for a site was progress.[16] The money available for community research is progress.[17] There is also progress evidenced in a recent statement by Commission Executive Director Richard J. Gimello that hearings have persuaded him that two incinerators would be wiser than the one originally proposed in the draft hazardous waste management plan.[18] However, there is a long history of "decide–announce–defend" to be overcome before we achieve what communication theorists call "two-way symmetric communication" and politicians call "a piece of the action."

VIII.   Involve the Community
in Direct Negotiations to Meet its Concerns

The distinction between community input and community control is a scale, not a dichotomy. Planning expert Sherry Arnstein describes an eight-rung "ladder of public participation," as follows: manipulation; therapy; informing; consultation; placation; partnership; delegated power; citizen control.[19] She adds:

> Inviting citizens' opinions, like informing them, can be a legitimate step toward their full participation. But if consulting them is not combined with other modes of participation, this rung of the ladder is still a sham since it offers no assurance that citizen concerns and ideas will be taken into account.[20]

A really meaningful participation program, Arnstein argues, involves some framework for explicit power-sharing with the community.[21]

In hazardous waste facility siting, today's community has two kinds of power: (1) the legally guaranteed right to provide input at many stages of the siting process; and (2) the political ability to delay, harass and quite possibly stop that process. The first, as Arnstein points out, is not enough to reassure a community that feels little trust for those at whom the input is directed.[22] That leaves the other source of power, the *de facto* veto.

This sort of analysis has led many observers to propose siting legislation that accords greater power to the community. Indeed, one state, California, makes siting virtually contingent on community acceptance.[23] Others, such as Massachusetts and Connecticut, do not go so far as to provide a *de jure* community veto, but do require the community to negotiate with the developer, with binding arbitration in the event of deadlock.[24] Still other states permit local regulation of the facility, but grant to a state agency the authority to override community regulations that make siting impossible.[25] As Morell and Magorian note, "expanded public participation procedures in a preemptive siting process are a far cry from such a balance of state and local authority."[26]

While New Jersey's Siting Act does not require negotiations with the community, it certainly does not foreclose the option—an option far more useful to the community than mere input, and far more conducive to siting than the *de facto* veto. The most productive option is probably negotiation between the developer and the community, with or without a mediator. If they are able to come to terms, the Commission could incorporate these terms in its own deliberations while still retaining its independent responsibility to protect health and environmental quality. If they are *un*able to come to terms, the Commission could retain its preemptive capabilities and the community its political ones. For the community, then, the incentive to negotiate is the likelihood that it can secure better terms from the developer than it can get from the Commission in the event of deadlock. For the developer, the incentive is the considerable possibility that there will be no facility at all unless the community withdraws its objections.

What is negotiated? What the community has to offer is of course its acceptance of the facility. What the developer has to offer is some package of mitigation (measures that make an undesirable outcome less likely or less harmful), compensation (measures that recompense the community for undesirable outcomes that cannot be prevented) and incentives (measures that reward the community for accepting the facility). The terms are value judgments. For example, a developer is likely to see as an incentive what the community sees as mere compensation. The distinctions among the three nonetheless have great psychological importance. Communities tend to see mitigation as their right. Compensation for economic costs is seen as similarly appropriate, but compensation for health risks strikes many people as unethical. Incentive offers, especially where health is the principal issue, may strike the community as a bribe.

Of course some forms of mitigation, compensation, and incentives are built into the Siting Act; among the most notable provisions are the five percent gross receipts tax[27] and the provision for strict liability,[28] which permits compensation for damage without proof of negligence. Clearly a still more attractive package is needed to win community support. What can help the parties in negotiating the package? I suggest training in negotiation for community representatives. An impartial mediator might also be provided, perhaps from the Center for Dispute Resolution of the Public Advocate's Office. Finally, a clear statement from the Siting Commission on how it will deal with a settlement if one is achieved would be useful.

Much will depend, of course, on the delicacy and skill of the developer. Compensation, in particular, should be tied as closely as possible to the damage to be compensated. A straight cash offer may be hotly rejected, whereas a trust fund to protect water quality would be entirely acceptable. Similarly, cash for damage to health is much less acceptable than cash for damage to community image. Where possible, compensation and incentive proposals should come from the community or mediator to avoid any suggestion of bribery. Some risks, of course, are so terrible that they are, and should be, unacceptable regardless of the compensation. No negotiation is possible unless the community agrees that a hazardous waste facility does not pose an unacceptable risk.

A great advantage of negotiation is that it encourages an openness about goals and concerns that is inconceivable in an adjudicatory process. Citizens concerned about property values may find themselves in a hearing talking instead about safety—but in a negotiation they will talk about property values. Similarly, a developer in an adjudicatory proceeding tends to understate risk. In a negotiation the community will insist that if the risk is so low the developer should have no objection to bonding against it. Suddenly both the developer and community will have an incentive to estimate the risk accurately. This pressure to be open affects not only the compensation package but the actual facility design as well. If developers must contract to compensate those they injure, they will be more likely to take the possibility of injuries into account in their planning than if they are merely instructed to "consider" social costs.

IX. Establish an Open Information Policy, But Accept Community Needs for Independent Information

Former EPA Administrator William D. Ruckelshaus was fond of quoting Thomas Jefferson: "If we think [the people are] not enlightened enough to exercise their control with a wholesome discretion, the remedy is not to take it from them, but to inform their discretion." Ruckelshaus usually added, "Easy for him to say."

Part of the problem of informing the public about hazardous waste facility siting is that the skills required to explain technical information to the lay public are uncommon skills. They are especially uncommon, perhaps, among those who possess the requisite technical knowledge. There are techniques to be learned: a standard called "communicative accuracy" to help determine which details may be omitted and which may not; various sorts of "fog indexes" to measure readability and comprehensibility; and other ways of simplifying, clarifying and dramatizing without distorting. The range of media available for the task also extends well beyond such standbys as pamphlets and formal reports.

The desire to explain technical issues in popular language is at least as difficult to acquire as the ability to do so. Experts in all fields prefer to confine their expertise to fellow professionals; "if laypeople misunderstand me I will have done them a disservice, and if they understand me what will have become of my expertise." All fields ostracize their popularizers. When the information is uncertain, tainted with values, and potent ammunition in a public controversy, the case for professional reticence becomes powerful indeed.

Nonetheless, it is essential to the success of the siting effort that information policy be as open as humanly possible. Unless legally proscribed, *all* information that is available to the Commission should be available to the community. The Commission should also make available simplified summaries of key documents and experts to answer whatever questions may arise. It is particularly important that all risk information be available early in the siting process. Failure to disclose a relevant fact can poison the entire process once the information has wormed its way out—as it invariably does. The standard is quite simple: any information that would be embarrassing if disclosed later should be disclosed now.

Even the most open information program, however, can expect only partial success. Individuals who are uninvolved in the siting controversy will not often bother to master the information, since there is nothing they plan to do with it. Individuals who are heavily involved, on the other hand, generally know what side they are on, and read only for ammunition. This is entirely rational. If changing one's mind is neither attractive nor likely, why endure the anxiety of listening to discrepant information? When many alternatives are under consideration, as in a negotiation, information has real value and helps the parties map the road to a settlement. When the only options are victory and defeat, objective information processing is rare.

Even in a negotiation, information carries only the limited credibility of the organization that provides it. As a rule, the parties prefer to provide their own. The Siting Commission would be wise to facilitate this preference. Rather than insisting that *its* information is "objective" and berating the community for distrusting it, the Commission can guarantee that all parties have the resources to generate their own information. The information should be generated as early as possible, while positions are fluid. Finally, the Commission should make sure the community has a real opportunity to use the information it acquires—ideally in negotiation. Information without power leads only to frustration, while the power to decide leads to information-seeking and a well-informed community.

X. Consider Developing New Communication Methods

There are a wide variety of all-purpose methodologies for developing
means to facilitate interaction, communication, trust and agreement. Some
are a bit trendy or "touchy-feely"; some are potentially explosive—all require
careful assessment and, if appropriate at all, careful design and implementation in the hands of a skilled practitioner. The list that follows is by no means
exhaustive. These are tools that are available to the Siting Commission, to a
developer, to a community group, or to anyone interested in making negotiation more likely or more successful.

1. *Delphi methodology.* This is a formal technique for encouraging
    consensus through successive rounds of position-taking. It is
    appropriate only where the grounds for consensus are clear—for
    helping the community clarify its concerns, for example, but not for
    helping it reach agreement with the developer.

2. *Role-playing.* Playing out the stereotyped roles of participants in a
    controversy can help all sides achieve better understanding of the
    issues. Under some circumstances this can greatly reduce the level
    of tension. There are many variations. Most useful for facility sit-
    ing would probably be exaggerated role-playing, in which partici-
    pants burlesque their own positions. This tends to produce more
    moderate posturing in real interactions. Counter-attitudinal role-
    playing, in which participants take on each other's roles, tends to
    yield increased appreciation of the multi-sidedness of the issue.
    Both require some trust, but much can be learned even from role-
    playing without the "enemy" present.

3. *Gaming-simulation.* This is a variation of role-playing, in which the
    participants interact not just with each other but with a complex
    simulation of the situation they confront. Game rules control how
    the participants may behave and determine the results—wins,
    losses, or standoffs. Participants learn which behaviors are
    effective and which are self-defeating. As with any role-playing, the
    participants may play themselves or each other, and may undergo
    the game in homogeneous or heterogeneous groups. Massachusetts
    Institute of Technology has recently developed a hazardous waste
    facility siting gaming-simulation.

4. *Coorientation.* This is a tool to help participants come to grips with
    their misunderstanding of each other's positions. A series of ques-
    tions is presented to all participants, individually or in groups. First
    they answer for themselves, then participants predict the answers of
    the other participants (those representing conflicting interests).

Responses are then shared, so that each side learns: (a) its opponent's position; (b) the accuracy of its perception of its opponent's position; and (c) the accuracy of its opponent's perception of its position. The method assumes that positions taken will be sincere, but not that they are binding commitments.

5. *Efficacy-building.* This is a collection of techniques designed to increase a group's sense of its own power. In some cases this includes skills-training to increase the power itself. In other cases, the stress is on increasing group morale, cohesiveness, and self-esteem. To the extent that community intransigence may be due to low feelings of efficacy, then efficacy-building procedures should lead to increased flexibility.

6. *Focus groups.* A focus group is a handful of individuals selected as typical of a particular constituency. This focus group is then asked to participate in a guided discussion of a predetermined set of topics. Often the focus group is asked to respond to particular ideas or proposals, but always in interaction with each other, not in isolation as individuals. The purpose of the focus group methodology is to learn more about the values of the constituency and how it is likely to respond to certain messages—for example, a particular compensation package in a siting negotiation. Focus groups do not commit their constituency, of course, but in the hands of a skilled interviewer and interpreter they yield far better information than survey questionnaires.

7. *Fact-finding, mediation, and arbitration.* These are all third-party interventions in conflict situations. Fact-finding concentrates on helping the parties reach agreement on any facts in contention. Mediation helps the parties find a compromise. Arbitration finds a compromise for them. These approaches assume that the parties want to compromise, that each prefers agreement to deadlock or litigation. They have been used successfully in many environmental conflicts, including solid waste siting controversies. The Center for Dispute Resolution of the Public Advocate's Office offers these services, as do several specialized environmental mediation organizations.

8. *Participatory planning.* This is the label sometimes given to a collection of techniques for making public participation more useful to the decision-maker and more satisfying to the public. To a large extent the value of public participation is in the agency's hands. It depends on how early in the process participation is scheduled, how flexible agency planners are, and how much real power is given to the community. Even if these questions are resolved in ways that

make participation more than mere window-dressing, the success of the enterprise still depends on technique: on how people are invited, on how the policy questions are phrased, on what speakers are allowed to talk about, what issues for how long, on who moderates the meeting, etc. Many techniques of participatory planning, in fact, do not involve a meeting at all.

9. *Feeling acceptance.* A classic misunderstanding between communities and agencies centers on their differing approaches to feeling; citizens may sometimes exaggerate their emotions while bureaucrats tend to stifle theirs. Not surprisingly, "irrational" and "uncaring" are the impressions that result. Feeling acceptance is a technique for interacting with people who feel strongly about the topic at hand. It involves identifying and acknowledging the feeling, then separating it from the issue that aroused it, and only then addressing the issue itself.

10. *School intervention.* In situations where strong feelings seem to be interfering with thoughtful consideration, it is sometimes useful to introduce the topic into the schools. Primary school pupils, in particular, are likely to approach the issue less burdened by emotion, yet they can be relied upon to carry what they are learning home to their parents. It is essential, of course, to make sure any school intervention incorporates the views—and the involvement—of all viewpoints in the community. Any effort to teach children a single "objective" agency viewpoint will bring angry charges of indoctrination. Existing curricula that are themselves multi-sided can augment the local speakers.

11. *Behavioral commitment.* People do not evolve new attitudes overnight; rather, change comes in incremental steps. The most important steps are not attitudes at all, but behaviors, preferably performed publicly so as to constitute an informal commitment. The behavioral commitment methodology, sometimes known as the "foot in the door," asks people to take small actions that will symbolize, to themselves and their associates, movement in the desired direction. Among the possible actions which can be taken: to request a booklet with more information, to urge rational discussion on the issue, to state that one is keeping an open mind, to agree to consider the final report when it is complete, to agree to serve on an advisory committee, to meet with citizens concerned about Superfund cleanup, etc.

12. *Environmental advocacy.* In a large proportion of successfully resolved siting controversies in recent years, respected environmen-

talists played a crucial intermediary role. Environmental organizations may need to play that role in New Jersey's hazardous waste facility siting. By counseling caution on industry assurances while agreeing that new facilities are needed and much improved, environmentalists position themselves in the credible middle.

A credible middle is badly needed on this issue, but it will take time. Now is not the time to ask *any* New Jersey community to accept a hazardous waste facility. From "no" to "yes" is far too great a jump. We should ask the community only to consider its options, to explore the possibility of a compromise. Our goal should be moderate, fair, and achievable: getting to maybe.

Notes

1. *See Superfund Strategy* (Apr. 1985) (Office of Technology Assessment).

2. BLACK'S LAW DICTIONARY (5th ed. 1979) defines "de facto" as a "phrase used to characterize a state of affairs which must be accepted for all practical purposes but is illegal or illegitimate."

3. N.J. STAT. ANN. § 13:1E-81 (West Supp. 1985) ("Eminent domain").

4. D. MORELL & C. MAGORIAN (1982).

5. Carney, *D.E.P.: The Record and the Problems*, New York Times, Jan. 27, 1985, § 11 at 6.

6. BLACK'S LAW DICTIONARY (5th ed. 1979) defines "de jure" as "descriptive of a condition in which there has been total compliance with all requirements of the law." Here the term refers to the actual legal authority of the state to site a facility over the objection of a municipality, whether or not that approach will ever be taken.

7. Starr, *Social Benefit Versus Technological Risk*, 165 SCIENCE 1232-38 (1969).

8. N. FREUDENBERG (1984).

9. N.J. STAT. ANN. § 13:1E 59.d. (West Supp. 1985); *see also* N.J. STAT ANN § 13:1E-60.c. (4) (West Supp. 1985).

10. *See* Starr *supra* note 7.

11. Slovic, Fischoff, Layman & Coombs, *Judged Frequency of Lethal Events*, 4 JOURNAL OF EXPERIMENTAL PSYCHOLOGY: HUMAN LEARNING AND MEMORY 551-578 (1978).

12. D. MORELL & C. MAGORIAN, SITING HAZARDOUS WASTE FACILITIES: LOCAL OPPOSITION AND THE MYTH OF PREEMPTION, at 74 (1982).

13. *Id.*

14. Goldensohn, *Opponents, Officials Charge Politicizing of Waste Site Debate*, *Star-Ledger* (Newark, NJ), Dec. 2, 1984, at 12.

15. M. KARLINS & H. ABELSON, PERSUASION, at 62-67 (2d ed. 1970).

16. *See* Dodd, *The New Jersey Hazardous Waste Facilities Siting Process: Keeping the Debate Open*, 9 SETON HALL LEGISLATIVE JOURNAL (1985).

17. *See supra* note 9.

18. *See Response to Comments on "Draft" Hazardous Waste Facilities Plan Issued September 1984* (Mar. 26, 1985) (copies available from the Siting Commission, CN-406, Trenton, NJ 08625).

19. S. ARNSTEIN, *A Ladder of Citizen Participation,* in THE POLITICS OF TECHNOLOGY, at 240-43 (1977).

20. *Id.*

21. *Id.*

22. *Id.*

23. *See* Duffy, 11 B.C. ENV. AFFAIRS, L. REV. 755, 755-804 (1984).

24. *Id.*

25. *Id.*

26. D. MORELL & C. MAGORIAN, *supra* note 12, at 102.

27. N.J. STAT. ANN. § 13:1E-80.b. (West Supp. 1985).

28. N.J. STAT. ANN. § 13:1E-62 (West Supp. 1985) ("Joint and several strict liability of owners and operators").

SAM GUSMAN

18 *Selecting Participants for a Regulatory Negotiation*

Three articles in recent issues of *Environmental Impact Assessment Review* have addressed various aspects of regulatory negotiation. Harter (1982) discusses the concept in the context of "a cure for the malaise" of rulemaking as currently practiced. He presents a group of recommendations regarding regulatory negotiation that were adopted by the Administrative Conference of the United States in June 1982. Kirtz (1982) describes a proposed experiment in negotiated rulemaking to be conducted by the U.S. Environmental Protection Agency. He presents a check list of criteria to aid in selecting rules most likely to be suitable for negotiation. Rodwin (1982) presents a critical and broad evaluation of the concept of direct negotiation of rules by affected parties. These are part of a growing literature that describes, analyzes, and criticizes the as yet untested concept of regulatory negotiation.

The focus of this article is exclusively on one particular aspect of regulatory negotiation, namely the selection of negotiators to represent parties with an interest in the regulatory issue. Selection of negotiators is a difficult and important problem from both practical and theoretical points of view. Selection can affect the legitimacy of the negotiating process which, at a minimum, depends upon the perception that all categories of affected parties are represented in a balanced way at the negotiating table. Selection must occur early during the regulatory negotiation process, during what might be called a

From Sam Gusman, "Selecting Participants for a Regulatory Negotiation," in *Environmental Impact Assessment Review*, Vol. 4 (1983), pp. 195-202. Reprinted by permission of the Plenum Publishing Corporation and Sam Gusman.

"convening phase." The process by which negotiators are elected can affect their willingness to participate. Thus, the appropriate selection of negotiators by a process they and others find acceptable is as important as, and intimately intertwined with, the selection of the issue to be negotiated.

Comparisons with Current Regulatory Practice

Current interest in regulatory negotiation is in large measure an outgrowth of dissatisfaction with the current federal regulatory process. The many sources of dissatisfaction include perceptions that costs are too high, that regulation (or lack of regulation) is unreasonable, or that the regulatory process (which may include appeals to administrative, judicial, and legislative channels) is too time consuming and complicated. Regulatory negotiation, an outgrowth and modification of current regulatory practice, does not have a perfect antecedent. Current practice is flawed. Regulatory negotiation will surely be found to be flawed also, but in different ways.

It is rational for the parties interested in a regulation to want to participate in a regulatory negotiation only if they see probable net benefits to their interests in comparison with current regulatory practice. The key question for participants is not whether the new and unfamiliar process of regulatory negotiation is perfect. It will be compared to current practice, not to some theoretical ideal.

Current regulatory practice gives all members of the public an opportunity to comment on proposed regulations. Stakeholders in a regulatory issue may carry their participation further, for example, by appeal through administrative and judicial channels. These kinds of participation require the expenditure of time, effort, and often considerable money as well. For this reason, stakeholders rich in resources can have greater opportunity than others to influence the outcome of a regulatory action. This potential inequality of influence is an imperfection of current regulatory practice.

However, regulatory negotiation could present even more serious problems of this sort. For example, regulatory negotiation processes that develop a "final" regulation would eliminate the current formal opportunity for public comment on an earlier "proposed" version and the procedural assurance that comments will be addressed by the regulatory agency. To offset this problem, regulatory negotiation has been suggested for development of proposed regulations which, after publication in the *Federal Register,* would be open for comment as per current practice.

Even with respect to the development of a proposed regulation, it could be argued that the direct or *de facto* exclusion of any stakeholder from a regulatory negotiation process constitutes an infringement of that stakeholder's relative opportunity to influence the outcome of the process, as compared with the opportunity afforded by current regulatory practice. At one extreme, since everyone and all future generations are potential stakeholders in many, perhaps all, regulatory action, it is obviously impossible to assemble all stakeholders for a regulatory negotiation. At the other extreme, it is equally impossible to assure that the regulatory agency staff who currently prepare a proposed regulation will have the knowledge and wisdom to take into account the interests of all present and future stakeholders.

Thus, the problem of adequate representation involves a comparison between two imperfect processes, though in both instances a subsequent period of opportunity for public comment is a partial safeguard. Regulatory agency staff are now expected to consider the interests of diverse present and future stakeholders (the public interest) during the drafting of proposed regulations. In a regulatory negotiation, agency staff is similarly responsible for the public interest and acts as a negotiator in its behalf. The negotiating process needs to be devised so that a decision cannot be reached unless agency staff concurs. The same "veto" power almost certainly would be demanded by the other negotiators, and should be granted to them as a condition of their participation. The other negotiators would probably represent the interests of organized stakeholders, such as regulated industries, public interest groups, and labor unions. Therefore, one can argue that agency staff would be able to concentrate even more attention on the stakeholders who do not or cannot speak for themselves.

Key Stakeholders

Many stakeholders have neither the interest nor the resources to become individually involved in the regulatory process. Many rely on organizations regularly participating in such activity. It is not unusual for organizations such as public interest groups, large corporations, industry trade associations, and labor unions to cooperate and rely on other groups with similar interests for representation on particular public policy issues. For example, not every environmental organization will become actively involved in every environmental issue; neither will every industry trade association. For many public policy issues it is possible to identify lead organizations to which other organizations and individual stakeholders turn for information and action.

Lead organizations usually cannot give legal assurances that the other stakeholders will actually follow their lead. Such cooperation is probably the consequence of an extensive though largely undocumented, informal network through which the staffs of organizations with similar interests communicate with each other and with constituencies. These lead organizations are called *key stakeholders* in this paper.

In practice, key stakeholders usually have offices in Washington and staffs that include lawyers with specialized expertise. They usually have sufficient resources to be implacable in pursuing their interests. It is not uncommon for their appeals of a regulatory issue through administrative and judicial processes to take many years. Nor is it uncommon for the apparent defeats they suffer to be recouped through later changes by Congress of underlying statutes. Thus, if any key stakeholder is dissatisfied with a regulation or the lack of a regulation, there is a good likelihood that the stakeholder will challenge the regulation, starting the lengthy—sometimes seemingly never ending—process of trying to change the situation.

Key stakeholders are an important part of the current political scene in Washington. They will undoubtedly continue to be powerful, and must be taken into account. Hypothetically, regulatory agencies might involve them in the drafting of proposed regulations. Key stakeholders then might have a sufficient sense of participation to overcome any "not invented here" anxieties about the proposed regulations. Regulatory negotiation is a process that can do this. It is a process that can give stakeholders direct access to the language of a proposed regulation and an opportunity to be sure that their points of view are not misrepresented. Key stakeholders could expect that direct participation in negotiating the language of a proposed regulation would offer less opportunity for distortion of their points of view than is the case in current regulatory practice in which only agency staff drafts proposed regulations.

There are, however, other features of a regulatory negotiation that can influence a key stakeholder's decision to participate. A stakeholder with the strength to prevail without negotiating is unlikely to want to participate. Also, an issue might be a facet of a more general proposition that the stakeholder opposes as a matter of principle. For example, negotiation of the details of operation of a uranium mine would probably not appeal to a stakeholder fundamentally opposed to the development of nuclear energy.

Regulatory Agencies as Key Stakeholders

In principle, a regulatory agency might be viewed solely as an agent of the public interest and devoid of its own institutional interest. To the extent this is not the case, it becomes a key stakeholder in its own right. This transformation can occur if agency personnel responsible for writing, reviewing, or approving a regulation see any personal or institutional advantage in the outcome of a negotiation, apart from the manner in which the outcome affects the public interest. For example, if the lead staff person or the responsible officer in the agency has ambitions or an ideological viewpoint that would be furthered or thwarted by the outcome of negotiations, it would not be surprising if this influenced the negotiating stance of the agency. Convening a regulatory negotiation may thus present more serious disadvantages for agency staff than for other key stakeholders, namely, perceived loss of power to draft proposed regulations unilaterally and the need to negotiate with other key stakeholders.

However, balanced against some loss of sole control of the process are many advantages, particularly the opportunity for the agency to resolve thorny issues by negotiation, with the expectation that private stakeholders who participate in a negotiated agreement will usually not challenge it later. In effect, the agency would be trading a perceived loss (of power) against a speculative but larger gain (of efficient and effective decision making). In the face of public dissatisfaction with current regulatory processes and Congressional interest in regulatory reform, it is not surprising that some agencies are considering demonstration trials of regulatory negotiation—but only some agencies and so far only in a very limited sense.

Selection of Negotiators

A mechanism must be devised to select negotiators who represent the interested parties. Direct negotiation of environmental issues has been successful with as many as about a dozen negotiators. It is conceivable that many more, perhaps hundreds, could be accommodated in a regulatory negotiation through a grouping of negotiators into coalitions that would choose representatives to sit at a bargaining table, and report back periodically to the other members of their coalitions. This would be a difficult process and is conceivably impractical. If the development of a proposed regulation by negotiation required the participation of hundreds of separate negotiators many regulatory topics would surely be discarded (at least at present) because of lack of experience in negotiating agreement among such numbers. There are, however, several ways to limit the number of negotiators.

One alternative is to have the regulatory agency or some other authority select the negotiators with due attention to maintaining a proper balance of interests and adequate representation of each different kind of interest in the negotiating group. This has the advantage of limiting the number of participants, but it offers no protection against objections to a negotiated agreement by those who were excluded from participation. Excluded parties might be antagonized by their exclusion and, because of heightened antagonism, object to features of the negotiated agreement they might otherwise have found acceptable.

A second alternative is to have the agency or some other authority designate the number of seats at the negotiating table, allocating several to each kind of interest group. A major disadvantage of this approach is that the allocation may be challenged. Also, there would still be the problem of dealing with excluded parties.

A third alternative is to have the agency establish a selection committee comprised of people who are balanced with respect to their affiliations and who represent all major interests. For example, the selection committee might operate by choosing negotiators from among those who volunteer, in response to a *Federal Register* notice. Those selected could be asked to represent not only themselves but also a group of others who volunteered, thus establishing a form of constituency relationship among interested parties. The negotiated agreement would be reached when all parties (the constituents as well as those at the table as negotiators) reach consensus. This approach might be challenged less frequently than the second alternative, but it would be more unwieldy. For many subjects it might be so unwieldy as to be impractical.

A fourth alternative is for the agency, an authority, or a balanced committee to identify the key stakeholders for the proposed regulation, that is, those key stakeholders with both the interest and the will to challenge an outcome if it did not accommodate their interests adequately. These key stakeholders would be selected as the negotiators. This is a modification of the first alternative, and has the advantage of emphasizing selection of negotiators likely to have both the resources and the will to challenge unwelcome outcomes. This diminishes but does not eliminate potential problems with excluded parties. This alternative still might be considered unfair by parties who are excluded or who believe they are underrepresented.

A fifth alternative is to limit attention to only those candidates for regulatory negotiation that are characterized by a small number of interested parties, say about a dozen or fewer. This could be a very small universe of proposed regulations. If regulatory negotiation were to be viewed as applicable only to this limited group of issues, questions could legitimately be asked about the desirability of giving so much attention to so limited a process. Nonetheless, regulatory issues for which there are limited numbers of interested parties might serve adequately for early demonstration of the regulatory negotiation process. Such demonstrations could provide valuable experience on which to base the design of regulatory negotiations involving larger numbers of parties.

There are, of course, other variations on these five themes but the criticisms of these five would probably be applicable to the variations. In any event, a whole different class of options opens up if the process uses a neutral facilitator, that is, a person (or persons) who can be expected to facilitate the process free of control (or the perception of control) by the regulatory agency or any other party. The facilitator would then be able, as a consequence of credibility as a neutral, to work toward *self-selection* of negotiators through use of interactive processes of consultation with interested parties. The following illustrates one way this could occur.

The agency could assemble a small, balanced *ad hoc* selection committee comprised of key stakeholders who would almost certainly be included as negotiators if a regulatory negotiation were to take place. The facilitator could meet with committee members, individually and as a group. He or she would ask who should be selected to be the negotiators and presumably state desirable conditions for the negotiator selection process. Some exemplary conditions might be the inclusion at the negotiation table of all parties with the interest and power to overthrow a negotiated settlement, the representation of all substantially different points of view, and the restriction of the number of negotiators to about a dozen. Through an iterative and personalized process of contacts, the facilitator would seek to identify a balanced group of negotiators who are willing to participate, and who are acceptable to each other and to all known key stakeholders. Those selected by this process would comprise a "preliminary" negotiating group. Their names would be published in a *Federal Register* notice that also invites attendance at a meeting of the "preliminary" group for the purpose of selecting still other candidates for participation as negotiators. Based on this meeting, the facilitator would determine by consultation with the "preliminary" group whether they wished to proceed with their present group, with substitutions, by addition of others, or not at all.

A decision not to proceed could occur for any of a number of reasons. For example, if one party believes that a second party's willingness to participate is cynical, based on a desire to use negotiations to postpone regulatory action, the first party would be unlikely to want to participate. A decision to proceed would imply a judgment by each member of the group that a negotiated agreement can probably be reached, and is not likely to be successfully challenged.

The facilitator could use some variation of the personalized process described above to convene a negotiating group. By agreeing to negotiate, the group already will have started on the path to consensus.

Conclusion

The goal of regulatory negotiation proposals is not to foster negotiation for its own sake. The goal is a practical one, to overcome some unsatisfactory aspects of current regulatory practice. Regulatory negotiation is simply a procedural device that may—if properly used—reduce dissatisfactions with that process and, more particularly, with the regulations it produces. Regulatory negotiation is based on a simple premise: people like to be powerful enough to have a meaningful voice in making the decisions that are important to them. The implication of this premise for the selection of negotiators is equally straightforward: involve interested parties in the negotiator selection process to the maximum extent that is practical.

References

Harter, P. 1982. Negotiating Regulations: A Cure for the Malaise? *Environmental Impact Assessment Review* 3,1: 75-92.

Kirtz, C. 1982. EPA Announces Negotiated Rulemaking Project. *Environmental Impact Assessment Review* 3,4: 367-372.

Rodwin, M.A. 1982. Can Bargaining and Negotiation Change the Administrative Process? *Environmental Impact Assessment Review* 3,4: 373-386.

S.A. CARNES, E.D. COPENHAVER, J.H. SORENSEN,
E.J. SODERSTROM, J.H. REED, D.J. BJORNSTAD, E. PEELLE

19 Incentives and Nuclear Waste Siting

Prospects and Constraints

Introduction

Whatever the future of nuclear power, high level nuclear wastes from operating nuclear reactors are abundant and continue to accumulate. The storage and disposal of these wastes present serious problems in the United States [1,2]. In recent years the importance of social and institutional issues in the siting of nuclear waste management facilities has been recognized [3,4].

Conflicts arising from social and institutional concerns are fairly common to the siting of airports, mental health facilities, prisons, and nuclear or coal-fired power plants [5,6], but the siting of nuclear waste management facilities has been and may continue to be particularly problematic. This conflict arises from many sources, but the extraordinary nature of a nuclear waste repository may require dealing with associated benefits, costs, and risks at a level of detail exceeding that necessary for more frequently developed facilities. The differences that distinguish the nuclear waste repository from other locally undesirable land uses, excepting perhaps chemical waste disposal facilities, are quite familiar: handling of hazardous material, long-term security requirements, suitability of only a few geologic formations, the sharp separation of benefits from costs for those experiencing both, and ownership of and responsibility for the repository by the federal government. These differences denote more risk, more long-term risk, a geographic concentration of risks, and

Reprinted with permission from *Energy Systems and Policy*, Vol. 7 (1983), pp. 323-351. Copyright © Crane Russak, New York, for *Energy Systems and Policy*.

353

reduced revenue opportunities for the host area, and indicate a need to redress the associated imbalances.

The nearly universal reluctance of states and communities to host waste facilities suggests that significant costs and risks, actual or perceived, have apparently been overlooked by facility proponents. A number of recent studies and policy initiatives have suggested the use of diverse incentives to increase local support and offset local opposition to such facilities in potential host communities [7-11]. Rarely, however, have incentives been systematically defined, identified, investigated, or evaluated. The object of this paper is to identify prerequisites to the use of incentives, suggest how incentives may be categorized, and identify criteria for evaluating the potential usefulness of particular incentives or sets of incentives.

Background

The range of social and institutional issues that currently hinders governmental attempts to resolve the radioactive waste management problem is extensive and includes institutional uncertainties, equity issues, and public acceptance [12]. Institutional uncertainties include dispersed authority, gaps in regulatory authority, governmental conflicts, diminution of institutional credibility, and waste management program inconsistencies and inconstancy [12,13]. In the latter case, for example, a number of actions have been proposed as official national policy since 1954 (see Table 1). These changes in policies and approaches have resulted in part from changes in national administrations (e.g., former President Carter's decision to reject reprocessing and President Reagan's recent reversal of that decision) and from changes in political institutions (e.g., increased public participation in waste management decision making), as well as from technological advances (e.g., waste solidification by calcination and vitrification). The consequences of inconstancy in waste management programs and policies have been uncertainty among the general public and distrust among citizens of potential host communities.

The need for so few high level waste sites and the nature of high level waste also raise concerns about equity. Equity issues involve problems of spatial equity, intergenerational equity, and what has been characterized as the labor/laity equity problem (i.e., the impact on waste management workers versus the general public) [12]. For instance, in the case of spatial equity the states have clearly indicated that wastes should be stored in the state in which they originate [9]. However, disposal is not feasible in every state because many states lack suitable geologic formations and because the cost of siting more than a few repositories may be prohibitive. The concentration of nuclear power plants along the eastern seaboard and the Great Lakes, together with

TABLE 1
Selected National High-Level Nuclear Waste Chronology and Related Events

1954	Atomic Energy Act included control of all nuclear wastes
1957	First commercial reactor built (Shippingport, PA)
1957	NAS recommends salt deposit disposal of civilian wastes
1966–1967	Operation Salt Vault Experiments, Lyons, Kansas
1966–1972	West Valley Nuclear Reprocessing Plant storing liquid neutralized high level wastes in carbon steel tanks (also used for defense wastes at Hanford, Savannah River)
1968	Public hearings made mandatory in licensing nuclear plants
1970	Calvert Cliffs decision forces AEC to include environmental impacts in licensing decisions
1970–1972	Proposed National Waste Depository, Lyons, Kansas
1972–1975	Retrievable Surface Storage Facility (RSSF) proposed
1975	Sierra Club and Ralph Nader helped focus national antinuclear movement
1976–1978	ERDA program proposed to identify sites for six commercial waste disposable pilot repositories
1976	Harris Poll shows nuclear waste disposal the major public concern over nuclear energy (67%)
1977	Commercial reprocessing of spent fuel rejected in United States, expanding the scope of the waste problem
1978	Thirty-three of 50 states have laws dealing with nuclear waste management
1979	Interagency Review Group on Nuclear Waste Management report
1979	Three Mile Island Accident
1980	DOE program to identify four to five sites suitable for mined repositories in different geologic environments with diverse rock types
1980–1981	Away-from-Reactor Spent Fuel Storage Facilities (AFR) proposed by federal government for interim storage
1980–1981	State Planning Council appointed to assist with the consultation and concurrence process in siting repositories
1981	Reprocessing ban lifted

the concentration of suitable sites for nuclear waste disposal in remote, sparsely populated, or arid areas of the United States, primarily in the West [14], creates the possibility of a serious spatial maldistribution of benefits and burdens.

Community acceptance of a repository is highly questionable, given these social and institutional problems and the critical, if not hypercritical, assessment of nuclear energy by the public [15]. Yet, acceptance of such a facility is essential if we are to site, construct, operate, and maintain a facility for an extremely long period of time. The major question facing facility sponsors is how to develop and maintain local constituencies for the repositories.

Most studies of radioactive waste repository siting have stressed federal/state relationships and have excluded the concerns and role of potential host communities. Strategies such as federal preemption [9], siting on federal reservations [16,17], state veto [6], the siting jury [18], the paths of least resistance [6,19], and the consultation and concurrence principle [20] ignore or at best minimize the importance of community involvement. Since siting is unlikely to occur without local acceptance, it is important that facility-related impacts be considered and assessed, and that these local residents be included in the process [21]. Incentives responsive to the concerns of local communities may facilitate community acceptance *if* certain basic principles, rights, or prerequisites are satisfied or achieved.

Siting Prerequisites

Public confidence in most institutions of government and business has shown a steady and substantial decline in recent years [22]. Restoration of this confidence, at least with respect to the siting of nuclear waste, might be achieved if a variety of concerns are addressed through the implementation of particular policies. Our judgment, based on an appreciation of our constitution and basic democratic and pluralistic principles and on experiences in siting hazardous and radioactive waste facilities, is that two concerns are of the greatest importance to the public: the integrity of public health, safety, and the environment and shared authority in decision making. In turn, these concerns may be satisfied if: (1) public health, safety, and the environment are protected; (2) a significant measure of local control in the siting and licensing process is recognized as legitimate; and (3) negotiations are recognized as a viable mechanism for reconciling differences and building consensus. It should be recognized that these prerequisites have empirical, analytical, and philosophical bases and are advanced as a means of addressing broad public concerns and minimizing some of the uncertainties that currently hinder the siting process.

PROTECTION OF PUBLIC HEALTH, SAFETY, AND THE ENVIRONMENT

The presence of adequate, reliable, and enforced regulations that protect the health, safety, and environment of residents near a proposed radioactive waste facility must be regarded as a vital element in the siting process. Much opposition to such facilities arises from the belief that waste management facilities may endanger health and safety. Both the degree and probability of risk from normal and abnormal operations of the proposed facility will inevitably be in dispute. The credibility of "experts" on both sides of the debate will be questioned by segments of the public. Existing regulations may not be known or understood, or their functioning may be discounted and viewed as unreliable. Agencies responsible for the enforcement of existing regulations may not be trusted or respected. Therefore, additional guarantees, over and above those presently mandated by federal or state law, are a reasonable subject for discussion by interested parties.

CONTROL AND AUTHORITY

Nonradioactive waste management and land use have traditionally been local prerogatives [23]. Only with the passage of the Resource Conservation and Recovery Act (P.L. 94-580) did the federal government begin to exercise significant control in these areas. Between the extreme approaches of federal preemption and state or local veto is a range of compromise approaches in which the different levels of government share power (e.g., consultation and concurrence [24], cooperative federalism [25], shared powers [9]). Once it is conceded that the potential host community has a legitimate role in the design and implementation of a siting strategy, the problem becomes one of determining the suitability of particular institutional arrangements for local decision making. Various local decision-making options are available for making that determination [26-28].

NEGOTIATION AS A MECHANISM FOR RECONCILING DIFFERENCES AND BUILDING CONSENSUS

It has been noted elsewhere that negotiation is the only major public participation strategy that focuses on the mediation of differences and thus has the building of consensus as a possible outcome [29,30]. For radioactive waste disposal, the central issue to be negotiated is under what conditions a repository might be sited within or adjacent to a community. As previously noted, most radioactive waste-management negotiations have been conducted only between federal and state/tribal jurisdictions. There are an increasing number of examples of negotiation processes that specifically incorporate local participation [31,32]. It seems clear, given the perceived instability and inconstancy of federal policy to date, that negotiations and any agreements that might result from negotiations would require substantial legitimation by various levels and branches of government (e.g., local and state governments as well as Congress *and* the Department of Energy) [33]. Otherwise, the credibility of any agreements would not likely be sufficient to convince local governments and their citizens to accept the facility.

While implementation of these prerequisites would not necessarily lead to positive siting decisions, they should lead to increased confidence at all levels and to the ability to take positive actions regarding the siting decision. If local participation in the siting process leads not only to increased knowledge and understanding of all dimensions of the construction, operation, and decommissioning stages of the repository but also to an awareness of the consequences of possible breakdowns in any of the systems, these prerequisites may well lead to resolute opposition to the facility. Local participation would also lead, however, to an enhanced identification of remaining technical and institutional problems and to potential solutions of these problems, including the possibility of employing relevant incentives.

Incentives for What? A Classification Scheme

Incentives are an integral part of a structured siting process, involving the creation of a mutually acceptable set of arrangements that make certain commitments and confer certain benefits for the acceptance of the proposed facility. It is important to distinguish incentive functions so that one can determine why a particular incentive might be offered, to whom it might be offered, and what institutional and administrative arrangements might be necessary to implement the incentive. Incentives can (1) mitigate anticipated adverse impacts of normal construction and operations through preventive or ameliorative actions, (2) compensate for actual damage due to abnormal or unanticipated events, and/or (3) reward communities for assuming a nonlocal cost or risk. Table 2 defines these types of incentives, identifies a range of options within each type, and provides examples of mechanisms that might be used for implementing the incentive. Table 3 lists some incentive packages currently used in siting other types of facilities.

An incentive might be developed to *mitigate* the risks or other negative impacts that may be anticipated to occur during normal construction and operation of a high level waste facility. This definition of mitigation is drawn from the field of social impact analysis as manifested through the environmental impact statement (EIS) process. It defines mitigation to be those actions taken in anticipation of projected adverse impacts of an intervention [37]. This definition is to be distinguished from that which denotes correction of actual adverse impacts.

Mitigation alone is unlikely to neutralize local opposition to waste facility siting, because it is not possible to predict all risks and costs accurately and completely and thus to eliminate these problems. Mitigation is largely based

TABLE 2
Incentives Classification System

Incentive Type	Brief Functional Definitions	The Range of Possible Strategies	Example of Corresponding Implementation Mechanisms
Mitigation	Actions geared toward preventing, reducing, or eliminating adverse impacts (costs and risks) before they occur	Buffers/land-use management Monitoring/detection Emergency preparedness Safety design Public education	Purchase of easements Establish dosimeter program Develop contingency plans Establish acceptable risk levels Distribute information brochures
Compensation	Payments for actual damages in the event of an accident or anomalous event	Socioeconomic impact mitigation Land value guarantees Trust funds Insurance programs	Develop job-training program Property dedication program Excise taxes on wastes Government-backed policies
Rewards	Actions designed to award benefits to communities assuming risks for which others derive benefits	Assumption of liability Direct monetary payments Bonus community services Tax incentives Subsidies (advance) Infrastructure development Linking Avoidance of other hazardous facilities	Contracts with local governments Payments-in-lieu-of-taxes (PILOTS) CETA-type programs Eliminate sales taxes Reduced interest rates Public works projects Federal appropriations Presidential order

TABLE 3
Incentive Packages Currently Used in Siting Other Types of Facilities

Facility	Types of Incentive Mechanisms	References
Black Thunder Mine, Wright, Wyoming	Building housing Building schools, other community facilities Cash grants State severance tax	34
Electricite de France, France	Price concessions on electricity to nearby residents Train and hire local workers Award significant share of contracts to local firms National company but subject to corporate taxes	11
Trident West Coast Submarine Base, Kitsam County, Washington	Joint planning DOD payments for community assistance Negotiations include public participation Coordinated or fast-track of other federal grants	35
Hazardous Waste Facility Mountain View, California	Very large buffer zones Joint planning	
Basin Electric, Wheatland, Wyoming	Guaranteed school bonds via nonprofit entity Joint planning State severance tax	34
Regional Hazardous Waste Management Facility (proposed), Hookset, New Hampshire	Negotiations currently being used to select incentives	36

on perceptions of the local population, and successful mitigation requires public involvement in determining the buffering, monitoring, and other options needed and in administering these options [38]. For example, monitoring for potential hazards could be utilized to help alleviate local fears or anxieties and to alert people to a problem should it occur. Radiation detectors could provide assurance to people that they were safe and would enable officials to detect potential problems. Given problems of institutional credibility, independent monitoring by the community financed by facility users may be required.

An incentive might also *compensate* for actual damage in the event of an emergency, accident, or other unforeseen anomaly. The traditional view of compensation involves a "make whole" concept or a provision for replacement costs [39]. Some impacts or damages may be compensable in theory but difficult to implement because of the problem of developing a precise compensation scheme [38,40]. Although the legal precedent for requiring compensation for redress of damages appears to be well established [41], implementation of that principle may be jeopardized due to our imperfect understanding of such phenomena as the health effects of chronic, low-level exposure to radiation [42,43].

One compensation measure is a trust fund in which a sum of money could be created with contributions by the government, industry, or both (e.g., Comprehensive Environmental Response, Compensation and Liability Act of 1980—Superfund). This could be a lump sum or a yearly contribution that accrues interest. The fund could be used to compensate people suffering damages should an accident occur or an anomaly be discovered. The processes by which the level of funding is established and by which compensation would be awarded and administered are likely to be complex. Recent proposed legislation in Tennessee, for example, would initiate a fund to be developed through hazardous waste generator fees with payouts constrained by a variety of scientific and institutional qualifications; these qualifications are included to establish the causality of the victim's injury and the effect of other legal remedies (e.g., tort litigation) available to a claimant [44].

Finally, an incentive might be used to *reward* a community for assuming risks and costs in order to meet nonlocal (i.e., national, state, regional, or international) needs. Assisting in solving national problems by assuming additional burdens is not in itself very compelling to local populations [45]. Some local costs and risks are less tangible than those potentially offset by mitigation or compensation and include such things as changes in community character, the stigma presently associated with garbage disposal or "dumping" activities, and residual risks to public health when the benefits are realized on a much broader scale. Rewards must be perceived as positive inducements and not as a form of conscription or being "bought off" on health and safety considerations.

In addition to direct payments, tax incentives, and other specific monetary rewards, reward systems include the linking of repository siting to the acceptance of other more desirable federal projects [39] or the avoidance of other hazardous facility sitings or undesirable land uses [16]. Interstate and regional compacts that distribute hazardous facilities are good examples of how the latter concept can be implemented [3].

Among these types of incentives, compensation and mitigation have been endorsed as useful mechanisms in alleviating many of the direct, quantifiable impacts of facility siting. For example, Resolution 5-4 of the State Planning Council on Radioactive Waste Management (SPC) notes that inasmuch as the federal government has responsibility for developing repositories, it should accept responsibility for socioeconomic impacts resulting from repository development by making payments to affected jurisdictions [3]; the antecedent status quo should be restored through mitigation and compensation. The reward type of incentive, which improves the status of the affected community, has had more limited application by governmental entities in past siting practices, but it is commonly a part of private sector siting agreements. The function of a particular incentive may vary with the situation. For example, some incentive mechanisms (e.g., community services) can be considered as mitigative or compensatory to the point that the preexisting community status is attained, but as rewarding once that status is surpassed.

The interchangeable and often casual use of these terms (i.e., incentive, mitigation, compensation, bonus, reward, and so on) has tended to blur distinctions among them, and some people may view all types of incentives as bribes. Particularly difficult to distinguish is the difference between a reward and a bribe. Whereas a bribe is an illegitimate use of money or favors to influence someone, often with a fiduciary responsibility, a reward is a legitimate benefit received for some worthy behavior or special service. Charges of bribery may result unless the siting prerequisites are satisfied (i.e., unless it is clear that public health, safety and the environment are nonnegotiable rights and that local governments have a meaningful role in the overall siting process). The extent to which negotiations are public and fair to competing interests may be critical to the public's evaluation of the incentive and the acceptability of the repository [46].

Can Incentives Work?

Evidence supporting the potential utility of mitigation, compensation, and reward in siting hazardous facilities or other unwanted land uses, including radioactive waste repositories, is quite limited. In addition to those examples noted in Table 3, for which no systematic data exist, a 1980 telephone survey of 426 randomly selected residents of three rural Wisconsin communities on the acceptability of hosting a nuclear waste repository has been analyzed [47]. Table 4a shows that when people were asked initially about their attitudes toward a waste facility, a substantial majority opposed locating one in their community. But 24 percent changed their initial opposition when they could stipulate various incentives for their communities. Table 4b indicates the incentive packages that induced the attitude shift. It should be noted that two seemingly unrelated items (access to information and power to shut down the facility) were particularly powerful elements of this incentive system.

TABLE 4a

Change in Attitudes Toward Hosting a Nuclear Waste Facility[a]

	Favor *(%)*	*Oppose* *(%)*	*Don't Know/ No Answer (%)*
Without incentives	22	71	7
With incentives	42	47	11
Shift	+20	−24	+4

[a] Respondents were presented with a limited list of possible incentives and were asked if an incentive or combination of incentives would represent a sufficient level of local control over a nuclear waste repository in their community and whether such an incentive(s) would induce them to accept a repository in their community. See Reference 47 for details on data collection.

Whereas the first four elements may be implemented relatively painlessly, implementation of the final element—power to shut down—may prove more problematic in terms of potential intergovernmental conflict and would indicate an area for negotiation.

Despite limits in this survey [47], findings suggest that nonmonetary incentives, such as independent monitoring and access to information, may significantly add to public acceptance of radioactive waste repositories. More-

TABLE 4b

Incentive Package(s) Influencing a Shift in Pro-siting Attitudes[a]

Incentive Package	*Percent Favoring a Repository In Their Community (%)*
No incentives	22
Substantial payments to your community	26
plus access to information	31
plus independent monitoring	34
plus representation on a governing board	36
plus power to shut down	41
plus other provisions	42

N = 77 (number of those within total sample of 420 who changed their position as various incentives were introduced)

[a] Incentives were offered additively. That is, people were asked if substantial payments to the community would be sufficient to accept a repository. If they replied in the negative, they were then asked if payments *and* information would be sufficient. The interviewer continued down the list until a cumulative package evoked an affirmative response, or the list was exhausted. The incentives were ordered to reflect what was judged to be an increasing level of community control. The results do not allow an assessment of the relative strength of each incentive proposed as a single mechanism. See Reference 47 for details on data collection.

over, results help confirm that packages of incentives may be of greater utility than single incentives, especially if they include measures that greatly increase community control of the facility. Finally, whereas a 20 percentage point shift in the acceptability of a repository appears to be significant, it does not produce a majority (much less a consensus) favoring the repository; in a *real-world* application of a potentially broader range of incentives, this shift might be much less or much greater. The determinants of such a shift can be analyzed only through a thorough evaluation of the incentive system in the context of a potential host community.

Evaluating Incentives

The different types of incentives previously identified are mechanisms that *may* aid in securing local acceptance of a high level waste repository. Given the diversity of possible incentives and the absence of relevant experience to assess their feasibility, we have developed a conceptual framework for evaluating their usefulness in high level waste repository siting. This framework builds upon the siting prerequisites previously noted and includes three sets of criteria that may be used to examine the advantages and disadvantages of particular incentives or sets of incentives. Although these criteria may at first glance be conceptually distinct, we suspect that there is substantial multicollinearity among many of the criteria. This could especially be the case depending upon the varying perspectives of evaluators (e.g., federal, state, and local governments) and the alternative rankings or weightings they may give the criteria. Figure 1 presents a simplified version of this framework, with the criteria appropriately grouped.

DESCRIPTIVE CHARACTERISTICS

Descriptive characteristics of an incentive include certainty, constancy, adequacy, and ease of administration. Certainty is defined as the likelihood that an incentive will be implemented as agreed. The confidence of a community that it will receive the incentive and its confidence in the sponsor's overall plan will be significant issues in the siting process. For instance, an incentive that provided a funding mechanism resistant to the vicissitudes of the budgetary process would assure communities that funds would be available to protect their interests over long periods of time. Several states (including Massachusetts, Michigan, Ohio, Pennsylvania, and Tennessee) have specified such guarantees in legislation dealing with the related problem of hazardous waste management [32]. The Price-Anderson Act and the Comprehensive Environmental Response, Compensation, and Liability Act of 1980 (Superfund) represent relevant federal counterparts.

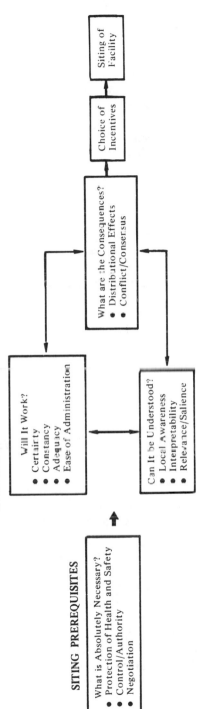

FIGURE 1. A framework for evaluating the utility of incentives for high level waste (HLW) repository siting.

As noted earlier, inconstancy in federal nuclear waste management policy has exacerbated the problem of public acceptance. The extent to which future policy and any incentives can ameliorate this condition is important in increasing the acceptability of federal policy generally and a repository site in particular. For instance, a system structured to guarantee delivery of the incentives, regardless of changes in the identity of the site, would reward the community for its initial acceptance of the repository; if the original site is kept, failure to deliver the incentive could result in a shutdown of the repository, forcing the selection of an alternative site(s). Measures to assure the locals of policy and program constancy would surely be a substantial topic to be negotiated during the siting process. As an evaluative criterion, constancy also connotes the steady availability of the incentive over time and is important with respect to temporal equity issues in radioactive waste disposal. Incentives supplied continuously would provide a stream of benefits to current and future community residents, whereas one-time disbursements (e.g., block grants) may favor the current generation.

Adequacy refers to the degree to which an incentive is large enough *or* sufficiently comprehensive to make the repository acceptable to a community. In view of the different functions incentives are designed to fulfill, adequacy may have a number of different dimensions or meanings: Is the potential compensation or reward high enough? Is the level of safety provided by the incentive system adequate? Are all likely risks addressed by the incentive system? Does the type of incentive chosen match the perceived need? People's perceptions of adequacy are highly variable, rendering a priori measurement of adequacy impossible. The *process,* then, by which this determination is made is critical in evaluating the incentive and involves the siting prerequisites previously noted.

Ease of administration has a variety of dimensions, including: (1) organizational requirements [48,49]; (2) the extent of bureaucratic interaction; (3) the degree of complexity of renegotiations [8]; and (4) the administrative costs of implementing the incentive [8]. For instance, under Point 1 above, state governments may need to pass or amend enabling legislation for local governments; local governments may have to invent new organizations and procedures for the development, negotiation, and operation of the incentive system; and implementation of the incentive may require the recruitment and/ or training of appropriate personnel and the provision of sufficient fiscal resources over long periods of time to ensure continuous operation of the incentive (and the facility). Each of these factors can alter significantly the ease and costs of incentive administration as well as the acceptability of the facility and related incentives. Simple, inexpensive administrative procedures are preferred, unless they negatively impact other important criteria.

LOCAL PERCEPTION OF INCENTIVES

It is equally important to assess how members of the potential host community would perceive and understand the incentives. The extent of local awareness of the facility and knowledge of its operational requirements, the ability locally to differentiate the purposes of the incentives and how they are to be implemented, and the relevance of the incentives to the needs perceived by the community are fundamental determinants as to whether the incentives will actually succeed in their purposes of reducing local opposition and developing support for siting the repository.

It is virtually certain that local residents will be aware of a proposed repository. Knowledge of its operational requirements, however, may overshadow awareness of a proposed incentive or any influence the incentive might have in shaping public support for or opposition to the facility. It is therefore important to consider both the repository and its associated incentive system as elements of a single package, so that public consideration and discussion of the possibility of participating in a siting process do not emphasize one over the other.

The interpretability of a given incentive refers to the availability to community residents of clear, credible information about the purpose and structure of the incentive and its proposed implementation. Interpretation of the function to be served by an incentive is not necessarily straightforward and may be partly a function of different statuses and modes and levels of participation among citizens. Some residents might interpret the offering of any incentive as an indication that the facility involves a greater risk than its developers have led them to believe, whereas others may be unable or unwilling to distinguish between the purposes of various legitimate incentives and perceive all incentives as bribes. Some very rational people may simply be confused by the whole problem. These kinds of responses may be less a reaction to *what* is being proposed than to *how* it is proposed, e.g., an incentive may be more likely to be interpreted as a bribe when the incentives proposal is initiated by facility sponsors than when developed as a reaction to a community's request [50]. The more the public understands an incentive's function (i.e., mitigation, compensation, or reward), the more likely the incentive will be capable of contributing to a focusing of community attitudes.

Finally, it is important that an incentive be relevant to the needs and concerns of community residents. Does the incentive address the risks and costs believed by community residents to be associated with the facility? If an incentive is viewed as addressing local concerns associated with a repository, the incentive may be more favorably viewed by the public and less likely to be viewed as a bribe. It is important that the range of relevant issues be identified by local interests and not be circumscribed by outside technical experts.

INCENTIVE CONSEQUENCES

The potential consequences of an incentive can be analyzed by assessing its distributional effects and its propensity to effect community conflict or consensus. We suggest that these effects are partly a function of other characteristics of the incentive and partly a function of the community's existing demographic, cultural, normative, social, political, and economic structure.

Distributional effects refer to how the benefits, costs, and risks of a repository are received or borne by different individuals and/or groups in the community and beyond. In simple terms, who benefits, who pays, and how do these effects accrue over time? The distributional effects of alternative incentives (i.e., mitigation, compensation, and reward) are likely to vary. Unless substantial care is taken in the design and implementation of incentives, their allocation among community residents may not be proportional to the differential costs and risks they would be expected to bear. For instance, some incentives may need to be distributed to residents adjacent to the repository, whereas others might be distributed more evenly to all members of the community. Development of an equitable distribution of incentives is likely to be an extremely complex and politically charged task. Its implementation would involve minimally an identification of risk takers and cost bearers over time, an assessment of their risks and costs, development of an incentive system responsive to varying risks and costs, and creation of implementation mechanisms assuring delivery of offsetting or rewarding benefits [47]. In the latter case, for example, efforts can be taken to assure equal access to the courts in the case of insurance schemes (i.e., compensation) through the establishment and maintenance of legal resources to protect the interests of the poor, those normally unable to use fully the judicial system in their own interest.

It can be expected that the siting of any hazardous facility will generate conflict and opposition [40,51]. It is conceivable that some siting incentives may generate conflict in the potential host community in addition to that generated by the proposal to site the facility itself. For example, if some residents perceive that the incentive is offered as a means of diverting their concern and attention away from the impacts of the facility, the incentive may exacerbate local opposition to the facility. However, the possibility of conflict due to a proposed facility and incentives should not obscure the significant role an incentive approach can have in developing community consensus supporting the siting of a repository. Such a consensus will likely have to address a number of diverse concerns regarding the repository. In the case of the

Wisconsin survey, increased support was predicated upon a multidimensional incentive system (e.g., transfer payments, access to information, and participation in repository operation). What appears to be critically important is creating the opportunity for all interested parties to be represented in siting and incentive design and implementation negotiations. In this way divergent attitudes and the reasons for those attitudes can be discovered, and the community can determine what package of benefits, if any, would be necessary to develop a consensus in favor of a repository.

Findings

Given the social and institutional background of nuclear waste siting, it is clear that alternative strategies focusing on public acceptance are needed. The purpose of an overall siting strategy would be the creation of a mutually acceptable set of arrangements that make certain guarantees and confer certain benefits in exchange for the acceptance of a proposed facility.

It is argued that this strategy should include three basic, nonnegotiable principles or prerequisites: protection of public health, safety, and the environment; a meaningful role for affected local governments in the siting process; and a recognition of negotiation or bargaining as an appropriate if not overriding element in the decision-making process. These principles are not novel; they derive from the underlying precepts of American federalism and pluralism and correspond to what is normally expected in the political process.

What is to be negotiated is the set of conditions under which a repository might be sited within or adjacent to a community, and these conditions have been characterized in terms of a balancing of actual and perceived benefits, costs, and risks associated with nuclear waste disposal. The unwillingness, to date, of communities to accept a waste repository indicates that this balance has not been achieved and that additional benefits are needed to strike that balance. Incentives, broadly defined and considered, have been suggested as potentially appropriate increments to normal benefit structures. Moreover, we have suggested that in addition to restoring a community to its preexisting status through the use of mitigation measures and guaranteeing such a status in the future through a compensation scheme, a community may be rewarded (i.e., be made better off) for its assistance in helping to resolve a serious national problem. Our categorization of incentives has been offered as a means of clarifying future debate on the possible use of incentives in siting dilemmas.

Although there is only limited and, for the most part, anecdotal evidence regarding the potential usefulness of incentives in siting locally unwanted land uses, the feasibility of future applications of incentives might be guided by attention to certain evaluative criteria. These criteria characterize incentives in terms of descriptive features (i.e., certainty, constancy, adequacy, and ease of administration), local perceptions of incentives (i.e., awareness, interpretability, and relevance), and the likely consequences of implementing incentives (i.e., distributional effects and sociopolitical conflict or consensus). It is not possible to prescribe appropriate values for these criteria a priori; it is possible, however, to anticipate alternative valuations from competing interests or stakeholders in the siting process. A siting strategy conforming to the prerequisites we have identified would allow for, but would not guarantee, negotiation of a mutually acceptable valuation of the benefits, costs, and risks of hosting a nuclear waste repository.

Conclusions and Policy Implications

The possibility that an incentive may have consequences contrary to its stated purpose means simply that, however attractive incentives may appear to be on the surface in helping to resolve the social and institutional problems of high level waste siting, they should not be adopted and applied without prudent analyses. These analyses can be approached in a variety of ways, but given the significance of local community acceptance of the repository, it appears essential that siting *and* incentives be assessed from a community perspective. The Nuclear Waste Policy Act of 1982 recognizes that "state and public participation in the planning and development of repositories is essential in order to promote public confidence" in the safety of disposal of radioactive waste and spent fuel [52]. The usefulness of the proposed approach may be judged most effectively by members of a potential host community. It may be fruitful to encourage community self-examination of the costs, risks, and benefits of repositories and prospective incentives. These independent assessments have been suggested by various parties [31,53], and potential models are available [32,54]. Application of an approach composed of meaningful community participation in repository siting and incentive design and implementation processes would help to corroborate or reject the approach offered here and would allow for relevant evaluations of the costs, risks, and benefits of high level waste repositories in a real-world setting. In addition, it would be possible to verify further the propositions that a package of incentives containing more than monetary payments is more responsive to local concerns than a unidimensional incentive and that inter- and intracommunity variation in perceived costs and risks dictate the composition of a multidimensional incentive package.

This approach, which focuses upon including the potential host community as a full partner in the siting process, appears to offer a means of resolving an important national problem. It may also be useful in addressing the siting of other "locally unwanted land uses" [5,6] and undesirable activities (e.g., chemical hazardous waste disposal facilities). It should be acknowledged that an incentive-based program is not a device that would supplant technological or other social considerations in the siting process. Instead, incentives are a means of helping to achieve the best possible technical solution, one which might not otherwise be implemented because of social and political constraints.

There are a number of potential problems, however, that should be acknowledged before testing this approach [47]. Full community participation would necessarily expand the political arena of the siting process. However, this arena already includes participants who have effectively vetoed siting of high level waste and other hazardous facilities time after time [47]. In the past this participation has been in a reactive mode; legitimation of community participation would give potential host communities an opportunity to participate in a positive manner.

We have not addressed the formidable problem of defining the zone of impact of a high level waste repository. This definition can be facilitated by future empirical research, but it is *essentially* a political definition that permeates the siting of virtually all hazardous facilities. Whether and how residents of communities adjacent to the host community or along the transport route should participate in the siting process and benefit from incentives are, perhaps, among the most difficult of the research and policy questions to be deliberated in the coming years.

Balancing the local and national burdens and benefits of high level waste repositories is but one of an array of equity issues in an industrialized society. It is not possible to understand and internalize all costs and risks and make appropriate allocations of benefits for each and every risky venture upon which society embarks. It seems clear, however, that for high risk ventures with few site options the need for incentives may be extensive.

References

We thank Drs. E. A. Hirst, R. B. Garey, R. B. Honea, R. B. Braid, T. J. Wilbanks, R. M. Davis, D. C. Parzyck, W. Fulkerson, and four anonymous reviewers for their critical review of a prior draft of this article. This article is based on a report prepared for the Office of Nuclear Waste Isolation, Battelle, Columbus, Ohio, and the U.S. Department of Energy, under Contract W-7405-eng-26 with the Union Carbide Corporation.

1. Roger E. Kasperson. 1980. Institutional and Social Uncertainties in the Timely Management of Radioactive Wastes. Testimony Prepared for the California Energy Commission for the Nuclear Regulatory Commission Disposal Rulemaking on the Storage and Disposal of Nuclear Waste, June 30.
2. Report to the President by the Interagency Review Group on Nuclear Waste Management TID-29442, Washington, D.C., March 1979.

3. State Planning Council on Radioactive Waste Management. 1981. Interim Report to President. February 24.
4. Todd R. LaPorte. 1978. Nuclear Waste: Increasing Scale and Sociopolitical Impacts. *Science,* 201 (July 7): 22-28.
5. J. H. Sorensen. 1982. Sweet for the Sour: Incentives for Siting Noxious Facilities. Paper presented at the 78th Annual Meeting of the Association of American Geographers, San Antonio, Texas, April 25-28.
6. F. Popper, Siting LULU's. 1981. *Planning,* 1 (April): 12-15.
7. Chauncey Starr. 1980. Risk Criteria for Nuclear Power Plants: A Pragmatic Proposal. Paper presented at the ANS/ENS International Conference, Washington, D.C., November 16-21.
8. David J. Bjornstad and Ernest Goss. 1981. Measuring the Impacts of Using Payments in Lieu of Taxes to Compensate Communities When Siting High-Level Nuclear Waste Isolation Facilities. Oak Ridge, Tenn.: Oak Ridge National Laboratory, draft.
9. Daniel Kevin. 1980. *Federal/State Relations in Radioactive Waste Management Oceans Programs.* Office of Technology Assessment, U.S. Congress Draft, December.
10. David B. Goetze. 1981. Resources for the Future, personal communication.
11. Remy Carle. 1981. Why France Went Nuclear. Public Power, pp. 58-60, 82, 85 (July-August).
12. R. Kasperson. 1980. The Darkside of the Radioactive Waste Program. In *Progress in Resource Management and Environmental Planning,* Volume 2, T. O'Riordan and R. Turner, ed., Chichester, New York: John Wiley & Sons.
13. Nancy E. Abrams and Joel R. Primack. 1980. Helping the Public Decide: The Case of Radioactive Waste Management. *Environment,* 22 (April): 14-20, 39-40.
14. Richard Ausness. 1979. High-Level Radioactive Waste Management: The Nuclear Dilemma. *Wisconsin Law Review,* No. 3: 707-767.
15. C. Hohenemser, R. Kasperson, and R. Kates. 1976. The Distrust of Nuclear Power. *Science,* pp. 25-34.
16. Current plans of the National Waste Terminal Storage Program call for exploratory shafts at three sites, two of which are located on federal reservations. See Suzanne I. Gray, *Framework for Community Planning Associated with Nuclear Waste Repository Siting,* ONWI-254. Columbus, Ohio: Office of Nuclear Waste Isolation, 1981.
17. U. S. Department of Energy. 1980. *Nuclear Waste Management Program.* Summary Document DOE/NE-008, Washington, D.C., Assistant Secretary for Nuclear Energy.
18. Kai N. Lee. 1980. A Federalist Strategy for Nuclear Waste Management. *Science,* 208 (May 16): 679-684.
19. Fred C. Shapiro. 1981. A Reporter at Large—Nuclear Waste. New Yorker (October 19).
20. State Planning Council on Radioactive Waste Management. 1981 *Recommendations on National Radioactive Waste Management Policies: Report to the President.* Washington, D.C.: State Planning Council, August 31.
21. Dillon's Rule, an axiom of the American federalist system which asserts that municipal governments are "creatures" of the state and that the extent of

municipal authority is determined by the state, might preempt a local role. See Robert L. Lineberry and Ira Sharkansky, *Urban Politics and Public Policy,* New York: Harper and Row, 1971, p. 113. In fact, however, the political reality of radioactive waste repository siting may be such that state preemption of local authority is not likely.

22. S. M. Lipset and W. Scheider. 1978. How's Business: What the Public Thinks. Public Opinion, 1:3.

23. S. A. Carnes, E. D. Copenhaver, et al. 1980. *Impacts of the Resource Conservation and Recovery Act on Energy Supply,* ORNL/OIAPA-15. Oak Ridge, Tenn.: Oak Ridge National Laboratory, October.

24. R. Reiser, H. Schilling, R. Smith, and J. Mountain, ed. 1980. *Consultation and Concurrence Workshop Proceedings, The Orcas Meeting.* East Sound, Washington, September 23-26, 1979, ONWI-87, Office of Nuclear Waste Isolation, Battelle Memorial Institute.

25. Randy Smith. 1980. Cooperative Federalism: A Reality for Successful Intergovernmental Accomplishment. In *Consultation and Concurrence Workshop Proceedings, The Orcas Meeting,* R. Reiser, H. Schilling, R. Smith, and J. Mountain, ed. East Sound, Washington, September 23-26, 1979, ONWI-87, Office of Nuclear Waste Isolation, Battelle Memorial Institute.

26. Terry N. Clark, ed. 1968. *Community Structure and Decision Making: Comparative Analyses.* San Francisco: Chandler.

27. Charles M. Bonjean, Terry N. Clark, and Robert J. Lineberry, ed. 1971. *Community Politics.* New York: Free Press.

28. Jane Hershberger. 1980. *A Comparative Assessment of Repository Siting Models with Respect to Intergovernmental and Public Relations,* IGS/RW-003. Berkeley, California: Institute of Governmental Studies, University of California

29. Lawrence Susskind. 1980. Citizen Participation in the Siting of Hazardous Waste Facilities: Options and Observations. Draft prepared for the National Governors' Association Sub-Committee on the Environment, November.

30. One example is the remarkable 1980 Hudson River Agreement which resolved numerous long-standing and seemingly intractable environmental and siting issues through mediated negotiations. See: Truman Temple. 1981. Peace at Storm King. *EPA Journal,* pp. 28-30, 37 (February).

31. National Governors' Association (NGA). 1981. *Siting Hazardous Waste Facilities.* Final Report of the NGA Committee, March.

32. National Conference of State Legislatures. *Compilation and Review of State Hazardous Waste Disposal Legislation* (unpublished).

33. E. Copenhaver, S. Carnes, J. Sorensen, E. Soderstrom, J. Reed, E. Peelle, and D. Bjornstad. Framework for Evaluating the Utility of Incentive Systems for Radioactive Waste Repository Siting. In *Advances in the Science and Technology of the Management of High-Level Nuclear Waste,* Peter L. Hofman, ed. Columbus, Ohio: Office of Nuclear Waste Isolation (forthcoming).

34. W. E. Blundell. 1981. Firms Seek to Avert Boomtown Problems by Providing Services. The Wall Street Journal, August 12.

35. Economic Adjustment Committee. *Preliminary Report, Community Impact Assistance Study.* 1980. Intergovernmental/Interagency Task Force on

Community Impact Assistance, President's Economic Adjustment Committee, February.

36. Peter Clark and Julia Wondolleck. 1980. Handbooks for Siting Hazardous Waste Management Facilities in New England. *Environmental Impact Assessment Review,* 1(3): 319-323.

37. For example, see U. S. Department of Energy, *Final Environmental Impact Statement Solvent Refined Coal—I Newman, Daviess County, Kentucky* DOE/ EIS-0073. Washington, D.C.: July 1981, pp. 4-161-163.

38. Lawrence S. Bacow. 1980. Mitigation, Compensation, Incentives and Preemption. Prepared for meeting, National Governors' Association Subcommittee on Environment, November 10.

39. William A. O'Connor. 1980. Incentives for the Construction of Low Level Nuclear Waste Facilities. In National Governors' Association (NGA), *Low-Level Waste: A Program for Action Appendix II,* Final Report of the NGA Task Force on Low-Level Radioactive Waste Disposal, Washington, D.C., November.

40. Michael O'Hare. 1977. Not on my Block You Don't: Facility Siting and the Strategic Importance of Compensation. *Public Policy,* 25: 407-458.

41. Robert McMahon, Cindy Ernst, Ray Miyares, and Curtis Haymore. 1981. *Using Compensation and Incentives When Siting Hazardous Waste Management Facilities: A Handbook,* SW 942. Washington, D.C.: U.S. Environmental Protection Agency.

42. National Academy of Sciences. 1980. *The Effects on Populations of Exposure to Low Levels of Ionizing Radiation* (BEIR III Report). Washington, D.C.: National Academy of Sciences Press.

43. United Nations Scientific Committee on the Effects of Atomic Radiation. 1977. *Sources and Effects of Ionizing Radiations.* New York: United Nations.

44. Gillock, Senate bill 1801, Tennessee State Senate, 1982.

45. Robert D. Brenner, 1980. *The Social, Economic, and Political Impacts of National Waste Terminal Storage Repositories,* ONWI/SUB/78/E512-01200-1. Center of International Studies, Princeton University, January.

46. Curtis Haymore. 1981. Disposal Costs, Financing Options. Paper presented at *Hazardous Waste Disposal: How, Where,—And at What Cost,* sponsored by Inside E.P.A. Weekly Report, Washington, D.C., June 18-19.

47. S. Carnes, E. Copenhaver, J. Reed, E. Soderstrom, J. Sorensen, E. Peelle, and D. Bjornstad. 1982. *Incentives and the Siting of Radioactive Waste Facilities* ORNL/5880. Oak Ridge, Tenn.: Oak Ridge National Laboratory, June.

48. Elizabeth Peelle, 1980. Testimony on *The Socioeconomic Effects of a Nuclear Waste Storage Site on Rural Areas and Small Communities.* Hearing before the House Subcommittee on Rural Development, Senate Committee on Agriculture, Nutrition, and Forestry, August 26. Washington, D.C.: U.S. Government Printing Office.

49. Gene I. Rochlin. 1980. *The Role of Participatory Impact Assessment in Radioactive Waste Management Program Activities.* Berkeley, CA: Institute of Governmental Studies, University of California, Berkeley, Report IGS/RW-002 (Draft) August.

50. Paul Rankin, National Solid Waste Management Association, Washington, D.C., personal communication on June 23, 1981.

51. U.S. Environmental Protection Agency. 1975. *Siting of Hazardous Waste Management Facilities and Public Opposition*, SW 809. Washington, D.C.: Office of Water and Waste Management, November. (Prepared by Centaur Associates).
52. Section 111 (a)(6), Nuclear Waste Policy Act of 1982 (P. L. 97-425).
53. Kathy Painter, National Wildlife Federation, Washington, D.C., personal communication on June 23, 1981.
54. Sam A. Carnes, Martin Schweitzer, and Benson H. Bronfman. 1982. Community-Based Assessment and Planning of Energy Futures: Final Report of the Decentralized Solar Energy Technology Assessment Program, ORNL/Report 5879. Oak Ridge, Tenn.: Oak Ridge National Laboratory, June.

MICHAEL O'HARE AND DEBRA R. SANDERSON

20 *Fair Compensation and the Boomtown Problem*

Rapid development of energy facilities in small communities imposes social costs on local populations while serving nationwide interests. The social pathologies arising from construction of energy facilities in rural locations have created an "energy boomtown problem" that has been widely recognized.[1] Both proposed and current solutions to the problem include prevention of localized costs brought about by better facility siting practices[2] and state or federal planning assistance for localities.[3] Other solutions seek to assist localities by improving their ability to raise revenue through existing means; for example, state enabling legislation might be changed to increase the local share of sales tax revenue and ease local borrowing restrictions.[4] Another class of solutions to the energy boomtown problem compensates communities for the costs imposed on them by energy development.[5]

In this article, the general "boomtown problem" and current compensation schemes are considered, and the appropriateness of subsidy schemes is analyzed on theoretical grounds. This analysis suggests that the effect of these subsidies as usually designed is to reward people who are not in fact injured by the development, and miss many of those who deserve aid. The misdirection is a result of carelessly identifying a community with the people who live in it at a particular time. An appropriate compensation plan requires that the affected groups of people be more carefully described. While the discussion

Reprinted with permission from *Urban Law Annual* (now *Washington University Journal of Urban and Contemporary Law*), Vol. 14 (1977), pp. 101-133.

that follows considers the problem specifically in the context of boomtown compensation programs, the analytical approach can be generalized to other geographically related programs.

The Energy Development Boomtown Problem

At first glance, the construction and operation of an energy extraction or conversion facility[6] in a rural location do not suggest a need for subsidies to the affected community. Economic development, of which an energy facility provides a dose enormous both absolutely and relatively, is something communities usually seek out and encourage. Offsetting these expected and realized benefits from energy development, however, are costs imposed on the localities that host either the developments or the newcomers needed to support them. In fact, it has been widely accepted that the rate of development in the "typical" boomtown is so great, and the changes in the quality of life it brings are so drastic, that accepted social indicators, such as employment stability, divorce rates, alcoholism and crime, are likely to record real pathologies: life in the boomtown is worse than it was in the village that preceded it.[7] Field interviews in several western states and the literature on boomtowns reveal several types of problems.

1. *Social Disruption.* Sudden changes in the nature of a community impose a new social structure on the old one and cause social conflict. Rates of alcoholism, drug abuse, mental illness, divorce and juvenile delinquency increase.[8] The Gillette, Wyoming divorce rate is now twice that found in the surrounding county.[9] Children have low achievement levels and increased truancy; assaults increase.[10] Rock Springs' Mental Health Center had a ninefold increase in cases when population approximately doubled between 1970 and 1975.[11] The Center reports that most of its new cases are long time residents having difficulty managing drastic changes caused by the large population influx.[12] They are more likely than the newcomers to become alcoholic or suffer from mental illness.[13]

2. *Inadequacy of Public Services.* Public services, especially those constrained by the size and condition of capital goods, often falter under the pressure of rapid population growth accompanying energy development. Prior to the energy boom, facilities may have been barely adequate—perhaps in poor condition or operating at capacity for a small population. A rapid influx of people requires service expansion and improvement or the addition of previously nonexistent services, but few boomtown areas are forewarned about

coming developments or the need to enhance their fiscal capacity. A variety of examples can be found:

> Eight out of ten water wells in one oil boomtown go dry because of increased water consumption;[14]
>
> Two Texas boomtowns discharge almost raw sewage because of over-loaded treatment plants;[15]
>
> A kindergarten meets in a condemned building because of a shortage of space;[16]
>
> County protective officers, facing increased countywide demands, reduce previous city coverage and force several small towns to create municipal police forces;[17]
>
> A Texas coal boomtown must more than double its number of firemen and almost double the amount of its firefighting equipment and facilities in order to remove a State Insurance Board penalty (based on the city's lowered firemen/population ratio) and to provide expected services.[18]

3. *Shortage of Private Goods and Services.* During a boom, the private market rarely keeps pace with the demand for goods and services, especially housing. In some cases, housing shortages can restrict energy development: one hundred families recently found no housing when transferred to an oil boomtown and had to be transferred back to their previous positions.[19]

4. *Inflation.* Excess demand triggers inflation in prices, wages and rents. While price increases are welcomed by the storeowner whose costs usually do not rise as quickly as revenues, and increased housing prices are a blessing to the landlord, inflation is particularly harmful to the senior citizen and others on fixed incomes who cannot take advantage of rising wages. High construction wages, combined with a general labor shortage, cause other wages to rise. This can hurt the agricultural economy (though agricultural workers benefit from higher wages if their employers don't go out of business).

   Increased costs can also affect provision of local public services. Two boomtowns[20] had to increase salaries by 40% in order to hold experienced employees. Increased costs for building materials raise municipal costs just when public facilities need to be expanded.[21]

5. *Revenue Shortfalls.* Even though growth expands sales and property tax bases, revenues increase more slowly than costs in the short run. Despite a 19% increase in sales tax revenue, Mt. Pleasant, Texas, a coal boomtown, has already increased property tax rates several

times.[22] Even with a 68% increase in its local sales tax revenue, Pearsall, Texas, an oil boomtown, finds itself short of operating funds.[23] These revenue shortfalls are due to (i) delays between the time development begins and the time the locality realizes either property or sales tax revenue; (ii) delays in raising capital for constructing and improving public facilities; (iii) capital needs beyond local government's legal bonding capacity; (iv) location of high-tax-yielding properties outside the communities hosting the newcomers and the resulting public costs.

6. *Resources Lost to Other Uses.* Industry and its workers are notably consumptive of three resources needed by the agricultural economy: water, land and labor. As new industries use efficient collection techniques and cities exercise eminent domain over water rights, less is available for agriculture. In the energy development regions of some states, groundwater use is unregulated by state permits.[24] Increased consumption by energy development may mean water shortages for cities and agricultural producers drawing from the same aquifer.

   Easily irrigated land near stream beds is particularly valuable to agriculture but it is also valuable to energy developers because, for example, coal is nearer the surface.[25] Strip-mining reduces agricultural output by removing land from production for at least ten years. Food processing industries fail in oil boomtowns because agricultural producers face a shortage of inexpensive labor, created by high drilling salaries that attract unskilled and semi-skilled farm workers.[26]

7. *Aesthetic Deterioration.* Boomtown development sacrifices amenity to economy and ease of construction. Trailer courts are laid out without paving or landscaping. Commercial establishments are built of sheet metal and often located in unsightly strips along major roads. Many residents consider aesthetic deterioration a problem, particularly if they considered the area attractive before the boom. Part of the aesthetic problem is caused by the size of new developments: many new neighborhoods, in which trees and shrubs have not had a chance to grow, look barren and dwarf established parts of town.

8. *Fundamental Change.* An important cost of boomtown development has nothing to do with conventional indicators of stress or inadequacy, since it results from change itself rather than what the town changes to. The original residents of a boomtown chose their community, or chose to remain, because it was the best place for them, or at least the best they could afford. When development occurs, the appearance, social structure, friendship patterns, style of life and

nearly everything else about their community changes. The community that supported them simply disappears. The injury such disappearance causes is only partly mitigated if the "new" town is clean and orderly; transporting an Eskimo to New York is only slightly less stressful if he is taken to Park Avenue rather than Harlem.

THE RATIONALE FOR DIRECT ASSISTANCE

Some boomtown costs can be prevented through better company or community planning. An alternate facility site may destroy less farmland; a new technology may require less water for processing coal; a town with excess public facility capacity could absorb a population increase without strain. But even the best planned and operated facility will force costly changes upon the surrounding communities. Preventing these costs may be unavoidable, impractical, or too expensive, that is, exceeding the cost of suffering. For example, the cost of preventing social costs to old-timers by building a whole new town for immigrants would probably exceed the benefits obtained. In these cases tolerating the costs rather than preventing them may be efficient.

Unfortunately, these costly changes often take place in energy boomtowns without compensation. The resulting decrease in the quality of life suggests that citizens of the community are bearing an unfair share of the costs of providing energy to ultimate consumers. "Costs" in this sense may be monetary, as is the case when taxes increase following construction of the facility, but they may take many other forms including damage to the natural environment, increases in the crime rate, or a change in the community's social structure due to a large influx of construction workers and their families.[27]

It is important to note at this point that not all boomtown costs are best reduced by compensation or subsidy. Some result from what an economist would call market failure, and are, or should be, dealt with by programs which involve no direct transfers of funds. For example, the inability of developing communities to finance newly needed capital facilities like sewage treatment plants or schools, or housing, often results (i) from state limitations on local borrowing, and (ii) from federal limits on lending interest rates. These limitations impede the functioning of a free capital market. Without these constraints, economic theory shows that towns or builders could borrow the right amount of funds at an efficient interest rate (one which reflects the real risks of the loan or bonds). If the market failure produced by these constraints becomes more costly than other problems they present, then the appropriate boomtown relief strategy is to relax them.[28]

A wide variety of boomtown relief programs are fundamentally concerned with correcting market failures. Typical of these are state loans to local communities, planning services, bonding limit extensions and better state planning.[29] Programs of this kind are separable, both conceptually and in fact, from subsidies that transfer resources to boomtowns or their residents, and the remainder of this article will have almost nothing to say about them. In general, we think anything a government can do to make the market in energy development work efficiently is probably a good idea and programs of this kind are, if anything, under-appreciated. In the discussion that follows, however, our concern will be with programs that transfer money or services to boomtowns.

Assuming that boomtown development is made as efficient and equitable as possible by introduction of programs to correct market failures, what theoretical basis underlies transfer programs? The decision to mine coal or convert it into electricity involves a comparison of the costs involved (bulldozers, labor, insurance, land acquisition, etc.) with the benefits (sales, for the most part). If some of the costs are ignored, too much coal will be mined or burned—it will appear "cheaper" than it really is. Thus efficiency requires that decision-makers consider the costs of their energy development including the cost of inputs like small-town amenity which they consume in the production process.[30] The obvious way to ensure that these costs are considered is to make energy developers pay for them, and then pass them on to consumers in the form of higher prices.

However, efficiency does not always require that the sufferers be paid.[31] Rather, in most cases, payment may be justified by the equity principle that people should be compensated when they suffer private loss for the public gain.[32] Our collective desire for coal does not justify confiscation of the amenity of a small-town inhabitant. In summary, since the energy development is providing economic and other benefits, such as furthering energy independence, on a national or at least statewide scale, and since the price energy consumers pay should reflect all costs of production, equity and efficiency suggest that the beneficiaries of the development compensate the losers (the community) for their associated costs.

EXISTING BOOMTOWN PROGRAMS

To put present compensation schemes in context, important flows of funds, some of which are zero under present policy, are displayed in Figure 1. In this diagram, resources from the different, but not exclusive population groups are transferred through the developers and the different government units to various recipients. Each population pays taxes (T_n, T_s, T_c) to its appropriate level of government. Federal and state governments spend some of these dollars and transfer a portion to lower levels of government (A_{fs}, A_{sc}, A_{fc}). These transfer payments are designed to increase the recipient's ability to provide certain goods and services deemed important by the giver.

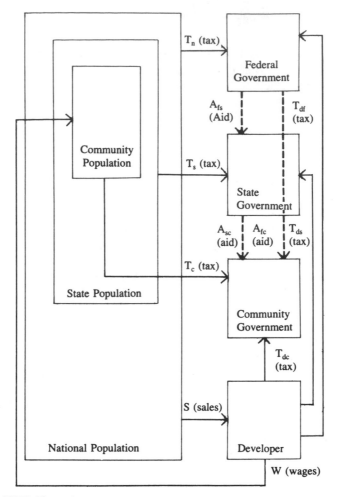

KEY: Figure 1

T_n = Federal government revenues from income tax, mineral lease revenues

T_s = State government revenues from sales taxes, property taxes, mineral lease revenues, possibly income taxes

T_c = Community government revenues from sales taxes, property taxes, user fees

S = Developers' sales of energy resources to consumers nation-wide

T_{df} = Federal taxes and payments required of developers

T_{ds} = State taxes and payments required of developers, such as severance taxes, conversion taxes, corporate income taxes, permit fees

T_{dc} = Community taxes and payments required of developers, such as property taxes, building permit fees, sales taxes

A_{fs} = Federal transfer payments to states

A_{sc} = State transfer payments to local communities

A_{fc} = Federal transfer payments directly to local communities

W = Developer's costs of doing business (including wages, capital costs, and land costs) exclusive of payments to governments.

FIGURE 1. Compensation Types

The governments also receive revenue from energy developers (T_{df}, T_{ds}, T_{dc}) who buy labor with wages (W) and receive revenue through sales to the national population (S).

Local communities usually shoulder much of the responsibility for pro viding public services. In cases of normal population growth, local communities can provide these services since their revenues (T_{dc}, T_c, A_{sc}, A_{fc}) expand at approximately the same rate as expenses. However, in cases of rapid energy development, service needs expand much faster than the local revenues. When energy facilities are outside a community's boundary it receives no direct benefits at all from the development ($T_{dc} = 0$). Community tax revenues (T_c) generally lag population growth.

Every existing compensation program can be described as changing the amount of funds flowing along one of the arrows of this diagram. Where state and federal governments feel responsible to assist localities, they may tax their populations or developers to finance compensation to communities.[33]

Several programs have been developed at the local, state and federal levels to adjust the total of costs and benefits for energy boomtowns to zero or above. These programs vary in several ways, but they can be conveniently sorted out according to the source of their funds.

1. The community government may use its authority to require the developer to make payments equalling the development's net costs to the community ($T_{dc} = $ Costs).[34] Most local governments lack sufficient authority, either *de lege* or *de facto,* to effectively imple ment such a policy.

2. The state government can transfer revenue from both the state population (T_s) and from the developer (T_{ds}) to the community government (A_{sc}). T_s includes income, sales and property taxes, while (T_{ds}) comprises severance taxes, conversion taxes and permit fees. Community payments (A_{sc}) can be channeled through grants, loans or state provision of services.[35]

3. With similar mechanisms, the federal government may transfer revenue from the national population (T_n) and from developers (T_{df}) to the community government (A_{fc}).[36]

4. Another approach involves federal and state cooperation. Instead of directly compensating the community government, the federal government may transfer revenue to the state government (A_{fs}), with the expectation that the state will transfer all or a portion of the aid to the appropriate locality (A_{sc}).[37] Federal controls over the state's allocation range from federally established distribution formulae to federally recommended but non-binding priorities for the revenues' use.

5. Federal and state governments can use their authority, on behalf of the community government, to require developers to compensate communities directly (T_{dc}).[38]

Several criteria can be applied to programs of this kind. They ask whether the program is (i) transferring the right amount of funds (ii) from the right source (iii) to the right recipients. Criteria of the first type comprise an extensive literature on cost-benefit analysis.[39] The difficulty of knowing how much compensation to pay rests for the most part in assessing prices for goods, such as aesthetic quality or family stability, which are not conventionally traded in markets and for which money prices cannot be observed. We will not consider this problem here as boomtowns do not present special difficulties in cost-benefit assessment.

Whether the right people are paying for boomtown compensation (the right people are *prima facie,* but rebuttably in special cases, energy consumers) is a question of applied economics. Again, although technically challenging, this problem is not peculiar to boomtowns and we will examine it no further.

The remainder of the article will, however, consider what kind of program is likely to reach the right recipients—the people who are made worse off by the development of a boomtown. We will see that giving money to a boomtown government, as nearly all existing and proposed programs do, is unlikely to reward the proper individuals. Even giving the town facilities, as a developer might do under programs of type 5 above,[40] misdirects the subsidy. To see why this is the case, we must look at the boomtown's population, and the dynamics of its development, in detail.

BOOMTOWN DYNAMICS

In order to design programs that reach the right recipients, the static model of boomtowns (Figure 1) must be replaced with a dynamic one (Figure 2) that depicts in more detail the *changing* characteristics of boomtowns. Figure 2 disaggregates the decisions made through a boomtown's history, and the impacts these decisions have, over six populations and over time. The six populations include:

  i. The energy facility developer and its shareholders,
 ii. The community residents who remain through the development process,
iii. The immigrants who arrive as development proceeds,
 iv. The outmigrants (those members of the community whose decision to leave is related to the development),

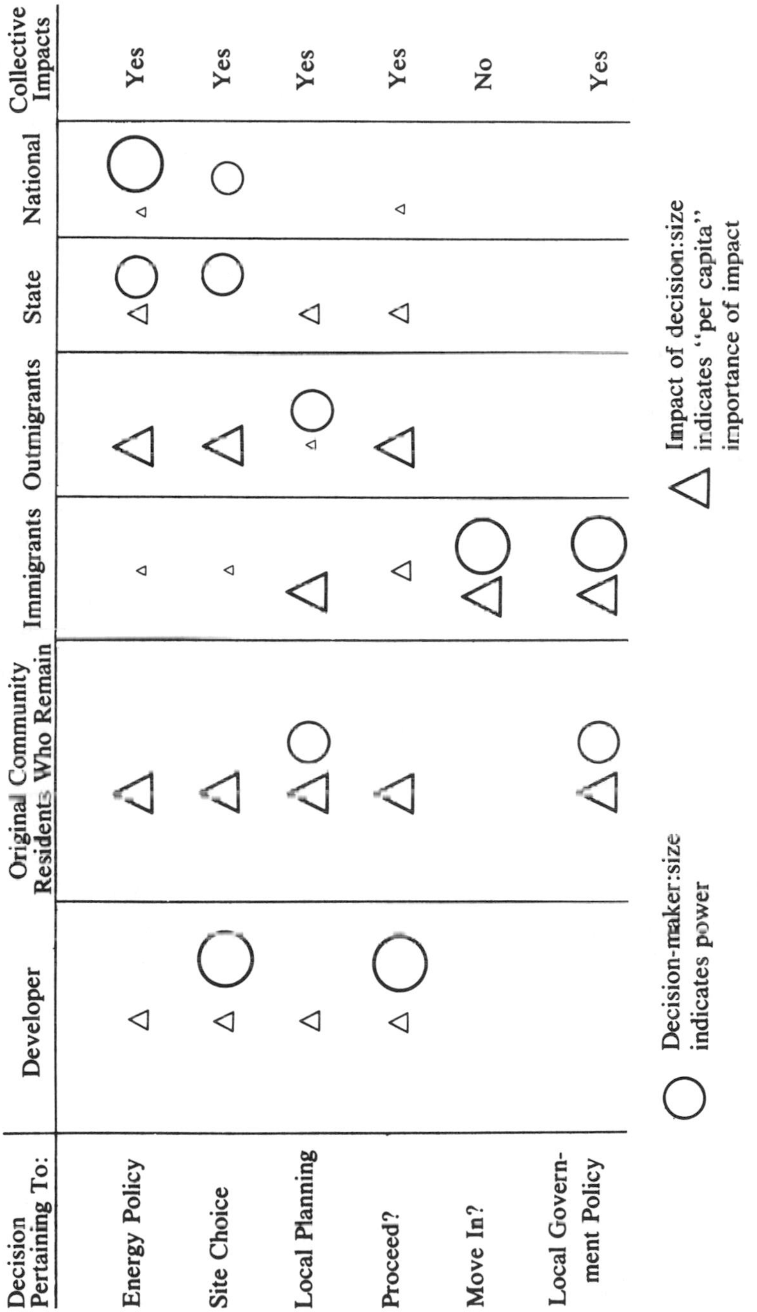

Decision Pertaining To:	Developer	Original Community Residents Who Remain	Immigrants	Outmigrants	State	National	Collective Impacts
Energy Policy	△	△	△	△	○△	○△	Yes
Site Choice	△	△	△	△	○	○	Yes
Local Planning	△	○△	△	○△	△		Yes
Proceed?	△	△	△	△	△	△	Yes
Move In?			○△				No
Local Government Policy		○△	○△				Yes

△ Impact of decision:size indicates "per capita" importance of impact

○ Decision-maker:size indicates power

FIGURE 2. Decision Map

v. The population of the state, and
vi. The population of the nation.

These six categories of people are subpopulations of the three major populations listed previously.[41] The categories are not necessarily exclusive nor do
their memberships necessarily coincide with a single government's constituents. At different times people may be found in more than one category.

The circles in Figure 2 are decision symbols, and vary in size to illustrate the power the respective decision-makers have in the choices taken at
each stage.[42] The triangles indicate the groups affected by the decisions at
each stage, and vary in size according to the "per capita" *importance* of the
impact.[43] Figure 2 can be read as a narrative from top to bottom. Initially the
state and national populations determine their respective energy policies
within which future development must occur. In the next stage, the energy
company, with a varying amount of state and national participation, chooses a
location. Next the entire initial population of the community, including both
those who will remain through the development process and those who will
leave (i) construct a set of local restrictions within which development can
occur, and (ii) do the initial planning which will guide the community's
response to the changes brought by development. The company makes a "go/
no-go" decision which presumably involves a prediction of the profitability of
the development under the restrictions developed in the previous stage.
Members of a potential immigrant population decide whether to move to the
community. When the development stage comes to an end and the operation
of the facility enters a steady state, the remaining original residents and the
immigrants (the new permanent population of the community) determine local
government policies with regard to public services, tax levels and the other
normal business of government.[44]

"Impact triangles" without "decision circles" are significant since, wherever possible, decisions should be made by those affected by them.[45] A look
at Figure 2 in this light brings the problem of the boomtown into perspective;
every triangle not associated with a circle promises dissatisfaction for the
affected population unless two things are simultaneously true:

1. The population empowered with the decision desires to act in the
   interest of the affected population, and
2. The population empowered with the decision is informed as to the
   desires of the affected population.

For example, the choice of a site is usually made predominantly by the
developer. The consequences of choosing one site over another, assuming a
spectrum of reasonably comparable sites, will probably be fairly small in the

company's terms, but for a particular community the consequences of being chosen will be enormous. We can expect that a bad decision is likely to occur if the developer is ignorant of the desires of the community. The next stage of decision, local planning, shows five populations affected by a decision taken by only two of them, but the decision-making populations have a great deal at stake. In this case it is likely not only that they will misunderstand or ignore the desires of the other two, but that the deciders' and the sufferers' interests will actually diverge; both conditions for a "correct" choice will be absent.[46]

At this point it may be useful to review the sources of the "boomtown problem" in light of the foregoing analysis. The process threatens a suboptimal outcome in any of several places. Notice that 3, 4 and 6 below are evident only in light of a dynamic rather than a static analysis.

1. National and state energy policy, which is presumably designed to serve an aggregate of the interests of the whole population, may be set with insufficient sensitivity to the large per capita costs imposed upon specific small groups which have little voting power. Despite the best will in the world on the part of the governmental decision-makers, such costs may occur for purely structural reasons. Notice that until specific sites are chosen for energy facilities, the citizens of many small rural communities respectively face only a small probability of being selected, so even if one wished to be responsive, it would be impossible to identify the particular towns whose population will in the end be affected.

   Even recognizing local costs, a Kaldor-Hicks criterion[47] will probably be used in a particular siting choice. Under this criterion a "correct" choice would accept the imposition of local costs if the (nationally distributed) benefits outweighed them. Most analysts believe this rule to be justified even though the sufferers are not compensated out of the gainers' benefits.

2. The next chance for costly error lies in the selection of sites. A developer may well be insensitive to differences in the desire for development of the communities among which it is choosing.

3. After a site has been selected, planning for future services must inevitably be conducted without the participation of future immigrants, even though they are the people who, by sheer number, will suffer the lion's share of the consequences. The immigrants not only have no political voice in the process at this point but cannot even be identified.

4. The consequences of the planning process for the portion of original residents who have the characteristics of being mobile and are thus potential outmigrants is especially interesting.[48] If the restrictions the

community places on the development are so onerous that the company chooses not to proceed with the projects, this portion of original residents has a future essentially unchanged from their present
condition and won't be driven to relocate. On the other hand, if the
development proceeds and they decide to relocate, the success or
failure of the planning restrictions they help to generate will be of no
consequence to them.[49]

5. Some projects ought not to go forward, even by the Kaldor-Hicks
    test, but if the developer makes the decisions, these projects may be
    carried out in spite of the large social costs they impose on the com-
    munity residents.

6. Finally, there is reason to believe that the large number of immi-
    grants to an energy boomtown may have markedly different tastes in
    government services, taxing policy and social conventions from the
    original rural population. Age differences, particularly between the
    retired farmers and ranchers living in small town centers and young
    construction workers, or contrasts in occupations and lifestyles can
    combine with the preponderant voting power of the immigrants to
    produce dissatisfaction with local policies among old-timers.[50]

The suboptimality of much boomtown development, especially that
resulting from causes 1, 2, 4 and 6 above, takes the form of unnecessary or
unfair costs which are imposed on particular groups of people. In the next
section we will consider the problem of identifying such groups and the costs
they suffer.

Identifying Compensable Costs

There are several reasons why governments may institute subsidy programs in addition to compensating suffering caused by development or other
government actions. In fact, most transfer programs are directed to recipients
who are thought worthy because of their condition rather than because of the
reasons for it. Income equalization programs and other forms of welfare subsidize people who are poor, ill-housed or ill-fed. Fortunately, all such criteria
are irrelevant to our discussion. Whatever subsidies are thought wise by
society for the poor or otherwise deprived, a different set of decisions should
determine compensation programs for costs caused by boomtown development. In other words, we are assuming that the poor, the ill-housed, and other
targets of entitlement subsidy programs in boomtowns should receive government aid or be denied it just as though they lived in New York or Kalamazoo.
Our concern is to identify people who deserve compensation for specifically
boomtown-related injury. Conversely, if property falls $5,000 in value

because a strip mine spoils the view, the owner should not be found less deserving of $5,000 in compensation just because he is richer or healthier than another who suffers an equivalent loss.

COMPENSATION CRITERIA

To determine who is and is not deserving of compensation, a test of injury will be applied to the various boomtown populations disaggregated in the previous section. The test is a simple one applied to the change in opportunities, including those not chosen, individuals experience with the occurrence of boomtown development. We argue that an individual is better off if he has more options (residential locations, jobs, friends, lifestyles) to choose from, and worse off if some are foreclosed. A Paretian criterion[51] can be formulated more precisely:

> A state of affairs S_2 is preferable to S_1 in the view of an individual if it offers him more choices, but does not foreclose any that S_1 provided.

If a state of affairs provides new choices but eliminates others, this criterion will not help us. But an "independence of irrelevant alternatives"[52] corollary can be stated:

> If a state of affairs S_4 offers an individual a choice which state S_3 forecloses, S_4 is preferable to S_3 in the individual's view if he did not choose any of the foreclosed options under S_3 and chooses one of the new options under S_4.

For example, if we are prohibited from sleeping under bridges by a proposed ordinance which also prohibits stealing bread, we will favor the ordinance since it allows us the new, desirable option of keeping our bread but forecloses an option we don't take advantage of anyway.

Figure 3 illustrates the above criteria with the symbolism of decision analysis. The utilities of the choices in each state of affairs are defined ordinally such that the choice made by the individual is exactly the choice with the highest utility. The variables A, B, C and D have positive values, and they or their combinations represent the amount of the utility of each choice. By our first criterion, State 2 is preferred to State 1, as it offers an additional option without foreclosing any options previously available. By our second criterion, State 4 is preferred to State 3. The only option lost, valued at A-B, would not have been chosen in State 3. The new option made available in State 4, valued at $A + D$, is preferable to the choice with utility A, found in both states.

Not all circumstances can be compared by these rules; if my favorite television program is replaced by another that I choose to watch, it's not clear

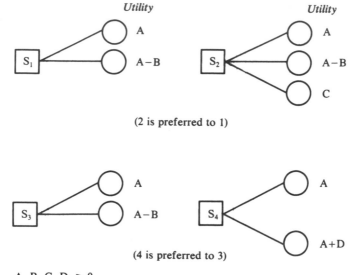

(2 is preferred to 1)

(4 is preferred to 3)

A, B, C, D, ≥ 0

FIGURE 3. Choice Criteria

whether I am better or worse off. Nor will these criteria help us determine the *amount* of compensation appropriate for a deserving individual unless a scheme is developed in which the victims can display meaningful exchange behavior.[53] But they can be applied to the populations discussed above to rule out compensation for some of them. If someone's post-boom circumstances are no worse than his pre-boom condition by our criteria, there is nothing for which to compensate him.

COMPENSATION IN THE BOOMTOWN

The change in state that the boomtown development brings to the original residents of the community is illustrated in Figure 4(a). Before energy development is threatened or occurs, individuals face two basic options. Those who are present have most recently chosen option 1, whether implicitly or consciously. Development adds a new option. They can live in the boomtown, enjoying or suffering (according to their taste and fortune) financial changes and changes in the quality of life. However, the development forecloses option 1. They can no longer choose the original town with its unmovable and unique friendship patterns, landscape and traditions.

Among outmigrants, individuals who leave town because of the development, the pre-boom state of affairs is preferred according to our second criterion. Notice that B, "before," includes an option that A, "after," does not, and the individual chooses that option under B. Also, the option which A offers that B does not is not the one he chooses under A. This means at least to a first approximation that the boomtown has imposed costs on the individual by forcing him into a less preferred set of choices. We say first approximation because as the primes in Figure 4(a) indicate, moving out of a boomtown may be quite different from moving out of the original town. For example, the boom development may have increased land values so that the emigrant can sell his property for an amount of money so large that he would have sold at that price and left had the option been available under B. If we think this to be true, though it is presumably not the case for renters or small property holders, then we cannot be confident that the boomtown has injured the individual, though we can no more be sure that he has gained.

A similar argument applies to an individual who remains after the changes brought by development. Since the boomtown has offered him a new

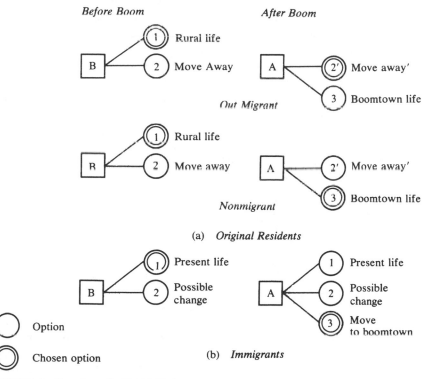

FIGURE 4. Boomtown Residents' Choices

option, which he accepts, and foreclosed the one he chose under the old state of affairs, his condition may be improved, damaged, or indifferent after development.

The immigrant who arrives to do construction work or to enter secondary sectors such as retailing, after a town starts to boom, displays different sets of choices as shown in Figure 4(b). Before the development occurs, he chooses between his present life and whatever other options are available to him. After the development, all these options remain but a third option is added. Furthermore, each immigrant has chosen option 3. By our first criterion the boomtown has improved his condition.

The analysis in the paragraphs above indicates the importance of distinguishing the populations of a boomtown. Some of the original residents of the community may be damaged by the development in a way that justifies subsidy, though others may be advantaged by the development or indifferent to it. But the newcomers often claimed to suffer social costs from boomtown life are not plausible candidates for subsidy through any boomtown-related program.[54]

This distinction has its roots in a fundamental difference between the "move-in" decision and other decisions, as noted in the last column of Figure 2 above. Most of the decisions, whether made by a group or an "individual" (for example, the developer), affect all of those involved in the same way: either everyone in town loses his "rural life" option (Figure 4(a)) or no one does. The "move-in" decision, on the other hand, is made by each potential immigrant. The quality of the boomtown is little affected by any of their individual decisions and they do not have to suffer its effects collectively. These individual decisions as to participation in the boomtown insulate immigrants from suffering the bad consequences of the decisions of others. No collective decision on the part of the townspeople can protect each townsperson in the same way.

DISAGGREGATION OF AFFECTED POPULATIONS

Policies to ameliorate conditions in boomtowns, to the extent that they involve money transfers to their populations, should recognize the distinctions we have drawn in the section above. In particular, "boom-town-specific" impact compensation is clearly not appropriate for the immigrants. They should be regarded as candidates for assistance on the same basis as other groups in the state and national population, and the conventional rules for justifying aid should be applied.[55] To anyone familiar, even at second hand, with the conditions in some boomtowns, this conclusion may seem harsh. Some qualifying observations are in order, though the basic result is not diminished. Certainly, the analysis provided above is weakened if the immigrants don't know what they are getting into. We have no way to assess the extent of this problem, but our rejection of subsidy programs for these people is accompanied by endorsement of "fair recruiting" practices and, if necessary, regulations, to ensure that immigrants know what conditions they can expect.

Furthermore, life in the boomtown may be suboptimal for structural reasons that can only be overcome by collective action beyond the abilities of a suddenly expanded, inexperienced local government. We expect public goods such as police protection and street maintenance to be under-provided by the market.[56] We should similarly expect that a government forced to operate beyond its capacities will not provide them optimally. Confidence that boomtown residents would happily pay for better government services, but cannot obtain them for administrative reasons, would support intervention by a higher and relatively less overstrained level of government to provide such services. This kind of assistance is not intrinsically a subsidy program, since the administrative services might be paid for through local assessments, but when local planning assistance is provided most efficiently by simply giving it away, our argument would not discourage it.[57]

As we have seen,[58] the original residents of a booming town cannot be excluded on equity grounds from development-related compensation. Some may profit from the change, but some will suffer, and the relative size of the two groups is difficult to ascertain, especially before the development occurs. While most people who stay after development may receive economic benefits such as new or better jobs, increased retail business, or land value appreciation, the unpriced social costs that are packaged indivisibly with the economic gains could well outweigh them. Furthermore, special costs are visited on particular subpopulations.

Despite the complexity of this packaging, costs and benefits can be identified with particular categories of people. People often face increased costs because they suffer inflated cost of living and reduced service quality *without* increases in income, wealth or the quality of new services. The examples below portray some categories of people likely to deserve compensation.

1. *People on fixed incomes:* Most retirees and handicapped people depend on a fixed income. Many female-headed households draw a large share of their income from welfare payments. If the local cost of living increases, these people suffer financially and therefore experience a declining quality of life.[59]

2. *Workers in surplus-labor categories:* Workers in occupations for which there are a surplus of workers will not participate in the wage inflation felt in other occupations for which there is a shortage of workers.[60] Thus, real incomes of the former workers will decrease as the cost of living increases while their salaries remain constant. In

particular, working women are seldom allowed to enter the high-paying construction field. Inflation, higher rents and a declining quality of life also hurt them when an influx of construction workers' wives may create a downward pressure on the wages and benefits paid for traditionally female-occupied service sector jobs.[61]

3. *Farm laborers:* In cases of extensive strip-mining, agricultural laborers may lose their jobs and those leasing farms may lose not only their farms but also their homes.

4. *Owners of agricultural-related industries:* Increased energy development has meant locally decreased agricultural production. Industries dependent on local produce may suffer decreased revenues or even go bankrupt. For example, in southwest Texas, planned construction of a food processing plant was delayed because area farmers could no longer sign contracts guaranteeing the needed supply of produce.[62]

5. *Consumers of particular services:* The decreased quality of services consumed by all residents—such as roads, police protection and fire protection—creates costs for everyone, but other services impose costs directly on selected groups of residents. For example, school children suffer more than adults from overcrowded schools, the elderly from overcrowded health facilities and overburdened doctors.

Not everyone within these categories automatically deserves compensation, since they may also be in categories of people who benefit. Property owners usually gain from increased property values, and owners of commercial establishments gain additional profits from increased business. Workers in occupations facing worker shortages—skilled labor, middle and upper managers—benefit from increased wages and job opportunities. Some unemployed people may find work which pays more than unemployment compensation. In cases where significant portions of land have not been disturbed, a shortage of agricultural laborers may increase salaries. And residents who learn to prefer an increased variety of social interaction may consider crowding and the arrival of newcomers as a benefit rather than a cost.

Despite these special cases, the conclusion of this analysis can be simply put: the only residents of a boomtown who should be subsidized or compensated under a boomtown program are found among the original residents. This has important policy implications for the conventional panoply of boomtown aid programs sketched above.

Compensation Alternatives

In light of the foregoing analysis, aid programs which direct funds to the government of boomtowns, especially after development has begun, can be seen to suffer from a fundamental flaw. By confusing a town with the people who live in it, this legislation generally directs aid to a population that includes a preponderance of recipients who ought not to be served: immigrants. Alternatively, the programs might be looked at as entitlement subsidy programs, directed towards people who are, for whatever reasons, deserving of amelioration by payments. In this view they are absurdly narrow, excluding all the people who qualify on grounds of their condition but happen not to live in boomtowns. In this section we will propose a conceptual framework that seems suitable for the design of "boomtown impact programs" and will also show that whatever compensation is paid should go to individuals rather than to local governments.

BOOMTOWNS AS DISASTERS

Nearly all of us willingly insure ourselves, paying a small, certain premium, against large, unlikely losses of various kinds. In some cases, rather than instituting an explicit voluntary insurance program, we agree to tax ourselves for relief payments to be disbursed whenever some of us suffer natural calamities like floods, earthquakes, or hurricanes.[63] If we accept that, on grounds of national interest which dominate any local costs, natural resources will be developed even though suffering is caused to those who live near them, the occurrence of a boomtown can be viewed as a natural disaster deserving compensation as "insurance."

To make this analogy clearer, consider two rural communities engaged in agricultural pursuits. One is struck by a devastating tornado, while the ground beneath the other suddenly turns to coal. Mining of the coal, and its consequent boomtown effects, are inevitable from the town's point of view. Both towns are similarly affected by natural forces beyond their control; the difference between the tornado and boomtown cases, if any, lies in the possibility that the coal-affected town has more warning that its coal will become economically attractive. But even this distinction is a weak one, since most natural disasters are foreshadowed probabilistically—floods occur in flood plains, tornadoes in tornado belts, and earthquakes in seismic zones.

Granting that state regulation and energy developers have some opportunity to divert boomtown "disaster" from one coal field to another, at least in the short-run, we suggest that an energy boomtown "happening to a community" is analogous for public policy purposes to a natural disaster, and that the insurance model justifies payment of compensation to the sufferers. Such payment should be made with care, and the allocation will inevitably be imperfect,[64] but the only important qualification boomtowns impose on the disaster relief model follows from the fact that energy development is beneficial to identifiable parties, the consumers and the developer. Therefore, the "premiums" for insurance should probably be collected from them, for example by an excise tax which forces the price of the developer's product up, for reasons of efficiency noted above.[65]

We have taken pains to defend the disaster insurance model because it points out the narrowness of the impact of boomtown development in a way complementary to the analysis above. Just as tornadoes don't happen to people who arrive after they occur, the compensable costs of a boomtown are not imposed on immigrants. Similarly, we note, in anticipation of the argument below, that disasters do not happen to governments, but to individuals, and correctly designed disaster relief programs provide subsidized loans, or grants-in-aid, to the individuals and not to their governments' treasuries.[66]

INDIVIDUAL COMPENSATION VERSUS INTERGOVERNMENTAL TRANSFERS

The boomtown disaster is visited, whatever its intensity, uniquely on a town's original residents, including those who find new conditions so distasteful that they leave. In order to direct compensation towards its proper objects, it is important that it *not* be provided directly to the community's government. There are several reasons why we prefer compensation payments directly to individuals.

1. *Spatial mismatch*—Many people who suffer from a boomtown do not live in the jurisdiction of the government in which the development "mostly" occurs. There are people on unincorporated land within "impact distance" of rural energy developments. Similarly, larger units of government are likely to include many individuals who are not affected adversely, but who would benefit from an intergovernmental transfer. It is rare that the constituents of any local government are the same group as the persons affected in a boom.

2. *Temporal mismatch*—Few governments can usefully spend a large windfall so as to dispense the benefits of the expenditure very quickly. Furthermore, many of the perceived needs of a rapidly growing community involve capital expenditures like school buildings. If the local government uses compensation receipts in ways which produce benefits over time, the newcomers, who we have demonstrated should be excluded from such benefits, will inevitably participate in the services delivered. Unless these benefits are wholly public goods, this participation will be at the expense of the original residents who were the intended beneficiaries of the whole amount of the subsidy. Not only will the newcomers passively draw off an unwarranted share of these benefits, but since they can be expected to exert significant and possibly dominating influence in the conduct of government after development occurs, they will presumably turn

capital investments they inherit towards the particular types of benefits that they prefer and which are unlikely to match the desires of the old-timers.[67]

3. *Poor discrimination*—Few government services are purely public goods, but most have the non-excludability property at least in part.[68] Local government's attempts to distribute the benefits of compensation receipts are unlikely to make the allocation of benefits match the differential costs suffered by citizens. If it hires more police, crime will be reduced for everyone, including those who actually benefited from the boom; if it reduces taxes, it will reduce them for everyone. If the "spill-over" benefits are obtained as a free bonus from a government program which adequately compensates the real losers, well and good, but there is nothing in our understanding of the kinds of costs boom developments impose to suggest that improved government services are an especially apt compensation for those costs. Furthermore, an important class of sufferers, those who leave as a consequence of the boom and take their votes with them, have only the most tenuous claim on local government's sympathies.

4. *Flexibility*—We find conclusive the fact that while compensation paid to government is likely to miss its intended targets for reasons 1 to 3 above, compensation to individuals does not inhibit the provision of government services as compensation when the sufferers find that appropriate. If they feel that government can best spend all or part of their payments, they can tax themselves and give the responsibility to government. They can even provide benefits to the newcomers through capital investment, if they so desire. Thus, individual compensation assures that the money so paid will go wherever it best serves the interests of the payees, even to government, whereas compensation paid to government gives no such assurance.

We excused ourselves from detailed consideration of allocating compensation payments among individuals, but a general observation can be made. Such allocation should be done through entitlement rules constructed in general terms, and not in view of any particular boomtown's history. It is preferable to construct a schedule of "boomtown disaster relief" under which individuals qualify for fixed payments insofar as they meet specific qualifications like "retired person," "non-landowner" or "agricultural supplies retailer." These categories of gainers and losers discussed in the previous section[69] are not exclusive and any compensation scheme designed to identify *net* costs must consider the magnitude of gains and losses for each category,[70] balancing expected costs and benefits in order to determine an individual's eligibility for compensation.

The size of the compensation should also be included in the compensation schedule and should cover real dollar costs, environmental costs, aesthetic costs and social costs predicted, at the time of the boom, to be imposed by energy development. Future unexpected benefits should not mean compensees must repay the compensation. The compensation should *not* be made in view of the residents' subsequent good or bad experience during the boom itself. The compensation is for suffering, current and predicted, which is imposed at the time the boom becomes a certainty, and any subsequent advantage a citizen gains from the development is appropriately considered his own. It is entirely appropriate for a boomtown resident to take his compensation and build a fortune as a shovel merchant. Similarly, the farmer who loses his compensation through unwise investment may qualify for income transfers paid to poor people statewide or nationally, but the misfortune is not a boom-related one.

Conclusion

Design of an appropriate boomtown compensation program in light of our analysis inevitably requires detailed consideration of gains and losses like those sketched above,[71] an analysis that will require empirical research not yet performed. The program's specific characteristics should depend on a balance between the costs of missing deserving parties, or wasting resources on undeserving people who slip through the net on the one hand, and the cost of research and administration on the other. What is important about the design process is that it begin with a theoretically valid framework limiting the search to correctly specified groups of potential recipients, and that it be focussed on individuals and not geographical or government units. As we have seen, unless the analysis starts with individuals and moves towards geographical or governmental aggregation only when efficiency demands it, it is likely to miss entirely important distinctions among the people the aid program intends to serve.

Our narrow conclusion, then, is that boomtown compensation programs should be focussed as finely as seems worthwhile on certain members of the original resident population, and should not be directed to residents of post-development boomtowns nor through local governments. Our broad conclusion is that the shorthand by which we refer to the people in a place by the place's name, or even worse, confuse them with their local government, is a trap for the unwary and one that can lead to major errors in policy design. It would be a wise humility for analysts to go back to first principles, repeatedly murmuring if necessary, mantras like

Cities don't suffer, people do.
A government is not a polity and a polity is not a person.
How would I feel if they did it to me?

Notes

The authors appreciate the research assistance of Alden Drake, the members of the Energy Impacts Project staff (cited as authors *passism*) and Lawrence Susskind for valuable review and criticism. Remaining errors are ours. This research was supported by the U.S. Energy Research and Development Administration (whose views are not necessarily those presented here) under contract No. E(49-18)-2295.

1. J. Gilmore and M. Duff, Boomtown Growth Management: A Case Study of Rock Springs–Green River, Wyoming 1-29 (1975); Office of Community Planning and Dev., U.S. Dep't of Housing and Urban Dev., Rapid Growth from Energy Projects: Ideas for State and Local Action (1976); Gilmore, *Boomtowns May Hinder Energy Resources Development,* 191 Science 535 (1976). *See generally* K. Toole, *The Rape of the Great Plains* 80-125 (1976).

2. *See, e.g.,* Industrial Development Information and Siting Act, Wyo. Stat.; § § 35-502.75 .94 (Supp. 1975); Coastal Zone Management Act Amendments of 1976, Pub. L. No. 94-370, 90 Stat. 1013 (1976) (amending 16 U.S.C. § § 1451-1464 (1972)). Other sources are collected and annotated in R. Little and S. Lovejoy, Western Energy Development as a Type of Rural Industrialization: A Partially Annotated Bibliography (1977).

3. Gilmore, *supra* note 1.

4. Wyoming Legislative Select Committee on Industrial Development Impact, Interim Report and Recommendation (1974).

5. For examples, see notes 35-38 and accompanying text *infra.* For a rationale for federal aid to boomtowns and their states, see J. Monaghan, Managing the Impacts of Energy Development: A Policy Analysis from a State Government Perspective (April 1977) (address delivered at National Governor's Conference, Washington, D.C.).

6. These facilities include strip-mines, coal-fired electricity generating facilities, coal gasification plants and oil drilling operations.

7. Little, *Some Social Consequences of Boom Towns,* 53 N.D. L. Rev. 401 (1977); J. Gilmore and M. Duff, *supra* note 1; Gilmore, *supra* note 1.

8. Little, *supra* note 7.

9. *Id.*

10. *Id.*

11. J. Gilmore and M. Duff, *supra* note 1, at 12. *But see* Mountain West Research, Inc., Construction Worker Profile: Final Report 55 (1975) (Prepared for the Old West Regional Commission, Billings, Montana) (reporting only a 90% increase in cases).

12. Mountain West Research, Inc., *supra* note 11, at 55.

13. R. Foster, State Responses to the Adverse Impacts of Energy Development in Wyoming (1977) (Energy Impacts Project, Laboratory of Architecture and Planning, M.I.T.).

14. D. Sanderson, State Responses to the Adverse Impacts of Energy Development in Texas II-4 to 8 (1977) (Energy Impacts Project, Laboratory of Architecture and Planning, M.I.T.).

15. *Id.*

16. *Id.*

17. *Id.*

18. P. Burke, An Impact Evaluation Report, City of Mount Pleasant, Texas 30 (1976) (General Land Office, Austin, Texas).

19. D. Sanderson, *supra* note 14, at II-21.

20. Mt. Pleasant, Texas and Pearsall, Texas. *Id.* at II-10.

21. *Id.*

22. *Id.* at II-11.

23. *Id.* Hanna, Wyoming presents another example of inadequate tax base growth. In the first three years of its boom, property assessed valuation rose 66%, but the per capita tax base fell from $562.12 to $499.87. Its tax rate was already at the statutory maximum. Outside subsidies were required to maintain adequate public services. Nellis, *What Does Energy Development Mean for Wyoming?*, 33 HUMAN ORGANIZATION 229, 236 (1974).

24. For example, in Texas the voluntarily formed Water Conservation and Subsidence Districts are the only entities with power to regulate the spacing and extraction rates of water wells. Seldom do these special districts restrict water extraction. D. Sanderson, *supra* note 14, at III-7. Both Colorado and North Dakota face court tests of the state's right to regulate groundwater use. C. Lu, State Responses to the Adverse Impacts of Energy Development in North Dakota 16-18 (1977) (Energy Impacts Project, Laboratory of Architecture and Planning, M.I.T.); L. Monaco, State Responses to the Adverse Impacts of Energy Development in Colorado 33-34 (1977) (Energy Impacts Project, Laboratory of Architecture and Planning, M.I.T.).

25. D. Sanderson, *supra* note 14 at II-22 to 24; R. Foster, *supra* note 13, at 10.

26. One town which has experienced this is Dilly, Texas. D. Sanderson, *supra* note 14, at II-22 to 24.

27. The previous section of this article highlights these costs imposed on boomtowns and particularly their long time residents. *See generally* J. Gilmore and M. Duff, *supra* note 1; P. Burke, *supra* note 18; R. Foster, *supra* note 13; Gilmore, *supra* note 1; R. Little, *supra* note 7; D. Sanderson, *supra* note 14.

28. Another example of market failure is the inability of boomtowns to obtain professional planning services. If the labor market in city planners worked perfectly, every town could buy as much planning as it needed. Because planners are difficult to divide among towns and often unwilling to move to rural places, it may be appropriate for the state government to provide planning services to developing communities. If it charges for the service, it will be operating a market-failure-correction scheme. If it gives away the service, it will be running a subsidy program as well.

29. For an overview of typical relief programs, see OFFICE OF COMMUNITY PLANNING AND DEV., U.S. DEP'T OF HOUSING AND URBAN DEV., RAPID GROWTH FROM ENERGY PROJECTS: IDEAS FOR STATE AND LOCAL ACTION 30-34 (1976).

30. One calculation finds social costs about one and one-half times the amount of direct costs in the production of electricity from coal. *See* E. Peelle, Internalizing Social Costs in Power Plant Siting: Some Examples for Coal and Nuclear Plants in the United States 1 (November 17, 1976) (Oak Ridge National Laboratory, paper presented at the International Meeting of the American Nuclear Society, Washington, D.C.).

31. The analysis of problems of this kind is the task of externality theory in welfare economics. Whether sufferers from an externality (an economic effect external to a decision-maker's balance sheet) should be compensated for efficiency's sake is not generally a simple matter. For a thorough discussion, see W. Baumol and W. Oates, THE THEORY OF ENVIRONMENTAL POLICY (1975). For a less technical introduction, see R. Dorfman and N. Dorfman, ECONOMICS OF THE ENVIRONMENT (1972).

32. In law, where government action is involved, the problem is addressed in discussions of the "taking issue." Principal papers on the legal issues involved include F. Bosselman, D. Callies and J. Banta, THE TAKING ISSUE (1973); Costonis, *"Fair" Compensation and Accommodation Power: Antidotes for the Taking Impasse in Land Use Controversies*, 75 COLUM. L. REV. 1021 (1975); Michelman, *Property, Utility and Fairness: Comments on the Ethical Foundations of "Just Compensation" Law*, 80 HARV. L. REV. 1165 (1967); Sax, *Takings, Private Property, and Public Rights*, 81 YALE L. J. 149 (1971). These articles concentrate on questions of land use but deal also with the larger issues.

33. One important justification for government impact programs was suggested previously in our discussion of the rationale for direct assistance. That is, since the larger polity benefits from the development, it should share in the induced costs. Additionally, a government might justify these programs on the theory that, since its policies either directly or indirectly cause these costs, it should therefore "pay" for them, or because the payments may induce local support for regionally beneficial but locally noxious projects.

34. In Washington, the Skagit County Commissioners conditioned site zoning approval on a contract rezone agreement under which Puget Power and Light Co. must meet 35 conditions to "reasonably and adequately mitigate the impacts of the construction of the project on the community." E. Peelle, *supra* note 30, at 11-18. Tax prepayments are calculated to cover education and law enforcement costs. *Id. See* Myhra, *Energy Development*, in PRACTICING PLANNER 12 (Sept. 1976). Because of their limited control over developments, few community governments are capable of directly demanding payments equal to the costs they absorb. Most taxing schemes must be imposed equally on all residents and not just on developers. More important, a single community's competitive position vis-à-vis a major energy company is weak. If it demands much more in local aid than the government of an alternate site, the developer may simply go elsewhere. For one view of developer-community relations, see S. West, Opportunities for Company-Community Cooperation in Mitigating Energy Facility Impacts (1977) (Energy Impacts Project, Laboratory of Architecture and Planning, M.I.T.).

35. For example, Wyoming has imposed a special coal severance tax to create a fund from which communities affected by coal production may obtain grants or loans to finance public water, sewer, highway, road or street projects. The tax will expire when $120 million has been collected for the fund. WYO. STAT. §§ 39-227.1, .10

(Supp. 1975 & Supp. 1977). Other compensation programs are authorized by the Wyoming Joint Powers Act, Wyo. Stat. §§ 9-18.13 to .20 (Supp. 1975), and the Wyoming Community Development Authority Act, Wyo. Stat. §§ 9-826 to 848 (Supp. 1975). *See* R. Foster, *supra* note 13, at 20-25.

North Dakota has imposed a privilege tax on coal conversion facilities. A percentage of the tax is returned to the county in which the facility is located. N.D. Cent. Code §§ 57-60-01 to 96 (Supp. 1977). North Dakota has also imposed a coal severance tax, with the proceeds allocated to coal impacted communities. N.D. Cent. Code §§ 57-61-01 to 10, 57-62-01 to 05 (Supp. 1977). *See* C. Lu, *supra* note 24, at 24-30. Both the Wyoming and North Dakota programs are designed to compensate communities for the adverse *fiscal* impacts imposed by energy developments. They do not attempt to compensate for all local energy development costs. Their programs focus on front-end capital requirements and link impact payments with revenues gained from increased energy development.

36. Only one federal compensation program provides aid directly to localities (A_{fc}) without going through state decision-making bodies. Under the Payments to Local Governments for Entitlement Lands Act, 31 U.S.C.A. §§ 1601-1607 (Supp. 1977), the federal government pays to any unit of local government up to 75 cents per acre of "entitlement lands" located in that unit's boundaries. *Id.* § 1602(a). If the land is located in two jurisdictions, *e.g.,* a town and a county, the smaller jurisdiction receives the payment. *Id.* § 1602(d). The payment is reduced according to the amount of other revenues collected from the federal property. *Id.* § 1602(a)(1). The objective of this payment is to compensate localities for foregone tax revenue. The only restriction on funds which go directly to localities is that they be used for a governmental purpose. *Id.* § 1601. Payments are made whether or not the lands are leased. *See* S. Brody, Federal Aid to Energy Impacted Communities: A Review of Related Programs and Legislative Proposals 40-44 (1977) (Energy Impacts Project, Laboratory of Architecture and Planning, M.I.T.).

37. Through the Mineral Lands Leasing Act, 30 U.S.C. §§ 181-287 (1971), *as amended by* 30 U.S.C.A. §§ 181-287 (Supp. 1977), 50% of the revenue from federally owned mineral leases is returned to the states in which the leased land is located. *Id.* § 191. Under the Act as amended, the state legislature has the responsibility of directing use of this revenue for planning, public facilities and public services giving priority to those subdivisions of the state socially or economically affected by mineral development. *Id.*

Communities receive only a portion of the revenue collected originally from mineral leases within their boundaries. For example, Wyoming gives some directly to host counties and places bonuses in an "impact and emergency account." Wyo Stat. §§ 9-577 to 580.1 (Supp. 1975). *See* R. Foster, *supra* note 13, at 34-36. Colorado places its revenue in an Oil Shale Trust Fund, the interest from which is distributed to affected communities. Colo. Rev. Stat. § 34-63-104 (Supp. 1976). *See* L. Monaco, *supra* note 24, at 37-38.

Another example, the Coastal Energy Impact Program (CEIP), requires that all of the money eventually pass through to the affected communities. The Coastal Zone Management Act Amendments of 1976, Pub. L. No. 94-370, 90 Stat. 1013 (1976) (amending 16 U.S.C. §§ 1451-1464 (1972)), allocate $1.2 billion for grants and loans to states and local areas affected by coastal energy development. It determines the interstate distribution of the funds and places restrictions and requirements on each state's intrastate allocation. Local areas must be able to demonstrate that they have exhausted other forms of assistance before applying for CEIP grants. *See* S. Brody, *supra* note 36, at 27-33.

38. For example, the Wyoming Industrial Siting Council requires developers to assist communities in providing public services should public revenues fall short of the demands placed on them by the energy development. WYO. STAT. § § 35-502.75 to .94 (Supp. 1975). In this situation the state uses its legal authority to force developers to provide local benefits (T_{dc}) which localities could not negotiate on their own. *See* R. Foster, *supra* note 13, at 30-34. In one instance, the Wyoming Industrial Siting Council conditioned the license for Missouri Basin Electric's proposed Wheatland power plant on the provision of financial assistance designed to reduce impacts. Direct payments and technical assistance help provide many public and private services, totaling approximately $19.3 million. (Up to $15 million may be recoverable through sale of the housing project). E. Peelle, *supra* note 30, at 9-18.

There are several other relevant examples. The defeated Synthetic Fuels Bill (H.R. 12112) would have permitted the U.S. Energy Research and Development Administration (ERDA) to require a development company to compensate community costs imposed by a federal demonstration project. *Proposed Amendments to the Federal Nonnuclear Energy Research and Development Act of 1974: Hearings on H.R. 12112 Before the Subcomm. on Economic Stabilization of the House Comm. on Banking, Currency and Housing*, 94th Cong., 2d Sess. 3-40 (1976). *See* S. Brody, *supra* note 36, at 34-36. The Federal Power Commission has assumed authority to force developers to mitigate adverse impacts imposed upon host communities. *See* E. Peelle, *supra* note 30, at 5. The Nuclear Regulatory Commission has required TVA to make direct payments to communities affected by the proposed Hartsville Nuclear Power Plant. *Id.* at 11.

39. The word "extensive" is to be emphasized. Introductions to the field can be found in E. Mishan, ECONOMICS FOR SOCIAL DECISIONS (1973); E. Stokey and R. Zeckhauser, A PRIMER FOR PUBLIC CHOICE (1977).

40. *See* note 38 and accompanying text *supra*.

41. *See* Figure 1 *supra*.

42. For example, on the assumption that immigrants substantially outnumber the remaining original residents of the community, they are expected to be more powerful in making local government policy in the post-development phase. Similarly, national energy policy dominates state policy for reasons of budget and constitutional precedence.

43. We use the term "per capita" somewhat loosely, to indicate the relative change in the utility of a member of a particular population. Notice that the size of this symbol does *not* vary with the *size* of the population.

44. An important source of boomtown problems is often a mismatch between the governments with taxing or regulatory authority over development and the populations affected. A common example is a facility located in a school district different from the one in which its employees reside; the plant's district has enormous potential tax revenues but few school children while the residents' district has large educational

obligations but a small tax base. UNITED STATES ENERGY RESEARCH AND DEVELOPMENT ADMINISTRATION, MANAGING THE SOCIAL AND ECONOMIC IMPACTS OF ENERGY DEVELOPMENT (1976). Our narrative decision model does not display this mismatch for reasons of clarity, but the reader should recognize the likelihood that consequences of development are not compartmentalized geographically to follow local government boundaries.

45. We violate this principle willingly only when we are forced to by practical considerations, as when a population voluntarily relinquishes its decision-making power in a repetitious or highly technical matter to an administrative unit of government.

46. Real examples of such mismatches are easy to find. In fact, the existing structure of most state compensation programs invites dissatisfaction of the affected population since the state officials, who serve the statewide population, decide on impact payments to the local, affected population, and the interests of the state government can conflict with the best interest of local energy impacted communities. Local officials cite this conflict as a reason to restructure compensation programs. For example, energy boomtown officials and developers in North Dakota argue that Coal Impact Funds should be given directly to boomtowns, since they know their needs better than any state agency. *See* C. Lu, *supra* note 24 at 28-30. They also argue that a larger portion of the Coal Severance Tax and the Coal Conversion Tax revenues should go to affected communities, since current compensation does not cover their costs. *See The Beulah Beacon* (Beulah, N.D.), September 23, 1976, at 1, col. 4. However, state officials prefer distributing benefits among all state residents rather than just compensating boomtowns. *See* C. Lu, *supra* note 24, at 28-30.

47. The Kaldor-Hicks criterion favors a change in the current societal state if those benefiting *could* compensate those losing in such a way that some would be better off and none worse off, even if the compensation would not actually occur. The underlying assumption is that, in the long run, the total net benefits of a series of choices will be equally dispersed across the total population. *See generally* E. Stokey and R. Zeckhauser, *supra* note 39; Zeckhauser and Schaefer, *Public Policy and Normative Economic Theory,* in THE STUDY OF POLICY FORMATION (R. Bauer & K. Gergen, eds.) 58-60 (1968).

48. *See generally* S. Goldstein, PATTERNS OF MOBILITY, 1910-1950, THE NORRISTOWN STUDY (1958); I. Lowry, MIGRATION & METROPOLITAN GROWTH: TWO ANALYTICAL MODELS (1966).

49. A cynic would predict latent outmigrants to (i) favor proposals only if they diminished the likelihood of construction and (ii) have no interest in proposals which would actually improve the local quality of life if the development proceeded. Their utility structure in any case is distinctly at variance with the interests of residents who expect to remain through the project's future history. However, until the day they leave, their formal political position is indistinguishable from that of the residents destined to remain. The local political scene in this critical phase is further confused because all residents may find it strategic to pretend to be "conditional outmigrants." The "real" outmigrants may be hard to distinguish from the remainers, and some people may not even know their own status.

50. Young boomtown immigrants in Hanna, Wyoming, show a preference for more public services than do old-timers of all ages. In the 30-years-and-under age group, newcomers show stronger preferences for retail shopping facilities, good schools, sanitary facilities, youth organizations, civic-service groups, and recreational facilities. In the over-30 age groups, newcomers and old-timers have more similar preferences. Newcomers and old-timers also differ politically. While old-timers in Hanna are staunch Labor Democrats, newcomers are more likely to be Independents. For more differences in these two groups, *see* Nellis, *supra* note 23; Mountain West Research, Inc., *supra* note 11, at 126.

51. According to the *Pareto criterion*, State A is better than State B if someone is better off in State A and no one is worse off. The *Pareto optimal* state would be that state for which no other state can be considered better by the Pareto criterion. See Zeckhauser and Schaefer, *supra* note 47, at 43.

52. R. Luce and H. Raiffa, GAMES AND DECISIONS 127 (1967).

53. Such a scheme is applied to the siting decision, and its importance is discussed, in O'Hare, *"Not on My Block You Don't"—Facilities Siting and the Strategic Importance of Compensation,* 25 PUBLIC POLICY 407 (1977).

54. Again, they may deserve government aid for a variety of reasons, but if so it will be under programs directed at people sharing their conditions generally and not only those who have such needs in boomtowns.

55. Note, however, that boomtown workers may fare poorly in the competition for direct assistance dollars from any level of government, since their incomes are large and low income has traditionally been a necessary condition for general assistance programs from government. Migrant farm workers, slum dwellers and some minority groups will probably be found in greater need. Furthermore, boomtown immigrants obviously prefer their boomtown condition to their previous circumstance. If they were not found worthy of assistance before, it is hard to see why they should suddenly become eligible.

Our lumping together all immigrants and declaring them ineligible for compensation may appear too simple. Consider immigrants who follow energy booms, staying in one location until work runs out. The boom/bust cycle associated with energy development "causes" the cessation of work in one location, and these people may appear to have only one choice other than unemployment, *i.e.*, moving on to the next boomtown. By our criteria, these people *may* deserve compensation from the previous energy boom, but not from one they have just joined. If one were to consider the costs and benefits from all of their moves, however, they probably would still show a net benefit. In deciding their first move to an energy boomtown (*i.e.*, the decision to adopt a career that requires such mobility) they probably knew the job would be temporary and they would have to move within a few years. The cost they placed on their eventual move was included in their personal calculation of the costs and benefits associated with this option and the boomtown lifestyle. One survey comparing newcomers and old-timers in a coal boomtown shows that newcomers tend to be younger, more mobile, better educated, and significantly better paid. Many newcomers know their positions are temporary and expect to move when the coal is depleted. Even prior to their most recent move, the newcomers tended to be a highly mobile population. *See* Nellis, *supra* note 23, at 232-33.

56. *See generally* W. Nicholson, MICROECONOMIC THEORY, Ch. 23 (1972).

57. This said, we should note a consideration that challenges *all* attempts to ameliorate the conditions of boomtown life. As reports from the Alaska pipeline project relate, the well-paid work on the "slope" and to some extent, in any boomtown, offers an opportunity for capital accumulation not otherwise available in American society. *See* W. Griffith, *Blood, Toil, Tears and Oil: Effects of the Alaskan Pipeline, N.Y. Times,* July 27, 1975, (Magazine), at 8. There are risks (lotteries and investment) which offer (actuarially unfair) low probabilities of very high returns, but few chances exist for a working man to accumulate enough capital *with certainty* to start a business or otherwise change what used to be called his "station." The boomtown allows those who wish to trade two or three years of suffering for large rewards to do so, but if boomtown conditions are made more attractive the wages associated with them can be expected to decline to match wages in established communities. Several researchers are developing the premise that wage differentials between boomtowns and stable communities are considered a premium to compensate workers for the boomtown's poor quality of life. Preliminary findings suggest a $.04 per week salary premium for each dollar decrease in per capita public capital stock. *See* Cummings and Mehr, *Investments for Urban Infrastructure in Boomtowns,* 17 NAT. RESOURCES J. 223 (1977). It is not obvious that boomtown workers using current conditions as a means to step over a convexity in their utility-of-money curve would consider it a favor to have the option to do so foreclosed. *See* H. Raiffa, DECISION ANALYSIS 94-97 (1968). In fact, we should at least entertain the possibility that boomtowns where life is onerous, but pay is high, serve a social purpose analogous to the function of the frontier in Turner's interpretation, and that this purpose might not only mitigate the societal cost of boomtown pathologies but even justify them! *See* F. Turner, THE FRONTIER IN AMERICAN HISTORY (1920).

58. *See* Figure 4(a) and accompanying text *supra.*

59. Limited empirical evidence shows that the income of aged residents in industrializing rural communities decreases relative to non-aged residents in the same community and to both aged and non-aged residents in stable rural communities. *See* Clemente and Summers, *Industrial Development and the Elderly: A Longitudinal Analysis,* 28 J. GERONTOLOGY 479 (1973).

60. For example, the city manager in Mt. Pleasant, Texas, a coal boomtown, estimates that 20% of the city's population will face an increased cost of living without experiencing any increase in income and wealth. Within this 20% he includes unskilled laborers facing no increased demand for their labor. *See* D. Sanderson, *supra* note 14, at II-27.

61. Clemente and Summers discuss the relative benefits received by women in rapidly growing rural communities. *See* F. Clemente and G. Summers, Large Industries in Small Towns: Who Benefits? 7-8 (1973) (Working Paper RID 73.9, Center for Applied Sociology, University of Wisconsin, Madison, Wisconsin).

62. D. Sanderson, *supra* note 14, at II-23.

63. For a general discussion of federal programs compensating communities for disasters and government action, see S. Brody, *supra* note 36.

64. *E.g.,* the town carpenter may be given relief payment for his house after a tornado even though the destruction it wreaks on his neighbors is a bonanza for him.

65. *See* notes 30-31 and accompanying text *supra.*

66. However, many existing programs ignore this precept. *See* S. Brody, *supra* note 36.

67. *See* note 50 and accompanying text *supra.*

68. The classic example is a park, A's enjoyment of which, until congestion sets in, leaves no less for B. The correct admission fee (price) for such goods is the marginal cost of providing them, or zero, so compensating A with a park inevitably benefits B as well. E Mansfield, MICROECONOMICS 424-26 (1970).

69. *See* notes 58-62 and accompanying text *supra.*

70. For example, a person on a fixed income may own his own home. Increased benefits from home ownership may not be sufficient to cover increased costs—food, clothes, taxes, medical services. This home owner may be eligible for compensation whereas a salaried home owner may not. Although home owners generally benefit from increased property values, those living near a facility or residential roads which become thoroughfares may face decreased property value.

71. *See* notes 58-62 and accompanying text *supra.*

LAWRENCE E. SUSSKIND AND STEPHEN R. CASSELLA

21 *The Dangers of Preemptive Legislation*

The Case of LNG Facility Siting in California

In 1977, when the accumulation of well-intentioned regulations made it difficult to site a liquified natural gas (LNG) facility in California, the legislature, with the full support of Governor Edmund G. Brown, Jr., passed a law, Senate Bill 1081 (Chapter 855, Statutes of 1977), that said, in effect, "not withstanding any previously enacted legislation or regulatory requirements, California will designate an LNG terminal site within a year." The state's attempt to preempt local regulatory authority, to say nothing of the legislature's willingness to circumvent its own facility siting, coastal protection, and environmental impact assessment laws, seems to have failed. This case study describes the circumstances leading up to the enactment of S.B. 1081 and analyzes the dangers associated with preemptive legislation. Had California confronted the real weaknesses in its energy facility siting process, the state could have identified positive steps that would have accelerated site selection without triggering the staunch opposition that now threatens indefinite delay.

Natural gas is a very important component of California's energy supply. When the governor and the legislature found themselves hamstrung in their attempt to site an LNG terminal, they sought to "cut through the red tape." While their frustration may have been justified, efforts to preempt laws and

From Lawrence E. Susskind and Stephen R. Cassella, "The Dangers of Preemptive Legislation: The Case of LNG Facility Siting in California," *Environmental Impact Assessment Review,* Vol. 1 (1980), pp. 9-26. Reprinted by permission of the Plenum Publishing Corporation and Lawrence E. Susskind.

regulations designed to protect public safety ought to be based on more than a temporary shift in administrative priorities or frustration with procedural delays. If there is a generally shared view that previously enacted laws and regulations were poorly conceived, then it should not be difficult to win public support for modifications of those laws and regulations. If earlier intentions have been met or are no longer relevant to the coalitions involved, it should be possible to shift resources and rechannel political energies toward new objectives. If new information or scientific findings suggest that previously set standards are no longer pertinent, it is likely that a technical challenge aimed at implementing appropriate modifications will succeed. In the case of California's effort to site an LNG facility, none of these conditions held. The governor was primarily concerned about convincing the private sector that he was not opposed to further economic and energy development. State energy officials were motivated, for the most part, by a fear that Canadian natural gas supplies might be cut off. Private industry stoked these concerns with dire predictions about energy shortages and job losses. State legislators were looking for a way to respond to constituents fearful of the risks associated with siting an LNG facility "in their backyard."

Instead of seeking ways to improve previously enacted statutes or to facilitate their speedy and effective implementation, the legislature and the governor sought to preempt them. Instead of searching for new ways to work with local officials and resident groups likely to be adversely affected by the siting of an LNG facility, the legislature and the governor blocked their involvement. In their headlong rush to override previously enacted regulatory requirements, the governor and the legislature short-circuited mandated environmental reviews, leaving those opposed to the proposed facility and those likely to be adversely affected by it no choice but to seek redress through the courts.

Natural Gas and LNG

Natural gas, the most commonly used fuel gas in the United States, is composed primarily of methane and higher molecular weight hydrocarbons. It is an attractive fuel source because it burns so cleanly, because its pipelines are convenient, and until recently, because it was available at a reasonable price (Shreve and Buick 1977). While domestic production of natural gas declined between 1973 and late 1978, abundant reserves exist abroad. Nearly 25 percent of all energy used in the United States in 1978 was derived from natural gas.

Liquified natural gas is natural gas cooled to -259 degrees Fahrenheit. The liquid takes up only 1/600th the volume of the gas. This facilitates storage and shipment. It also multiplies the explosive properties of the gas.

The current fleet of LNG tankers in use poses a potential threat fifty times that of the atomic bomb dropped on Hiroshima. Still larger tankers, that could carry twice as much LNG, have been proposed. LNG terminal sites pose even greater hazards than tankers at sea. If an accident were to occur, a vapor cloud drifting over a populated area could ignite and cause catastrophic damage.

The odds of an LNG accident occurring are highly disputed. There are currently more than 150 plants in the United States and Canada where natural gas is liquified and stored during seasons when the demand for natural gas is low (Drake and Reid 1977). These "peak shaving" plants have excellent safety records (Lom 1974). When the demand for natural gas rises, LNG is revaporized and distributed through existing pipelines.

There are currently three LNG receiving terminals operating in the United States—at Everett, Massachusetts; Cove Point, Maryland; and Elba Island, Georgia. More than 100 LNG shipments have been made to these terminals over the past eight years without an accident. In 1976, more than 4.7 billion cubic feet of LNG were imported, mostly by tankers from Algeria, but also by truck from Canada. Gas company representatives also point to Japan's flawless safety records when documenting the risks inherent in the use of LNG. Japan imports 80 percent of its gas in liquid form.

The only major LNG accident in the United States occurred in October 1944. An LNG storage tank at a peak shaving plant in Cleveland, Ohio, ruptured and leaked 4,200 cubic feet of LNG into the streets and sewers. It ignited, killing 130 people, injuring 225, and causing $7 million in property damage. The accident stopped almost all LNG use in the United States for twenty years. Not until the mid-1960s, after significant advances in LNG technology were made, did utilities begin using LNG again.

LNG is viewed, in some quarters, as an attractive solution to the country's energy supply problem. Federal government projections suggest that LNG might supply as much as 15 percent of all our natural gas needs by 1985 (more than forty tankers would have to enter U.S. harbors on a regular basis to make the necessary deliveries).

The Importance of LNG to California

Twelve million people in Southern California are served by natural gas; nine out of ten homes use gas for water heating; three out of four use gas for cooking. In addition, more than 190,000 industrial and commercial consumers depend on gas and are not equipped to use alternate fuels. Also, given the smog problem in Southern California, other economically competitive fuels are much less attractive because they do not burn as cleanly (California State Legislature Assembly Subcommittee on Energy 1976).

Up until the late 1960s, adequate gas was supplied to Southern California via intrastate wells, two interstate pipelines, and imports from Canada. In 1970, 642 billion cubic feet of natural gas came from California wells, 1,262 billion cubic feet came from Southwestern U.S. pipelines (in Texas, Oklahoma, and New Mexico), and 294 billion cubic feet were imported from Canada. By 1975, California marketed production had dropped to 368 billion cubic feet, Southwestern U.S. pipeline gas had fallen to 1,159 billion cubic feet, but Canadian imports had risen to 365 billion cubic feet. End-use sales over this five year period fell by 14 percent because supplies were inadequate (California State Legislature Assembly Subcommittee on Energy 1976).

One reason it was difficult to secure adequate supplies in the mid-1970s was that California had difficulty competing with intrastate buyers in the producing states. Interstate regulated prices were set at one-third to one-half the price of gas sold in the intrastate markets of the producing states. Deregulation, however, increased supplies from the Southwest and made it profitable to tap gas from offshore wells in the Gulf of Mexico (which until recently had to be sold at the cheaper prices of the interstate market). In 1977, Pacific Lighting Corporation estimated that at best deregulation would only increase supplies from ten to twenty percent (California State Legislature Assembly Subcommittee on Energy 1976).

In 1976, Southern California Gas Company and Pacific Lighting Corporation predicted that California's failure to obtain new supplies of natural gas would cause serious industrial and commercial dislocations. They predicted that the curtailment of deliveries to customers without the capacity to use alternate fuels would occur as early as the fall of 1979. Industry forecasts estimated that as many as 700,000 people would be unemployed as a result. An increase in the supply of LNG was perceived as the only means of preventing industrial shut-downs and maintaining the level of regional employment. The dire unemployment prognoses did not come to pass, but they were very much in the headlines in 1977 when S.B. 1081 was before the legislature.

The Effort to Site an LNG Plant Along the Coast

In 1972, the Pacific-Alaska LNG Company, a subsidiary of Pacific Lighting Corporation, made the first application to site an LNG terminal in California. At the time, the uncertainties associated with acquiring the permits necessary for constructing and operating an LNG facility in California were unknown. Federal, state, and local agencies played reactive roles, waiting to evaluate the site selections presented by private industry. Pacific Lighting Corporation and Southern California Gas Company actually wanted to build two LNG terminals to ensure continuity of service. In September 1973, while environmental impact studies (to accompany the initial application to site a facility in Los Angeles) were being prepared, Western LNG Terminal Associates, another subsidiary of Pacific Lighting Corporation, filed an application with the Federal Power Commission (FPC) to begin environmental studies at three sites: Los Angeles (as a terminal for Alaskan LNG), Oxnard (as a terminal for Indonesian LNG), and Point Conception (as a contingency site). Each proposed facility was intended to handle 4 billion cubic feet per day of natural gas.

Los Angeles.   Pacific Lighting Corporation and Southern California Gas Company favored Los Angeles as a site for an LNG terminal. The proposed terminal was to be in a protected harbor with high berth availability (Gatzke, Landis, and Pollock 1978). Minimal environmental impact was expected because the site was in an already developed area. For these and other reasons, Los Angeles would be the least costly site to build. Pipeline costs would also be minimal because of the proximity of existing lines (Resource Planning Associates 1977).

In May 1972, Pacific-Alaska LNG Company submitted an application to the Los Angeles Harbor Department. A few months later, the Board of Harbor Commissioners appropriated $220,000 to compile data and to undertake experimental work that could be used in preparing a Draft Enviromental Impact Report (EIR). A Draft EIR was completed in November 1974. Pacific-Alaska LNG Company applied to the FPC for a permit to purchase, liquify, ship, and store natural gas in Los Angeles. The utility company hired Science Applied, Inc., to conduct a risk assessment and an analysis of safety systems. That report was finished in December 1976 and helped to justify the proposed Los Angeles terminal site.

Opposition groups formed in the neighborhoods surrounding the proposed site. The San Pedro and Peninsula Home Owners Coalition and the Point Fermin Residents Association adamantly opposed the project. They argued that the risk of an accident was too great and that the construction of the terminal would adversely affect property values. They objected primarily on the grounds of safety, indicating that they were not opposed to LNG in general, only to the proposed site.

In September 1976, the FPC issued a Draft Environmental Impact Statement recommending the elimination of Los Angeles Harbor as a potential site. The FPC felt that the area's vulnerability to earthquake damage (because of its nearness to the Palos Verde fault) exceeded acceptable limits.

Despite the potential earthquake exposure, the Los Angeles City Council's Industry and Transportation Committee approved in December 1976, by a vote of twelve to two, Western LNG Terminal Associates' application to lease land on Terminal Island. The following day, the Italian oil tanker

San Sansenina exploded and burned in Los Angeles Harbor. Shock waves from the explosion were felt in several sections of the city, alerting people to the possible risks of dangerous cargoes.

Within a few days, the City Council formed a Hazardous Cargo Task Force to prepare a risk assessment for Los Angeles Harbor. Meanwhile debate began in Sacramento over the advisability of siting an LNG terminal in a densely populated area such as Los Angeles. The risk assessment prepared by Science Applied, Inc., became the center of this debate (and was later attacked at state assembly subcommittee hearings). Assemblyman Terry Goggin called for a one-year delay in the selection of an LNG terminal site. In the meantime, the Los Angeles City Council approved a twenty-five year lease for an LNG terminal by a vote of thirteen to two.

In Sacramento both the state and the assembly considered bills to streamline the energy siting process. Debate focused on the overall safety of LNG, the dangers of siting a terminal in a densely populated area, and the need to build a terminal before natural gas shortages occurred causing serious unemployment and industrial dislocations.

In August 1977, the Los Angeles City Council voted to oppose any state legislation that would prevent the construction of an LNG terminal in Los Angeles Harbor. Nevertheless, in September 1977, the state legislature passed and Governor Brown signed S.B. 1081. This law preempted existing state and local siting laws, superceded mandated environmental reviews, and prohibited the siting of an LNG terminal in a densely populated area. Thus, after more than four years and countless studies, the state legislature passed a law that disqualified Los Angeles as a possible site for an LNG terminal.

Oxnard. The proposal to site an LNG terminal at Oxnard lacked local support (Bingham, Freeman, and McCreary 1978). In April 1977, a poll by a local newspaper, the *Ventura Star Press*, found people four to one against the proposed facility. Many residents and the state Department of Food and Agriculture were concerned that prime agricultural land would be destroyed by further industrialization that would be encouraged because of the availability of new natural gas supplies. In addition, Oxnard residents were worried about the catastrophic consequences of an LNG accident. Located within four miles of the proposed site were twenty-seven schools with a total of approximately 20,000 students.

The Ventura County Concerned Citizens, the Ventura County Environmental Resource Agency, the Environmental Coalition of Ventura County, and the local chapter of the League of Women Voters argued that an LNG plant should not be located in such a densely populated area. Consultants hired by the adjacent town of Port Hueneme charged that the Oxnard site was not safe for other reasons. Port Hueneme residents were in the unenviable position of potentially suffering all the negative consequences of a proposed LNG terminal (e.g., high risk of accidents, pollution, and loss of property values) with no say in the decision and no chance to secure any of the property tax benefits. The Sierra Club opposed the site because two important defense installations were within four miles of the proposed site: the Pacific Missile Range and the Naval Construction Batallion Center. An LNG terminal would be a good target for a sabotage operation.

Still, the Oxnard site offered a number of advantages. While additional berth space would be needed for LNG tankers, no unusual construction costs were anticipated. In addition, the terminal, if approved, could be built before predicted natural gas shortages occurred.

In March 1975, Western LNG Terminal Associates filed an application with the city of Oxnard for a special use permit to construct an LNG terminal and regasification facility. Soon thereafter, the city hired Socio-Economic Systems to prepare an EIR for the project. The Oxnard City Council decided it should have more firsthand knowledge about LNG receiving terminals, so several of the representatives, at their own expense, flew to Japan to visit a similar facility. Members of the Planning Commission went to San Diego to see an LNG peak shaving plant.

The hotly disputed Draft EIR was released in August 1976. The city's Public Works Department and the Environmental Resources Agency charged that the Draft EIR was inadequate because it did not thoroughly address disaster possibilities, possible mitigation measures, or possible impact on wildlife or air quality. Socio-Economic Systems prepared an addendum to the Draft EIR. The final EIR was approved by the Oxnard City Council by a vote of four to one in June 1977.

In the meantime, two new groups formed to oppose the LNG project: the Campaign Against Utility Service Exploitation (CAUSE) and Citizens United for Responsible Energy (CURE). But, as in Los Angeles, local decision making was entirely preempted by the passage of S.B. 1081. The Oxnard site was excluded from consideration because of the high population density surrounding it. Many local officials, on both sides of the LNG controversy, were outraged by the state's usurpation of local powers.

Point Conception: Prior to the passage of S.B. 1081, Point Conception was the least favored of the three proposed sites (Nickell, Smith, and Smith 1978). From the start, the only apparent advantage of Point Conception was the very low population density surrounding the site. On the other hand, weather conditions at Point Conception were sure to hinder vessel access. Berths for LNG ships were minimal and Point Conception was not close to any existing pipelines for natural gas. The need for extensive pipeline rerouting and expansion of berth spaces made Point Conception the most costly of the three sites. In addition, the risk of an accident was increased by the proximity of the site to a seismic fault (Resource Planning Associates 1977).

The nearby Santa Barbara oil spill in 1969 made Point Conception residents extremely sensitive to the risks of energy-related accidents. Local opposition had previously formed to prevent oil company development in Santa Barbara County. Several new groups formed to oppose the LNG terminal: the Point Conception Preservation Committee, the Bixby Ranch Landowners Association, and the Hollister Ranch Landowners Association. They did not want to gamble on an LNG accident, and they wanted to protect the rural character of the area.

In August 1976, Western LNG Terminal Associates filed an application with the Santa Barbara County Planning Department for a change in the County General Plan to allow for development of an LNG terminal at Point Conception. The Santa Barbara County Office of Environmental Quality hired Arthur D. Little Company to prepare an EIR and with Resource Planning Associates to prepare a gas supply and availability study. An assessment of state energy needs (and gas supplies) had already been completed by the utility companies, but the Office of Environmental Quality wanted an independent analysis.

In March 1977, the Planning Department formed a Citizen's Advisory Task Force on LNG to review the EIR and other relevant materials and to advise the Board of Supervisors regarding the siting question. The passage of S.B. 1081 undercut further local effort.

The city of Los Angeles would have accepted an LNG facility. At least, its elected officials seemed inclined to do so. The city undertook a fairly sophisticated analysis of the risks and impacts likely to be involved. Opposition groups formed in the neighborhoods surrounding the proposed site, but the City Council was not swayed by their arguments. The proposed Oxnard site lacked local support. Residents feared the facility and worried about the effects of further industrial development associated with new cryogenic industries. Oxnard also commissioned an elaborate impact review. Local officials made an extraordinary effort to educate themselves about the technology and the risks involved. Point Conception was the least favored of the proposed sites. Even the industry representatives were not especially pleased with the costs involved in preparing the site. A number of groups concerned about protecting the rural character of the area banded together to oppose the facility. The County commissioned not only an elaborate impact assessment but its own analysis of state energy needs as well. In sum, there was no evidence to suggest that existing laws, administered locally, were not adequate. Concerned groups had more than ample opportunity to express their views. Local officials had no difficulty coping with the technical complexity of the issues involved.

The Pre-S.B. 1081 Siting Process

Prior to the passage of S.B. 1081, utility companies did all the long range planning and decided which technologies were appropriate. The utilities selected sites, acquired land, and then sought federal, state, and local approval. Public agencies participated in the siting process only after the utility companies submitted applications for the required licenses and permits.

Throughout the 1970s, the increasing politicization of environmental concerns led to the adoption of numerous regulations aimed at protecting environmental quality. The addition of each new regulatory review created a new opportunity for interest groups to question, delay, and possibly stop proposed energy projects. The passage of the National Environmental Policy Act (NEPA) and the California Environmental Quality Act (CEQA) reinforced the popular notion that adverse environmental impacts should be taken into account in choosing project locations and that individuals should be given ample opportunity to indicate all the ways in which they might be affected by these impacts.

Even today, the EIR/EIS review processes do not come into play, for the most part, until after sites are selected and land is acquired by private applicants. This means that the public, and especially those adversely affected by a facility, are put in the position of "spoilers." The public review process (both before and after S.B. 1081) begins when the utilities feel they have just about completed their work.

Because the processes of impact assessment and site selection occur sequentially, site selection takes almost twice as long as it would otherwise. And, in the end, site approval is by no means guaranteed. A lawsuit filed at the end of a multilayered review process can delay and ultimately "kill" a project, suggesting that not everyone who should have participated in the "bargaining process" from the beginning was, in fact, involved or that the mechanisms for balancing competing interests in the course of the review process were not adequate to the task of achieving consensus.

Although the Pacific Lighting Corporation first considered the Point Conception site in 1968, it did not contact Santa Barbara County until eight years later when it submitted a request for general plan and zoning changes. During those eight years, the utility conducted in-house studies of alternative sites. But the public evaluation process, requiring a similar consideration of alternative sites, could begin only after the zoning change request had been submitted.

In addition to the problem of sequential private and public reviews of alternative sites, five other problems contributed to the delay and confusion associated with the pre-1081 siting process: (1) the lack of an overarching state energy policy deprived decision makers of a backdrop against which to evaluate specific projects; (2) the lack of a proper forum within which to consider the full range of costs and benefits of proposed projects meant that the impacts were often misconstrued; (3) a lack of agreement concerning the range of technical analyses required to make an informed siting decision left groups arguing about the facts and not just their different views; (4) the failure to develop a credible energy needs assessment left each project vulnerable to the charge that it was unnecessary; and (5) the failure to ensure timely and adequate public participation at each step in the siting process aroused more adverse feeling than might otherwise have been directed at a particular project. The legislature should have been addressing these problems, not merely the problem of delay.

No State Energy Policy: Very few states have an energy policy that can provide a framework within which to consider particular project or site proposals. Without such a policy that enumerates production and conservation objectives, disagreements over the desirability of alternative energy sources or the relative desirability of alternative technologies will be played out every time a new project is proposed. Centralized policy formulation is difficult, but in the absence of a state policy, continual debate about the broad issue of energy confounds the effort to make site specific decisions. Efforts to judge proposed LNG terminal sites in California become occasions to debate the relative merits of LNG as an energy source for the state.

No Forum In Which to Weigh Benefits and Costs: Private utilities linked the need for an LNG terminal to the maintenance of regional employment in Southern California. They charged that unless an LNG facility was built quickly there would be serious job losses. Facility siting agencies, however, are rarely charged with implementing employment policies. While some jobs may have been lost, it's not clear that building an LNG facility was the best or only way to save them. The task of the energy agency is to maximize energy supplies, with some consideration of the direct cost implications for rate payers. It would be inappropriate for the energy agency to seek the most effective way of promoting job development regardless of the implications for energy supply. In selecting sites for energy facilities, the private sector rarely weighs the full costs of environmental damage against the benefits associated with each site. All too often, costs of only one kind are compared to a narrow range of benefits in one policy arena, while other costs and benefits are considered in other arenas.

The primary users of the additional natural gas sought for California will be the residents of Southern California, regardless of which terminal site is selected. Yet, the people likely to be adversely affected by an accident or by the impacts of a new facility will probably be those who live in the area immediately surrounding the new installation. Thus, not only are different sets of costs and benefits considered in separate policy arenas, but benefits to one political jurisdiction and costs to another are rarely considered together.

Different Views About the Role of Technical Analysis: The Los Angeles City Council failed to consider potential seismic hazards (identified subsequently in the EIS) when it made its decision to approve the proposed LNG project. The project was ultimately rejected by the FPC because of this hazard. The representatives from the Oxnard City Council who visited the LNG terminal in Japan did so in an attempt to better understand the technologies involved in LNG processing. In preparing an EIR for the proposed Point Conception site, Santa Barbara County evaluated the project so thoroughly that the process of impact assessment became surprisingly costly and time consuming. The assessment produced twenty-five volumes of technical reports and included an extensive review of alternative sites along the entire coastline, both on and off shore, and reconsidered the overall need for natural gas in California. Each municipality in which a proposed site was located defined differently the kinds of technical analyses it needed and judged the technical findings differently. State agencies, as will be discussed below, also made very different judgments about the required data and studies. In some instances, disputes over the appropriateness of a particular site could be traced to a reliance on different types of data.

Lack of Credible Needs Assessments: The process by which utilities and state and federal agencies assess energy needs often lacks credibility. A great deal of criticism has been directed (both in California and elsewhere) at forecasting methods that do little more than extrapolate from past trends, that are internally inconsistent and insensitive to end-use needs, and that consider only a limited range of technical options. A lack of agreement on the need for additional energy supplies makes consensus on particular projects difficult to achieve.

Inadequate Public Participation: In California, the adequacy of public participation in the consideration of alternative sites has been challenged. In Los Angeles, the City Council ignored the objections of people living adjacent to the proposed site. In Oxnard, the residents of the adjacent town of Port Hueneme were not included in the review process. The only option for residents who feel that their interests are not adequately considered is to bring legal action in an effort to stop construction. One way of gaining a legal and political foothold from which to mount such a challenge is to point to an inadequate process of public participation. It need not be argued that a more adequate process of public participation would have resolved disagreements. Just a claim that "due process" has been ignored will yield sympathy for a political challenge to a particular siting decision.

The Intent and Passage of S.B. 1081

In July 1976, the Assembly Subcommittee on Energy held LNG hearings on the safety, reliability, and financing of LNG. The hearings were held in Los Angeles and chaired by Assemblyman Terry Goggin. Testimony was given by representatives from the utility companies, all levels of government, environmental groups, the shipping industry, and the financial community. By January, Goggin had introduced Assembly Bill 220 "to enact the California Natural Gas Act of 1977 which would provide for the siting of loading, regasification, and storage facilities for liquified natural gas pursuant to the issuance of a special LNG site and facility certificate by the California Coastal Commission."

In March 1977, Assemblyman Dannemeyer introduced an alternative bill that would give the Public Utilities Commission (PUC) instead of the Coastal Commission "exclusive authority with respect to approving an application to locate a liquified natural gas facility in a particular location." Dannemeyer's bill was opposed by local officials in Los Angeles, Oxnard, and Point Conception.

In September 1977, Governor Brown signed a compromise bill, Senate Bill 1081 (Chapter 855, Statutes of 1977), sponsored by Senator Alquist. Overall project approval authority was delegated to the PUC, removing all consideration of costs and benefits from local hands and from the hands of the Coastal Commission and locating them exclusively in an energy agency. The bill included a detailed timetable for decision making and mandated remote mainland siting of California's first LNG terminal.

The decision about acceptable levels of risk was essentially settled by establishing population density requirements in rings around hypothetical terminal sites: no more than 27 permanent residents would be allowed within one mile and no more than 1800 permanent residents within four miles of an approved site. This was the aspect of the law that eliminated Los Angeles and Oxnard from further consideration.

Under S.B. 1081, utilities were required to make application to the PUC requesting approval of an LNG terminal site. The PUC established safety regulations. The state Energy Commission was required to complete a natural gas needs assessment. Sites were researched and recommended by the Coastal Commission; that is, the Coastal Commission identified, evaluated, and ranked sites for an LNG terminal and submitted its recommendations. These were supposed to be submitted by 31 May 1978, although that deadline was missed. S.B. 1081 gave the PUC final decision-making power. The PUC was supposed to approve only the top ranked site unless construction could not be completed in time to meet LNG needs. In that case, the PUC was empowered to choose a lower ranked site.

This altered the role of the Coastal Commission. Formerly, it analyzed utility company proposals. Under S.B. 1081, it was required to select sites that will, in all probability, have environmentally degrading consequences.

Because of the density restrictions, Point Conception was the only site of the three proposed in September 1974 that could still be considered. Consequently, the PUC and the utility companies viewed it as the favored location for the LNG receiving terminal. Of all the possible remote sites, Point Conception would be available most quickly, and most of the environmental studies that the utilities would normally undertake had been completed prior to the passage of S.B. 1081. In addition, S.B. 1081 required that Point Conception, the site favored by the utility companies, be included in the Coastal Commission's ranking of sites.

After the enactment of S.B. 1081, opposition to an LNG terminal at Point Conception increased dramatically. The Bixby Ranch Landowners Association filed suit in federal court to enjoin state officials from implementing S.B. 1081, alleging that it was unconstitutional for the state government to designate an LNG site since a federal statute gives exclusive siting power to a federal regulatory agency. This challenge was dismissed. The Santa Barbara Board of Supervisors voted four to one to intervene in the federal siting hearings in Los Angeles (at which representatives recommended the study of offshore sites). The Point Conception Preservation Committee, Santa Barbara Citizens for Environmental Defense, the Hollister Ranch Owners Association, and the Sierra Club also pushed for offshore site consideration because of their concerns about safety and their worries that a terminal would encourage additional development.

The pre-S.B. 1081 siting process in California was similar to siting processes in most other states. Siting decisions were made on a one-by-one basis without any reference to an overall state energy policy. The full array of costs and benefits associated with each technology at each proposed site were not considered simultaneously. Public participation in the setting of energy policy priorities and in the evaluation of proposed sites was limited. The state government waited for private industry to suggest sites and then more often than not, deferred to the industry's needs assessments and site analyses. S.B. 1081 did little to respond to these shortcomings, nor did it give the state what it needed most—a more effective way of mediating among the conflicting concerns and desires of different interest groups.

The Attempt to Implement S.B. 1081

Pacific Lighting Corporation and the Pacific Gas and Electric Company mounted an extensive campaign to site the facility at Point Conception. They hired Winner/Wagner Associates, a public relations firm, to promote Point Conception as the number one site. But, if anything, the utilities' campaign had a negative effect on the Coastal Commission's ranking. The Commission evaluated eighty-two sites including eighteen nominated by the public. Only four sites were included in the final ranking released on 31 May 1978 by the Coastal Commission:

1. Horno Canyon on the Camp Pendleton military reservation in San Diego County
2. Rattlesnake Canyon in San Luis Obispo County
3. Point Conception in Santa Barbara County
4. Deer Canyon in Ventura County

The criteria used by the Coastal Commission in selecting and ranking sites includes: potential impacts on marine and land resources, public access, public service impacts and requirements, impacts on archaeological resources, and impacts on public views. In addition, remoteness and the potential cost of the facility were important considerations. The Coastal Commission included terms and conditions for each recommended site to ensure that adverse environmental impacts would be minimized and that public health and safety would be protected. The staff reported that "there is no possible remote onshore terminal site that will not cause major adverse impacts to natural marine wildlife resources, public recreation areas, and other resources protected by the California Coastal Act of 1976" (*Los Angeles Times* 1978a).

The Coastal Commission's recommendations encountered tremendous resistance. The Navy and the Marine Corps were opposed to the site at Camp Pendleton because they felt it would endanger the lives of the 44,000 base residents and the people who used the heavily traveled Route 5. In addition, Camp Pendleton "is the only remaining beach in Southern California suitable for Marine and Navy amphibious training. To build an LNG terminal there would cause maritime hazards" (*Los Angeles Times* 1978b). Pipelines from the terminal would infringe on troop maneuvers. The existence of the San Onofre nuclear power plant five miles away further complicates the use of the Camp Pendleton site.

A native American Indian group opposed the Rattlesnake Canyon site. Archaeologically significant materials had been discovered on that site; these would inevitably inhibit construction. Adverse wind and wave conditions would necessitate the construction of a $175 million breakwater. In addition, Rattlesnake Canyon is within five miles of the Diablo Canyon nuclear power plant.

The utility companies were angry that Point Conception was ranked third, rather than first, on the Coastal Commission's list. An active earthquake fault had been discovered near the site during the commission's selection process. The Coastal Commission had eliminated another site, Las Varas, from consideration for the same reason, but retained Point Conception because S.B. 1081 required that the Coastal Commission rank the site selected by Western LNG Terminal Associates before the enactment of S.B. 1081.

Deer Canyon in Ventura County, ranked fourth, was considered most likely to create adverse environmental impacts. Its proximity to the popular Leo Carillo State Beach and Point Mugu State Park made it a particularly undesirable selection.

Ultimately, even with the discovery of the fault, the PUC felt that California's pressing need for natural gas made Point Conception the only possible site that could be constructed in time to prevent gas shortages. On 31 July 1978, the PUC provisionally authorized, by a vote of five to zero, Point Conception as California's first LNG terminal site and granted a permit for the $570 million project to Western LNG Terminal Associates.

The PUC felt that Camp Pendleton and Rattlesnake Canyon, the two sites ranked higher on the Coastal Commission's list, would take too long to build. Camp Pendleton's use was being resisted by the Department of Defense; extensive delays were expected. In addition, the Department of Defense felt it was near too many people as well as too near the San Onofre nuclear power plant. Rattlesnake Canyon was found unsuitable because of the need for an expensive breakwater to deal with the hostile marine environment.

In November 1978, the state Lands Commission approved a thirty year lease for the proposed LNG terminal at Point Conception. The Federal Energy Regulatory Commission (FERC) was the only remaining regulatory body that needed to approve the site before construction could begin. FERC hearings opened in mid-December 1978.

Meanwhile, in May 1978, a group of approximately fifty Chumash Indians occupied the proposed LNG site at Point Conception. They claimed that the site was on a sacred Indian burial ground. Kote Lotah, leader of the Indian group said, "this land is our western gate to the spiritual world, like the gates of heaven" (*Los Angeles Herald Examiner* 1978). An anthropologist testifying at the FERC hearing compared construction of an LNG terminal at Point Conception to "selling popcorn in a cathedral or building a terminal at the center of Mecca" (*Oxnard Press Courier* 1979). In response to these claims, the chief archaeologist for the Institute of Archaeology at the University of California, Los Angeles, stated that "no human skeletal remains have been found during excavations at the proposed site and that a search of available literature has revealed no reference to burial grounds at or near the proposed terminal location" (*El Monte Mid Valley News* 1979). In addition, a University of Santa Clara anthropologist testified that he could find "no inherent contradiction between traditional Chumash religious values and the placement of an industrial facility in the Little Cojo area [Point Conception]" (*El Monte Mid Valley News* 1979).

Seven months later, on 13 August 1979, Judge Samuel Z. Gordon handed down a 355-page opinion noting that the Indians' argument seemed specious and urging the Department of Energy "to bless the Point Conception plan" (*New York Times* 1979a). The U.S. Air Force requested that hearings be reopened because of the proximity of the Vandenberg Air Force Base. The Air Force was concerned about the possibility of a rocket or jet falling on the LNG terminal.

On 12 October 1979, the FERC approved the siting of the LNG terminal, having dismissed the Air Force's concerns. Thus, after six years and more than a dozen state and federal regulatory reviews, Pacific Gas and Electric Company and Pacific Lighting Corporation received a green light to build the LNG terminal at Point Conception. They were required to do further seismic, wind, and wave studies, but these were not preconditions to the permit.

The Chumash Indians, together with the Hollister Ranch Owners Association, the Bixby Ranch Landowners Association, the Sierra Club, and Santa Barbara Citizens for Environmental Defense filed an application for a rehearing by the FERC. The rehearing was denied. Then, in December 1979, while undertaking various trenching studies at the Point Conception site, Western LNG Terminal Associates announced that they had discovered two additional faults. The Chumash Indians and the Santa Barbara groups filed an action in the Federal Circuit Court of Appeals. They contend that the rights of the Chumash Indians have been denied, in violation of the American Indians Religious Freedom Act. They also assert that two preconditions for the approval of an LNG plant under the terms of the Natural Gas Act have not been met, namely, fundamental findings of need and safety. The issue of need is once again open to review. Deregulation of natural gas prices appears to have caused a glut of natural gas in California. When prices were deregulated, domestic suppliers "discovered" substantial additional supplies. The issue of safety is, of course, open to review in light of the new seismic dangers discovered subsequent to FERC approval. Finally, these same groups contend that the EIS prepared for the Point Conception site was inadequate under the terms of both the National Environmental Policy Act and the Historic Preservation Act. The Council on Environmental Quality has sent a letter to the FERC indicating that the EIS was indeed inadequate.

If Western LNG Terminal Associates' study of sea conditions and seismic dangers requires alterations in the original terminal design (for instance, if a sea wall has to be built), the plaintiffs in the federal suit are likely to demand that a new EIR as well as a new EIS be prepared. Western LNG Terminal Associates has offered the Chumash tribe sixty acres of land adjacent to the proposed terminal site if they will agree to drop the suit, but they have refused the offer.

The LNG facility siting process is not yet over in California. Court action could drag on for years. FERC approval may be withdrawn in light of the new seismic dangers recently discovered on the site. The site that the PUC thought was "best" may, at the very least, be unnecessary and, at worst, too dangerous to build on. The siting process mandated by S.B. 1081 did not yield the definitive decision its drafters intended. The technical analyses and the balancing of costs and benefits, which should have been part of the siting process, appear to have been inadequate.

Conclusions

S.B. 1081 preempted municipal participation in the LNG siting process. Los Angeles might well have accepted an LNG terminal. Officials in that city obviously calculated the risks of an accident differently from the members of the state legislature and officials in Oxnard and Santa Barbara. S.B. 1081 also put the Coastal Commission in a difficult position, requiring that body to propose an LNG terminal site incompatible with its general mandate to protect the coastline. In the end, the Coastal Commission's rankings were ignored by the PUC, suggesting that the full range of environmental costs was never balanced against the economic advantages sought by those who called for quick action to avert possible LNG shortages.

The ready availability of adequate natural gas supplies in California in January 1980 raises questions about the utilities' call for quick action in the first place. The recently announced U.S. agreement with the Mexican government regarding American importation of Mexican LNG raises further doubts about the credibility of the needs assessments that spurred the passage of S.B. 1081 (*New York Times* 1979b).

S.B. 1081 not only sought to speed up the regulatory review process, but it also sought to short-circuit required environmental reviews. Had environmental impact review requirements been pursued by the state, further seismic studies might well have been prerequisite to granting of a permit, and archaeological findings and issues of concern to particular interest groups might have been reviewed more carefully. Perhaps further study and negotiation could have suggested mitigation measures or compensation acceptable to the Chumash Indians and the environmental groups in Santa Barbara. While it is difficult to imagine how the results of a siting process could ever please everyone, it is not hard to see how efforts to preempt normal procedures and guarantees stimulate suspicion, ill will, and lawsuits that might otherwise not arise.

Environmental regulations, public participation requirements, and rules regarding the consideration of certain technical analyses have been adopted because they are important. We depend on the government to guarantee public safety. Efforts to "cut red tape" threaten to undermine the delicate system of checks and balances through which we determine levels of risk and weigh costs and benefits.

There are, undoubtedly, ways of eliminating delay caused by dilatory administrators, but efforts to preempt regulations because of current anxiety about dwindling energy supplies ought to be resisted. As it turned out, there was no immediate shortage of natural gas in California (as the industry claimed there would be). There is now sufficient time for California to complete a careful review of its state energy objectives and to implement a siting review that balances as wide a range of costs and benefits as possible and provides the requisite opportunities for public participation at each step in the policy-making and siting process. This should happen even if the FERC fails to reverse its earlier decision or if pending legal action is unsuccessful.

The facility siting problem still remains in California as well as in other states. New ways must be found to bring all the parties with a stake in each siting decision to the bargaining table. Their negotiations must be informed by technical analyses that they believe to be credible. Negotiations must seek to balance state-wide needs with local concerns. Existing regulations must be accepted as constraints on the bargaining. Negotiations of this sort, perhaps involving mediation, may produce the definitive siting decisions for which California is searching.

References

Bingham, G.; Freeman G.; and McCreary S. 1978. The "Local Story": Oxnard's Response to the Proposed LNG Terminal (unpublished paper). Department of City and Regional Planning, University of California, Berkeley, California.

California State Legislative Assembly Subcommittee on Energy. July 1976. *Liquified Natural Gas Hearings.* Testimony of Joseph R. Rensch, President, Pacific Lighting Corporation.

Drake, E. and Reid, R.C. 1977. The Importation of Liquified Natural Gas. *Scientific American,* vol. 236, no. 4.

El Monte (Calif.) Mid Valley News, January 3, 1979.

Gatzke, A.E.; Landis, J.; and Pollock, P. 1978. Los Angeles Harbor LNG Terminal (unpublished paper). Department of City and Regional Planning, University of California, Berkeley, California.

Lom, W.L. 1974. *Liquified Natural Gas.* New York: Halsted.

Los Angeles Herald Examiner, December 12, 1978.

Los Angeles Times, May 8, 1978a.

Los Angeles Times, May 9, 1978b.

New York Times, September 9, 1979a.

New York Times, December 29, 1979b.

Nickell, M.; Smith, M.; and Smith, P. 1978. Chronology and Context of Local Decision Making for the LNG Terminal and Processing Plant in Santa Barbara County (unpublished paper). Department of City and Regional Planning, University of California, Berkeley, California.

Oxnard Press Courier, January 18, 1979.

Resource Planning Associates, Inc. 1977. The LNG Decision in California: Reliability, Cost, Safety, and Siting. Prepared for the California Energy Resource Conservation and Development Commission, RPA Reference No.: RA-76-37B.

Shreve, R.N. and Buick Jr., J.A. 1977. *Chemical Process Industries.* New York: McGraw Hill.

NICHOLAS A. ASHFORD

22 *The Limits of Cost-Benefit Analysis in Regulatory Decisions*

Cost-benefit analysis can be a useful tool, but some regulatory reformers would have us apply it as an indiscriminate, decision-making *rule.* I would like to offer some words of caution—on methodological flaws and on possible political misuse of the results—that may be summarized as follows:

- There are important differences between economic regulation and environmental, health, or safety regulation that must not be overlooked.
- Costs are easier to express than benefits, but their quantifiability makes them no more certain or reliable.
- Benefits include improved quality of life and good health as well as positive economic side-effects, but they defy accurate estimation and their recipients are not a well-organized lobbying group.
- The comparison of costs and benefits is beset by serious methodological difficulties and requires the analyst to make value-laden assumptions; yet cost-benefit analysis appears, deceptively, to be a neutral technique.
- Insistence on cost-benefit decision rules and other regulatory "reform" efforts may be undemocratic attempts to reorient legislative mandates.

Reprinted with permission from *Technology Review,* M.I.T., Alumni Association, copyright 1980.

Crucial Distinctions

Economic regulation seeks to improve the workings of the market by encouraging competition, economic efficiency, and a diversity of goods and services. Regulation addresses itself to this goal by attempting to ensure that the price mechanism operates efficiently to properly allocate goods and services among economic sectors and between producers and consumers. Economic regulation, therefore, properly carried out, is expected to reduce prices.

Health, safety, and environmental regulation, on the other hand, attempts to ameliorate the adverse consequences of market activities—and technology in general—by reducing the attendant social costs. This regulation attempts to internalize the social costs of production by ensuring that the prices of goods and services reflect true costs to the society. Although prices can be expected to go up in response, Charles Schultze (in his now-famous work with Alan Kneese entitled *Pollution, Prices, and Public Policy)* has cautioned us not to regard as inflationary those price increases that internalize social costs.

The assumption that all price increases are inflationary (indeed, inflation was so defined by an early executive order of Gerald Ford) ignores the crucial distinction between economic and environmental regulation. With economic regulation, associated price increases may well be inflationary and an indication that government efforts need to be re-examined. But with environmental regulation, price increases may be a measure of success. Environmental regulation is not really an instrument of economic policy; it is an instrument of *social* policy concerned with the nature and distribution of the effects of industrial activity. Therefore, environmental regulation cannot be judged by economic criteria alone.

Even if such criteria are (inappropriately) used, inflation is still a phony issue in the national debate over environmental, health, and safety regulation. Actual estimates of the effects of such regulation on the Consumer Price Index—by several groups, including the president's Council on Wage and Price Stability and the Council on Environmental Quality—place the effect at well below 1 percent in a time of double-digit inflation.

Inflated Numbers

Because the costs of complying with regulation can be easily monetized, it is often assumed that they are reliable estimates of true costs. But in many instances the costs are not only uncertain, they are also unreliable. Agencies depend to a large extent upon industry data to derive estimates of compliance costs, and I do not believe I am being too unkind in questioning the bias of those estimates. The regulatory agencies generally do not have access to information, especially on alternative products and processes, that enables them to come up with the best estimates of compliance costs.

Compliance costs estimates often fail to take into account three crucial issues:

- Economies of scale are inevitably realized by increased production of compliance-related technology.
- A regulated industrial segment is able to learn, over time, to comply more cost-effectively—management scientists call this the "learning curve."
- Compliance costs based on present technological capabilities ignore the important benefits, both to the regulated firm and the public, that come from technological innovation.

Environmental regulation has often been called "technology-forcing," so costs of compliance should not be based on static assumptions about an industry and its technology. Otherwise, a large overestimation will result, as in the case of the OSHA vinyl chloride standard. The actual (and minimal) economic impacts were in stark contrast to ominous preregulation predictions.

Understated or Unstated Benefits

The "science" (or perhaps the "art") of estimating numbers of prevented cancer cases, chronic disease cases, or even injuries is in its infancy. Because of the accepted view of cancer causation, many health professionals believe there is no safe exposure to a carcinogen. Safe levels for chronic toxins (which are not carcinogens) are often derived from either acute human exposures or high-dose animal experiments, and techniques for extrapolating to lower doses for chronic human exposure are imperfect. Therefore, benefit calculations for a particular maximum exposure level (allowed under a specific regulation) are often not very meaningful.

Theories of accident prediction do not serve us much better. We scarcely need reminding of the unanticipated risk that attended the incident at Three Mile Island, or the failure to predict design defects in the DC-10.

Both costs and benefits of regulation are beset by uncertainty; however, the uncertainty surrounding the benefit calculations is usually much larger. It is fair to say that the state-of-the-art in benefit estimation is much less developed than the methodologies for calculating compliance costs. In addition, there is no organized interest group that systematically pursues benefit estimations in the same way that compliance costs are researched. And the tendency by analysts to rely on hard numbers—softer numbers are harder to believe—places the estimation of benefits on insecure ground.

It must also be realized that the benefits derived from direct regulation are only a part of the benefits of the regulatory process. Indirect, or *leveraged*, benefits are derived from the pressure of regulation to induce industry to innovate—to deal preventively with previously unregulated hazards and to find ways to meet the public's need for a cleaner, healthier environment while maintaining industrial capacity. Put another way, the positive side-effects accompanying regulation need to be included in a complete assessment of the effectiveness of the regulatory agency's strategies.

Comparing Apples and Oranges

Even if we could accurately estimate the amount of disease or injury prevented by regulation, and the costs of doing so, two difficult tasks remain:

- Monetizing health benefits that may accrue far into the future (or even monetizing current accident-prevention benefits); and
- Comparing those benefits to current compliance costs.

A human life or a lost limb does not have an established market value. Payments to workers to assume risky occupations prior to being injured (*ex ante* valuations) are different from the values placed on the injured workers by their families after the injuries have occurred (*ex post* valuations). Which valuation is correct? The work of Fischhoff, Kasperson, Kunreuther, and others amply demonstrates the inability of people and firms to consistently evaluate long-term, low-probability risks. These characteristics leave market valuation of the benefits of regulation in great doubt.

There is another crucial problem with regard to valuation. Economic efficiency reflects the maintenance of current economic arrangements, and it is naive to talk about workers who sell their wages off for their health as if the transaction took place in an unconstrained market. A worker does not have a large bundle of economic goods, and this affects his or her selling price. If you think it is unfair for poor people to sell their wages off more cheaply than wealthy people, then you do not like the working of the market. If you do not care, then you are willing to allow the working of the market mechanism. It inevitably comes down to the fundamental issue of the distribution of wealth.

Some analysts still insist on expressing health, safety, and environmental benefits in monetary terms, although this practice is changing. The successor to evaluating a change of net social welfare in dollars is the benefit-to-cost ratio—e.g., the number of fatalities prevented per dollar expended. The problem with this index is that it can never really be applied. The benefits of regulation include deaths prevented, diseases and injuries prevented, pain and suffering prevented, hospital costs prevented, and so on. The benefit part of the ratio is composed of many elements of different character—how do we decide, for example, how many serious injuries are equivalent to one death? In addition, how do we properly "discount" the costs and benefits that accrue, each differently, over time?

The present value of the net effects of any given regulation, or the *ranking* of the effects of alternative regulatory regimes, can change markedly depending upon the discount rate used in the cost-benefit calculation. For example, using a discount rate of zero for future health benefits (i.e., not discounting future health benefits) may make a regulatory choice tenable, while using a discount rate for health benefits comparable to the discount rate for capital expenditures may show a proposal to be undesirable. Further, since the consequences of many regulatory actions may be to impose compliance costs today in order to bring about health benefits far into the future, the choice of discount rate can make one regulatory option look better or worse than an alternative. Since there is no consensus on what that rate should be, the policymaker's preference for a particular regulatory option can be hidden in the choice of a discount rate.

An even more serious limitation of a simple comparison of costs and benefits is that it ignores equity implications—costs and benefits are often borne by different groups of people. Thus, the aggregation of costs and benefits is value-laden—it is a political decision, conscious or unconscious, to ignore equity.

Finally, the comparison of costs and benefits of a regulation must in turn be compared against what might happen in the absence of that regulation. If we estimate the benefits and costs of adopting a safety standard for a consumer product, for example, we must ask whether the manufacturer could make the product somewhat safer in the absence of regulation—in response to product liability lawsuits, for example. It might not be correct, therefore, to attribute to regulation either all the costs expended or all the benefits conferred.

Whose Mandate?

There are a number of different benchmarks that the regulatory decision maker might use to arrive at a particular strategy and hence be called on to defend. They include economic efficiency, cost-effectiveness, health-effectiveness, distribution consequences (equity), and specific mandates embodied in various pieces of legislation. In some legislation, the discretion on how to "balance" various considerations is broad; in others, it is more narrowly defined. In many instances, criticism of a particular decision to regulate is really a criticism of the balance struck by Congress in empowering an agency to act. Attacks on the FDA's ban of saccharin or on OSHA's standard for occupational exposure to benzene, for example, are really attacks on the legislative mandates. By asserting that a standard is not cost-effective or that it is too expensive, critics are attempting to force an evaluation of the proposed regulation against different benchmarks.

A more serious concern, however, is that assessment of an agency's economic impact, by groups such as the Council of Economic Advisors or the Council on Wage and Price Stability, may really be strategies to reorient various legislative mandates to their own point of view. It is certainly undemocratic, if not dangerous, for our society to let any one group of people— whether scientists, lawyers, or economists—set national priorities, and we must try to avoid such a "tyranny of experts."

There are no facile rules of thumb, no quick fixes, no simple indices of correctness in environmental regulation. A search for a facile decision rule— imposing upon the regulatory decision makers a requirement to undertake analyses that are overly quantitative and restrictive—would in reality *absolve* regulators from accountability rather than force them to articulate the hard choices. What can be expressed in a cost-benefit equation is only a small part of the picture. Efforts to improve regulatory decision making might best be focused on ensuring that government, workers, consumers, and industry have better access to information—on the nature and extent of health hazards, and on the technological capabilities of industries to respond to regulatory controls.

Suggestions for Further Reading

I. General References

Anderson, Richard F. and Michael R. Greenberg, "Hazardous waste facility siting: a role for planners," *Journal of the American Planning Association,* 48 (Spring 1982) 204-218.

Barton, Stephen E., "Property rights and human rights: efficiency and democracy as criteria for regulatory reform," *Journal of Economic Issues,* 17 (December 1983) 915-930.

Blowers, A., *Something in the Air: Corporate Power and the Environment* (New York: Harper and Row, 1984).

Braithwaite, John, "The limits of economism in controlling harmful corporate conduct," *Law and Society,* 16 (1982) 481-503.

Cox, Kevin and R.J. Johnston (eds.), *Conflict, Politics, and the Urban Scene* (New York: St. Martin's Press, 1982).

Cullen, J.D. and P.L. Knox, "The triumph of the eunuch: planners, urban managers, and the suppression of political opposition," *Urban Affairs Quarterly,* 17 (1981) 149-172.

Daneke, Gregory A., "The future of environmental protection: reflections on the difference between planning and regulating," *Public Administration Review,* 42 (May/June 1982) 227-233.

Dragun, Andrew, "Externalities, property rights and power," *Journal of Economic Issues,* 17 (September 1983) 667-680.

Duberg, John A., Michael L. Frankel, and Christopher L. Niemczewski, "Siting of hazardous waste management facilities and public opposition," *Environmental Impact Assessment Review,* 1 (March 1980) 84-93.

Fatkin, Harry, "NIMBY: the siting challenge," *Environmental Forum,* 3 (November 1984) 49-53.

Forester, J., "Planning in the face of power," *Journal of the American Planning Association,* 48 (1982) 67-80.

Kamieniecki, Sheldon, Robert O'Brien, and Michael Clarke (eds.), *Controversies in Environmental Policy* (Albany: State University of New York Press, 1986).

Kasperson, Roger E., *Equity Issues in Radioactive Waste Management* (Cambridge, MA: Oelgeschlager, Gunn and Hain, 1983).

Kates, Robert W. and Jeanne X. Kasperson, "Comparative risk analysis of technological hazards: a review," *Proceedings of the National Academy of Science,* 80 (November 1983) 7027-7038.

Kemp, Ray, "Planning, legitimation and the development of nuclear energy," *International Journal of Urban and Regional Research,* 4 (1980) 350-371.

Keystone Center, *Siting Non-Radioactive Hazardous Waste Management Facilities, An Overview* (Boulder, CO: Keystone Center, September 1980).

Lake, Robert W., Ursula Bauer, Yvonne Chilik, and Lisa Disch, *Paths to Participation: The Public Role in Hazardous Waste Management* (New Brunswick, NJ: Rutgers University Center for Urban Policy Research, forthcoming, 1987).

Lester, James P. and Ann O'M. Bowman (eds.), *The Politics of Hazardous Waste Management* (Durham, NC: Duke University Press, 1983).

Mitnick, Barry, *The Political Economy of Regulation* (New York: Columbia University Press, 1980).

Morell, David and Christopher Magorian, *Siting Hazardous Waste Facilities: Local Opposition and the Myth of Preemption* (Cambridge, MA: Ballinger Publishing Co., 1982).

Mumy, G.E., "Long-run efficiency and property rights sharing for pollution control," *Public Choice,* 35 (February 1980) 59-74.

Murray, William and Carl Seneker, "Implementation of an industrial siting plan," *Hastings Law Journal,* 3 (May 1980) 1073-1089.

National Governors' Association, "Siting hazardous waste facilities," *The Environmental Professional,* 3 (1981) 133-142.

O'Hare, Michael, Lawrence Bacow, and Debra Sanderson, *Facility Siting and Public Opposition* (New York: Van Nostrand Publishing Co., 1983).

Popper, Frank, "Siting LULUs," *Planning,* 47 (1981) 12-15.

Seley, John, *The Politics of Public Facility Planning* (Lexington, MA: Lexington Books, 1983).

Sussna, Stephen, "Remedying hazardous waste facility siting maladies by considering zoning and other devices," *The Urban Lawyer,* 16 (Winter 1984) 29-69.

Tapscott, G., "States try various means to site landfills," *Solid Wastes Management,* 25 (1982) 52-54.

Tarlock, A. Dan, "Siting new or expanded treatment, storage, or disposal facilities: the pigs in the parlors of the 1980s," *Natural Resources Lawyer,* 17 (1984) 429-462.

White, Irvin L. and John P. Spath, "How are states setting their sites?" *Environment,* 26 (October 1984) 16-20 ff.

Williams, Bruce and Albert Matheny, "Testing theories of social regulation: hazardous waste regulation in the American states," *Journal of Politics,* 46 (1984) 428-458.

Williams, Edward A. and Alison K. Massa, *Siting Major Facilities: A Practical Approach* (New York: McGraw-Hill, 1984).

II. Public Participation

Arnstein, Sherry, "A ladder of citizen participation," *Journal of the American Institute of Planners,* 35 (July 1969) 212-224.

Barber, Daniel M., *Citizen Participation in American Communities* (Dubuque, IA: Kendall Hunt Publishing Company, 1981).

Berry, Jeffrey M., "Beyond citizen participation: effective advocacy before administrative agencies," *Journal of Applied Behavioral Science,* 17 (1981) 463-477.

Checkoway, Barry, "The politics of public hearings," *Journal of Applied Behavioral Sciences,* 17 (1981) 566-582.

Checkoway, Barry, "Public hearings are not enough," *Citizen Participation,* 1 (1980) 6-7, 20.

Cunningham, James V., "Power, participation, and local government: the communal struggle for parity," *Journal of Urban Affairs,* 5 (Summer 1983) 257-266.

Darke, R., "Public participation and state power," *Policy and Politics,* 7 (1979) 337-355.

Davis, Charles, "Substance and procedure in hazardous waste facility siting," *University of Wyoming Journal of Environmental Systems,* 14 (1984-1985) 51-63.

Fainstein, Susan S. and Norman I. Fainstein, "Citizen participation in local government," in *Public Policy Across States and Communities* (JAI Press), pp. 223-238.

Farkas, Alan, "Overcoming public opposition to the establishment of new hazardous waste disposal sites," *Capital University Law Review,* 9 (Spring 1980) 451-465.

Fuerst, J.S. and Roy Petty, "Due process—how much is enough?" *The Public Interest,* 79 (Spring 1985) 96-110.

Gittell, Marilyn, *Limits to Citizen Participation* (Beverly Hills, CA: Sage Publications, 1980).

Hadden, Susan G., "Technical information for citizen participation," *Journal of Applied Behavioral Science,* 17 (1981) 537-549.

Hendrickson, Mark L. and Stephen A. Romano, "Citizen involvement in waste facility siting," *Public Works,* 113 (May 1982) 76-79.

Luke, Ronald, "Managing community acceptance of major industrial projects," *Coastal Zone Management Journal,* 7 (1980) 272-293.

Payne, B.A., *Organizational Approach to Estimating Public Resistance at Proposed Disposal Sites for Radioactive and Hazardous Wastes,* Report No. CONF-8209104-2 (Washington, DC: U.S. Department of Energy, 1982).

Petersen, James C. (ed), *Citizen Participation in Science Policy* (Amherst, MA: The University of Massachusetts Press, 1984).

Rosener, Judy B. "Making bureaucrats responsive: a study of the impact of citizen participation and staff recommendations on regulatory decision making," *Public Administration Review,* 42 (July/August 1982) 339-345.

Rossini, Frederick A. and Alan A. Porter, "Public participation and professionalism in impact assessment," *Journal of Voluntary Action Research,* 11 (January/March 1982) 24-33.

Stone, Clarence, "Systematic power in community decision making," *American Political Science Review,* 74 (December 1980) 978-990.

Susskind, Lawrence E. and Michael Elliot, "Learning from citizen participation and citizen action in Western Europe," *Journal of Applied Behavioral Science,* 17 (1981) 497-517.

Thomas, John C., "Citizen participation and urban administration: from enemies to allies?" *Journal of Urban Affairs,* 5 (Summer 1983) 175-182.

Vedlitz, A., J.A. Dyer, and R. Durand, "Citizen contacts with local governments: a comparative view," *American Journal of Political Science,* 24 (1980) 50-67.

White, Louise G., "A hundred flowers blossoming: citizen advisory boards and local administrators," *Journal of Urban Affairs,* 5 (Summer 1983) 221-230.

III.   Mediation, Negotiation and Compensation

Bacow, Lawrence S. and Michael Wheeler, *Environmental Dispute Resolution* (New York: Plenum Press, 1983).

Barton, Stephen E., "Conflict resolution and necessity, practice, and ideal," *Journal of Planning Education and Research,* 4 (December 1984) 96-102.

Bingham, Gail, *Resolving Environmental Disputes: A Decade of Experience* (Washington, DC: The Conservation Foundation, 1986).

Bingham, Gail and Daniel S. Miller, "Prospects for resolving hazardous waste siting disputes through negotiation," *Natural Resources Lawyer,* 17 (1984) 473-490.

Boyle, Susan B., *Siting New Hazardous Waste Management Facilities Through a Compensation and Incentive Approach: A Bibliography*, Council of Planning Librarians, 1983.

Clark, Peter B. and Wendy M. Emrich, *New Tools for Resolving Environmental Disputes* (Washington, DC: Council on Environmental Quality, 1980).

Colosi, Thomas, "Negotiating in the public and private sectors: a core model," *American Behavioral Scientist*, 27 (November/December 1983) 229-254.

Duensing, Edward and Yvonne Chilik, *The Negotiation of Environmental Conflicts: Techniques, Case Studies, and Analyses*, Public Administration Series: Bibliography P-1942 (Monticello, IL: Vance Bibliographics, June 1986).

Duffy, Celeste P., "State hazardous waste facility siting; easing the process through local cooperation and preemption," *Boston College Environmental Affairs Law Review*, 11 (October 1984) 755-805.

Fisher, Roger, "Negotiating power: getting and using influence," *American Behavioral Scientist*, 27 (November/December 1983) 149-166.

Fisher, R. and W. Urry, *Getting to Yes: Negotiating Agreement Without Giving In* (Boston: Houghton Mifflin, 1981).

Goldmann, R.B. (ed.), *Roundtable Justice: Case Studies in Conflict Resolution* (Boulder, CO: Westview Press, 1980).

Groves, D.L., "A model for conflict resolution," *International Journal of Environmental Studies*, 22 (1984) 173-181.

Kennedy, W.J.D. and H. Lansford, "The metropolitan water round table: resource allocation through conflict management," *Environmental Impact Assessment Review*, 4 (1983) 67-78.

Lake, Laura (ed.), *Environmental Mediation: The Search for Consensus* (Boulder, CO: Westview Press, 1980).

McCarthy, Jane E. and Alice Shorett, *Negotiating Settlements: A Guide to Environmental Mediation* (New York: American Arbitration Association, 1984).

McCrory, J.P., "Environmental mediation: another piece for the puzzle," *Vermont Law Review*, 6 (1981) 49-84.

McEwen, Craig A. and Richard J. Maiman, "Arbitration and mediation as alternatives to court," *Policy Studies Journal*, 10 (June 1982) 712-726.

Meeks, Gordon, Jr., *Managing Environmental and Public Policy Conflicts: A Legislator's Guide* (Washington, DC: National Conference on State Legislatures, 1985).

Mernitz, S., *Mediation of Environmental Disputes: A Sourcebook* (New York: Praeger, 1980).

Patton, Leah K. "Problems in environmental mediation: human, procedural, and substantive," *Environmental Comment* (November 1981) 7-11.

Raiffa, Howard, *The Art and Science of Negotiation* (Cambridge, MA: Harvard University Press, 1982).

Rubin, Jeffrey, "Negotiation: an introduction to some issues and themes," *American Behavioral Scientist*, 27 (November/December 1983) 135-148.

Sorenson, John F., "Sweet for the sour: incentives in environmental mediation," *Environmental Management*, 8 (July 1984) 287-295.

Sullivan, Timothy J., *Resolving Development Disputes Through Negotiation* (New York: Plenum, 1984).

Susskind, Lawrence E., "Environmental mediation and the accountability problem," *Vermont Law Review*, 6 (1981) 1-47.

Susskind, Lawrence E., "Mediated negotiation in the public sector: the planner as mediator," *Journal of Planning Education and Research*, 4 (August 1984) 5-15.

Susskind, Lawrence E., Lawrence Bacow, and Michael Wheeler, *Resolving Environmental Regulatory Disputes* (Cambridge, MA: Schenkman, 1985).

Susskind, Lawrence E. and D. Madigan, "New approaches to resolving disputes in the public sector," *Justice Systems Journal* (Summer 1984).

Susskind, Lawrence E. and C. Ozawa, "Mediated negotiation in the public sector: mediator accountability and the public interest problem," *American Behavioral Scientist*, 27 (1983) 255-279.

Susskind, Lawrence E. and A. Weinstein, "Toward a theory of environmental dispute resolution," *Boston College Environmental Law Review*, 9 (1980) 311-357.

Talbot, A.R., *Settling Things: Six Case Studies in Environmental Mediation* (Washington, DC: The Conservation Foundation, 1983).

Index